Jack,

With appreciation for your own...

to this and for your own work,

Martin

JOURNAL FOR THE STUDY OF THE OLD TESTAMENT SUPPLEMENT SERIES
274

Editors
David J.A. Clines
Philip R. Davies

Executive Editor
John Jarick

Editorial Board
Robert P. Carroll, Richard J. Coggins, Alan Cooper, J. Cheryl Exum,
John Goldingay, Robert P. Gordon, Norman K. Gottwald,
Andrew D.H. Mayes, Carol Meyers, Patrick D. Miller

Sheffield Academic Press

Biblical Form Criticism in its Context

Martin J. Buss

Journal for the Study of the Old Testament
Supplement Series 274

Copyright © 1999 Sheffield Academic Press

Published by Sheffield Academic Press Ltd
Mansion House
19 Kingfield Road
Sheffield S11 9AS
England

Printed on acid-free paper in Great Britain
by Bookcraft Ltd
Midsomer Norton, Bath

British Library Cataloguing in Publication Data

A catalogue record for this book is available
from the British Library

ISBN 1-85075-876-X

CONTENTS

A SYMBOLIC FORM OF THIS STUDY

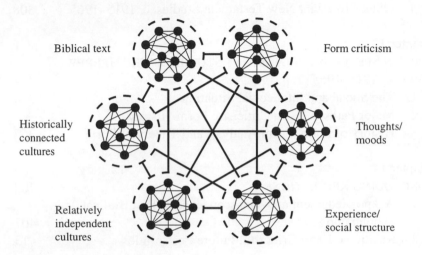

Explanation of the network of networks:

Biblical form criticism examines the relations of the biblical text to thoughts and
moods expressed and to 'life' (social structure and personal experience).

In doing so, it takes account of other cultures, whether historically connected or
not, with their respective relations to both thoughts/moods and social structure/
experience.

As a procedure, form criticism is itself related to the same considerations,
especially to thought (philosophy) and to social structure.

All of these complexes, which have imprecise boundaries, contain more or less
extensively interconnected elements.

In relation to each other, the various complexes, like their parts, have a certain
independence even as they are connected; in other words, the relations between
them are neither entirely accidental nor deterministic.

PREFACE

One can go forward by looking back. The present history is designed to support a forward movement—not by denying appreciation to what has already been done, but rather by pointing to new opportunities that can arise in a pursuit of what has not yet been done extensively. In fact, in preparing this history, I have often been deeply impressed by the quality of older work. In many ways, it seems that one can build on earlier foundations, even though criticism of previous work is also appropriate. Such a situation is fortunate, for it implies that it is not necessary to begin from scratch and, further, that our own present work, too, may in the long run be helpful for future generations.

The history presented exhibits a certain pattern, but that does not mean that everything has been made to fit that pattern. Rather, individual studies have their own attractions. Furthermore, it is a central principle of relational theory, which I accept, that reality does not cohere altogether. The complexity that results from a lack of a precise fit makes it more difficult to absorb the material than would otherwise be the case; but this is a history, not a novel (there is at least a relative distinction between those genres). At the same time, the work is not a chronicle, a progression of unrelated items. Rather, in selecting particular items for discussion, I have attempted to convey a sense of intellectual/social movements. Thus, not just microhistory (by decades) but also mesohistory (by centuries) and macrohistory (by millennia) are objects of the study.

Since this is a history rather than a theoretical treatise, reflective considerations are scattered throughout the volume. Not all readers will want to read all portions equally well; consequently, I have attempted to discuss theoretical issues in such a way that a knowledge of the whole is not necessary to make sense of comments made in individual parts. Still, for a reasonably complete picture of the theoretical framework, one will need to dip, at least, into every chapter.

I do believe that so-called fact and theory are not independent of each other. Similarly, as will become apparent, I believe that ideas and social life are interdependent, although they do not rigidly determine each other. Nevertheless, I hope that many readers will find the survey useful even if they are not interested in, or persuaded by, the contextual vistas.

ACKNOWLEDGMENTS

Permission by Trinity University Press for my reissuing, in revised form, 'The Study of Forms', in J. Hayes (ed.), *Old Testament Form Criticism*, 1974, and by W. de Gruyter for my use of 'The Idea of *Sitz im Leben*—History and Critique', *ZAW* 90: 157-70, is gratefully acknowledged.

In producing this work, I have been aided by a great many persons. These include, with long-term and extensive involvements, Nancy Buss and John Hayes. (In fact, the dictionary of biblical interpretation edited by Hayes, to appear soon, provides many data, including secondary references, that can complement the present, more selective, history.) Others who have helped in important ways—such as by reading and commenting upon portions of the history—include: John Dearman, Phillip Callaway, Julie Palmgren, Donald Hantula, Sharon Terr, Lauren Rio, LaShun Simpson, W. Rhett Lawrence, Janet Mabry, James Joyner, William Griffin, Tammi Turner, Michael Janis, Stephen Christian, Steven Fitzgerald, Eric Probst, Sarah Dille, Amy Oh, Jignasha Amin, William Vetter, Eric Koch, Vernon Robbins, David Blumenthal, Manfred Hoffmann, Sean Wee, Traci McMeans, John Snavely, Adrienne Ash, Shelise Henry, Luke Johnson, Thomas Flynn, Sarah Melcher, Carleen Mandolfo, Jacqueline Lapsley, Timothy Sandoval, Jill Schatz, Kamla Alexander, Dung Bui, Jane Gatewood, Justin McCarthy, Barbara Llanes, Mark Roncace, Peter Trudinger and, last but not least, Nickie Stipe. Thanks to all!

ABBREVIATIONS

ABD	David Noel Freedman (ed.), *The Anchor Bible Dictionary*
AcOr	*Acta orientalia*
AJA	*American Journal of Archaeology*
AJT	*American Journal of Theology*
ARG	*Archiv für Reformationsgeschichte*
ARW	*Archiv für Religionswissenschaft*
ATR	*Anglican Theological Review*
BA	*Biblical Archaeologist*
BASOR	*Bulletin of the American Schools of Oriental Research*
BibInt	*Biblical Interpretation: A Journal of Contemporary Approaches*
BJRL	*Bulletin of the John Rylands University Library of Manchester*
BSac	*Bibliotheca Sacra*
CBQ	*Catholic Biblical Quarterly*
CW	*Die Christliche Welt*
DBSup	*Dictionnaire de la Bible, Supplément*
ET	English translation
EvT	*Evangelische Theologie*
ExpTim	*Expository Times*
HDB	James Hastings (ed.), *A Dictionary of the Bible* (5 vols., 1898-1904)
HibJ	*Hibbert Journal*
HTR	*Harvard Theological Review*
HUCA	*Hebrew Union College Annual*
HZ	*Historische Zeitschrift*
IB	*Interpreter's Bible*
IDB	George Arthur Buttrick (ed.), *The Interpreter's Dictionary of the Bible* (4 vols., 1962)
IDBSup	*IDB*, Supplementary Volume
Int	*Interpretation*
JAOS	*Journal of the American Oriental Society*
JBL	*Journal of Biblical Literature*
JBR	*Journal of Bible and Religion*
JPOS	*Journal of the Palestine Oriental Society*
JQR	*Jewish Quarterly Review*

JR	*Journal of Religion*
JRH	*Journal of Religious History*
JRT	*Journal of Religious Thought*
JSOT	*Journal for the Study of the Old Testament*
JSSR	*Journal for the Scientific Study of Religion*
KD	*Kerygma und Dogma*
LB	*Linguistica biblica*
LW	*Lutheran World*
NedTTs	*Nederlands theologisch tijdschrift*
NRT	*La nouvelle revue théologique*
OTS	*Oudtestamentische Studiën*
PAAJR	*Proceedings of the American Academy of Jewish Research*
RAC	*Reallexikon für Antike und Christentum*
RB	*Revue biblique*
RE	*Realencyklopädie für die protestantische Theologie und Kirche*
RFT	*Relational Form: Transmodern Views* (working title of a manuscript)
RGG	*Religion in Geschichte und Gegenwart*
RHR	*Revue de l'histoire des religions*
RTP	*Revue de théologie et de philosophie*
SEÅ	*Svensk exegetisk årsbok*
SJOT	*Scandinavian Journal of the Old Testament*
ST	*Studia theologica*
TBl	*Theologische Blätter*
TLZ	*Theologische Literaturzeitung*
TP	*Theologie und Philosophie*
TRu	*Theologische Rundschau*
TRE	*Theologische Realenzyklopädie*
TSK	*Theologische Studien und Kritiken*
TZ	*Theologische Zeitschrift*
VD	*Verbum domini*
VF	*Verkündigung und Forschung*
VT	*Vetus Testamentum*
VTSup	*Vetus Testamentum*, Supplements
ZAW	*Zeitschrift für die alttestamentliche Wissenschaft*
ZDPV	*Zeitschrift des deutschen Palästina-Vereins*
ZKG	*Zeitschrift für Kirchengeschichte*
ZKT	*Zeitschrift für katholische Theologie*
ZNW	*Zeitschrift für die neutestamentliche Wissenschaft*
ZTK	*Zeitschrift für Theologie und Kirche*

Chapter 1

INTRODUCTION: RECOGNIZING FORMS

1. *The Notion of Speech Forms*

The study of literary (including oral) forms, or form criticism, can be
defined as the study of patterns of speech. According to Hermann
Gunkel, literary types are constituted by a complex of: (1) thoughts and
moods, (2) linguistic forms (sounds or written symbols) and (3) a
normal connection with life.[1] The folklorist Ben-Amos has called these
three aspects 'the cognitive, expressive, and behavioral levels of
genres' (297). Inherent in the notion of genre, of course, is that one is
not dealing with a purely particular item. *Characteristic of form criticism, then, is attention to the relations of the three aspects mentioned in
patterns that are general, that is, actually or potentially repeated.*
(According to the conception adopted by the present writer, whether
anything is general or a pattern does not depend on how often it appears
but on whether it is viewed as something that is not limited to, or even
necessarily exhibited by, a particular. What is assumed then is not an
Aristotelian essence, that is, a set of characteristics exhibited by members of a certain group, but a possibility which may be actualized.[2])

The term 'form'[3] has presented some difficulty in literary discussions, since it sometimes designates only the external (audible or
visible) features of a text, in contrast to what is called the content—the
objects, concepts or emotions to which the expression refers. To be
unambiguous, such a restrictive use of the word 'form' requires the use

1.   See below, 11.2.d.
2.   On this issue, see philosophical observations below (7; 11.3.a; 12.4; 13.2.d)
and in *RFT*. Strict nominalists (see below, 4.3.c) would treat such structures as only
mental, entirely constructed or purely conventional; others would treat structures as
grounded in reality (with its possibilities), while acknowledging that free construction and an element of arbitrary conventionality enter into their appearance in
thought and behaviour.
3.   For a useful overview of its meaning, see Orsini.

of a qualifying adjective, so that one can speak of 'linguistic', 'metrical' or 'acoustical' form. Without an explicit or implicit qualifier of this sort and with a greater sense of unity, 'form' can refer to a pattern with several facets. Within the phrase 'form criticism', in fact, it properly denotes a holistic design of speech, including its perceptible (physical) phenomena, its (referential) content and its (sociopsychological) role.

To understand something means to recognize the dynamics of its form, that is, to see how its parts or aspects relate to one another.[4] Relations may be logical (for thought), effective (for action) or spatiotemporal (e.g. for aesthetic apprehension). In so far as a recognition of them shows a coherence or appropriateness, it can be called 'insight'.[5] Some interpreters limit scholarship to external descriptions, being sceptical of, or not concerned with, insight. The position defended here is that a relational analysis leading to comprehension is not only possible but also desirable, engendering enjoyment and an enrichment of existence.

The recognition of form as a complex of relations constitutes one of three aspects of interpretation which can be called 'form', 'faith' and 'fact'. They can be distinguished, but never separated. Formal analysis—seeking to comprehend the nature of relationships—necessarily draws on faith, which is orientated toward reality as a whole and thus goes beyond that which can be understood. At the same time, formal analysis interacts with historical study, which deals with particular historical actualities, or so-called facts; these involve, in part, accidental and non-meaningful data.

A theoretical frame for an analysis of types of speech has been given by Wittgenstein, whose philosophical investigations led him to

---

4.   It is true, there is also a conception of 'understanding' according to which it means no more than a perception of the thought of another person; that is a nominalist conception not adopted here (see Buss 1993: 76). The importance of 'understanding' for form criticism, although without an express explanation of what that means, is emphasized by Tucker (1) and in the title and exposition of G. Lohfink.

5.   An important study of insight is by Lonergan, who described it as the grasping of terms and relations mutually establishing one another (1957: 12) and characterized 'form' on the basis of relations between things (432). From the point of view which will be called 'relational' in the present work, however, Lonergan (with a largely Aristotelian-essentialist outlook) did not make adequate allowance for a multiplicity of forms in an object in relation to different observers. (Lonergan is followed by B. Meyer.)

recognize the existence of different 'language games', each representing a special 'form of life' (11). The comparison with games is useful, since language structures have rules that govern their successful operation. A language form cannot be purely singular, for a sign whose meaning is not shared does not communicate, just as it is impossible to play a game without a shared structure. In revealing order, form criticism is comparable to telling someone the rules of chess or tennis. These can change over a period of time, but at any given time they transcend what can be observed on any single occasion, since a particular instance of a game exhibits moves, scores, etc., that are variable even within a stable structure.

To a considerable extent, rules of languages and games are merely conventional in the sense that they contain arbitrary or accidental components. Some general patterns, however, can be observed in different languages and games, indicating that not everything is fortuitous. A reflective analysis then probes for the rationale of a structure, that is, the reasons why its individual aspects are effective in relation to the dynamics of the whole. For instance, one can ask, just what it is that makes tennis or chess an exciting game which has continued over many years? Such an analysis can not only help to defend a traditional pattern but also provide suggestions for improving a system, perhaps in the light of new circumstances.

2. *Subconscious and Reflective Awareness of Forms*

Although all beings exhibit forms, that does not necessarily mean that they are aware of them. Purely physical and organic objects are, presumably, not conscious of their own patterns.

On the human level, the carrying out of rules of behaviour, such as those of speech, is often done subconsciously. A system is subconscious when a speaker or hearer is sufficiently aware to act meaningfully in relation to it, whether through correct usage or in an appropriate response (such as laughing at a joke or accepting an implicit offer of friendship), even when the rules for the communication cannot be articulated. For instance, a child learns grammatical patterns well enough to operate with them, but they are not in full awareness; thus, in order for them to be known directly, they have to be taught in school.

An important kind of minimal or implicit awareness appears in the universally observable phenomenon of classification. As far as can be determined, all languages include terms for types of speech-events, such as prayers, commands or greetings. These represent a rudimentary sort of form criticism.

A word of caution, however, is in order. It is quite possible to make pragmatic distinctions without explicit labels, and classificatory terms are not always used in a precise or invariable fashion. In fact, it is likely that categories are commonly constructed and recognized not in terms of abstract definitions but with reference to typical members of the group (thus, Rosch). Characteristics that define a class, then, can be vague or probabilistic in that they appear frequently but not always (Stevenson, 182-205).

The task of form criticism is to go beyond subconscious knowledge. It brings patterns of speech into full, reflective awareness. Since these patterns embody significant structures of one's own as well as of other cultures, the study of literary forms lays bare and clarifies major movements of human life in which one actually or potentially participates.

3. *Reflexive Awareness*

Human reflection comes to still another level of awareness when it is itself analyzed, with attention to its own interests. What is examined then is not literary form but form criticism. The present essay is an attempt to proceed in this way. Its hope is that by employing analytical, historical and theological/philosophical perspectives, the kind of questions that can be asked and the procedures that can be carried out to answer them will become clearer.

Fortunately, in carrying out this attempt, one can avail oneself of the help of a large number of histories of exegesis. Until recently, to be sure, most of them had their primary interest in the development of historical criticism, which they considered to be the truly valuable approach. Differently, a history focusing on formal study deals more directly with structural and functional issues.[6] Still another kind of history deals with the specific content of texts (such as their theology). These three kinds cannot be rigidly separated; the primary focus of the present study, however, is on formal analysis, with other aspects

6.   An important early history of formal study is that of Alonso Schökel 1963: 3-54 (revised 1988). A number of relevant recent studies with a more or less limited focus will be listed at appropriate places below.

mentioned only in order to indicate what the fuller picture is like.

One limitation of histories of biblical study so far—whether focusing on history, form or content—is that they have paid only a small amount of attention to the philosophical, social and psychological dimensions of the interpretive process. In a preliminary way, these issues were treated in Buss (1974), an antecedent to the present study. A decade later, Reventlow described in detail the social context of a considerable portion of early Protestant exegesis (1984); however, he connected the context more with the substantive positions taken than with the nature of the questions posed, as the present study seeks to do. Philosophical aspects of interpretation have been discussed somewhat widely, although not systematically (e.g. by Kraeling, 1955). During the last few years, there has been an explosion of studies asserting the social and cultural relativity of exegesis and demonstrating this relativity in constructive interpretations.[7] Only a few studies, nevertheless, have applied this perspective to the history of biblical interpretation,[8] and even fewer have shown how the social and intellectual context affects an assessment of form.

As will be seen, 'form' can be understood in varying ways. The varying conceptions reflect divergent philosophical positions, which are linked with different social orientations and with changes in patterns of perception, as they are studied in psychology.[9]

Are the philosophical, social and psychological aspects of interpretation secret, hidden from the consciousness of the interpreters or hidden by them from others? In part yes and in part no. Specifically, the philosophical and psychological aspects of exegesis have often been recognized only vaguely, especially after c. 1700, as intellectual life gradually became more specialized, so that intellectuals were not necessarily well versed in all the different dimensions of thought. For instance, although it is well known that historical criticism was interested in particularity, interpreters did not often state explicitly a connection with particularist philosophy (which at that time still included psychology).

---

7. Including Segovia and Tolbert; Smith-Christopher.

8. A large number of studies by Klatt, Rabenau, Rogerson and Long (to mention just a few) have dealt with what may be called 'microsocial' relations; they are important (in part in order to avoid simplistic assessments), but they often do not raise questions concerning major social movements that affect interpretation.

9. See Rosch (already cited), below on Piaget, and in some detail *RFT*.

The social implications of interpretation, however, have been, as a rule, quite conscious and deliberate, since social (including political) processes are common overt concerns. Thus, in the nineteenth century the conflict over historical criticism involved the political issue of freedom versus order, a fact that was conscious on both sides (professors lost jobs over this).[10] Furthermore, both before and during that century, historical consciousness and critical attitudes toward the Bible were involved in colonialism (conquering 'lower' races, sometimes even thought of as non-Adamites), the rise of capitalism and a rejection or restriction of royalty (see Chapter 6).

Interpreters have usually been quite proud of their political views, considering them to be the right ones. Thus, social orientations do not need to be unmasked, as though they were hidden,[11] although they may need to be recovered by historians living in later centuries when those issues are no longer as obvious as they were to writers and their audiences in their own time.[12] Sometimes, it is true, there may be a need to point out to scholars that there is a connection between their politics and the orientation they apply in scholarship, for they may be aware of each aspect of their outlook only separately, and it is often appropriate to indicate that a given scholarly outlook is self-serving.

The form-critical assumption of a correlation between life, thought and verbal expression will thus be borne out for the process of form criticism itself, in that social life, theoretical assumptions and specific interpretations are connected. To be sure, the correlation between scholarship and its context is not rigid, just as the correlation between the three aspects of literary form is not rigid but probabilistic.[13]

10. For example, W. de Wette and H. Ewald. For others, see Harrisville and Sundberg (47, 100, 264, 266).

11. Contra Buss (1974: 3) and others. The Bible and Culture Collective (1995: 302) thinks that especially dominant groups hide their views; the opposite is more likely to be the case, since minority (and especially subversive) positions need to be restrained in public statements.

12. Sometimes this involves finding statements made by the writers in which political issues are expressly addressed, but often the social dimension is indicated within the interpretation of texts.

13. See Chapter 14 below.

Chapter 2

BIBLICAL PATTERNS

Since it is not possible to enter into many specific details, statements in the present work that refer to 'the Bible' without qualification are intended to be true irrespective of whether one means by that term the Jewish Bible (*Tanak*) or some version of the Christian Bible. In their character, statements that will be made are neither purely descriptive (especially since there is no such thing) nor strictly religious. Rather, they are theoretically reflective. It is true, they are held in conjunction with a non-authoritarian Christian theology;[1] but they would probably be true also in an atheistic, agnostic, Jewish, or traditional Christian framework, for, contrary to the strongly holistic theories of science, many assertions that can be made are at least roughly commensurable within different frames.[2] The adjective 'biblical' refers to some or much of the Bible, but not necessarily to all of it.

Such an abbreviated way of speaking, incidentally, is not limited to references to biblical literature but applies also to what is said about Plato, Augustine, Maimonides, Luther, Muilenburg and others who are discussed. It is not possible to represent adequately their many writings, but an attempt is made to highlight themes that are typical for each of them.

---

1. 'Authoritarian' here means an attitude that accepts, without justification, the words of a finite being (including the Bible). A good example of a non-authoritarian Christian approach is Kwok; see further below, 13.2.d.

2. Cf. *RFT* on Hesse; similarly, Levenson (104). P. Davies argues for different disciplines based on different theological assumptions; but he hardly favours having different 'societies of biblical literature' (there would have to be quite a few of them), for he acknowledges that there is no neutral position (16, 26, 48, 83, 126) and he values conversation (52). For instance, in Watson, with which he disagrees on the whole, Davies can undoubtedly savour the analysis of the Joseph story.

1. *Implicit Philosophy of Reality and Speech*

a. *Revelation and Intellectual Apprehension*

The Bible contains little theoretical reflection about language or about any other issue, since it does not consider any phenomena in a primarily conceptual manner.[3] The reason for this lies in the fact that its thrust is more religious than philosophical.

The primary emphasis of the Bible is that of a comprehensive pragmatics, taking account of a reality that is larger than oneself.[4] This kind of orientation transcends what can be handled intellectually, for an intellectual representation is part of oneself (i.e. of one's mind) and thus necessarily less complex than oneself. Accordingly, any apprehension of what is greater or more inclusive than one's own being must admit that it is inherently partial and must include an element of intuition (i.e. a somewhat unclear sense). Furthermore, while one can typically control what is less complex than oneself by outsmarting it, an apprehension of what is greater requires a strongly receptive attitude towards it (according to traditional terminology, one receives 'revelation'). Since the content of what is received in this way is more than can be rationally grasped, it must incorporate considerable mystery; but, as will be discussed, it can include rather than negate a limited intellectual apprehension.[5]

Specifically, biblical revelation presents to its hearers a challenge to their will and feeling, with a cognition that elicits commitment and joy. It encourages them by assuring them of their worth, but it also makes them face the side of reality they prefer to ignore, such as the presence of a tendency to place a greater value on oneself than on another. In this sense, revelation uncovers or unmasks existence.

3.   G. Kennedy (1980: 120) has characterized the rhetoric of the Hebrew Bible as 'preconceptual'; he is correct in so far as he points out that biblical thought does not focus specifically on conceptuality, a significant but limited vision of the real.

4.   In contrast, what is normally called 'science' is partial in procedure. (See, for example, Wieman, 160; Ramsey, 37; Kaufman, 35; Pannenberg 1990, chapter 7.) According to E. Johnson (231, largely following Rahner) 'a certain "logic of the infinite"' connects the finite with the infinite without one being absorbed into the other.

5.   Buber described a holistic I–thou relation as without specific content, apparently in an overreaction against the danger of attaching ultimate significance to what can be grasped or handled. For a more positive role of reason and factuality within a holistic apperception, see below 2.2 and *RFT*.

In its negative side, biblical speech is a forerunner—indeed, a cause—of what has come to be called 'ideological criticism', which typically identifies self-justifying conceptions as unduly self-serving.[6] Most of such criticism in recent times, it is true, has been directed at uncovering the problematic side of other persons or groups, not of oneself.[7] In contrast, much of the criticism present in the Bible was directed against members of the speaker's own community—a community which then preserved those words. Thus, while the Bible has room for kings and is largely androcentric, it also criticizes royalty, together with much of what is often valued by and in males, such as a high degree of self-assertion.[8] (Moderate self-assertion is supported in wisdom literature, in which women play a considerable role, so that this literature may counter women's, and men's, temptations not to assert themselves adequately.)

Just one example—one not as well known as others—can illustrate the situation. Israel had a tradition that it escaped from slavery in Egypt. This tradition does not simply vilify Egypt, as one might expect it to do. Rather, it half-excuses the oppressive Pharaoh (he did not know about Joseph and God hardens his heart repeatedly) and tells of his daughter's compassion for baby Moses. Furthermore, it pictures all of the Egyptian people—not just the Hebrews—as 'slaves' of Pharaoh (Gen. 47.19) and attributes this sad condition to the Hebrew Joseph, who saved the land from starvation in such a way as to make the Pharaoh owner of everything.[9] In short, the biblical story describes the

6.   This, to be sure, is only one kind of ideological criticism; see, for example, Gottwald.

7.   That is observed by O'Brien (121). Marxists have made a major contribution in terms of ideological criticism but tend to exempt themselves from it. (Marxist governments do make generous use of enforced self-criticism for the control of underlings.)

8.   Saiving Goldstein, 100-12, pointed out that Protestant theologians have one-sidedly focused on typically male sins, ignoring what she considers the more typical female sin of 'underdevelopment of the self'. Her critique also largely fits the Bible, although the Bible supports moderate self-assertion.

9.   This phase of the story is well described by F. Watson (60-77) (although without relating it to the Exodus account). It is true, one can argue that the story's description of Joseph's contribution to the oppressive power of Pharaoh is due to a desire to play up Hebrew importance in world history, but the point of the story seems to be to account for oppressive conditions in Egypt. A morally paradoxical view of history is expressly stated in Gen. 50.20.

evil that was experienced by the Hebrews as something for which they
had partial responsibility.

b. *The General/Reasonable and the Particular/Arbitrary*
In the Bible, God is the prime reality greater than human beings. That
means that God can be helpful or critical or both. For instance,
Horkheimer (1968: 374 [1935]) has observed that the concept of 'God'
nurtures the idea that there are norms critical of what occurs in nature
and society.

Greatness might be expressed in the form of sheer force. However, in
biblical literature God is not, as a rule, presented as exercising arbitrary
authority. For instance, even in the story of Job there is a reason for
God's action, although the hero is never told it. A central biblical
attribute for God is 'rightness' (*ṣedeq/ṣedaqah*),[10] which establishes
common welfare with equity. In short (this point cannot be argued here
in detail), the divine way includes reasonableness, although that is not
its only aspect.[11]

Since sheer particularity is arbitrary, while that which is general
(recurring) can be suspected to have reasons (which need not be 'good',
i.e. something of which one approves), it is well to look at biblical
ideas concerning generality and particularity. These two categories will
become important for the history of interpretation.

Indeed, although biblical writers did not address philosophical questions in the formal way for which Greeks are noted, one can deduce
their position in regard to ontological issues from statements in which
they are dealt with implicitly. True, biblical writers did not all agree
with each other. On the contrary, different opinions, or at least
emphases, appear in the Bible, just as they do in Graeco-Roman tradition. If one places them together, however, as has traditionally been
done, a complex pattern appears. This involves a combination of concerns with the general and with the particular, one that runs throughout

10. The whole topic of righteousness cannot be discussed here, but see
H. Schmid (1968: e.g. p. 8); Ho; Gossai (stressing relationality).

11. While reasonableness is not the only component of the meaning of *ṣedeq*, it
is included as one; see also (in a Christian version) 1 Jn 2.29; 3.7. In fact, biblical
laws are relatively high in giving reasons (cf. views by Maimonides, Gemser and
others, as reported below, 4.2.a, and 13.1.c). Beyond the rational, however, stand
such themes as the (particular) election of Israel (Deut. 7.7-8) and perhaps the
threat expressed in the exegetically difficult Exod. 4.24-6.

the Bible, although sometimes one side or the other receives primary billing.

To begin with, God is spoken about in the Hebrew Bible sometimes by means of a general designation ('Elohim', the plural form of a word, indicating God's role in relation to all human beings) and sometimes with the use of an individual name (YHWH, primarily in relation to Israel). In quantity of appearances, YHWH predominates, but Elohim provides a frame. In the New Testament, God's personal name is not used, but deity is individualized in Jesus.

Commands in the Hebrew Scriptures prescribe not only particular acts but also, and especially, types of action. The range of the applicability of laws varies. Some, especially ritual ones, are apparently intended only for Israel; others, especially those dealing with inter-human relations, are either directed towards all human beings or, more commonly, open-ended in their range. (The range and rationality of laws came to be discussed extensively in later Jewish literature, as will be seen.) The New Testament presents a general call for love as well as some other general rules or principles. (Whether, or to what extent, they are 'rules' or only 'principles' has been heavily debated in Christianity.)

Prophetic speech in the Bible is predominantly particular. That is understandable, since both evaluations and predictions, which form the primary contents of prophecy, are by their nature particular. Nevertheless, those prophecies that are preserved in the Bible have a quite general application, since they deal with human life at a very basic level (e.g. oppression). Of course, there would have been little point in preserving those words if they had not had a wide relevance.

The literature called 'wisdom' is often thought to be general or rational rather than particular in outlook. That is correct in the sense that it has little concern for Israel as a special entity. However, royal chronicles, which are particular in nature, were probably kept by courtiers who thought of themselves as 'wise' persons.[12] Furthermore, a major branch of wisdom focused on the partial irrationality of existence (Qoheleth and Job), so that wisdom certainly cannot be identified with a point of view that considers reality to be rational. In fact, one must distinguish clearly between 'reason'—in the sense of a reflective human process that does not rely primarily on receptive intuition—and

---

12. Of course, if the book of Proverbs provides the standard of what is considered wisdom, then narratives are not covered, but that premise is open to doubt.

a belief in 'reasonableness', in the sense of coherence or order, as a feature of reality. It was reason, as defined, rather than a belief in reasonableness that was characteristic of wisdom.

In short, a duality of the general/reasonable and the particular/arbitrary runs through much of biblical literature. It is not the case that one aspect or the other is limited to a certain portion of it; rather, they intertwine. There is also no evidence that one of these two dimensions of reality was thought to be more basic than the other.

It is argued elsewhere (in *RFT*, summarized in Chapter 7 below) that the idea of relations integrally combines those two dimensions. As a matter of fact, relationality is important in biblical, as in other, literature and culture. Yet in the Bible the concept of relationship is not addressed theoretically as such, as distinct from the specific kind of relation into which something enters. Communication, a special form of relation, however—especially, speech—receives express attention.

c. *Speech*

Speech is a central theme in biblical tradition. In regard to this, two major types are represented: a divine form and a human form. They are associated respectively with two different (although not separate) ways of human existence. God's speaking to human beings expresses a dimension of existence in which one is receptive, while human speaking represents a form of life in which one is active.

Specifically, divine speaking constitutes a major part of priestly and prophetic traditions in Israel. Most of the instructions transmitted by priests are represented as coming from God. Promises, threats, and related forms of speech expressed by prophets were largely attributed to the same source. In line with ancient views of the power of blessings and curses—reflecting in part the observation that speech has social effects—Israelites believed in the creative and redemptive power of divine utterances (Gen. 1.3; Isa. 55.11; etc.—cf. Rabinowitz), and Christians came to identify God's word with Jesus.

The speech of human beings, in contrast, is an important topic of what Israelites called 'wisdom', which represents the humanly active and reflective side of life (although reflection was not as strongly developed among them as in Greece). Specifially, the Hebrew terms for 'mouth', 'tongue', 'lip' and 'word' appear repeatedly in the books of Proverbs, Qoheleth, Job and Psalms with reference to human speech, while in non-wisdom books these words are largely used in a figurative sense, applied to God, swords, fire and the like.[13] In the New Testament, exhortations about ordinary speaking (different from non-rational 'tongues') occur especially in contexts explicitly related to wisdom (Col. 4.6; Jas 3.1-12).

The concern with human speech in wisdom combines an enlightened self-interest with an orientation to the social good (e.g. Prov. 10.21; 18.13). An enjoyable character of what is said is declared in Qoh. 12.10: 'The assembly speaker sought to find pleasurable words'. The pleasure here referred to appears to be largely, although not only, that of the content,[14] so that content and aesthetic form were not separated.

2. *Implicit Recognition of Forms of Speech*

Biblical literature not only used the symbol of divine speech and spoke about human speech in general but also showed an awareness of specific categories for speaking. For instance, it employed names for literary genres, such as the song, dirge, parable, oracle or laws (Liedke; Cooper, 3-7).[15] As is quite natural, the labels applied to types of speech were often not very precise. For instance, although the terms for laws or instructions tended to designate different kinds of inculcations, they were used with considerable freedom.

The fact that the classifying of speech played a major role, at least at the subconscious level, is further shown by the way the Bible is organized. The Scriptures, namely, are an anthology arranged by literary genres according to a typology that was presumably accepted by those who transmitted or gathered the texts. For instance, virtually all of the extant proverbs occur in two books (Proverbs, Qoheleth), the vast majority of psalms in just one, and love songs in another. This canonical arrangement may have had an important sociological component. Since many of the literary types were associated with particular kinds

---

13. On proper speaking according to Proverbs, cf. Bühlmann; non-proper, deleterious speech is included in the overview of Shupak. For rhetoric in Near Eastern schooling, see, for example, the Egyptian Merikare 32, and Crenshaw (1985: 607, 609).

14. Similarly, Stoic and other ancient rhetorical perspectives placed a major emphasis on rectitude (cf. Rahn, 148; Kustas, 27); cf. below for Graeco-Roman rhetoric.

15. Craig (122) presents evidence that biblical writers discriminated between prose and poetry, although not rigidly.

of persons who acted as their primary bearers, each of these bearer groups could crystallize their own contribution.[16]

Arrangement by genre, as a matter of fact, was not unusual. For instance, Mesopotamian collections were ordered to a large extent by types of speech (cf. Wilson, 59-60). A canon of Greek literature, formed in Alexandria and elsewhere, included for each genre the writers and works judged to be the best.[17] Apparently, both in Greece and in Israel the canonical collection provided a set of ideal forms or models for each of several dimensions of life, as expressed in literature.

For the major categories, Israelites employed the image of personal prototypes: Moses for laws, David for psalms of lament, Solomon for wisdom (including human love).[18] Thus, although an interest in individuals is also evident in biblical literature (thus, for example, Gunkel 1912), individualism was avoided in favour of attention to literary types or structures. Even in the area of life in which individuality played the greatest role—prophecy—a number of figures were treated as authors of groups of sayings that are best seen as traditions rather than as the words of a single person.[19]

In the Hebrew canon, the different literary types are not arranged haphazardly.[20] Rather, those expressed in the form of divine speech appear primarily within its first two divisions (Pentateuch and

16. Classifications of Greek poetry took account of the kinds of occasions with which genres were, at least originally, connected (D. Russell 1981: 153; Cole, 37). A similar kind of classification has been observed for contemporary folklore (e.g. in India [Flueckiger, 39]).

17. See Marrou, Part II, chapter 7; Kennedy 1994: 64. The poetry attributed to Pindar was arranged by genres at least by Alexandrian times; furthermore, as in some later arrangements, the genres were sequenced according to whether they were religious (god-directed) or relatively secular (Pfeiffer 1968: 184), in a way that parallels the Hebrew division between priestly/prophetic and other writings.

18. In Greek tradition, as in the Israelite, poetry was often attributed to 'mythical protocomposers', which provided a certain typological order (Nagy, 49, 72).

19. In Greece, too, 'classical' poetry, such as that of Pindar, was thought of as having 'transcendent occasionality', i.e. as being directed towards a particular situation but nevertheless archetypal (Nagy, 76).

20. Far from mysteriously (*pace* Barton in Sæbø, 81). According to Frye (315), the Bible is 'probably the most systematically constructed sacred book in the world', but other canons (Hindu, Buddhist, etc.) have a fairly clear structure also. See below, Chapter 4 (*passim*), 8 (Goldman) and 13.2.b, for analyses of canonical arrangements.

Prophets). In content, they contain a revelation involving ultimacy—in dynamic terms, Origin and End. Of these two divisions, the Pentateuch—largely priestly in character—is devoted almost entirely to the theme of the origin, or sacred past, of the world and, in particular, of Israel; its laws form a part of the charter which is an integral aspect of origin myths (Malinowski, 43). The prophetic part, containing evaluations and announcements, is concerned with the issue of whether the divine will is, or will be, fulfilled. The third division largely contains literature styled as human speech to or about God or even without any reference to deity. Its topics, especially those classed as wisdom, revolve predominantly around limited matters dealt with according to moderate standards (in contrast to the extreme ones applied by some prophets). The social location of the third part is among the 'wise' (largely, lay people) and lower clergy (singers—especially Psalms, Lamentations, Chronicles).

It is important to observe that the three divisions of the canon overlap in character[21] even as they clearly differ in their primary patterns.[22] This overlap has an important theoretical side, for it indicates that receptivity and activity are not altogether separated in the biblical structure.[23]

Within the New Testament, gospels and letters each form a group. One of the gospels, Matthew, is arranged according to literary types, including ethical instructions, miracle stories and parables.

In the New Testament, furthermore, identifications of author and addressee have an implicit literary-typological significance. The gospels are anonymous (except for the fact that Luke's personal 'I' appears in the introduction), letting the figure of Jesus shine forth in speech and action. The letters, in contrast, are attributed to apostles,

---

21. An overlap can be seen in the presence of a divine response to Job, which largely has the negative function of showing the limits of human reason, and in the use of oracles—either quoted or with a general application (unlike those of the prophetic books, which are specific)—in Psalms. Conversely, there are wisdom elements in the first two divisions of the canon, including historical narratives and certain ethical and observational elements. In Hosea, for instance, divine speech and human speech—which correspond roughly in their contents to Buber's two types of relation—are intermingled (Buss 1969: 60-71; cf. Macintosh and, for the Pentateuch, for example, Frymer-Kensky).

22. The Septuagint's order, which may or may not be a Christian creation, has a somewhat different but also form-critically sensible structure.

23. That, in fact, they *should* not be separated is argued in *RFT*.

who (as was true for Israelite prophets) repeatedly stand not simply as individuals but as the fountainheads of traditions. The addressees of letters can represent a type of person—for example, Timothy as a clerical leader.

Biblical literature thus contains an implicit recognition of speech patterns and employs them as an organizing principle. In later years, as will be seen, Jewish and Christian interpreters applied literary analysis consciously, under the influence of Graeco-Roman writings. That was readily possible, since societies or cultures can learn from one another when they have a similar range of concerns but have not developed them equally.

Chapter 3

GRAECO-ROMAN THEORIES OF FORM

1. *Philosophy*

Greek philosophy (literally translated, 'love of wisdom') developed in close analogy to, and in contact with, the Near Eastern (including Egyptian) educational tradition.[1] The word *sophia* even has a range of meaning virtually identical with that of the Hebrew *ḥokmah* ('wisdom'), in that it denotes any skill, but especially a mental one. The Greek sophists of classical and imperial times were in many ways counterparts of the 'wise' in Israel—educators, speakers, thinkers and advisers.

A certain tension, it is true, developed between some of those who were called 'sophists' and other philosophers. According to a charge laid against them, the sophists were orientated primarily towards immediate practical ends and were interested in the success of their specific tasks without paying adequate attention to theory and ethics. The charge may be unfair, however, and we will not make a distinction between sophism and philosophy here.

Greek philosophy (much of it preserved only in fragments and secondary reports) was heavily concerned with whether, or to what extent, reality is a unity or a multiplicity and whether being (firmness) or becoming (change) is primary.[2] The very earliest thinkers (before Socrates) did not foreground the term 'form', which came to be important in later philosophy; but they set the stage for subsequent thought concerning form or structure.

Thus, three philosophers living during the sixth century BCE in Asia

---

1.   See, for example, Burkert 1992 (add: reports about Thales and Pythagoras in Egypt); Thrams, 2-5, 7-15.

2.   Editions and translations of the essential texts have been furnished by Diels and Kranz (standard), Wheelwright (convenient for the non-specialist and relatively full), and various detailed studies.

Minor envisioned in different ways an original reality that is single but not rigid. (Specifically, Thales conceived of this reality as water. Anaximander thought of the ultimate as a non-concrete infinite/indefinite; derivative concrete beings, in his view, are in conflict with one another, an 'injustice' for which they are again absorbed into the ultimate. Anaximenes, taking up a position between these, identified the ultimate as air, which exists in different degrees of compression; this is even less rigid than water but not completely non-concrete.) Pythagoras (also in the sixth century BCE) believed that 'number' is basic; this involves both contrast (with multiplicity) and harmony—a duality appearing in mathematics and music.

Stressing the role of negativity, Heraclitus (c. 500 BCE) highlighted strife together with multiplicity and becoming, but he also believed that order lies behind and emerges from strife. Quite differently, Parmenides (c. 500 BCE or somewhat later) espoused a solid, unchanging unity. His student, Zeno of Elea, formulated paradoxes of motion, apparently in support of his teacher. (In contrast, Heraclitus had envisioned a coincidence of opposites.) Taking a mediating position, Empedocles (fifth century BCE) gave place to both strife and love, favouring the latter.

In the late fifth century BCE, Socrates gave close attention to the nature of what is designated by general terms, such as 'justice' and 'humanity' and names for literary types. His outlook, however, is known primarily through the eyes of Plato (early fourth century), who probably modified it considerably.

Although Plato's thinking was open-ended, the position attributed to Socrates in his middle-period writings (for example, in the *Republic*) is the one with which he has long been identified and which will be treated as that of Plato when no further qualification is made.[3] It took patterns, or forms, as paradigmatic models, which more truly have being than do particular objects, which are transient (*Timaeus*, 27-28).

Diverging from his teacher Plato, Aristotle (mid-fourth century BCE) held that general forms (which are designated by linguistic terms) are present in particular existents. He believed, further, that some of the characteristics of an object are 'essential', while others are 'accidental'. The essential ones are given in the definition of the 'species' to which an object belongs. This conception implies that there is only one correct

3.   See Gonzalez for interpretations that balance a view that Plato advocated definite positions with one that sees his dialogues as primarily exploratory.

formal analysis for a given object, a position that can be called 'Aristotelian essentialism', whether or not it altogether correctly represents Aristotle's view.[4]

Strongly particularist, standing at the opposite extreme to Plato, was Antisthenes (c. 400 BCE)—like Plato, at one time a student of Socrates. He is reported to have said that every object can be described only by its own formula. More moderately particularist was Epicurus (c. 300 BCE). He considered general concepts to be images standing for a group of similar objects. In the Middle Ages, his kind of view came to be described as one which holds that forms arise after objects, i.e. in a reflection on them, rather than their being prior to them (Plato) or in them (Aristotle).

Epicurus was a (partial) indeterminist. In this respect he differed from Democritus (a little before 400 BCE), who had joined a belief in atomism (i.e. reality is composed of particular atoms) with an acceptance of regularities to which the atoms are subject. It is useful to note that Democritus, according to ancient reports, derived his idea of atoms as solid units in part from Parmenides' notion of the whole world as a solid unit. As will be seen later, monist holism and atomistic pluralism indeed resemble each other in conception. Through his determinism, in fact, Democritus envisioned a kind of monism in which all of reality is solidly locked together.

Not altogether unlike Democritus, Zeno of Citium (c. 300 BCE), the founder of Stoicism, believed that existents are particular, yet pervaded by a universal *logos*.

The political views of these different thinkers were correlated on the whole with their conceptions of reality. A fluid or varied unity may well represent a traditional society with incipient literacy, as obtained in the sixth century (traditional societies by no means constitute rigid unities). Plato, with his emphasis on generality represented by transcendent forms,[5] leaned toward elitism, especially of an intellectual and moral kind. Aristotle, relatively more particularist, favoured a combination of oligarchy with democracy and placed value on the middle

4.   There is some vagueness in Aristotle's statements, and his position was not static (cf. Wians). Nevertheless, he did distinguish between 'essential' and 'accidental' properties, and he has long been understood in the way stated. For other views concerning definitions, see below, 6.1.b.

5.   It is true, Plato's forms are not strictly general structures, but their paradigmatic nature gives them a generally relevant character (cf. Spellman, 60).

class as a mediator between high and low (*Politics*, 1296f.). Democritus, envisioning law-abiding atoms, championed politically free democracy, and Epicureans, more free-wheeling, enjoyed voluntary friendship circles, with (moderate) pleasure as their standard. Claiming Antisthenes—who was born of a non-Greek slave mother—as a founder, Cynics rejected social conventions, but they did not do so in favour of a competitive individualism; rather, they wished to live close to nature and lived a simple life, giving up wealth and the pursuit of it. One of them, Diogenes of Sinope, thought that 'the only true commonwealth...is as wide as the universe'.[6] Zeno, the Stoic—who came from the East (his father may have been Jewish) and who received training from a follower of Diogenes[7]—stressed a universal perspective together with the individuality of existence; he advocated an internal liberation that realizes *logos*. (Thus, like others, he stood in contrast to some sophists[8] who had championed the idea that 'might makes right'.)

These variations illustrate a tendency for a primary orientation toward a strong generality (such as Plato's) to be associated with an aristocratic inclination, while an atomist outlook goes with individualism, often middle-class. A primary orientation towards, or inclusive of, the concerns of the lower class[9]—to be distinguished from voluntary poverty—was largely absent. However, Stoics (to cite one group) espoused, in theory, the equality of human beings and supported 'a humanitarianism that resulted in a little legislation and some charitable foundations' (Colish 1985: 37; Sandbach, 148).

Not only did the political views cohere quite well with metaphysical ones, they also correlated fairly closely with a given thinker's own position in society. Nevertheless, two reservations must be expressed. One is that we are not altogether, or reliably, informed about individual social situations.[10] Another is that the match between position and

6.   Diogenes Laertius, *Lives of Eminent Philosophers*, 6.72; on Cynics, cf. Downing.

7.   Later Cynics in turn learned from Stoicism (thus, for example, Koester, 148).

8.   Thus Callicles and Thrasymachus, as represented by Plato.

9.   Arguments are presented in *RFT* (cf. Chapter 7, below) that this kind of orientation requires both particularity and generality. Stoicism (and Cynicism?) did cover both of these aspects, but not as intrinsically joined as in later relational theory.

10.   The sociological issues here set forth are, of course, the subject of extensive debate. Useful overviews of philosophy with attention to its social situation are

thought is far from perfect, for human beings have ways of transcending their situation, such as through reflection[11] or (perhaps even more so) through some forms of religion. For instance, Plato, who came from an aristocratic family, rejected 'excessive wealth' and opposed giving 'special honour or a special education' to a wealthy or royal person beyond that given to a poor or private one (*Laws*, 696).[12] Stoics—who included notably a slave (Epictetus, c. 100 CE), on the one hand, and an emperor (Marcus Aurelius, second century CE), on the other—believed that governmental authorities are subject to the ethics of 'natural law' (with a call both for benevolence and for the permitting of free speech), so that many Stoics were, together with Cynics and others, critics of the powerful. This fact led to the expulsion of philosophers from Rome (even death for some) c. 70 CE.[13] Similarly, but in a religious way, Christianity (transnational like the empire) was able to assert itself as a counterweight to military power.

Many of these philosophers took some steps toward, or defended, sexual equality.[14] In terms of practice, that was especially true for Epicureans and Cynics in their semi-private circles. Nevertheless, all of the moves along this line were limited to such an extent that they had little or no public impact upon society. Even from within philosophical circles, virtually no writings or sayings by women are preserved.

Together with these more or less positive views of reality, there arose also a tradition of scepticism, especially from c. 300 BCE on.[15] One can

presented by B. Russell (for the West); Randall (for the recent West); Nakamura (for East and West); Helferich. Traditions about philosophers' backgrounds are in large part preserved by Diogenes Laertius (third century CE).

11. Thus also Foucault in his final years (see *RFT*).

12. One might say that Plato, in stressing intellectual/moral elitism, supported his own role as teacher, but he undermined this role by doubting that virtue can be taught (*Meno*, 93-94).

13. See Dawson (37) with references.

14. Cf. Snyder (105, etc.); Tuana (1994). Pythagoras included women in his circle. Plato proposed the presence of women among the guardians of the ideal commonwealth although he considered them relatively inferior to men (*Republic*, 455-56); Socrates/Plato reported receiving deep insight about love (in a rich and broad sense) from Diotima (*Symposium*, 201-12). In a collection of stories, Plutarch celebrated historically effective deeds by women. The Neoplatonist Hypatia (fifth century CE, murdered by Christians) was famous, but her works are not preserved.

15. If Protagoras and Gorgias are to be interpreted sceptically rather than relationally, scepticism or even nihilism would have started in the fifth century, possibly reflecting the breakdown of traditional order with the rise of democracy.

speculate that it reflects the political dissolution of local societies with the arrival of empire structures (thus also P. Green, 606). After several centuries, as the empire situation stabilized, scepticism receded, although it did not die out altogether.

As Western society developed during the Common Era, one or another of the philosophies described became prominent, although always modified by newer thought and with the absorption of themes from other traditions.

At first, versions of Platonism, mixed strongly with Stoic and to some extent with other traditions, dominated (see, for example, Procopé in Sæbø, 453-73). This complex suited the needs of people in the Roman empire and its aftermath, for in the empire local collectivities were superseded by a universal authority to which was joined considerable economic and spiritual privatism (Heichelheim, 160, 340, 343).

After c. 1150 CE, Aristotelianism became the primary orientation for a number of mediaeval and some Renaissance thinkers. It furnished a moderate point of view in a situation that had a limited amount of social order, with a slowly rising middle class.

From the fifteenth century on, positions resembling those of Democritus, Epicurus and Heraclitus were to enjoy popularity more or less increasingly, although not exclusively so, as elements of a relatively individualistic and conflictual culture. The mathematical view of reality championed by Pythagoreans flowered in the growing rule of mathematics in science during the same period, but it largely became a means of calculation.

From the late nineteenth century on, as a next step, an outlook not unlike that of the presocratic Empedocles (with positive and negative relations) and also incorporating some elements of other Greek philosophies came to be formalized in relational perspectives, which drew even more heavily on Jewish, Christian, non-'Western' and women's orientations. (See Chapter 7 and *RFT*.) These relational views seek to be inclusive of classes, genders and cultures without destroying differences. A sceptical and even nihilist line emerged along with it, however.

It can be noted, then, that the various points of view that have become dominant at different times in Western thought were already

(Pyrrho, c. 300 BCE, had some knowledge of philosophies of India but seems to have gone further than they did in the direction of scepticism.)

present in some form in classical Greek tradition. Each had a certain, although not absolute, affinity with a given stratum of society; their dominance varied since the relative prominence of one social stratum or another changed in history. Furthermore, the range of opinions in ancient Greece was matched to some extent by the range of views in early written traditions of India and China.[16] One can thus conclude that major philosophical standpoints, such as in regard to generality and particularity, are tied less to a specific space and time than to other factors, including among these a thinker's social orientation. Similarly, in the realm of religion, the different perspectives present in first-century CE Judaism—relatively this-wordly, moderately eschatological and dramatically apocalyptic—held largely by different social groups, each have a close parallel in present society with a primary location in a corresponding social circle. In other words, major orientations are transhistorical (i.e. according to a perspective that gives attention to history but not only to that).

2. *Theories of Types of Speech Acts*

In the fifth century BCE, Protagoras mentioned four types of sentences or discourses: request, question, answer and command.[17] A more elaborate analysis along this line was made by the Stoic Apuleius (second century CE) in a work on 'interpretation' that was to influence mediaeval thinkers. Apuleius pointed out that arguing or disputing speech is only one of several varieties. Other kinds include commanding, wishing, admiring and lamenting (Sullivan, 22).

3. *The Study of Literature, Including Especially Poetry*

The examination of literature (i.e. mostly poetic works that had been transmitted from the past) was a basic part of Graeco-Roman education. In this system, the study of language (reading and writing) and of

16. For instance, within Hinduism the early schools Nyaya and Vaisesika and later the thinker Ramanuja accepted particularity (in addition to generality) more so than did others. In some cases, parallels are due to mutual influence, for the 'Eastern' (east of Persia) and 'Western' lines have not been altogether independent, even though they have been largely so. The parallels, however, should not be overdrawn, for Indic and Chinese philosophies also contained special concerns not well represented in Greece.

17. Diogenes Laertius, *Lives*, 9.53.

literature was called 'grammar' (i.e. knowledge of writing); it preceded 'rhetoric' in the educational process.[18]

Literature (especially Homer) was thought to furnish not only entertainment but models for both language and thought. In other words, literature was treated as archetypal. Since the origin of poetry was attributed to inspiration, students were not ordinarily taught to produce poetry. Literary texts, however, were often cited as examples of linguistic usage, although with the warning that poetry is permitted irregularities that are not proper for ordinary speech or writing.[19]

The study of literary texts included both the explaining of individual words and sentences and a broader interpretation that could be called 'exegesis'. The latter term means, literally, 'a leading out' and designated the recognition of what one can learn about reality and ethics from a passage. Professional exegetes, for instance, were those whose primary task it was to interpret holy laws (Blass, 151; Schreckenberg, 1188) or to make sense out of an oracle.[20] The exposition of texts could be either moral or natural, or both. For example, figures in the epics could be seen as good (or evil) examples, or as representations of physical, social and metaphysical realities.

While this positive use of 'classical' literature was common in the educational process, it was not undisputed. In the sixth century BCE, Xenophanes criticized mythology for its immoral elements.[21] Accordingly, efforts were made to find acceptable, and indeed profound, meanings in Homer through the use of allegorical interpretations. These came to be carried out elaborately by Stoics and Neoplatonists.[22] Allegorical interpretation was facilitated by the belief—in good part justified—that poetry employs much symbolism.

Some, however—for example, a sophist in the fifth century BCE

18. See Marrou, Part II, Chapter 2 (as well as more recent overviews); thus also in the Middle Ages (Murphy, 136). Similarly, nowadays, the school subjects English, German, etc., cover both language and literature.

19. See, for example, Quintilian 1.5.17; 1.8.6; 10.1.28. For practice in writing, students paraphrased materials that were literary but not strictly poetic, such as Aesop's fables, aphorisms, and anecdotes (*chriae*) (Quintilian 1.9.3).

20. According to F. Siegert in Sæbø (131), this meaning of 'exegesis' led to one which designated 'some kind of demythologization according to the epoch's intellectual standards'.

21. Somewhat differently, Heraclitus objected to Homer's wish that conflict would vanish (C. Kahn, 204).

22. For the difference between Stoics and Neoplatonists, see below on Philo.

(D. Russell, 85-86) and Quintilian in the first century CE (*Institutes of Oratory*, 10.1.28)—believed that poetry was intended not for moral improvement but for pleasure. Epicureans especially, such as Philodemus (first century BCE), thought of poetry as mostly useless for either moral or factual knowledge. Still, Philodemus pointed out that literature does have, for both good and ill (!), some moral implications.[23]

The content, emotional effect and meanings of poetry were of deep interest to Plato. Like Socrates and others before him, he distinguished various genres: drama, epic, lyric, political speeches, laws, prayer, etc. (e.g. *Laws*, 700). In his middle period, he was unhappy about the moral character of epic and lyric forms and was ready to admit only 'hymns to gods and praises of famous men' into his ideal commonwealth (*Republic*, 607).[24] Later, he permitted and even encouraged poetry, but only with supervision and censorship (*Laws*, 653-54, 799, 817, 829).

Rather interesting in relation to religious issues is Plato's use of myths as an expressive form for contents that involve ultimates. A central category for the ultimate dimension was for him the soul, so that its eternity in both quasitemporal directions ('origin' and immortality) was an important theme in myths he created.[25] His argument that a story, not literally true, should be taught to citizens in order to give them a reason for their various roles (*Republic*, 414-15) embraced the role of foundation myths in societies. (The role of origin stories, including their relatively non-literal character, was known in the ancient world.)

Plato's followers treated poetry more positively than he. Among them, Plutarch (c. 100 CE) furnished a literary and moral defence of Homer without much reliance on allegory. He did so by elaborating the long-held view of poetry as a kind of writing that presents fiction, i.e. things not strictly true.[26] He argued that the depiction of interwoven good and evil has an educative value, for it furnishes both positive and negative examples and, further, underscores Euripides' point that virtue

23. G. Grube (196); Asmis and others in Obbink (27, 31, etc.).
24. Cf. Pappas (209-16) for details.
25. See especially *Timaeus* for creation, the *Statesman* for world cycles with their dependence, *Meno* for the soul's pre-existence, *Gorgias* for immortality, and *Phaedrus* for love and the soul's journey through the heavens.
26. See Pratt for Greek poetics (Hesiod, Plato [e.g. *Republic*, 377], etc.). According to Virgil (first century BCE), poetic truth aims not at 'material usefulness' but at 'the quality of human experience' (Perkell, 139). Theon (first century CE) characterized a *mythos*, 'fable', as 'a false story that resembles truth' (*Progymasmata*, Preface, 1).

and vice are always mixed together—contra Stoics, who idealize heroes.[27]

Plato's immediate student Aristotle both extended and modified his teacher's observations about literature, in the slender and incomplete *Poetics*. Like Plato (*Republic*, 393-94), he characterized poetry as furnishing 'representation' (*mimesis*), namely, the portrayal of a more-or-less typical human reality, not literal truth in regard to individual events. However, whereas Plato, at least in the *Republic*, feared that the dramatization of harmful emotions would strengthen them, Aristotle regarded their portrayal as allowing one to deal with them adequately.

Aristotle, in line with his concern for the forms that are shared by species, engaged in careful classification. He divided artistic genres by giving attention to three considerations: the medium or means used (language, rhythm, or a combination of these two), the matter or object presented (primarily, the social role of persons depicted), and the manner of presentation (direct in dramatic speech and action, indirect in narration, or mixed). Some of these variables cut across each other, so that the system of artistic genres exhibits not so much a hierarchical structure as a multidimensional array.

Typologies similar to Aristotle's existed both earlier and later (Donohue; O'Sullivan, 151). For the different poetic genres, some fairly elaborate rules emerged, especially in the Peripatetic (Aristotelian) tradition.[28] These were partially reflected in Horace's *Ars Poetica* (first century BCE).[29] Nevertheless, the inspirational element of poetry continued to be stressed.

A comprehensive system of classification was offered in the Coislinian Treatise (perhaps first century BCE, but probably much later). It listed both 'non-imitative' and 'imitative' genres. The first, 'non-imitative' group has as its two major subdivisions 'history' (covering all factual knowledge) and 'instruction' (divided into didactic and theoretical varieties). The other, 'imitative' (or 'representational') group includes

27. 'How to Study Poetry' (*Moralia* 14-37); similarly also pseudo-Plutarch, 'The Life and Poetry of Homer'.

28. Aristotle's *Poetics* was not widely known before the Renaissance, but that does not necessarily mean that it was without influence, for quite a few ancient ideas percolated anonymously and the Peripatetic school carried on his philosophy. Cf. below for his *Rhetoric*'s indirect impact.

29. Frischer argues that Horace's work is satirical rather than serious, but that thesis is quite speculative and does not represent the way the work was understood.

stories and dramas; the latter are subdivided into comedies, tragedies, mimes and satyr-plays.

4. *Rhetoric*[30]

The knowledge of proper speech became important in the fifth century BCE, when democratic forms of government arose in Sicilian Syracuse and in Athens.[31] With this development, lawsuits had to be addressed to large juries, and political speeches were needed to sway the assembly. The development of rhetorical theory was spurred by these practical ends, although display oratory also arose early in Sicily, especially since democracy was fragile and practical oratory was not always called for (Enos, 48-52).

Over the centuries, a number of technical terms evolved (cf. Lausberg; Martin). Recurring elements of thought became known as 'places' (Greek, *topoi*, with the singular *topos*, from which the English 'topic' is derived); the Latin phrase *loci communes* (English, 'commonplaces') later became current for standard themes in logic, theology, etc. The process of recognizing appropriate topics is called 'discovery' (*heuresis*, in Latin *inventio*). Elements of expression included the overall 'arrangement' (*taxis*, in Latin *dispositio* or *collocatio*) and 'diction', involving specific verbal patterns (*lexis*, in Latin *elocutio*). Different forms of expression were recognized as having 'appropriateness' (*prepon*,[32] in Latin *aptum*) for particular contents and for certain occasions or 'times' (*kairoi*).

Plato opposed a manipulative form of rhetoric, which was understandably dominant. He wanted rhetoric to serve truth and ethics, including self-criticism.[33] In part following him, Aristotle stressed logical aspects of rhetoric, although not exclusively so.

In accord with his interest in essential forms, Aristotle provided a thoughtful systematization of rhetoric. In this he gave attention to the

30. A number of rhetorical texts are partially translated in Matsen *et al.* Overviews by biblical scholars that can complement the present one have been furnished by B. Mack, Bullmore and R. Anderson.

31. The details of this development are disputed (cf. Schiappa) but not important here.

32. Already, Aristotle, *Rhetoric*, 1408a.

33. Cf. Ueding and Steinbrink (20). Kennedy (1994: 38-39) remarks that the high ideal did come 'at the cost of practical effectiveness', as is illustrated by the death of Socrates.

character of the speaker, the emotional reactions of the audience, the relevance and reasonableness of the argumentation, the choice of verbal patterns and sequential arrangement. He outlined three major rhetorical genres, related, as he said, to three kinds of audiences and exhibiting three different kinds of content. Specifically, forensic or legal speech is addressed to evaluators of past events and deals with justice; epideictic speech (praising or censuring someone) addresses observers of a person in the present and deals with honour; deliberative oratory (advice) speaks to persons about to make decisions regarding the future and concerns itself with what is useful or expedient. Each of the three major genres was divided by Aristotle in accordance with its mood, whether positive or negative: forensic speech includes accusation and defence; epideictic, praise and blame; advice, persuasion and dissuasion.[34]

Aristotle carefully considered the nature of topics (content) not merely as conventional matters, but as kinds of intrinsically persuasive arguments. He saw that certain topics are general in the sense that they can be used for various purposes, that some are particularly relevant for a certain genre without being ruled out for others, and that certain thematic aspects of one genre can be closely related to corresponding themes of another one. For example, the uses of maxims and comparisons are widely applicable; a word of counsel may be very similar to praise except for a difference in phrasing (1367b). He thus avoided rigid compartmentalization, although one of the difficulties of his analysis is its failure to allow adequately for transitional or mixed forms.

In subsequent centuries, Greek and Roman handbooks developed more specific rules for public speaking. Such rules could become unrealistically elaborate and rigid, especially in times when autocratic government prevented the extensive use of deliberative speech in practical affairs so that rhetoric became largely a matter for display. Quintilian (first century CE), however, insisted on the flexibility of rules (2.8).

In the third century CE, a rhetoric attributed to Menander gave

34. Aristotle's *Rhetoric* may not have had very much direct influence BCE, but it had an indirect one (R. Anderson, 41) and in major ways reflected a broad tradition. The *Rhetorica ad Alexandrum,* standing in the sophistic tradition which Aristotle partially opposed, had a seventh category, investigation, which is not restricted to any of the main genres. It may be noted that categorizations similar to Aristotle's are implied in Arabic systems of genre terms, which are heavily based on mood and reference point: self-praise, praise of others, praise of women, blame of others, confession of sin, admonition, lament over the dead, thanksgiving, etc. (see, for example, Ahlwardt, 31).

detailed attention to the relation between various types of speech and the occasions for which they are designed. It illustrated this connection by referring to the Jewish practice of gathering in Jerusalem for praise, probably drawing this information from Philo or Josephus, or perhaps from both (Russell and Wilson, 73).

5. *Types of Style*

Prose and poetry were not separated sharply but were often viewed as part of a continuum,[35] although what was called strictly 'poetry' was often restricted to what had metre. The presence of different degrees of poetic or artificial features within various kinds of speech led to theories concerning levels of style or 'types of speaking' (*genera dicendi*). A high style of speaking with much metaphor, rhythm, etc., was seen to stand close to poetry (Aristotle, *Rhetoric* 1404a). Quite a few rhetoricians—including Aristotle (*Rhetoric* 1404a) and Epicureans (R. Anderson, 51)—wanted to keep such poetic elements at a minimum within rhetoric. However, Aristotle recognized that poetic style enhances the emotional character of speech (1408b).

A major characteristic of poetry already mentioned is variation from standard language. Such variation is already apparent in word or sentence formations, often for metrical reasons (Quintilian 1.5.18; 1.7.14; 10.1.29). It takes place, further, in the use of what came to be called 'schemes' (Latin, *figurae*) and 'tropes'.[36] According to Quintilian's systematization, a 'trope' means an alteration of a word or phrase from its usual meaning (especially, metaphor); a 'figure of words' is a special verbal arrangement (such as rhythm or unusual syntax); and a 'figure of thought' form is a deviating thought such as question, irony and apostrophe (address of someone unreal or not present). Allegory was usually classified as an extended metaphor, sometimes as a figure of thought.

Typologies of literature and expression by stylistic criteria, it may be

35. See already Bethe and Wendland in Gercke and Norden (450), and again, for example, Enos (85). According to Proclus, the Grammarian (sometime during the second to fifth centuries CE), 'the virtues of prose and poetry are the same, but differ in degree' (D. Russell, 201).

36. Cf. the statement by De in regard to Sanskrit poetics, that a 'figure' (*alamkara*) 'connotes an extraordinary turn given to ordinary expression, which makes ordinary speech...into poetic speech' (1963: 23).

noted, are not unusual and were pursued, for instance, also in ancient India.[37] The Chinese Ssukung Tu (ninth century CE) characterized 24 modes of poetry on the basis of such criteria (Hymes, 29). In recent times, Joos has distinguished between the frozen (often written), formal (informational), consultative (informational with interaction), casual and intimate styles; his discussion revealed that the use of these styles is closely connected with variations in content and in the speaker's or writer's relation to the audience. Officially differentiated styles are characteristic of socially stratified societies (cf. Albert, 35-54).

Quite widespread in the Graeco-Roman world were descriptions of three kinds of style. These were repeatedly identified as high, middle or low in level. A little differently, a work of uncertain date (between 300 BCE and 100 CE) attributed to Demetrius presented four kinds of style that involve three levels: magnificent (high), charmful (mid-level), simple (low) and energetic (a form identified as independent of level).

As stated in detail by Demetrius (and more briefly earlier by Aristotle, *Rhetoric* 1408a), the level of style employed is to accord with the importance (in part, social) of the subject matter discussed. For example, a depiction of great battles or of heaven and earth is appropriately presented in magnificent form, but the description of a cottage calls for simple style (*On Style* 75, 190).

What are the marks of high style? For some, such as in *Ad Herennium* 4.8.11 (first century BCE), they are as much ornateness as possible. In line with such thinking, Demetrius assigned allegory, the most elaborate scheme, to magnificent style and an employment of proverbs and fables primarily to the charmful, intermediate style. Since allegory was thought to be a feature of high literature, it was natural that interpreters, including Stoics, would engage in allegorical interpretations of poetry that was held to be religiously and morally important, such as Homer.[38] Parallelism (especially antithetic in content,[39] sometimes simply in terms of a bipartite sentence organization) was accepted as the only major artful form in the simple style of Lysias (fourth century

37. Sanskrit poetics (from BCE beginnings to fairly modern times [De 1960, etc.]) has given attention to: (1) the different kinds of emotions evoked by literature; (2) figures or tropes; (3) style values (e.g. well knit, lucid, forceful, agreeable); (4) suggestivity (*dhvani*; cf. Vellanickal). Of these considerations, especially the second and third are similar to those of Graeco-Roman theories, but Indian analyses became considerably more elaborate.

38. Cf. Reventlow (1990: I, 38-43).

39. Thus already Aristotle, *Rhetoric*, 1409b (see Krašovec, 1-3).

BCE; Jebb, 166). It was not treated as especially characteristic of poetry, as was done later in biblical studies, but as one of the more ordinary figures.[40]

Nevertheless, opinions varied about just what constitutes the form and function of high style and, in general, how styles are to be used. Dionysius of Halicarnassus (first century BCE) considered 'grand' style to be 'austere'—unpolished, jagged and somewhat archaic, its opposite being 'smooth'. His own preference was for a mixture of the two (*On Composition*, 22-24). Seven major 'ideas' (forms) in style—clarity, grandeur (with the wide-ranging subdivisions solemnity, roughness, vehemence, brilliance, florescence and abundance), beauty, rapidity, character, sincerity and force—were described by Hermogenes (second century CE), without express reference to levels. His ideal was that these forms would be 'blended together' (225). Quite a few other rhetorical theorists also favoured, or at least permitted, mixtures and variations in style (e.g. *Ad Herennium* 4.11).

The style values expressed by Greek rhetors (speakers and theorists) had a relation to politics. In the early period of Greek democracy, orators such as Gorgias attempted to apply in public speaking the poetic style of the earlier aristocratic (Homeric) period. In the fourth century BCE, an effective but 'humble' prose style was used by Lysias, major philosophers and others. Demosthenes (in the same century) varied his style, while Aristotle took, on the whole, a moderate position in this regard; politically, both of these men stood between aristocracy and democracy. During the time of the Hellenistic empires, an elaborate sort of oratory flourished, but a number of theoreticians in the early centuries CE urged a style that is quite sparse, in an Atticism that venerated the past (Kennedy 1994: 230f.).

In Rome, a similar development took place. A poetic prose preceded the classic (sometimes fairly simple) oratory, which reached a high point in the final years of the republic near the turn of the era. Cicero (first century BCE), moderate in elaboration, placed primary emphasis on content and morality. He recognized the need for adjustment of style to both occasion and person (*Orator* 74), as well as to weightiness of topic (101), but he related variety in style especially to purpose: a plain style is appropriate for intellectual proof, a moderate one serves pleasure, and a vigorous kind 'moves', that is, it leads to emotional

40. E.g. Demetrius (22-24), on antithesis, and Dionysius of Halicarnassus (23, end), on parallelism in sound and structure.

persuasion (69).[41] A more highly ornate tradition for speech became widespread under the emperors. A faction that argued, in contrast to this, for a fairly simple style included the important first-century CE writer Quintilian. He did accept the need to consider, in addition to other factors, the social ranks of both the speaker and the addressee (11.1.43-45) in choice of style. His 'grand' style, however, was 'robust', or forcible, while florid style (traditionally aristocratic) was ranked as intermediate. It is likely that philosophical (especially Stoic and Cynic) opposition to autocracy was connected with a favouring of simplicity,[42] although no simple equation can be made.

During the Roman period, some Jewish influence appeared in a work that made only a small impact in its own time (c. 100 CE) but became influential much later. Entitled *On the Sublime*, it treated impressive or moving style without limiting itself to traditionally high literature. Among its examples stood the love poetry of Sappho. For proof that the source of profundity and impressiveness lies in mental power rather than in ornateness, the work cited, as one of two examples, Gen. 1.3: 'God said: "Let there be light" and there was light' (9.9).[43] The author did not want to limit style to the sparse Atticism favoured by Caecilius, a theorist with whom he was in conversation. However, he located the origin of current poor style in a 'craze for novelty' (5)[44] and in love of wealth, honour and extravagant pleasure, which leads to an acceptance of bribes and greed for the neighbor's possessions (7, 44). Notable emphases of the work include the emotional source of poetry and imagination as a part of mental vigour.

Certainly, Graeco-Roman and Judaeo-Christian traditions did not live in watertight separate compartments. Since, furthermore, they varied internally, it would be misleading to think of them as having

41. The style levels relevant to weightiness—low, temperate and impressive—were not the same as the kinds differentiated in regard to purpose, although there was a similarity between them.

42. E.g. Stoics favoured a simple style in rhetoric, as major republican leaders had done (Kennedy 1994: 91, 147).

43. This passage and some other parts of the work have affinities with Philo and Josephus (Arieti and Crossett, 57). The fact that Moses is described as 'no ordinary man' suggests that the author (or interpolator?) belonged to the same faith, unless he is simply falling in with Caecilius (who was Jewish) at this point.

44. D. Russell (in Kennedy 1989: 329) implies that a polemic against 'novelty' was common in rhetoric at that time.

each a differentiating 'essence'.[45] Their differences, and the differences between these and other traditions, are relative rather than absolute. Nevertheless, it is true that the Graeco-Roman contribution was especially strong in the realm of reflection, while the importance of the Bible lay in faith.

45. A denial of continuity (as again by Bloom) is typically based on an essentialism which envisions divergent 'essences' of each tradition; essentialism, however, is, if anything, more Greek (specifically Aristotelian) than biblical, so that this kind of sharp contrast, besides being incorrect, is inconsistent for anyone valuing the latter.

Chapter 4

EARLY AND MEDIAEVAL ANALYSES

1. *Early Biblical Interpretation*

a. *General Developments*

Jewish and Christian exegetes learned extensively from established rhetorical and poetic theory. They rarely did so slavishly, however. Attempts were made to create special categories for biblical material when to do so seemed necessary or appropriate. Neither the borrowing nor the originating of concepts appears always to have been successful in hindsight, but is it otherwise in modern scholarship? In any case, it is clear that many of the ancient interpreters understood the need for recognizing forms of speech, and saw both similarities and differences in comparison with other traditions.

In many of the rabbinic traditions, such as those preserved in the Targums, the Talmud and the Midrashim during the first millennium CE, literary typology plays only a limited role. That does not mean that they one-sidedly favoured particularity. Rather, they exhibit a strong sense for relationships.[1] The notion of relationality—as will be discussed more fully below (Chapter 7)—includes both generality and particularity; it is, however, more flexible than a notion of classes that is based on the idea that each class exhibits an 'essence'.[2] Within biblical literature, seen as a differentiated although connected whole, several major categories were identified, as follows.

Exegetical procedures distinguished, at least implicitly, between prescriptions and narratives, in that different rules came to be constructed

1. Handelman (39; for the Bible, 31).
2. According to Neusner (1991: 103), categorization in the Mishnah is 'polythetic', i.e. one that recognizes cross-cutting categories on the basis of divergent criteria; this is in line with relational rather than essentialist logic (cf. *RFT*). Again, according to Neusner (1994: 279-82), the later *Sifra* on Leviticus derived polythetic classification from Scripture. (Other rabbinic traditions varied in their use, or lack of use, of categories; cf., e.g., Neusner in Sæbø, 311.)

for the interpretation of these two major types of literature.[3] As is indeed appropriate, legal (*halakhic*) exegesis (like legal hermeneutics in general [Faur 1986: 89]) was more precise than the other (*aggadic*) kind.

It was obvious that large portions of the Pentateuch are laws or, more generally, directives. The application of them to current conditions thus had natural affinities with the work of the Greek 'exegetes', mentioned above. As Daube has shown, the rules for legal exegesis were, in fact, similar to those employed in the forensic branch of Graeco-Roman rhetoric. It was a fundamental principle in both traditions that laws are formulated in an illustrative manner and that cases not explicitly covered are to be interpreted by analogy or deduction.[4] This approach to the formulation of law appears to have been common in the ancient Near East, so that the Talmud's use of models, instead of abstractly stated principles (Steinsaltz, 228), was in line with ancient usage.

A number of distinctions were made within laws. For instance, offences against God were not identical with sins against human beings (*Yom.* 8.9). The organization of the Mishnah (c. 200 CE), in fact, to a large extent separates ceremonial from social regulations. Within the social, a division was made both in arrangement and in terminology between capital and monetary cases (*Sanh.* 4.1), one that was comparable to the Roman contrast between public and private law (cf. Cazelles [see below, 13.2.c]; Jackson, 183).

The differentiation between offences against human beings and those against God was not necessarily identical with, but was nevertheless related to, another classification of law, one that involved the question of its rationality. Specifically, talmudic and other traditions made a distinction between those laws—largely social in character—that would be valid without special revelation (*mishpatim*) and those injunctions (*huqqim*)—largely ceremonial—that represent a more-or-less arbitrary legislation specifically for Israel.[5] This distinction makes sense, for one

---

3.   Seven rules for *halakhic* (legal) exegesis were attributed to Hillel (first centuries BCE and CE); Ishmael's 13 rules are quite similar to them. Thirty-two largely *aggadic* rules were formulated by Aqiba's student Eliezer (second century CE). To be sure, the distinction between *halakha* and *aggada* was not altogether precise.

4.   The rabbis responsible for the Talmud, however, used formal analogy less freely than did Samaritans and Karaites (cf. Lowy; Nemoy, 246-48); they relied heavily on oral tradition in furnishing details not specified in the biblical text. For the use of analogy in the ancient Near East, cf. Fishbane (247-49).

5.   *B. Yom.* 67b; *Sifra* on Lev. 18.4. See, further, Urbach (365-99) for rabbinic

can argue that, in so far as rituals are symbolic, they can be arbitrary in their specific form. However, this classification according to rationality did not attain rigidity, and there were differences of opinion in regard to it. For instance, some held the view that all laws have reasons even though they may not be known (see Urbach, 311-99).

This issue was important also—and indeed especially—to Christians, since it is relevant to the question of universal applicability. Christians, from the second century on, distinguished in the Hebrew Bible between: (1) universally valid moral principles; (2) historically conditioned juridical rules; and (3) ritual prescriptions for Israel.[6]

Non-legal (*aggadic*) Jewish exegesis was designed to reveal the richness and relevance of biblical literature (Fishbane, 282). Procedures applied in it included some that involved mysterious elements—such as exposition on the basis of the numerical value of letters or treating parts of words as abbreviations. Processes of this kind were used widely in the interpretation of dreams and oracles (Lieberman, 70-75) and thus implied an oracular conception of the texts to which they are applied.[7]

More generally, Jewish interpreters recognized the use of figures of speech as a feature of non-legal style. This can be seen, for instance, in the fact that the Aramaic Targums regularly rendered a Hebrew metaphor either by turning it into an express comparison (with 'like' or 'is compared to') or by furnishing what was believed to be its meaning (for example, 'a strong ass', as a description for Issachar in Gen. 49.14, is translated 'rich in possessions').[8] In this manner, they treated as metaphors most of the biblical anthropomorphic descriptions of God—such as by translating 'mouth' by 'word'—although sometimes expressions which can be considered to be anthropomorphic were

tradition (which was not homogenous). (See also below, 4.2.a.)

6.   Thus, basically, Justin in the second century (Stylianopoulos, 56-66). At about the same time, the Gnostic Ptolemy, in his Letter to Flora, divided the prescriptions of the Hebrew Bible into those that are 'pure' (especially, the Ten Commandments), those that are mixed with evil (e.g. 'eye for an eye') and those that are symbolic (ceremonial prescriptions). The distinction between moral, historical-judicial and ceremonial laws continued into the Middle Ages (cf. Rogerson 1988: 70-71) and beyond (Diestel, 295).

7.   Already at Qumran, non-ordinary interpretation was applied to texts classed as prophetic (M. Maier in Sæbø, 121). An assumption that the Bible is cryptic was applied in Jewish (and Christian) interpretation also to narratives, etc. (Kugel 1997: 18).

8.   As pointed out by Churgin (81-87); Vermes (26-66); Grelot (93).

rendered literally.[9] Part of the targumic tradition, further, avoided indirect ways of expression such as questions and exaggerations,[10] thereby, too, interpreting rhetorical figures.

Some portions of the biblical text were considered to be specifically poetic. In fact, the Masoretes had a special cantillation system for Psalms, Job and Proverbs, and there was a tradition identifying a small number of biblical 'songs' in other books (Kugel 1981: 133-34), together with instructions on how such poetry was to be written in columns (Y. Green). The generic distinction between law and poetry was made sharply enough so that David (as the author of Ps. 119.54) could be held culpable for calling divine statutes 'songs'.[11]

Since Graeco-Roman tradition generally regarded metre as a sign of poetry, biblical interpreters looked for evidence of it (Gray; Baroway). Josephus (first century CE) believed that the Psalms are formed in metre, especially with trimeters and pentameters, and that the Song of Moses is in hexameter style. This analysis reverberated widely and was extended by further Jewish and Christian discussions. Since it was known that hexameter verse represented the standard metre of didactic poetry, this form was identified especially—by Jerome (c. 400 CE) and others—in wisdom and wisdom-orientated literature.[12]

For an interpretation of texts of all types, an apprehension of a holistic sense of the Bible and of reality, including the present, was crucial. (From a later perspective, one might say that discontinuity was not sufficiently recognized; modern views, however, may have exaggerated distinctions and tensions within the Bible.) Individual passages were viewed in relation to others in sacred literature, as was done in Homeric exegesis (Mayer, *RAC*, VI: 1202). Cross-referencing, accordingly, occurred extensively in the midrash and was prescribed in both legal and non-legal exegetical rules (cf. Heinemann 1971; Patte; Boyarin). *Derash*, going beyond an immediate sense of the text, had as its basic

9. The Targums do not appear to avoid anthropomorphisms out of embarrassment; rather, they translate them like other metaphors into their meaning (cf. M. Klein). Such a rendition assumes, of course, that the expressions in question are figurative. The Targums' procedure is an interesting way of handling metaphors, which are not always easily translated into the language of another culture.

10. Drazin (13). Exaggeration was expressly recognized as a style form, for example, in *Sifre* to Deuteronomy (Neusner 1994: 63).

11. Cf. Kugel (1990: 10) (without accepting his interpretation).

12. Josephus (*Apion* 1.40) described wisdom writings by a term that could be used to designate didactic poetry.

principle the relating of one text to another. Often, especially in non-legal exegesis, the interpretations given—which were multiple—were quite fanciful in detail (playful in execution),[13] but they seem to catch the spirit of the faith as a whole.[14]

Christians similarly observed all-embracing structures (Gorday, 35), with a prime focus, of course, on the New Testament. According to the formulations of Irenaeus (second century) and Tertullian (c. 200 CE), the few and obscure passages should be interpreted in the light of the many and the clear, on the basis of which, with the help of tradition, one can establish an overarching 'rule of faith'.[15] For Irenaeus, this 'rule' was not identical to any one formulation—such as with a single credal, ecclesiastically established form[16]—for the 'rule' did not have for him altogether specific concreteness, as apparently came to be the case for the more particularist and thus more concretely orientated Tertullian.

A culturally inclusive perspective, although without denying the importance of borders, appeared in the view of such Jews as were willing to acknowledge elements of Graeco-Roman tradition partly on the ground that Western wisdom had been derived from the Bible (Hengel, 166-71, 299-300; Fischel; Sterling, 218). Even more so than Jews, Christians were enmeshed in Graeco-Roman culture, with its literary, rhetorical and philosophical traditions; these features were taught in schools, which Christians did not change much when they obtained power (Schäublin 1992: 149). That culture was regularly tapped by educated Christian leaders and could be officially acknowledged as of value, although subordinate in its relation to theology (cf. Lampe).

The physical world, further, was not excluded from the Christian vision. For instance, the fourth-century Syrian theologian Ephrem celebrated in his hymns the symbolic whole formed by the Old and New Testaments in conjunction with nature (*De Virginitate* 20.28-30).

A holistic view of the Bible did not prevent at least some interpreters from recognizing the peculiar stylistic patterns of individual books.

13. Cf. Seeligmann (1953: 159-67).

14. Kadushin (ix, xi), well describes a half-belief of specific assertions within an organismic unity. By accepting a larger unity, ancient exegesis differed in its multiplicity (cf. Eskenazi) from free play (cf. D. Stern; Fraade, 16). For *halakha*, a variety of interpretations needed to be much more limited, of course, than for *aggada* (cf. Halivni).

15. Margerie (I.ii.a; II.i.a); Kugel and Greer (155-77).

16. Hägglund, 1-44; Young 1993: 48-60.

Individual styles were noted, especially in discussions concerning the disputed authorship of writings.[17] Clement (c. 200 CE) argued that the 'complexion' of the letter to the Hebrews is similar to that of writings by Luke; he thus credited Luke with translating it from an original in Hebrew by Paul. Dionysius of Alexandria (third century CE) showed differences in phraseology and manner of reasoning between the Gospel of John and the Apocalypse. Eusebius (fourth century CE) argued that non-canonical books differ in content and style from apostolic writings.[18]

Especially notable for the recognition of particularity is the fact that Jerome, besides referring to common biblical speech patterns (Schade, 84), pointed out distinctive stylistic features for a number of biblical books. He described Isaiah's manner of expression as urbane or elegant (relatively high), rather than rustic (relatively low). He said that this literary form, as to some extent that of other prophets, uses a style—employed also by some classical orators—which is not metrical but which uses short clauses like those of poetry. Jerome regarded 2 Peter as coming only indirectly from the apostle, because of its divergence in style from 1 Peter.

Despite such recognitions of individual differences, however, texts were not approached simply for the message they had in the past. Rather, interpreters saw operative in them transtemporal principles relevant for themselves.[19] Indeed, a transhistorical interpretation is needed by anyone who takes a text as more than a curiosity (Dawson, 237).

b. *Exegesis in the Time of the Empire before Constantine*
The first systematic interpreter of the Bible was Philo Judaeus (early first century CE). He was deeply steeped in Greek philosophy, rhetoric and poetics, but his primary conscious orientation was clearly toward the Jewish Scriptures, which he expounds (thus also Dawson).[20]

17. To be sure, Pope Gregory the Great (near 600 CE) could say that it is not important to know the writer's identity since in any case the Holy Spirit dictated the text (*Morals of the Book of Job*, I, Preface, 2).

18. Eusebius, *Ecclesiastical History* (6.14.2 for Clement; 7.25.24 for Dionysius; 3.25.7).

19. Neusner has described such principles as 'all time rules of society' (1989: 182) or 'laws of history' (e.g. 1994: 383).

20. Philo's background in regard to Greek philosophy, rhetoric and poetics and his dedication to Judaism (including a closeness to the midrashic tradition) have been discussed extensively in recent years. Philo had a definite impact on Christian

Within biblical narratives, Philo distinguished between accounts of divine creation and the history of human beings with a description of the rewards and punishments they receive (*Praem. Poen.* 1f.; *Vit. Mos.* 2.47). He divided Pentateuchal law into general and specific legislation. With regard to its style, he observed the use of exhortations, especially in Deuteronomy (*Spec. Leg.* 1.299), and noted a personal touch in the second-person form of address in the Decalogue (*Dec.* 36-39). According to his analysis, the Pentateuchal narratives form a framework for the law, so that God as Creator can persuade and exhort rather than demand as a despot (*Op. Mund.* 3; *Vit. Mos.* 2.48-51). He listed threats and warnings as additional forms of speech that are related to the others in function (*Praem. Poen.* 4). Thus the biblical genres were seen as complementing one another.

Philo reflected deeply (with the help of Platonic thought) on the dynamic structure of biblical texts. In his view the process of creation, as of final salvation, is beyond time; thus, details of creation stories, when taken in their most obvious sense, are 'myths' (*Leg. All.* 1.2, 43; 2.19; *Agr.* 97; *Deus Imm.* 32). In a number of narratives he saw an allegorical meaning in addition to a literal one, so that they have a practical applicability for the current reader; in fact, he appears to have been the first to propose more than one sense for a text.[21] For laws he discussed social and religious reasons, with attention to symbolic meanings, without discarding a literal view of them as rules to be followed (cf. Borgen, 261). Philo's allegories will appear arbitrary to someone not sharing his world-view, but they represent a special form of analogy (Christiansen; Reventlow 1990: I, 48) and assume that reality does not consist of isolated fragments (Bruns, 102).

The use of allegory reflected a combination of religious, literary and social considerations. As was mentioned earlier (3.5), allegory was regarded by many as a feature of high style. Height could have both religious and social significance, and it was not uncommon to merge these two considerations. In the stratified authoritarian structure of an empire, furthermore, there was little room for a practical political rhetoric. Thus, as has been mentioned, much of rhetoric under empires exhibited an ornate style, although there was also an opposing line, in

thought (Runia) and, less clearly so, on Jewish thinking (cf. below on Saadia).

21. Thus, Tobin (155, 172). Philo's *Questions and Answers* (perhaps early and exploratory) seem to accept the reality of a temptation by a serpent (Gen. 2.4, 14), although not necessarily that of other elements of the story.

part connected with opposition to despotism. Philo participated in the aristocratic ethos but also resisted it. For instance, the main examples he gives for the sin of stealing involve oppressive actions by an oligarchy, even though he was himself a member of an upper class (*Dec.* 136, 171).[22]

In its transtemporal character, allegory resembles typology, which matches events separated by time. Typology was practised in Alexandria by a number of Jewish interpreters other than Philo and perhaps already at Qumran,[23] as well as soon after Philo in the New Testament. Philo's outlook stood close to the typological approach by accepting both historical and present-applied meanings, as was not done in philosophical interpretations of Homer and Hesiod.

With respect to the philosophical tradition, Philo's predominantly Neoplatonic allegory was similar, but not identical to, Stoic allegory. Stoics thought of ideas that are represented by literary figures in stories as abstract representations rather than as real, since for Stoicism reality is composed of material particulars (although pervaded by *logos*); but Neoplatonism thought of ideas as ontologically real—even personal (as described by Bernard, 276). An individual figure, then, for Philo, had not only a concrete-historical but also a real-transtemporal dimension.

Neoplatonic tradition flourished especially in Alexandria. Accordingly, among Jews and Christians the most intensive and extensive interest in allegories was expressed by Alexandrians, especially by Aristobulos (second century BCE), still moderate), Philo, Clement and Origen. Clement (c. 200 CE) justified this approach by observing that both Greeks and barbarians, when speaking of divine realities, expressed them in symbolic and metaphoric terms (*Stromata* 5.4). A highly spiritual view of the New Testament, sometimes together with a quite literalistic one of the Old, was developed by Gnostics, who were largely concentrated in Egypt (cf. Pagels, 42-61).

Definitely less symbolic in his approach was Tertullian (c. 200 CE), a Roman lawyer orientated professionally more to rhetoric than to the poetics in which allegorical interpretation was at home. Although he accepted the presence of 'enigmas, allegories and parables' in the Bible, he defended a fairly literal position in regard to such issues as the resurrection, with the aid of Stoic beliefs in the particular and

22. He exhorted the wealthy toward liberality (Williamson, 207).

23. See Siegert in Sæbø (189-97), and Instone Brewer (194-95). For various kinds of typology and allegory, not clearly separable, see Young (1997: 148-213).

material character of reality (*Against Marcion* 3.5; *On the Resurrection of the Flesh* 26). Also in other respects, Tertullian was relatively particularist, especially (as is well known) in his making a contrast between 'Athens' and 'Jerusalem'.

Origen (third century CE)—the first systematic Christian exegete[24]— pointed to the presence of 'various tropes of eloquence and different species of speech', whose pattern one should observe (Gögler, 358-67). Among genres whose meaning is non-literal, he listed parables and riddles (as had been done by Justin, *Dialogue with Trypho* 77, in the second century). He could, of course, point to statements in the Bible in which figurative speech is explicitly mentioned, such as Ps. 78.2.

Origen interpreted as purely symbolic specific details of the creation and flood stories, concrete elements of eschatological visions (cf. Trigg, 132, 246), large parts of the Gospel of John and some of the prescriptions of both Testaments (*First Principles* 4.2f.; Homily 8 on Numbers, Commentary on John, etc.).[25] He pointed to Plato's use of myth and argued that such a form of presentation is useful for the 'many' who are 'simple' (*Contra Celsum* 4.39; 5.15; 6.2). In most parts of the Bible he found both a historical and an allegorical meaning. The latter is important, he says, since biblical writings were designed not to tell about ancient history, but for 'discipline and usefulness' (Homily 2 on Exodus). While Origen was gladdened by the presence of many simple persons within the Christian community, he was disturbed by their failure to discern the spiritual meanings which he found.

Origen regarded all Scripture as imbued with divine reality and sought to grapple with it as a 'single body' (*First Principles* 4.1.7; Comm. on John 10.107). According to his own report, he learned from a Jew to view Scripture as a coherent whole with many different compartments (*Philocalia* 2.3). As he saw it, each of the different parts—or genres—presents its own subject-matter with its special usefulness for the recipient (Torjesen, 124-30).

In line with his conception of complementary genres, he interpreted

24. During the preceding century, brief quasi-literary observations concerning the gospels had been made by Papias and Justin (see Dormeyer, 7-16). For an introduction to the writings of early Christian exegetes, see standard patrologies, theological encyclopaedias and histories of interpretation; recent studies are too numerous to be mentioned here more than selectively.

25. In taking creation and eschatological descriptions symbolically, he was followed by Eusebius and Socrates Scholasticus (Chesnut, 243).

the three books attributed to Solomon as representing three kinds of philosophy (as they had been listed, for example, by Cicero), from which the Greek 'sages', he said, have learned: ethics in Proverbs, physics (i.e. observation of natural existence) in Qoheleth and metaphysics (a higher 'vision') in the Song of Songs (Preface to the Song of Songs). These generic identifications were accepted by many subsequent interpreters.

In major ways following rabbinic tradition (Koch 1994; Hirshman, 83-94), Origen interpreted the Song of Songs as a profound drama that expresses an ultimate love. It is archetypal, he said, in that 'other nations have derived from this work the genre of the wedding song' (Homily 1 on the Song of Songs).

The similarity of the genres of biblical literature with those of other cultures was well-known. In the third-century *Teaching of the Twelve Apostles*, it was presented as a reason for *excluding* the reading of other literature, on the grounds that the Bible is sufficient in representing the various types.

c. *'Pagan' Interpretations*

As the Bible, together with Jewish and Christian interpretations of it, came to be known by other thinkers, a number of them provided their own assessments of that literature. Some of these assessments are known through Christian responses to them; thus they do not constitute a hidden line within the history of exegesis, although their point of view was rejected.

Celsus (second century CE), whose home was in Alexandria, was aware of allegorical interpretations of the Bible, including especially those of Philo. In a similar way—although more thoroughgoingly—he characterized such stories as those concerning paradise and Jesus' birth as 'mythical', that is, basically untrue; yet he thought that giving them a symbolic interpretation was better than taking them at face value. He was, however, unhappy about the content of Christian thinking and remained critical of anthropomorphic descriptions of God as they appear in the Bible.

Somewhat later, a writer familiar with Origen (who had responded to Celsus), in a work 'Against the Christians', scornfully rejected an interpretation of the Pentateuch as something that contains enigmas and oracles with hidden mysteries. (However, Porphyry [third century], with whom that writer has been identified, engaged in extensive symbolic interpretations of Egyptian and Greek traditions.)

In the fourth century, Julian (the second emperor after Constantine, 361–63 CE) rejected Christianity and described New Testament stories as wickedly composed fabrications. Concerning Genesis accounts, he said that 'unless every one of these legends is a myth that involves some secret interpretation, as I indeed believe, they are filled with many blasphemous sayings about God', since they attribute unworthy characteristics to God.[26]

Utilizing historical-critical procedures current at that time in classical studies, along with structural and philosophical literary analyses, these figures anticipated the major conclusions reached many centuries later by Jewish and Christian historical critics (see below, 6.1.g). They could do so readily since they stood in an inner distance from the biblical materials. This distance had an explicit social aspect, for they objected to Christianity's predilection towards, and popularity with, children, women and social 'sinners' (thus, Celsus) or toward the poor (thus, Porphyry [?], 'Against the Christians')[27].

d. *Greek-Language Christian Readers in the Fourth and Fifth Centuries*
Early in the fourth century CE, Christianity became first an officially tolerated and then an established religion in the Roman empire. Christians thus lost some of their hostility towards the larger society, which had been expressed either in direct opposition to it or in a spiritualistic world-transcending interpretation of the Bible. Fairly ordinary rhetorical analysis—in a number of cases exercised by interpreters who had been formally trained in rhetoric—became influential in exegesis.[28] Especially notable is the fact that commentators learned from pagan exegetes to pay attention to the aim (*skopos*, Latin *intentio*) of a writing, which shows the type of speech to which it belongs, such as ethical instruction or teaching about nature. A statement of this aim and thus of

26. See already Stein; on the question of Porphyry's authorship, R. Hoffmann (21-22).

27. Celsus spoke in part on the basis of observing, or hearing about, an actual popularity of Christianity with children—who were gathered by missionaries—and with women, and perhaps also with social transgressors, in part perhaps (such as in the case of trangressors) on the basis of what the biblical text said in relation to such persons. The charge of 'Against the Christians' was at least partially based on biblical texts.

28. Cf. Young (1997: 170-76—although without reference to the political side of this).

the genre, was often provided at the beginning of a commentary on a given text.[29]

The Psalms almost cry out for a treatment that is concerned with their major types; several fourth-century exegetes presented such an analysis. For instance—carrying forward previous suggestions—Eusebius (on Psalms, Introduction) argued that the terms *psalmos* (Hebrew *mismôr*) and *ode* (Hebrew *shîr*) referred to differences both in musical performance and in content. The *psalmos* is recited with musical background, while the *ode* is sung; 'if an allegorical view may be taken', he judged tentatively, the former is orientated towards the believer's works, while the latter is a meditation on divine reality. Such a classification was continued by Basil (Homily on Ps. 29 [Hebrew 30]), Gregory of Nyssa (*On the Titles of Psalms* 2.3)[30] and others. Hilary of Poitiers elaborated this typology, with attention to the combination of these terms and to other biblical genres (cf. Margerie, II.ii.a.4). Probably more important was another set of characterizations emanating from Eusebius. They formulated for each psalm its *hypothesis* (in Latin translation, *argumentum*), that is, its subject-matter or intended point. This was stated by means of one or two phrases that describe the central content or the literary type of the psalm, such as 'prophecy of Christ', 'accusation of the wicked', 'victory hymn', or 'the incarnation of Christ'.

Like Eusebius, but in greater detail, Athanasius provided a synopsis for each psalm, which states in general what happens within it: requesting, exhorting, praising, and so on. According to reflections he presented on the functioning and typology of psalms (Letter to Marcellinus), they act as a mirror in which one's own emotion can be perceived; if it is a negative one, it can then be healed or corrected. Even more, they furnish models by which feelings can be learned and are exemplars for the verbal expression of emotions. Athanasius went on to list the psalms by groups formed by the following features, singly or in combination: narration, petition, thanksgiving, confession, exhortation,

29. See Birt (170); Bultmann (1984a: 131); Kerrigan (92-93); Daniélou; Kennedy (1989: 332) (for Neoplatonic commentaries); and below on mediaeval interpretation. Not all aspects of exegesis are relevant in the present context, but D. Russell (in Kennedy 1989: 298) has observed that Christianity learned 'a technique of close reading', so that 'to read St. John Chrysostom's Homilies on the Pauline epistles can be uncannily like reading Hermogenes or Syrianus on Demosthenes'.

30. Gregory also examined the overall arrangement of the Psalter, following Graeco-Roman commentators in this procedure (Heine, 27).

promise, praise, thanksgiving and so on. In more general terms, many exegetes (including Gregory of Nyssa) distinguished between 'prayers' of supplication and 'hymns' of praise.[31]

Similar analyses were made during the same period in regard to other biblical writings. Ambrose developed a theory of the intent of different genres (to teach, announce, castigate, persuade, etc.) and observed in Luke the literary form of historiography.[32] Epiphanius of Cyprus identified ten types of speech within prophecy (Diettrich, 10). In the literal part of his exegesis, Cyril of Alexandria (early fifth century) paid attention to prophetic style, with changes in speaker and addressee; to processes of reproof, exhortation and encouragement; and to the use of tropes and figures (Kerrigan).

Without specific reference to genres, Macrina taught her brother Gregory of Nyssa a semi-literal view of the resurrection as a restoration of humanity's 'original state'. This came to be very influential in subsequent Christian theology.

Chrysostom (fourth century) spoke, in his *Synopsis of the Sacred Scriptures*, of denunciations, entreaties, exhortations and predictions by the prophets, as well as of their visions and of such forms as proverbs. Discussing in a commentary the 'value' of Isaiah, he said that the prophet 'pronounces the judgments of God with much boldness, rebukes sinners, and...comforts whoever is exasperated with sinners' (Introduction, ET by Garrett).

Chrysostom and Theodore of Mopsuestia (c. 400 CE), leaders of the school of Antioch, were educated both by the theologian Diodore and by the pagan rhetorician Libanius. The latter was devoted to a simple ('Attic') style, which suited his active involvement in political rhetoric—often as a champion of persons treated unfairly—in Antioch, where local leaders played a major role in governance. (Chrysostom could draw on this city's tradition in his concern for social service;[33] cf. Brändle,107.) In line with this emphasis on relative simplicity, and probably influenced by it, members of the school of Antioch favoured

31. Earlier, Origen (like some others) had based a typology on the use of four words for prayer in 1 Tim. 2.1 (*On Prayer* 14); he interpreted the second of these as including praise, while the others involve petition to meet one's need, intercession and thanksgiving.

32. On Psalm 1; introduction to Luke; cf. Pizzolato (97-158, 328-30).

33. In both sermons and commentaries, he championed the poor quite radically (Kelly, 97-99; Kertsch, 65, etc.; but he was very harsh toward Jews, well represented in Antioch [Kelly, 63-66], and was also, like many others, misogynist).

an assumption that elaborate stylistic figures, such as allegories, are used sparingly in the Bible. For instance, they accepted the serpent's speaking in the Garden of Eden as partly literal, in that Satan used the serpent as a vehicle (Froehlich, 90, 97). Symbolism in John could be ignored (Simonetti, 73). A formal consideration, however, could lead Theodore to a critical judgment which denied the historicity of a presentation; thus he regarded Job, which he compared in structure to tragedies, as fictional (cf. Schäublin 1974: 77-81). Both Chrysostom and Theodore paid close attention to the rhetorical coherence and style of biblical writings, such as of Paul's letters (Bultmann 1984a: 52-82; Gorday, 107-32).

Theodore held that the writings attributed to Solomon were based on 'wisdom'—human intelligence (presumably guided by God)—rather than on 'prophecy', i.e. direct supernatural revelation. This was one of the reasons why his work was condemned by a council in the sixth century, but the idea re-emerged later in Thomas Aquinas and was current in Jewish tradition.[34]

Hadrian (fifth century), who in large part stood within the Antiochene school, wrote the first work to be entitled an 'Introduction' to the Scriptures. As Jülicher has already noted, its emphasis was not on history, as in more recent works with such a title, but on rhetoric and didactics (1894: 8). Besides pointing to tropes and other stylistic devices, Hadrian outlined the literary types of the Bible. He distinguished between prophetic (revelatory)[35] and historical (that is, 'enquiring') patterns; the second kind is available to the senses and is thus relatively secular. Each of the two major types are subdivided according to the three aspects of time—past, present and future. Acting on the assumption that the three divisions of secular rhetoric according to these temporal dimensions (as analysed by Aristotle) are already known, Hadrian described the three revelatory ones in some detail. The prophetic past is illustrated by the account of creation, the prophetic present by Elijah's knowledge of Gehazi's sin and the prophetic future by predictions, including those of fulfilment in Christ.

In contrast to most of Jewish tradition but in common with most Christians, Hadrian placed the Psalms under the heading of prophecy.

---

34. See Jarick (308) and elsewhere in the present volume for Maimonides, Thomas and others.

35. That 'prophecy…reveals what is hidden', not just the future, was said also, for example by Gregory the Great (Schreiner, 41).

This was done since Christians commonly believed that the psalms refer to Christ or, especially, embody the voice of Christ as a representative either of God or, most frequently, of human believers.[36] In regard to the style of Psalms, he viewed them as having metre for singing purposes, while other prophecies (i.e. those in the prophetic books) are 'prose-poetry' (two words are drawn together) and wisdom literature uses recitational *stichoi* (extended rows). Apart from the question of rhythm, prophetic forms are seen to include ordinary speech, visions and symbolic actions.

e. *Latin Interpretations*

Soon after 400 CE, Pelagius, a British exegete living in Rome, presented a canonical analysis along generic lines, not very different from what was implicit in earlier conceptions (*Argumentum omnie epistularum* [Howlett, 56-65]). According to that view, the Gospels—which contain 'examples and precepts of living'—correspond to the Pentateuch of the Hebrew Bible, and the Epistles of the New Testament—providing exhortation directed to particular circumstances but of value to subsequent times—correspond to the Prophets, in harmony with a typical Jewish understanding of these.

Writing over a period of about two decades before and after Pelagius's work, St Augustine, bishop of Hippo in Africa, furnished a systematic treatment of the language of faith in his handbook *On Christian Teaching*. Largely (although not altogether) Neoplatonic in philosophy, he had taught rhetoric for 13 years prior to his conversion. At first repelled by the lowliness of the style of the Latin Bible, he came to accept its form of expression for two reasons. On the one hand, the spiritual-allegorical approach he heard expounded in Ambrose's sermons, indebted to Philo and Origen, implied the presence of profundity, which would be understood by the mindful. On the other hand, he saw in the 'humble genre of speaking' the 'holy humility' of Scripture, by which it reaches the lowly multitudes (*Confessions* 6.8; cf. Strauss, 33).

For several centuries, Christian theologians had stressed the need for a lowly style both in biblical literature, to be understood as a divine accommodation, and in sermons (E. Norden 1913: 521-32; Rogers and McKim, 9, 11, 18). Such a perspective resembled and sharpened the

---

36. See Rondeau. Such an identification was made less so by Antiochenes than by others, but Hadrian was not a pure Antiochene.

outlook implicit in the diatribe, a form of popular exhortation by ethical philosophers (especially, Cynic and Stoic) who sought to lead hearers to an ultimate goal, a divine 'end' (*telos*; Capelle and Marrou, *RAC*, III: 991-93). Indeed, it can be frequently observed that faith in a supreme deity (or 'high god') includes a concern for the lowly.

Aware of the role of 'holy humility', Augustine expressed ambivalence towards the employment of rhetorical training. Thus he took a median position in regard to the use of pagan education.[37] The prologue to *On Christian Teaching* defends the use of this on the ground that human beings have received the basics of their language on the whole from secular sources; it argues that what can be learned from human sources should be 'learned without pride' (5).[38]

In its arrangement, the work discusses first 'discovery' (content) and then style, according to a traditional sequence representing their relative importance. In a theoretical reflection, the content of the speech of faith is compared with that of standard rhetoric. For the latter, a central concept is 'the useful', which Augustine understood as the means to an end. In contrast to it, he said, stand things to be 'enjoyed', loved for their own sake (1.3-4), ends in themselves. What is inherently enjoyable is the Trinity, the foundation of all things (1.5). Within this realm, a central *topos* is love for all human beings (1.20-30). Other topics of faith include the Church, Scriptures, eternity and incarnation. (Burke, a modern theorist of rhetoric, has well discussed the role of the topics of beginning, end, evil, sacrifice, word, and so on in Augustine's system of speech.)

With considerable care, Augustine presented a theory of signs, with implicit allusions to the philosophical tradition. Specifically, he characterized a sign, which can be a word or a non-verbal object or event, as involving a referent beyond itself, called up in the mind of the recipient.[39] (This triple nature of a sign—with a vehicle, referent and

37. In 362, Julian had prohibited Christians from acting as instructors in public schools, the curriculum of which was focused on Graeco-Roman tradition. This brought about major Christian protests. However, in 398, when Augustine began writing *On Christian Teaching*, the Council of Carthage forbade bishops to read non-Christian literature unless it was necessary (Swearingen, 179-80). Relatively positive toward the use of pagan literature was Basil a few decades earlier.

38. Numbers here represent those found in the body of the translation by D. Robertson Jr (1958) and in the margin of the translation of the edition by R. Green (1995).

39. 'A sign is a thing which causes us to think of something beyond the expres-

perception—was later formalized by C.S. Peirce.[40]) Signs are treated as necessary, although they are not identical to reality (Rist, 40; Stock, 278).

Augustine's formal observations include a discussion of narration and description. It notes that these two categories overlap, since the aim of some narratives is to describe presently observable locations or objects (2.45). In regard to the question of whether a statement is figurative or not, the primary criterion for a true meaning is whether it serves love (3.23-24). (Similarly, the main aim of Buddhist hermeneutics in the *Vajrayana* was 'to accelerate the cultivation of compassion' [Thurman, 123, 125].) The hermeneutical rules of the fellow African Tyconius (fourth century) are treated as useful, though fallible, guides to biblical symbolism (3.42-56).

Finally, Augustine brought up rules of style forms reluctantly, since they are only a means to an end and should ordinarily not be focused upon consciously (4.4). Examples from Paul and Amos demonstrate the use of verbal schemes, such as a climactic sequence of phrases or sentences (4.11-20). However, eloquence is shown to be independent of elaborate tropes and figures; thus Jer. 5.30-1 is an example of an eloquent passage that is all the more powerful since it is 'pure' (4.30).

Citing Cicero, Augustine referred to two kinds of style differentiation. One is related to content: high style is appropriate for high-ranking content (4.34). The other involves function: a vigorous style serves emotional persuasion. Augustine in effect abolished the first of these two standards in favour of the second. Specifically, he said that in a sermon—which deals with the high topic of God—even an item that normally ranks low (e.g. money) becomes high because of its role in the service of God (4.35). Having thus levelled the topics, he used the term 'grand' as a label not for a style for weighty topics, but for an emotionally moving style (4.38, 54-55). This conception of grand style

sion the thing itself makes upon the senses. Thus, if we see a track, we think of the animal that made the track; if we see smoke, we know that there is a fire which causes it; if we hear the voice of a living being, we attend to the emotion it expresses; and when a trumpet sounds, a soldier should know whether it is necessary to advance or retreat, or whether the battle requires some other response' (2.1, ET D.W. Robertson Jr).

40. At the end of the nineteenth century, Peirce formalized relational philosophy and set forth a triple view of signs (see *RFT*) that is closely similar to Augustine's, as has been noted previously (Stock, 290 n. 107).

was not completely novel,[41] but it provided a line that became influential for later Christian theories (Shuger). In terms of its characteristics, Augustine viewed as the most essential feature of grand style, not ornamentation, but 'a violent spirit' (4.42). This emotional style is illustrated by Gal. 4.10-20, while the more intellectual Gal. 4.21-6 exhibits low style (4.39, 44).[42] Like others before him, Augustine, favoured a mixture of styles (4.56).

Augustine recognized a multiplicity of true interpretations,[43] which he viewed not as mutually contradictory but as unified (Margerie, III.ii.d). At one point, he furnished a 'literal' interpretation of Genesis 1–3. Even on this level, without allegory, however, he interpreted the time indications in the first chapter as metaphoric.[44]

The question of symbolic interpretation was of similar importance to others of that time. Among these, Augustine's slightly older contemporary, Jerome—already mentioned for his interest in metre and individual styles—engaged both in relatively literal and in more allegorical exegesis. Especially for the latter kind, he made use of traditional rhetorical characterizations of forms of speech, such as that of the enigma, a 'dark saying' with a not-immediately-obvious meaning (D. Brown, 147-48).[45] Eucherius (fifth century) presented a list of biblical metaphors, including references to God's eyes, human bones, the city of Jerusalem, numbers and so on.

In the sixth century, influenced in part by the school of Antioch, Junilius Africanus's *Of the Parts of the Divine Law* discussed four species of teaching. They are history (narrating the past), prophecy (making manifest the concealed), proverbs (using figurative or artistic style) and 'simple' teaching (dealing with the present in a straightforward manner, such as in Qoheleth and New Testament letters).[46]

41. Cf., e.g., *On The Sublime*, probably not known to Augustine.

42. In calling the 'moving' style 'grand', Augustine conflates Cicero's two distinctions (see above).

43. For others who did so in early Christian centuries and later, see Lubac (I/I.2.1).

44. Earlier, he had given a more allegorical interpretation of Genesis.

45. Kamesar (48) suggests that a reason why Jerome turned to the Hebrew form of the Bible was to see its literary quality in view of the fact that translations failed to fulfil Graeco-Roman expectations.

46. Cf. above for Origen, whose view of Qoheleth had become widespread. The Epistles of the New Testament could be placed into the same category, since they do not claim direct divine revelation (differently, the sayings of Jesus in the

Several streams that had moved in part independently during the fourth and fifth centuries in different parts of the empire flowed together in the commentary of Cassiodorus (sixth century) on the Psalter, which can be regarded as carrying out a well-rounded form criticism. Its introduction delineated the character of sacred literature as a whole (with reference to Augustine), the characteristics of prophecy as a subdivision of it, the 'special eloquence' of the Psalms (viewed as a kind of prophecy) and their falling into groups[47] (in part following Hilary). The work dealt with the Psalms' content, style and role in the Church's praise. It envisioned a dramatic form for many of them, with alternating speakers. For individual psalms, it noted the use of 'figures' and the rhetorical disposition or arrangement (the opening, the close, and the sequence of themes). Reflectively, it often observed aptness of content and style (Schlieben, 44).

Besides showing rhetorical and 'grammatical' (including poetic) characteristics of the Psalms, the commentary pointed out logical and mathematical features (such as the number eight [on Ps. 8, Conclusion] and a division of the Psalter into 15 [7 + 8] groups of 10), as well as other matters that were treated by the traditional arts, including music and astronomy (Walsh, 4, 15-18). In representing the thrust of Psalms, its preface mentioned 'the tongue of hidden powers which brings the proud low before the humble, subjects kings to poor men and nurtures little ones with kindly address', together with the expression of 'amazed reverence', 'the weeping of those who make lamentations' and announcements of salvation and judgment.

That salvation is centered in Christ was held to be indicated by means of allegory (a 'figure, which says one thing and means another' [on Ps. 7.1]). Yet, in Cassiodorus's view, the reference to Jesus Christ is sometimes so obvious that only 'the mad wilfulness of Jews' fails to recognize it.[48] Of these two Christian interpretations, the first (the allegorical) one is the more defensible, since it acknowledges that the meaning found is an indirect one.

Gospels were regarded as divine speech). Cf. Evans (32).

47. The membership of groups is not well identified (O'Donnell, 145), but seven 'penitential psalms' are identified (on Pss. 6, etc.).

48. On Ps. 88.27f. (H 89.26f.): 'He will cry out to me, You are my father... And I will make him my first born...'

f. *The Social Context and Significance of Early Interpretation: A Generalization*

Various connections between exegetical processes and their social contexts have been noted. Can a generalization be made? Cautiously, one can say that the interpretations that have been treated, which emanated from the educated elite, largely presupposed an aristocratic–hierarchical society. In such a society—as also in many simpler ones—communal order is valued more than it is in the bourgeois society which came later. A philosophical expression of this was Platonism, which had already been associated with the aristocracy in Greece.

This is not to say that the interpretations slavishly accepted the given hierarchies. On the contrary, there were significant Jewish and Christian countermoves, as there had been countermoves in Greece and Rome (e.g. by Stoics and Cynics and even within Platonic thought).

One aspect of hierarchization was male domination, with an attendant devaluation of women in most writings; in fact, almost all exegetes mentioned were males.[49] How this limitation affected formal analysis is a question not easily answered. Nevertheless, a few possibilities can be raised. Specifically, one can speculate that a one-sided focus on commonality such as was prominent in the early period—just like a one-sided attention to particularity that came later—is in principle male-centred, for either or both of two possible reasons. One is that men, as they have been bred and trained in society, may tend to be more one-sided than women.[50] Another is that, on the one hand, pure commonality supports domination, an imposed structure, while, on the other hand, pure particularity favours forceful competition, a role that fits males, who are not pregnant or lactating. It will be argued later (Chapter 7) that a balance between generality and particularity provides for greater equality, sexually and otherwise, than does either perspective alone.

A prominent feature of the interpretative process in Mediterranean culture as it moved from a traditional to a more reflective one (aided by writing, which had both positive and negative effects)[51] was the

---

49. For reports about premediaeval and mediaeval Jewish women exegetes, see Eskenazi. Some Christian women interpreters will be mentioned below (writings by them are preserved from the Middle Ages on).

50. This possibility is discussed in *RFT*.

51. Writing supported both domination and a high degree of reflection, sometimes critical of domination. Cf. Buss (1996: 88) and *RFT*.

employment of what can loosely be called 'allegory'. That this process was not merely a happenstance can be seen from the fact that it took place in Confucian China in a way that was similar to its role in a good part of Graeco-Roman and Judaeo-Christian interpretations. In both contexts, the approach retained old traditions but gave them a moral or metaphysical interpretation.[52] Continuity was thus maintained even as new moral needs were addressed and new intellectual possibilities were actualized. Explicitly, a text's allegorical interpretation was justified as a way of showing 'usefulness'.[53]

At the same time, the actuality of the past was not denied by Jewish and Christian interpreters. Rather, it was preserved in the idea of multiple meanings. If an allegorical interpretation stands by itself, without presupposing another literal one—as it typically did in Graeco-Roman exegesis—it suppresses a distance between the past text and its subsequent application (Nichols, 65). Early biblical interpretations did not obliterate such a distance, although they may still have underestimated it. Of course, the temporal and social distance of those interpretations from the biblical world was as yet not very great.

2. *Mediaeval and Renaissance Jewish Interpretation (c. 900–1600 CE)*

a. *Types and Functions of Biblical Speech*
In the tenth century, Saadia Gaon ushered in a golden age for Jewish philosophy and provided through his exegesis a foundation for much of later Jewish interpretation and, indirectly, for that of Christians.[54] A large part of his cultural background lay in Arabic linguistic theory and philosophy, which had been influenced by several strands of Greek (including especially Aristotelian and atomistic) thought. A further stimulus—both positive and negative—came to him from the Karaites,

---

52. According to Wan (176), the task of Western allegory was basically epistemological, while that of the Chinese was moral; but the moral component was prominent, and probably primary, also in the West.

53. Thus, Gregory of Nyssa for the Song of Songs (Dünzl, 57).

54. For Saadia's writings, see Baron (306-29); Simon (303-304). For bibliographical data regarding other Jewish exegetes, see, for example, the *Encyclopaedia Judaica* (1971). Recent European-language translations include those of Moses ben Naḥman (Naḥmanides) on the Torah (by C. Chavel, 1971–76), Tanḥum Yerushalmi on Joshua (by H. Mutius, 1983), Abravanel on Amos (by G. Ruiz, 1984), Abraham ibn Ezra on Gen. 1-11 (by Rottzoll, 1996) and of a number of works, in excerpts, by L. Jacobs (1973) and A. Berlin (1991).

a socially marginal group which rejected the authority of rabbinic tradition and sought to approach the Bible directly. Saadia defended the tradition against them, but he was undoubtedly prodded by this movement, as well as by the general Arabic tradition (grammatical and in part particularist),[55] to give careful attention to a simple or 'plain' meaning of Scripture (the *pešaṭ*).

For his exegesis, Saadia stayed largely within an ordinary sense of the text, but this includes the use of figures of speech, which he examined in considerable detail (Commentary on Job, Introduction and *passim*; cf. L. Goodman). One (although by no means the only) motivation for his apprehending of figures was that he would be able to identify their presence whenever the most literal meaning goes against reason or experience. (This is an instance of 'charitable' interpretation, a process that is normally adopted in human communication; it makes the assumption that the person whose words are being heard or read is trying to make reasonable sense).[56] For instance, he interpreted in a figurative way anthropomorphic descriptions of deity and the speaking of animals (Bacher 1892: 50; Zucker, xv), in opposition to what was said in a number of Graeco-Roman and Muslim critiques of the Bible (Lazarus-Yafeh, 30-31, 136-37). Furthermore, he paid close attention to the way in which both small and large sections relate to one another and to what aim they are directed (Rosenthal, 88, 100, 116-18).

Saadia took careful note of the genres of biblical literature. He did this systematically in introductions to different parts of the Bible, in his *Book of Beliefs and Opinions* (3.6) and in a work (largely lost) which presented grammatical, rhetorical and poetical observations together with a list of Hebrew words according to beginning and ending letters as an aid to alliteration and rhyming.

In the Bible, he recognized three major types of speech—commandments, announcements of consequences and narratives—each with a positive and a negative aspect. In a manner somewhat reminiscent of Philo's analysis, he described the literary types as parts of a united whole; within this, the commandments are central, but narratives constitute the most effective means of inculcating obedience to God (Introduction to the Torah). He went on to outline the functional

55. Holtz (220), Rottzoll (xix) and others point out that the *peshat*, ordinary sense, was emphasized only after contact with Islam. For a brief report on Muslim thought, see below, 4.3.c.

56. Halbertal (27-32), following a philosophical tradition.

contribution made by each of several specific Pentateuchal genres, such as travelogues.

In one of his prefaces to the Psalter (ET Sokolow), he discussed 18 forms of speech. These include questions, commands, narrations by a divine or human voice about the past, present or future, and prayers by individuals or groups. He saw that the Psalms are cast for the most part in the form of speech to or about—rather than by—God, but he did not think of them as having emanated from human beings who wished to express their feelings. Instead, he held that they were revealed by God for spiritual and moral instruction and as guides for praying; they are thus models or prototypes, not now to be used as actual prayers.[57] In the temple in biblical times, he believed that they were sung by a definite class of people (such as a division of the Levites), at a certain place and time within worship (in the morning, at a particular festival, etc.) and in a specified manner (such as with a given melody). This analysis—with its focus on speech types, models and circumstances—exhibits important elements of a form-critical approach.

Within the book of Proverbs he identified 12 groups of sayings. One contains proverbs that are stated descriptively, but are meant prescriptively (e.g. Prov. 16.12); another, proverbs that contain comparisons (e.g. 27.9).

One aspect of form-critical analysis is to note the connection of texts with life. It can be stated not only in terms of occasions but, perhaps even better, in terms of purposes or functions. Saadia indeed held, like rabbis before him (see above), that especially the social laws of the Bible have intrinsic (non-arbitrary) and thus rationally statable human functions (*The Book of Beliefs and Opinions* 3.2).[58] In fact, Saadia found in 'most' ritual laws 'partially useful purposes', even though it is not necessary that there be such (*The Book of Beliefs and Opinions* 3.1. end).

Procedures similar to Saadia's were carried out soon after him by

57. In opposition to the Karaites, who advocated the use of biblical psalms in synagogue worship, Saadia sanctioned the 'reading' but not a 'praying' of biblical psalms. (See the discussion in Simon, 1-11, which, however, fails to bring out the fact that Saadia viewed the psalms as guidance for prayer.)

58. Cf. above, 4.1.a. Fox (126-29) denies that 'natural' law is held in the Hebrew Bible and by Saadia, since he defines 'nature' in a certain way and describes reason as 'unaided'; in terms of the conceptualizations adopted he is right, but even less applicable to Saadia is the conception of God as a despot (as Fox, too, rightly indicates [129]).

Karaite commentators, in part influenced by him and in part carrying on their own tradition. Qirqisani spoke of 'the perfection of the whole of Scripture in the way of account, address, statement and question, relating to fact, metaphor, generalization, advancement, postponement, abridgment', etc. (Nemoy, 59). Yefet ben 'Ali and Salmon ben Yeruḥam paid attention to the rhetorical genre of texts—such as with a thrust to explain, exhort, or disapprove—and indicated the dynamic movements by listing the lessons to be learned and thus the values to be gained by the reader (Vajda, *passim*; Nemoy, 86; Beattie, 48-49). They believed that the Psalms provided instruction in praise and exaltation, showing the 'laws' of prayer and furnishing some precise wordings to be used, especially in ritually obligatory prayers (Shunary, 159; Simon, 61-64, 73).

The apex of mediaeval Jewish philosophy was reached in the latter part of the twelfth century with Moses ben Maimon, or Maimonides. His view was in good part Aristotelian, as can be seen in his definition of species as a 'universal [i.e. general structure] which includes a number of individuals and constitutes the essence of each of them' (Efros, 51). Maimonides believed that the Hebrew word for such an essential form was *tselem* ('image'), while *to'ar* refers to external appearance (*Guide for the Perplexed* [written in Arabic] 1.1).

Maimonides' interpretation was not highly literal but instead analysed experiential and social processes, which are relevant to a form-critical analysis. In his view, divine revelation came to prophets in dreams and visions in which they heard or saw symbols of truth. Thus he held that certain narratives, such as stories of prophetic actions and about angels, represented visionary rather than actual occurrences (2.46).[59] Further, he argued for the presence of metaphoric speech in the creation account and in many other contexts (2.30, 47) and—as had already been done by a rabbi in the third or fourth century (*b. B. Bat.* 15a)—considered the book of Job to be a fiction (3.22). Such critical reflections, however, were not intended to be presented to 'the multitude of ordinary people' (Introduction; 1.17). His outlook thus had an elitist dimension, although Aristotelianism is on the whole less elitist than Platonism.

Taking a functional view, Maimonides focused on the purpose of the book of Job and, more extensively, on the purposes of Pentateuchal

---

59. He was anticipated (probably, influenced) in this by Abraham ibn Ezra's view of this kind concerning Hosea's involvement with Gomer (Lipshitz, 2).

laws and narratives. Laws, he said, aim at the welfare of body and soul, including as a purpose that of social cohesion (3.27, 49; Twersky 1980: 443-47). More so than most of the rabbinic tradition and Saadia, he believed that all laws have reasons, although these may not be obvious (3.26). That does not mean that the laws could have been known without revelation.[60] Rather, the point is that God exercises 'wisdom', not merely a purposeless will (3.26). He cited in support biblical passages which describe God's statutes as 'righteous,' or 'right' (Deut. 4.8; Ps. 19.10). In this sense, he could say that 'there is nothing as rational' as the scriptural commandments (Sáenz-Badillos, 71).

The structure of the canon was very clearly related by Maimonides to different kinds of revelation. While the prophets other than Moses received truth through dreams and visions, God spoke to Moses in the Torah directly, without 'imagination' (i.e. the use of images, which he considered to be characteristic of prophecy).[61] The Torah presents (general) law, but the prophets give (particular) exhortations.[62] Unlike both of these bodies of material, the Writings by David, Solomon, and so on, were inspired—moved in normal consciousness—by 'the Holy Spirit' (2.45). This theory of the canon was not new, but it led him to view the Psalms not as divinely revealed models (contra Saadia) but as truly prayer, directed from human beings to God (2.45).[63]

Among the defenders of Maimonides—controversial in some circles—stood David Qimḥi (c. 1200 CE). He characterized prophecies as 'critical instructions' or 'consolations' (Introduction to Isaiah; on

60. When Maimonides rejected the view of Mu'tazilite Muslims that some laws (especially the social ones) are 'rational' (Twersky 1972: 378), he probably had in mind their belief that those laws can be known through reason alone (Faur 1969: 301). Traditionalist, or 'orthodox', Muslims held that 'all duties are grounded on divine fiat alone' (Faur 1969: 303). Maimonides rejected that position, in this respect agreeing with the Mu'tazilites.

61. For details, cf. McKane (23-41) (but it is not appropriate to say that Maimonides 'excludes supernaturalism' [39, 41] merely because he gives an intellectual account of revelation).

62. This view allowed him to explain the directions of Ezekiel 46, diverging from the laws of the Talmud, as an 'exhortation' applying to a future moment (*Mishneh Torah*, VIII, treatise 5, ch. 2, §14, perhaps in line with earlier, less clear, interpretations).

63. A similar view of Psalms was held by Abraham ibn Ezra and was implicit in some earlier rabbinic and Karaite traditions (Simon, 82 [with n. 55], 187-216; Simon's judgment that Moses ibn Giqatilla denied an influence by the Holy Spirit [129] is based on less-than-clear indirect evidence).

Hos. 1.1; etc.) and described some of the psalms as commending, exhorting, making a comparison, and so on (e.g. Pss. 120.4; 128.1; 135.5). He made observations about figures of speech and sound patterns (Talmage, 106).

During the thirteenth century, a mystical tradition—in a broad sense Platonic, but also influenced by Maimonides—emerged in strength. This tradition tended to view the literary form of the text as an external feature, a garment which clothes the true meaning (e.g. the Zohar, 3.152a, described narratives as a covering for divine precepts)[64] and strongly stressed a symbolic interpretation. Its strength lay in pointing to what can be called the mythical aspect of biblical literature, including the theme of origin. For instance, Moses ben Naḥman recognized the protological character of Genesis stories, in that they deal with the creation of the world and treat the patriarchs as representatives of their offspring, 'as a kind of creation of their seed' (Introduction to Exodus).

The mystics were not antirational.[65] Rather, one of their interests lay in showing the wisdom, including purpose, underlying the laws, so that they would not be obeyed simply servant-like (Abraham Abulafia).[66]

The allegories set forth in mystical exegesis could be viewed as dangerous for the ordinary believer (e.g. by Baḥya ben Asher, c. 1300 CE, Introduction to the Pentateuch). A fundamental assumption, however, was the unity of the Bible; thus, Abraham ben Isaak ha-Levi Tamakh (fourteenth century) made explicit in his introduction to the Song of Songs that the occult interpretation harmonizes what is said in the Song with its larger scriptural context.

A rational functional perspective with less mystical overtones was prominent in the work of two fourteenth-century interpreters. Joseph ibn Kaspi, conversant with Arabic thinkers, held that Scripture was written in a way that appeals to the literal-minded masses in order to support political stability (*The Silver Goblet*, 152, 154a; cf. Herring). Levi ben Gershon (Gersonides), treated the book of Job as a philosophical dialogue (in many ways as Maimonides had done). For other biblical writings, Gersonides listed at length the lessons to be learned, treating characters as models for good and evil. He denied the literal

64. Similarly, Segal (24), for allegories in general.

65. On 'philosophical mysticism' in Islam and medieval Judaism, see Blumenthal.

66. Abraham Abulafia also said that Hebrew, unlike other languages, 'is not the result of convention'. See Idel (11, 55, 110).

character of time indications in the creation stories (Staub) and—in accordance with a suggestion made tentatively by Tanḥum Yerushalmi (thirteenth century)—believed that the statement that the sun stood still (Josh. 10.14) metaphorically expresses the speed and comprehensiveness of Joshua's victory.

Functional reflection continued in the fifteenth century. Providing a reason not for the details of ritual but for the fact of ritual, Isaac Arama argued that animal sacrifices serve to integrate repentant inadvertent sinners (Gate 55 in his commentary on the Pentateuch).

Especially noteworthy analyses of the purposes of biblical contents were made by Isaac Abravanel (c. 1500 CE). He furnished extensive treatments of social and political elements of biblical literature, with a critique of monarchy (on Deut. 17.15). In his exegesis, he regularly stated the 'intention' or rhetorical force of larger or smaller sections (such as, for Amos 4.1-6.14, to criticize).

Like others before him,[67] Abravanel believed that poetic portions of the Bible—even if they occur in the Pentateuch and the Prophets—were not given by direct divine revelation (such as in a dream) but were inspired by the Holy Spirit under conditions of normal human consciousness.[68] This meant, contrary to some other views,[69] that poetry is not especially close to prophecy but that the revelatory character of all biblical poems is similar to that of the materials in the third division of the canon, which are often poetic.[70]

Abravanel was more ready than Maimonides had been to believe that items reported happened literally (Reines, xxiii, 96). For instance, among reported prophetic symbolic actions, he interpreted non-literally most of those actions that are reported in first-person speech by the

67. See above, 4.1.a, and Simon (80) for Yefet ben 'Ali.

68. Commentary on Exod. 15 (A. Berlin, 127; cf. Cooper, 160).

69. In Jewish tradition (according to D. Pagis in Kugel 1990: 140-50), *non-biblical* poetry was associated with (non-Israelite) prophecy, apparently on the basis of a far-flung tradition concerning the relation between poetry and prophecy (see below, 4.3.a). It seems, further, that at Qumran Psalms were treated as prophetic (Maier in Sæbø, 122, 126), and Christians often classed Psalms as prophecy (see above, 4.1.d, for Hadrian).

70. On this, cf. Malherbe (38, 51). A little earlier, Shem Tov ibn Falaquera (thirteenth century) had placed the poetry of Exod. 15 and Deut. 32—'prophetic', since it is in the Pentateuch—higher in revelation than Wisdom writings 'composed through the Holy Spirit'. Abravanel, however, seems to have regarded the poetic form of Exod. 15 as (merely) 'inspired'.

prophets themselves (they may represent inner experiences), but he accepted as actual events those that are reported in third-person speech by others (cf. Bitter, 91; similarly, although calling on style rather than on experiences for explanations, Buss 1969: 53).

In 1573, Azariah de' Rossi gave expression to the central principle of form criticism: 'the *words* of the poem must be correct for the *voice* [content, including especially mood], just as the voice must be correct for the required *occasion*' (italics supplied; A. Berlin, 150). A major question raised by this statement is, what is meant by 'correct'? Is it merely an arbitrary convention, or are there intrinsic connections? As we have seen, Jewish thinkers discussed biblical texts partly in terms of their social functions (thus there would be intrinsic connections) and partly in terms of God's free will for Israel. It is likely that Azariah had in mind at this point intrinsically appropriate correspondences.

b. *Grammar, Rhetoric and Poetics: Special Observations*
As a part of literary analysis, the study of Hebrew grammar developed by leaps and bounds. Obviously, Jews had known since biblical times how to speak Hebrew, but only from the tenth century on were the rules of the language systematically formulated. At first, features of style were not sharply distinguished from those of grammar or lexicography; for instance, metaphoric meanings could be included in a dictionary. Yet gradually the different aspects of language came to be treated separately.

In regard to anthropomorphic language, Judah ibn Quraysh (c. 800 CE) adapted the adage of Rabbi Ishmael (second century) that Scripture 'speaks in human language'. In older use, the formula had referred to the grammatical construction in which an infinite absolute precedes a finite verb.[71] Judah and others after him used the adage to justify a metaphoric interpretation of anthropomorphic descriptions on the grounds that these state the reality of God in human language (Bacher 1902: 167; Hirschfeld, 25).

Responding to advances in linguistics, a number of major mediaeval commentators placed their primary emphasis on basic grammar; yet they gave attention also to coherence and style. For instance, Samuel

---

71. See *b. Ber.* 31b; *Sanh.* 90b; *Keri.* 11a; *y. Ned.* 36c, with several examples; *Sifre* to Num. 15.31. The fact that this grammatical construction became rare in late biblical and Mishnaic Hebrew (Polzin 1976) may have contributed to Aqiba's literal interpretation of it, which the saying rejects.

ben Hophni (c. 1000 CE) pointed out persuasive devices in Judah's speech to Pharaoh (Gen. 44.18-34) and formulated the rule that in the Torah the sequence of presentation can be ignored (Sarna 1993: 24). Solomon ben Isaac or Rashi (eleventh century) pursued the coherence of texts largely in terms of their content, filling in missing details with the aid of rabbinic lore; occasionally (e.g. in his introduction to the Song of Songs), he made reference to stylistic features. His grandson Samuel ben Meir (twelfth century) showed a 'profound sensitivity to form' (Japhet and Salters, 48-49) in noting literary features (such as repetition and anticipation [on Gen. 1.1]) and the units of a discourse. Following in part in the footsteps of his grandfather, he outlined the 'ways of Scripture', that is, grammatical and stylistic patterns, including those that involve the organization of passages (M. Berger, 77, 83).

Abraham ibn Ezra (early twelfth century) listed five methods of exegesis: (1) expansive commentation (e.g. by Saadia), which—resembling some of ancient Homeric exegesis ('leading out,' see above, 3.3)—discusses not merely the words of the text but the subject-matter presented by it; (2) the Karaite procedure, which ignores the oral *halakhic* tradition of the Talmud and tries to understand the Bible without its aid; (3) fanciful allegorical interpretation; (4) free-wheeling, often mutually contradictory, midrash; and (5) grammatical interpretation. He accepted as valid only the last of these five. It included for him (as in the normal use of 'grammar' at this time) attention to stylistic features, such as word economy, chiasmus, resumptive repetition, irony, metaphor and moderate allegory.[72] Sometimes, although sparingly, he provided brief characterizations of genres. For instance, he pointed out relationships between the parts of a book and observed that Isa. 40 'comforts', while Isa. 59 'reproves'.

Analyses that focused on the literal or 'plain' meaning of the text raised questions which involved interpreters in problems of historical criticism, since on that level there appear certain tensions in the text, or contradictions, which, in fact, had been noted by pagans and Muslims (Lazarus-Yafeh, 28-29, 135-39). Thus, during the eleventh and twelfth centuries theories with at least a mild criticism of traditional historical views arose.[73] For the most part, however, difficulties encountered in

---

72. Sarna (1993: 12); Gómez Aranda (xxxxvi-lvii). Strickman (xvi-xvii) lists a number of stylistic observations by Abraham ibn Ezra, although without references to their occurrence.

73. Judah ibn Balaam and Joseph Bekhor Shor envisioned multiple traditions

the text were solved through an appeal to assumed Hebrew rhetorical usages—such as ellipsis or a readiness to deviate from temporal order (Sarna 1971: 346; 1993: 10-11). For legal interpretation, midrash (looking to the interlinking between texts and valuing tradition) remained normative.[74]

Several writers furnished systematic analyses of rhetoric and poetry. Jonah ibn Janaḥ (eleventh century) dealt with metaphors and other tropes both in his grammar and in his dictionary. Moses ibn Ezra (c. 1100 CE) wrote a significant work on Hebrew poetry and rhetoric, in the last chapter of which he listed a large number of stylistic devices, including metaphor, allusion, comparison and hyperbole. Like Saadia, he denied that metre is to be found in the Bible, but he explicitly regarded Psalms, Job and Proverbs as poetic (as the Masoretes had done implicitly) and noted deviations from ordinary prose in other biblical books. He could even say that 'prophet' is the Hebrew word for 'poet', although he certainly did not mean to imply that biblical prophets are 'only' poets (Heschel 1962: 387).

Judah ha-Levi (twelfth century) accepted the presence of songs in the Bible, but reasoned that the Scriptures rejected metre in order to permit the recitation to follow closely the meaningful rhetorical pattern marked by Masoretic accents. These, according to him, indicate either a pause or a continuation, and distinguish question from answer, the beginning from the body of speech, haste from calm and command from request (*Kuzari*, 2.70-73; cf. Cassel 1922: 172-73).

A number of other interpreters discussed the nature of poetry in the Bible (A. Berlin, 87-162). Saadia characterized a considerable portion of biblical literature as 'poetic prose' (Cooper, 150). The majority opinion was that biblical poetry was not strictly metrical, for, as Samuel ibn Tibbon (twelfth century) pointed out, poetic conventions vary.[75] Several writers indicated that there are levels or degrees of metre and that flexible ones are present in biblical literature, so that some of it

for the Decalogue or other Pentateuchal materials; Isaac ibn Jashush, Moses ibn Giqatilla, Joseph Kara and Abraham ibn Ezra raised questions about the date of texts (Bacher 1894: 260-66; 1902: 167-69). Whether special sociological conditions (an urban situation or involvement in trade—notable in connection with later advances in historical criticism) favoured such a development remains to be investigated.

74. See Lockshin and cf. above, 4.1.a.

75. For the (different?) view of Josephus and some others, see above.

could be sung.[76] At least two noted that in Aristotle's conception poetry is not strictly identified by linguistic form; in that light, it is possible to see that the Song of Songs is truly poetic since it is designed to 'glorify the exaltation of its subject and to draw emotions to the truth of its content' (Moses ibn Tibbon [ET Cooper, 156]; similarly, Abravanel [Cooper, 159]). In 1573, Azariah de' Rossi came to characterize the 'metre' of biblical poetry as one that is based on 'ideas' or semantic units. He observed that this feature is translatable.

Parallelism as a repetition or resumption of thought or structure was recognized as a stylistic device in varying degrees by Saadia (Ecker, 337), Jonah ibn Janaḥ (Bacher 1889: 39), Moses ibn Ezra and others.[77] None of them regarded it as specifically poetic, in distinction to rhetoric. After all, parallelism was viewed in ancient theory as one of the most prose-like of artificial forms of expression.[78] Joseph ibn Kaspi (early fourteenth century), however, made a careful analysis of antithetic parallelism in Proverbs, one of three books given a poetic cantillation by the Masoretes.

Judah Messer Leon presented, in 1475/76, a systematic rhetoric illustrated by examples drawn from the Bible.[79] This work, *The Book of the Honeycomb's Flow*, was based on the conviction that the sacred writings stand in continuity with other literature but surpass it in excellence and can serve as models.[80] In a classical Graeco-Roman manner, its analysis covered types of speech, kinds of reasoning and stylistic tropes.

In sum, mediaeval and Renaissance interpreters included in their work reflective literary analysis, using procedures and concepts drawn from rhetorical and poetic traditions and giving consideration to social functions. They did so, clearly, in order to understand the text in its

76. Moses ibn Tibbon, thirteenth century; Moses ibn Habib, Isaac Abravanel and Yohanan Allemanno, fifteenth century and beyond.

77. Kugel (1981: 173-78); A. Berlin (72, 76, 78); Magonet (17-18).

78. See above 3.5, on Lysias (and already Buss 1974: 10, 17, with a reference to Heschel 1962: 375, leading back to earlier reports—apparently missed by Kugel 1981, who, however, saw that mediaeval writers thought of parallelism as less than poetic [132]).

79. The work is not arranged as a commentary; but an index (as in the edition and translation by Isaac Rabinowitz, 1983) makes the work readily usable as an exegetical resource.

80. The work thus allowed for interaction with classical non-Jewish rhetoric (Tirosh-Rothschild, 232).

significance for life. Unlike what was beginning to happen in Christian and secular culture (to be discussed soon), they did not—at least not yet—adopt a particularist position that stresses pure arbitrariness and thus potentially creates a gulf between past and present. Particularity was important for Judaism, but it was balanced by attention to generality, a belief that beings share something and do not stand in isolation. Aristotelianism, championed by Maimonides, moved towards providing a balance, but it retained a traditional rigidity in its idea of essence.

3. *Literary Patterns in Mediaeval Christian Exegesis*

a. *Rhetorical and Poetic Considerations*

Christian thought of the Middle Ages was deeply occupied with the relationship between faith and culture. Although these two were not identified with each other, they were treated as closely connected, so that biblical exegesis continually interacted with theoretical ('secular') analyses of literature.[81]

A major development in rhetorical theory lay in the formulation of the art of preaching, which in its moral orientation was comparable to the ancient diatribe. Handbooks for this genre placed major emphasis on discovery (topics), including attention to the needs of various kinds of people or circumstances; they did not neglect elocution and rules of exegesis. The themes discussed were naturally orientated toward the Bible, but could also be drawn from non-Christian material. Thus the important *Sum of the Art of Preaching* by Alan of Lille (c. 1200 CE) employed illustrations from Graeco-Roman philosophers and myths in addition to making numerous references to biblical literature.[82]

The poetic and expressive characteristics of the Bible were appreciated by philologists and commentators, who saw lines of continuity between sacred and other writings. For instance, Isidore of Seville (seventh century) quoted the repetitious sentence 'Let Reuben live and not die' (Deut. 33.6) as an example of the category of 'amplified' expression (*Etymologies* 1.34).

The Venerable Bede (c. 700 CE) devoted a work to the schemes and

---

81. For bibliographical data see Spicq; Stegmüller; Hardison (1974: 259); Evans (xi-xv, 193-95).

82. In regard to poetry, Alan furnished a 'Neo-Platonic defense of metaphor' (J. Simpson, 243).

tropes of the Bible.[83] As earlier Jewish and Christian writers had done (cf. Droge), he regarded these as older and better than those of the Graeco-Roman tradition. Specifically, he held that all of the pagan forms are included in the Scriptures but that these have in addition some special procedures, such as the method of teaching morality by referring to human beings who are imperfect (R. Ray). In regard to the teaching by means of imperfect figures, he may not have been aware of Plutarch's anticipating such a theory for Greek literature (see above, 3.3).

In the fourteenth century, Boccaccio considered it at least possible that Hebrew poetry was historically primary. He stressed a similarity between biblical and Graeco-Roman writers in their use of fables, either in a purely imaginative form or mixed with history. All poetry, in his view, 'proceeds from the bosom of God', although the inspired poet needs to know grammar and rhetoric (*Genealogy of the Gentile Gods* 14.6-9).[84] Behind this outlook stood an extended tradition that related non-biblical poetry to prophecy and held that it shares in divine inspiration.[85] The latter, further, overlapped with the even broader one that envisioned poetic truth different from a purely factual one (see above, 3.3).

Biblical literature was widely held to have several meanings, just as this was thought to be true for poetry (e.g. Dante, *The Banquet* 2.1).[86] This belief, one can note, is in part correct, for it is a mark of great literature that it speaks in manifold ways and transcends a specific

---

83. Koch (1964: 16), already, mentioned Bede's reference to genres (drama, narrative, etc.) in the Bible.

84. This thesis played a role in defending his own poetizing (Kuczynski, 120-21).

85. A classic discussion of mediaeval and Renaissance 'Bible poetics' is that of Curtius (221, 231). For greater detail, see Buss (1963: 390) (on Israelite, Arab and Greek views relating poetry to prophecy); Hardison (1974: 278-97, 406, 449) (referring to Alexandrians, Fulgentius [c. 500 CE], Petrarch [fourteenth century] and others); Lindhardt (97-99, 153) (on several theorists in the fourteenth century, including Mussato and Salutati); Klopsch (34-35, 46-47, 84-86) (with reference to twelfth- and thirteenth-century Christian views); Kugel (1981: 182) (on thirteenth- and fourteenth-century Jewish statements); Kugel (1990) (essays on Graeco-Roman, Jewish, and Muslim views, sometimes ambivalent, concerning a relation between poetry and inspiration).

86. Cf., e.g., Treip (34, etc.), for allegorical interpretation of general literature in the Renaissance.

situation.[87] The different senses were each assigned an appropriate use. For instance, the moral ('tropological') meaning of Scripture, with applications to the life of human beings, was regarded as important for preaching purposes (e.g. by Guibert of Nogent, c. 1100 CE, on sermons), while allegory was valued especially for hymns of praise (Freytag, 152). In formulating new interpretations, the general tendency was to add them to previous ones rather than to replace them (Matter, 201).

Quite a few mystics or near-mystics drew upon biblical words, including those in the Song of Songs and those dealing with Christ's crucifixion. They absorbed them into their bodies (even though metaphorically), so that the boundary between text and life and between the external and the internal was breached (Lochrie, 56f.). Notable among such mystics were a number of women, such as Gertrude the Great of Helfta (thirteenth century) and Julian of Norwich (c. 1400). With a direct relation to the ultimate, they could state their interpretation with calm, but high, confidence.[88]

About this time, in fact, women began to publish under their own names. Their writings were to a large extent theological (Demers, 88), presumably since at this time they had more status in the religious than in the secular realm, with convents as important centres of scholarship. Their role in the educational system, however, continued to be different from that of men. Accordingly, they were somewhat less involved than were men in the theory of style (a major part of the traditional grammar and rhetoric, taught primarily to male youngsters)[89] and especially less in the construction of commentaries (an important means of formal biblical instruction). Instead, they moved for the most part directly to the meaning of Scripture.[90]

---

87. Cf. *RFT* for Jameson's application of the fourfold sense to literature.

88. Thus, for example, Hildegard of Bingen (twelfth century), with a prophetic consciousness (Newman, 17), explaining biblical passages in *The Book of the Rewards of Life*, said simply, 'This means that...' Hadewijch of Brabant even spoke of Christ as coming humbly to her for oneness (Vision 7). See also below for Teresa of Avila. (Research on this topic has been aided by N. Stipe.)

89. However, Hadewijch and Julian of Norwich were two, among others, who knew classical poetics and rhetoric.

90. Women writers did present loosely structured but reflective expositions, such as those by Hildegard of Bingen, dealing with many biblical passages in *The Book of Life's Merits* and, more systematically, with the Gospels.

Thus, Angela of Foligno (thirteenth century) said that it was 'not so much the great commentators on the Scriptures who were to be commended, but rather those who put them into practice' (209-10). Her mystical experience led to what is ineffable, but the experience allowed her to understand 'how the Scriptures were written; how they were made easy and difficult; how they seem to say something and contradict it... I see all this from above' (214). This is transrational (not less, but more than, rational).

The richness of literary forms in the Bible was impressively described by Ulrich of Strasbourg in *The Highest Good* (1.2.8-9; thirteenth century). The Scriptures, he said, are 'historical'—since they recount events with general significance—and 'poetic', with the use of images; they are didactic, juridical, thoughtful, emotional, prophetic (revealing past, present and future) and musical (metrical). They combine certainty with uncertainty, clarity with mystery, delight with horror; their style is usually simple, but sometimes ornate to show that the simple form is not due to lack of ability. Their multiple themes reveal divinity, display beauty[91] and announce many kinds of good.

b. *Comprehensive Literary Analyses*

Mediaeval exegetes developed systematically the various features of literary analysis which had been established in preceding centuries. Prologues to pagan, Christian and biblical writings pointed out several of the following aspects of a work: its circumstance, its literary form or 'quality' (especially, its poetic or rhetorical genre), the kind of philosophy to which it belongs (e.g. ethical instruction), its aim and its value for the reader.[92] This scheme drew on an intellectually eclectic background.

In such introductions, especially during the eleventh and twelfth centuries (such as those by Rupert, Hervaeus, and Langton), a distinction was regularly made between intention, on the one hand, and goal and utility, on the other.[93] 'Intention' referred to the thrust or rhetorical

91. The notion that beauty (or fitness) is exhibited by the content of the Bible had previously been developed by Anselm (*Why God Became a Human Being*, 1.1, 3; 2.8, 9; c. 1100 CE), among others.

92. See Spicq and Minnis; cf. also Moses bar Kepha on John (ninth century). (Ethiopian prologues to the book of Hebrews presented the 'reason' for it [Cowley, 268, 270, 275].) Jerome's prologues, which contained some of this kind of information, were often reprinted in the Middle Ages.

93. Such a distinction was standard in prologues to non-biblical writings; see

character of the verbal act, such as to exhort, commend, provoke or instruct, together with its central point in content. 'Goal' (*finis*) or 'utility' referred to a consequence desired by the author or valuable for the reader, such as the achievement of moral good or eternal life. Recently, a similar differentiation has been made by J.L. Austin, employing the terms 'illocution' (or 'force') for what is done *in* a text (such as, to exhort) and 'perlocution' for what is done *by* it (its result). In close harmony with mediaeval terminology, although probably without knowing it, van Dijk (174), has called rhetorical force 'intention' and a desired result 'goal'.[94]

The aim or rhetorical thrust of a text furnished, as is usual, one of the important criteria by which types of literature were identified. Thus, Peter Abelard's prologue to Romans[95] described the literary structures of the canon in light of the prevalent view that the intention of rhetoric is both to teach and to move; each Testament includes teaching (of a central kind, primarily in the Pentateuch and Gospels) and genres that move the audience toward following it, especially exhortation (as in prophecy and Epistles) and narratives. This canonical view was not far from others that had been set forth. For instance, Moses bar Kepha (Syriac, ninth century) had distinguished between the Gospels which present the story of salvation and the Epistles which show its usefulness to believers (Reller, 225).

The mode of treatment employed by a biblical writer was discussed by a number of commentators. This involved a variety of stylistic forms, including the amplification ('exaggeration')[96] of divine deeds, expressions of appreciation for persons addressed in order to put them into a mood to listen (with Cicero, *De inventione* 1.22) and a dramatic manner (Abelard and Peter Lombard on Romans, prologues

Huygens (67-68, 78). In biblical commentaries of the twelfth century, the distinction appears, for instance, in those by Rupert on Job, Honorius on Psalms, Hervaeus on Paul's letters, Wolber on the Song of Songs and Stephen Langton on Chronicles. 'Goal' (*skopos*) and 'usefulness', etc., were important already for Origen (cf. above) and Gregory of Nyssa (Heine, 126; Meissner, 225).

94. He stated the distinction as follows: 'Whereas an 'intention' has the action itself as scope, a purpose will be taken as a mental event in which the agent represents the goal(s) of the action'.

95. Similarly, the *Commentarius Cantabrigiensis* emanating from his school.

96. Exaggeration, or 'hyperbole', was noted as a stylistic device, for instance, by Theodore of Mopsuestia (S. Hidal in Sæbø, 554).

and comments on 1.7-8;[97] Gerhoch on Psalms). Metaphors could be found in the story of creation (Abelard, *Hexaemeron*, with a reference to Plato).

To reflect on the source, mode and usefulness of an object such as a scriptural work and to understand its fittingness was called 'meditation' by Hugh of St Victor (*De meditando*).[98] Indeed, the prevailing focus of commentaries was not on a description of independent elements but on a recognition of patterns cohering both internally and externally (in relation to life).

In the thirteenth century, a number of exegetes stated the major aspects of exegesis in terms of Aristotle's four 'causes'. 'Efficient' cause designates the author; 'material' cause, the contents; 'formal' cause, the pattern of the text; and 'final' cause, the result to be reached. The formal cause, which represents in an Aristotelian outlook the dynamic pattern of an object, included for them the thrust or force (Austin: illocution) of a verbal act along with its stylistic mode.

A major figure applying this pattern was Thomas Aquinas. Viewing organization by parts as an important aspect of form, he divided individual chapters into sections, usually subdividing these one or more times, and carefully noted the logical and rhetorical relations between the many parts. For each large or small portion, he described what the author 'does' (thus, usually) or 'intends' (e.g. on Isa. 1.2; 40.1; Mt. 2; Jn 1.1), whether to explain, show, thank, request, exhort, urge, prohibit, threaten, rebuke, commend, promise, raise and solve a question, or bewail. Stylistic forms noted include the following: visions, parables, the format of letters and ornate words.[99]

Thomas pointed out the variety of literary kinds in the Scriptures. In his introduction to the Psalter, he listed as biblical modes or forms narratives, admonitions, exhortations, prescriptions and disputations (Job

97. According to Colish (1994: 194), Lombard did unusually well in carrying through with a rhetorical analysis of Paul.

98. Abelard, Lombard, Gerhoch and Hugh wrote in the twelfth century.

99. E.g. on Isa. 1.1, Mt. 13, Romans, Lamentations. Like others, Thomas distinguished between the 'form of the treatise' (largely: division into parts) and the 'form of the treatment' (mode). The latter (the mode) is described by the Letter to Can Grande, 9 (c. 1300, attributed to Dante) in a way that closely fits Thomas's analyses as follows: it can be poetic, fictional, descriptive, or digressive, etc., and includes definition, proof, refutation and the giving of examples.

and epistles) and divided the Psalms into entreaties and hymns of praise. He spoke of the Song of Song's 'quasi-comic style'—the term 'comedy' was taken beyond drama in the Middle Ages—and described the Song's mode as one that exhibits desire and contemplation rather than the process of approval or disapproval which is pronounced in other parts of the Bible. In accordance with their literary character (and in harmony with the thought of Maimonides and other Jews), the third division of the Hebrew Bible was believed by Thomas to present, not specifically direct divine revelation, but an inspired form of wisdom, as that is exercised in an exploration of philosophical problems (prologue to Job).

For Thomas, the four 'causes' of a text are integrally connected with one another. For instance, in the prologue to Jeremiah he noted that the symbolic mode of the book is related to its authorship in that it reflects Jeremiah's prophetic office. He defined the literal meaning of a text as the one intended by the author; this can be parabolic or metaphoric (*Summa Theologica* 1.1.10; and on Gal. 4.24). In fact, according to Thomas, building on earlier reflections (Evans, 57-58), this literal meaning is the only one given by the words themselves; other meanings are not directly those of the text, but those of the objects to which the text refers (such as of the ark in the flood story as a symbol of the Church)[100] or are applications of it to another occasion (Domanyi, 67-70). The writer's goal or final cause was seen in relation to the immediate recipients of the writings. The recipients were, however, envisioned by Thomas not purely as individuals, but as representatives of certain kinds of people: Gentiles (Romans), Jews (Epistle to the Hebrews), church leaders (Timothy), civil leaders (Philemon).

Aristotle's philosophy placed greater value on particularity than Platonism did. In biblical studies (including the work of Thomas), that interest showed itself in an increased emphasis on the historical context of writings, a fact that has been chronicled in previous histories and will not be treated again here in detail. Organizationally, Aristotelianism was associated at this time especially with the new universities, which were supported by an emerging bourgeoisie as largely self-governing city guilds, training professionals who operate at a social level

---

100. This came also to be the view of Nicholas of Lyra but was far from clearly that of Hugh of St Victor in the passages described by Turner (103-104) in an otherwise helpful overview.

below that of nobles.[101] Aristotelian academic exegesis came to be known as 'scholastic'.

The scholastic pattern orientated towards the four Aristotelian 'causes' was followed widely for more than 100 years. Already before Thomas, his former schoolmate Bonaventure (thirteenth century) had developed it extensively in his commentaries, despite qualms he had about the new dominance of Aristotelian philosophy.[102] His treatment of the principles of interpretation listed the genres that appear in the Bible—narration, precepts, exhortation, threat, promise, supplication, praise, etc.—and proposed that in their variety they are effective for different types of people (*Breviloquium*, prologue, 5).[103] During the fourteenth century, the pattern of four causes was applied with less thoroughness by Nicholas of Lyra and John Wyclif.

All of these analyses (perhaps especially those of Thomas) may be useful even for today's form criticism. In fact, N. Lohfink (1983: 239-41) has noted that the approach pursued in the current series entitled *The Forms of Old Testament Literature* is reminiscent of Thomas's commentaries.

c. *The Rise of Modern Particularism*
Up to this point, Platonism and Aristotelianism had provided the dominant philosophical climate for interpretation. Towards the end of the Middle Ages, however, a different perspective, labelled the 'modern way', gained ascendance.[104] It held that reality is composed of particular objects and that general categories are secondary in relation to these. This outlook was called 'nominalism', since it regarded general terms simply as names that are applied to similar objects. The designation nominalism, to be sure, is somewhat imprecise and potentially

101. Of course, two-way causation is possible; Daly (17) suggests that the discovery of the full Aristotelian corpus was one of the factors which aided the rise of the universities (and thus, one can add, supported the rise of the bourgeoisie).

102. A leading role in the move toward Aristotelian philosophy was made by Bonaventure's and Thomas's teacher Albertus Magnus whose commentaries use a number of the exegetical procedures applied more systematically by his students.

103. According to the *Summa Theologica* begun by Bonaventure's teacher Alexander of Hales and completed within his school, a multiplicity of scriptural modes is appropriate in view of different subject-matters and different audiences; fables have truth with respect to that which is their purpose (Introductory Treatise, 1.4.3-4).

104. It often built on Aristotle's view, taking further some aspects of it.

misleading nowadays, since mediaeval thinkers used the term 'name' to designate a concept, not merely a concrete word; thus, most mediaeval versions of it set forth a moderate position known, more precisely, as 'conceptualism' (something general exists only as a concept).[105] Radical nominalists—as they have surfaced occasionally then and later—disavow even general concepts and think of linguistic terms as labels for groups of different sizes (a group being a particular entity composed of smaller ones, just as a house is composed of woods, nails, etc.).

Nominalism, as a philosophical tradition that began in the Middle Ages, is a variety of what can be called 'particularism'. This latter term (used also by Dewey 1938: 518 and Armstrong, 14) covers a number of points of view, ancient and modern, which in one way or another have regarded particulars as the primary reality. To provide stylistic variation, the present study will use the two terms in alternation as rough synonyms.

The word 'particularism', it should be made very clear, does not refer to a focus on particularity if that focus is balanced by an acceptance of generality, but rather to an outlook that favours the former one-sidedly. As was stated by Werblowsky, 'particularism (as an "ism") is different from the affirmation of particularity' (42). The polar opposite is 'generalism', which may apply to Platonic thought.

It is likely that a completely thoroughgoing particularism cannot be consistently communicated to someone else, for communication implies some sort of sharing and thus some kind of generality. In fact, all nominalist systems appear to falter in their consistency (see *RFT*). Thus, one has to speak of greater or lesser degrees, as well as of different kinds, of particularism.

The antecedents of the nominalist movement were complex. Its philosophical background lay in strains of Greek and Muslim thought.[106] Furthermore, biblical faith probably made a contribution to

105. Since for Plato universals were 'ideas', conceptualism has some affinity with Platonism; on the border between these two philosophies stood Peter Abelard (Copleston, II: 151).

106. Greek philosophy was in part indirectly mediated by Muslims. In Muslim thought, one strand—which became recognized as 'orthodox'—was strongly particularist and insisted that God's, so-to-say arbitrary, will determines ethics. (To be sure, the belief that the Qur'an is eternal, coeval with God, balanced this outlook.) Another strand, which was more rational, made an impact on a number of Jewish and Christian thinkers, including Thomas Aquinas. It also contained particularist elements; in fact, rationalist philosophers (especially Averroes, twelfth century CE)

it (cf. Glover), for an interest in particularity represents one side of biblical perspectives on existence (see above, Chapter 2). A relatively early Christian thinker who leaned toward this side was Tertullian, who highlighted a tension between rationality and faith, the latter standing under the authority of the institutional Church.[107] Indeed, without the use of general reason, authority readily becomes a standard.

An explanation of why nominalism became prominent in the fourteenth century (with some antecedents during the previous 200 years) requires a sociological analysis. The most relevant context was probably furnished by a decline in feudalism, with a the rise of relatively independent cities, among whose citizens a bourgeois culture, emphasizing individuality, gradually developed.[108] A movement in this direction in the academic popularity of Aristotelianism has already been mentioned (in fact, early nominalists often cited Aristotle even as they went beyond him).

William of Ockham (fourteenth century CE) formulated especially clearly a version of the new way of thinking. According to Ockham, direct ('intuitive') perception of particulars[109] is prior to conceptualization (or 'abstraction'); indeed, 'everything outside the soul is particular' (*Quodl.* 1.13). This position stood in contrast to that of Hugh of St Victor (twelfth century), who in his hermeneutics (*Didascalicon* 3.9) had directed that one begin with universals, or general terms, and proceed from there to individuals by making distinctions. (The term 'universal' designated at that time what hereafter will be 'general', i.e. something shared by more than one actual or potential object; in an Aristotelian framework, the term applied to something shared by all

quoted the opposing side, so that they contributed to a knowledge of particularist ideas by Christian mediaeval theologians. (The influence of these discussions on Christian mediaeval philosophy is discussed in Sharif, 232, 547, 1359, 1362, 1368.)

107. Cf. Stuhlmacher (84). Tertullian, to be sure, was not altogether against rationality (Ayers, 7-60; Steiner, 208-14).

108. See, for example, Ferguson; Roebuck (61) (on the prevalence, by the thirteenth century, of semi-independent cities with special 'civil liberties'); Feld (15). Already in ancient Israel, the buying and selling of real estate in walled towns had rules different from the ones applicable to the countryside, with permanent alienation of property (Lev. 25). Cities and their attendant middle class declined during the later Roman period but rose gradually during the Middle Ages (see Berman, 333-404, with references). In England, semi-independent towns were known as 'boroughs'; the French word 'bourgeois' is allied to this term.

109. Prologue to the *Ordinatio*, q. 1; cf. Boehner (xxiv, 268).

members of a certain kind. A different conception of universality will be mentioned below, Chapter 6).

In regard to natural order, according to Ockham, the ideas by which God created the world are particular—not general, as earlier thinkers had held with the aid of reference to the 'kinds' mentioned in Gen. 1.11-12, 21, 24-25 (*Sent.* 1.35.5). In other words, an ordered arrangement by kinds is posterior to, not prior to, individual existents, which, rather, are primary.

A major value for particularism is freedom in the sense of an absence of either internal necessity or external restraint—whether for a human individual or for a nation or for God. Ockham, giving shape to this value, defended the rule of the king against the pope, thus supporting nationalism. At the same time, he limited the king's authority to acts that further the good of the people, to whom he owes his power (*Dialogus* 3/2.2.26-28), thus defending individual freedom.

God's freedom was guarded by saying that the ultimate standard of goodness is what God freely wills, without necessity or reason as a guide or restraint, although God wills adherence to reason, as a secondary factor.[110] In the absence of an operation of necessity for God, Ockham emphasized God's power (Dupré, 123).

Ockham's outlook—as is true for all forms of nominalism—meant that there is a major distance between rational thought and both theology and ethics. For instance, he believed that no feature of God's reality can be proved (*Quodl.* 5.1).[111]

Nominalism's emphasis on freedom in the sense of independence has a converse: a denial that relations are 'real' beyond being matters of thought.[112] In its view, a relation comes into play only as one thinks about the two individual existents, who alone are real.[113] Ockham set forth such a position to a large extent, but it constituted a problem for the doctrine of the Trinity, which he accepted on the basis of the

110. See *Sent.*, 1.2.1; 1.43.1; 2.9, 19; 3.12; 4.9.

111. All that he thought provable is that there are one or more beings that are greatest in reality (there can be several such if they are equal).

112. Already al-Ghazali (a leading Muslim particularist) had held that relations exist in the mind, not in extramental reality (Sharif, 615).

113. Most nominalists do admit particular relational qualities adhering in individuals, such as Ann's being a mother of Robert, which is a feature ('quality') of Ann and is different from Susan's being a mother of Steven. (For instance, L. Valla, to be mentioned below, 5.1, downgraded the category of relationality to one of 'quality'.) But nominalists do not envision real relations between individuals.

Church's authority. Ockham's solution was to assert that God's reality is different from that of the world, so that relations can be real within God, even though they are only thought elsewhere (Adams, 215, 276; Henninger, 132). Moreover, Ockham accepted as real the relatedness of beings to God (Mojsisch, 591), agreeing in this with Thomas Aquinas (who, at the same time, had already held that God's relation to other beings—the converse relation—is not real since God is self-sufficient).[114] Thus relationality was in part retained within the religious realm.

The particularist outlook required a new concept of form. For Ockham, form was no longer a general category but rather the specific shape of a given material. He also denied the existence of a unified form of the whole for an object; an object is, rather, to be viewed as a composite of its parts (Moser, 57-65).

Ockham did not publish any biblical commentaries, but his exegetical approach included the view that only the original meaning of a text is significant (Schlageter, 254-63). This view radicalized the interest in the historical meaning of the text, then growing among both Jewish and Christian interpreters.[115] In conjunction with Ockham's overall philosophical perspective it pointed in the direction of historical criticism, which came to overshadow the study of form as a general and holistic pattern.

Somewhat later in the fourteenth century, John Wyclif sharply rejected particularism on the ground that it forms the basis of selfishness (*On Universals*, 3). Nevertheless, he moved towards an emphasis on individuality by espousing a version of physical atomism (Kenny, 4) and by arguing for the exclusive authority of the Bible, which is available to any Christian apart from an ecclesiastical structure (*Of the Truth of Holy Scripture*, chs. 3, 7f., 15). He was thus somewhat of a transitional figure.

At this time, the Bible was coming under open attack on the basis of anomalies in its materials. Against such attacks, Wyclif insisted that Scripture has its own logic and grammar and that, indeed, its pattern of thought and its mode of speaking (rather than individual words) should be a standard for believers. This verbal-logical structure represents, he

---

114. *Summa*, 1.28.1; E. Johnson (225).
115. See above, 2.b, for Jewish exegetes. Within Christianity, Hugh and, more still, Thomas (cf. above) took major steps along this path.

said, Christ as the Word (*Truth*, 1-3, 6, 9, 16).[116] Biblical logic involves above all, according to Wyclif, a transcendence of ordinary temporal concepts (Jeffrey 1985: 281). In regard to the Bible's style, Wyclif discussed at length its use of symbolic language (*Truth*, 1, 4, pointing out, again, that fictions can convey truth) and made such observations as that the book of Isaiah includes a tragic and a comic part.[117] Contrary to established Catholic doctrine, he came to believe that the eucharistic words about the presence of the body of Christ are not to be taken realistically.

116. In fact, Wyclif envisioned 'Scripture' as a metaphysical 'book of life', of which Christ, truth of whatever kind and the codices of the Bible are different versions; the codices by themselves, without the presence of the other aspects, are not truly 'Scripture' but only witnesses to it (Oey, 90-93, 203-204).

117. Benrath (67). Wyclif often followed literary categorizations by Peter Aureoli, who anticipated Ockham's perspective in many ways but still engaged in an extensive classification of biblical literature (see his *Compendium*; Benrath, 13, 23, 66).

Chapter 5

POSTMEDIAEVAL EXAMINATIONS OF FORM

The period from c. 1475 to c. 1700 can be regarded as that of early modernity, although the modern way of nominalism had been set forth already before then by Ockham and others. The period was marked by a continuing, gradual rise of the middle class. Gutenberg's achievement in printing (c. 1455) both contributed to, and was furthered by, the rise;[1] a similar circularity of effects was true for Columbus's journey in 1492. In philosophy, particularist perspectives gradually gained ground, especially (although not only) in Protestant circles.

Socially, feudalism crumbled in the face of an emerging city life, with an intercontinental commerce that often involved robbery of other groups at gunpoint. Yet both capitalism and republican forms of government, the next major arrangements, remained limited in extent. One political phenomenon was that of absolute monarchy, which focused on the king or 'prince' as a great individual.[2]

Some Jewish contributions during the early part of this period have already been mentioned. The primary focus in the present section is on Christian work, especially on Protestant interpretation. The very word 'Protestant' indicates an emerging interest in difference (with deviation from what is established) in contrast to a 'catholic' (general and inclusive) outlook. A full flowering of a particularist attitude, however, did not take place in biblical exegesis until about 1775, in high modernity.

---

1.   See *RFT*.

2.   Thus Jean Bodin (in 1576, with subsequent revisions) and Jacques-Benigne Bossuet (*Politics Drawn from the Very Jacques-Benigne Words of Holy Scripture*, 1679). Both considered royal authority to be 'absolute', but Bodin took it to be subject to 'divine and natural laws' (1.8 [1583: 362; 1992: 13], and Bossuet held it to be subject to God and reason. The expressly nominalist Hobbes also supported royal authority (see below, 6.1.c).

1. *Catholic and Protestant Interpretations, 1500–1575*

About 1500 CE, Western Europe witnessed a number of cultural movements that are commonly known as constituting a 'Renaissance'. In good part it involved the revival of a knowledge of Greek and the rediscovery of some Graeco-Roman classics—all of this aided by the use of print. Protestant reliance on the Bible was closely connected with the new attention to old texts. More was happening, however, than a renewal of old culture, for society was changing.

One phase of this development is known as 'humanism'. It considered the earlier Aristotelian scholasticism to have been rather dry, and drew instead on a mixture of philosophies, including Platonism, Pythagoreanism (fascinating to Reuchlin and others [cf. Røstvig]) and Epicureanism. The particularist strain, present in Epicureanism, showed itself in an application of historical criticism to the Bible (at this point in the form of text criticism).[3]

a. *Catholics in the Period of 'Humanism'*

A richly textured conjunction of theology with general culture was developed by Erasmus early in the sixteenth century. His exegesis of the Bible was strong in the application of grammar, including linguistics, and rhetoric. Of these approaches, the linguistic one dealing with the original Greek form of New Testament texts was relatively new in Western Christian tradition. The other orientations were, of course, already well established, but Erasmus gave them a number of fresh twists (see Chomarat, 509-710; M. Hoffmann, 32-36).

Carrying previous observations further, Erasmus recognized the pervasive presence of 'rustic' (simple and rough) style in the Bible; in fact, he valued its restraint in expression. Thus, he praised the rhetorical art of Jesus in speaking to ordinary people as well as that of other biblical speakers or writers in addressing their own audiences. In regard to typologies, he observed that Holy Writ includes compositions belonging to different genres, with different styles (on Ps. 33 [Hebrew 34].2).

---

3. Lorenzo Valla, important for his analysis of the history of the biblical text (in a 1444 MS discovered and published by Erasmus) as well as for historical criticism in regard to other materials, had a definite interest in Epicureanism (*De voluptate*, 1421); like Ockham, he both used 'singular' terms in his logic and downgraded the category of 'relation' (P. Mack, 68, 74, 79-86, 93).

In *Mode of Praying* (1523), he distinguished between praise, thanksgiving and request, with numerous examples from biblical literature.

Anticipating Robert Lowth, Erasmus noted three kinds of parallelism, according to whether the meanings are the same, related or opposite. For comparison in this, he referred to Quintilian's rhetorical theory and to bucolic poetry.[4]

Two other Catholic interpreters of the same time, John Colet and Jacob Cajetan, made important contributions. Like earlier commentators, they treated the details of the creation account as figurative. Colet called Moses a 'poet', who can 'invent something, even to a degree unworthy of God, if only it may be of advantage and service to humanity'—such as to depict God's creation as though it formed a sequence of events (Letters to Radulphus).

b. *Luther and Melanchthon*

Martin Luther's initial training was largely nominalist (cf. McGrath 1987: 117). As he wrestled to a new way of understanding faith, he broke with the kind of nominalism in which he had been schooled, but he did not leave the orbit of this philosophy altogether.[5] Most notably, he revived and developed the idea that words create reality; one can thus describe his outlook as a variant of what Jean Piaget has called 'nominal realism'.[6]

Although Luther emphasized both written and oral speech as a foundation for faith, he gave little attention to rhetorical or poetic considerations, especially in works directed to the general public. There are several discernible reasons for this restraint in literary analysis. One is that Luther was trained more in law than in literature. Another lies in

---

4.   On Ps. 1.5, as pointed out by Chomarat (672-73); cf. below, 5.2.d, on Lowth.

5.   In an informal statement (T, 6419), Luther said that he was at one time a nominalist, with the implication that he was no longer that, at least not of the kind he cited (on the two major kinds, see for Calvin below). He did, however, base 'rightness' on God's 'will', not on God's wisdom (Lorenz, 56). Both Erasmus and Boyle (260-82) have placed Luther close to Stoicism; that is correct in so far as it points to the fact that Luther, like Stoics, espoused a moderate form of particularism. Frei (1-3) called his outlook, like that of Calvin, 'realistic', in the sense that it focuses both on actuality and on representational transtemporality. (Luther's works are here cited by 'W' for the main part of the Weimar edition, 'B' for its division on Bible translation, and 'T' with its number for table talk.)

6.   See *RFT* and above, 2.1.c, for biblical versions of this.

the fact that printing had opened up a wide readership which often did not have the benefit of a literary education. Addressing such a public, Luther presented almost exclusively the practical and experiential meaning of the biblical text without giving professional guidance on how one would determine such a meaning. Thirdly, a theological/ philosophical reason for the restraint in literary analysis is that Luther, like Ockham, kept rationality, and thus reflective literary study, at some distance from faith.

In oral or written comments designed for a limited circle, Luther did make use of rhetorical and, even more, of poetic concepts.[7] For instance, he described the book of Job as a free dramatic rendering of an actual occurrence, resembling a comedy of Terence (T, 475). In fact, Luther appreciated much of classical culture, including its poetry, even as he distinguished faith sharply from culture (Blöchle). Still, he was reserved in the identification of poetic or rhetorical figures, and often accepted a quite literal meaning for a narrative or statement, such as within the story of creation (W, XLII: 92). Scepticism towards the use of symbolism was a reason for his rejection of the Apocalypse as apostolic (B, VII: 404).

Rather than dealing extensively with style, Luther focused on the content and power of what is said, especially by God. He described the world, including human beings, as 'words' in the creative language of God (W, XLII: 17) and said that through faith human beings are changed into God's word, that is, into the righteousness declared in that word (W, LVI: 227). His two major categories, gospel and law, however, were not identified with genres of the kind that are determined by style or manner of presentation. Thus, the Epistles of Paul were thought by him to represent 'gospel' as much as, or even more than, the books that are normally given that title (W, X/IA: 10; XII: 260).

7.   See especially H. Bornkamm (30-37); Krause (191-202); Junghans (87-89, 207-19, 240-73); Hagen (1993: 111, 150); Buchholz (49-50, with references). Luther did not, however, make an effort to distinguish between the different 'figures' (Brecht, 134). In terms of intended audience, one must make a distinction between: (1) comments not intended for print; (2) publications in Latin; and (3) German works. For instance, his observations in Latin lecture notes about poetic style in Hab. 2.11, 13 (W, XIII: 72, 410) either do not have a parallel in his German commentary on Habakkuk or else are recast there in a way that explains the Hebrew usage of 'twisted words or parable' (W, IX: 416). The example just given shows that Luther did sometimes present literary observations for the general public, but in a manner that does not presuppose a formal relevant education.

Like a few interpreters before him, Luther rejected an assumption that there are multiple senses. Specifically, he virtually identified the 'literal' meaning of a text with its practical ('tropological') meaning (Ebeling 1951: 228-29; 1962: 44-90), by focusing on its 'purpose', downplaying mere 'historical faith'.[8] This identification was supported by the fact that in Luther's view Christian *practice* is centred in *faith*, by which he meant the absorbing of God's activity and word so that an event which is proclaimed is a reality in the believer's existence (thus already in 1514; W, III: 397, 9-11 [Lohse, 62]). The identification of the literal with the practical, unfortunately, has a shadow side in that Luther (as is true for others recognizing only a single meaning) was often unduly tempted to attribute to a text a meaning for faith that was hardly its historical one, without acknowledging the hiatus.

Luther's scepticism towards symbolism and multiple senses had a social aspect. He believed that the Bible is clear for all faithful readers, so that it is unnecessary to ask the pope for a determination of its true meaning. This view stood in contrast with that set forth by Vincent of Lerin (*Comminatoria,* 2; fifth century), who argued that the depth of the Bible requires an ecclesiastical authority to declare its correct sense.[9] Moreover, an innerworldly asceticism, typical for parts of the middle class, contributed to Luther's opposition to a luxuriating in symbolism.[10] Specifically, in a critique of others who contrasted spirit with letter (and who were on the whole either traditional or radical rather than moderate in politics), he asserted that 'enthusiasm is the origin, power and strength of all heresies' (W, L: 246; Ebeling 1962: 313).

Luther's interpretation of the Psalms, to which he turned repeatedly, shows how his thinking developed over the years. In early lectures (1513-15) prior to his break with the Catholic Church, he regularly identified the speaker of a psalm with Christ (as had often been done before then, at least in part, and specifically so by Faber Stapulensis in

8.   Harrisville and Sundberg (17, 231).

9.   Closer in time to Luther (in 1503), Silvester Prierias argued that the literal sense is reachable by human investigation, but then that other meanings are given authoritatively by the Church (Oberman, 291). McGrath (1993: 145, 157) points out that Luther, more than left-wing reformers, gave some room to the authority of church tradition. In fact, in 1522, in the midst of his arguments for the clarity of Scripture (cf. Buchholz, 59-85; Lohse, 212-13), Luther placed explanatory notes with his translation of the New Testament (M. Edwards, 110).

10.   On the social situation, with attention to printing and a strong urban context, cf., in addition to special studies, Ozment, 203.

1509, pursuing a prophetic sense as the only truly literal one [Preus, 137-45]). Later, Luther treated the Psalms (somewhat like Athanasius) as models for the words and feelings of a believer, and described most of them as containing a general exhortation, thanksgiving, or lament and as utilizing indefinite phrasing for a wide applicability (B, X/I: 102; W, XXXI/I: 68; Raeder1977: 31-34). He could combine both kinds of interpretation by saying that in the Psalms one has the experiences of Christ and of his body, that is, of the Church—not just those of 'one or two' individuals (B, X/I: 98). He used Ps. 101 as a model for princely behaviour (W, LI: 200-64).

Towards the end of his life (c. 1532; W, XXXVIII: 17-18), Luther provided a fivefold classification for the Psalms: prophecy, moral teaching, consolation, supplication (with complaints and laments) and thanksgiving (including praise). This ordering adapted a four-fold 'typification' (*Vergattung*) of the Psalms (1526) by Martin Bucer, who had treated supplication and consolation as subdivisions of one category, just as some twentieth-century scholars have connected psalms of confidence with laments. Luther was not rigid in his classification but pointed out that many psalms incorporate two, three, or more of the elements listed.

Systematically form-critical was the work of Philipp Melanchthon, Luther's friend, professor of classics and law (with a good knowledge of Greek and Hebrew), theorist of rhetoric and a poet. Especially well known is the fact that he organized theology, conceived as a kind of rhetoric, around *loci communes* or 'topics' (1521). His work on general rhetoric (1519) referred to biblical writings as good examples of speech (Schneider, 81, 85). This influential work absorbed some nominalist ideas, but Melanchthon was far from a thoroughgoing particularist (cf. Schneider, G. Frank).

In biblical exegesis, Melanchthon made extensive use of rhetorical and logical concepts, giving attention both to types of content and to style.[11] For instance, Romans was described as judicial rhetoric (1519; Schneider, 133-36). He characterized 1 Corinthians as 'familiar correspondence' (rather than as an essay), as A. Deissmann was to do much later (1522, ET J. Donnelly). For prophets, their tragic or consoling

---

11. An increase in attention to logic (as compared with what Erasmus did) was due to strong influence by Agricola (on whom see below; cf. the analyses of Schneider and M. Hoffmann in Wengert and Graham).

character was noted (e.g. introduction to Isaiah).[12] The Psalms were classified by types grouped into three major genres, corresponding roughly to Aristotle's rhetorical divisions (which were praising, advising and judging): gospel teaching or prophecy, persuasion (including consolation and petition) and law or precepts (e.g. on Ps. 110, lecture of 1542). Biblical proverbs were compared with those of other nations (1529, 1550).

In an early sketch for a commentary on Romans (Bizer, 20), Melanchthon outlined the major literary genres of Scripture as law, promise and history. History, he said, gives examples for the other two. Soon after that (in 1519/20), he analysed Matthew as 'history' in the way he had identified that genre in his work on rhetoric: it collects *exempla* which teach basic truths pointing to a central thesis (Schneider, 149). He also described narratives of the Hebrew Bible in terms of genre, giving notice to fables and to ethical topics (Maurer, 213).

c. *Other Protestant Reformers*

Huldreich Zwingli, an early Protestant leader influenced by Erasmus and Stapulensis and conversant with J. Reuchlin's Hebrew grammar of 1518 largely based on Qimḥi's (Hoburg, 105), took extensive account of stylistic figures and tropes.[13] Following an intimation by Erasmus (later modified by Erasmus himself) and a specific suggestion by Cornelius Hoen, he interpreted the word 'is' in the formula of the Lord's Supper as meaning 'signifies' (from 1524 on). A similar—symbolic or spiritual—view of the sacrament was accepted by virtually all leading Reformers of that time except Luther. For instance, Thomas Cranmer argued that Scripture is full of figurative speech (including metaphors and parables) and employs it especially when speaking of the sacraments (*Defence* 1550, 3.12).

The opposite path (less figurative than had been common earlier) was taken by the Protestant Erasmian S. Castellio in his understanding of the Song of Songs as an erotic poem. He regarded the Song as

---

12. Works by Melanchthon, as of those by other interpreters, are cited here in a form identifiable by those who are familiar with the respective writers; this may be by topic, date or both; an overview of his commentaries is furnished by Wengert in Wengert and Graham.

13. Zwingli also engaged in rhetorical classification, for example on Gen. 48.3 (1527), Exod. 15.11 (1527), and Psalms (1525, 1532).

'lascivious and obscene' and therefore condemned it, according to a report by John Calvin, which gave Castellio's condemnation of it as the reason for his not being admitted to the ministry (Bainton 1963: 8-9).

More or less systematic literary analysis was practised widely by early Protestant writers. Heinrich Bullinger discussed in detail how to treat prophetic and other texts in terms of rhetorical principles (1525 [Hausammann, 161-76]) and then furnished above all a commentary on Romans along those lines. Caspar Schwenckfeld, with mystical tendencies, applied some rhetorical principles to the Bible, which he regarded not so much as the word of God as a witness to it (*Holy Scripture,* 1551). Wolfgang Musculus argued that all of Scripture is inspired but that it contains different literary types with varied functions. The four major genres he identified are the historical, legal, prophetic and sapiential[14] (prefaces to Genesis and Isaiah, 1554, 1557).

Calvin, who shared with Luther a training in law, was occupied with the practical meaning of the Bible. Yet he also attended to its compositional structure, as he had already done at age 20 in a commentary on a work by the Stoic Seneca (Parker, 60, 89).

Calvin's theology absorbed major particularist themes. Especially, his stress on God's undetermined 'will', according to which 'salvation is freely offered to some' (*Institutes* 3.21.1),[15] recalls the emphasis on God's freedom by late-mediaeval nominalists. Some of these believed in God's predestining some human beings for salvation and others for damnation (McGrath 1986; Hensley), picturing God as acting independently of what anyone else does. (Another group of nominalists gave considerable room to human freedom in preparing themselves for salvation. This kind of nominalism was rejected by Luther and Calvin.) Nevertheless, Calvin did not hold to a pure nominalism. For instance, he could speak of God's 'wisdom' (*Inst.* 1.5.2), with the implication that God's activity is not entirely arbitrary.[16] Furthermore, he believed that all truth has the Spirit of God as its foundation (*Inst.* 2.2.15), so that he did not separate non-Christian reason from faith.

14. The sapiential was called 'parabolic' on the basis of use of the Hebrew word *mashal*, following a widely established terminology.

15. Final version, 1559, ET J. Allen.

16. The 'wisdom' of God had long been emphasized by those who did not envision God as arbitrary; such wisdom can, of course, be considered to be an aspect of God and need not form an external restraint upon divine action (see, for example, above, for the view of the mediaeval Jew Abulafia).

The Psalms were for Calvin, as for Luther, a 'mirror' of the soul, showing its 'anatomy', i.e. emotions; furthermore, they give instruction in prayer and in enduring suffering (preface to Psalms). The laws of the Bible were regarded by him both as a mirror of the human situation—impelling one to seek grace—and as rules and thus models for action, established by divine authority (*Inst.* 2.7.7-17; 8.41). The use of biblical narratives is to bring about confidence and reverence ('Last Four Books of Moses', preface); biblical persons and events form exemplars for human life (Ganoczy and Scheld, 155).

For individual biblical books and their parts, Calvin indicated the nature of the literary thrust, such as to exhort, recommend, criticize, threaten, console, defend oneself, complain, give thanks or incite to praise. Thus, the book of Jonah was taken as both historical and didactic. Describing a public social situation, Calvin referred to ceremonies of thanksgiving (on Ps. 22.23). He identified Psalm 79 as a collective 'complaint and lamentation of the church'.

The style of biblical writings was of subordinate interest to Calvin but not ignored. Like Jerome, he referred to the fine diction of some of the prophets, assessed as 'not inferior in eloquence' to pagan authors, as well as to the simpler speech of other biblical writers (*Inst.* 1.8.2; similarly, on Mic. 1.2 [cf. Armour]). The marriage of Hosea was interpreted by him and by other Protestants—more regularly than by Jewish and Catholic interpreters—as figurative (Bitter). He rejected allegorical interpretations if these are taken to represent the author's meaning, but he accepted extended applications or comparisons (on Gal. 4.22), and he believed Christ to be adumbrated in figures and types of the Hebrew Bible (cf. Wolf, 69-73; *Inst.* 4.15.9).

Calvin regarded anthropomorphisms and other problematic forms of expression as an accommodation of the Holy Spirit to human capacity. In fact, accommodation to human capacity was a major theme of his interpretation of the Bible, both in regard to language (so that his view of divine dictation did not violate the human writer's individuality) and in regard to content, taking an evolutionary view of sacred history.[17]

d. *Flacius: A Synthetic View*
Matthias Flacius, a Lutheran Hebrew specialist who had carefully studied Aristotle, formulated, in Latin, a *Key to the Holy Scriptures*

17. Krusche (163-74); Rogers and McKim (137); T. Parker (91-94); Opitz (108-290); Puckett.

(1567; cf. 1968).[18] This extensive and often excellent work includes an exegetical and theological lexicon, an outline of sacred hermeneutics, a linguistic grammar, a detailed discussion of tropes and schemes and close analysis of individual styles, including those of the prophets (in terms of oratory), Paul and John.

General requirements for an understanding of the Scriptures, according to this work, are faith and moral commitment—the Bible is not a dead book (hermeneutical precept 3)—and a willingness to employ dialectic and rhetoric. Specific procedures set forth centre on the relatedness of the parts of a passage or book to its dominating concern so that it is seen as an organic whole. 'Scope' (aim) is defined as that which gives unity to a work. Determination of the scope and organization of a work can be aided by attention to genres, which form complementary groups, each potentially with a characteristic impact on the 'life of human beings' (precepts 20-24).

Flacius went on to present perceptive analyses of the genres of biblical literature, as follows: sacred history differs from secular history by dealing with primary (ultimate) causes and events. The prophets point out penalties, correct their audience and provide hope through promises. The psalms are either directed from human beings to God—in requests or thanks—or from God to humanity—teaching, promising, admonishing, or consoling. (Genres, however, can by mixed.) Wisdom is related to philosophical disputations. The book of Proverbs is partly religious and partly civil, drawing largely from experience. Paul's writings reflect different rhetorical genres; they cover many general concerns, although they also show the characteristics of personal letters.

Both in theory and in execution, Flacius's work thus constitutes a high point in biblical form criticism.

2. Reconstruction in Poetics and Rhetoric, c. 1500–1775

The literary character of the Bible was discussed not only by theologians but also by many others who were concerned with speech and

---

18. Cf. Raeder (1991). More limited in extent was a work by Niels Hemmingsen on 'method' (1555). In this work and in commentaries, Hemmingsen treated the author (still considered relatively unimportant), the occasion, the 'principle point or question' and the procedure used in dealing with this (Hagen 1990).

literature. In fact, the legitimacy and scope of poetry and rhetoric in general were matters of lively debate.[19]

a. *Poetics in Dispute, c. 1500–1675*

Doubts about the value of poetic productions on moral or social grounds had emerged from time to time in ancient and mediaeval times (cf. Hall, 43). They became even stronger in some Protestant circles (especially Puritan)[20] from the middle of the sixteenth century on. The economic pressures of a middle class played a role in this questioning attitude, since poetry and drama lead to 'idleness' rather than to virtue (Fraser, 3, 15, 76, 180). For instance, Samuel Daniel pictured an opponent of poetry as saying that this 'busy world' or 'wiser profit-seeking age' requires something better than songs (*Musophilus*, 1599, lines 10-13).[21] In 1693, the philosopher John Locke opposed the teaching of poetry to schoolboys, on the grounds that its pursuit does not usually yield 'gold and silver' (*Some Thoughts Concerning Education* 174). Thus it is not surprising that Locke's commentaries on several of Paul's letters contain little notice of literary form.[22]

A positive connection between poetry and religion, however, was made in pious songs and plays, making reference to the Bible. Indeed, poetic versions of biblical content became even more popular then than they had been earlier.[23] Such productions were typically based on the long-standing belief, expressed, for example, by Edward Leigh in

---

19. Cf. Norton (I, 62-312), largely for England.

20. However, as Knott (5) points out, Puritans had 'no monopoly on plainness'; Locke, to be cited, was Anglican. (Furthermore, Knott rightly observes the Puritans' recognition of figurative language in the Bible.)

21. Similarly, with affirmation, Adam Smith (*Lectures on Rhetoric and Belles Lettres*, 21 January 1763) stated that prose, supported by the wealth created through commerce, is 'naturally the language of business, as poetry is of pleasure and amusement'.

22. Locke did note some special characteristics of Paul's style (like Richard Simon, whose work he knew), but he regarded Paul's avoidance of stylistic ornaments as an advantage (preface to Paul's Epistles, c. 1700).

23. Poetic versions had been produced previously, for instance, by Juvencus and Proba (fourth century, the latter a woman), Alcuin (eighth century), and increasingly during the Middle Ages by both Jews and Christians. Sedulius (preface to *Pascalis Operis*, fifth century) referred to David as a model for Christian poets; similarly, among others, J. Lydgate (c. 1413; Kuczynski, 135f.). See, for example, essays in Kannengiesser; for German psalms poetry, I. Bach and H. Galle 1989.

1657,[24] that biblical literature provides a model for poetry. Especially numerous were metrical renditions of psalms, which were produced by persons in many stations of life, including Queen Elizabeth.[25] In English alone, more than 300 covering the entire Psalter appeared by 1640 (Lewalski, 39).

Major literary artists who created renditions of biblical works or themes included Leone de' Sommi (an Italian Jew), Clémont Marot (whose version of the Psalms was completed by T. de Bèze), Martin Opitz and András Horvát (Hungarian). Among Puritan poets who did so were Edmund Spenser, Philip Sidney, his sister Mary, Countess of Pembroke (her renditions of the Psalms were long unpublished but are rated by Steinberg 1995 as superior to others),[26] George Wither and John Milton (with an awareness of both Jewish and Christian interpretations of the Bible [see, for example, Christopher, Rosenblatt]). Many of these figures reflected on the close relation between the Bible and other literatures, not infrequently in defence of their own poetry.

For instance, a number of Italians continued, although more cautiously than others earlier, to connect poetry with theology.[27] Among them, the dramatist de' Sommi attributed the origin of the theatre to Moses, the author of Job according to Jewish tradition (C. Roth, 262). Sidney's *Defence of Poesie* (1595)—strongly Protestant but also humanist, with an affinity to Neoplatonism (Waller, 76)—cited the parables of Nathan and Jesus in support of imaginative literature ('the application most divinely true, but the discourse itself fained', E3); poetry praising 'the excellencies of God' represented to him the highest type (C1). For the German Martin Opitz, 'poetry was originally nothing other than hidden theology' (*Das Buch von der deutschen Poeterey*, 1624: B1). Similarly, poetry as a divine gift to humanity and as a characteristic of the Bible was the main theme of the anonymous Spanish

24. *Annotations on Five Poetical Books of the Old Testament*, A6.

25. Sixteenth century, associating herself and associated by others with David (Holland, I: 145; Hannay, 92-5). Others included Pope Urban VIII (seventeenth century), and the Jewish doctor-poet Abraham Zanti (c. 1700 CE; Wogue, 305). Cf. Seybold, 225-28.

26. During the Renaissance, women came to write more extensively than before, though not only the amount but also the kind of writing (and publishing) they did was still restricted (Hannay, x; M. Lamb, 4-17).

27. Savonarola inveighed against equating the two. Cf. Weinberg (336, 567); Hardison (1962: 7).

work *Panegyrico por la poesia* (1627) (Curtius, 532-42).[28]

Poets such as these could engage in specific analyses of biblical literature. For instance, George Wither provided for his *Preparation to the Psalter* (1619) an introduction with attention to style, content and genres; he recommended the 'funeral elegy' of 2 Sam 1.19-27 as 'a pattern for our funeral poems' (*The Hymnes and Songs of the Church*, 1623: 23). Partially following analyses by biblical scholars,[29] Milton valued the biblical Song of Songs as a 'divine pastoral drama', the Apocalypse as a tragedy (with a chorus) and Job as a model for epic literature (*The Reason of Church Government*, 1642, II, Introduction).

At the same time, the movement commonly called 'neoclassicism' tended to separate secular and biblical poetry. This movement, very influential then, formulated rather precise rules for literary genres. It did so in part on the basis of such as could be found in Aristotle and Horace, but it was by no means simply traditional; rather, it went beyond older writers in the formulation of rules, rejecting adherence to authority (Calinescu, 28-35). Furthermore, in another move to modernity, it gradually decreased the linkage of levels of style with social status. The rules, however, presupposed, and further supported, a gap between sacred and secular literature, for they were not obeyed by biblical forms. In fact, Nicolas Boileau, an important neoclassicist, opposed the mixing of biblical and pagan themes in a single work, as had occurred earlier (*L'art poétique* 3.199).[30]

b. *Rhetoric in Transition, c. 1500–1675*

During this period, general rhetorical studies frequently took account of biblical forms.[31] For instance, Thomas Wilson's influential *Arte of Rhetorique* (1553) analysed the story of David and Goliath as an

---

28. A little earlier, in the second half of the sixteenth century, an appreciation of the poetic qualities of the Bible had been expressed by Luis of Leon (see Alonso Schökel 1963: 6-8; 1988, 1.3). For further English-language examples, see R. Zim in Prickett (1991: 64-135).

29. Johann Mercer (1573), not unlike earlier commentators, had described the Song of Songs as a drama and Job as following the pattern of tragedy. In his views regarding Song of Songs and the Apocalypse, Milton stood close to David Pareus (1628).

30. For others who kept religion and literature separate during the following century, cf. Norton (I: 53-56).

31. Cf. Shuger (80) for the period after 1575 (apparently underestimating this use in earlier years).

example of demonstrative speech. As is appropriate for a narrative, this biblical account answers the following traditional seven questions in relation to the action: 'who', 'what', 'where', 'with what help', 'where-fore', 'how', 'at what time'.

Attention to schemes and tropes continued and perhaps even increased.[32] Richard Sherry's *Treatise of Schemes and Tropes* (1550) gave as the reason for examining such figures that a knowledge of them leads to a better understanding of literature. Employing a useful ana-logy, he compared ignorance of their varieties to entering a garden without knowing the names and properties of herbs and flowers.

Such literary forms indicate, of course, a continuity between biblical and other writings. Accordingly, Joannes Susenbrotus (1540), Sherry and Henry Peacham (*The Garden of Eloquence*, 1577) drew from both biblical and other writings for their illustrations. Dudley Fenner (1584) substituted biblical examples for the classical ones in Ramus's work on which he largely relied. John Barton produced a rhetoric 'exemplified out of holy Writ' (1634).

At the same time, a major new development was taking place in the teaching of rhetoric. Rudolph Agricola (fifteenth century) and Petrus Ramus (sixteenth century)[33] championed the removal of content ('invention' and arrangement) from rhetoric, since that subject over-lapped with matter treated in logic. This move left for rhetoric primarily style and delivery. That had the terminological consequence that 'rhetoric' came to designate the external characteristics of speech or the means by which something is expressed. This narrow conception of rhetoric had antecedents, for there had long been a tradition of rhetori-cal theory which, unlike that of Aristotle, gave primary attention to the expressive side of speech. The overt exclusion of content from rhetoric, however, was something new.[34]

An important ground for the separation of treatments of style from

32. In the early and middle part of the sixteenth century, systematic treatments of schemes and tropes in the Bible were presented by Santes Pagnino (1526, Roman Catholic [Kugel 1981: 227]) and Bartholomaeus Westhammer (1528, before the English break with the Catholic Church, and 1551, etc. [Dyck, 162]). Many studies in biblical interpretation between 1400 and 1900 referring to 'figures' (as well as to 'types') are listed in Jeffrey (1992).

33. Ramus became a Protestant and was killed for his new faith; his rhetoric and logic was then widely followed by Protestants.

34. The study of logic could, in fact, absorb all of rhetoric, as in Isaac Watts's *Logic* (1725), which defined logic as the study of reasoning and communication.

those of content was the conviction, expressed by Ramus, that one can speak about a given object in any manner.[35] This idea undercut the traditional notion of aptness, which had been central to traditional rhetoric; that is, it was no longer held that certain forms of expression are the ones that are appropriate for a given topic. Ramus did continue to believe in a correlation, to some extent, between style and content, but he held now to a weaker kind of appropriateness than had been common earlier (Ueding and Steinbrink, 92).

A combination of social and theoretical developments can account for the rise of Ramism and for its widespread influence after 1570. On the social side, it is likely that a decline in aristocratic sensibility played a role, for two reasons. One is that levels of style had often been associated with social levels.[36] In a non-aristocratic society, this association becomes less important. Another reason is that a middle-class-orientated society tends to be more individualistic than an aristocratic one, so that rules about what is appropriate would be less rigid.

Intellectually, such acceptance of variability was readily supported by particularist philosophy. In fact, although Ramus was not a thoroughgoing nominalist,[37] he adopted important features of nominalist logic.[38] That the elimination of 'discovery' (content) from rhetoric is integrally connected with this kind of philosophy is corroborated by the fact that the similarly particularist Epicurean Philodemus seems to have urged the same step (Kennedy 1994: 94-95).

The de-emphasis of aptness fostered freedom, since prescribed matchings were no longer in effect. It meant, however, that style could be understood as ornamental rather than as integral to a work (C.D. Lewis, 18; also, George Puttenham, *The Arte of English Poesie*, 1589, III).

35. Ueding and Steinbrink (92) (the exact location of this statement in Ramus's corpus is not made entirely clear).

36. In Graeco-Roman culture, the association between high style and high social level held sometimes, although not always (see above, 3.5). In the Middle Ages, the association was standard, for example in instructions for letter writing that advised the use of an elaborate style when addressing persons of high status (Ueding and Steinbrink, 68, 91). It still held true for Scaliger (sixteenth century; Ueding and Steinbrink, 94).

37. His famous 'one method' moved from the general to the particular (Gilbert).

38. Most notably, this involved the employment of statements about individuals (such as 'Socrates'), which had not been a part of Aristotle's logic (see *RFT*). Ramus could treat individuals as species and vice versa (Ong, 203-205).

With a gradual decline of aristocratic rule, furthermore, high-style rhetoric was often attacked or, at least, avoided. Especially from the end of the sixteenth century on, verbal schemes were downgraded in favour of figures of 'wit and thought' (Croll, 54, 204; Barner, 247). That was especially true for the speech of middle society, since much of court style remained fairly elaborate, and lower-class preaching—strongly emotional—was full of mystical expressions (Lewalski, 253).[39]

Unadorned objectivity in language became important in philosophy, science, and historiography (Shapiro, 119-62, 227-66). Renewed philosophical criticism of rhetoric sharpened an old opposition between philosophy and rhetoric (cf. Ijsseling, 67). For science, straightforward prose was expressly made the standard during the seventeenth century. (Thomas Sprat, in his *History of the Royal Society*, 1667, 2.20, called it the language of 'artisans, countrymen, and merchants'.) In history writing, an older convention that permitted and even encouraged an imaginative reconstruction of dramatic aspects of an event, such as of a speech that would have been made, was rejected from c. 1574 on (W. Nelson, 40-42, 105).[40] The temper which led to this rejection, together with the subsequent loss of an awareness of the earlier convention, had major implications for the way many readers of the Bible came to take events narrated in it, namely as precise reports.

With a lack of consideration of content, following Ramus, and now also with a lack of an interest in different kinds of style, some rhetorical treatments finally limited themselves largely to delivery, the manner of presentation itself (from Thomas Sheridan, 1756, on; cf. Kennedy 1980: 228-29).

In contrast to an earlier need to defend the Bible's relative simplicity, the newly emerging preference for unadorned rhetoric created the problem of how to explain such artful constructions as do occur in the Bible. One option was to think of these as reflecting a sacred (perhaps ideal) style. With at least a hint of that possibility, schemes and tropes were discussed under the heading of 'sacred rhetoric' in *Philologia*

39. However, already from the end of the sixteenth century on, German court style moved toward simplicity (Ueding and Steinbrink, 94), apparently under the influence of the new bourgeois tendency. On plain style in preaching, see, for example, E. Davis (2-4).

40. To be sure, already Lucian of Samosata (second century CE) had opposed even 'the least amount of untruth' in *How to Write History* (7).

Sacra (1623) by Salomon Glass, a biblical scholar, and in *Centuria Sacra* by the clergyman Thomas Hall (1654, with 'about one hundred rules' for scriptural interpretation). In a very comprehensive manner, Johann Alsted, *Triumphus Biblicus* (1625; Dyck, 166) presented a 'sacred rhetoric', a 'sacred poetics', and a 'sacred logic'. Bishop John Prideaux's *Sacred Eloquence* (1659)—a guide to preaching based on the Bible—derived its very organization from a holy number; it had seven parts (each again divided sevenfold): tropes, figures, schemes, pathetics (passions), characters, antitheses (contrasts) and parallels. The widespread use of typological interpretation also often sought to explicate a special 'language of Canaan' (Lowance).

c. *Sublimity (c. 1675–1775)*

The emerging interest in relatively simple style led to a fascination with 'sublimity', a style that is in one sense high (significant) but in another sense simple (non-elaborate) and, in any case, emotional. It had been described in the work *On the Sublime*, which, like other analyses of style, straddled the fence between rhetoric and poetics (above, 3.5). This treatise had been copied often enough to survive, but (because of its non-aristocratic character?) had received little notice before the appearance of several editions and translations of it from 1554 on. Widespread attention came to it when Boileau published a free translation in 1674, the same year in which he published *L'art poétique*, which represented the culmination of neoclassicism. That year, then, marks an important watershed in the history of criticism, for the theme of sublimity came to supplant neoclassical rules.

Boileau himself, in reflections on *The Sublime* after 1674, made the observation that sublimity is a style that is both moving and simple—embodying a union of what had sometimes been considered opposite characteristics (Brody, 91). Augustine and others had already argued for a grand rhetorical form that is emotional without being elaborate, so that the idea of a non-elaborate but moving style was far from novel.[41] This idea, however, now captured widespread imagination and was applied to literature ('poetry') as well as to rhetoric.

Sublimity, then, became the supreme word of eighteenth-century

---

41. See Shuger for mediaeval and especially postmediaeval rhetorics. Major rhetorical treatises later than 1554, cited by her, already make use of *On the Sublime*, as well as of Hermogenes and other classical rhetoricians who did not identify grandness with elaborateness.

criticism. The meaning attributed to this word ranged widely, indicating varying degrees of dignity and simplicity, but always implying a strong feeling (cf. Monk). The concept naturally fitted biblical literature, which had furnished an illustration for it from the start. Joseph Addison (*Spectator*, 160 [1711], 333 [1712]) applied it to the Psalms and other parts of the Hebrew Bible; Campegius Vitringa, to Isaiah (1714, Introduction); François Fénélon (*Dialogues*, 1718), to Moses, psalms, and the prophets; and Anthony Blackwall (*The Sacred Classics*, 1727), primarily to the New Testament. Johann Turretin employed it in his lectures on method (published 1728; *Opera*, II: 105). Sublimity played a considerable role in Lowth's *De sacra poesi Hebraeorum* (1753), which then influenced subsequent works. At the end of the eighteenth century the theme was taken over by Romanticism, which further developed the stress on feeling. A relatively late use was that of Samuel Pratt, *The Sublime and the Beautiful of Scripture* (1828), with an emphasis on the touching simplicity of its narratives.

d. *Lowth*

Robert Lowth's lectures on the 'sacred poetry of the Hebrews', delivered originally at his inauguration as professor of poetry at Oxford (1753), were grounded in classical studies, but they were also in touch with newer developments of his day. In combining older and newer perspectives, they furnished a level of form criticism that has not yet been surpassed by any work dealing with the entire Hebrew Bible.

Lowth delineated the methodological basis of his work succinctly and with sophistication. He distinguished between an unnecessarily prescriptive approach, which states rules for a prospective composer of poetry, and a critical procedure, which recognizes the principles of literature. A producing 'genius', he said, does not need to be conscious of, or concerned about, the rules of the art; the purpose of criticism, however, is 'to perceive and comprehend clearly the reasons, principles, and relations of things'. Like other sciences, that of poetry is based on observation and points out what is 'conducive to the attainment of certain ends' (Lecture II).[42]

The fact that Graeco-Roman categories and regulations are not always reflected in the form taken by biblical literature was viewed by

---

42. Outside of biblical studies, Lowth is well known for his furnishing a long-influential prescriptive grammar in 1762.

Lowth not as a defect, but as an advantage[43]. Lack of adherence to arbitrary rules shows that biblical poetry is truly good literature, deeply emotional and universal in character. Since poetry 'appears to be an art derived from nature alone, peculiar to no age or nation, and only at an advanced period conformed to rule and method, it must be wholly attributed to the more violent affections of the heart, the nature of which is to express themselves in an animated and lofty tone' (I). The Greek view of poetry as a divine gift fits very well the sacred writings, 'the only specimens of primeval and genuine poetry' (II).

A major portion of Lowth's work is devoted to aspects of poetic style. The primary features of Hebrew poetry are the 'sententious' arrangement in lines, the 'figurative' use of images drawn from various spheres, and the 'sublime' expression of high mind and vehement passion. Together these form the 'parabolic' character denoted by the Hebrew word *mashal* (IV-XVII). Lowth was well aware of the fact that style involves not only 'diction', but even more what can be subsumed under content, namely 'sentiment' and 'mode of thinking' (IV). The first topic, or 'common place', of sacred history is the contrast between chaos and creation; this also acts as a recurring motif for 'any remarkable change in the public affairs' (IX).

Purpose is so closely connected with content and expression that 'nature and design' (XX) fuse into a single concept. In general, the purpose of sacred poetry is to lead human beings to virtue and piety, exciting 'the more ardent affections of the soul...to their proper end' (II). More specifically, its 'office' is 'to commend to the Almighty the prayer and thanksgiving of his creatures and to celebrate his praises'— human expression toward God—and, in a reverse direction of speech, 'to display to mankind the mysteries of the divine will, and the predictions of future events' (II).

Lowth went on 'to distribute the Hebrew poems, according to their different species, into different classes' (II). Specifically, he divided them into prophetic, elegiac, didactic, lyric, idyllic (hymnic) and dramatic forms. Like more recent form critics, he recognized the existence of schools of prophecy and the connection of their activity with music.

---

43. A similar argument, with appeal to an 'Oriental' style, had been made by his predecessors in the chair of poetry at Oxford (e.g. Thomas Warton the Elder, *Poems on Special Occasions*, 1748; see Hepworth, 29-57) and by Augustin Calmet, *Commentarium literale*, I/I, 1734: 329, 331 (first French edition, 1716), the latter also contrasting artificial with natural poetry.

Lowth analysed the basic pattern of funeral recitation (*qîna*) with reference to the inequality of its lines (which had long been recognized) and to Amos's application of the genre. The Song of Songs (interpreted allegorically) is described as semi-dramatic, for it contains alternations of speech and a chorus but lacks a connected story or fable. Similarly, according to Lowth's useful judgment, Job lacks a strict plot and contains a 'representation of those manners, passions and sentiments, which may actually be expected in such a situation' (XXXIII).[44]

One of the major differences between Lowth's and most earlier approaches is that some portions of the Bible which had been previously regarded as rhetorical—especially, prophetic materials—were treated by him as poetic. His position as professor of poetry undoubtedly influenced that orientation; but his view can be understood as an outgrowth of preceding developments, which can be sketched briefly, as follows.

First of all, 'figures'—which include parallelism (in content or clausal structure, or both) had been recognized since classical times as poetry-like characteristics present within speech (see above, 3.5). Thus, a view of parallelism as poetic in an extended sense had been standard for a long time. By Lowth's time, scepticism toward the use of high, poetry-like style in ordinary speech had emerged. Even clausal parallelism, long considered the artful style furthest removed from poetry, had gone out of favour for public speech, although extensive parallelism continued in certain, largely plebeian, traditions (of which Martin Luther King's 'I Have a Dream' [1963] is an especially effective recent example).[45] The parallelistic structure that is present in much of prophecy could thus be perceived as specifically poetic rather than as what might be expected in rhetoric.[46]

Equally important for treating parallelism as poetic was an increased

---

44. Lowth refused an intellectual solution to Job; 'neither the nature nor the object of the poem required a defence of the Divine Providence, but merely a reprehension of the over-confidence of Job'. He did not state equally clearly a critique of Job's friends. (For discussions concerning Job during Lowth's time, including a controversy in which he was engaged, see J. Lamb.)

45. Cf. e.g. Pipes (157) on African–American rhythmical preaching.

46. Parallelism as a rhetorical (low-level poetic) device had already been recognized by both Jews (see above) and by Christians, including among these Nicholas of Lyra and Luther (Raeder 1977: 289). S. Glass listed a form of it among tropes, under the name of *epexegesis* or *exergasia* (1636, *Philologia Sacrae* 5.2.7). Lowth, too, considered it 'agreeable' 'even in prose' (1753, III).

acquaintance with literary traditions other than the Graeco-Roman, including the native American, Indic, Norse, Finnish and Chinese. Some of these employed parallelism rather than metre in poetry (that is, in literature transcending ordinary speech).[47] Thus, the idea of what could be counted as characteristically poetic style was modified.[48]

In fact, even without such information, there had already been some specific steps towards treating parallelism as poetic. Erasmus had moved in that direction and had described three types of parallelism in Psalms.[49] The Jewish scholar Immanuel Frances stated in 1677 the basic principle of parallelism in content by speaking of 'the doubling of language in different words' and had described this feature—perhaps the first one to do so explicitly—as poetic (A. Berlin, 165). He also said

47. Parallelism is a rather common feature of literature in oral cultures. Specifically, the similarity of Finnish with Hebrew poetry with regard to the use of parallelism was discussed shortly before Lowth (Steinitz, 15f.).

48. The notion that poetry need not be metrical had been held in some Graeco-Roman and, even more, in mediaeval Jewish discussions and had appeared in other contexts at least from the end of the sixteenth century on (e.g. Sidney, *Defence of Poesie*, 1595, C2). Lowth argued that Hebrew poetry did employ metre, but that its precise form can no longer be recovered.

49. See above on Erasmus. A move to treat parallelism as poetic (besides the fact of his finding it in Psalms) can be discerned in Erasmus's suggestion that parallel clauses may be accompanied by different musical instruments (on Ps. 33 [H34].2); perhaps he was stimulated by Philo's description of an antiphonal singing of hymns (*Vita*, 83-87, etc.), which Lowth cited (lecture 19). The nature and degree of Erasmus's impact on the subsequent interpretation of parallelism remains to be investigated more fully. One can note, however, that much of Erasmus's work was widely known (Campion, 151) and that, like Philo and in a sense like Erasmus, a number of exegetes associated parallelism with singing by alternating choirs; thus, Johann Gerhard (c. 1630; see Salomon von Til, *Digt-, Zang- en Speel-konst*, 1692, II, i, 8), Marc Meibomius (c. 1700; cf. Kugel 1981: 267), Johann Carpzov (*Introductio ad libros poeticos biblicorum* [first edn, 1720], 2.1.10), and Lowth (*Isaiah*, 1778, Introduction). Alessio Mazzocchi—a contemporary of Lowth (see Bonamartini), who may have learned of Philo's notion of antiphony through A. Calmet's commentary, to which both he and Lowth refer—saw *epexegesis* as a typical feature of poetic books in the Bible (*Spicilegium Biblicum*, VI, on Psalms, c. 1720). Christian Schoettgen had already moved toward characterizing *exergasia* as poetic by expressly identifying rhetoric (i.e. stylistic flourishes) with poetic features (*Horae Biblicae et Talmudicae*, 1733, §5; Kugel 1981: 268), as was, in fact, implicitly an old view (see above, 3.5). For Lowth, parallelism was not the primary distinguishing mark of poetry (see his introduction to Isaiah, 1778), but it came to be widely viewed thus within biblical scholarship.

that biblical poetry regularly has a break in the middle of each line, thereby indicating that a poetic line typically has two parts, which together form some sort of structural parallelism. Perhaps without a knowledge of either of these two writers, Lowth, in a work on Isaiah (1778, 25 years later than his lectures on Hebrew poetry), distinguished (much like Erasmus) between synonymous, antithetic and 'synthetic' kinds of parallelism. In the third of these kinds, a verse or line has two parts which are not parallel in meaning but are separated by a caesura (as Frances had observed).

Among reasons for considering prophecy as poetic, it is worth remembering that Christians had long treated the Psalms—which are poetry—as prophetic, and non-biblical poetry had often been associated with some sort of prophecy.[50] It was, then, not altogether difficult to reverse the characterization of poetry as prophetic and look on prophecy as poetic.

Finally, a major motive for interpreting prophetic words as poetry may have been a readiness to understand them as more than prosaic predictions, namely functionally as critiques or encouragements (Lowth 1753, XX). This line had been anticipated, at least implicitly, by John Dennis (*The Grounds of Criticism in Poetry*, 1704, Preface).[51] A functional-poetic interpretation of prophecy may have been perceived at that time as the most noteworthy implication of Lowth's analysis, since it contributed to a 'critical' (less traditional) view of Scripture.

3. Form in Professional Biblical Exegesis, 1575–1775

A large number of commentaries and other kinds of biblical study were printed during the two hundred years from 1575–1775.[52] Often still

50. See above, 4.3.a. Thus, again, Lowth (ch. 18).

51. Dennis viewed the literature of the Hebrew Bible other than the 'ceremonial and historical'—presumably including the prophets—as poetic. For poetry in general, Dennis did not want to abandon rules altogether but to formulate such as are better than the neoclassical. Thus, he outlined nine literary rules, which serve the traditional ends of poetry (primarily, to reform manners and, secondarily, to please) by—this was new—'exciting passion'.

52. For the many exegetes of this period, the surveys by Diestel, Wogue, J. Schmid and Freiday complement one another. Additional details can be found in G. Meyer (with an index in vol. 5), S. Davidson (679-91) and in standard reference materials. Extensive bibliographies appear in several works of that time, especially in those by Carpzov.

written in Latin, they show an extensive awareness of the classical tradition and of early Christian writers. Indeed, they remained to a considerable extent under the influence of older questions. One relatively new interest was linguistic grammar, which had become strong in Christian circles during the fifteenth century; this motivated many exegetes to give careful attention to mediaeval and Renaissance Jewish commentaries. Thus a sense of continuity with older exegesis was still strong.

Rhetorical and poetic forms, in fact, continued to be of interest to biblical scholars throughout this period. For instance, biblical 'usages', including special prophetic patterns, were analysed by Francis Ribera (c. 1590, Catholic), and Johann Rambach devoted a major portion of his *Institutiones Hermeneutica Sacra* (1723, Lutheran) to tropes and figures and to other literary features.

A major element of commentaries of this time was a detailed description of the internal progression of a text. Sometimes, the patterns envisioned were derived from classical rhetoric. Often, however, such an 'analysis' (as it was called) primarily applied a logic drawn from Ramus.[53] These two procedures were similar to each other, but a primarily logical analysis did not cover the pragmatic and emotional aspects of the text.[54]

A definite reduction in rhetorical sensitivity occurred at the end of the sixteenth century. It is illustrated by the disappearance of the observation that Paul's appreciative words towards his audience in Rom. 1.7-8 serve the function of 'capturing the good will' of his readers, one of the tasks of an introduction inculcated by Cicero. The recognition of such a function of Paul's praise appeared regularly until the sixteenth

53. Although a careful examination of these analyses cannot be made here, it appears that, while traditional rhetoric was still influential for Christoph Koerner (on Psalms, 1578), it was less so for most of the later commentators, including R. LeBlanc (on Psalms, 1665–76, Catholic). An expressly 'logical' analysis was applied by the Ramists Johann Piscator (for many biblical works, 1589-94), Robert Rollock (for Epistles, 1593–1605), and William Temple (for 20 psalms, 1605), by Pietists such as A. Francke (cf. Diestel, 349, 412), and by J. Rambach (*Institutiones*, 1723, 3.3). Virtually identical with a logical one was the 'real' (as distinct from a 'verbal') analysis of the Dutchman Hermannus Venema (on Psalms, 1767–81).

54. Logic had already been stressed, although not exclusively, by the early particularist Peter Aureoli (thirteenth century; F. Stegmüller 1951: 207-19) and by Melanchthon, indebted to Ramus's predecessor Agricola (see above).

century but largely ceased thereafter.[55] The omission can in part be linked to an adoption, by many Protestants, of Ramist rhetoric, which lacked that element; but it occurred quite widely among both Catholics and Protestants, so that it clearly reflected a general change in attitude. The Scriptures obviously came to be taken in a rather straight-faced fashion, with factual (or logical) rather than pragmatic (rhetorical or poetic) truth as the standard.[56]

Especially notable for the period under discussion is an interest in history, exhibited by Catholic, Protestant and Jewish works alike.[57] It showed itself in reconstructions of the chronologies of events narrated and of the details of ancient objects described,[58] and in attention to development both within the Bible and after it in transmission, translation and interpretation. Thus, Johann Bengel (*Gnomon*, 1742, Preface, 5) counted six ages of exegesis up to his time and described the most recent one as 'critical, polyglott [concerned with versions], antiquarian, homiletic'. Often, the points of view adopted were rather literalistic. For instance, the details of the creation accounts were accepted at face value by most Protestants and Catholics.[59] A number of scholars,

---

55. One finds it in Abelard and other mediaeval writers, in Bullinger (1525), Melanchthon (1532; 1540), Calvin (1540), Petrus Vermigli (1561, Catholic), Ambrosius Catharinus (1566, Catholic), Joachim Camerarius (1572, a student of Melanchthon) and R. Rollock (although less sharply so; 1593, Protestant). Thereafter, the idea of capturing good will appears to be missing from most analyses of Romans, including those of Guilielmus Estius (c. 1610, Catholic), Andrew Willett (c. 1620), Hugo Grotius (c. 1640, Protestant), Matthew Poole (1676), John Locke (1705?), Matthew Henry (c. 1710), Natalis Alexander (1746, Catholic) and John Wesley (1755); some of these, it is true, present only disconnected annotations of the text, but this very format itself reflects a disinterest in structure. A mild acknowledgment of the rhetorical role of praise does occur in the commentary by J. Cocceius (c. 1650, Reformed) and a stronger one in an English edition of G. Diodati's annotations (1648); but C. a Lapide (first edn, 1614; Catholic) and S. von Til (*Opus analyticum*, c. 1700; a student of Cocceius) expressly rejected this functional element as primary.

56. According to Rashkow (117), furthermore, translators reduced the moral complexity of texts.

57. Thus also Baird (115). The interest in history is very prominent in Protestant and Catholic commentaries. The study of Jewish (including biblical) antiquity was furthered by Azariah de' Rossi and Abraham ben David de Porta-Leone (c. 1600 CE).

58. As noted by Childs (1994: 331).

59. As already by Luther and Melanchthon and then by most of the commenta-

however, saw biblical history in a different, so-called 'critical' light, as will be discussed further, below.

In regard to forms of expression, the historical orientation showed itself in an increased attention to differences in style between individual books of the Bible. Commentaries and systematic introductions regularly described the variations in language and presentation exhibited by individual authors. For instance, Richard Simon spoke of the 'particular' style of biblical writings (*Histoire critique de Vieux Testament*, 1678, 1.4; etc.). In fact, in secular criticism, 'style' came to be defined as the manner of expression characteristic of a person or group (Lempicki, 235). The recognition of such differences within the Bible naturally created a problem for a belief in its being dictated by God, a relatively literalist belief that came to be emphasized in some circles. The problem, however, could be solved by assuming with Calvin that the Holy Spirit adjusted the style employed to fit not only the content, but also the particular writer and audience.[60]

Along with such rivaling historical interests, nevertheless, the classification of literary types continued[61]. During the early part of the seventeenth century, the Catholic Cornelius a Lapide prepared lists of maxims (*gnomae*), adages (pithy sayings), hieroglyphs (e.g. Hos. 1.2), enigmas (Hos. 2.2), paradoxes (Jn 1.1), parables, counsels (Mt. 5.3), precepts, promises, threats and miracle stories, as they appear in the prophets and Gospels, and described the style of the Song of Songs as 'comic and bucolic'.[62] Johannes Cocceius (c. 1650), Protestant, pointed

tors of the following 200 years (Johann von Marck wrote 854 pages on the history of paradise, 1705); exceptions include Grotius's symbolic view of the serpent in Gen. 3.1 (c. 1640) and Henning Witter's interpretation of Gen. 1.1–2.3 as a poem (1711). That a literal interpretation of origin stories is in part a modern Western development can be gathered from comparative studies (e.g. Finnegan, 29, 35, 63).

60. Analyses of individual styles were too widespread to be listed. For theories of divine accommodation to individuals, see, for example, Johann Hülsemann (c. 1650 [Dyck, 160]); John Owen, rejecting the Jewish distinction between kinds or degrees of revelation (on Hebrews, 1668, Introduction, I, 27-30); Johann Majus, against Simon (*Selectiores dissertationes*, 1708, I, 4); and Bengel (*Gnomon*, Preface, 12). Most earlier interpreters had been less specific in describing divine inspiration, even when they used the word 'dictation' (after all, ancient dictation was not always verbatim).

61. Formal analysis, however, could also be absent or sporadic, such as, it seems, in works by Robert Bellarmin (c. 1600, Catholic) and John Lightfoot (seventeenth century, Protestant).

62. See his introductions to the major and minor prophets, four Gospels and

out in his commentaries the type of speech (*genus orationis*) appearing in a text, often noting that the title of a whole book or of one of its parts gives an indication of it.

A little later, Baruch de Spinoza—not a biblical scholar, but eventually influential in that field—observed, somewhat in passing, that the style of New Testament Epistles is argumentative, rather than that of an authoritative fiat found elsewhere in the Bible (*Tractatus theologico-politicus*, 1670, XI). His coreligionist Immanuel Frances identified 12 types of poems: praise, thanksgiving, prayer (petition and confession), prophecy, praise of the righteous, condemnation, words of joy or reproof, justification of complaints (including joy), allegorical love poetry, lamentation over the temple or over mocking enemies; most poems, he said, combine such types (A. Berlin, 168).

According to the Protestant August Herman Francke (*Manuductio*, 1693, 1.3), histories, prophecies, psalms and epistles exhibit different logical patterns. Matthew Henry spoke more than once of several 'ways of writing', i.e., histories, laws, prophecies, songs, epistles and proverbs (e.g. on Proverbs, c. 1700). J. Turretin (1728; *Opera*, II: 95-96), also Protestant, declared that the Christian Bible, including the New Testament, contains four genres, 'or better' four types of matter: historical, prophetic, moral and dogmatic,[63] each with special hermeneutical rules. He noted that the aim of Genesis 1 is to commend the observation of the sabbath (96), in other words, that it is a foundation story. Quite commonly, in fact, commentaries indicated a text's 'purpose' and thereby its rhetorical kind (exhortation, request, etc.).[64]

Song of Songs (c. 1625). 'Enigmas' also appear in lists of tropes by S. Glass (1636) and August Pfeiffer (*Hermeneutica Sacra*, 1684, 13.4).

63. Earlier, J. Gerhard (Protestant) placed literary types similarly under 'matter' rather than 'form' (*Loci theologici*, 1610, 1.2, 52 [the 1639 edition is quite different]); though his view was largely Aristotelian, the notion of form as inner structure has here partially broken down. A more traditional analysis can be found in Carpzov's *Introductio* (1721), which divides the literature of the Hebrew Bible into histories, poetry (subdivided into tragic [Job], eucharistic, moral, mystical [Song of Songs] versions) and prophecy.

64. 'Purpose' was usually, as was true earlier, called *scopus*, sometimes *propositum* (e.g. William Ames on Psalm 5, 1635). The Aristotelian 'four causes' were applied by Nicolai Seraius (on the Psalms, 1612, Catholic). A number of writers used the notion that scriptural purposes are spiritual as an argument against a literal interpretation of physical descriptions, as had already been done in older works (see Rogers and McKim, 225; Hooykaas, 68-71).

The Psalms, in particular, were again often classified. Widely recognized within them were the following types of speech: petition, lament (or 'complaint'), consolation, praise, thanksgiving, instruction, exhortation and (less regularly) reflection. Giovanni Diodati (1644, French Reformed) grouped these forms according to whether they address God, human beings, or oneself, while other structures (also found in the Psalms) represent God speaking to the faithful or to God's enemies.

Some scholars observed that biblical texts, such as psalms, could be 'mixed' in form;[65] this opinion implies that typologies, while significant, do not reveal the essences of texts. An essentialist outlook was thus being replaced by a different one which was to dominate the succeeding period.

4. *The Old and the New in Hermeneutics*

a. *Secular Hermeneutics*

The early modern period was rich in systematic descriptions of the science of interpretation, or 'hermeneutics', both sacred and secular.[66] Some of those orientated towards sacred Scripture have already been mentioned.

A high point in secular contributions was reached by Johann Chladenius in his 'Introduction to the Right Interpretation of Intelligent Speeches and Writings' (1742), with a brief reference to sacred writings. This was written in German, while a previous hermeneutics by him had been in Latin; the language-change reflected the author's participating in a major transition. The work provided a significant balance of old and new features of interpretation. Specifically, it stated the need to give attention to the circumstances of time and place (§10)—a relatively new emphasis—and—as an old interest—to seek to discern the 'purpose' of a writing (i.e. a desired 'movement' in the 'soul' of the recipient, 154) as one that varies according to the 'type' of the book

65.   On Psalms, for example, C. Koerner (1578), Anthony Gilbie (1581, applying Théodore de Bèze) and the Protestant poets George Wither (1632) and Arthur Johnston (1637); François Dupuis (1530, Catholic) had listed overlapping categories for the Psalter. Mixed literary forms in the Bible, more generally, were described by John Brown (*Essays on the Characteristics of the Earl of Shaftesbury*, 1751, 3.8).

66.   For the secular ones especially (from the sixteenth century on), see, for example, Lutz Geldsetzer's introduction to the re-issue of Chladenius's hermeneutics in 1969.

(727). Combining the older generic view with a newer interest in subjectivity, the work pointed out in its analysis of the genre of historical narration that events are seen differently by different persons so that an account always represents a 'perspective' (*Sehe-Punckt*, 309).

b. *Women's Hermeneutical Contributions*

Women's contributions of this period are noteworthy both for their social significance and for their hermeneutics.[67] It is true, in amount they were still quite limited. Within Protestantism, as in Catholicism, women were active in a number of ways (see, for example, Wittenmyer; P. Russell, 185-211; Demers, 72-79), but without producing systematic expositions of Scripture. Presumably, a major reason for that lack was that academic teaching was not a role in life for them, especially because Protestants abolished convents.[68] When Catholic and Protestant expositions were produced, however, they contained, not surprisingly, both traditional and newer elements. The following examples can indicate some of their range, which overlaps that of rhetorical and poetic analyses already surveyed.

The Catholic Teresa of Avila (c. 1570) wrote meditations on the Song of Songs on the basis of a careful reading of the text. To a wonderment why the Song's 'style'—love poetry—is employed, she responded with the question, 'What more was necessary than this language to enkindle us in His love'? (1.4), thus reaffirming the idea of an appropriateness of language to one's intention. Her exegesis did not engage in analysis for its own sake but was orientated pragmatically ('I shall be able to say only...what serves my purpose' [1.9]). In the process, she exhibited both tentativeness ('I am not thinking I am right in what I say') and confidence ('the Lord teaches me' [1.8-9]).

Not altogether different from these meditations, but more radical, was a very lengthy commentary on the Bible by the unorthodox ('quietist') Catholic Jeanne-Marie Guyon (c. 1713-5). 'The Holy Scriptures', she said, 'have an infinite profundity and many different senses...The great men of science are attached to the literal sense and other senses', but the Saviour has explained to her the 'mystical, or interior' sense (1790 edn, lxvii). For instance, Genesis 1 was seen by

---

67. Cf. Lerner, *passim* (especially, Chapter 7).

68. Cf., e.g., how the *Fraumünster* ('Woman Cathedral') in Zurich was led by women from 853-1524 CE, but thereafter, as a Reformed institution, by males (Vogelsanger).

her as a *belle figure* of 'regeneration, or of the soul overwhelmed by the naught of sin'. Striking are both her confidence and her interiority. The interiority was in line with a traditional role for women, but she held it to be appropriate also for males.

Shortly before then, in 1683, Jane Lead, in the Theosophist tradition and a founder of the Philadelphians (Philadelphia is 'the city of love'), conveyed revelations that she had received about the Book of Revelations, 'unsealing' its secrets 'not hitherto' understood. She expected soon a literal coming of the end, but the focus of her exposition was not on specific events but on the character of the New Jerusalem and its temple as 'Love-Power and Wisdom' (99). Jerusalem was for her 'a figure of the Principle of Light, where all Natures and Properties are harmonized...all faculties are spiritualiz'd and...reconciled to each other in a sweet Love accord'(2). Indeed, women constituted a rather high percentage of those exegetes who gave to the Book of Revelation a 'symbolic'—rather than (according to Gunkel's later distinction) an 'allegorical'—interpretation, that is, a vision that sees the end in holistic-single terms instead of relating images of the book to a series of concrete events.[69]

Of course, an inner, personal dimension does not exclude an outer, social one. Specifically, Margaret Fell, co-founder of the movement of the Quakers, who hear an inner voice, had argued for a public role of women beyond the private or domestic realm. In *Womens Speaking Justified, Proved and Allowed of by the Scriptures* (1666), she defended the thesis that all can be speakers for God. The fact that she relied on the authority of the Bible was a traditional side of her work; a relatively new one was her historical sensitivity in arguing that the restriction of women's public speaking in 1 Cor. 14.34, which runs counter to what is otherwise known about women leaders working with Paul, addressed local conditions. Her work thus represented a growth both in egalitarian and in historical consciousness.[70]

69. See A. Wainwright (203-11), for such interpreters, and below, 11.1.a, for Gunkel. On Lead, see also Demers (79-89); incidentally, her full first name (Jane), which would have identified her as a woman, did not appear in the work cited.

70. It is true, neither the egalitarian nor the historical element were altogether novel. Major arguments for women's equality had been presented from the end of the Middle Ages on, by both women and men (cf. Lerner). That scriptural passages should be interpreted according to their 'occasions' or 'circumstances', in such a way that one can take account of variations in themes, had been said, for example by Calvin (*Institutes*, 3.18, 14; 4.16, 23).

Chapter 6

FORMAL ANALYSIS DURING THE REIGN OF HISTORIOGRAPHY
(c. 1775–1875)

1. *The Triumph of Historicism*

a. *A New Orientation: Particularist Modernity*[1]
The eighteenth century witnessed the victory of an interest in particularity, with an emphasis on personal freedom and an envisioning of characteristic differences between human 'individuals', 'nations',[2] 'races',[3] 'religions'[4] and 'times', with a preference for the 'new'.[5] Such an orientation had begun to play a significant role in preceding centuries, as has been seen. It now came into fuller play. Although radical particularism was never adopted (as probably cannot be done consistently), various versions of it were prominent, with concerns for autonomy, whether of the self or of a nation.

A recurring theme of the movement in this direction was freedom in the sense of a denial of authority of an empire over a nation with its own language and culture, of an aristocracy over the middle class, or of

1.   Ferré (101), too, describes particularism (in Ockham) as 'the Modern spirit'.
2.   John Dryden spoke of 'the Genius of the Age and Nation' (*Works*, XVII: 188 [c. 1677]). Similarly on national features: Anthony, Earl of Shaftesbury, *Characteristics of Men, Manners, Opinions, and Times*, 1711; D. Hume, *Of National Characters*, 1742; Madame de Staël, *De la littérature considerée dans ses rapports avec les institutions sociales*, 1800 (with an interest in national differences). Cf. I. Berlin, 147-49, for views of nationality prior to Herder; Tilgner, 23, 37, 43, for later ones; Oden, 12-15, on nations viewed as individuals.
3.   See below, section c.
4.   A belief common among intellectuals during the seventeenth century, that there is a universal natural religion—better at one time than now—gave way in the eighteenth century to a belief in multiple religions, often thought to be moving in the direction of progress (cf. *RFT*).
5.   Rightly, T. Rendtorff (13); Adam.

a traditional idea over the mind. Nationalism already played a major role at the end of the Middle Ages and during the Reformation; anti-aristocratic notions developed in various ways in the following period. Independence of thought (rejecting tradition) became valued increasingly after 1600. The widespread emphasis on 'reason' during the Enlightenment of the seventeenth and eighteenth centuries was directed against heteronomy, including the authority of the Bible or Church.[6] Romanticism, which followed, increased still more an emphasis on self-determination, individual and national; it thus even became hostile to reason, especially in so far as it might be claimed to provide standards for behaviour.

A major turn took place in conceptions of reason, in fact. Particularism, as has already been mentioned, treats ethics and faith as being based on a 'free', in a sense arbitrary, decision (e.g. God's). That leaves for reason only an instrumental or calculating function, the furnishing of means towards an end; one can call it 'cold' reason. According to Thomas Hobbes (a strong nominalist), 'reasoning is nothing but *reckoning*, that is adding and subtracting' (*Leviathan*, 1651, I, v). The split between science and rhetoric has already been mentioned. During the Enlightenment, especially during its early part (seventeenth century), reason was often still undifferentiated from emotion and value. A falling apart of reason (thought) and will or feeling, however, gradually became pronounced, although they were typically thought to cooperate, with each side making its contribution.[7]

Indeed, as was said earlier in examining Israelite 'wisdom' (2.1.b), a use of 'reason', in the sense of an active apprehension rather than a receptive intuition, must be distinguished from an apprehension of 'reasonableness', that is, a coherence that exhibits appropriateness. Modernity was high in stressing assertive reason but low in allowing for reasonableness or appropriateness in reality (a point to which we will return). It did hold to regularity, especially in the non-human

6. Cf. Reill (4-5); Kopper (12, 82). Thus already, very clearly, Spinoza (*Tractatus Theologico-Politicus*, 1670, VII, near end). Subsequently, for example, Anthony Collins, *A Discourse of the Grounds and Reasons of the Christian Religion*, 1724: v (inspired by the nominalist Locke), stressing the 'right and duty to think for [one]self', even while learning from others (vii).

7. See Horkheimer (1947); MacIntyre (54); Taylor (cf. listings in the index for 'disengaged reason'); Toulmin (31-42 [rationalism was strong in the seventeenth century], 48, 115, 134, 148); Tuana (1992: 34-56). The Kant of the second 'critique' (1788) differentiated 'practical reason' from 'pure reason'.

world, but this perception supported mastery of the environment, embodied in technology. Mathematics, treated as a form of calculation[8] rather than as a vision of contrast and harmony (as in Pythagoras), was useful both for this and for commerce.

The early part of the Enlightenment (before 1700) gave to an older interest in universality a tolerant slant, placing value in all human thought, including various forms of religion, in opposition to an authority that claims exclusive revelation.[9] This idea of universality was supported by a continuing essentialism, according to which objects (such as human beings) have an essence that is shared by all in their class. The theme of universality continued thereafter; but, when it did so, it often appeared in a nominalist frame, within which it becomes monistic universalism, which amounts to a conception of particularity writ large. As Werblowsky (42) rightly stated, 'universalism is very often little more than a euphemistic name for the imperialist-expansionist pretensions of a particular religion or ideology'. (The Christian tradition has often tended in this direction, although it has also included an accepting version of universality.)[10]

It must be seen that particularity can be applied to several levels, including those of the human individual, the human group (class, nation or religious community), humanity as a whole and, finally, the universe (if conceived as a uni-verse). An application to the universe was clear in the thought of Spinoza; namely, as a particularist he adopted a view of 'substance' as an independent reality[11] and then argued, with good logic, that there can be only one such, specifically God, who includes all of reality. A conceptual correspondence, in ancient Greek thought, between the rigid monism of Parmenides and the atomism of Democritus (both of them think in terms of a solid unit, although they differ in regard to its size) has already been noted.

In regard to history, thus, two major kinds of historical perspectives arose, one close-to-monistic, the other close-to-monadistic (a monad

8.   An important development in mathematics at this time was called 'calculus'.

9.   E.g. Catholic and deist broadmindedness flourished at least in some circles (see *RFT* for Nicholas of Cusa [1453], Hubert of Cherbury [1624], etc.).

10.   See below, 6.1.e; 12 (for a number of twentieth-century thinkers); 13.1.b.

11.   *Ethics* (1674), I, definition 3. This definition was indebted to Aristotle, but Spinoza interpreted 'independence' more radically than Aristotle had done, taking relations to be mental only. He did allow for secondary differentiation within the whole.

being a small isolated unit). The version approaching monism, which included the views of Hegel and Marx, envisioned a pattern of upward movement in human or even universal history. According to this idea, cultures other than one's own are viewed as lower steps on a single ladder which leads to a higher ideal state. This perspective had room for historical rationality with a goal within the unified whole.[12] The other, rather monadistic, kind of historicism was orientated towards individuals or groups. It was reluctant to give an 'explanation' of human events or expressions, because it held that culture embodies freedom for the individual or group (Droysen).[13]

Both conceptions of history—the progressivist and the individualistic or nationalistic one—were based on an idea of freedom that stressed independence, either in relation to the past or in relation to other beings or groups. The rejection of tradition was strong enough that, especially in the upper strata of society, there was a gradual turning from an orientation toward the past as the repository of ideal norms to a future-orientated perspective. During the seventeenth and eighteenth centuries (with a midpoint for this process near 1700), in fact, one can almost see Western Europe making a physical turn, away from facing towards the past as 'before' it to a fronting towards the future.[14]

Such evolutionary views, which began with reference to the human realm, were then also extended to the non-human. In particular, Charles Darwin's accounting of organic evolution by his theory of natural selection (1839) applied the principle of competitive aggressiveness within and between societies, which ruled in his human world.[15] In later editions of his work, Darwin joined the concept of natural selection with Herbert Spencer's observation that complexity increases in evolution, by holding that an increase in complexity also represents an increase in fitness. This idea further supported the notion of progress.

12. Hegel's conception of reason was not just 'cold', with love included (MacGregor, 294).

13. Ferry has called only a determined reason-orientated view of history 'historicist' (182); such a narrow definition is not adopted here.

14. In Italy (cf. Vattimo in *RFT*), and cautiously in England among the nominalist *moderni*, the process began already before them.

15. Darwin's notebooks 'make plain that competition, free trade, imperialism, racial extermination, and sexual inequality were written into the equation from the start', as a context in which he operated (Desmond and Moore, xxi, cf. 141, 180, 191, 267, 653). Progressivism, as then envisioned, probably played at least a partial role in stimulating Darwin's theory of evolution (in part contra Hodge).

(More recent analyses, however, indicate that a correlation between complexity and an ability to survive is doubtful, so that the idea of progress becomes questionable for this reason as well as for others.)[16]

b. *Philosophy*

Postmediaeval philosophy was largely, although far from entirely, particularist. (Aristotelianism and Platonism, at the same time, remained influential until the eighteenth century.) For instance, Francis Bacon (*Novum Organum*, 1620) did much to inaugurate the new spirit by challenging the authority of tradition,[17] advocating power over the rest of nature, and arguing in favour of 'induction', that is, the derivation of general ideas from particular phenomena.

Hobbes, a quite thoroughgoing nominalist,[18] and Locke, similarly nominalist, pointed out (in 1656 and 1690) that classifications are relative to one's point of view and do not express essences inherent in objects.[19] Anti-essentialism thus became characteristic of 'modern' thought, but it must also be noted that Aristotelian essentialism did not lose its hold altogether.

Eighteenth- and nineteenth-century nominalism could be 'materialist' (treating matter as fundamental), 'idealist' (considering mind to be basic), or dualist (accepting both mind and matter as givens, although not necessarily with equal status). The idealist kind usually incorporated the moderate nominalist ('conceptualist')[20] belief that structures have a place in the mind. However, George Berkeley (early eighteenth century) was a radical nominalist who denied that general structures exist even in the mind. He was able to avoid sheer anarchy, for as a Christian (he became a bishop), he could trust in God to hold things

16. An increase in complexity is a large-scale feature of both inorganic and organic evolution, connected with a growth in 'entropy' (see *RFT* and below, Chapter 7); a favouring of 'fitness' (i.e. survivability) operates locally.

17. Similarly already in the thirteenth century, Roger Bacon objected to following 'unworthy authority' and 'custom' and made an appeal for the use of observation as a source of knowledge (*Opus Majus* 1.1).

18. However, he was not a 'radical' nominalist, for he acknowledged general structures as secondary (mental) realities.

19. Hobbes, 'six Lessons to the Professors of Mathematics' (1656), lesson 2; Locke, *Essay Concerning Human Understanding* 3.3.20; 3.6.32 (1st edn, 1690). Locke did believe in the 'real' essence of an object, but considered it to be unknowable.

20. See above, 4.3.c.

together. In contrast, the 'objective idealist' Hegel, a century later, held that God and the human self virtually coalesce in 'spirit/mind' (*Geist*), which forms the basis for all of reality and reaches a reflective awareness in Hegel's own thought.[21]

Dualistic philosophies, such as that of René Descartes (early seventeenth century), were probably the ones that were most widely accepted. They often treated matter (semi-monistically) as a block within which determinism rules, while holding that the mental realm includes many 'free' (monadic) units.

Indeed, most postmediaeval thinkers (dualist or not) believed in the operation of general principles or regularities in the non-human world. Such regularities were typically viewed not as innate characteristics of beings (as in Aristotelianism) but as reflections of 'laws' laid upon them contingently by God.[22] According to this conception, the regularities have no ground other than God's fiat (they are not intrinsically 'reasonable'), so that they must be discovered by experimentation rather than reached or supported by reflection about what is appropriate. This position had practical implications; it supported an attitude of control over objects for the following reasons: A control of objects is facilitated by their being regular (predictable), and an exercise of control is emotionally easier when objects are thought not to have their own innate movements which might need to be respected, but as being passively dumb matter (even animals were described as machines).

For instance, Hume (eighteenth century) viewed particulars as the ultimate constituents of the world and was sceptical about fundamental relationships of reality.[23] Thus, in regard to causality, he could observe—somewhat like Ockham (Klocker, 8, 15)—only a regularity

---

21. This conception implied that structures and relations are real since the mind in which they exist is real; it thus provided a stimulus for later relational theory, which accepted the reality of relations without tying them specifically to mind.

22. See F. Oakley and H. Jonas in O'Connor and Oakley (60-83, 247-58) (pointing to a background in mediaeval Muslim and Christian particularism); McGrath (1987: 19-20) (for mediaeval nominalists); Barrow (61-62) (with a comparison by Newton in 1693 that implies a particularist view of politics); Klocker (11) (on Ockham); Wyatt (126) (on Calvin). Malebranche (c. 1700 CE) went further by holding that natural events are 'occasions' of God's actions (although these are typically regular). His slightly younger contemporary, Leibnitz, held that particular 'nomads' do not affect each other but have been set into a pre-established harmony.

23. That does not mean that he rejected relations in nature altogether, but his precise position is subject to dispute.

in sequence, not an inner connectivity between events.

In accepting regularity in this way, most of nominalist philosophy resembled the deterministic particularism of Democritus (and of Stoicism) more than the indeterministic one of Epicurus. However, positions close to the latter kind appeared also, especially from the end of the eighteenth century on, such as in 'utilitarianism' (emphasizing pleasure, as did Epicurus) and in Romanticism.[24]

c. *Politics*

On the political front, the major alternatives within particularism are: (1) unrestrained self-assertion; (2) authority; and (3) prudential compromise. Unrestrained self-assertion means chaos, unless it leads to the victory of one, who then exerts a power-based authority. Compromise, the third option, can be regularized by the notion of a 'covenant'; this, however, implies a degree of mutual respect based on some commonality,[25] so that it is not purely particularist. Anarchism, embodying the first option, was sometimes advocated, but not widely so. Instead, royal authority and covenant formed the two prime theoretical bases for politics in early modernity. These two conceptions were often combined;[26] in fact, kings and relatively individualistic burghers repeatedly made common cause against the traditional aristocracy and the Church.

Gradually—especially early in Great Britain, where nominalism was relatively strong—sovereignty came to be assigned to the people. Their representatives were then expected to 'legislate', that is, constantly to create new laws. To be sure, a sense of divine order usually still lay in the background. Many particularists, specifically, limited human

---

24. Francis Bacon favoured aphorisms over systematic theory (*The Advancement of Learning*, 1605, 6.2), and Pierre Gassendi (seventeenth century) was a notable Epicurean. Romantics (around 1800) objected to rationality and strict lawfulness (e.g. Friedrich Schelling, *Werke*, II, 1927: 589 [1800]). 'Utilitarianism' had strong nineteenth-century advocates, with an ethical ideal of maximizing enjoyment replacing the older ideas of natural law or natural rights.

25. This point is controversial, but it seems to be borne out by history. A way to falsify it would be to point to a single (reasonably successful) example of a society with no assumption of commonality or shared worth. Jane Mansbridge rightly pointed to the need of going beyond pure 'adversary' democracy (1980).

26. Hobbes combined both of these conceptions in *Leviathan* (1651), by saying that members of a state agree to accept a sovereign's absolute authority. Combinations with more moderate conceptions of royal authority are mentioned by Harris (112) for the period from the sixteenth to the eighteenth centuries.

arbitrariness by the belief that sovereigns (whether they are royal or popular) are subject to moral laws laid down contingently but universally by God.[27] As reflections of God's will, moral laws were thus conceived in much the same way as were physical laws (contingently universal), except for the fact that human beings were thought to have enough freedom to be able to violate the laws applying to them.

In regard to culture beyond the borders of one's nation, an interest in difference or novelty became widespread. An early example of this was a fascination with the 'strange' or 'sheerly other', which in the late Renaissance replaced a mediaeval tendency to explain differences on the basis of analogy (Mullaney, 43-44). Appealing to this fascination, exotica came to be collected and displayed in reasonably well-to-do households (e.g. J.Z. Smith, 15-44).

With more serious implications for those affected was the idea that humanity contains different races or even different species, which may not all be truly human. It was generally believed that there are major intellectual, emotional and moral differences between such races or species. This belief provided Europeans with justification (sometimes prospectively and sometimes retrospectively) for subjugating others, including native Americans and Africans.[28] Indeed, it is probably not accidental that European culture during the period of colonial imperialism was marked by philosophical particularism, just as was Muslim

27. See above, Chapter 5, for Bodin and Bossuet in relation to royalty. Even Hobbes (*Leviathan*, 1651, Chapter 26) recognized what he called 'natural law'—contingent (a result of God's decision) but universal—in addition to special divine laws. (*Pace* Cooke, a non-theistic natural law theory was not possible in a nominalist framework.) Such an interpretation of natural law abandoned the old (e.g. Aristotelian) idea that it is inherent in the nature of realities. In fact, less orthodox than others, Hobbes believed that both God's positive law (in the Scriptures) and the law of nature (as it applies to social processes) are 'law' only through human assent (*Liberty, Necessity, and Chance*, no. 14). Far from being 'bourgeois', as Marxists have thought (cf. Bobbio, 10), the idea of natural law was prebourgeois and was gradually (although not always) abandoned, at first through redefinition; Marx's rejection of natural law is an instance of his heavily bourgeois orientation. See further, below, for the anti-natural-law historical school, reflected by C. Schmitt, Ritschl and Barth.

28. For views concerning different human races and species, see W. Stanton (15); Gossett (15, 44-46 [on views, from 1520 on, about Negroes and others as human beings not descended from Adam], 44-46); J.Z. Smith (47); Popkin (115-65); Fox-Genovese (59). Cf. below for I. de Peyrère on pre-Adamites; for the continuation of such ideas into the 1860s, see Pobee (60); R. Edwards (258).

culture, which experienced expansion and economic power before then.[29] (It is, incidentally, not true that a republican form of government militates against empire formation, as one can see from the conquests by Rome, England, the US from its beginnings on, and others.)[30] Even though particularism is not necessarily, or alone, hegemonic, it does readily move in that direction in the absence of a recognition of commonality that implies a shared worth.

Connected with the Dutch East India Company, Grotius (early seventeenth century) developed a system of international law for the restraint of war, but it applied only to competitions within Christian Europe (Hinsley, 165) and was not widely accepted even for these. In fact, from the fifteenth to the nineteenth centuries, theories of what constitutes 'just war' were on the whole downplayed in favour of a Machiavellian view of state sovereignty; accordingly, European countries, fighting with each other, advanced in war technology, while non-European countries, where more restraint of war was practised, fell behind in this, so that they readily became victims when Europeans turned against them (Keegan, 382-92). In fact, Hegel was sufficiently group-particularist that he not only shared in the racism then common but also believed that the very existence of states calls for war and that war is not governed by any law other than world history, which means that the outcome of war is in a deep sense right (he opposed international organization [Hösle, 581]).

While imperialism marks a deplorable aspect of modernity, this complex also had positive sides. As is often the case, then, the development had many different facets, in which good and evil grew together.

For instance, after 1700 the emerging emphasis on freedom, in the sense of a rejection of external authority, contributed to an opposition to slavery (which was also especially vicious at that time)[31] and to its abolition during the nineteenth century.[32] Furthermore, individualism

---

29. In fact, Locke was a colonial administrator. The philosophical outlook supporting older conquests is less clear. Nazism, too, was particularist; see below.

30. Contra a self-serving opinion, discussed, for example, by Troeltsch in 1915 [Platte, 186, differently 237]).

31. Before its abolition, 'negro slavery...at least in the British colonies and the United States, was the most brutal form of slavery ever known', according to Westermarck (704); even if it was not the very worst form ever (this judgment has been disputed), it was certainly near that.

32. See Gay (407-18); B. Davis (46-47, 526). More pragmatic connections

gave support to the spread of republican forms of government and, via competitive capitalism, to the Industrial Revolution, which brought about numerous benefits despite the terror it wrought for many. In regard to gender, the self-assertive competitiveness of this period highlighted a traditionally male manner, but an increased readiness for change, and actual changes in social conditions encouraged the possibility of a new role for women.[33] The idea that there is a basic difference between men and women continued and sometimes was sharpened; yet there was also, on the way towards greater equality, a drive by women and (to a lesser extent) by men to moderate or deny many of the distinctions that had been made between them.

d. *'Bourgeois' Aesthetics, Industry and Morality*

The interest in novelty observed already in several aspects of modern culture extended to aesthetics, within which it had earlier been decried by the author of *On the Sublime*. For instance, Lord Kames, an important aesthetician as well as a promoter of industry, believed that novelty in art is 'the most powerful influence' for raising emotions (*Elements of Criticism*, 1762, Chapter 6). He noted approvingly that surprise awakens self-love, which he valued positively. At this time, a new literary form, the 'novel', permitted the delineation of individual characters, including their change (growth), within the story.

Kames's orientation toward novelty and thus variety in aesthetics was not an isolated theme but rather an integral part of a certain conception of reality. Like Voltaire, he believed that humanity includes more than one species. Closer to home in Scotland, he was a member of a group of important thinkers that included Adam Smith, David Hume, Adam Ferguson and William Robertson. In contact with similar work elsewhere (such as in France), some of these thinkers—especially, Ferguson and Robertson—furthered historiography with developmental theories between 1750 and 1780; Smith constructed a theoretical model for a new economy valuing self-interest. In general, the group held that

between the antislavery movement and capitalism (see Bender) may well have obtained also, but should not be overstressed. An ideology, such as one that values freedom from external control, can have both admirable and problematic sides.

33. See Fraisse; DeGiorgio; Lerner. The exact nature of predisposing social conditions is debated. In Christianity, women played prophetic roles especially outside the larger established Churches (cf. below on J. Lee.)

conflict engendered by self-love leads to progress.[34] A clear picture of these bourgeois characteristics of egotism and continual involvement in change was later drawn by Marx and Engels, who themselves adopted the bourgeois ethos of movement through struggle (*Manifesto*, 1848).[35]

The fact that the outlook described had sociologically a middle-class orientation was conscious for at least some of its intellectual leaders. Thus, Hume valued the 'middle station of life' for being conducive to greatest virtue and wisdom (1742 [Carabelli, 49]) and for having as its members those who support liberty with an interest in securing their property (1752 [1955: 28]).[36] Kames relied on the same stratum for the standards of good taste (*Criticism*, ch. 25). In Germany, Herder similarly viewed the middle class as the pillar of a state—the source of its intellectual and cultural activity—and advocated the emerging historiography as useful for an age dominated by commerce and education (IV: 483; XVIII: 108; XXIII: 429; XXIV: 174). In ancient Greece, as noted earlier, philosophical particularism had already been associated with a middling status.

The middle-class orientation involved, on its practical side, an enhancement of commerce and industry. In fact, the increase in sensitivity for linear time was probably related to this, for the accumulation of capital required a consciousness of the time-value of money ('interest').[37] Connected with industry was the goal of gaining control over the environment, facilitated by an inner distance between humanity and other beings.[38]

It is not possible to argue here for the relative priority of philosophical, social and technological factors.[39] All that can be indicated is they

34. Wheeler (127). Self-assertion is regarded as central for modernity also by Blumenberg (144).

35. Althusser, among others, failed to note this fact sufficiently, despite some remarks by him in this direction (14). Marx's indebtedness to bourgeois thought is better shown, for example, by M. Seliger in Thadden (46-47).

36. Cf. *A Treatise of Human Nature* (1739, 1.4.1) (merchants' activity forms the model for probable knowledge). (Hume, to be sure, did not favour the middle class altogether, but sought to balance it with traditional leadership.) Property was a central notion already for Locke; its connection with individuality was at that time still fairly conscious in the language ('proper-ty'; cf. German *Eigentum*).

37. Cf., e.g., Quinones (3-7); Schoeps (52); D. Lowe (35, 109).

38. For the relation between domination and alienation, see Horkheimer and Adorno (essay I) (they call the Enlightenment 'nominalist'), and Keller (97).

39. Mann described history in terms of four relatively unrelated forms of

were connected, often with mutual effect. For instance, the middle class both contributed to and benefited from conquests, republican government and a readiness for change. The frank espousal of competition favoured those who had the ability and power to compete. It stood, however, in potential conflict with a moral order that calls for the advancement of the common good; it was thus contrary both to traditional feudal designs and to radical visions favouring the poor, for both of these orientations claim a moral order not compatible with pure competition (cf. Troeltsch, I, ch. ii, §9; Mannheim).

e. *Religious Considerations*

Adam Smith valued self-interest and believed that 'benevolence' counteracts this to only a very limited extent.[40] It is true, he also highlighted the role of sympathy, in which one projects by imagination one's own feelings upon others in comparable circumstances. The sympathy he described, however, supports both ambition and distinctions in social ranks, for honour in the eyes of others causes both envy and an 'admiration' that causes 'obsequiousness to our superiors'.[41] Smith did speak, especially in later editions, of an impartial morality that transcends narrow self-interest and social recognition, but he located its prime basis in 'the love of what is honourable and noble, of the grandeur, and dignity, and superiority of our own characters';[42] even this is thus self-orientated. In economics, he developed the thesis that self-regarding competition (at least in moderate form) would actually lead to a greater good for all through the operation of an 'invisible hand'. This thesis held that the invisible hand operates automatically, without special divine or governmental involvement; Smith's view thus represented a practical atheism, while also making unnecessary extensive royal action, which had been important for Hobbes, who believed that the egoism of individuals needs to be restrained.

In fact, atheisms of various kinds (theoretical or only practical) became widespread in high modernity, with a sense of the absence or death of God (Miller, 30f.). Especially males, whose aggressive side

---

power: economic, ideological, political and military. This multiple view is useful but insufficiently integrated. An attempt at a general theory is presented in *RFT*.

40. *The Theory of Moral Sentiments* (6th edn, 1790), e.g. 3.3.5. (The 1st edn appeared in 1759; it was somewhat modified.)

41. Smith, *The Theory of Moral Sentiments*, 1.3.2.

42. Smith, *The Theory of Moral Sentiments*, 3.3.4.

was emphasized, were alienated from Christianity and Judaism, although they continued to occupy the leadership positions of most religious organizations.[43]

Although modernity came to be largely antireligious, it must be remembered that its interest in particularity stood in continuity with what was one aspect of Christian (and Jewish) faith, nurtured, one-sidedly, in mediaeval nominalism. In fact, there were a number of linkages between bourgeois consciousness and Christianity—despite the fact that there were divergences between them—especially the following two.

One frequently discussed tie-in between Christianity and modernity is the phenomenon that a belief in progress resembles Christian (and Jewish) eschatology in envisioning a better world. The Christian outlook, especially in the form that it took in Paul's thought, had already had a tendency toward monistic universalism, with evolutionary elements (such as treating the Hebrew Bible as a step towards Christian faith).[44] Of course, this similarity does not mean that Christian ideas were the only cause for the modern belief in progress, which, on the contrary, differed sharply from biblical faith; but in historical reality there are always multiple causes at work, in this case including Christian ideas.[45] For a number of colonial conquests, in fact, Christianity (understood in a monistic-universalistic way) provided an ideology which stated as an aim for the conquests the conversion of those subjugated.[46]

43. In Catholic countries, anticlericalism and non-attendance at church were specifically male phenomena (De Giorgio, 169). In the US (according to Douglas), 'the minister and the lady were appointed by the society as the champion of sensibility' (12) in tension with 'the most powerfully aggressive capitalist system in the world' (6), handled by lay males. (E. Stanton [in *The Woman's Bible*, I, 1895: 8] said that woman was, perversely, 'the chief support of the church and clergy; the very powers that make her emancipation impossible'. To be sure, there were also some women who opposed the Bible [mentioned by Gestefeld in *The Woman's Bible*, I: 146f.]).

44. Monism was absent from Jesus' teaching, it seems. (The fact that Paul tended toward monistic universalism does not, of course, mean that all of his viewpoint was without value.)

45. Blumenberg's highlighting of the anti-Christian character of modernity fails to deal adequately with multicausality.

46. See again Prior (50-57). (Oddly, in comparing Christianity with Judaism [285], Prior loses sight of the Christian monism that has justified conquest, as described by him earlier.)

Another tie-in lies in the fact that Christianity has a tendency to distinguish between the life of faith and the life of the social world apart from faith; it typically (perhaps most sharply in Calvinism) takes a quite pessimistic view of 'fallen' human actuality, considering it to be strongly self-centred. Bourgeois ideology can be understood against this background, although in two quite different ways.

One of these bourgeois ways was exhibited by Adam Smith—located in Scotland, where the Calvinist notion of human depravity was especially common. In a sense, he adopted the view that human beings are (after the fall, prior to regeneration) basically self-centred,[47] but he differed from this view by holding that such an orientation is good, as has already been seen to be true for the Scottish group to which he belonged. His ethos—characteristic especially of the upper portion of the bourgeoisie—has subsequently been described as follows:

> The middle class person was one—most often male at this time—who saw the opportunities and took them for himself: he grasped his own individual capacities as his only true endowment and resolved the use of that endowment to enter into a life-time of continual self-expansion, self-expression and self-enrichment. To accomplish those ends, the middle-class person had to become a calculating, willful and often ruthless individual...competing shamelessly against his rivals... Bereft of the inherited standards of status of worth that predominated in a simpler age, the middle-class person was caught up in a mad race for self-esteem and self-glory based on his mastery and development of unique personal characteristics.[48]

Another bourgeois way was taken by earnest Christians and Jews, as well as by some persons who had intellectually but perhaps not emotionally abandoned the faith they once had. They accepted competitive capitalism as 'realistic', that is, as suiting the unfortunate self-centredness of human beings. They permitted that system to hold sway in the public world, in which, with appropriate qualifications, they could exercise a calling and engage in service; but they found primary fulfilment in the private realm, including the family and the sphere of religion.[49] They, too, were individualistic, but in a more spiritual way;

47. A position of this kind has appeared recently again in the rather traditionally Christian work of René Girard. Hobbes had held a similar view.

48. D. Frank (127-29), for this type, as it continued c. 1900 (it is quite widespread still, and variations of it occur also outside the modern West).

49. This description is based on extensive knowledge (in person or through biographies, etc.) of persons in capitalist society. For the ideal of service among

they belonged often, although by no means only, to the lower bourgeoisie. They formed a group that had and still has the reputation of being well-behaved and without whose cooperation the capitalist system probably cannot work (the more strongly grasping one alone would probably self-destruct).

These two divergent, but complementary, perspectives (together with numerous intermediate ones) have, since the eighteenth century, conjointly supported capitalism. Modifications of those two views c. 1900 led to social democracy, which is no longer pure capitalism even though it incorporates elements of it (see Chapter 7 below).

Definite moves towards transcending capitalism were already made during the nineteenth century. One such was atheistic. This included the position of Karl Marx. Marx shared with his bourgeois contemporaries an emphasis on strife. But he was sharply critical of the individualistic and middle-class-orientated version of that emphasis, even though he thought of that version as a necessary stage through which history must pass on the way towards the dictatorship of the proletariat. However, he believed that conflict constitutes a central motor of history and was sceptical of the possibility of transcending one's group, thinking that claims to altruism are, for the most part at least, a mere cover for selfishness.[50]

A very different move toward transcending individualistic modernism—ultimately probably more significant—was religious. It was significantly formulated by Catharine Beecher. She participated in the modern ethos by valuing 'free investigation and discussion' (*An Appeal to the People in Behalf of their Rights as Authorized Interpreters of the Bible*, 1860: 344)—willing to go against tradition—but she did not abandon faith. As an educator of young women, she set forth a 'mental and moral philosophy' that granted more importance to 'experience' and 'reason' than most theologians have done, and more to the Bible than most philosophers did,[51] thus going counter to the nominalist split between reason and faith. Perhaps she was aided by the fact that she

---

secularized persons, cf. Yeo (94-102). Troeltsch, among others, has seen the co-presence of the two perspectives (IV: 302-11 [1907]), describing the connection between Calvinism and capitalism better than Weber (I: 607-794 [1911]). An antithesis between the two perspectives apparently grew gradually, as more persons lost 'faith'.

50. Cf. *RFT* for some discussion of Marx.

51. *The Elements of Mental and Moral Philosophy*, 1831 (see, for example, iv, commenting on philosophers' disregard of the Bible).

was by profession neither a theologian nor a philosopher; if so, she illustrated the fact that often an intellectual breakthrough is led by a partial outsider.[52]

Although Beecher remained reserved about a political role for women, she entered forcefully into the realm of intellectual debate.[53] In particular, she rebelled against the doctrine of 'total depravity',[54] according to which human beings have, since Adam's fall, 'such a depraved nature that every moral act is sin and only sin until God regenerates each mind'. She judged this doctrine to be contrary to the Bible and to a sensitive education of children.[55] By arguing that human beings are not fundamentally isolated, she was in 1860 an early (perhaps the earliest) proponent of relational philosophy, as that became important in subsequent decades and during the twentieth century.[56]

f. *Revision in the Notion of Form: Historical versus Generic Criticism*
The social and philosophical reorientation of modernity brought about new conceptions of form, although Platonic and Aristotelian versions

---

52. A combined view of philosophy and theology had a history on which she could draw. Nevertheless, her synthesis in major ways went beyond that. For the role of partial outsiders, see below on Gunkel.

53. She accepted women's subordinate status in 1837 (*An Essay on Slavery and Abolitionism*, 99), but moved beyond that position, especially in regard to public discussion (as noted by L. Mott already in 1856 [Greene, 231-32]). Her education of young women furnished a foundation for subsequent, more political, feminism. In fact, already in 1829 she noted that women's education was outrunning their opportunities (*Suggestions Respecting Improvements in Education*, 54-55).

54. This doctrine was accepted by her father Lyman Beecher (*Views on Theology*, 1836: 195f.); it was rejected not only by Catharine but also by her brother Edward, perhaps in response to a personal struggle in Catharine (Harveson, 157). Actually, that doctrine went beyond Calvin, although he was one who expressly developed the theme of human depravity; Calvin, namely, did not believe depravity to be total, but allowed for the operation of divine grace, even among those who are not elected to be saved, for the sake of the 'preservation of the universe' (*Institutes*, 2.3.4.4-5). C. Beecher labelled the rejected view 'Augustinian'.

55. *Appeal* (1860: 4). At about the same time, H. Bushnell issued his well-known call for the 'Christian Nurture' of children (1st edn, 1847; final edn, 1861). These two works, it seems independently, reacted against roughly the same theology in partial harmony with a more liberal one emerging in New England.

56. *Appeal* (101); cf. *RFT* and below, Chapter 7.

continued.[57] Thus, whereas Aristotle had distinguished between those qualities that constitute an essence and other qualities that are accidents and had used 'form' to designate the essence, Hobbes, rejecting essence, defined 'form' as follows: 'Form is the aggregate of all accidents, for which we give the matter a new name' (*English Works*, IV, 1840: 309 [1682]). Immanuel Kant located form in the perceiving mind, which orders sense-perceptions in part on the basis of 'pure' forms innate in mind.[58] 'Form', he said, is the 'manner in which we recognize an object' (19).[59]

Very widely, form was thus treated as an external (sensuously perceived) aspect of existence. In treatments of literature, it was set in contrast to content—a contrast that would not have made sense in a Platonic or Aristotelian framework.[60] The fact that the distinction between form and content had a social base was sometimes recognized; for instance, the aesthetician Robert Zimmermann, who supported the distinction, showed that historically and theoretically it is closely connected with individualism (*Aesthetik*, I, 1858: 65). It is true, once form and content were distinguished, attempts could then also be made to correlate them.[61]

Of course, there were also contrary voices. For instance, in his relatively classicist period, the poet Johann von Goethe constructed a morphology with a holistic view also for plants (1790, etc.). He shared, however, the developmental interest of his time in that the central focus

57. Emerton (1984) traces a variety of such ideas of form (more or less modified) in science before c. 1800.

58. In the mind, according to Kant, the 'pure' forms of space and time are present even (at least theoretically) apart from empirical input.

59. As formulated in a lecture on logic, as it was copied by Pölitz in 1789 (similarly, according to lecture notes for other years). According to Kant (*Logik*, §2), 'the matter of conceptions is the object, their form is generality'; this generality is mental.

60. Whyte (232) dates the beginning of the devaluative use of 'form' to the middle of the seventeenth century. The reorganization of rhetoric by Agricola and Ramus (fifteenth and sixteenth centuries) had already moved towards a separation of form from content.

61. For instance, Hegel distinguished 'form' as sensuous representation from 'content' (or 'idea'), and valued the latter ultimately more highly (lectures on aesthetics, 1823-26, for example at the end of the introduction), but he held, approaching monism, that in a true work of art the two constitute an 'identity' (Wicks, 108, etc.).

of this appoach was on metamorphosis, or transformation, the growth of forms in an organism.[62]

For the study of human life, certainly, history became the central concern. In accordance with the generally prevailing outlook, the new historiography emphasized divergence and change (Ebeling 1959: 253) and aimed to be factual, untrammelled by an authoritarian tradition. In order to overcome a distance in time and character, Friedrich Schleiermacher (1959: 109 [1819]) called for contact with the different other through 'divination'. This is aided but not fully determined by a comparison of this other with oneself and with third persons.[63] Sometimes, a call for objectivity included the theme of self-denial by the investigator, which is the intellectual form of an inner-worldly asceticism characteristic of some forms of bourgeois culture.[64] Interest in history and particularity was revealed also in creative literature and in the visual arts (Wölfflin, 19, 233; Richardson, 45).

From a dominantly particularistic perspective, the study of literary genres was called into question or sharply revised. Traditional criticism had viewed genres as 'species' of literature, each with their own essence. Now it became standard to focus on individual items and to consider literary genres only as convenient groupings of these or as largely arbitrary conventions followed by them. For instance, Schleiermacher considered special hermeneutics, which deals with genres, to be merely an 'aggregate of observations', without theoretical significance (1959: 79 [1819]).[65] Often, both critics and authors

---

62. Similarly, his friend Friedrich Schiller, also fairly classical, stressed a holistic and universal form (*Über die ästhetische Erziehung des Menschen*, 1795, 12.5; 22.5). Perhaps influenced by Goethe, August Schlegel spoke of an 'organic form' which is 'meaningfully external' (*ein bedeutsames Aeusseres*) but which grows on the basis of an inborn constitution (*Vorlesungen über dramatische Kunst und Literatur*, 1809, lecture 12 [1923, II: 112]). A somewhat different idea of inner form was taken over by some from Shaftesbury (seventeenth century), who in good part continued a classical position (see, for example, Orsini). In regard to the Bible, Goethe accepted a divine 'inner' meaning (*Dichtung und Wahrheit*, 3.12) together with a varied particularity in specific matters (Schottroff, 1984: 463-85).

63. Cf. Ellison (79-89). It is similar to the 'intuition' of particulars according to Ockham.

64. See Wach (I: 140, 161; II: 251, 328; III: 126-27) on Schleiermacher, Leopold von Ranke and others in the nineteenth century.

65. In lectures of 1831/32 (*Einleitung ins neue Testament*, section 2) he continued to acknowledge a need for 'special hermeneutical' rules for individual genres, but he did not furnish an analysis of them.

rebelled against the assumption of rules for a work of art. Thus, genre theory, which had frequently dealt with such rules, became increasingly vague. After 1815, its usefulness was often rejected, and every work could be declared individual in character (Wellek, II: 266, etc.). In fact, several of the more significant reflections on genres that emanated from this period (especially those by Hegel and Ludwig Uhland) were not published by the authors themselves, perhaps because the topic did not fit the discussion of that time.

In so far as genre theory did continue, one of its traditional aspects—consideration of the social status of the protagonists—was abandoned because of a new, more egalitarian, social attitude. Thus, of Aristotle's threefold classification of the arts, only two distinctions remained significant, namely, 'means' (language, rhythm, and so on) and 'manner of representation' (epic [narrative], drama and lyric).

Such types as remained in the discussion were not viewed as exclusive structures to be applied precisely. Even ancient theory had not insisted on pure genres, although the ideal of purity had been discussed from time to time. Now, combinations of different features could be frankly accepted or positively valued (Scherpe, 121-28, 161-69).

g. *Biblical Historical Criticism*
With regard to the Bible, a major sense of difference between its period and the present emerged. (For instance, Bishop Berkeley, an archnominalist philosopher, thought that the Bible's being written 'at distant times' made some of it difficult to understand for persons who 'live in other times'.)[66] Consequently, in biblical interpretation a 'figural' understanding of events or persons that sees transtemporal meaning in them was greatly reduced (Auerbach, 495). Individuals spoken about were now less often taken as a reflection or impress of fundamental religious processes. That was especially true in academia, for typological interpretation continued to flourish outside of it in both 'white' and 'black' communities.[67]

In academic biblical studies, 'historical criticism' came to be the primary approach. It involved an assertion of freedom, in the sense of

66. Euphranor (for Berkeley) in *Alciphron* (1732, sixth dialogue).
67. For the African American tradition, cf., e.g., V. Wimbush and D. Shannon in Felder (91, 120); T. Smith. A 'white' example: typology (in good part future-orientated) played a major role in *The True Explanation of the Bible, Revealed to Joanna Southcott* (1804).

independence, for both thought and practice.[68] On the practical side, it supported the legitimacy of new political and economical processes. This support is indicated by a strong association of early historical criticism with the libertarian tradition of the commercially flourishing Dutch republic[69] and with nominalist philosophy in England, where republican forms hemmed in royalty and colonial commerce was strong.[70] To be sure, a sceptical view of the Bible was largely limited to a relatively high (so-called 'well-educated') social stratum, within which it flourished at first informally (outside of academics).[71] For

68. Freedom was a central theme, for instance, for Spinoza (seventeenth century) and for Johann Semler's *Abhandlung von freier Untersuchung des Canon* (1771-75), which marks the beginning of full-scale historical criticism of the Bible in Germany. On challenges to biblical authority in England, France, etc., prior to the eighteenth century (also by common people), cf. Hill (210-14); Woodbridge (86). In Germany, at least, the theme of freedom was associated with a rejection of 'Judaism' (including much of the Hebrew Bible) as normative for Christianity—Judaism being considered relevant, rather, for a particular time and place (thus, in Semler's work and in Peter von Bohlen, *Die Genesis*, 1835, vif.; cf. Bickerman, 19, 25; Lüder, 141). One strand in early historical criticism was Roman Catholic, in part because the Bible's authority was less crucial for Catholics than for Protestants; in nineteenth-century Germany, however, the Catholic hierarchy succeeded in restraining its open expression (Friedrich Bleek, *Einleitung*, §10).

69. So, Andreas Masius, Jacques Bonfrère, Grotius (who wrote for the Dutch East India Company), Isaac de la Peyrère (cf. Popkin, 115-65 for the implication of his theory concerning pre-Adamites in regard to the differential treatment of human groups [e.g. with an influence on Voltaire, cited above]), Spinoza (his distinction between piety, with ethics as content, and philosophy, dealing with 'nature' [in *Tractatus theologico-politicus*, 1670, XIV]—important for his criticism—was typical for nominalism), Jean Le Clerc, C. Vitringa (cf. De Vries, 10f.). Other critics, such as R. Simon, knew one or more of these. Descartes, whose impact on biblical historical criticism was indirect through some of these, had done much of his writing in this location.

70. Thus, Hobbes, *Leviathan* (1651), focusing especially on the Pentateuch, and Collins, a follower of Locke (who was a colonial administrator), especially on Daniel (1726, etc.).

71. See Hayes (1995: 44). The strong advance of historical criticism in nineteenth-century Germany (after beginnings elsewhere) was in large part due to a high level of academic freedom, especially as an ideology, fostered perhaps by political divisions within the German-speaking area, with rivalry between states in terms of the fame of their universities. (Similarly, Bray, 227. In Great Britain, there was less emphasis on a university-trained clergy [e.g. Milton opposed it]; Rogerson 1985: 138 indicates that there were many fewer theological professors there. Furthermore, during the nineteenth century, historical criticism in England seems to

socially lower-positioned persons, it was often a literalistic approach to the Bible which furnished an element of freedom, since it did not require the help of a clerical or academic elite.[72]

On the whole, in newly leading circles—the main beneficiaries of the new economy—the authority of Scripture fared poorly. Especially the Hebrew Bible, with its legal structure including the prohibition of usury or interest (cf. B. Nelson), was under suspicion. Voltaire criticized religion for inhibiting commerce, industry and the luxurious arts (Schwarzbach, 233). Thomas Paine attacked the Bible both for its content and for its manner of presentation; he objected to its 'obscene' narratives, found Ruth 'foolishly told', and judged the stories about Jesus as largely legendary (*The Age of Reason*, 1795, 1.1, 2, 7).[73]

The fact that a number of the major theses of the emerging historical criticism—including a post-Mosaic date for the Pentateuch, a Maccabean date for Daniel, and the unreliability of stories about Jesus—had been set forth by early critics of Christianity[74] shows that it was not so much the discovery of new data but rather an attitudinal change that lay behind the new outlook on the Bible. This new attitude can be said to have had many advantages, for a great many modern developments, including the abolition of royalty and of the prohibition of interest ('usury') and a critique of patriarchy, would hardly be possible without such a change in attitude,[75] although two of these steps—critiques of royalty and (implicitly) of patriarchy—can also find some support within biblical literature.[76]

have been impeded by a split between general culture and the Church [Rogerson 1995a: 69]).

72. In fact, Pietists and similarly literalistic groups, following a version of empiricism, placed considerable emphasis on personal experience.

73. Paine cited the biblical criticism of Faustus of Mileve (rejected by Augustine), Abraham ibn Ezra and Spinoza, and was probably aware of the extensive criticism then flourishing in France and England (Davidson and Scheick).

74. Cf. Stein (28, 33); S. Ackerman. Some, but perhaps not all, of these points were made by 'Porphyry' (not mentioned by Kraus [1969]), one-sidedly focusing on the contribution of Protestant Reformers to historical criticism; see on 'Porphyry' above, 4.1.c. Julian observed a difference between the Synoptics and John in regard to Jesus' divinity.

75. Soon after 1850, in fact, attempts to find support in the Bible for women's rights was abandoned by many (although not by all) in the US (Hardesty, 84-85).

76. Biblical reservations towards royalty are well known. For biblical criticism of males, see above, 2.1.a. The liberation of women can be covered by the theme of liberation for the oppressed, and feminists indeed found various support in the

The participation of women in biblical exposition during the period c. 1700 to 1875 was still largely limited to the role of educating children and young women (Demers, 90-120). A notable work that stood on the border between addressing the public and speaking to the private realm was an extensive study by Grace Aguilar (Jewish) concerning 'The Women of Israel' (c. 1845). Aguilar—believing in a divinely ordained equality of the sexes, although intending to be low-key about this—placed her hope especially in women to hasten the day of the Lord through home instruction of 'their sons' and through their 'spiritual elevation' socially and 'yet more domestically'.[77]

Women did not participate directly in the early application of historical criticism to the Bible, presumably in good part because of their virtual limitation to the private realm, especially within the major religious traditions. One can also ask whether aggressive masculinism had in principle something to do with the historical-critical approach, at least when that is not balanced by another one. While this question is not easily settled, it does appear to be the case that, for whatever reason, a one-sided orientation towards separateness (as perhaps also a one-sided emphasis on generality, current earlier) has been more typical of men than of women; will that continue to be the case?

2. Analysis of Biblical Literature: General Treatments

If one adopts Hobbes's nominalist conceptions of form as the 'aggregate of all accidents, for which we give the matter a new name' (cited above, 6.1.f), much of historical criticism falls under the heading of form criticism. We shall exclude this line, however, from the present survey for two reasons. One is that the history of historical criticism has already been covered quite a few times. Another is that, if 'form criticism' is taken so broadly that it includes particularist criticism, then it becomes synonymous simply with 'criticism'. We will thus restrict the term to those approaches that allow for the possibility of real, not merely conceptual, generality.

Although formal analysis, as defined, was not the prime focus during

Bible; for instance, the African American Jarena Lee, who heard a vivid voice calling her to preach, felt supported in this by the account that women were the witnesses of Jesus' resurrection (*Religious Experience and Journal of Mrs. Jarena Lee*, 1849: 10-11).

77. Chapter on the wife of Manoah (Eskenazi, 98) and near the end of the work (in the 1854 edition, at least).

the period under discussion, a number of relevant contributions appeared. Sometimes they were made in connection with historical study, with adjustments called for by historical criticism. At other times they emanated from persons who either did not accept the new ethos or were unwilling to be limited by it; that happened especially near the beginning and end of the period.

a. c. 1775–1800

Herder, knowing Lowth, was still interested in literary classification, but in his descriptions generic terms are quite fluid and melt into one another.[78] An interest in Asian and other cultures (cf. Willi) provided him with the comparative perspective which is almost a necessity for a criticism concerned with literary patterns. He did not, however, harmonize the various traditions. Rather, one of his most notable theories was the particular character of peoples, each with their special spirit or culture.

In examining the 'spirit of Hebrew Poetry' (1782–83), Herder employed a considerable number of formal terms, not as a basis for differentiating the texts into separable classes (because of a disinterest in distinguishable genres already mentioned) but for the sake of characterizing them. In the Bible, he found picture speech, poetry about persons (in fact, Hebrew history is poetry, since it is 'painted as present', 234), fables, riddles, word play, joyful song, praise, victory songs, blessings, royal psalms and national songs. Psalms are classed according to their complexity. In his preface to another work (1787), he grouped elegies according to concern about a general state of affairs, for individual problems, or for one's country (*Sämmtliche Werke*, XII: 331-35).

Herder's analysis gives a fairly secular impression and makes little allowance for the basic religious dimensions which were outlined in earlier studies.[79] An early sketch not published by him did furnish an

---

78. Cf. Wellek (I: 200); Kathan (2, 93); C. Bultmann (23-32). Herder's interpretation of the Song of Solomon was influenced by Opitz, who had divided the song into a series of poems. Like Opitz (cf. above), he composed paraphrases of biblical materials (1771-73); indeed, his work generally bears the mark of a poet and literarily sensitive person. 'Form-critical' (Bayer, 43) observations by Herder's slightly older associate Johann Georg Hamann, with a strong interest in language, were very limited in extent.

79. That does not mean that he rejected revelation altogether; he was a preacher c. 1771–75 (Zippert).

extensive treatment of Gen. 1.1–2.3, an 'old oriental poem explaining the arrangement of the week from the creation of the world' (1769; VI: 70). But it denied that this is a divine oracle about creation (VI: 74), giving credit instead to human insight. What Herder did publish declared that the tendency of Israel and of other ancient nations to derive everything from God was that of a child, contrary to the will and enquiry of an adult human being (XI: 361).

Johann Gottfried Eichhorn, in his famous Introduction (1st edn, 1780; 4th edn, 1824), spoke sometimes of genres, although in a very vague fashion. He tended to view expressive form as external, calling it a 'clothing', *Einkleidung*, of the word (Sehmsdorf, 63, 91; cf. Herder, XI: 9). Of more interest to him than generic theory were questions of the time and circumstance of a writing. Indebted to both Herder and Eichhorn, Karl Stäudlin described such forms as visions, fables, elegies and songs of joy as an *Einkleidung* (1783, etc.; cf. J. Schmidt). Johann Hess, too, viewed myth as an *Einkleidung*.[80]

Generic classifications were included in the hermeneutics of Georg Bauer (*Hermeneutica Sacra*, 1797) and of Gottlob Meyer (*Versuch einer Hermeneutik des Alten Testaments*, 2 vols., 1799–1800). Like Turretin (cf. above), they treated under 'general hermeneutics' principles that apply to the whole of the Bible or to any literary work, and under 'special hermeneutics' principles of interpretation relevant to the thrust of different genres. The genres treated included myth, history, poetry and prophecy, which were further subdivided. Meyer sought to reach 'the most general form [namely, the logical form] of human thinking' expressed in a writing; this logic includes several kinds of judgments. Peculiarities of the Orient and of Christianity were noted by him as well. In these important works at the end of the eighteenth century, one can see a culmination of earlier perspectives together with an openness to the newer historical ones.

b. c. 1800–1875

During the nineteenth century, the theme of a connection between poetry and religion was continued by a number of non-theological literary figures and critics, including William Blake, William Wordsworth,

---

80. *Bibliothek der heiligen Geschichte* (1792: 165). A briefer, and more classical, analysis of 'the poetry of the Hebrews' with attention to its 'kinds' was furnished by Hugh Blair, *Lectures on Rhetoric and Belles Lettres* (1783, lecture 41).

Samuel Coleridge, Percy Bysshe Shelley and William Hazlitt.[81] Connecting the variety of religions with nationalities and combining variety with unity, Blake formulated this principle: 'The Religions of all nations are derived from each nation's different perception of the Poetic Genius, which is everywhere call'd the Spirit of Prophecy' ('All Religions are One', 1788). Coleridge, by then relatively conservative in his social and literary views, declared in posthumously published 'Letters on the Inspiration of the Scriptures' (I [c. 1820]) that in the Bible 'I have found words for my inmost thoughts, songs for my joy, utterances for my hidden griefs, and pleadings for my shame and my feebleness'. Influenced by Coleridge and by others with a Platonic streak (see Crosby), the theologian Horace Bushnell predicted that 'the Scriptures will be more studied than they have been, and in a different manner— not as a magazine of propositions or mere dialectic [logical] entities, but as inspirations and poetic forms of life' (*God in Christ*, 1849: 93).

Women entered the discussion at important points. Sarah Grimké (Quaker) made the form-critical argument that God's statement to Eve that 'your husband...will rule over you' is a prophecy, not a command (although the English translation used said 'shall' for 'will').[82] In accordance with this analysis, Elizabeth Wilson defended 'the equality of the sexes at the creation and [!] since the fall'.[83] C. Beecher, in *Common Sense Applied to Religion: or, The Bible and the People* (1857), provided a chapter on the 'Interpretation of Language'. In this, she dealt with association and abstraction and with 'figurative' and 'symbolic' language, including allegory, hyperbole and irony. She set forth the rule that, 'when the literal meaning expresses what is not consistent with the nature of things or with the writer's other declarations, then the language is *figurative*' (279). This principle was traditional; more liberal assessments by her in regard to theology have already been reported (6.1.e).

African American 'spirituals' and addresses—like other songs and sermons—contained an implicit hermeneutics. Specifically, it has been observed that this tradition exhibits 'a hermeneutic characterized by a

81. Cf. Prickett (1986: 43-62; 1991: 190-214); Norton (II: 136-75); B. Shelley. Was this relationship explored for the Bible also by non-theological critics outside the English world?

82. *Letters on the Equality of the Sexes, and the Condition of Women* (1838, I). Cf. Selvidge (44-54), and below, 6.3.a.

83. *A Scriptural View of Women's Rights and Duties* (1849, I).

looseness, even playfulness, vis-à-vis the biblical texts themselves. The interpretation was not controlled by the literal words of texts, but by social experience. The texts...seized and freed the imagination'.[84] Since slave narratives made much use of symbols and metaphors (Coleman, 96), their authors and hearers must have recognized such features in the Bible.

Comprehensive views of the forms of biblical literature were largely limited in this period to persons whose interests ranged beyond biblical scholarship, especially toward Near Eastern cultures or to literature in general. A number of such treatments were directed toward general readers, who would not have been interested in the details of historical criticism, which were the prime focus of academic study of the Bible.[85] A majority of the relevant works were conservative in historical matters. Some of them continued the tradition of dealing with both general and special hermeneutics, the latter dealing with specific genres.[86]

Literary analyses included, specifically, Johann Wenrich, *De poeseos Hebraicae atque Arabicae* (1842), examining lyric and narrative types as well as prophetic forms, and Claude Plantier, *Etudes littéraires sur les poètes biblique*, covering Moses (the Pentateuch), Job and Solomon, David (Psalms), and prophets (1842, 2nd edn 1865).[87] Plantier lauded the 'sublimity' of biblical style and described Isaiah as a prophet with 'high irony', 'vehemence' in feeling, topographical colour and logical order. For Proverbs, he pointed out parallels with 'profane moralists' in content and literary forms; in comparison with biblical wisdom, however, Marcus Aurelius and Epictetus were, in his opinion, one-sidedly severe and less able to win the heart.

George Gilfillan, author of many studies of English literature, treated

84. V. Wimbush in Felder (88). For a more recent period, too, it has been noted that 'black dependence on Scripture is not slavish or literal' or one that accepts inerrancy, even when quite orthodox (H. Mitchell, 50, 113; G. Davis, 2).

85. In Germany, works with general literary observations included J.H.A. Gügler, *Die heilige Kunst oder die Kunst der Hebräer* (1814); Friedrich Lisco, *Die Bibel* (1853); and Heinrich Steiner, *Ueber hebräische Poesie* (1873). According to the last-mentioned, Hebrew poetry surpasses others in immediacy, freshness, depth and liveliness (40).

86. Georg Seiler, *Biblische Hermeneutik* (1800 [ET 1835]); Johannes Pareau, *Institutio interpretis Veteris Testamenti* (1822) (cf. below); J.E. Cellérier, *Manuel d'herméneutique biblique* (1852 [adapted ET 1881]).

87. A third edition of 1881 responded to other studies.

biblical 'poetry' in a broad sense by giving attention to histories, prophecies and New Testament writings in *The Bards of the Bible* (1851).[88] He declared that 'the proof of great thoughts is, will they translate into figured and sensuous expression?' (II); as he saw it, to the Hebrew poet 'the poetical and the religious were almost the same' (II). He divided Hebrew poetry into two main classes: the Song, subdivided according to mood, and the Poetical Statement, which he ordered by content (III). Influenced by Herder and Gilfillan, LeRoy Halsey (*Literary Attractions of the Bible, or, A Plea for the Bible Considered as a Classic*, 1858, in the US) enthusiastically recommended the 'poetry' and 'oratory' of the Bible. He believed that biblical productions surpass other literatures in the lyric and didactic departments (89). Isaac Taylor, who wrote many works of Christian reflection, argued that the poetic style of much of the Hebrew Bible was appropriate for the foundation of faith, while postexilic prophecy and the New Testament presented revelations in prose suited for a view of the 'awful realities of another life' (*The Spirit of Hebrew Poetry*, 1861: 209).

Discontent about the state of affairs in biblical scholarship was expressed in 1856 by Ernst Meier, professor of Near Eastern languages and literatures. While valuing the new freedom of thought and the recognition of differences, he deplored a lack of attention to the complete nature of humanity (including its aesthetic and social aspects) and a tendency for many 'Introductions' to contain 'an inorganic, arbitrary collection of learned memoranda'.[89] Therefore, he sought to combine two facets in his study: a historical side, with relations to concrete conditions and to laws of development, and an aesthetic side, in continuation of the work of Lowth and Herder (viii). Meier did not furnish generic analyses as such (although he called for a history of genres, iv) but discussed poetic forms at appropriate points in his history. He observed, for instance, that prophetic literature, like didactic poetry in general, includes a mixture of lyric, satiric, narrative and instructional forms (248). Looking ahead, he projected a three-stage history of biblical interpretation, in which a 'dogmatic' period and a 'free' one would be followed by one which sees together the divine and human sides of the Bible.

88. Also published in 1853 with the title *The Poets and Poetry of the Bible*.
89. *Geschichte der poetischen National-Literatur der Hebräer* (iii, v, xv-xvi). Already during the previous two centuries, biblical study was often very fragmented.

A. Wünsche and Gunkel (see below) later listed as partial anticipations of their approaches not only Meier's study but also a relatively popular one by Carl Ehrt on Hebrew poetry. Ehrt furnished an 'attempt to present Hebrew poetry according to the nature of its materials' (1865). In his view, biblical genres include secular and religious types; among them, nature poetry has both secular and sacred aspects. The author left for another occasion an analysis of the poetry according to its forms. It is noteworthy that this work, dealing officially with content rather than with form, was accepted by Wünsche and Gunkel as anticipating their own aesthetic analyses; clearly, in their later time, form came to be thought of as something that does not stand in contrast to content.

Succinctly but with sensitivity, the Orientalist Theodor Nöldeke furnished, for a wide audience,[90] a series of essays on 'Old Testament literature' (1868). He covered its major types (history, poetic narratives, lyric and didactic poetry, prophets, etc.).

Two important Jewish literary introductions appeared during the ten years preceding 1875. Julius Fürst produced a 'history of biblical literature' (2 vols., 1867–70)—designed for the 'hearts of the Bible-loving people' (I: viii)—with detailed analysis and documentation. Following a historical outline, this work (unduly neglected by later scholars) is full of observations regarding the literary character of books and of poetry and speeches contained in them. For instance, speeches by Moses and Joshua are related to the genre of prophecy, with its subdivisions (I: 459-70). Characteristics of Hebrew literature observed by Fürst include a relative unconcern with individual authorship or with precise historical situations and a readiness to modify speeches and poems in tradition (II: 224-26). In 1872, David Cassel presented an aesthetically sensitive history of Israelite literature as the first part of a comprehensive survey of Jewish literature; Gunkel acknowledged it as a partial precursor of his approach (1906a: 49). While the work did not advance the field substantially in a technical sense, it would be useful even today as a meaningful introduction.

---

90. Eberhard Schrader, in the eighth edition of de Wette's Introduction (1869: 9), described this work as 'relatively popular'. In fact, Nöldeke expressly wrote for a general readership. Meier had clearly attempted to meet, as well, an 'urgent need in scholarship' to reach out widely (iii).

3. *Treatments of Individual Kinds or Bodies of Literature*

Naturally, some studies during the period of c. 1775–1875 focused on specific kinds of writings. A view of some of their highlights will give a picture of the general nature of the discussion.

a. *Myth*[91]

At the end of the eighteenth century, the concept of myth came to play a prominent role in biblical studies, in part as a result of theories for Greek literature put forward by Christian Heyne, classical philologist and professor of eloquence. Biblical and other scholars were aware that the term applied especially to accounts of the origin of the world or of humanity (thus, notably, Wilhelm Teller, in his edition of Turretin's lectures, 1776: 689). Heyne, however, defined myth as the oldest form of literary expression—highly figurative in character—so that the term designated simultaneously the character and the age of a narrative.[92] This dual conception was followed by Eichhorn (since 1779), Johann Gabler, Georg Bauer (in works not individually cited here), G. Meyer (in his hermeneutics), and others, including the Roman Catholic Johann Jahn ('Introduction', 2nd edn, 1803, II/I, §§18-20).

M. Hays (Unitarian) undermined, in 1798, a belief in the inequality of the sexes by referring to an interpretation of Genesis 2–3 as 'allegorical, or mythological', an interpretation which was already held by 'many of the primitive Christians' (i.e. by the Gospel of John or by early theologians?). In the usage of 'eastern nations', she explained, 'their most sublime instructions were couched under the veil of fable and allegory'.[93]

Following the philosopher Jacob Fries, Wilhelm de Wette viewed

91. See Rogerson (1974), with bibliography and information presupposed here.

92. The thesis of myth as an old literary form is a variation on the theme (propounded by G. Puttenham, *The Arte of English Poesie* [1589, 1.3], and Giambattista Vico, *Scienza nuova* [1725, 3rd edn, 1744], among others) that the earliest literature was poetic. A rather positive version of this view was expressed by John Caunter, *The Poetry of the Pentateuch* (1839), dealing with the blessings, etc.; its first chapter is entitled: 'Poetry probably coeval with the Creation. Intellectual superiority of the primitive races'.

93. *Appeal to the Men of Great Britain in Behalf of Women* (7; Selvidge, 88-95). Similarly, in her essay 'On the Equality of the Sexes' (1790), Judith Sargent Murray (Universalist?) called the stories of the Bible 'metaphorical' (Selvidge, 141).

myth as a relatively permanent manner of speaking about the divine and argued, furthermore, that it is more useful to understand a myth on its own terms than to pursue a small-scale curiosity seeking to reconstruct events that lie behind it (*Beiträge*, II, 1807: 400; in later works, however, de Wette toned down his references to myth and engaged in extensive historical reconstruction).[94] With a more history-orientated conception of myth, David F. Strauss, who was indebted to Schelling, held that the mythical form applied to traditions about Jesus even though they arose during a relatively advanced stage of literary production, since they developed orally and thus without a conscious deviation from the facts (*Das Leben Jesu*, 1835, §§9, 12).[95]

Johann George, in 1837 (*Mythos and Sage*, 91), noted again, as Teller had done, that myths represent, not an early kind of thought, but thought *about* early history ('origins'). In contrast, the biblical historian Heinrich Ewald accepted a definition of 'myth' on the basis of content as a 'story about gods' (in the plural) and thus regarded it as not applicable to the literature he studied (since c. 1843). On the whole, in fact, the term 'myth' receded in use during the nineteenth century.

b. *Poetry*
An interest in poetry remained alive. Thus, discussions of poetic form—i.e. rhythm—occurred frequently, either within commentaries or in separate works.[96] At least two studies (Karl Justi, *National-Gesänge der Hebräer*, 1803-13, and H. Ewald, *Die Dichter des Alten Bundes*, I, 2nd edn, 1866: 29-46) furnished subdivisions of poetry, according to content.[97] Ferdinand Ranke devoted a study to poems mourning the death of a person or nation (*Das Klaglied der Hebräer*, 1863).

As was indicated above, a distinction between epic, lyric and dramatic forms continued in literary criticism, together with a recognition of their flexibility and of mixtures; in biblical studies, this contrast

---

94. That de Wette (still) had definite, even primary, universal and literary interests is well brought out by Rogerson (1992, 1995b).

95. A little differently, in *Hermann Samuel Reimarus* (1862: 286), Strauss spoke of the Jewish *stylus theocraticus* which refers events to their ultimate (divine) causes.

96. E.g. John Jebb, *Sacred Literature* (1820) (especially on the New Testament); Joseph Saalschütz (a Jewish Orientalist), *Von der Form der hebräischen Poesie* (1825); *Form und Geist der biblisch-hebräischen Poesie* (1853); Michel Nicolas, *La forme de la poésie hébraïque* (1833).

97. Ewald had less subdivision in the 1st edn, 1839.

appeared in numerous discussions regarding the Song of Songs and Job. The Song of Songs was now appreciated as love poetry and was regarded by a majority of scholars as a drama involving the contest between a shepherd and a king for a woman's affection. The victory of the former appealed to an anti-aristocratic sensibility and to an orientation toward Romantic love (based on individual emotion).[98] In regard to the book of Job, classifications of it as a drama (sometimes even again as a tragedy) or epic or as a didactic poem had significant advocates, but more frequently it was thought that the book exhibits features of one or more of these forms without falling strictly under any one of them.[99] E. Reuss was one who believed that Hebrew poetry lacked a true epic or drama, a situation which he held to be due to the basically subjective and individualistic character of Hebrew poetry.[100]

In regard to the Psalms, there was considerable ambivalence towards classification. Many commentators did not present a systematic grouping of them, emphasizing almost exclusively a reconstruction of their historical setting. Some exegetes did furnish classified overviews, but often, it seems, for more practical than theoretical reasons, such as to enable the reader to locate a given topic (thus, expressly, Andrew Fausset in 1871). Only a few had an intrinsic interest in a description of the patterns of the texts.

Among these, Moses Mendelssohn, standing on the border between the older and the newer (historical) orientations, found in the Psalms representations of three kinds of lyric poetry: song, elegy and ode (the last being devoted to a definite subject and culminating in personal reflection, III/I: 337-39 [1779]). His typology, accepted by Johann Augusti (in 1806), was criticized by W. de Wette in his Psalms

98. An interpretation of the Song of Songs as involving a triangle began in 1771 (with partial mediaeval Jewish anticipations [Ginsburg, 88]). The anti-aristocratic orientation is made explicit in Friedrich Böttcher's thesis that the Song, with its favouring of the shepherd, was directed by a tenth-century North Israelite against despotic rule in Jerusalem (*Die ältesten Bühnendichtungen*, 1850).

99. An argument in favour of a dramatic interpretation was the presence of a prologue and epilogue; but the conservative scholar Heinrich Hävernick (*Handbuch*, III, 1849) argued that the prologue and epilogue are more integrally a part of the book than they are for a classical drama. (For overviews of relevant opinions, see the Introductions of de Wette, 8th edn by E. Schrader, and of F. Bleek; de Wette himself called Job a tragedy, but such a characterization had been more frequent earlier.)

100. 'Hebräische Poesie', *RE*, V, 1856: 600.

commentary (1811) as excessively 'formal-aesthetic', since Hebrew poetry is 'formless and special'.

De Wette preferred to divide the psalms into groups based on content:[101] (1) hymns honouring God; (2) psalms dealing with the people of Israel; (3) Zion and temple songs; (4) royal psalms; (5) laments (including individual and communal psalms, out of which type, he said, have grown general and didactic poems and psalms of thanksgiving); and (6) religious and moral psalms. In his more general 'Introduction', he provided alongside this a classification by 'degree of enthusiasm' and 'nature of mood': (1) hymns and odes; (2) songs; (3) elegies; and (4) poems of instruction.

De Wette's outlook was basically individualistic: 'Every writing requires its own hermeneutic; it can be known and understood only in its own form' (*Beiträge*, II, 1807: 25). He regarded most of the psalms as the 'living effusion of an emotion-filled heart'. He did note that many of them, especially among the laments, were quite similar to one another; such 'imitations' he regarded as not truly poetic (1811: 2, 21-22).[102]

A partial similarity with de Wette appears in Friedrich Bleek's Introduction (1860). He distinguished, at least roughly, between 'general' psalms (including didactic poems and hymns of praise) and those which are 'historical' or 'personal'. He believed that the majority of the Psalms, especially the older ones, are of the personal-historical kind and represent the 'living expressions of the poet's feelings', although it is true that for purposes of general use the collection of the Psalter had excluded songs that were highly particular, such as David's elegy concerning Jonathan (reported in 2 Samuel).

Several different classifications of the Psalms were provided by conservative scholars.[103] One, based on their 'subjects', was outlined by

101. The version of de Wette's typology reported here is the one found in later editions. In the first edition, the laments were called 'psalms of misfortune', more obviously representing content. 'Content' (*Inhalt*) is the basis of the classification specified in his Introduction (1817, etc.).

102. Similarly, he believed (probably in good part correctly) the non-Pauline letters of the New Testament imitated a 'model for that genre' furnished by Paul (Introduction to the New Testament, 4th edn, 1842, §60).

103. E.g. Friedrich Umbreit, *Christliche Erbauung aus dem Psalter* (1835), related the Psalms to the Lord's Prayer, on the basis of which Friedrich Oetinger, *Einleitung zum neutestamentlichen Gebrauch der Psalmen* (c. 1748), had already divided the Psalms into seven genres. Hengstenberg's division by moods, to be

Thomas Horne (*Introduction*, 1818, and so on). It lists as types 'prayers', psalms of 'thanksgiving', 'praise and adoration', those which are 'instructive', 'more eminently and directly prophetical', and 'historical' psalms. In a partial contrast to this, Ernst Hengstenberg's commentary (1842) grouped the psalms according to mood: joyful, sad and calm (i.e. didactic).[104] A third typology related psalms to different stages of temple ritual, with the assumption that not individual experience, but the 'typical was at the foundation of the ritual' (Eleazor Lord, *The Psalter*, 1860: ix). Gunkel later attempted to combine these various criteria of thought, mood and cultic situation—together with lexical and grammatical considerations—in his classification.

c. *Other Texts*

Prophecy was more rarely subdivided into types of speech. Sometimes, however, there appeared characterizations by content or thrust, mentioning threats, promises, exhortations, laments, etc.[105] An important achievement was the delineation of apocalyptic as a literary complex with characteristic features different from those of other prophetic writings (especially, Friedrich Lücke in 1832).

Jewish scholars furnished significant treatments of biblical laws and regulations. The orthodox Samson Hirsch ordered them into six groups, modifying Maimonides' more elaborate classification, as follows: *toroth*, 'teachings preparing spirit and emotions for life' (the unity of God, faith, love, etc.); *'edoth*, 'symbols (*Denkmäler*) for the truths grounding Israel's life' (sabbath, festivals, tefillin, etc.); *mishpatim*, 'expressions of righteousness towards human beings'; *huqqim*, laws of righteousness towards earth, plants, animals and one's own body, feelings, spirit and word (including food laws, sexual abominations and

---

mentioned, was simpler than Matthew Parker's earlier rendition of Psalms according to eight emotional patterns (*The Whole Psalter Translated into English Metre*, 1567).

104. This division was followed in the Introductions of H. Hävernick (1849), Karl Keil (1853, with reservation) and S. Davidson (vol. II of Horne's tenth edn, 1856).

105. Ferdinand Hitzig (Protestant) in treating Jeremiah (1841) and the Minor Prophets (1838): *Strafrede* (Jer. 2.1–3.5), *Drohrede* (Jer. 34.8-20), *Strafandrohung* (Amos 1.3–2.16), *Ermahnung* (Zeph. 2), *Klage* (Hab. 1.2-17). Johann Scholz (Roman Catholic), *Einleitung* (1848, III: 231): *Belehrungen, Ermahnungen, Verheissungen, Drohungen*. J. Fürst (Jewish), in the work discussed above (I: 460): *Mahn-, Straf-, und Drohreden*.

vows); *mizvoth*, 'commandments of love'; and *'abodah*, 'divine service' (prayers, blessings,etc.). He did not believe that one can fully understand the reasons for the commands, but his arrangement and discussion of the stipulations provided a rationale for them (*Horeb*, 1837: 441, etc.). The liberal J. Fürst (1867 [cf. above], I: 288) noted briefly that Mosaic law, like Solon's in Greece (which he dated a little later), covered law, religion and morality. Taking a moderate position, Samuel Luzzato reflected on the functions of the stipulations, both in regard to their very existence as a form of speech (they were issued, he said, when a need for express laws arose in a growing society) and in regard to their aim. For the latter, he envisioned two fundamental goals— social welfare, or virtue, and the maintenance of Jewish religion.[106]

For the New Testament it was common to note a division by form between historical books, letters and a book in prophetic style; or, one could distinguish between historical and didactic books.[107] The relations between forms however, were not analysed. The issue of whether Paul's thanksgiving was designed to 'capture the good will' of his readers (in Rom. 1.8, etc.) was often left undiscussed. A number of writers did point out such a function, although sometimes in a mild form—such as, that Paul sought to clarify the relation between himself and the readers. Yet others rejected his having that intent and emphasized that Paul opened his heart to express his true feelings.[108]

d. *Attention to Special Styles and Purposes*
Especially prominent in the nineteenth century were examinations of the stylistic peculiarities of individual books, writers and sources.[109]

106. See 'The Foundations of the Torah', published in 1880 after Luzzato's death in 1865 (ET in Rosenbloom, 147-209).

107. The former division appears in Introductions to the New Testament by Leonhard Bertholdt (1812–19); K. Credner (1836); S. Davidson (1848); F. Bleek (1875); the latter in those by Johann Hug (Catholic, 1826); E. Reuss (5th edn, 1874).

108. Giving the rhetorical function: Johann Koppe (1805) and Christian Böhme (1806) (both of these wrote in Latin, showing their connection with traditional scholarship); Adam Clarke (1821); Eduard Köllner (1834); Moses Stuart (1827). More cautiously: Friedrich Tholuck (1824); W. de Wette (4th edn, 1847); Benjamin Jowett (1859). That Paul was expressing a genuine feeling was emphasized by Wilhelm Benecke (1831); Johann Reiche (1833—a 'pouring out of the heart'); Conrad Glöckler (1834—'really from the heart'); Hermann Olshausen (1835); Friedrich Philippi (2nd edn, 1856—a view into Paul's heart); John Godwin (1873).

109. Relevant studies—not the primary concern of the present overview—are too

Such stylistic forms are general in the sense that they appear more than once in a given work, but they mark a work off from others which are similar in purpose but by a different author.

When the aim of a work was discussed, it was most commonly stated in terms of the purpose of a particular writing in its own situation rather than in terms of a generic thrust, which had been the primary emphasis earlier.[110] In fact, the notion of 'special hermeneutics' was extended beyond the recognition of genres to an understanding of single works. This was done by G. Meyer (in his hermeneutics, I, 1799, §7), by Friedrich Krummacher (using as successively narrowing focuses of 'special hermeneutics' the following: a people with its language, a period, an author and a work[111]), by Lücke,[112] and, even more radically, by de Wette (as we have seen). Since, however, in practice it is not feasible to furnish rules of interpretation for each work, the enterprise of special hermeneutics was gradually abandoned, and often with it also any close attention to the nature of rhetorical aims or poetic functions.

One widespread opinion, in biblical as in other studies, was that the highest goal of interpretation is not to understand the text but to understand the person who produced it. Krummacher, who argued for this position (*Über den Geist*, 9), believed that great writers express high originality (although, to be sure, one can be original without being great), so that they produce from 'within themselves', without a formal law (32).

numerous and varied to be surveyed here. One can mention, however, the Introductions by de Wette and S. Davidson (1848-51) as well as Christian Wilke's *Die neutestamentliche Rhetorik* (1843: chapter 8), among the more inclusive ones.

110. The importance of noting purpose (*Zweck*) and intention was stressed by Albert Immer, *Hermeneutik des Neuen Testamentes* (1873), with close attention to the particular situation, although with traces of the earlier tradition of special hermeneutics by genres.

111. *Über den Geist und die Form der evangelischen Geschichte*, 1805: 5-23.

112. *Grundriss der neutestamentlichen Hermeneutik*, 1917: 7-8.

Chapter 7

'FORM' AFTER 1875 OUTSIDE BIBLICAL STUDIES

At the end of the nineteenth century (after c. 1875), a major change
took place in Western Europe and in the US, so that twentieth-century
society and culture (including scholarship) became in many ways quite
different from what they had been earlier. Given the complexity of the
development, a detailed discussion of it is reserved for another volume
(*RFT*).[1] The following summary presents some of the highlights of the
emerging situation.

The new era has been called (e.g. by Toynbee) 'postmodern'. This
one term, however, has come to cover at least three major lines which
have run throughout the twentieth century. One is 'antimodern'. It
opposes the disorderliness that is inherent in modernity, especially
individualism and a strong sense of historical change. The second is
'transmodern'.[2] It believes that the features of modernity mentioned are
valuable but that they are problematic when they are emphasized one-
sidedly. The third is 'ultramodern'.[3] It attempts to eliminate the ves-
tiges of concern with generality that had continued in the modern age
so that it moves from moderate nominalism to extreme nominalism; it
readily eventuates in scepticism or nihilism, especially when held without a belief in God, for then reality has no coherence at all.[4] Although

1.   *RFT* presents a context for biblical study. It is furnished on the basis of
questions and themes that emerge in biblical scholarship, so that the discussion
involves a give-and-take.

2.   The term 'transmodern' is due to a suggestion by the French social thinker
Ferry, who presented a similar (although very brief) overview of three lines. The
term is used with virtually the same meaning by P. Ray. Others have described this
line as 'constructive' or 'affirmative' postmodernism.

3.   The term 'ultramodern' was coined by the architectural theorist Jencks for a
form of the postmodern he opposed. His own view is transmodern, according to the
terminology adapted here.

4.   A delineation of three lines is, of course, an oversimplification (see below

the three are not sharply separated, they can be distinguished as follows: antimoderns value coherence over a lack of it; ultramoderns are orientated primarily towards a lack of coherence; transmoderns give to both aspects approximately equal weight.

The central theme that emerged in the transmodern line is the importance of relations, highlighted, for instance, by Peirce and Buber. A concern with relations as such was not novel; however, an overt focus on relationality as a key idea was new. One of the characteristics of relations, as discussions during the century showed, is that they combine particularity with generality. Thus the one-sided emphases on generality prior to the high Middle Ages and on particularity thereafter were overcome, at least temporarily (whether this combination will hold cannot be said, for one cannot predict the future).[5]

A simple example can illustrate the theoretical situation. Let us take two acorns. According to an argument that might support a nominalist conception, they have no qualities that are exactly alike. Size, colour, weight, flavour, and so on, may be very similar, but since they will always be slightly different they have no precise property in common. That is indeed a persuasive observation. Let us look, however, at relations. Both of the acorns are lying on the ground; the relation 'on-ness' (or being-next-to) is thus shared (it occurs more than once). Furthermore, both acorns came from an oak tree. This relation thus, too, recurs. In other words, relations are the sorts of realities that are general, not limited to a specific occasion. Some relations are even universal, relative to a certain group; for instance, coming from an oak tree is true of all acorns. In fact, since all acorns can be treated within nominalism as a single group object, this kind of universality can be

for some overlaps); but using 'postmodernism' as a name for all three is a still greater simplification which creates all sorts of problems, such as in The Bible and Culture Collective's account of Schüssler Fiorenza's critique of ultramodernism (1995: 260-67). Like others, George Aichele rightly emphasizes that postmodernism is very varied (15). Boer (with a good brief summary of Ockham [133-34]) recognizes the connection of the nominalist wing of postmodernism with 'modern' capitalism; apparently, however—and this is not unusual—he does not know that (transmodern) relational philosophy already embodies a step beyond both essentialism and nominalism, in line with what he seeks (149).

5.   In the high Middle Ages, as one orientation was about to give way to its opposite, the joining of generality and particularity in Aristotle's philosophy was widely accepted for a while but then passed. The juncture of the two aspects in relational theory is more integral but may not hold.

accepted within nominalism, although nominalism cannot deal with a more contingent generality. (In twentieth-century non-nominalist logic, relations are usually symbolized by capital roman letters, which refer to repeatable phenomena, while lower-case letters refer to particulars.)

The foregoing analysis does not necessarily go beyond nominalism. For one can argue, as nominalists do, that relations are not real but only thought; that is, the fact that the acorns are on the ground and that they come from an oak tree does not represent a reality but a reflection upon the reality of several particular objects placed together in one's mind. One of the problems with assuming real relations, in fact, is that they must hover *between* objects, a possibility that nominalists have explicitly rejected. This very assumption, however, is made in the kind of philosophy that can be called 'relationism'. It holds that betweenness is just as real as are particular objects.

According to this theory, then, relations, which can recur, are real. At the same time, the theory holds that the particular objects, the items that stand in relations, are also real, even to the extent of having a semi-independent existence, for real relations must have endpoints with some independence, so that they are not simply absorbed into a larger whole. Thus it is said that relations 'both combine and separate'.

The fact that relations involve both a degree of connectedness and a degree of separation has an important consequence for the theory of causality. It is captured in the notion of probability, including conditional probability and correlation (the degree to which the likelihood of one event is affected by the occurrence of another one). Apart from the extremes of 0 (for no connection) and ±1 (for determinism), a probabilistic correlation measures an association that involves both a degree of predictability (connectedness) and an element of unpredictability (partial independence). Nominalism can handle only the extremes— monadism (radical pluralism) and monism (tight connectivity within a large unit). Essentialism, another option, considers some associations as necessary ('essential') and others as accidental. Most relationists, in contrast, have, from the very beginning, believed in (partial) indeterminacy in regard to all associations. In fact, the idea of causality (which, as a relation, was a problem for nominalism)[6] requires a partial indeterminism, for if a connection is rigid, we do not really have two related items but two parts of one item, and if the items are fully independent,

---

6.   See above, 6.1.b.

there is no causal relation between them even if they appear in a regular sequence.

The implication of such a view for a notion of form should now be clear. Relational theory rejects not only the Platonic idea of form, which downgrades the importance of particulars, but also the Aristotelian conception of it, which focuses on essences, and, further, the nominalist one, for which form is either a heap of accidents or else a strongly unified whole. Form is held instead to be *a complex of relations* which are each shared (at least potentially) with some other existents and can thus be understood, but which together form a whole that evades complete understanding; for, since relations even within a whole require some distancing between the items related, a real whole cannot be completely unified.

In relation to an observer, the 'other' is thus considered to be neither completely strange nor completely familiar. Furthermore, relationism supports neither antirealism—such as is expressed in the belief that language creates what reality there is (scepticism)—nor a position that the observed is simply independent of the observer (objectivism), for it believes that all of reality is connected.

Since relationism (like nominalism) makes no distinction between essential and accidental features, a given object can be classified in terms of several different forms, according to one's principle of selectivity, which depends on one's purpose. However, while nominalism holds that a form or structure is in the mind of the observer rather than in the object, relationism holds that form emerges interactively as an aspect of a reality revealed to a subject with its questions, thus formed cooperatively by object and observer.[7] For instance, colour is neither in an object by itself nor in the perceiving subject by itself, for the perceiver's sensations are formed by a history of interaction, even if a particular instance should be imaginary. A thoroughgoing relationism, in fact, holds that an object does not have any properties purely 'in itself', but that all properties are relational, although some of them are

---

7.   It is correct to say that a reader-orientated approach rejects the idea of a 'disinterested reader' (McKnight, 15), but one should not say that it implies that one cannot 'obtain verifiable knowledge by applying certain scientific strategies' (McKnight, 15); for knowledge is at least approximately verifiable in relation to a given framework of observation, and science, too, is relational. Appropriate is Segovia's statement that meaning resides 'in the encounter or interchange between text and reader' (Segovia and Tolbert, II: 8).

potential rather than actual properties (e.g. colour, before there is a being to perceive it).[8]

What has been described on its intellectual side had a very important social dimension. Relational theory was associated with the social welfare movement that arose in strength at the end of the nineteenth century, as well as with a more pronounced role for women and with ecological concerns, which were connected with each other from that time on. Feminism's impact on society and culture was both direct and indirect (via males with whom women were associated).[9] In fact, social democracy embodied in many ways an image of the state as a mother rather than as a father. Thus a traditionally feminine role was projected into the public realm, to be supported by men as well as by women, while, at the same time, women adopted styles and roles that were more openly self-assertive.

This large social movement, with its several aspects, accepted much of modernity but at the same time sought to go beyond many aspects of it. For instance, it accepted individualism to a large extent but was not content to let it be all-important. It saw that a view (and activity) of life that supports the downtrodden requires solidarity, not merely competitiveness. Such solidarity means sharing power, not simply an exercising of beneficence.[10]

The change in orientation was reflected in the meaning given to the word 'freedom'. An old, somewhat elitist, use of that word had meant by it freedom from fleshly, selfish drives and pursued, as an expression of such freedom, the contemplation of general ideas that reach beyond oneself. In the modern age, another meaning for 'freedom' (it was not new as such, but it was newly highlighted) referred to an avoidance of external restraints; it valued independence and thus particularity. Socially, it undermined traditional hierarchies and supported instead persons with the ability to compete, who readily constitute a middle class. Going beyond this position, freedom came to be thought of in

8.   The idea of possibility is problematic for nominalism (since the ontology of this includes only actual particulars), but it is important for relational thinking.

9.   Three examples (more on them in *RFT*) can illustrate this impact: the first clear statement of relationism seems to have come from a woman (C. Beecher); Peirce, a crucial figure for relational theory, had input in this regard from his feminist first wife (née Fay); Dewey's association with and learning from women is well known.

10.   The 'social democracy' of this outlook thus differs from Aristotle's stand, which balanced aristocracy with a middle status.

transmodernity as a fulfilment of potentials for all, including those who are not powerful in the struggle of life. This kind of freedom would involve community along with individuality, generality and particularity together.[11]

Along with social development, it seems that a change in the thinking style of individuals has taken place. Working in twentieth-century Switzerland, Piaget observed a shift in adolescence from 'concrete thinking' to 'formal thought', which he characterized as relational. Although Piaget was inclined to think that this transition marks a change in mental development independent of culture, it is likely that individual development in this case, as in others, absorbs the movement of culture. On both cultural and individual levels, there is here a move through and beyond the concreteness that is typical of nominalism—such as is shown in a concern with objects or facts, or of ideas that are placed 'in' a mind like a container—towards a thinking that is concerned with relations.[12]

During the twentieth century, relational theory has taken a number of theoretical steps. Especially notable is the development of communication theory. In this the insight arose that 'information' requires entropy, or 'uncertainty', as a precondition. In other words, communication is enriched by variety and partial unpredictability. In fact, experiments have shown that aesthetically—and perhaps in other respects—human beings prefer to receive a maximum amount of information. That means that they thrive in a context that provides as much entropy as they are able to handle as a precondition for information.

One important consequence of such interaction is that a growth of entropy is not contrary to a growth of communication but, rather, potentially supportive of it as long as there is an element of connectivity between beings that partially hooks them together. Since the growth of entropy is a long-range trend, there becomes possible a long-range view of history, which discerns a tendency towards a joint growth of entropy and communication on all levels of existence, from the physical to the human. This view is not one-sidedly optimistic, for

11. *Pace* Brueggemann (13, 15), preferring particularity (however, Brueggemann has made use of the human sciences more than have most biblical scholars, and he may have since modified the view cited somewhat).

12. Cultural and individual developments in other times and places appear to be somewhat different; for instance, they may have less of a concrete focus as one of their steps.

communication is not necessarily something good, to be valued; nor is that view determinist, for entropy and (even more so) communication are probabilistic phenomena.[13] Yet the conception does allow for some kind of progress. One would need to be antimodern in order to deny the possibility of progress altogether (the possibility is largely implicit in feminism and is usually assumed in science and technology). The truth of the matter appears to be that both good and evil can progress—often, together[14]—and that it is a challenge for human beings to align themselves on the side of the one, while opposing the other.

The notion of an expansion of communication furnishes a useful angle on historical development. The development of writing was closely associated (both in support and in protest) with the rise of hierarchical orders, although it is possible to have hierarchies without writing. The medium of print both resulted from and enhanced an emerging prominence for the middle class. Transmodernity, in turn, has been associated with means of communication beyond printing (such as radio and telephone), as well as with an increased use of writing and print by groups that previously operated largely orally.[15] These correlations should be treated with care; for instance, it is not certain that a given medium (e.g. print) has a specific effect. Still, it appears that enhanced possibilities of communication—first among an elite, then more widely, and now very inclusively (even globally)—have played a significant role in the historical process.

On the social level, a counterpart to the duality of entropy and communication is the recognition that a combination of connectivity and semi-independence is important also for groups. Sheer difference would ground a strife that leads to the physical obliteration of the other, but a strong conformity obliterates the other culturally. In fact, a degree of independence is needed for a sense of identity. Yet even differences cannot be observed without communication, which, together with the

13. This view does not represent a 'grand narrative' in Lyotard's specific sense of that phrase (which is monistic), but it rejects Lyotard's own grand narrative, according to which modernity leads integrally to dissociative ultramodernism.

14. This can be conceptualized in a communicational framework, for not only is entropy or uncertainty (unpredictability) a prerequisite for information, but information appears to generate new kinds of entropy. Although entropy and information should not be equated with evil and good respectively, the interplay between them has similarity with the interplay between those two poles.

15. For instance, the women's movement was in part propelled by increased literary education for women (cf., e.g., C. Beecher's comment cited above, 6.1.e).

surprise element that constitutes 'information', assumes a degree of commonality.

The 1960s witnessed a conjunction of communal interest with a drive for quasi-mystical personal freedom, sometimes going to impractical extremes but furthering positive liberation in regard to race, gender and economic welfare in the US (and elsewhere). Established society thereafter turned against what it rightly or wrongly considered to be excesses. Nevertheless, the outlook that blossomed at that time (after earlier beginnings) continues in a substantial portion of the population. According to a recent survey by P. Ray, persons he calls 'transmodern'—whose primary values are both personal growth and social service, feminism, intercultural (including interreligious) appreciation, spirituality (often non-traditional), simplicity and ecological concerns—constitute about a quarter of the US population (60 per cent of these are women), while two other, larger, segments of society are formed by 'traditionalists' and 'modernists'. (The latter, which form the largest group in his survey, are orientated towards social-material 'success', either as something already largely achieved or as something to be struggled for; this group apparently includes sceptical 'ultramodernists', for it expresses more cynicism than do the others, especially more than do the transmoderns.) Even traditionalists and modernists accept, to a large extent, some of the newly established values, such as racial and sexual equality and attention to ecology.

Whether transmodernity will lead to a post-capitalist society remains to be seen. In fact, it is somewhat on the defensive currently, pressed by both antimodernism and ultramodernism.[16] Not much will be said here about antimodernism, but the ultramodern line deserves a word.

Nietzsche, especially through jottings in his very late, near-mad years, inspired much of twentieth-century extreme-nominalist scepticism and nihilism.[17] He alone can hardly be charged with this development, for his words would not have had any effect if they had not struck a resonant chord, which they did for many. It can be debated whether the emerging sceptical/nihilist line—represented to this day almost entirely by Eurocentric males—constitutes the last gasp of the

---

16. The communal aspect is opposed by ultramodernism, and the personal aspect by antimodernism and Marxism. Continuing modernist capitalism opposes both aspects, since quasi-mysticism is not competitive. Ray's survey, however, shows that transmodernity is not dead.

17. In his lucid time, Nietzsche himself was not nihilist, nor fully sceptical.

bourgeois world (as Marxists have argued) or whether it is an effective defence against a new viewpoint, for, if nothing is true, the new is undercut and existing privileges can continue.[18] In any case, scepticism/ nihilism (as was already true for the lucid Nietzsche), has often been opposed to social democracy and to feminism or has (at least) been ambivalent about them (as befits scepticism!); it played a major role in Nazism.

Although ultramodernism is opposed to transmodernism, a number of thinkers have intertwined elements of both lines. They include notably Heidegger, Foucault, Derrida and Rorty. In fact, Derrida said expressly that one should not choose between the two lines but combine them according to the principle of undecidability (427-28). Such a combination is not altogether illogical, for (as has been seen) entropy—highlighted by scepticism—lies in the background of communication. Nevertheless, for conceptual clarity and for a commitment to human welfare, it is important to disentangle the two threads. In fact, most women writers and quite a few male ones—including most non-Westerns dealing with this conception—have discriminated between them, accepting the relational and rejecting the sceptical/nihilist thread. (In the words of Ellen van Wolde [1996: 182], it is 'not so much that everything is relative [in a sceptical sense] as that everything is relational'.)

Another mixed tradition is that of Marxism, which combines modern with transmodern elements. Specifically, it continues a nominalist frame, focusing on social classes and on universal human history in a fairly rigid way,[19] although it does contain looser relational elements. It one-sidedly emphasizes force, either in a class struggle or in establishing conformity under the leadership of a party, at least in its Leninist version. Despite its undeniable idealism and some important contributions—especially in the overthrowing of old political structures—Marxism thus has, together with Nazism, starkly contributed to the horror side of the twentieth century.

It seems that the main serious problems of the twentieth century have arisen from one-sided particularism. They include, among those that had begun already well before that century, rapacious (unrestricted) capitalism, colonialism, and exclusivist religious wars and pogroms.

18. In the history of thought, scepticism has apparently been after (not before) a paradigm shift.

19. See above, 6.1.a.

Nevertheless, it is possible to learn some valuable points from (partly nominalist) Marxism and (largely nominalist) Nietzscheanism, just as one can learn from other traditions.

In fact, transmodernity does not altogether devalue the past, whether recent or distant. Rather, relational theory has drawn on a far-flung set of ideas. Some of these are Christian and Jewish. Others come from China, India, Africa, Greece and elsewhere. The relational outlook is thus a truly international and interreligious one.

One of the striking features of this intellectual complex is that most of the philosophical adherents of a relatively pure form of it have had religious interests of an inclusive sort.[20] In fact, a relational conception draws together ethics and factual knowledge rather than dividing them from each other.

Although relationism has not won universal or even near-universal assent from philosophers, it has been influential during the twentieth century in most of the disciplines of scholarship, including physics, linguistics, rhetoric, sociology and psychology, often pursuing human ideals. It is thus clear that a major paradigm shift has taken place.

Biblical studies, too, as we will see in Chapters 8–13, have received the impact of the new outlook, although relational theory was not absorbed as well as might be helpful. One eminent figure was Gunkel. He drew together the linguistic form, the content (both in thought and feeling) and the social situation of literary genres. In line with the emerging interest in holistic form, scholarly endeavours indebted to his synthesis have been called 'form critical'.

Gunkel's tri-aspectual vision of genres was powerful enough so that it helped to inspire key figures in a number of disciplines—including anthropology (Malinowski, etc.), text linguistics (Zellig Harris), literary studies (through an apparent impact on the Bakhtin circle) and, quite possibly, philosophy (specifically, Wittgenstein).[21] It is true, Gunkel envisioned the connections between phenomena too tightly, so that those stimulated by him needed to modify his conception by permitting

20. They include Peirce, Husserl, Cohen, Buber, Dewey (in a quite liberal way), Whitehead, Wittgenstein (but both his degree of religiousness and his being relational rather than sceptical are debated), Jaspers, Hartshorne, Ricoeur and West, among others. The following women thinkers with religious interests (in addition to expressly theological ones) should probably be considered to be relational: Weil, Arendt, Irigaray and Hesse. Some relational thinkers, however, are not, or do not appear to be, religious (and vice versa).

21. See *RFT* for details.

greater flexibility and unpredictability. What happened, then, is that those who adapted Gunkel's idea brought it in line with relational theory, which provides a kind of insight, the standard for which is not a recognition of strict coherence but one of moderate and varied connectivity.

Chapter 8

JEWISH ANALYSES OF FORM, C. 1875–1965

In introducing his overview of biblical literature (1886), Gustav Karpeles made a statement which reflected a new attitude toward biblical study, namely, a desire to go beyond the outlook of historical criticism. According to his description of the situation in exegesis, there have been two major approaches: one that is allegorical-typical-dogmatic and another that is rational-historical. A third one, 'aesthetic' or 'literary-historical', exhibited by Herder and gradually gaining ground, was, in his judgment, likely to become dominant in the future. More than the others, he said, it is compatible with all reasonable orientations, although not with theological craziness or strenuous atheism (19). For the beginning portion of his history of Jewish literature, Karpeles then surveyed the Bible's historical books (which are not necessarily comparable to a 'modern work of history', 31), poetry and prophecy.

A little earlier, H. Graetz, in a commentary on the Psalms, had analysed their types (1882). He recognized three major genres (*Gattungen*): laments, hymns and didactic psalms. Four additional genres (bringing the total to seven) were identified as subdivisions of the major ones: request, penitence, thanksgiving and reprimand (*Rüge*). He noted that the forms overlap to some extent (13) and that the reprimands resemble prophetic speech. Furthermore, cutting across the divisions observed are distinctions between a focus on individuals, the nation or the king (14f.). This is a quite reasonable analysis. C.G. Montefiore, in *The Bible for Home Reading* (1901), furnished a classification that was a little different: Psalms of Prayer in Seasons of Trouble, Psalms of Happy Communion With God, Psalms of Thanksgiving, Royal Psalms, Didactic Psalms and Psalms of Praise. He similarly did not view the groups as rigid (489). Kaufmann Kohler discussed 'The Psalms and their Place in the Liturgy', placing them largely outside the temple (1897). In the process, he referred to hymns of Babylonia, Persia and

India and thus indicated that this kind of expression is not limited to Israel.

In a major sweep, Amos Fiske described 'The Jewish Scriptures' (1896), 'The Myths of Israel', specifically the 'tales and myths' of Genesis (1897) and, finally, 'The Great Epic of Israel', that is, 'The Web of Myth, Legend, History, Law, Oracle, Wisdom and Poetry of the Ancient Hebrews', each type treated individually (1911). More concisely, S. Bernfeld (1921) described the 'literary forms' (94) of the Bible. He believed that in them 'there is confirmation of the experience that every time when new thoughts, new problems and new moral demands arise, a new language is created also' (94). In his view, the prophets began with poetry designed for readers but then moved towards oral rhetoric (thus partially already Amos, more extensively Jeremiah and others).[1] Morris Jastrow, Jr, whose scholarship ranged far in ancient Near Eastern and Jewish studies, explicated Qoheleth as 'A Gentle Cynic' (1919), the book of Job (1920) and the Song of Songs (1921), with attention to literary structures. He provided a typology for the Song of Songs and compared Qoheleth with other writings.

The important Jewish philosopher H. Cohen held that *Gestalt* is the 'unity of body and soul', in which form and content are identical (cf. Hamburger, 93). Thus, in an essay on the style of the prophets (1924: 262-83 [1901 MS]), he discussed content and style of this literary type as inseparably connected (263). The style of the prophets, he said, designates the relation between religion and ethics (264); love is a basic element of it, although anger—sometimes in jarring proximity—also plays a major role (271-74). The 'end of days' spoken of by prophets 'is the end of these days, which are not the days of God' (272). 'The prophetic style', thus, 'has created the ideal of world history' (283).

In Cohen's philosophy, the triad I-you-it was important.[2] He did not himself apply an analysis along its lines to biblical literature, but others were to do so soon thereafter.

Among these, his student F. Rosenzweig reflected on the appearances of 'I', 'we' and 'you' in the Bible, including Genesis, the Song of Songs and Qoheleth (1921, 2.1 end; 2.2). In 1928 (1937:167-81) he

---

1.   Earlier, Michael Heilprin had devoted two volumes to 'The Historical Poetry of the Ancient Hebrews', from Gen. 4.23-24 to Hosea (1879–80); he spoke of 'legends', etc. Horace Kallen described 'The Book of Job as a Greek Tragedy', similar to Euripedes (1918).

2.   See *RFT*.

analysed the form (*Naturform*) of biblical stories as 'dialogical'; that is, their narration neither obliterates the distance between past and present nor treats the past as an external message or event but, rather, grows within a discussion—presenting an answer, counterstatement, or addition to antecedent speech. The narratives have not only an artistic 'point' but also, in interaction with this, a thematic 'key word' (*Stichwort*, not necessarily expressed by a literal word), without which they would be only aesthetic. Message and command go together. Rosenzweig indicated that a dialogue structure is observable also in other genres (*Stilgattungen*) of the Bible (psalmic lyricism, prophetic rhetoric, legal casuistics) and—as he said is probably true for all aspects of the Bible taken one at a time—also in other literature.

Buber had already had an illustrious career in religious and social studies when he published the relationally orientated *I and Thou* in 1923 and then engaged in a translation of the Bible together with Rosenzweig.[3] He believed that stylistic form is integrally connected to content within an indissoluble gestalt (II: 1095-96, 1184 [1936]). In a 'form-critical' (II: 452 [1942]) analysis of style, he explored the genre or 'type of form' of biblical speech (II: 1195, 1150 [1936]) and gave attention to the repetition of words. In his view (II: 1184-85 [1936]), the Bible contains, not timeless third-person sentences, but utterances addressed to a thou as a report, legal saying, prayer, confession, etc. Its narratives are only in small part 'chronicle-like', but in most of them there 'lives a calling, time-binding, exemplifying and warning voice'. Contextual connections are significant, but 'most important', he believed, is not what the historian has to say about the circumstances of a text but what the text has to say about its connection with a situation.

M. Buber published a considerable number of biblical studies applying these principles (II [1926–51]; cf. Kepnes). One of them (on the 'wisdom and action of women') concluded with the following words, which combine a general with a particular perspective: 'Jews, too, know about the eternal Antigone. In their own, Jewish manner' (II: 923 [1929], on 2 Sam. 21.10). A major contributor to relational philosophy, he believed that 'biblical humanism' focuses not on phenomena by themselves but on relationality (II: 1091 [1933]).

Another significant thinker was A. Heschel. (He was appointed by Buber in 1937 to serve as his successor in an organization devoted to adult Jewish education, subsequently became a leading theologian in

---

3.   See *RFT*. Buber incorporated an openness toward Taoism and Zionism.

the US, and, in the 1960s, participated actively in the civil rights movement.) In 1936 he presented a phenomenology of prophecy, that is, a description of the structure of the prophetic word as it appears to a thoughtful observer entering imaginatively into that ancient world.[4] He based it on the 'literary givenness' of the phenomena, focusing attention not on the multiplicity of data but on their intrinsic connections within a gestalt (4). He observed that the prophets were concerned with God as standing in an emotional-personal 'relationship to the world' (131, 161-62). This 'pathos' of deity is not a blindly stormy or arbitrary 'affect', without reason; its inner law, rather, is ethics (132, 136). It is not egocentric but directed toward someone and thus inherently relational; there is, indeed, 'no separate history of God or people' (133). Precisely since the primary movement comes *from* God, it is directed *towards* human beings, 'anthropotropic' (114). The divine involvement means that there is a being concerned with everyone and everything, in particular with the problems of the poor (146).

Less strongly philosophical, although imbued with a theoretical spirit, were several other literary analyses. In a brief study on 'The Bible as Literature' (1929), Samuel Daiches, who was relatively traditional, expressed the opinion that readers have found in the Bible 'hope, support and guidance for every situation in life, whether the life is that of an individual, or of a nation, or of the whole human race', thus giving voice to the concept of life situation (23). Just as God creates the world through speaking, so, he said, the 'Bible speaks to us' and creates a 'world of goodness, love, and faith' that is not otherwise available (24).

The literary critic E. Auerbach wrote a penetrating study under trying war-time circumstances, with limited access to scholarly publications. He compared biblical narratives with Homer and found the biblical more mysterious (with a depth that is not fully expressed), more orientated to a history running from creation to an end, and more inclusive

---

4. A key concept for phenomenology, following Husserl, is 'possibility' (implied by the word 'imaginatively', above); the question of reality or truth (such as whether God is really related to the world in the manner described) is suspended. Furthermore, phenomenology is concerned with the content of thought (what thought is about), not with the thought processes themselves (see *RFT*). Heschel followed its procedure, he said, in order to avoid both objectivism and subjectivism, which are one-sided and serve theological and psychological dogmatism, respectively (2). The work represents, in retitled form, Heschel's 1935 dissertation in philosophy, *Das prophetische Bewusstsein*.

socially (7-29). These three characteristics are connected with each other (as he hinted, although he did not fully develop the connections).

S. Goldman, a reform rabbi, judged that a 'masterly combination of the universal, particular, and symbolic is present' in the stories of Genesis (1949:106). He observed that (in comparison with other surviving bodies of literature) the Hebrew canon is unusually well organized (1948:27, 30); numerous subsequent references to the Bible showed to him that it is an 'eternally effective book' (104).[5]

In fact, Jewish scholars participated in an ethos which—from the 1930s to the 1960s—focused on patterns or structures, whether of language, thought, or institutions. Thus, Y. Kaufmann delineated the structure of *The Religion of Israel* (Hebrew 1937–56) with major attention to thought. Theodor H. Gaster outlined a Near Eastern, including Hebrew, 'seasonal pattern' in ritual and literature (*Thespis*, 1950). M. Tsevat (1955) showed linguistic patterns that are characteristic of psalms—a macro-genre—and Stanley Gevirtz gave attention to language 'Patterns in the Early Poetry of Israel' (1963). Quite a few of the many contributions by Julian Morgenstern[6] dealt with literary or ritual structures. Judah Palache, teaching from 1924 on in a Protestant theological faculty upon appointment by the city of Amsterdam (which had the right of election [Bauer, 105]), deeply influenced subsequent Protestant literary analyses in the Netherlands, especially through reflections on the nature of narratives (ET in Kessler, 3-22 [1925]).

D. Daube, who participated (c. 1935) in a seminar led by the New Testament form critic C.H. Dodd and then became a specialist in Roman law, correlated the different aspects of language with each other. In 1956, he discussed several 'Forms of Roman Legislation', associating linguistic formulations with their respective functions. Although his analysis was not altogether successful, since style and function are not matched perfectly, the work is noteworthy for its interdisciplinary use of form-critical procedure as it had been developed within the biblical field. In a very important study on 'the Exodus

---

5.   Other literary studies were presented by Gresham Fox (*The Bible as Religion and Literature*, 1934), Solomon Freehof (see Preminger and Greenstein), and R. Gordis (with important studies of Qoheleth, Song of Songs, Lamentations, Job, etc., including also a general overview of the literature of the Tanakh, 1971: 3-44 [1949]). Also literary in a sense was the work of U. Cassuto (1934, etc.), who argued that YHWH and Elohim represent God's name and title respectively, rather than the usages of different documents lying behind the Pentateuch.

6.   Cf. references to them in Eissfeldt (1965); Rowley (1967).

Pattern of the Bible' (1963), Daube showed that the Exodus story reflects in terminology and imagery the 'social practice' of the dismissal of a slave, either to freedom or to a new master, and that laws and other narratives reflect, in turn, the pattern of the Exodus account. He thus correlated linguistic phenomena, content, and social life and identified a general pattern, present in narratives as well as in laws.

A postcritical (not anticritical) way of teaching the Bible was presented in 1953 by Zvi Adar, a prominent Israeli theorist of education, in what is one of the finest general introductions to the Hebrew Bible written during the twentieth century (ET: *Humanistic Values in the Bible*, 1967). Adar distinguished between a traditional religious approach, a critical (primarily historical) approach, and a third one which he called 'humanistic-educational' (1967: 33). The traditional approach holds that the Bible's significance is general in such a way that its applicability today is not different from its past meaning (44). The critical approach, in contrast, 'endeavors to keep the Bible within the limits of its own time' (44). The first of these involves an unquestioning acceptance of 'dogma' (26, 38). The other is so absorbed with the circumstances of the Bible that it fails to give attention to what the text says (44-45). The third approach is 'open' in two ways: it is available to persons who are not biblical scholars (425) and it does not automatically accept whatever appears in the Bible (428). In it, a reader is not 'dominated' by the Bible (47). Furthermore, since there is no concern with 'imposing anything', there is, also, no need to 'vindicate' Scripture (429).

Adar did not specify a procedure by which a reader might determine the value of a biblical point of view. He affirmed 'a common human experience shared by the people of the Bible and by us' (31) but also paid attention to changes over time in social organization. Since he regarded an understanding of the Bible in its own time (44) as a step towards its application in the present, he must have envisioned the forming of an analogy that recognizes a correspondence between past and present relations; but, as is typical for many works directed towards the general reader, much was left to intuition.

Adar believed that the Bible is important for current general education 'because it does lay bare the deeper meaning' of human existence, with its 'greatness and meanness...conflicts and strivings' (429). It is 'great literature because it reveals the innermost depths of the human soul' (45); indeed, its excellence as literature may be based on the fact that 'it was written...not for the sake of art but for the sake of life' (46). Within the biblical *paideia* (educational culture), he identified five principal 'aspects' (47) or 'literary forms' (419): historical narrative, prophecy, law, poetry and wisdom literature, each treated in detail. He observed different movements within the several literary forms in regard to whether God speaks to human beings or whether these speak either to God or to each other (34, 424). He valued the prophetic 'passion for justice' but cautioned against equating it with a specific political programme (25, 422). Reflecting typical Israelite-Jewish self-criticism, he pointed out that the Bible 'attacks overriding national pride' (17) and that the inclusion within it of Qoheleth and Job, with their 'penetrating inner criticism', furnishes the best possible proof of the Bible's greatness (425).

Adar did not set humanism in opposition to religious faith. Rather, in his study of 'The Biblical Narrative' (1959 [Hebrew 1957]), he stated that 'the religious spirit emerges precisely because the stories...are human in the extreme' (260). Indeed, much of Judaism, like ancient Israel, does not draw a line between 'religion' and the rest of life. Thus, readers theologically more traditional than Adar should also be able to appreciate his rich analysis.[7]

Important contributions to the literary study of the Bible were made by M. Weiss from 1961 on. Among his antecedents, he mentioned Buber and Rosenzweig, as well as Dilthey, who conceived of poetry as an 'organ of an understanding of life', and Boeckh (see below in connection with Gunkel), who saw that understanding involves recognizing not phenomena as such but their relationships (M. Weiss 1961: 256, 267). Better than Gunkel did, he treated forms as present in, rather than as lying behind, the text (261). He had a strong interest in the particularity of texts, but he utilized general literary principles (e.g. that of 'perspective'); his analysis of Ps. 46 led to the conclusion that it has a 'universal character' (300).[8]

---

7.   In *Jewish Education in Israel and the United States* (1977), Adar pointed to a somewhat similar approach in Conservative Judaism in the US, such as that of the Melton Project (including N. Sarna, *Understanding Genesis*, 1966). Brueggemann, *The Creative Word* (1982), resembles Adar (1953) in approaching the canon as education.

8.   Other literary contributions by him included a work in 1962 (Hebrew; revised ET: *The Bible From Within*, 1984); *VT* 1963: 456-75; etc.

It should be noted that structural-literary analyses were done especially by those who were not specifically biblical specialists. Those who were specialists were, like their Protestant counterparts, caught up heavily in historical investigations.

Nevertheless, it is clear that Jewish contributions since 1875 have combined particular with general perspectives. This fact is not a startling one, for such a combination has been typical of Jewish work from the start. A purely general approach would dissolve Jewish identity. A purely particularist one would eliminate the relevance of the past and would set Judaism into a sharper opposition to the rest of the world than is envisioned in most of the biblical tradition. What was new, however, was that the two aspects were joined in the manner in which they are combined in twentieth-century relationism. In fact, the philosophers and theologians among them (Cohen, Rosenzweig, Buber, Heschel) were leaders in the development of relational theory.[9] Noteworthy, moreover, is the fact that many of the Jewish writers had a broad orientation—towards ancient Near Eastern studies,[10] philosophy, literature, education, and so on—so that they were able to set the Bible in relation to various realities and issues.

9.   See further in *RFT*.
10.   Cf. B. Levine in Sperling *et al.* (106) (see that volume for other studies by Jewish scholars, too numerous to be listed here).

Chapter 9

ROMAN CATHOLIC VIEWS OF LITERARY FORM, C. 1875–1965

In a similar way, Roman Catholic thinking was moving towards an integrative-dynamic view of the Bible. A view widely accepted among Catholics in the middle of the nineteenth century, advocated especially by J.B. Franzelin, had been that divine inspiration pertains specifically to the ideas of the Bible, not to the way in which they were expressed, so that content and literary form were separated (Burtchaell, 88-120). This differentiation resembled the distinction between content and external form widely made within a particularist perspective, but it was sufficiently Platonic-Aristotelian in its philosophical conception that a text's thought (called 'content' by others) was described as the 'formal word', while its concrete phenomena (called 'form' by nominalists) were labelled 'matter' (98). The theory had a number of advantages: it allowed for a human contribution to the shaping of the text; it could explain minor discrepancies in the Bible; and it permitted an acceptance of inspiration for the Latin Vulgate equal to that of the original Hebrew and Greek text. It had the disadvantage, however, of downgrading linguistic structure.

A major contribution to an approach going beyond that of Franzelin was a theory of inspiration which arose within Neo-Thomism, a theology which fitted an increased interest in social and intellectual cohesion. Thomas Aquinas was made standard for Catholic theology in 1879 by Pope Leo XIII, whose support for major social concerns is well-known. The philosophy of Aristotle standing in the background of Thomas Aquinas supported organic integration, both for society and for literary expression. In regard to the inspiration of the Bible, Neo-Thomism envisioned not a division of labour between God and humanity, in which each is active in respect to a different aspect of the text, but an employment by God of human authors as instruments (as Thomas had said). Such an employment involves an enhancement

rather than an overpowering of human insight and speech. Since the
Holy Spirit is infinite, rather than a finite being who competes with
other finite beings, its 'primary' causation can bring into play secondary causes (i.e. human beings)[1] without restricting their freedom
(thus, Eugène Lévesque in 1895/96 [Burtchaell, 132]).[2]

As ideas and verbal expressions were drawn together by this theory
of inspiration, the notion of literary genre became important once more.
Specifically, it played a significant role in Leo XIII's encyclical *Provi-
dentissimus Deus* of 1893. In a quite traditional manner, the encyclical
pointed out that the Bible contains 'alleviation of evil [i.e. words of
comfort], exhortation to virtue and invitation to the love of God'; for
morality, there appear 'most holy precepts, gentle and strong encouragements, splendid examples of every virtue and finally the promise of
eternal reward and the threat of eternal punishment' (Megivern, 196).[3]
The document said, with Augustine, that 'there is in the Holy Scripture
an eloquence that is wonderfully varied and rich, and worthy of great
themes'. Furthermore—this point was partially new, although a number
of older directives along such lines were cited—it urged preachers to
immerse themselves and their communication in biblical language,
which is more powerful than merely human speech (196-98). The
encyclical rejected the view (accepted a little earlier by some Catholic
interpreters) that the Bible can err in matters other than those of faith
and ethics (215), a view that reflected the nominalist separation of religion and ethics from other kinds of truth. Nevertheless, it asserted that
some scientific matters that are 'useless for salvation' are not included
in 'what the sacred writers, or rather the Spirit of God speaking through
them...wished to teach' (213). Thus, it became a challenge for Catholic

1.   Religious people, including theologians, have long asserted that an event
can have both a 'primary' (divine) and a 'secondary' (ordinary) cause.
2.   This theory was formulated sharply by Schell: God does not need to limit a
human being as another human being would do; rather, God, as life itself, enhances
the human being in its own activity, so that the content and verbal form of the text
are equally human and divine (1889, 98, 103-108). (Schell's work, not as strongly
Thomist as some, was placed on the Index of forbidden books in 1898, but it had
been, and continued to be, influential.) For other similar views, see Burtchaell (124-
30); Rahner (68). (Rahner, further, initiated a collective theory of inspiration, with
which the social orientation of form criticism was congenial [Vawter, 106].)
3.   Page numbers in Megivern are given here, to indicate the relative location
of statements within the encyclical; the translation, however, diverges at some
points from Megivern.

biblical scholars to determine what communicative intention is embedded in a text or, in other words, what is its genre.

The idea of genre had been touched upon implicitly by François Lenormant in 1880, describing the early chapters of Genesis as a 'Book of Beginnings' similar to other ancient Near Eastern sacred books.[4] He referred to the symbolic interpretations of Alexandrians (including Origen) and of Cajetan (sixteenth century, mentioned above) as antecedents of his view (xx). He did not, however, carefully characterize a genre, and he continued to make a distinction between religious/ethical and other truth (ix). Moreover, his work was fairly radical in historical questions so that it was placed on the Index of forbidden books.

Relevant also to the issue of genres was a massive work by Gustavo Strafforello in 1883, which presented parallels to biblical proverbs from all over the world. For Strafforello the existence of parallels was not bothersome but rather underscored the position that biblical literature—including the proverbs of the Hebrew Bible and of Jesus, the 'tragedy' of Job, the 'idyll' of Ruth and the songs of prophets and psalms—are 'archetypical' (I: vii). A view of this kind had already been held in early times (see above, for example, for Origen).

More theoretically, the challenge of genres was taken up by Marie-Joseph Lagrange in a formulation that became widely accepted. On a basis of a Thomist view of inspiration, he wrote: 'It will always be very important to consider whether the sacred author [of the Gospel] really had the intention of writing a continuous history... It is God who teaches, but the teaching of the hagiographers is one, the teaching of the prophets another, the teaching of Jesus Christ and the apostles another; different from each other are teaching through history, teaching through allegory, and teaching through discussion' (1895: 569-70). In fact, each form 'must be interpreted according to its own rules' (1903, III), as had indeed long been held in special hermeneutics.

Similar views, often in the train of Lagrange, were expressed by other scholars in France, Germany, England, and the US.[5] Especially detailed was Franz von Hummelauer's overview of narrative genres (1904). These involve the fable, the parable, epic poetry ('probably'

---

4. *Les origines de l'histoire après la Bible et les traditions des peuples orientaux*, 1880-82, I: xviii.

5. Perhaps also elsewhere; see studies discussed by Burtchaell, Fogarty, Seidel.

historical), religious history (incidents true but selected for the purpose of edification), 'old history' (written according to the artistically free canons of ancient history), 'popular tradition' (with a historical kernel), 'free narrative' (although historically true, e.g. Ruth), midrash (for edification) and prophetic or apocalyptic narrative (with the motif of fulfilment and symbols). According to Hummelauer, a consideration of ancient standards of history writing is appropriate, since early theologians had already compared biblical with classical historiography (18). Like Lagrange and others (Burtchaell, 108, 158; Fogarty, 86), Hummelauer connected a writer's 'intention' with the nature, or genre, of a text (44); this intention is the standard for the 'truth' of a text, which is not equivalent to its 'historical value' (49).

Much more sceptical than Hummelauer with regard to historical questions was Alfred Loisy. Loisy opposed a distinction between inspired and non-inspired aspects of the Bible (in 1892, cited by Lagrange 1895: 565); but instead of regarding the Bible as wholly true in relation to its intention, he described biblical truth as 'relative', relevant for its own time (1903: 127, 135 [1892], 162 [1893]). He did not believe that a statement can be true at all times nor—if a universally true statement should exist—that it would be understandable at any time (136, 157). He was thus more historicist than were others. Furthermore, as is typical for a particularist, he separated what a historian can determine about the 'objective value' of an event from what faith says (39-41 [1903]). He presented, however, useful reflections about biblical genres. In his judgment, ancient Babylonian 'myths' exceed Israelite 'legends' poetically, both in imagination and in language, but the Israelite stories exceed the others religiously and morally; he observed that biblical narration has a strongly 'didactic' cast and is 'submerged in the Law' (1901: 212). In the New Testament, including the Gospels, he saw reflections of Christian preaching and ritual (1902 [a controversial work which he published without seeking an imprimatur]). After his excommunication in 1908,[6] he spoke of biblical 'myths'. From 1920 on, he built on work by Protestant form critics; specifically, he viewed New Testament literary forms largely in terms of church 'catechesis'.

6.   Before then, Loisy had already lost a job and some studies by him were placed on the Index. Although in 1893 he submitted to Leo XIII—whose encyclical was in good part stimulated by Loisy's writing—he was not thereafter willing to accept ecclesiastical authority.

Alarmed especially by Loisy and other 'modernists', but also by more moderate figures, the Catholic Church cracked down hard on a large number of scholars in the last days of Leo XIII and, even more, under his successors Pius X (pope from 1903–14) and Benedict XV. The Pontifical Biblical Commission ruled in 1905 (23 June) that a non-historical (non-literal) interpretation of a text may be given only if it can be firmly shown that the sacred writers themselves intended it. During the next ten years, the commission declared obligatory a number of traditional beliefs, including the substantially Mosaic authorship of the Pentateuch. Biblical scholars were thus driven towards relatively non-controversial topics or towards reporting primarily the opinions of others. The pressures for the new scholarship, however, could not be contained altogether. Indeed, partial steps toward liberalization were taken under Pius XI, who was pope from 1922–39 (see, for example, Robert and Tricot, 89-90).

In a striking study (1925), Thaddaeus Soiron presented an analysis of the 'gospel as human life form'. Clearly influenced by Protestant form critics, although without express reference to them, the study shows how form criticism can be carried out (differently from many Protestants) for the sake of its own aim, rather than as a means for speculative historical reconstruction, and by understanding 'life' (cf. Gunkel's 'life situation') as an integral process rather than as a collection of externally described organizational arrangements. It was thus in many ways better than what was written by Protestants.

According to Soiron, the Gospels must be understood as 'works of literature' according to the standards of ancient historiography. They do not furnish a historical-chronological report without gaps. Rather, they wish to show the 'meaning of the mission of Jesus' (5, 25). The reports are truthful, but they are formed according to stylistic patterns which involve certain numbers, keywords, and systematic arrangements (12-27). As 'good news', they have a practical purpose: the 'formation of life' (28). Their background lies in 'life circles' within which this formation has already begun (29). They answer questions which early Christians posed concerning the 'life of Jesus' (29). These questions revolve around the topics of messiahship, the 'life of the new righteousness', and the legitimation and apostolate of the new righteousness (30-52). In describing the life of Jesus, the Gospels present the 'life form of humans' (54, 70); its foundation is poverty in spirit (66). Christ is the typical, exemplary realization of human nature at its deepest,

which—by dethroning the 'I', in poverty, lowliness and suffering—
becomes a carrier of divine life (76). Thus there is the challenge 'to live
according to the form of the gospel' (77).[7] The study, then, was slightly
liberal in regard to the composition of the gospel, but it was essentialist
(as befits an Aristotelian-Thomistic view) in regarding the Christ presented by the gospels as the true essence of humanity.

A number of significant formal observations were made in the 1930s.
In a volume devoted to the topic of inspiration (1930: 75), Augustinus
Bea, rector of the Pontifical Biblical Institute in Rome, declared that
'each genre has its own truth', giving as examples a fable (Judg. 9.8-
15), an epic song (Ps. 103 on creation) and a dialogue (Job). H. Höpfl
stated in a discussion of biblical literary forms that 'one must admit...a
difference between ancient and modern history' (1934: 208). In an
impressive analysis of biblical poetry, Edward Dhorme treated its different genres and observed 'harmony, inspiration, elevation' in both
ideas and style (1931: 10).

In a reflective essay, J. Coppens called for renewed attention to the
'aesthetic or literary aspect' of exegesis. 'There was a time', he said,
'when it was favored to approach the sacred Books from a literary point
of view'; writers 'sought to inculcate a taste for them by praising, even
describing minutely, all their beauties'.[8] Critical theories led to a
neglect of this aspect. 'Yet, a literary and aesthetic comprehension of
the sacred Books' is helpful not only for a philological understanding
of them but also for the religious life and preaching of clerics; the
Scriptures have a remarkable power of expression, useful even for the
present (1938: 789).[9]

A. Robert and A. Tricot included in their general introduction to the
Bible (1939) an overview of genres, ordered according to the different
parts of the Jewish and New Testament Scriptures. Robert said that by
'literary genres' one means 'general forms of thought and expression

7.   The analysis is marred, unfortunately, by a repeated critique of Pharisaism
which accepts at face value the Gospels' description of this orientation. (That fault
has, of course, been widespread.)

8.   Perhaps Coppens was thinking of Plantier (1842, third edn 1881), together
with earlier writers.

9.   In 1959: 164-76, connecting form with content, E. Beaucamp described the
Bible's 'religious sense of the universe' with reference to its poetic descriptions,
which exhibit realism, a sense of movement and life, and personification.
L. Krinetzki (1965) discussed Israelite prayer (including psalms) for a general audience, with attention to genres, in line with Gunkel's analysis.

current in a given time and place' (24).[10] For him, there is a 'tight connection between thought content and literary presentation', which are, like body and soul, 'distinct, but intimately united'; 'the literary study of the Bible, if it is well understood, is then not simply a study of the vocabulary and external forms of the thought but a study of the doctrine. And conversely...a theological synthesis constructed outside the literary question risks being artificial and inexact' (189).

According to Tricot in that work, the formation of New Testament literature was conditioned by practical needs for Christian 'propaganda' and 'catechesis', so that the Gospels are not, strictly speaking, biographies (192, 195, 221). In his opinion, the genres of the New Testament were different from Graeco-Roman forms; they did not follow sharply defined rules but were 'popular' (222).

A year later (1940), E. Schick published a detailed form-critical study of the Gospels, advocating positions very similar to those of Tricot, although they apparently were reached independently. He, too, believed that the Gospels, though historical, were not truly biographies (51-52).[11] Like Tricot, he argued—against some Protestant reconstructions of the tradition which assumed that forms in their original setting in life were simple or 'pure'—that pure literary forms appear precisely *not* in material that stands close to life.[12] He held, furthermore, that names given to literary genres should not imply a judgment about the historicity of the materials they cover.

Thus, while Catholic Hebrew Bible scholars used the notion of literary genres to a large extent (although not entirely) as a means of developing a new view of history, Catholic New Testament specialists pursued form criticism primarily as a structural and functional investigation.[13] The reverse situation obtained among Protestant form critics, among whom New Testament scholars especially (even more than Hebrew Bible specialists) attempted to present a historical view in what was called 'form-history' (see below). The Catholic Hessler (1992: 65) has commented, wisely, that in focusing on 'compositional structure'

10. One genre he identified (since 1934) was the 'anthological' one; it makes extensive use of earlier written products, coming close to a pastiche (cf. Seidel, 263, for him and his followers).

11. Schick (13) cites Lagrange (1928: vi), stating that the Gospels do not furnish materials sufficient for a modern-style 'life of Jesus'. Lagrange, however, compared Mark with ancient biographies (1911: cxiv).

12. Similar criticisms were made by Benoit and Szörényi (see below).

13. Thus also, for instance, J. Dupont (93).

rather than on prehistory, Catholic New Testament scholars were 'ahead' of their Protestant colleagues.[14]

An openness towards newer approaches accelerated under Pius XII, who became pope in 1939. His encyclical *Divino afflante Spiritu* (1943) did not differ sharply from earlier pronouncements; for instance, it continued to condemn the belief that the truth of Scripture is limited to issues of faith and morality, and that physical and historical matters have no connection with these (Megivern, 317). Yet the tone was different. It urged the interpreter to determine—'with all care and not neglecting any light which recent investigations provide' (presumably including works by Protestants)—the special character and circumstances of the biblical writers, and the oral or written sources and the 'forms of expression' used by them, in order to determine what they intended to say (331). It affirmed that new knowledge is possible and that scholars—including (by implication) church officials—cannot determine *a priori* what ancient 'literary types' were like; indeed, twentieth-century study has made clearer 'what forms of speaking were used in those ancient times, whether in poetic descriptions or in the formulation of precepts for life and of laws or in the narrating of historical facts and events' (332). The question of intention—whether biblical writers 'intended' to use these forms, as the Biblical Commission had required in 1905—was subtly downplayed in favour of a determination that certain literary forms were in fact employed.[15] What was relatively new in the encyclical was not a recognition of literary types—in itself not a controversial issue—but a historical understanding of them. Thus, attention to literary form constituted a bridge that connected historical phenomena with theological meanings.

More important, perhaps, than the encyclical itself was the way in which a more accepting policy was applied. In 1948, the Pontifical Biblical Commission gave greater latitude for dealing with the issue of the Mosaic authorship of the Pentateuch and declared the question of the literary genre and historicity of the first 11 chapters of Genesis to be an open one. Not long thereafter (12 August 1950), Pius XII warned that scholars were taking excessive liberty as a result of this declaration; repression did take place, but freedom of enquiry nevertheless

14. Hessler referred to Soiron, Willibrod Hillmann (with a study of the passion narrative in 1941) and Schick.

15. A 'wish' or intention to employ these forms is attributed only to the ancient writers in general, not to biblical writers specifically.

continued to grow, as biblical scholars proceeded with a mixture of restraint and boldness (cf. Fogarty, 248-56).

In 1949, K. Schelkle presented an impressive 'form-critical' and 'theological' study of the passion story. Schelkle believed in the substantial accuracy of the reports of the last days of Jesus, but he held that they were presented within a theological perspective. The passion of Christ, with which the resurrection is connected intimately, represents 'the form and life of the Church', or the 'archetype of the Christian life' (195, 217); Schelkle showed how the pattern entered into the preaching and cult of the Church.[16] Reflecting on procedure, he said that 'it is insufficient to append to the sentences of Scripture historical and archaeological notes and to attempt to understand what is "objectively" contained in them'; rather, it is in line with the intention of the text to 'make its kerygmatic content...live, to make the power of the word effective for today and now' (299). Yet he rejected the view, voiced by some Protestants, that the historical life of Jesus is unimportant; indeed, he denied a sharp distinction between a 'supposedly objective' historical criticism and faith (299), as is made by particularist historicism.

Quite a few other Catholic studies orientated toward genres appeared after the 1943 encyclical. H. Cazelles showed, in 1946, that the divergent forms of Hebrew law represent different functions (see below in connection with relevant Protestant discussions). A pervasive shift in outlook[17] can be seen, for instance, in relation to the book of Jonah. Prior to 1943, only a few twentieth-century Catholic scholars (like some early Christian and mediaeval Jewish writers) had treated it as nonhistorical (see Feuillet 1949, 1113-19); by the 1950s, this interpretation was quite widespread (with Feuillet's support). A Spanish congress was devoted to the topic of literary genres (Congreso de Ciencias Eclesiásticas 1957). R. Schnackenburg described gospel narration as a proclamation of good news rather than as 'mere historical reportage'; through the Gospels, he said, the words of Jesus became a 'continuing and immediate address' to subsequent hearers (1963: 31-

16. The study refers extensively to Protestant scholarship, but surprisingly not to Soiron (1925), with a similar literary and theological analysis. Soiron had been cited by Schick (known to Schelkle) but only for his compositional analysis, not for his structural examination of the 'life' of Jesus. Schelkle himself was ignored by the Catholics Schnackenburg (1963) and Hessler (1992: 65).

17. The story of the shift was recounted and the new attitude was itself expressed in Levie (1958).

32). The term 'address' here probably echoes the dialogical view developed by the Catholic thinker Ferdinand Ebner (similar to Buber) and others.[18]

The way was thus well prepared for Vatican II, a liberalizing council which began under John XXIII (pope from 1958–63) and issued its declarations under Paul VI; in fact, biblical scholarship stood in the vanguard of its movement. In 1965, the council formulated a 'constitution' on revelation with a major emphasis on the Bible (*Dei verbum*). This stated: 'In determining the intention of the sacred writers, consideration must be given, *inter alia*, to literary types, for truth is set forth and expressed divergently in texts with various kinds of history, in prophetical and poetical texts, and in other kinds of literary expression... To understand what the sacred author wanted to affirm' requires attention 'to the accustomed native modes of perception, speech, and narrative which flourished at the age of the sacred writer' and to the modes of communication employed at that time (§12). This perspective does not imply a downgrading of Scripture. Rather, the constitution urges 'frequent reading of it' not only by the clergy but also—with a partially new emphasis—by the laity (§25).

The council also issued statements on 'social communication' (especially, the mass media with their advantages and problems), on relations between the Catholic Church and other groups (Christian, Jewish, and so on) and on various internal issues, including liturgy (liberalized). The overall thrust of the council was an opening up of the Church to the rest of the world, engaging in communication with it. Such a movement can be seen, for instance, in the writing of A. Bea, an important contributor to the formulations of Vatican II (as earlier to that of *Divino afflante Spiritu*). In addition to his focus on the Hebrew Bible (already mentioned), he had a pronounced ecumenical perspective; expressing this, he spoke of a 'polarity' of unity and freedom among human beings (1964: 6).

A significant writer on literary forms from before the time of the council on was L. Alonso Schökel, who began his career by teaching and writing about non-biblical literature.[19] In 1960, he defined genres

18. See *RFT*.

19. Early publications by him dealt with the history of Greek and Latin literature (1945 [seventh edn, 1965]), the formation of style (1947 [fifth edn, 1968]), modern poetry (1948), twentieth-century Spanish poetry (1950) and the pedagogy of comprehension (1954); for these and for subsequent publications concerning the

on the basis of three features: content, structure (organization) and style (1960a: 13). This analysis lacked Gunkel's 'life situation' as a defining aspect but employed the concept of 'internal form', which designates the intuitively grasped heart of a text.[20] Soon thereafter, he produced an overview of Hebrew stylistic forms, together with a history of a recognition of them in biblical study (1963, revised in 1988).[21]

In a well-rounded work soon after Vatican II (1966), Alonso Schökel discussed the three 'dialogical functions' of language described by K. Bühler,[22] as well as 'monological' forms (e.g. in Qoheleth). He regarded the psalms that address God as part of a genuine dialogue, inspired so as to teach people to pray (2.5).[23] Other topics covered in this study included the 'three levels of language' (common, technical and literary), as they are found in the Bible, and relations between speech and writing.

In sum, Catholic biblical scholarship succeeded in combining particularity (as examined in critical historiography) with generality. It did so with the aid of a notion of genres that was supported by Aristotelian philosophy, which has room for both of those dimensions. A difficulty with this path is that Aristotelian essentialism involves some definite intellectual (and perhaps social) problems that have already been discussed in part. Many of the Catholic analyses reported, however, do not depend on strict essentialism; rather, the concept of genres presented in *Divino afflante Spiritu* (1943) was historical since it referred to special ancient forms.

Indeed, the more recent studies (especially after 1965) on the whole reflect a movement from essentialism towards relational thought. Already Bea's reference in 1964 to a polarity of unity and freedom expressed the duality of partial connectedness and partial separation of relational theory (see above, Chapter 7). Similarly, Alonso Schökel's

Bible until 1983, see Collado and Zurro (14-21).

20. A 1954 article in the same journal dealt with the literary genre of the Gideon story.

21. Alonso Schökel's history is valuable as a first of its kind; his assertion, however, that in the Middle Ages and Renaissance the Bible was neither 'the object of literary study' (except in the few works listed) nor 'a model for poetic composition' (1988: 2) appears to be based either on a still-limited knowledge or on a narrow meaning of those phrases. A history of stylistic and generic analyses by Catholic writers from early times on was furnished by Muños Iglesias (1968).

22. See *RFT*.

23. Cf. the points of view of Saadia and Maimonides (above, 4.2.a).

1966 work was relational rather than essentialist, since it considered a variety of factors—not just a single classification according to essences. Subsequently, he made this approach more explicit by observing that Israelites did not make a clear distinction between genres (1988: 8) and that the Bible exhibits patterns other than these commonly labelled 'genres' (e.g. the Exodus pattern, 194), so that patterns can be identified in different ways depending on the criteria employed.

Chapter 10

THE BIBLE AS LITERATURE: PROTESTANT ANALYSES
LARGELY BY OR FOR NONSPECIALISTS, C. 1875–1965

Near the turn of the century, a major change took place in Protestant interpretation, but much of this turn was concentrated in works that stood outside academic biblical scholarship. They were produced by scholars who were not biblical specialists or by biblical scholars who addressed a public beyond the academic circle. Their broad involvements led them to be more sensitive to changes in society and culture than was professionalized scholarship. Within the profession, in contrast, established procedures and goals could become habits that continued even though they no longer met social needs.

The new movement presupposed the spirit and major conclusions of historical criticism. However, instead of dealing with further details along that line (which may have very little social and personal significance), it took a step beyond that. This move was difficult for Protestant specialists in biblical study, who largely continued to adhere to nominalism, to which they had become used. Nevertheless, as we shall see later, Protestant academics, too, moved in the new direction, although with some difficulty.

1. *Arnold*

Matthew Arnold, professor of poetry at Oxford just as Lowth had been, engaged in a literary approach to the Bible. His primary interest was the content—especially, the thrust or kind of content—to be found in literature; specifically, he characterized literature as 'a criticism of life' (III: 209 [1864], etc.). This emphasis on content rather than on external form resembled classical (Aristotelian) literary theory. His work involved major social concerns. With a conviction that a human culture requires greater equality than obtained (II: 8 [1861]; VIII: 289, 304

[1878], and so on), he took a strong interest in public education. Accordingly, he concerned himself with the teaching of the Bible to the general public, 'the little-instructed—the great majority' (III: 43 [1863]).

In opposition both to literalistic interpretation and to an intellectualist shunning of the Bible, he argued that its language 'is not scientific but *literary*'; it is 'the language of poetry and emotion, approximate language thrown out, as it were, at certain great objects which the human mind augurs and feels after' (VII: 155 [1875]; similarly, VI: 189 [1871]). He considered that some of the clergy were 'not conversant enough with the many ways' in which human beings 'think and speak' to be able to recognize this fact (VI: 316 [1871]). His niece, Mary Ward, said more specifically that the Bible offers not 'facts' but 'testimony' (Prickett 1986: 238; 1991: 217).

Arnold accepted the validity of historical criticism, but he rejected the view (stated by the historically orientated critic Edmond Scherer) that a knowledge of the author's character and temporal situation leads 'spontaneously' to a right understanding of a work (VIII: 175 [1877])[1]. Against historicism, Arnold asked (III: 73-74 [1863]), 'which is the true science of the Bible'—that which helps human beings to be 'transformed by the renewing of their mind' (Rom. 12.2) or that which helps 'settle the vexed question of the precise date when the book of Deuteronomy assumed its present form' (a desideratum expressed by a biblical critic of his day)?

Arnold's substantive contribution toward understanding the Bible, it is true, was limited. The rich analysis presented earlier by Lowth had to a large extent evaporated in the particularist atmosphere of the nineteenth century; a newer one, which would require the efforts of many persons, had not yet been constructed. Still, Arnold observed fruitfully that the Hebrew Bible 'is filled by the word and thought of righteousness' (VI: 180 [1871]). The word 'God' receives a functional definition in light of the literature within which it appears; it designates 'the not ourselves which makes for righteousness' (VI: 196 [1871]; VII: 193 [1875]). Thus, although he did not show the intermediate steps that can lead to this conclusion, he set forth a central thrust of the Bible.

---

1.   Arnold was untypical at that time (before 1890 [G. Watson, 134]) in questioning—at least partially—the value of historical criticism for apprehending literature.

2. *Moulton*

Following Arnold, Richard G. Moulton held that literature deals with 'Life'; he called it the 'science of life' and believed that all forms of literature—including the 'most frivolous', as well as the sacred Scriptures—deserve attention (W. Moulton, 43 [1890], 34-35 [1912]). Carrying on Arnold's programme of general education, he played an important role in the movement which extended university education in England and the US off-campus and to non-resident students, in a democratizing effort to include 'poorer' persons (W. Moulton, 20) and women. His major specializations were the plays attributed to Shakespeare (it was not crucial for him what individual wrote them) and the writings of the Bible.

Although Moulton regarded literary development as important (1885: 37) and dealt extensively with the evolution of forms in some publications, he eschewed an 'exclusive historic spirit' (1899: vi). Thus, he was concerned with 'analysing literature as it stands for the purpose of discovering its laws', just as botany or economics deal with the phenomena and principles of vegetable life or of commerce (cf. Lowth's methodological basis); to apply a scientific approach to literature was not a problem, for 'art is a part of nature' (1885: 21, 36, as was held by others with a populist orientation [see *RFT*]). As was common at the end of the nineteenth century, he continued to use the term 'inductive' for scientific procedure even while describing science according to a newer conception of it as a process which involves the testing of hypotheses (1885: 25); the term 'inductive' thus meant for him an approach both empirical and systematic.[2]

In contrast to Wordsworth, who had held that every poet must be examined as a pure individual, Moulton judged that 'inductive criticism is mainly occupied in distinguishing literary species' (1885: 32). Specifically, in his view, 'literary morphology' is an 'inquiry into the foundation forms of literature' (1899: v). Its 'underlying principle is

---

2. Cf. *RFT*. Moulton considered his position to be 'unfashionable' (1896: vii) but to stand in the vanguard of a new movement (1885: 20, 267), as indeed proved to be the case. Controversial before 1900 (Gayley and Scott, 5-6, 27-29, 57, 70), it became not atypical after 1900, as quite a few pursued a 'types approach' or downplayed individual authors (see Ehrenpreis, *passim*—cf. there pp. 30-33; Gayley and Scott, 391; Wellek, IV: 148, for similar views expressed before 1900).

that a clear grasp of the outer literary form is an essential guide to the inner matter and spirit' (vi); in other words, literary form is connected with content and life. Since 'different classes of writing' have 'different effects' (1885: 267), it is important to consider 'purpose' or 'intention', but a work's purpose need not have been conscious for its author (26). In fact, it is a 'disturbance in literary appreciation to have the personality of an author interposed between the reader and the work'. The light shed by 'historical surroundings' is 'least important just where the literature is most worthy of study', that is, in 'the masterpieces of literature, which are for all ages and all peoples' (1896: viii).

Moulton believed that the morphological method is especially applicable to the Bible, since a long oral transmission and the prevalence of floating literature (with unclear authorship) make a reconstruction of sources virtually impossible (1899: 98). He accepted the major results of historical criticism but argued that the value of the writings is independent of their date, which is often quite uncertain. Thus, the literary study of the Scriptures is 'a common meeting ground' for all readers, including the conservatively devout who accept traditional datings and those who do not grant any authority to the Bible (iv). After all, the Bible is 'an *interesting* literature' (in Moulton *et al.*, 7).

It is impossible to summarize briefly the wealth of Moulton's observations, which made free use of previous analyses and anticipated some that arose later, perhaps independently. The combination of styles which is characteristic of prophecy (noted a little after him by Gunkel) is termed 'rhapsody'. Very short oracular sayings lying side by side in some prophetic books (observed also by Gunkel) are characterized as 'sentences' which can be united in 'cycles'. Deuteronomy contains 'spoken rhetoric'; the Epistles, 'written rhetoric'. Many of the psalms are said to belong to rituals. Such psalms include 'accession hymns', which use the phrase 'Yahweh is king',[3] and 'votive hymns', in which a personal strain merges with general praise (1899: 197). Psalms moving through several moods are labelled 'liturgies' (198; similarly Gunkel later). The word 'idyll' describes Ruth and other works because of their

---

3. A number of conservative and other exegetes (including Calvin) had interpreted the phrase as referring to an entry into rule, past or future; Thomas Kelly Cheyne (*The Origin and the Religious Contents of the Psalter*, 1891: 71, 341), spoke of 'enthronization' and 'accession psalms', without connecting them with a festival. Moulton seems to have been the first to regard this group as a whole (not only Ps. 47) as 'ritual' hymns. (Cf. below 13.2.c, on Mowinckel.)

'homely' subject matter. Wisdom literature is identified as a form of 'philosophy' (as had long been done).[4]

In terms of sustained profundity, Moulton's observations do not equal those of Lowth. Nevertheless, they represent a step beyond Lowth in that, reflecting historical criticism during the intervening years, they breathe a less classical (Graeco-Roman) spirit.

In comparison with Arnold's analysis, a noticeable lack lies in the fact that Moulton's work gave little attention to the legal and ethical aspects of the Hebrew Bible (as was true also for Lowth). This lack is surprising in view of the fact that Moulton devoted a volume to the moral system implied—not necessarily expressly stated—in Shake-speare. The deficit in ethical description can perhaps be explained by the goal of the educational programme in which Moulton was involved, namely, to teach sensitivity rather than the rigid moralism typical of the religious segment of middle-class culture (see *RFT* on this literary goal, and above, 5.2.a, on the reserve towards poetry that was typical of both the religious and the success-orientated segments of the middle class).[5] Moulton, however, remarked that the prophets were often 'in opposi-tion to the secular government', 'not the counsellors who guided, but the agitators who roused to resistance' (1901: 259).

W.R. Harper, a Hebrew Bible scholar who became the inaugurating president of a revived University of Chicago in 1891,[6] persuaded Moulton to join the university for its first year of classes (1892/93). He

---

4.   Most of this analysis appeared already in the first edition (1895). In regard to wisdom as philosophy, cf. also above for Origen, Theodore, Junilius Africanus, Thomas Aquinas and J. Pareau (1822); further, E. Reuss, *La Bible* (VII, 1878); W.T. Davison, *The Wisdom Literature* (1894); Karl Kautzsch, *Die Philosophie des Alten Testaments* (1914—part of the popular 'religiohistorical' series in which Gunkel participated).

5.   The two segments of the middle class overlapped, of course, as do most groups. In fairness to middle-class persons, it should be pointed out that they cannot afford the more free-wheeling outlook of the well-to-do and thus find it useful to construct rules (e.g. regarding sex—including dancing—and various kinds of drugs, from alcohol on, and in support of a work ethos) to guard against the anomie of poverty; pleasure, including poetry, is a potential threat for them. In Arnold's judgment, the 'harsh, unintelligent and unattractive' culture of the middle class would not appeal to the 'masses' to which he wished to bring education, so that it would need to be bypassed (II: 26 [1861]).

6.   As president of Chicago, Harper insisted on a relatively high degree of aca-demic freedom, also with regard to political matters, but (like most) not perfectly so (Danker, 168).

became there head of the Department of General Literature, which focused on literature in translated form. Moulton had, in fact, advocated the study of Graeco-Roman literature in translation, taking a middle path between the older elitist education requiring Greek and Latin and a progressivist inclination to abandon classical literature altogether. His treatment of the Bible similarly represented an approach that was not bound to tradition but was appreciative also of the old and had faith in the power of great literature to reach all human beings.

When Moulton visited the United States in 1890/91, a movement for increased Bible teaching in a variety of settings had already begun there, and he stirred up further interest in that. After a series of lectures by him—he was perhaps the best-liked Extension lecturer—the audience voted to declare that 'he has led us as a prophet of the coming time, when the Bible shall be a branch of study in all our colleges, and when all culture, and all literature shall acknowledge the Bible as the world's chief book' (S.P. Cook, 156).

The old—e.g. mediaeval—view that the Scriptures represent literature at its highest was thus resurrected in a moderate form in the context of an interest in general education. This integrative view stood in contrast with the separation between biblical and other literature, which was made by some in the seventeenth century (cf. above) and was continued in the following centuries in conservative Protestant circles. It also went counter to the historical orientation which insisted on the distinctiveness of national (or regional) traditions. These perspectives stressing difference—typically middle-class—were transcended in the notion of 'the Bible as literature'. In that phrase, the word 'literature' did not refer to a special form of writing, such as fiction or poetry, although it excluded a specialized one that is dryly intellectual (as a scientific essay might be). Instead, it indicated a continuity between biblical and other productions and the possibility of a free human approach.[7]

Within a few years, Moulton was able to put together a team of 20 writers in addition to himself to produce a cooperative volume entitled *The Bible as Literature* (1896). Of the contributors, 19 were located in the US and one was a Scot; about 12 were primarily biblical scholars.

---

7.   Barr (1982) has argued, with partial justification, that B. Jowett's prescription in 1860 to 'interpret the Scriptures like any other book' was literary rather than historical in conception; Jowett, however, did not distinguish between a literary approach and a historical one.

All of them were significant scholars in the sense that they produced works of their own before or after this. One of them, Milton Terry, had written an extensive 'Biblical Hermeneutics' (1883), which had given, in a largely traditional manner, detailed attention to 'special hermeneutics'—that is, to considering styles (poetry, symbolism) and genres (fables, riddles, proverbs, dreams, prophecy, and so on)—but which also contained angles not typical of older Protestant hermeneutics, such as a recognition of non-biblical scriptures or canons. Another contributor, John Peters, published simultaneously a little volume on 'What One Parish Is Doing for Social Reform' (1896), reflecting his involvement in such reform.

3. *Briggs*

A manifesto for the literary study of the Bible had been issued already in 1882 in an essay by Charles Briggs (revised in *Biblical Study*, 1883). Briggs noted that attention to literary forms languished after Lowth and Herder, but he observed that relevant observations were made by de Wette, Ewald and Reuss (although they 'have given their strengths to other topics') and, more recently, 'in the school of Kuenen'[8] and by Arnold. Thus there 'lies open...one of the most interesting and inviting fields for research', which elicits enthusiasm in the young, including young scholars (1882: 66-67, 76; 1883: 229, 240).

According to Briggs, the Bible contains both prose and poetry, between which it is not possible to draw a precise line (1882: 67). The prose portions include history, orations (including those of the prophets), epistles and fiction. These 'general forms...present the greatest variety of form, the noblest themes, and the very best models. Nowhere else can we find more admirable aesthetic as well as moral and religious culture'; this should be taught in schools together with Greek and Roman writings, for these 'lack the oriental wealth of color, depths of passion, heights of rapture, holy aspirations, transcendent

---

8.   It is not clear whom he had in mind as members of the 'school of Kuenen'; however, Kuenen's 'historical-critical introduction' (Dutch 1861–65 [ET 1886]; 2nd edn, 1887–93) contained literary observations (for instance, in discussing the 'form of Israelite poetry' in vol. III, he noted that poetic speech differs in both content and style), and Henricus Oort and Isaac Hooykaas produced, with the assistance of Kuenen, *The Bible for Learners*, which dealt extensively and in a reflective fashion with biblical 'legends' (including 'myths'), etc. (ET, 6 vols., 1873–79).

hopes, and transforming moral power' of the Bible (1882: 76; 1883: 239). The Bible's poetry is 'simple and natural', 'essentially subjective', 'sententious' and 'realistic'. It can be divided into Lyric, Gnomic, and Composite classes (1883: 250-53, 284; for the 'composite' kind, cf. both Moulton and Gunkel on a combination of styles in prophecy). In composite poetry, such as in Isa. 52.13-53, 'we have the climax of Hebrew poetic art, where the democratic and heroic elements combine to produce in the larger whole ethical and religious results with wonderful power'; it uses, he said, 'the epic, dramatic, and pastoral elements in perfect freedom, combining them in a simple and comprehensive manner' in such a way that the 'forms of beauty and grace...do not retard the imagination in admiration of themselves, but direct it to the grandest themes and images of piety and devotion' (1882: 70; 1883: 294).

Biblical literature clearly was not understood by Briggs in purely aesthetic terms. On the contrary, in a controversial address, 'The Authority of the Bible', delivered and published under the same title in 1891, he argued that 'many principles' embodied in the Pentateuchal codes 'are invaluable hints for the solution of the social problems of our day'[9] and complained that 'we bury the sublime ideal' of the Sermon on the Mount; he projected that if someone would, like Jesus, 'rebuke sin in high places and trouble the people with his unapproachable holiness', then 'Christian theologians and ecclesiastics' would call for that person's death (58-60). In fact, Briggs was soon criticized sharply both for his liberal historical criticism and for espousing what was considered to be an unrealistic idealism that will undermine society (Chambers, 492). He was defrocked but did not lose his teaching position.[10]

In that address and later, Briggs acknowledged three sources of 'divine authority': the Church, Reason and the Bible, with the Bible

9.   In 1882 (77) Briggs gratuitously criticized a Rabbinic emphasis on law and ritual, but this remark was dropped in 1883. His 1891 statement undoubtedly alludes to the 'social question' of that time.

10.   After considerable controversy aroused largely (although not only) by the address, Briggs was suspended from the Presbyterian ministry in 1893 until such time as he may repent; the reasons for that action included both his historical criticism and his theory of sanctification—in some ways less Presbyterian than Methodist or perhaps Catholic—which he held in conjunction with his ethical idealism.

standing in the position of climax.[11] His recognition of the authority of the Church countered individualism; at the same time, his acceptance of reason as a source of divine authority supported the free exercise of insight. Reason was defined in a 'broad sense' to include metaphysical reflection, conscience and 'religious feeling'.

It is characteristic of much of the literary study of the Bible that it encourages a direct encounter with the text in such a way as to reduce reliance on professional scholars. Briggs was no pure individualist in this regard. Rather, giving room to both personal and professional elements in interpretation, he said that 'the ordinary reader may enjoy [the Bible, like Shakespeare and Homer] as literature without being a critic—but the labors of critics are necessary' for a presentation of such literature to readers (1883: 216).

Briggs's description of literary features of the Bible was expanded in his *General Introduction to the Study of Holy Scripture*, 1899 (oddly, without reference to Moulton). His subsequent publications, however—including a commentary on the Psalms co-authored with his daughter Emilie Briggs—gave only limited attention to formal analysis, perhaps since they were addressed primarily to a scholarly audience.

4. *Harper*

A key organizational figure for the lay study of the Bible was William Rainey Harper, who had a passion for adult education in biblical literature as well as more generally. From 1882 on, he edited a journal devoted to biblical study by non-specialists[12] (in it appeared the 1882 essay by Briggs). Simultaneously, he organized a Hebrew Summer School and a Hebrew Correspondence School. Before heading the University of Chicago, he provided leadership for the Chatauqua summer and travelling programmes—with a strong but not exclusive emphasis on the Bible—which eventually reached a goodly portion of the the the US population. In many ways, including his own enthusiastic teaching (e.g.

11. In this view, Briggs stood close to Anglicanism and to the associated J. Wesley (eighteenth century), for whom Scripture, reason, Church and experience were authoritative together in a unified way (S. Jones, 102). After his suspension from the Presbyterian ministry, in fact, he was ordained as an Episcopalian in 1899.

12. It began as *The Hebrew Student*, continued in 1883 as *The Old Testament Student* (with *Hebraica* as a separate journal for specialists), in 1889 as *The Old and New Testament Student* and in 1893 as *The Biblical World*.

at Yale), he contributed to a movement to introduce and enhance the teaching of the Bible in colleges and universities.[13]

Harper's educational vision was populist and valued inclusiveness, in terms of both economical class and gender.[14] To be sure, his record on including women was not unmixed.[15] However, K. Budde, who visited in Chicago during 1898, took note of Harper's expression of pride in having opened the door wide to women (Budde 1907: 826).

Like most populists at that time (see *RFT*), Harper did not make a sharp distinction between the physical sciences and the humanities. Nor did he accept a gulf between Christianity and other religious traditions. Accordingly, the journal he edited represented Judaism and non-biblical religions in freestanding quotations, discussions and book reviews. Its first volume in 1882 contained a Hindu parallel to Prov. 31 (about the 'virtuous woman'), 'Beams from the Talmud' (three times), an article on 'Russia and the Jews', and a discussion of a verse from the Qur'an. After the World Parliament of Religions in 1893, the journal furnished a regular series of 'Comparative Religion Notes' (cf. Shepard, 49-50). As Harper saw it, the Scriptures present the highest truth, but all of reality and all knowledge is of one piece. Indeed, he believed that God works through and in natural order; an important

13. Such teaching remained prominent until religion courses in colleges became more varied c.1960. (Student interest in the Bible remains high, however, although few colleges continue this area as a requirement.)

14. For his summer and correspondence courses, he kept prices very low (with the aid of financial support he raised). Women took part in the Hebrew Summer School at least from 1882 on, as was reported in his journal. For the University of Chicago, as it was reconstituted in 1889, a decision was made from the very beginning that the sexes would have equal opportunity at all levels. Caroline Brey-fogle received there a BA degree in 1896 (communication by the university registrar) and a PhD in Hebrew Bible in 1912 on the basis of a dissertation on the *The Hebrew Sense of Sin in the Pre-exilic Period*, which was published that same year. (In 1910: 418, Breyfogle expressed a feminist ambivalence toward the Bible by observing that the prophetic movement 'against the Baal, the Ashtaroth, and the qadeshah serving at the sanctuary' was 'in the interest of public morality. But it reacted against woman, sweeping away her last independent stand and possibility of a career'.)

15. He initially needed to be persuaded about the wisdom of including women as students in the university, but he energetically recruited women faculty; during the period of 1900–1902, he favoured segregating women students (L. Gordon, 87, 113—incidentally, both inclusion and segregation involved pragmatic besides ideological considerations).

insight is to 'discover ever more clearly the essential harmony of the Divine activity as revealed in the Scriptures and the laws of human reason, and…to find the same God and the same Divine methods in human life everywhere' (1890: 264). Harper, in fact, denied all disorder and arbitrariness in deity (263). That position can be held to be one-sided, just as one can think that for the position he opposed, one that accepts God as present primarily in what is unusual and incomprehensible.

Harper considered himself and his journal to be 'conservative', but this was true only in the sense that a positive attitude towards past tradition was maintained. In fact, Harper accepted historical criticism in reasonable measure. He believed literary criticism, however, to be of equal or greater importance (1893: 244). He held that the biblical narrative will increase in appreciation and influence when 'it is clearly understood that it is *story*, rather than *history*' (1899: 90, 91).

From 1887 on, Harper's journal offered 'Inductive Bible Studies' consisting mostly of questions. In addition to carrying an overtone of scientific procedure, the word 'inductive' meant here that students were asked to arrive at answers by studying the biblical text itself instead of spending much of their time in reading scholarly opinions (some of which may be rather speculative).[16] Strictly speaking, of course, his procedure was not inductive, since the questions were formulated by the teacher, who was guided by a certain understanding of the text. Nevertheless, the process stressed cooperation between teacher and student. In some classes that used its philosophy (e.g. at Amherst College [Burroughs, 1891: 24-25]), students were asked to make observations and to formulate questions stirred by the text, before the teacher presented any questions. Earlier already, Briggs (1883: 77) had employed the term 'inductive' to designate literary description in contrast to historical placement. These uses of the term had an affinity with Moulton's in 1885. In any case, the term 'inductive' came to be used widely for close-to-the-text structural or formal analysis.[17] The term's

16. In fact, Harper had long favoured the acquisition of Hebrew by 'induction', i.e. by learning grammatical forms as they arise in the text.

17. A similar usage continued in the twentieth century for the study of non-biblical literature. The task of arriving at general principles which is implied in the term 'induction' (moving from particulars to generality) was sometimes expressly stated by Harper and others, but it was not carried out frequently, except in reaching towards the general theme of a book under discussion.

implication of a partially democratic procedure expressed the fact that the literary analysis had an egalitarian political agenda.[18]

In addition to publishing study guides, Harper presented his own substantive analyses, which he called 'constructive'. In these, published as articles between 1900 and 1905, the literature of the Hebrew Bible was arranged by major genres and, within such types, by period.[19] Above all, he treated separately the 'prophetic element', the 'priestly element' and the 'sages' of the Hebrew Bible (see F. Brown 1908: xxvii); he remarked that 'the three great divisions of Old Testament literature' reflect the roles of a priest, prophet and sage mentioned in Jer. 18.18 (1916: 9). Although the studies did not contain a detailed analysis comparable to Gunkel's 'Introduction' to the Psalms, they included observations about styles, roles, contents and minor genres.

These studies were not done for idle purposes, but rather in order to recognize and enhance life. In fact, Harper gave three reasons for regarding the Bible as 'a book of life': it is 'instinct with human life'; it has the purpose of 'lifting and purifying' life; and 'behind it lie the inexhaustible potencies of God's life' (1891: 5). W. Chancellor wrote, in Harper's journal, much in his spirit, as follows: 'Our thought concerning the Bible is tending to become critical, scientific, philosophical—in a word, literary…History is the record of deeds; literature, the embodiment of life. We have both in the Bible. The study of history gives knowledge; that of literature instructs in wisdom' (1888: 11). He illustrated this thesis through an analysis of the book of Amos, in which oppression of the poor is a major theme (14).

5. *Others*

Briggs, Moulton and Harper were not alone after 1880 in observing the literary qualities of the Bible. The great poet, Walt Whitman, although not notably religious, declared in an essay, 'The Bible as Poetry', that the Bible still contains 'the fountain heads of song', with 'the finest blending of individuality and universality' (II: 545-49 [1883, 1888]). F. Bowen, author of a considerable number of volumes in philosophy

18. As has been stated, for a recent phase of literary study, by Greenstein (1989: 22).

19. They may reflect earlier teaching; two series of them (on priestly and prophetic elements) were also published separately in book form. (Harper also published one technical work, a commentary on Amos and Hosea; in this, he argued that Amos incorporated 'wisdom' [1905: civ]).

and history, published in 1885 a sensitive treatment of biblical literature using the following headings: narratives, parables, philosophy, poetry, history and institutions. The union of content and expression which he pursued can be seen, for instance, in the following statement: 'This sympathy with all living things, but especially with the weak, the needy, and the unfortunate, is the source of what is tender and pathetic in Hebrew poetry' (101). J. Genung, author of respected handbooks on rhetoric and poetics, discussed in 1891 'The Epic of the Inner Life' (i.e. the book of Job) as Hebrew poetry. Later, he wrote on other aspects of wisdom literature and produced a general survey of biblical genres (1919). He called his spirit 'constructive, as distinguished from the purely critical' (1904: vii).

Influenced by Moulton, Genung and others, the prominent Congregational minister Lyman Abbott presented a moving account of the 'Life and Literature of the Ancient Hebrews' (1901). His theology was strongly incarnational (seeing 'God as dwelling in matter', 11); accordingly, his literary analysis was founded on 'the theological assumption that God's revelation...is in and through a human experience' (17). He proceeded largely by types but also emphasized evolutionary development. Since 'literature is an interpretation of life' (201), he treated content (including concern for the poor and oppressed, 345) as an integral and central part of the literature.[20]

Genres played a considerable role in S. Curry's 'Vocal and Literary Interpretation of the Bible' (1903). Curry reasoned that, for the effective public rendering of a text (such as in a worship service), the reader must be linked 'in unity with the aspirations, the sorrows, and joys' of humanity and thus 'must appreciate the universal forms, which in every age and clime have been the necessary expression of human feeling' (57).

Inspired by Harper but more traditional in historical matters, Wilbert W. White sought to stimulate first-hand study of the Bible. For this purpose he founded in 1900 a school which came to be known as the 'Biblical Seminary in New York'.[21] It was intended to devote much of

---

20. To be sure, Abbott's social views on some crucial topics (women's status and racial relations, as stated in other volumes) were rather conservative by present standards, but he had a partial sympathy with socialism and was liberal in criticizing the punitive treatment of criminals.

21. Later, 'New York Theological Seminary' (with N. Gottwald as a prominent member).

its curriculum to the study of the Scriptures, treating theoretical and practical theology in direct conjunction with it. White and his followers called their method 'inductive' in order to characterize a scientific and independent spirit, as was stated by G. Burroughs (Eberhardt, 120). The group featured a 'compositive' method which consisted in studying the internal and external connections of a text (145-53). In the process, they observed closely relationships between parts on various levels, up to the Bible as a whole as a complex of literary structures (Sweet, 1914: 71-95), including genres.

This tradition's procedure was outlined with special care in a volume by R. Traina (1952), which, at least until very recently, has continued to be in print—not surprisingly, since it is one of the best practical hermeneutics ever written, both for lay persons and for scholars.[22] It calls for examining relations between textual portions on different levels (from phrases to books) and for observing 'general literary forms' (68-71). It recognizes both mood (31) and logic (129). 'Rational' analysis involves the asking of 'why' questions, seeking both 'reasons' (grounding in reality) and 'purposes' (96, 104-108). The final step of this hermeneutics is 'correlation'—relating phenomena within the Bible with each other and with 'life-as-a-whole' (226).

Emanating in part from the White tradition, H. Kuist advocated, in a sophisticated theoretical manner, a 're-creative criticism' going beyond historical reconstruction (1947: 56-60).[23] It attends to structural relations (including a number of 'laws of composition', such as repetition, radiation, contrast and interchange) and to subjective participation. 'Form'—'expressive organization'—'releases [for the reader] what is vital in the subject matter of Scripture' (91, 108). Both 'freedom to think' and 'commitment', including a 'social conscience', he said, are integral parts of this interpretive process (113-34, 155).

Harper's student C.F. Kent followed in his teacher's footsteps by furnishing structural analyses of biblical literature. Characteristically, he believed that if the book of Proverbs 'is to fulfill its mission to the

22. Traina's volume, it is true, contains a number of elements that will be questioned by many readers—for example, the insistence that the Scriptures should be studied 'inductively' since they are 'objective' (their truth being external to the interpreter, 7), the statement that 'the Old Testament is preparatory and partial' (157) and the implication that the resurrection of Jesus is historical (170-71). Yet with its attention to 'life', with express reference to psychology and at least potentially or implicitly involving sociology, it is unusually well-rounded.

23. A critical approach is not rejected. I have been a student of Kuist.

present age, order must be evolved out of chaos' (1895: 4). He pursued that aim through classification, with a primary emphasis on theme, and provided what can be called a survey of the 'topics' of Israelite wisdom. Eventually, he covered the entire Hebrew Bible according to the principle stated as follows: 'For practical purposes a logical arrangement is more important than a chronological. The canons of scientific literary classification, in which community of theme, point of view, authorship, and literary style are the guide, must first be applied...When kindred narratives, laws, prophetic address, and proverbs have been grouped together, it is then possible and practical to arrange the material within each group and subdivision in its chronological order' (1904: vii).

Kent's programme corresponded closely to Gunkel's concern for a coherent order, for genres and for a two-dimensional (both synchronic and diachronic) history of literature. Since Gunkel's formulations appeared either at the same time or later, the resemblances must be regarded as reflecting a common intellectual situation, unless Gunkel was indebted to Kent.[24]

Unlike Gunkel, Kent did not examine the form and history of the literature in careful detail. Thus, his studies represent more an arrangement of data than a finished product of scholarship. He did have a strong practical interest—notably, to meet the needs of students at colleges and universities. He viewed his time as a period of the rediscovery of the Hebrew Bible (1906: 3), especially on account of its social orientation. He regarded humanitarian laws as 'the high-water mark of Hebrew thought and teaching' (1902: 208), spoke of 'Moses' assertion of the rights of the industrially oppressed', and believed that the prophets' social principles would form a common ground on which theological conservatives, radicals and persons from different religious traditions can unite (1917: vi, 3).

The literary structures of the Bible became also the concern of a large number of other studies appearing in England, Canada and the US, which can be mentioned only briefly.

Some of them were written by professors of English, such as John Gardiner (*The Bible as English Literature* [i.e. in translation], 1906),

---

24. Kent spent two years in Germany, but too early or too far removed from Gunkel's sphere (1891/92 in Berlin, 1896/97 in Breslau [G. Dahl]) to allow for a dependence on Gunkel. Gunkel, however, apparently had a knowledge of the US scene by 1904 (see below 11.1.b).

Edward Baldwin (*Old Testament Narrative*, 1910; *The Prophets*, 1927; *Types of Literature in the Old Testament,* 1929) and William Phelps (*Reading the Bible*, 1919; *Human Nature in the [Hebrew] Bible*, 1922; *Human Nature and the Gospel*, 1925 [dealing with the interweaving of content, life, and literary form]). Some were by an author of novels and other literature: Mary Ellen Chase, *The Bible and the Common Reader*, 1944; *Life and Language in the Old Testament*, 1955; etc. The promi-nent critic H.L. Mencken described the Bible as 'unquestioningly the most beautiful book in the world' (1930, 5.10). J. Powys's *Enjoyment of Literature*, 1938, devoted two chapters to the Bible.[25] (According to Powys [11], 'the power of the Bible does not lie in its doctrine, does not lie in its spirituality, does not even lie in its righteousness. It lies in its supreme emotional contradictions, each carried to its uttermost extreme, and each representing, finally and for all time, some unchang-ing aspect of human life upon earth'.)

A number of literary-structural analyses came from writers with a fairly traditional historical orientation. For instance, Stanley Leathes discussed 'The Structure of the Old Testament' (1873), with different roles played by the historic, prophetic, poetic and legal elements. E.W. Bullinger furnished a very detailed overview of the 'Figures of Speech Used in the Bible' (1898). Robert Girdlestone presented a genre analy-sis or 'Grammar of Prophecy' (1901); his quite comprehensive survey of styles, recurrent formulas and patterns of speech included the obser-vation that the future is 'expressed in terms of the past' (creation, Sodom and Gomorrah, Exodus, David, and so forth [66-73]). Some Protestants found, like Catholics, that a theory of genres led them to a new view of inspiration. Thus, James Orr, in *Revelation and Inspiration* (1910), presented a view concerning that topic that was very much like Neo-Thomism.[26] He observed that biblical literature appears in many types, including partially that of legend (173-74). Building on Orr, Bernhard Ramm (*Special Revelation and the Word of God,* 1961: 68) concluded: 'scripture does refer to history, but from the perspective of

25. Somewhat similarly, the comprehensive overview of literature by H. and N. Chadwick gave room to a discussion of 'Early Hebrew Literature' (1933, II: 629-777).

26. See above for this Catholic view. Orr argued that 'inspiration does not annul any power or faculty of the human soul, but raises all powers to their highest activity, and stimulates them to their freest exercise. It is…a life imparted to the soul which quickens it to its finest issues' (169).

literature and not scientific historiography; to law, but never in isolation from literature; and to theology, but always in the form of literature'.

Other relevant analyses by religious writers were more liberal theologically and historically. One, by Louise Seymour Houghton, *Hebrew Life and Thought* (1906), dealt with 'folklore', 'poetry', 'love stories', etc. (she found the 'question of laboring classes' to have been as important then as in her own time). Several were based on sermons or furnished sermon guides: Stopford Brooke, *The Old Testament and Modern Life* (1896) ('The events are legendary, the human life is not'; the stories are treated not as 'history' but as 'noble tales of human life, in the same way as we might preach on the story of Ulysses...Hercules...or King Arthur', although the biblical ones are 'more worthy for preaching purposes', 17-18); Frank Seay, *An Outline for the Study of Old Testament Prophecy, Wisdom and Worship* (1919) (for 'young preachers', with major attention to literary forms); Ernest Howse, *The Lively Oracles* (1956) (following after his *Spiritual Values in Shakespeare*, 1955).

A number of studies were produced by professors of religion, including biblical specialists.[27] Arthur Culler, with a broad orientation, examined biblical writings as 'Creative Religious Literature' (1930), comparing them with others similar in structure or theme, such as Negro spirituals or pessimistic literature. James Muilenburg, of whom more will be said, had taught English prior to receiving a graduate degree in biblical literature.

This listing is far from complete, both in regard to general studies and in regard to the many more that were devoted to individual books or complexes, such as the parables of Jesus.[28]

27. Among them stand: A.R. Gordon, *The Early Traditions of Genesis* (1907); *The Poets of the Old Testament* (1912); *The Prophets of the Old Testament* (1919); George Adam Smith, *The Early Poetry of Israel in its Physical and Social Origins* (1912); Henry Fowler, *A History of the Literature of Ancient Israel* (1912); Julius Bewer, *The Literature of the Old Testament* (1922, revised 1933—with a good bibliography); Laura Wild, *A Literary Guide to the Bible* (1922); J.G. McIvor, *The Literary Study of the Prophets* (1925); Margaret Crook, *The Bible and its Literary Associations* (1937—coauthored); *The Cruel God* (1959) (on Job); Elmer Leslie, *Poetry and Wisdom* (1945); Lindsay Longacre, *The Old Testament: Its Form and Purpose* (1945); Edgar Goodspeed, *How to Read the Bible* (1946).

28. M. Reid (1959), Gottcent (1979), and Preminger and Greenstein (1986) excerpt or annotate works by biblical and other scholars, including a number not mentioned here.

It is noteworthy that several of the authors cited—including Houghton, Wild, Innes (still to be discussed), Crook and Chase—were women. This reflects the fact that women were now entering more fully into academic life than before, although they were still largely positioned on its margin.[29] Contributors to *The Woman's Bible* (1895–98), were among those who made some structural-literary observations. These were not always in direct support of the cause of women (e.g. on Job and Proverbs, II: 98, 100 [Elizabeth Cady Stanton]), but they repeatedly served that cause either by reading a biblical passage in such a way that it does not inculcate the oppression of women[30] or by relativizing the authority of the Bible, such as by identifying the stories as 'legends', 'myths' or 'parables' (I: 56 [E. Stanton]; II: 166 [Lucinda Chandler]).

6. *General Reflections on the Bible as Literature Movement*

The basic outlook of the general movement was stated by C. Dinsmore, who also engaged in the study of other literatures:

> The Bible in recent times has passed through two distinct phases and is entering upon a third. There was a period when it was regarded as an infallible authority, the divine element was emphasized and the human overlooked; then came the age of the critic with his eager search for authors, dates, and documents; his main contentions having been established, his battle is losing its heat and absorbing interest. Now we are entering upon the era of appreciation. Educators are beginning to realize that Hebrew literature is not inferior to Greek and Roman in cultural value (1931: v).

29. Wild, Crook, and Innes did have academic positions; cf. below, 13.1.a.

30. For instance, E. Stanton judged that Gen. 3.16, on women's subordination, is a prediction (I: 17; cf. earlier S. Grimké) rather than a curse. U. Gestefeld viewed the Pentateuch as a 'symbolical description' of the spiritual development of human beings, who have both a male (external) and a female (internal) aspect (I: 144-46; cf. Guyon, earlier); such an interpretation may, of course, be used to restrict women to the private realm, but Gestefeld treated the 'male' and 'female' dimensions as aspects of all human life. Similarly, L. Chandler, with a symbolic interpretation according to which the masculine represents 'force' and the feminine 'love', said that the ideal person embodies 'a perfect balance' of the two (II: 167). Earlier, the more conservative Hannah Whitall Smith had discussed the image of 'God as our mother' in her guide to reading the Bible (*The Open Secret*, 1885: 117-38, referring especially to Isa. 66.13).

The biblical scholar and Islamicist Duncan MacDonald judged similarly that 'the analysis and dating of documents...have run themselves to a stop'; he believed that 'because of it all, the Old Testament has fallen on evil days' and that the Hebrew Bible should instead be seen as 'giving a mirror to life and all varieties of living' (*The Hebrew Literary Genius*, 1933: xxi-xxii).

It is clear that members of the literary movement that has been surveyed did not pursue an externally formal point of view but envisioned linguistic form, content and life as constituting an integral unity. This fact was apparently overlooked by the conservative T.S. Eliot in his criticism of the movement as insufficiently religious.[31] T.R. Henn, virtually the last representative of the movement, said that the Bible (with 'parallels and analogies in every literature') 'reflects and communicates' the 'conflict' of human beings with themselves and with their situation (1962: 18, 23). Discussing themes and styles in their connection with each other, he observed that the 'diverse and multiform' visions of the Bible, confronting nature and history, enabled human beings to 'see high things' that embodied 'terror or exaltation or delight, behind which lay the mystery of God' (23).

Social ethics was a major interest for these studies. For instance, a significant development can be seen in their treatment of Amos. Prior to the end of the nineteenth century, it had been common to describe Amos either generally as favouring righteousness or specifically as

31. Eliot was unhappy about those 'who have gone into ecstasies over "the Bible as Literature"' (1975: 98 [1935]). His anti-populism and extreme conservatism (at one time rejecting money [Ackroyd, 76, 109, 143, 171, 221]) kept him from recognizing the spiritual quality of the Bible as Literature movement, which had a social-democratic cast. Similarly, C.S. Lewis said that 'those who read the Bible as literature do not read the Bible', presumably since they do not acknowledge 'the religious claims of the Bible' (1950: 23-24). One can wonder whether Eliot and Lewis actually read more than the titles of the relevant volumes, since the volumes themselves exhibited definite religious interests, although often not traditional ones. (For instance, Wittgenstein was turned off by the title of such a work so that he 'wouldn't want to look at' it [Rhees, 119]. Josipovici, 26 shows that Lewis's criticism was inconsistent.) Even Albert Cook, *The Bible and Prose Style* (1892), was much less superficial than its title may suggest, for it describes the style as 'conformable to human nature', with 'sensibility, intellect, imagination and will' (xvi); thus, W.H. Auden's warning about reading the Bible for its prose (quoted in Carroll, 143) is hardly relevant in regard to Cook. (Of course, the Bible is not 'merely literature', if one defines that narrowly; furthermore, since it is critical of everything, it is 'anti-literature' even as it is literature [Fisch 1988: 2].)

opposing the luxury of the rich.[32] Differently now, many of the works mentioned expressed considerable sympathy with Amos's denunciation of oppression of the poor and weak. This shift reflected a turn c. 1900 from a middle-class revolt against the aristocracy to a concern for those injured by bourgeois society.

The shift in political focus was, in fact, integrally connected with the rise of a newer kind of literary study. The newer perspectives, both political and literary, toned down the emphasis on competitive discreteness (as in capitalism)[33] and on struggle (as especially in Marxism) for which historical criticism was an intellectual expression. The older orientation was not, for the most part, rejected by the literary critics; but it was balanced or overshadowed by other, more cooperative and thus more general, concerns.

The emerging perspective was strongly relational. Although it is true that the studies did not all fit a single mould, it can be observed that they often combined generality with particularity, as relational theory does, and that they gave attention to relations both within the text and between the text and human life. The dimension of generality was prominent in that they focused on literary types, which were identified in terms of both organization and theme, although genres were never treated as rigid. The element of particularity appeared in their referring to variations within types and to fluidity in the borders between genres, as well as in their recognition of special characteristics of the biblical literature as a whole which make it unique—as any sufficiently complex whole is unique while sharing many of its features with other complexes. The fact that texts were seen in relation to life meant that the description was not neutral but moved into the area of moral assessment. Discussions of connections between phenomena implied that what is to be considered good is not simply arbitrary.

All of these principles were well expressed in *The Bible as Literature* (1930) by K. Innes, a British professor of English concerned with literature and other aspects of culture. She was active in Quaker life, as a number of previous women contributors had been. Noting that the Bible contains narrative, poetry, 'proverbial wisdom and reflection', prophecy and a 'book approaching dramatic forms', she said that 'its

32. E.g. Herder (XII: 114) contrasted luxury with work-orientated moderation.

33. For example, Henn compared the view of Job's friends, who argue that people get what they deserve, with that of *laissez-faire* capitalism, obviously devalued by him (1970: 212-13).

contents must clearly be studied as separate types of literature' which represent the 'library of a unique ancient people' (18)—thus referring both to types and to uniqueness. According to her analysis, storytellers do not need to 'conform to definite rules and regulations which the critic lays down', but in the 'stories, which from their permanent and universal appeal through the ages have established their claims as the "classics", we can find common features without which…they would not be great' (23)—acknowledging flexibility together with generality. Furthermore, she believed that the 'form of literary expression can never be detached from that which a writer wishes to express' or from life. This union of literary form, content and life is revealed in the fact that the prophets' 'expression of moral indignation and moral fervor' exhibits stylistically an urgency on the basis of Deity's word and an 'intensity of feeling, which frequently carries them, as it were, outside themselves, whether in denunciation, in grief, or in rapture' (169-71); with the aim of persuasion, as 'great lovers of their land' and of God's 'chosen people' (192), they relate war and peace to righteousness with judgment and hope (193, 201).

Similar literary studies appeared outside the English-speaking world. It is not possible to examine them here, but it is worth mentioning that literary typologies ('legend', 'idyll', 'romance') played a role in Ernest Renan's *Histoire du peuple d'Israel* (1887–93), a work that became known also to Wittgenstein. Another relevant example is furnished by the insightful study of 'Humor and Irony in the New Testament, Illuminated by Parallels in Talmud and Midrash' (1965, in English) by an Icelandic literary figure, Jon Jónsson.

From the 1950s on, a large number of theological analyses, stimulated by Wittgenstein and other language philosophers, were concerned with the nature of religious language. Two examples must suffice to represent this movement. Hutchison held that at the center of all religions lie 'basic symbols' that provide an orientation toward 'ultimate meaning…answers to the question, "Whence? Whither? Why?"' (1956: 39). Stuermann, dealing with 'logic and scripture', described five 'functions' of language found in the Bible, including the logical (such as the informational content of history), the ceremonial, the directive, the expressive and the poetic (closely related to the expressive) and held that the poetic was the most pervasive one (1962: 113-27).

Contributions to the Bible as Literature movement did not usually furnish the details with which specialists deal. Thus they have largely remained outside the academic tradition. Is that a reason why they were virtually unknown—or, at least, not mentioned—by scholars of the Bible who pursued aesthetic approaches after 1965? However, because of their breadth of perspectives covering the different aspects of literature and life, the older studies seem humanly superior to many later works in their thoughtful attention to the interplay between linguistic form, content and life. Furthermore, studies in the Bible as Literature movement lacked the questionable assumptions that were introduced by Gunkel; they thus followed relational principles better than did scholarly traditions that emanated from him, as will be seen. Thus, despite a certain technical simplicity, they represent a more truly sophisticated form criticism than others to which that name is applied.

Chapter 11

GUNKEL IN HIS CONTEXT

1. *The Intellectual and Social Framework*

a. *Beyond Particularist Historical Criticism*
In Germany, a call to go beyond particularist 'historicism'[1] was made
by the systematic theologian Martin Kähler (1892: 4). He did not reject
as erroneous, but sought to go beyond, an outlook that places literature
into its own specific time (*Zeitgeschichte*, 1892: 19; 1937: 168 [1896]).
He advocated a 'transhistorical' (*übergeschichtliche*) perspective,
which sees that which has general validity in connection with the particular, so that history is not viewed in terms of isolated entities (1883:
13-14). For instance, he did not identify Christ simply with the earthly
Jesus.[2] Holding that historiography is not without presuppositions, he
denied that the purpose of the Gospels was to present documents for an
objective biography of Jesus and argued that the Gospels should be
read for their *kerygma*, 'message' (1892: 14; 1937: 25, 28 [1896]). The
significance of the Hebrew Bible lay for him in its complete form rather
than in versions reconstructed by historical criticism (1937: 140, 175
[1896]). Kähler characterized briefly a number of Israelite genres—
especially, stories of creation (a process lying beyond history) and
sagas, which combine historical realities with poetry (1937: 157-58,
244-45 [1896, 1904]).[3]
    Hermann Gunkel, Kähler's junior colleague in Halle, similarly

1. The term 'historicism' as a derogatory one had been coined a few years
earlier by the economist K. Menger (see *RFT*).
2. Kähler developed this point with increasing clarity in subsequent editions of
the 1883 work (1893 and 1905).
3. This analysis was somewhat unusual at that time only in that it was placed
within a relatively conservative theological framework or form of expression. For
instance, Herman Schultz used the terms 'myths' and 'sagas' for those two major
kinds of stories (*Alttestamentliche Theologie*, I, 1869: 30-44), as did Gunkel.

viewed as insufficient a *zeitgeschichtliche* historiography that treats literary works primarily in connection with their own specific temporal circumstances.[4] Thus, he examined the symbols of the New Testament book of Revelation in relation to those of older Israelite, Jewish and Babylonian stories (1895). He highlighted the 'traditions' of themes and expressions that continue over a long period of time, specifically those that involve the fundamental religious categories of Creation and Chaos, Origin and End. In his view, a temporal interpretation of the individual symbols of the Apocalypse in terms of particular phenomena of the first century CE treats them as though they were allegorical in the way in which Adolf Jülicher (1888) had analysed allegory, as a literary form in which each element has a specific referential meaning.[5] It is better, he believed, to understand Chaos, End, and so on, as continuing religious perspectives. The continuity of the symbols used for them over a long period of time indicates that they are not simply reactions to specific events. Specific social developments, he admitted, do affect the expressions of particular writings (398).

Gunkel's view was (and is) difficult to grasp for someone who regards reality as primarily factual-spatiotemporal, with no room for an eternal or ultimate reality.[6] Gunkel, in fact, had deep religious sensitivities or at least an empathy for such; he recognized, for instance, that spirit-filled persons confront a power which they experience as not their 'I' (1899: vii; cf. M. Arnold's description of religion). He expressed the hope, in a declaration not typical of prefaces to academic studies, that his scholarly work would aid a 'knowledge of the ways of God' and thereby contribute to the building of God's kingdom (1895: x).

Although Gunkel shared with Kähler a strongly religious orientation, he differed from him by pointing to a continuity between the Bible and

---

4. On *Zeitgeschichte* as one-sided: Gunkel (1895: 233, etc.; 1900b: 343—not rejecting all *Zeitgeschichte*, 359); letter to Jülicher, 1906 (Rollmann, 278). (Gunkel [1892a: 155] cited Kähler approvingly on the topic of history.)

5. 1895: 74 (reference to Jülicher), 234. Cf. J. Lead in 1683 (above, 5.4.b).

6. Wellhausen (and others) expressed legitimate criticisms about some of Gunkel's reconstructions, to which Gunkel reacted with what appears to be undue sensitivity (cf. Klatt, 70-74). Nevertheless, the difference in their perspectives extended beyond the accuracy of historical analysis to a divergence in their conception of history. (Cf. Smend [1991: 124]. It should be noted, however, that Wellhausen was not atomistic. Gunkel gave him credit for presenting a coherent view [acknowledged similarly by Polzin 1977: 126-49] as well as for literary sensitivity [1900a: 60; 1904c: 22; 1906a: 99; 1907b: 80; 1914a: 390].)

other cultures. Like Kähler, Gunkel was interested in 'biblical theology';[7] for him, however, as not for his colleague, biblical theology, properly executed, is a 'history of religion' (1904c: 24; 1927a: 1091). In this regard he agreed with Albert Eichhorn, a church historian at Halle and centre of a religiohistorical circle dealing with Israelite and early Christian literature, as well as with the Orientalist Paul de Lagarde. (Both of these religiohistorical figures also questioned— somewhat like Kähler, although in their own way—the value of being concerned with a biography of Jesus.[8])

Gunkel believed that individual traditions each have their own peculiarity (e.g. 1910a: 11) but that history has an overarching unity, moving towards a goal recognizable only by faith, and that within its connectedness everything is both special and comparable (1910a: 10). Divine revelation occurs in history, thus understood, in such a way that its truth does not form 'an exception in the life of humanity' (1905a: 63). Israel is not 'altogether peculiar and *fundamentally* different from all other nations' (1905a: 57), nor does Christianity form a special half of history (1910a: 13).[9] Nevertheless, comparison also makes clear for Israelite and Christian forms of religion their greatness and originality (1899: viii; 1910a: 14).[10]

Gunkel saw religion largely in ecstatic terms. His first publication dealt with the experiential and expressive activity of the Holy Spirit in early Christianity (1888). Subsequently, he described the 'secret experiences' of Israelite prophets, as reflected in their speech (1917a

7. See, for example, the subtitle of Gunkel (1888).

8. Eichhorn described as inadequate a 'historical criticism' which attempts to reconstruct the life of Jesus instead of understanding the Gospels in relation to Christian ritual and faith (1898: 25). P.de Lagarde, a still earlier advocate of the study of 'religion' (to the point of being anti-Christian), regarded as 'devil's work' the writing of a 'biography' of Jesus, i.e. a historical reconstruction of his life (1920: 65 [1873], against D. Strauss); he, too, stressed religion as 'life'. (Gunkel was a student and friend of Lagarde, but far from a full follower of his; see Klatt, 24.)

9. Similarly, A. Eichhorn's habilitation thesis No. 18, in 1886 (Gressmann 1914a: 8). Eichhorn admired the philosopher Herman Lotze (Gressmann 1914a: 19), who described religion as expressing faith in a goal of history and himself affirmed a movement in history, although very cautiously; did Lotze's outlook then also influence Gunkel?

10. Carl Clemen, *Die religionsgeschichtliche Methode in der Theologie* (1904: 39), too, argued that the general and the special character of Christianity can both be recognized only through a comparison.

[1903]). Other analyses followed similar lines—without neglecting the social dimension of faith—and there is reason to suspect that he himself experienced ecstacy. He believed that religious experience is more universal than are interpretations of it expressed in the form of religious beliefs (1899: ix).

Against the atomizing 'historical criticism' of his day, Gunkel preferred what he considered to be a truer 'historical' approach, one which recognizes movement in existence but sees in this movement (and in existence itself) the operation of 'rule and order' (1905a: 59), even, in its religious thrust, a 'higher historical necessity' (1903: 96). He envisioned regularity not only in the material world, as had long been done, but also in human life:

> Historical exegesis is based on the fundamental conviction that the life of humanity does not proceed according to arbitrariness and accident but that eternal orders have governance within it. Bound thus together by order and law, the mental life of a people—indeed, of all peoples together—is a great unity, and everything individual is understandable only in this connection (1904c: 25-26).

Great individuals, also (better: they especially), exhibit the secret order of God, which is the same in all multiplicity (1904b: 1109-10).

This view of history, propounded in 1903, 1904 and 1905,[11] resembles that expressed by Harper in 1890 and is similarly open to the charge of neglecting the role of the irrational in events. In fact, about 1910, quite likely in response to the philosophical movement which became a basis of indeterminist physics, Gunkel—like Troeltsch, whom he probably followed—came to allow for the possibility that natural connections sometimes disappear; he noted that science or scholarship would reach its limit at such points (1914a: 395).[12] In this

---

11. Gunkel's view of history is discussed in O'Neill (1991: 247). Hegelian perspectives entered into it, although in modified form (cf. Klatt, 34 and below on Gunkel's Hegel-orientated mentor Lasson). Quasi-Hegelian was Gunkel's envisioning (1907b: 81) a slow but inexorable progression of Spirit.

12. There is considerable similarity between Gunkel's 1903–1905 ideas and those expressed and reported (with reference also to Gunkel) by Troeltsch, who was closely associated with the religiohistorical circle (II: 729-53 [1898], 673-728 [1904], 193-226 [1908]). Troeltsch moved, about 1910, towards an increased acceptance of 'contingency' (II: 769-78); in this he appears to have been motivated by new developments in physics to give heed to William James (and thus indirectly to Peirce) as well as, probably, to Henri Bergson (cf. II: 726 [1904]; see *RFT* on Peirce

revision, however, he did not identify God's activity especially with the breaks in the order.

Gunkel's conception of history allowed him to refer for purposes of comparison not only to earlier but also to later literature and to that of more or less distant locations, including Persia, India, China, Japan, Polynesia, Africa, the Americas and various parts of Europe.[13] He was interested not in tracing the diffusion of themes (1904b: 1109) but in gaining insight through 'analogy' (1904b: 1109; 1904c: 27; 1905a: 60; 1910a: 12f.; 1926: viii).

In this emphasis on analogy, Gunkel followed an approach practiced and championed by the anthropologist Adolf Bastian as well as by A. Eichhorn and the historical theorist Troeltsch.[14] (Since such a comparative procedure was typical of the religiohistorical school generally, it is perhaps more clearly labelled 'religiophenomenological'.) Giving attention to comparable structures was, in fact, an interest for Gunkel from early on; for example, when Bernhard Weiss observed lectures by Gunkel to students in 1891, he was struck by an occurrence in them of 'the mutual illustration of kindred phenomena', which led to an assessment of fundamental reasons (*letzten Gründe*, Rabenau, 438).

With such an understanding of historical reality, Gunkel distinguished between *Literarkritik*, 'literary criticism' (or simply *Kritik*) and *Literaturgeschichte*, 'literary history'.[15] He described the two procedures as follows: '*Kritik* deals with relatively external problems according to the time and author of the individual writing, while *Literaturgeschichte*, entering more deeply into the nature of things, seeks to recognize the history in which the entire literature has arisen'[16] so that

and others). The mystery of individuals was indicated by Gunkel already (1903: 12).

13. See the indices of Gunkel (1901a; 1910b; 1911—even for a general audience!; 1926, on Genesis and Psalms; 1917b, on the folktale; also, 1906a: 100).

14. Analogy rather than diffusion was emphasized for anthropology by Bastian in the latter part of the nineteenth century (cf. Buss 1974: 35f.). Analogy was stressed for historical theory by Troeltsch (in 1898, etc.; see above) and in practice by Eichhorn (see Klatt, 21f.).

15. In current English usage, the meanings of those terms have almost been transposed, so that the German form is used here to avoid ambiguity. In German, the distinction between the two terms is heightened by the fact that *Literaturgeschichte* makes reference to literature (which can be oral, e.g. Gunkel 1907b: 67), while *Literarkritik* refers to written productions (which may not be viewed as aesthetic).

16. 1917a: 106; similarly, 1904c: 20-22; 1905a: 41; 1913c: 2642.

the individual phenomenon is seen in its inner connectivity (1929: 1677, in his general overview of 'biblical literary history' in *RGG*).

Gunkel accepted *Literarkritik* but believed that it had reached its limits both in terms of what knowledge can be reached and in terms of what is useful for understanding. Its major points, he said, had at one time agitated people, but further effort along that line was becoming boring (1907b: 82). On the whole, he believed, it had achieved what it could, in that general agreement had been reached (and, he implied, is reachable) only in its major points (1904c: 21; 1906c: 30). Specifically, he listed four primary conclusions as the only ones to be widely accepted: the Pentateuch in its available form was not written by Moses but is based on later sources; most of the Psalms do not emanate from David; Isaiah 40–66 stems from the Persian period; and the book of Daniel was composed in the time of the Maccabees (1905a: 42). In support of Gunkel, it can be pointed out that critical scholarship has not moved beyond those agreements since his time.

Gunkel did present source-critical analyses in his commentary on Genesis, but he warned that they are uncertain (1901a, preface). Furthermore, Gunkel took over from Wellhausen the idea that individual oral stories lay behind the Genesis narrative.[17] However, his pursuit of this idea was clearly not grounded in a critical curiosity that seeks to establish historical 'facts' but in a desire to reach beyond the written text towards 'life'—emotional, practical, popular and social in character.[18] He seems to have thought of this 'life' transhistorically, somewhat along the line in which A. Dieterich (a key figure in the religiohistorical school) thought of popular existence as an 'eternal' common-human background for more elaborate cultures (1904: 2). Attention to oral life would thus provide a brake on historical criticism rather than act as an extension of it.

Most importantly, Gunkel argued that philological, archaeological and critical study is only 'preparatory work' for a 'living understanding' (1901a, preface; 1901b: 141; 1907b: 82) and that, in fact, 'critical

17. See Gunkel (1901a: xix, 1-2; 1902: 2; 1910b: xxxiii). Wellhausen had envisioned that independent oral stories lay behind Genesis, although (like Koegel subsequently [see below] and Gunkel after him) he allowed for their belonging to common 'circles of conception' (1889: 9 [first publication 1876]). See below for Wellhausen's impact on Bultmann.

18. That his motivation in reaching toward the oral context of biblical literature was to show its connection with 'life', thus characterized, is expressly stated (1917c: 109); it is implicit in many other statements.

and chronological' problems (in detail) are insignificant for understanding what a text 'means', even when it is treated, rightly, as a historical phenomenon (1904a: vii). Similarly, Moulton's observations about the uncertainty and unimportance of precise datings—closely paralleled by Gunkel (1906a: 52)—had supported his own going beyond such questions. In any case, it was Gunkel's judgment that primary attention should be given not to a further determination of historical-critical issues but to aesthetics and religion (1904c: 22; 1910a: 7).

b. *Aesthetics and Religion*
In his aesthetic interest, Gunkel did not stand alone in German Protestantism.[19] F. Baethgen had published a lecture on the two aesthetic dimensions 'charm and dignity' as they appear in the Hebrew Bible (1880). A. Jülicher had argued that the parables of Jesus are stories with only one point, rather than allegories referring to a sequence of phenomena (1886).[20] Emil Kautzsch wrote for a general audience *The Poetry and the Poetic Books of the Old Testament* (1902). Gunkel was associated personally or through scholarly contact with all three of these writers and declared himself especially indebted to Jülicher.[21] H. Dechent issued an insistent call for 'more Herder' (i.e. for greater literary sensitivity) in biblical scholarship, preaching and religious education (1904). E. Bittlinger argued that a poetic or symbolic interpretation would do more justice to religious (including biblical) speech than had been done by traditional allegorical exegesis, which had 'materialized' it by giving it specific concrete applications (1905).[22]

19. A move in that direction, appreciated by Gunkel (e.g. cited in 1901a: i; 1904c: 22; 1927b: 8), had been made by E. Reuss, positioned on the border between French and German culture. Reuss's translation and introduction for a general audience ordered the material by major genres and included a good number of literary observations (French, 1874–79). Also relevant was K. Floeckner 1898 (with references to Reuss, Nöldeke, and some others).

20. Jülicher (1899, I: vii, 300, 318) modestly disclaimed novelty for this view, mentioning G.H. Ewald, B. Weiss, Alexander Bruce and others, as preparing the way. For subsequent criticism, see below (12.1).

21. Kautzsch taught from 1888 on in Halle, where Gunkel was located from 1889-95. Baethgen was senior colleague to Gunkel for a year in Halle and from 1895 on in Berlin (Klatt, 37). Gunkel described Jülicher's 'precious' work as the first one devoted to a biblical genre (1904c: 22; 1906a: 99) and emphatically expressed his own indebtedness to it (see 1895: 74 [cf. above, 11.1.a] and a 1906 letter published in Rollmann, 280; *pace* Klatt, 112).

22. Bittlinger described allegorical interpretation as having engaged in undue

Eduard König, more conservative than these writers, gave a careful account of biblical stylistics, including rhetoric and poetics (1900). He classified elements of style according to the 'sphere of life' to which they are related: the intellect (distinctions and clarity), volition (definiteness and liveliness), or the aesthetic sense (beauty—including a harmony of content and form—and euphony). This division of stylistic features resembled to some extent the distinction between intellectual 'figures of thought' and verbal 'figures of speech' in Graeco-Roman theories of style. In another work (1907) König dealt with the poetry of the Hebrew Bible according to its stylistic form, content and spirit. In this analysis, too, literary genres—epic, didactic, lyric and oratorical[23]—were set in relation to psychological processes (45-46). Hebrew poetry was grouped into the following types, both pure and mixed: epic-lyric, epic-didactic (Job), purely didactic, purely lyric and drama-like (Song of Songs). In 1927, he characterized psalms according to whether they are epic-lyric, descriptive (e.g. praising), didactic, essentially lyric or expressing a will (requesting, etc.). He argued (probably with some justice) that psalm headings express distinctions of this sort.

The year 1906 witnessed the appearance of several significant literary studies. One of them, by August Wünsche, which Gunkel treated as being similar to his own work,[24] discussed at considerable length the 'Beauty of the Bible' in a manner which took account of its religio-ethical character (1906a: ix, etc.); Wünsche arranged the literature according to its genres (prophecy, songs of praise about Yahweh's actions, curses and blessings, lamentations, etc.). Besides thus giving

materializing more so than in inappropriate spiritualizing (17, etc.). This characterization of allegory is similar to Gunkel's reference to allegory in 1895, reported above. König (1916: 120-34), in turn, criticized both Bittlinger and Gunkel for 'poetizing'.

23. König's analyses along such lines (including the listing of description as a type in 1900: 1) are similar to those that have been made in general nineteenth- and twentieth-century rhetorics (see *RFT*).

24. Wünsche (1906a: viif., 3-4) mentioned as his predecessors Lowth, Herder (with a special emphasis on him), Justi, Umbreit, E. Meier, Cassel, Ehrt, Steiner (1893), Baethgen, Kautzsch and Dechent (all of them have been reported in the present work). Upon seeing Wünsche's study, Gunkel (1906a: 99) accepted as his own antecedents several of these persons (Herder, E. Meier, Ehrt, Cassel, Kautzsch and Wünsche himself), thereby showing that he saw his own work as standing close by Wünsche's. (For references to Herder by Briggs [1882] and by Karpeles [1886], see above. Gunkel cited Lowth, on Isaiah, in 1895: 98.)

attention to what he called 'material beauty', he described in another volume the imagery of the Hebrew Bible as a major aspect of its stylistic 'formal beauty', here using 'form' in a narrow sense (1906b: iii). Earlier (from 1883 to 1906), he had provided comparative overviews of riddles, fables, traditions about a tree or water of life, and stories about creation and fall. Also in 1906, O. Frommel—a poet, novelist and Christian thinker about art—dealt with the 'poetry of the gospel of Jesus'. Jesus, in his view, was 'prophet and poet in one person', expressing religious experience symbolically (26, 115). He described the 'poetic forms' employed by Jesus, including rhythm and images (38-156), and, more importantly, Jesus as an 'artist of life'; specifically, he said, the 'artwork of his life' consisted in sacrifice and selfless love (157, 175). Gunkel expressed appreciation of the warm sensitivity of Frommel's study and, at the same time, a hope that the aesthetic character of the Bible would receive an analysis that is more scholarly than Frommel's; he recommended attention to genres as a step towards that end, giving Jülicher's work as an example (1907a). Furthermore, in that same year K. Budde published a detailed 'history of old Hebrew literature' (1906). Gunkel praised it for moving beyond criticism—in the sense of asking for the date and authorship of books—to a coherent 'literary history' (1907c). Gunkel himself presented in 1906 a comprehensive overview of 'Israelite literature', with primary attention to its genres (1906a).

It is thus clear, in regard to developments both in Germany and elsewhere, that a major change in outlook took place at the turn of the century. In fact, there is reason to believe that not only Budde[25] but also Gunkel[26] had contact with the Anglo-American Bible as Literature movement before 1904.

---

25. Budde visited Harper in 1898 and published a literary analysis of Hebrew poetry in English in 1902 (see below, 11.2.c).

26. Gunkel did not cite Moulton. However, nine of Gunkel's early studies of psalms appeared in English in Harper's journal (*The Biblical World* 21 and 22, 1903) before they were gathered, in German, in 1904a (two of these studies, along with two others, had appeared still earlier in *CW* 15, 1901). Thus it is likely that Gunkel's statement (1904a: viii), that 'in Germany there has hardly been a fundamental effort to describe the aesthetic-literary character' of the psalms, indicates for him (as already noted for Budde) an acquaintance with the Anglo-American movement. Translations of the introduction to 1901a and of 1901b and 1903 appeared in the US virtually simultaneously with the German. Did Gunkel know Briggs's or Moulton's analysis of composite liturgies, which anticipated his own?

Gunkel's point of view, however, was quite unpopular in German theological academic circles. It was opposed, on the one hand, by religiously conservative persons[27] and, on the other hand, by scholars favouring a continuing pursuit of fact-orientated historical criticism. Indeed, Gunkel's academic career was rocky and probably would have foundered without support from governmental authorities, which transferred him from New Testament to Hebrew Bible studies (for Christians, a safer field).[28] The German honorary degree he received in 1911 was a doctorate of philosophy, not of theology; the DTheol he obtained during the same year was awarded by a Norwegian university (Klatt, 193).

It is true, one of the reasons for Gunkel's difficulties lay in his personality, in that he made claims for his own importance and was ready to express criticism of the viewpoints of others, especially orally and in letters.[29] (An inclination to be outspoken has been reported similarly for

27. That was true for most of his life (cf. M. Dibelius 1932: 147).

28. On the opposition and on ways it was overcome, see, for example, Klatt (15, 45, 193, 223-26); Rabenau. Apparently as a result of government pressure, Gunkel was given a place in Halle in 1889, but he was soon prohibited there from lecturing on biblical theology (Smend 1989: 164). Gunkel's relation to the government varied; for a while before World War I, it has been suspected that he was opposed in high places as a 'radical liberal' (Klatt, 193), but after the war he benefited from a favourable attitude by the democratic government. It must be noted, however, that Gunkel received support at crucial points from Wellhausen and Budde, through letters of which he probably had no knowledge (Klatt, 167; Smend 1989: 170). Still, for a later time, it is reported (at second hand) that Budde was vehemently opposed to him (Hülsebus, 144), although Gunkel had contributed to Budde's Festschrift in 1920 in response to an invitation which Gunkel appreciated as an indication that in scholarship there are, appropriately, 'opponents' but not 'enemies' (1920: 69—clearly, he welcomed the invitation as a sign of peace from the Wellhausen–Budde circle).

29. Gunkel made strong claims and criticisms already about 1888 (Rabenau: 434-36; Lüdemann and Schröder, 29), later also in relation to co-workers (Klatt, 198) as well as orally against Wellhausen (Baumgartner 1959: 376). In 1895 (and similarly in 1901?) he had a nervous breakdown at the conclusion of a deep involvement in his work, so that he spent two months in an institution (Klatt, 81, 193; cf. O. Dibelius 1961: 60). Although much of his sense of isolation was justified, it is possible that he also suffered from a degree of paranoia (which may, of course, have propelled him in his work); yet his writings have an elevated, warm and largely appreciative tone (psychologically a defence perhaps, but in any case an intense expression of a vision and commitment). In two items directed to the public, he spoke for self-transcending peace and for other-regard, with reliance on

W.R. Smith and Briggs, objects of heresy trials.[30]) Problems in advancement, however, were experienced also by other religiohistorically orientated scholars, and it is clear that the opposition to him was not based entirely on personal factors. Indeed, persons tend to become controversial primarily when they *both* hold unpopular opinions *and* express their views forcefully.

A major difference of opinion existed in regard to the question (mentioned earlier) whether aesthetic description can be scholarly. As Gunkel reported, his opponents considered an aesthetic approach not to be scholarly (*wissenschaftlich*);[31] they thus represented the particularist tradition, which treats aesthetic appreciation as a private matter.[32] Gunkel, however, argued that beauty can be analysed intellectually in a systematic ('scientific', *wissenschaftlich*) manner and that—in contradistinction to a dilettante or purely popular approach—it is not enough to engage in exclamations concerning the beauty of the Bible (1906c: 32-33; 1909b: 1191). Since, as we have seen, Gunkel contrasted *Literaturgeschichte* with externally minded *Kritik*, it is clear that he believed that scholarship can reach an inner structure, not merely observe externals. This belief differs from the nominalist one according to which form, including aesthetic quality, is external to an object.[33]

Making the assumption (shared with the Anglo-American Bible as Literature movement) that aesthetic or literary quality is not merely superficial, Gunkel declared that an aesthetic treatment, if it is sensitively and fully executed, will lead not away from but towards the religious content of a work. 'Form' and 'content', in his somewhat scathing words, are not as distinct as a 'Philistine' thinks (1904c: 23; similarly, 1906b: 4). He observed that in biblical writings, as in others, aesthetic and religious qualities can be linked (1904a: 104). A

divine aid, in struggling as a co-worker with God (1892b; 1906d: 649—the latter a poem).

30. See contributions to Johnstone (40, 60-62, 277), for Smith, and above for Briggs; cf. below for K. L. Schmidt and others in conflict with government.

31. 1907b: 83; 1927b: 23; similarly, reports by Gressmann (Klatt, 73) and Baumgartner (1963: 7). At least partially continuing the line of these opponents, E. Otto praised K. Koch for leaving behind Gunkel's 'aesthetic subjectivism' (1988: 5).

32. See *RFT* on literary criticism and above, (10.1), on E. Scherer.

33. The nominalist view that form is external to the object broke with essentialism and thus prepared the way for a relational view, but it was not yet identical with this, for in particularism relations are considered secondary.

significant element associating aesthetics with religion is the fact that both have an experiential character not limited to rational (calculating) thought. This 'living' character of religion was, in fact, important for the religiohistorical school.

Does the possibility of a disciplined approach to literary structure imply, further, that scholarship can penetrate into the heart of religion? Gunkel indeed believed that it can; in this, too, he went contrary to nominalism (for example, in Ockham), which sets faith in sharp contrast to reason. By making clear a text's religious content (1904c: 29), he intended to 'serve life'.[34]

His commentary on the Psalms, Gunkel said, was predicated on the assumption that in the psalms there ring 'bells of eternity, whose sound reaches even into our days and can never end' (1926: vii). He believed that it is possible to 'learn to pray' from the psalmists, although only in partial ways (1922: 109). Previously (1903: 11), he had declared that— despite a necessary consideration of historically relative elements—the 'proper theme' of New Testament scholarship is 'not the always-past but the always-present', which has grown out of the past. A recognition of shared reality requires, in Gunkel's view, receptivity (as does religion itself). An entry into the life of the pious authors, with their feelings (pain, exultation, etc.), is the gift of 'hours of experience' in which 'the melodies of the past…begin to sound more clearly and loudly … in the heart of the present person'; 'one can prepare oneself for such hours of inner hearing, but one cannot force them', so that it is necessary to 'wait for them', although that means that exegesis proceeds more slowly than it might otherwise (1926: vii).[35] Besides such inner hearing, however, a scholarly interpretation needs an honest effort to 'employ the discipline of calm and conscientious reflection' (viii).

In addition to the symbol of hearing, Gunkel used that of seeing,

---

34. See below for his impact on K. Barth. O. Dibelius's claim (1961: 59) not to have heard about revelation from Gunkel, although he was fascinated by him, presumably reflects a particular conception of what constitutes revelation. (O. Dibelius, later a leader in the confessing church, was conservative enough to declare himself antisemitic in 1933 [Gerlach, 42] and in 1945 to express the wish to exclude all 'foreign' elements from the Church, considering Nazism such an element [Greschat, 45]).

35. Similarly already (1904c: 23—'long, repeated, loving contemplation', to which one should devote one's 'best hours') and in a 1925 letter (formal observations 'come as a gift—all of a sudden they are there' [Rollmann, 286]).

representing something a little more active.[36] Characteristic of seeing is a simultaneous perception of phenomena, linked together in a constellation.[37] Gunkel described his perception of psalms accordingly:

> At first, the individual poem flows together in the soul of the re-creator [*Nachschaffenden*] out of the individual observations made. Then the individual pictures of psalmists fall into religious types, and all these must fuse finally into an overall picture of the history of religious poetry (1926: vii).

This report gives the impression of an inductive procedure; the typology used by Gunkel, however—including praise, thanksgiving and lament—was for the most part already quite common (as he pointed out, 1906c: 32; 1927d: 89) and thus did not emerge from the data for him. Gunkel himself pointed (1907b: 80) to the constructive (rather than simply inductive) nature of apprehension: 'the picture of the past [to be described by the historian] is not contained in the sources; rather, these provide only the raw materials [like stones for a building]. Thus the historian...must...construe' it. Although the notion of construction may no longer have been prominent in Gunkel's mind in 1926, the term 're-creator' still gives room to activity by the recipient of a text. (Compare H. Kuist's theme of 're-creation'. Both Kuist and Gunkel drew on a literary critical tradition, widespread since the end of the nineteenth century [see *RFT*], which emphasized a personal and active involvement by a reader or hearer.)

Thus, in Gunkel's view, an interplay of subject and object, of reason and feeling, and of activity and receptivity is required for an appropriate understanding. He aimed to join precise scholarship with aesthetic and theological orientations. Of these two, the theological was primary for him;[38] his aesthetic sensitivity, however, is reflected in the fact that he published several religious and a few nationalist poems.[39]

One can ask, of course, whether his aesthetic and religious goals were accomplished with a degree of success. In answer, it is possible to say that he made major strides but that much, of course, remained to be

36. Cf. Buss (1961: 105), with the contrast somewhat overstated.

37. To some extent, that is true of hearing, too, of course; the difference is only a relative one.

38. 'We are not aestheticians but theologians' (1904c: 24).

39. The religious poems, at least, appeared anonymously (*CW* 20, 1906: 409, 433, 601, 649, 913 [listed in his bibliography, H. Schmidt 1923: 214-25]); for others, see Klatt (220).

done.[40] His limitations are understandable. After all, he wrote prior to the intensive work that took place in the field of literary criticism during the twentieth century. More importantly, a careful comparative study of faith—with attention to its psychology[41] and sociology and with a conception that recognizes its depth but is not authoritarian—had hardly begun in his day. In any case, for whatever reason, his theology lacked the sharp edge that is needed to address life adequately, or, for that matter, to run a successful ecclesiastical organization.

One major criticism that can be made of his analyses is that they are unduly sunny. They do not take adequate account of the judgmental and tragic aspects of biblical literature, which represent the problematic side of life. They also do not call attention to those features of the Bible that a reader today may want to reject.

There is no reason to believe that a shortcoming in critique is inherent in aesthetics.[42] Literature can be horrifying (for example, Franz Kafka and horror movies), and artists have often been at the forefront of social criticism (see, for example, Weinel [1914: 164], for expressions at that time in sympathy with the proletariat). Literary critics can represent terror in and by a text (Trible 1984). However, Gunkel's weakness in critique (although he was socially more critical than many others, as will be seen immediately) expressed a certain almost childlike naïveté.

c. *Outreach and Social Concern*

Like other members of the religiohistorical circle, Gunkel had a strong interest in reaching the general public.[43] His work was designed to aid the 'practical work of the church' (1913a: vii), but he also sought to address non-ecclesiastical audiences. Already in an early review, he

---

40. His most outstanding literary analyses were probably those dealing with the Elisha stories (published as a volume in 1922).

41. Gunkel voiced the hope that a complete history of ecstatic 'spirit' might be written some day but he judged that in addition to relevant historical studies an advance in the field of psychology would be needed for that (1899: xi).

42. As will be seen below, the aesthetically orientated H. von Soden and M. Albertz were among the stronger critics of Nazism; it is possible (although, of course, not certain) that the same would have been true for Gunkel.

43. To some extent they were forced into such an outreach by financial pressures brought about by a lack of academic support, but this lack of support was itself in good part a consequence of their broad orientation. See N. Janssen in Lüdemann and Schröder (1987: 109-36).

urged biblical scholars to speak to the public (1892a: 158). A little later, he issued a 'cry of distress' occasioned by the appearance of a popular work which was not well grounded in scholarship. He considered the fact that it filled a vacuum to be a 'call for repentance' to professional biblical scholarship, which had buried itself in 'uninteresting, i.e. unimportant, particular data' through a 'dealing in minutiae' by *Literarkritik*, instead of becoming devoted to 'the primary issue', religion, seen within an 'international' (i.e. intertraditional) perspective (1900a: 60-61).

The broad outreach of the religiohistorical circle to which Gunkel belonged was exercised through both lectures and publications. Many of the lectures took place within the university extension movement; this had officially begun in England in 1873 and in Germany in 1892 (Klatt, 85). Gunkel thus shared a social situation with Moulton, whose work was in many ways similar to his. The lectures and extension courses had a special appeal to school teachers, including those who taught religion, so that public education became a significant sphere of influence for Gunkel and his associates.[44]

General-audience publications included a series entitled 'Religiohistorical Books for the People', and two sets of commentaries, one for the Hebrew Bible and one for the New Testament.[45] The commentaries, lacking technical matters (such as secondary literature and Hebrew), highlighted aesthetic and religious characteristics, although they included historical considerations. In regard to historical issues, Gunkel (1911: vi) rejected the idea, 'proposed simultaneously by persons holding different perspectives, that the biblical books should be interpreted in the way in which the final...redactors may have understood them';[46] he wanted, rather, in treating Genesis, to give attention

44. A good example of the open spirit of this appears in Weiser (1925), recently available again in print.

45. Gunkel contributed three volumes to the Books for the People (1906b on Elijah, 1916b on Esther, 1917b on folk tale motifs); they also have scholarly significance. To the general-audience commentaries, Gunkel contributed one on Genesis (its preface rhapsodically addresses the Bible as 'teacher of humanity') and an introduction to prophecy, which has been influential in scholarship. A further step, going beyond exposition toward application—with a strong social concern inspired in part by Friedrich Naumann—was taken by F. Niebergall (1912–22), referring, for example, to the prophets' 'critical patriotism' (II [1915!], iv, 29, 129).

46. See above for Kähler's emphasis on the final form of the text. Who among more liberal interpreters may have had a similar focus is not clear.

to all levels, from the earliest oral to the final written one. In tone, the publications were neither conservative nor radical; on the whole, they sought both to maintain continuity with and to go beyond past tradition (cf. Klatt, 89).

The outreach towards the public was intimately connected with the circle's commitment to a social sense, with an interest in general welfare.[47] Gunkel's political commitments along these lines were not stated systematically but were implied in his strong attachment to the pastor/ politician F. Naumann, a leading advocate for Christian involvement in the newer social concerns.[48] To the encyclopaedia *Die Religion in Geschichte und Gegenwart*, of which he was a co-editor, Gunkel contributed an article on the Hebrew aid to the poor (1909a) and one on 'individualism and socialism in the Old Testament' (1912). In laws, psalms and prophecy he saw strong moves to counteract oppression by the rich and powerful (1904a: 133; 1906a: 77, 89; 1909a; 1912: 500f.; 1913b: 1945; 1922: 83).[49] One can argue, of course, that he was simply reporting the biblical content; but a personal interest in the issues is

47. See, for example, Gressmann (1914a: 24, 39); Eissfeldt (1930: 1900). W. Bousset, a prominent member of the school, was a Social Democrat. A. Jeremias, religiohistorical in outlook and long a pastor (shunned by the theological academia?), published a study on the 'social task of the church' (1918).

48. See Klatt (265-66). Naumann could call his outlook 'Christian-social' or 'national-social'; the latter term might place him as a forerunner of the Nazis, but in 1906 he was expelled from a nationalistic organization because he supported 'Judaism and Social Democracy' (see, for example, reports in *CW* 47, 1906: 885, 933).

49. Gunkel distinguished between cultic psalms of lament, not preserved in the Bible, focusing especially on illness (1906a: 65), and 'spiritual' songs, which were 'lyrics of "the poor"' (89). Aware of Egyptian 'poetry of the poor' and attending to hints in prophetic literature, he believed that an Israelite poetry of the poor began already before the exile (e.g. 1906a: 89); in fact, observations of this sort (in 1913b: 1945) were repeated in their second edition, Gunkel's final word on the subject (1930, in *RGG*). The pre-exilic appearance of the poor in psalms was downplayed in the part of his *Einleitung* that was edited by Begrich (1933: 209; but see 262-63, which probably indicates Gunkel's view). (Mowinckel [1962, II: 86], perhaps in part on the basis of a recollection of what Gunkel said when they were together, wrote that he pointed to lower classes as embodying the 'poor'.) It is true, Gunkel's treatment of social criticism by the prophets (1917a: 79-83) is relatively reserved and quotes a statement by Troeltsch that the prophetic ethic 'has no thread in common with … democracy and socialism in their modern sense'; did Gunkel exercise caution in wartime, although daring to raise the topic at that time?

evident, for instance, in the encyclopedia articles, which appear to have been especially created for his contribution.[50]

He supported nationhood—also for Jews, it seems—but in a form which is democratic and does not rely only on force, with a perspective transcending one's own group.[51] In arguing for the thesis that divine activity involves natural processes (1914a: 395), he said that a desirable provision of aid to children in a troubled family would not be left to the working of a divine miracle; clearly, he assumed—as a point of view also for his audience—that social action would be applied as a form of divine activity.

Social agitation at the turn of the century included a concern for women's rights. An indirect involvement of Gunkel's circle in this movement, at least, is shown by the fact that works dealing with feminism were published in association with the religiohistorical studies on the Bible. More than one work advocating women's rights appeared in the series *Lebensfragen* ('Questions of Life') edited by Gunkel's

50. The article dealing with the Hebrew concern for the poor was the only one on the topic of the poor in the first edition of *RGG*; in the second edition, it became part of a more comprehensive article, which disappeared in the third edition, after Gunkel's death. The article on individualism and socialism in the Hebrew Bible was the only one that combined those two topics in *RGG*, apparently on the basis of Gunkel's interest.

51. During World War I, he published writings which pointed to or implied parallels between Israelite and German struggles; for instance, he wrote on 'Israelite heroes and war piety' (1916a, dedicated to his son who served in the war [cf. G. Mitchell 1995: 113-19]) and Esther (1916b, a popular commentary the logic of which supports Zionism, to counteract pogroms and to aid inner Jewish development [1, 91]). A short article by him was emotionally supportive of the war (1917d: 2) and he wrote poems for soldiers (Klatt, 220). However, he also declared that 'Jesus weeps' because of the war (1914b) and that 'the last word is...peace' (1916a: 47); he pointed out that Amos transcended nationality (1917a: 48) and that optimistic prophecy (which he had compared with German confidence in war, 1917a: 36) led to Judah's downfall (1917a: 66). In an unpublished essay of 1915, Gunkel advocated political freedom for the 'common' person, the true 'hero' of the war (Klatt, 266); in fact, the war ended with an overthrow of the monarchy. Although he was decidedly not a pacifist, he criticized privately a reliance by the German government purely on force. (See Klatt, 222. On the glorification of power in Germany at that time, cf. discussions reported by O. Dibelius [35], and both Nietzsche and Spengler, examined in *RFT*.) After the war, Gunkel had close ties to the democratic government in Berlin and was sympathetic toward criticism of the early Nazis (Klatt, 220-26, 266; Smend 1989: 172; Baumgartner 1959: 375). In 1926: 253, he referred to a 'pogrom mood' threatening a diaspora Jew.

student H. Weinel.[52] Women—including school teachers, playing a role relatively new for them—constituted a major portion of the audience of the public-interest lectures given by Gunkel and others.

Although it seems that Gunkel himself never addressed the question of the women's movement explicitly, he stood close to the movement. Three women students—Margarete Plath, Else Zurhellen (later Zurhellen-Pfleiderer) and Hedwig Jahnow—both contributed to his work and published studies of their own, some of which will be discussed below.[53] Of these, Jahnow had a Jewish heritage and perished in a concentration camp in 1944.[54]

2. *The Form-Critical Programme*

a. *Two-Dimensional Literary History as a History of Genres*

The statement of a theory is, of course, much more useful for life than is a mere collection of data.[55] This was probably a major reason why Gunkel looked for patterns in the materials he studied. In any case, with regard to the book of Genesis, he was dismayed that traditional commentaries contained primarily separate bits of information; he considered these as no more than a step towards an understanding of the 'meaning' of the Hebrew Scriptures, his primary concern (1901a,

52. See below on Weinel. Within Hebrew Bible studies, the possibility of an early matriarchy was discussed extensively in Germany and elsewhere by persons with an orientation toward the history of religions, especially in the train of W.R. Smith.

53. See Baumgartner (1963: 12), reporting that Gunkel taught at a women's school while in Berlin, and Hülsebus (138-39), reporting that members of a women's school took courses at the university (may both reports be true?). Plath aided Gunkel by 1899 (Gunkel 1899: xi) and began publishing herself in 1901. Zurhellen wrote a MS on Genesis stories of which Gunkel made use (1902: 2). Jahnow wrote her 1923 work at Gunkel's suggestion; in 1926 she received (presumably for this work) an honorary degree from the University of Giessen, where Gunkel was positioned. See further on these women below.

54. See Bail and Seifert in Jahnow *et al.* (26), reporting that her family had converted to Christianity. (These authors should have added 'in Germany' to their statement that Jahnow was the only woman writer then dealing with the role of women in the Hebrew Bible in a scholarly manner [27]; cf. above for Breyfogle.)

55. In contrast, K. Marti (1906: 1060), with a particularist outlook, said that the aim of historical criticism is to present 'facts' (*Tatsachen*) 'as objectively as possible', avoiding 'theories', including questions of 'revelation'.

preface).[56] Similarly, for psalms, he saw a need for 'bringing light and order into the multifarious data and showing their inner structure'—the way the data have significant relations to each other—instead of treating the individual texts in an isolated manner (1927b: 8, 168).

From about 1904 on,[57] Gunkel located order explicitly in a 'history of literature' with two axes, the synchronic and the diachronic. At any one time, different genres stand side by side; each of them undergoes a development. Coincidentally or not, C.F. Kent set forth a similar programme explicitly in 1904, after more implicit versions had been presented earlier by Moulton, Harper and himself.

Consideration of the two axes together involved the formation of a cross-sectional perspective, which came to be highlighted in twentieth-century linguistics, sociology, anthropology and literary study, in contrast to the evolutionary one, which had dominated the preceeding period.[58] In Germany, the conception of a 'literary history' that highlights the role of genres and thus combines synchrony with diachrony had been set forth in an influential essay by B. ten Brink (1891: 26). Thus, Gunkel's two-dimensional view was by no means unusual then.

For instance, of special relevance for Gunkel's work was the fact that the notion of a two-dimensional history of literature with a focus on the development of literary types became dominant at the end of the nineteenth century in classics. The standard methodological work advocating such a history of literature was by August Boeckh.[59] As was true for some other significant treatments of genres earlier during that century (especially those of Hegel and Uhland), this work consisted of lectures that were not published near the time they were given but appeared

---

56. In 1892a, Gunkel had defended biblical scholarship against a conservative critic (A. Bender) who argued that scholarly *Kritik* turned the Bible into 'chaos' and neglected 'history'; here he accepted much of Bender's complaint.

57. See 1904a: viii; 1904c: 23; 1906c: 32; etc.

58. The two dimensions had both been acknowledged earlier, but the theme of evolution had been central in attention from the eighteenth century on. (See *RFT*.)

59. 'Literary history is the result of a generic interpretation of all writings, in a given cultural sphere' (1877: 144; cf. 130, 156, 250, 527-28). Boeckh's orientation towards genres was acknowledged by Christ (1898: 2); his work was called 'basic' (*grundlegend*) by Gercke (Gercke and Norden 1910: 36). More recently, Betti (1967: 419) has referred to the significance of Boeckh for genre criticism and, similarly, Jäger (1975: 105) to Boeckh's fundamental importance in pointing to both synchronic and diachronic connections. (On Gunkel's knowledge of Boeckh, see further below.)

only posthumously. When they became public in 1877, the time was ripe for a synthesis of concerns with both history and genres. Indeed, quite a few histories of Graeco-Roman genres were produced during the last decades of the century and soon thereafter.[60] A number of these histories discussed the relation of literary genres to popular forms of speech, with their oral occasions, as came to be done by Gunkel.

Gunkel had several lines of connection with classics, so as to receive a procedural bearing from that field. One was that his 'advisor' Adolf Lasson (Jewish in background)—to whom he dedicated his early study of psalms (1904a) as he began his interest in a genre-orientated 'history of literature'—highly valued Boeckh's outlook, having studied under him.[61] Direct contact by Gunkel with classics is attested, for by 1900 he received specific suggestions from the leading scholar of Greek literature, U. von Wilamowitz-Moellendorff, who was located, like Gunkel then, in Berlin.[62] Although Wilamowitz-Moellendorff favoured individuality in literature, he recognized the importance of genres and argued in a widely known essay (1900) that E. Norden had paid insufficient attention to them in his work on prose forms (1898).

Another point of contact between Gunkel and this field lay in the circumstance that the classicist Hermann Usener and a circle around him stood in a close working relationship with the religiohistorical circle (Gressmann 1914a: 29). Usener called for a recognition of the forms (*Formenlehre*) of mythology, with an interest in images, and was followed in this by A. Dieterich (1903; 1905: ii). Dieterich encouraged a continuation of the study by classicists of the history of styles, motifs and aims of prayer (1905: 484). (Gunkel referred to works by Usener and Dieterich in 1895: 283 and 1903: 6.)[63]

Especially important for Gunkel's relation to classics was the fact that P. Wendland, a student of Usener and friend of Dieterich, analysed literary and religious forms of Hellenistic Judaism and of the New Testament as well as of other Greek traditions. With a major emphasis on the rhetorical tradition, Wendland repeatedly pointed out the role of

60. See Gercke and Norden (425-50, 585-87) and the bibliography of Wilamowitz-Moellendorff (1905).

61. See, for example, *Philosophen-Lexikon*, II, 1950: 23.

62. 1900b: 334, 355, 364, 372, 378. See, further, below. Gunkel's readiness for personal contact appears also in the aid he obtained from a scholar of Persian (1904a: 258).

63. Other work by Dieterich became important for M. Bakhtin, who appears to have received an impetus also from Gunkel (see *RFT*).

standardized ways of expression; for instance, he spoke of 'firm forms' (*feste Formen*, 1896: 707) and of 'firm topics [*Topik*] and stereotyped form-speech [*Formensprache*]' (1904: 344, in a standard New Testament journal).[64] Gunkel was stimulated by him, it appears, in his own recognition of stereotyped forms of expression (*Formensprache*, 1906a: 99; 1907c: 850; 1909b: 1191; 1924b: 182; etc.). Wendland, in turn, knew (and praised) Gunkel's commentary on Genesis.[65] Since the two lived near each other,[66] it is likely that they were personally acquainted.

It was not Gunkel's practice to refer to writers for their methodological contributions.[67] He had a substantive reason, however, to cite a work by O. Gruppe, which dealt with the cults and myths of Greece, the Near East and India (1901a: 91), so that we know that he was familiar with it. In that work Gruppe discussed the relation of cultic hymns and myths to more 'artful' ones, considered to be more strictly intellectual or aesthetic in character (*Kunsthymnen, Kunstmythen*). Concerning the relation between popular (including cultic) and 'educated' poetry, Gruppe wrote this: 'The populace gives to artistic poetry form and receives in return spirit. The poetry of the educated is like a mint in which the coin circulating among the people is cast ever anew' (1887: 67). He held that non-cultic religious poems can be connected secondarily with ceremonial contexts, after having been free from such a

64. Dilthey had used the term *Formensprache* for 'schemes of aesthetic perception' (VI: 276 [1892]). The term (modified in meaning) may have come to Wendland via Usener, who was a long-time friend of Dilthey and adapted also other terms used by Dilthey (Bremmer, 464, 470f.).

65. In Gercke and Norden (1910: 441-42), Wendland recommended Gunkel's work on Genesis as a valuable model for classics. (It should be noted that in this work Gunkel did not yet mention or produce a history of literature; his analysis, rather, was praised by Wendland for a considerable number of literary observations with attention to oral forms.)

66. Wendland served as *Gymnasium* (pre-university) teacher in Berlin from 1890 to 1902. Gunkel was located in that city from 1895 to 1907, teaching not only in the university but also in a *Lyceum*—the women's counterpart to a *Gymnasium*—if Baumgartner (1963: 12) is correct. A. Lasson taught until 1897 at a *Gymnasium*, while holding the position of *Privatdozent* at the university (*RGG*, III, 1912: 1976). Thus, these figures shared a social location. O. Gruppe, to be mentioned, was also located in Berlin.

67. Also his indebtedness in specific interpretations is often unclear, since Gunkel was reserved in documentations (in part to aid the readability of his work [1901a, preface]).

connection (546). Such a theme re-emerged in Gunkel's view that hymns can return to the cult from which they (by style) originated (1906a: 97; 1913b: 1942).

It is clear, then, that Gunkel received important impulses from classics in regard to form criticism. This point must be emphasized since dependence on classics and other fields has been denied by his biographer, Klatt.[68] Similar views of genres were also current in other areas of scholarship from which Gunkel learned—including studies of the ancient Near East, Europe (e.g. traditional Germany) and India. (See below for details, as they involve the social situations of genres.)

Specifically, it is likely that the earliest influence upon Gunkel in terms of a recognition of genres came from Germanics. As a student in Göttingen in 1881, Gunkel attended lectures on German historical grammar by W. Müller, who had prior to that time published a discussion of Germanic cult practices. Müller's analysis of myth and legend, published later (in 1889) but perhaps already mentioned in lectures, undoubtedly made an impact on Gunkel's Genesis commentary; Gunkel, for instance, used the same example of an etymological aetiology (1901a: xiii, as in W. Müller, 4).[69] Around the turn of the century, if not before, Gunkel came under the direct or indirect influence of L. Uhland's analysis of early German genres, about which more will be said.

The field of Germanics, in fact, had helped to introduce the concept of genres into biblical studies already prior to Gunkel. On the basis of a knowledge of both Germanic and Near Eastern studies the Wellhausen follower K. Budde had presented analyses of Israelite genres together with their life contexts (as Gunkel repeatedly acknowledged).[70] Budde

---

68. Gunkel's student W. Baumgartner reported the connection with classics, mentioning Wendland and E. Norden as relevant scholars (1932: 390; 1963: 6). Klatt (112) is right in saying that Norden is not one from whom Gunkel would have received his method (in fact, in a later edition of his 1898 study, Norden acknowledged the appropriateness of Wilamowitz-Moellendorff's criticism of it for a lack of attention to genres), but Klatt appears to have been unfamiliar with the work of other classicists reported in Gercke and E. Norden (1910).

69. In general, Gunkel's interpretation of sagas stood close to the scholarly tradition of Karl Otfried Müller, Heinrich Dietrich Müller and Wilhelm Müller. In Halle (during the early 1890s), the Germanic scholar O. Bremer was a member of his friendship circle (Klatt, 21, 23).

70. 1906a: 99; 1906c: 32; and often orally thereafter (Smend 1994: 369). Cf. further below in regard to the question of a *Sitz im Leben*, as well as Gunkel's

may, in fact, be regarded as the founder of form criticism of the Hebrew Bible in so far as that procedure is viewed (as many have done after Gunkel) as a branch of historical criticism. There was an important difference between these two scholars, however, in that Budde remained largely within the particularist tradition, while Gunkel wished to recognize general and natural processes and connections. In that outlook, he stood close to Moulton, Harper and Kent.

An important strength of the two-dimensional (synchronic and diachronic) view of literature towards which Gunkel moved with a recognition of genres, lay in its providing a better-balanced view of history. If surviving literature is treated diachronically without regard to a continuing simultaneity of genres, it is possible to obtain the impression that types of speech such as prophecy, psalms, law and proverbs succeeded each other, since particular specimens of each can be dated to certain periods. In fact, such an outlook had been proposed repeatedly in biblical studies before Gunkel. His recognition, however, that different types of speech are co-present in a society, representing different aspects of it, undermined a purely developmental view. Gunkel illustrated this point orally by arguing facetiously that the absence of reference to small children in the Song of Deborah shows that there were none such in early Israel (Stauffer 1961: 31). He pointed out (most systematically in 1927d) that the major genres of psalms must have been pre-exilic, even if the preserved examples of each come from a later period, in part since similar genres appeared already in Mesopotamia and Egypt.

Already in 1895, Gunkel argued that a false view of history is obtained if exclusive reliance is placed on the dates of surviving writings. If relevant elements are attested earlier (for example in Mesopotamia), one must assume that there were intermediate links, constituting a tradition.[71] In regard to the Psalms, Gunkel concluded that it is neither possible nor important to date the individual psalms precisely but that attention can and should be given to the development of the genres on the basis of a number of indications (1927d: 90). The

---

appreciation for Budde's history of Israelite literature already mentioned. But personal tensions have been reported (see above).

71. Similarly, against relying altogether on the time of surviving literature (1907b: 83; 1914a: 388-90; 1927c: 534). Furthermore, Gunkel believed that excessively sharp *Kritik* had unnecessarily declared some texts to be secondary and thus late (1910a: 10).

difficulty experienced in dating precisely texts such as psalms was regarded by Gunkel as appropriate in relation to poetry, for 'all poetry and especially that of the Psalms loves, in accord with its nature, an indeterminate form of expression' (1927b: 1).

Furthermore, attention to the synchronic dimension of genres aids the recognition that major forms of speech are relatively universal (highly transchronic), even though they undergo a history, and that differences often represent a variety that continues. Indeed, Dilthey, of whom Gunkel may have had some indirect knowledge, argued in his analysis of historical understanding that human beings can be comprehended only on the basis of structures shared with others; accordingly he outlined major 'types' of world perspective (VII: 141, 147; VIII: 73-165). Gunkel stated, similarly, that the several genres of psalms express different 'types of piety' (1926: x).[72]

In applying a distinction between the synchronic and the diachronic dimensions to biblical materials, Gunkel made important advances. Nevertheless, he did not carry through such a dual view as well as he might have done, as the following account will show.

In the introduction to the first edition of his commentary on Genesis (1901a), Gunkel analysed a number of narratives as aetiological, that is, as explaining phenomena that are current in the narrator's time.[73] Although he believed that for many of the stories this aetiological purpose (which is a synchronic issue) also reveals their origin (a diachronic matter), he cautioned that that would not be true in all cases, for purpose and origin must be distinguished (1901a: xvi).[74] In 1902 (x, xxviii), he stated even more strongly that an aetiological element of a narrative is often secondary, so that it does not constitute the kernel from which the narrative arose. In fact, he judged—probably correctly—that the question of origin cannot be determined on the basis of internal evidence (xxviii).

He failed, however, to move far enough toward a distinction between

72. No direct dependence on Dilthey is presupposed by the correspondences (as rightly pointed out by Klatt, 122, with regard to other examples of similarity between the two figures); but it is nevertheless a possibility, at least by means of oral transmission, for example through Wendland (see above) or through Lasson.

73. In this, he followed a large number of older studies (e.g. Nöldeke, *Die alttestamentliche Literatur*, 1868: 10).

74. The recognition that aetiological features are at least sometimes secondary had been reached shortly before then by Mogk (1897) and by Dähnhardt (1898: iv)—also by others? It was widespread in folklore studies after 1900.

synchrony and diachrony. He continued to accept an evolutionary scheme for narrative types. At first (in 1901a: vii), for example, he accepted the theory held by a number of writers, that myths (including aetiologies)[75] are the oldest form of narrative out of which other kinds have arisen. After abandoning this theory, in part since it was being abandoned by others, Gunkel adopted in its place the theory of Wundt (1905: 328, 340), according to which folk tales rather than myths represent the earliest kind of narratives.[76] This theory was still evolutionary, but it envisioned a different sequence for the rise of narrative types; it was thus not fully two-dimensional. Gunkel applied this theory in the third edition of his Genesis commentary (1910b) and in his study of 'folk tales' in the Hebrew Bible (1917b).

A position different from the evolutionary one of Wundt in 1905, just cited, was presented, also in 1905, by E. Bethe. Bethe argued that the three major narrative types then widely discussed—myths, sagas and folk tales—differ in function, not in the historical sequence in which they have appeared. He did not furnish an empirical grounding for his position; that may be a reason why Gunkel, who knew and appreciated his work at least by 1917 (1917b: 6), did not accept his view. In 1926, however, a position similar to Bethe's was set forth by B. Malinowski (who at one time had studied under Wundt); he observed in a Melanesian culture that myths, sagas (non-founding ordinary memories) and tales (stories about events accepted as imaginary) form complementary structures, each with their own role in society. In moving toward a structural-functional view, Malinowski appears to have been aided by Gunkel's emphasis on a life setting for genres, mediated to him by A. Gardiner (see *RFT*). Gunkel himself, however, did not see the implication which his own form-critical approach, with its attention to social roles, had for an assessment of narratives.

Nevertheless, Gunkel saw that the major genres are on the whole contemporaneous with each other: prayers (with their most important subdivisions), narratives, instructions, etc. At the same time, he

---

75. Aetiologies were often regarded as myths (a point apparently overlooked by Rogerson [1974: 61] in charging Gunkel with inconsistency).

76. In Wundt's terminology, 'myth' became a general term, covering 'fairy tales' as a subdivision; 'myth' in a narrower sense was called *Göttersage* by him (as noted by Gunkel 1917b: 7). Gunkel, however, continued to use the word 'myth' for stories about gods and, moreover, did not assume that folk tales (*Märchen*) form the basis of all stories (cf. Rogerson 1974: 60-61).

recognized—properly in principle, even if not always correctly in detail—that genres undergo changes, in both major and minor ways. Thus, he distinguished 'history writing' from 'saga', which is oral and older.[77] In his survey of psalm genres (1927b, 1933, completed by Begrich), he attempted to trace their history, as it is reflected in surviving texts.

b. *Steps in the Development of Gunkel's Concept of* Sitz im Leben
A synchronic view of genres, according to which different genres coexist, suggests, as has already been indicated, that each genre plays a certain role in life and that each may thus be used only or primarily in certain kinds of contexts. This position was developed extensively by Gunkel. For the social location of a genre he used the term *Sitz im Leben*. The focus on the issue is probably Gunkel's most impressive contribution, which spilled beyond biblical studies to other disciplines. To be sure, his ideas on this topic were not unproblematic, so that they needed to be modified both by biblical scholars and by others indebted to him. In any case, however, a careful look at his conception is in order.

To begin with, there is a need for terminological clarification. The term *Sitz im Leben*, as it was employed by Gunkel, refers to the home— origin or normal location—of a genre, not to the context of a particular text. The word *Sitz* means (a regular) 'seat' or 'residence' and thus refers to the 'home' of a genre, in contrast to the usages of individual instances or applications of it, which, according to Gunkel, may appear outside the normal context. Some later writers, at first New Testament and then also Hebrew Bible scholars, including K. Koch in his introduction to form criticism, have applied the term also to the setting of a particular text, such as of a psalm or parable;[78] such a usage introduces an element of imprecision, for it is far from clear how a particular text can have a general occasion, although it is certainly true that a text can be used on several occasions and that it can be intended for repeated use. (Quite a few conundrums, such as whether a text changes its *Sitz*

77. 1906b: 5 (the written-oral difference is not the only one he mentions).
78. See below 12.3.c; 12.4 for New Testament scholars from 1924 on. Within Hebrew Bible scholarship, this usage appeared in Birkeland (1933b: xviii, xix, 258, 244); Bernhardt (1959: 41); Koch (1964, §§3-5, 13); Sawyer (1967: 142-43); Lapointe (1970: 16); Fohrer *et al.* (1973: 196—in some tension with pp. 93-95?); J. Barton (1992: 840).

im Leben or whether it is liturgical or just literary, etc., are in part a result of confusion engendered by, or reflected in, that imprecise usage of the term.) Furthermore, the attribution of a *Sitz im Leben* to a particular text deflects from a reflective facing of the question, 'To what kind of human dynamics does this kind of text relate?'; instead, it simply answers a factual question.

Gunkel's conceptualization of a *Sitz* developed gradually. The first step, in his work on creation and chaos (1895), made the point that certain features of expression have a literary[79] home from which they can move into other genres. Specifically, he derived some elements of prophetic style from the style of hymns and proposed that theophanic descriptions had their basic location (*Sitz*) in poems regarding Sinai (1895: 99, 104). The notion of a 'place in literature' (Alonso Schökel 1960b: 162) thus does not represent a secondary development after Gunkel but marked the starting-point of his thinking about a *Sitz*.

Much earlier, in 1740, when genres still stood in the centre of interest, Johann Breitinger, in a study of comparisons and parables (*Gleichnisse*), had spoken of their *Sitz* or *Platz* ('place')—that is, natural location—within certain literary types.[80] In concept and terminology, Breitinger thus anticipated Gunkel's first step. One can then wonder whether Gunkel, who was interested in relatively old German tradition (Klatt, 17, 265) and came to write an article on *Gleichnisse* in the Hebrew Bible (1910d), knew this study. Conceivably, Julicher, whose analysis of parables was important for Gunkel in his 1895 study and whom he acknowledged as a progenitor of his genre-orientated work (see above), referred him to Breitinger's study, since it included an illustration from the Hebrew Scriptures (351).[81]

A second step by Gunkel placed emphasis on the social occasion with which a literary piece or genre is associated, its *Situation*. Key portions of a relevant passage in the introduction to Genesis (1901a: xviiif.) are as follows: 'If we want to understand the stories better, we

79. The words 'literary' and 'literature', in Gunkel's usage, referred not only to written expressions but also to oral materials (e.g. 1906a: 53), as in Gruppe (iv) and Paul (216).

80. *Critische Abhandlung von der Natur, den Absichten und dem Gebrauche der Gleichnisse*, 1740: 58, 117, 160-89, 201.

81. Jülicher did not cite Breitinger, at least not in the second edition of his work (1899—the first edition of 1886 is not available for inspection); that lack, however, may be due to the fact that Breitinger did not deal with the parables of Jesus.

must imaginatively place before our eyes the situation' in which they were told. Of such situations one hears in Exodus 12 and 13, and so on, referring to questions of children concerning a sacred custom or symbol. 'The usual situation, however, which we have to imagine, is this: during an evening of leisure the family sits at the hearth', adults and especially children listening to stories from the days of old. For certain poems, however, 'we may think of another situation', namely, a festival.[82] In subsequent years, Gunkel employed the word *Situation* to designate a behavioral setting, either that of a particular poem[83] or the normal or original one for a genre.[84]

A third step taken by Gunkel contrasted expressions in a practical oral situation ('life') with artificial written usage. The phrase *Sitz im Leben* made its first appearance, still non-technical in force, within a discussion of this contrast:

> The oldest genres, which are based on an active connection with life processes (*die ihren Sitz im Leben haben*), are orientated toward definite (*bestimmte*) listeners, and strive after a definite (*bestimmte*) effect, are for these reasons almost always completely pure. But when writers take charge of a style, deviations and mixtures enter in many ways as they aim for clever, complicated effects (1906a: 54).

More technical perhaps is the phrase *Sitz im Volksleben* ('seat in folk life') in the following statement: 'Whoever wants to understand an ancient genre, has to ask...where it has its seat [*Sitz*] in folk life' (1906a: 53). In the same year he published this statement: 'Every old literary genre originally has its *Sitz* in the life of the people of Israel at a quite definite place (1906c: 33).[85]

---

82. The body of the Genesis commentary, which was probably written prior to the introduction (1901a: 72, 203, 208, 215), employed the word *Situation* in a much less technical sense, as did a publication by Gunkel appearing in 1900 (1900b: 359). In these cases—as in normal German usage of that time—*Situation* referred either to historical circumstances or to a condition or event depicted by a text, such as by a narrative (cf., e.g., Wellhausen 1897: 141; Cornill 1896: 228). It is thus possible to date the beginning point of Gunkel's use of the word *Situation* for recurring circumstances—and, with it, the emergence of his notion of a life context for genres—to 1900 or 1901.

83. 1904a: 31 (*Situation und Gelegenheit*), 42, 75; 1927b: 104 and so on. An older meaning (i.e. events pictured) still appears in Gunkel (1904a: 8, and so on).

84. 1904a: 40, 240-41, 264, 266-67.

85. In 1904/5 lectures taken down by Bultmann, much of this conceptualization was present, but not yet the term *Sitz im Leben* (De Valerio, 88-93; it is also not

By 1909, the new terminology and conceptualization has crystalized:

> Since these old genres originally existed not on paper but in life, the original units were as short [as they appear in the text] in accordance with the low facility of a hearer and especially of those ancient hearers to receive it. The '*Sitz im Leben*' indicated by us also explains why these oldest genres have a quite [or, completely] pure (*ganz reinen*) style: they are designed for a definite situation (*bestimmte Situation*) and correspond to it thoroughly (1909b: 1193).

The crucial and amazing passage just cited contains quite problematic assumptions. Are situations and genres in oral, including 'primitive', life clearly demarcated from each other so that situations and genres are simple or 'pure', as he said from 1906 on?[86] Is there in life a rigid, rather than only a probabilistic, association between events and words? Indeed, Gunkel presented no evidence for this inflexible picture of life. His conceptualization in this third step, in which the term *Sitz im Leben* first appears, was, in short, highly questionable.

Not yet burdened with the questionable assumptions of the third step was a statement by Gunkel (1906c). It described a situation in terms of speaker, listener, mood and desired effect (33).[87] This complex does not require a specially organized occasion but is constituted by the roles of the participants.[88] As further discussion has shown, Gunkel would have been wise not to go beyond such a conceptualization in terms of roles.

Since Gunkel's term *Sitz im Leben* was associated with unacceptable assumptions and, furthermore, has come to be widely used for the situation of a particular text so that it has lost its specific shape,[89] it is preferable and clearer now to use instead the less problematic term 'life

---

possible to determine Gunkel's precise conceptual frame from this version).

86. See below, in the discussion of his ideas of genres.

87. According to H. Schmidt (1903: 395), references in Erbt (1902) to 'place [*Ort*, i.e. kind of location], listeners and circumstances' and to different styles reflect what Gunkel had said in lectures of which Erbt learned through oral and written reports by Gunkel's students. Erbt's work thus helps one trace Gunkel's development.

88. That Gunkel's formulation (1906c: 33) described roles (rather than organized occasions) has been well pointed out by H.P. Müller (1983: 271-83); however, Gunkel spoke in the same work of a 'definite location' (33) and a 'pure' genre (36).

89. It has even become widely used for particular (historical) contexts; cf. Güttgemanns (1970: 167-68).

situation'.[90] This term can indicate the dimension of generality implied
by the word 'life' without affirming the doubtful assumptions that
Gunkel made. It can be applied both to a genre (an abstract entity) and
to a given text in so far as this is seen not 'as' a particular but 'as' the
expression of a transindividual genre, one with relevance also for the
present.[91]

c. *The Background of the Concept of Life Situation*
Although Gunkel was unusual in visualizing a rigid association
between expression and context in oral life, the idea that social occasions served as a background for literature was current and even dominant in a large number of disciplines. These included those that dealt
with biblical, Germanic, ancient Near Eastern, Graeco-Roman and East
Indian literatures.

1. *Biblical Studies.* In biblical studies, the recognition that various
genres, including popular ones, are reflected in the Hebrew Bible was,
in fact, reached prior to Gunkel. Building on observations by Lowth
and on newer ones concerning ceremonies in the modern Near East by
J.G. Wetzstein (in 1873), Budde, in several items from 1882 on, analysed the natural place in 'life'[92] and the metaphorical adaptations of
some Israelite genres, specifically the love song and dirge. Budde held
that Wetzstein's contribution lay in his being able to show for the songs
in Canticles 'a definite, firm place (*eine bestimmte, feste Stelle*) in the
life and in the customs of the people' (1898: xvii), namely, wedding
festivals.[93] Secondary employments of genres (important in Gunkel's
conception) were called *contrafacta* by Budde, adopting for them a
term for German hymns modelled after secular poems.[94] (He was well
acquainted with, and even active in, the field of Germanics.) After

90. The term 'life situation' (*Lebenssituation*) was used (equated with
'function') by H. Ringgren (1966: 643).
91. See below, 12.4, for a fuller discussion of this point.
92. The dirge represents 'an element of old Israelite life'; it operates in 'real
life' (Budde 1883: 183). Lowth and Wetzstein were cited in Budde (1882: 3, 25).
93. Wetzstein had been preceded by E. Renan in 1860, not cited (not known?)
by him. Wetzstein's view was adapted by the Jewish scholar, K. Kohler (*Das Hohe
Lied* [1878: 9], speaking of a 'wedding play'—known to Budde?). The same thesis
appeared in E. Stanton, *The Woman's Bible* (II, 1989: 100), without documentation.
94. Budde 1893: 482; etc. (For further bibliography, see: *Karl Buddes Schrift-
tum*, 1930.)

publishing a number of relevant studies which became quickly known, he presented (in 1902, in Hastings' *Dictionary of the Bible*), a brief general survey of various kinds of Hebrew folk poetry in relation to 'family life', 'the life of the community', 'religious life' and 'national life' (10-11). Gunkel gave credit to Wetzstein and Budde for furnishing a 'living view of Hebrew genres' (1906a: 99; 1913a: 32 [1906]).

Not tying psalms specifically to any given ritual occasion but holding that some of them were 'composed from the first for liturgical use', W.R. Smith pointed out that they express feelings arising 'in circumstances which frequently recur in human life' (1881: 178). This analysis stands close to Gunkel's valid second step. Somewhat later—then occupying the position of professor of Arabic (having been dismissed from his chair for Hebrew Studies)—Smith stated that 'by far the largest part of the myths of antique religions are connected with the ritual of particular shrines, or with the religious observances of particular tribes and districts' and drew from this phenomenon the conclusion that in almost all cases myths were derived secondarily from the cult (1889: 19). Like Gunkel after him, Smith thus went beyond available evidence to overemphasize a concrete setting as an originating point for literature. (He was cited by Gunkel on the topic of cultic actions at least by 1927b: 12.) Both of these two scholars, it turned out, made a significant impact on scholarship at large; they had unduly bold positions, but their positions were modified by others.[95]

2. *Germanics*. Connections between Gunkel and the field of Germanics have already been mentioned (including, as a possibility, a knowledge of Breitinger). At the end of the nineteenth century the most outstanding history of early German literature was a work by R. Koegel, known for its attempt to reconstruct a picture of ancient German poetry and life with major attention to its genres. Its procedure was stated as follows: 'Whoever wants to penetrate the nature of our oldest poetry must hold before the eyes their connection with the old pagan festivals, with their sacrificial dances and processions' (1894: 6). This statement is similar in aim and wording to Gunkel's 1901 formulation quoted above; in this and other respects, the study furnished a significant antecedent to Gunkel's Genesis commentary.[96] A shorter version of Koegel's study

95. Smith provided inspiration for James Frazer, Durkheim and others (see Beidelman, 47-48, 57-58).

96. A connection between Koegel and Gunkel is supported by the fact that they

had appeared as part of the *Grundriss der germanischen Philologie*, the standard series of the field, edited by Paul. In the methodological portion of that series, H. Paul described 'processes that are repeated with a degree of regularity at certain times and on certain occasions (*bestimmte Anlässe*)' and observed that 'the creation and delivery of poetry is in many ways bound to a definite occasion (*bestimmte Gelegenheit*), to the cult, to the festivals and plays of the people' and that 'oratory arises from public religious, political and juridical life', while great writers have a varyingly close 'connection with life' (1891: 154, 216-17).

Paul and Koegel gave credit to Uhland, a major poet and an analyst of popular poetry then widely regarded as superior to the brothers Grimm in sophistication. About 1840, Uhland had prepared an important analysis of popular poetry; left incomplete—perhaps because it did not fit the spirit of that time—it was published after Uhland's death in 1862 among his collected works. (These were cited by Gunkel in 1917b: 55). Uhland classified the poetry according to genres and related at least several of these to their 'special home place (*besondere Heimatstätte*) where they grow and from which they stem' (III: 383, similarly 13). The occasions on which they are used he called *Anlässe im Volksleben* (III: 10, 12, 15, 181); a group of these form a 'sphere' (*Gebiet*) of life (III: 12, 383).

Gunkel quoted a poem by Uhland (in 1900c: 95). This fact does not necessarily imply that he knew Uhland's analytic studies by then. However, the use of the term *Volksleben* in crucial passages,[97] together with a close similarity in conception, suggests a direct dependence of Gunkel upon Uhland at least by 1906. Perhaps, Gunkel's image of storytelling during a winter evening (in 1901a: xviii, cited above) was derived from Uhland (I: 352), although that is far from certain. More important are other terminological and conceptual parallels between them, some of which have just been noted.[98]

used the word *Kranz*, 'garland', to designate a circle of poems or stories which presuppose each other although they are individually artistic wholes (Koegel 1894: 133-34; Gunkel 1901a: xx-xxi, xxvi, 146-47, 266, 357).

97. Also *Stelle im Volksleben* (1909b: 1193, partially similar to Budde; similarly, 1927d: 88).

98. Terminological similarities (in addition to items already mentioned) include Gunkel's statement that a genre has *ursprünglich ihre eigentümliche Stätte* (1924b: 183) 'from which it stems' (1910c: 48; cf. Zimmern, below) and the phrase *Gebiete des Lebens* appearing in Erbt (1902), which reflects lectures by Gunkel (see above on Erbt).

Since there were quite a few other relevant studies—partially dependent on Uhland[99]—it would be difficult to know which, in particular, had a direct impact on Gunkel. Most likely, there were several such.[100] One theme widespread in Germanic studies since the end of the eighteenth century was that of a split between popular ('living') and intellectual literature, which became crucial for Gunkel in 1906, as has already been shown.[101] The split was generally lamented, since it was believed that great art requires the interaction between the two strata.

3. *Studies of the Ancient Near East*. A major stimulus for the concept of situation came from investigations of ancient Near Eastern literature. For instance, A. Jeremias proposed for certain works a cultic 'situation', designating thereby, it seems, a particular context and thus approximating some of Gunkel's early usage of the term (1887: 7; 1891: 775 [the lexicon in which this appeared was used heavily by Gunkel]). H. Winckler spoke of a Babylonian 'Easter' festival (1901: 31, 53), as did Gunkel, who was associated with him in Berlin (1901a: xv, xix). Genres, styles and occasions—separately or together—were noted by others as well.[102]

Especially important for Gunkel was the work of H. Zimmern, his colleague at Halle until 1894, who contributed to his study on creation and chaos (1895) and also aided subsequent analyses by him (acknowledged by Gunkel, 1901a, preface; 1903: vi; 1905b: x). Zimmern's dissertation (1885) established the kinds of occasions on which Babylonian penitential prayers could be used by means of two kinds of

99. E.g. C. Beyer 1883: 87, etc. Klatt (108) refers to a study (critically) dependent on Uhland.

100. W. Scherer (1887: 7-16—with a knowledge of Uhland's work) is virtually a model for Gunkel (1906a: 55-56, 60-66); since it was a rather standard work, it may well have been known to Gunkel, who cited Scherer (1888) in 1902 (xxiv).

101. A list of writers on the subject would include Herder, Jacob and Wilhelm Grimm, Schlegel, Uhland, Vilmar (his history of German literature appeared in many editions), Paul (1891: 224), Elster, and Dieterich (1902: 172). Especially from Vilmar on, the words *Riss* ('split') and *Gebildete* (the 'educated') were used almost monotonously in discussing this, as in Gunkel (1906a: 53—cf. 1905b: 4).

102. Other relevant observations included those of L. King (1896: xxii-xxiii) and Jastrow (1898: 294). It is possible that the notion of a life context of literary genres was also in the mind of Erman, an outstanding Egyptologist with whom Gunkel was in personal contact; however, Erman apparently never explicitly discussed this issue (cf. *RFT* on A. Gardiner, associated with him).

evidence: cultic directions and narrative reports mentioning the use of a given type of prayer in connection with certain circumstances (2). Gunkel later similarly listed narratives and laws among evidence for reconstructing the contexts of verbal expressions (1910c: 48; 1913b: 1931). In 1905 (4, 7, 13) Zimmern set Babylonian hymns and prayers in relation to the 'situation from which they stem'[103]—specifically to cultic processes 'in connection with various important courses of action of private and public life' and especially in relation to a magical use in which most of them have 'their original *Sitz*'. The word *Sitz* is here associated by Zimmern with 'life' (*Leben*), as was not done by Gunkel until a year later.[104]

4. *Classics*. The notion that genres were adapted, for artistic purposes, from prior usages in popular situations was common in standard works on Graeco-Roman literature.[105] A. Couat (1882) described Alexandrian Hellenistic poetry as based on genres which had once served a social function; he observed that older, such as pre-Hellenistic, poets could sacrifice originality to the conventions of tradition in order to meet public needs (515-16). Similarly, R. Reitzenstein—a member of a scholarly circle not far removed from that of Gunkel—analysed in a well-known study (1893) several Alexandrian genres as used outside the social contexts in which they originated, for display or entertainment. R. Hirzel, in examining the history of the dialogue, noted that an interest in the history of genres at that time lay 'in the air'; he began with a brief discussion of the oral forms of 'real life' (1895: vi, 26). In part inspired by W.R. Smith, several classicists—including notably J. Harrison (e.g. 1913)—derived Greek dramatic forms from religious rituals (this thesis was subjected to considerable criticism later).

Gunkel's direct or indirect connections with the classicists Boeckh, Gruppe and von Wilamowitz-Moellendorff have already been mentioned. Wilamowitz described Attic drama in terms of its connection with a 'definite occasion' (*bestimmte Gelegenheit*), namely, the

103. Cf. Uhland and Gunkel (1910c: 48), cited above. Was the use of the word *Situation* by Zimmern—and perhaps the echo of Uhland—indebted to Gunkel, orally?

104. Zimmern may have derived the word *Sitz* from Gunkel's use of it for a literary home in his 1895 study to which Zimmern contributed.

105. See, for example, Sellars (1889—cf. Gercke and Norden, 560); Christ (1898).

Dionysus festival (1959, III: 1; cf. I: 108 [1895]). In his 1905 survey of Greek literature—part of the same series to which Gunkel contributed a year later his overview of Israelite literature—he pointed out that the Greek orator sought to serve 'life' and that Menander (third century CE) set forms of speech in relation to occasions; he cited Menander's discussion of Jewish praise in Jerusalem (150-51). If Gunkel did not already know of Menander's reference to the singing of hymns at Jewish festivals, he probably became aware of it through this citation.

5. *Indology*. Gunkel's interests also ranged to India. In fact, comparisons between Near Eastern and Indian hymns were not uncommon in the last decades of the nineteenth century. Indian traditions are especially amenable to form criticism, since they contain not only literary materials but also extensive directions for the carrying out of various private and public procedures. It was thus natural that scholars concerned with the culture of India examined its verbal and active aspects in their relation to each other. For instance, Gruppe, in the work known to Gunkel, presented a discussion of Brahman hymns in relation to both a cultic and a more purely literary use (283-314). Hermann Oldenberg, in 1894 and 1903 studies cited by Gunkel (1906a: 102; 1910b: xxviii; 1911b: 328), dealt in detail with Vedic rites for 'occasions' (*Anlässe*) of public and family life, together with the basic elements of their literary expression, although he insisted the literature was not always connected with ritual.

The Indologist Maurice Bloomfield, writing in English, employed the word 'situation' for the recurring context of religious expressions, including hymns (1886: 469; two essays in *JAOS* 15, 1893: xxxix, xlv [another part of that same journal volume was used by Gunkel and Zimmern in 1895: 25, 401]; *The Atharva-Veda*, 1899: 57). Such a use of the word 'situation' for a recurring context did not, perhaps, appear elsewhere—especially not in German—prior to Gunkel's use of it from 1901 on.[106] It is possible that Gunkel encountered Bloomfield's work as he was preparing his studies of psalms, for which it was relevant. It is possible, of course, that a coincidence has occurred or that an intermediate (oral?) vehicle served as linkage.

---

106. This judgment relies on a general knowledge of literature and sense for the German language. (See a note above in section 2, for Gunkel's more typically German use of *Situation* prior to 1901.) For the somewhat similar use of 'situation' by M. Bloomfield's nephew, the linguist L. Bloomfield, see *RFT*.

6. *A General Theory of Folklore*. Finally, it is appropriate to refer to a general analysis of folklore. A crucial role in forming Gunkel's perspective may have been played by Wundt, influential for Gunkel (cf., e.g., Klatt, 135). A major work by him, based not on field observation but on wide reading, distinguished between *ad hoc* songs and 'community songs'; community songs are 'restricted', in his words, to 'definite occasions' (*bestimmte Gelegenheiten*, 1905: 310), without, however, citing at all adequate evidence for such a restriction. Wundt's statement may have contributed to Gunkel's envisioning, from 1906 on, a firm connection between 'pure' popular genres and externally describable settings.

It is possible that some of the misapprehension by Wundt and Gunkel was caused by an ambiguity in the German word *bestimmt*; this adjective ranges in meaning from 'certain' (i.e. 'some') via 'definite' (i.e. 'specific') to 'fixed' (i.e. 'exclusive'). Wundt and Gunkel used the word in the sense of 'exclusive', while others, including H. Paul and Wilamowitz-Moellendorff, appear to have employed it somewhat more loosely.[107] In fact, Paul, in the statements cited, qualified the association by such phrases as 'with a degree of regularity' or 'in many ways'. In any case, a subtle but significant shift in conceptualization took place, apparently so for Wundt and clearly so for Gunkel.

In sum, Gunkel was deeply indebted to other disciplines for his basic idea of *Sitz im Leben*. His contribution—but also, in many ways, his problem—lay in the way in which he utilized this notion for his theory of genres.

d. *Gunkel's Conception of Genres*

As has already been indicated, central to Gunkel's outlook was his acceptance of both particularity and generality. Gunkel was concerned with generality in the forms of: (1) transtemporal continuity; (2) a

---

107. Even Budde, cited above, may not have intended the meaning 'exclusive'. How Gunkel himself glided across the different meanings of the adjective can be seen in the following sentence (1917a: 109): 'Whoever in the ancient world appears speaking or singing, does so on a *bestimmte* occasion, considers *bestimmte* hearers, and seeks a *bestimmte* result'; this sentence makes good sense (even for today) if *bestimmt* means something like 'definite', but Gunkel treated it as though it were true with the meaning 'fixed', and he continued from this assertion to the conclusion that expressions were standardized. In Gunkel's writings, the adjective could qualify the nouns *Stelle*, 'place', and *Gelegenheit*, 'occasion'; see, for example, 1909b: 1193; 1913a: 33 [1906]; 1913b: 1941; 1924b: 183.

shared humanity; and (3) social community. All three of these elements entered into his notion of literary genres. At the same time, he was intensely interested in the uniqueness of particular persons, texts and religious traditions. Uniqueness, he believed, is especially pronounced in great phenomena, which combine a variety of forms; for instance, Israel learned from other societies (1895; 1900a: 61) and Christian religion is 'syncretistic' (1903: 95). In fact, it is important, as has often been done, to distinguish between individuality and sheer particularity, in that individuality involves a synthesis, a combination of general forms within a unique constellation. Structures that contain many forms in their complex whole are indeed likely to be more special and at the same time share more features; for instance, human beings are more special than are most physical objects, since they have more features and thus more features to share.

Gunkel's interest in human particularity appeared in several ways. For instance, one justification he gave for furnishing a general history of literature was that only in such a way can great poets and writers be recognized as such (e.g. 1917a: 108). He took pains to examine each of the 150 psalms and viewed many of them as expressions of personal piety. Unlike some other scholars of his time, he believed that individual human beings were important in Israel from early on, although not as much so as they have become in recent times (1912; 1914a: 391; etc.). He even expressed a worry that in the historiography of his 'socialist time' there might be a tendency to neglect individuals unduly; in regard to these, he held that 'every person, even the most minor, has its mystery, of which one can give an outline perhaps, but which one cannot capture in a calculation' (1903: 12).

Clearly, Gunkel wished to acknowledge and point to the greatness and mystery of particular human beings and to the creativity of particular writings. Yet Gunkel's scholarship was designed to obtain an understanding, a process which requires a recognition of shared structures. Thus, the 'final goal' of his work was a 'knowledge of genres' in their history (1927d: 90).

In Gunkel's view, genres existed prior to particular compositions. In this, he reversed the judgment of de Wette, according to which psalms that express deeply individual emotions are the oldest ones, while other psalms are imitations of them (1811, see above). Indeed, the novelty of Gunkel's approach lay not in a new classification (his typology was not very far from de Wette's)[108] but in the way in which the role of genres was conceived. Gunkel believed that individual authors adapted pre-existing genres in creative ways. They could do so by incorporating elements of one genre within a text that belongs basically to another, or by producing texts in which different genres are mixed within a more inclusive whole, called a 'liturgy' (1906a: 86; 1913b: 1947; etc.). He observed (1906a: 86, etc.) that prophecy made wide use of different forms—often metaphorically—as had similarly been noted by Briggs, Budde and Moulton.

Not only are genres temporally prior to particular texts but they furnish to these their intrinsic structure, according to Gunkel. 'If we want to look into the inner life of the psalmists, we must begin with these genres that are given by nature', in his view (1922: 3).

In making a statement such as this, Gunkel moved into the proximity of Aristotelian essentialism, holding that a proper classification reflects the 'essential' nature of objects. It is true, Gunkel did not argue for a timeless essentialism for which the essence of literary genres is universal. Rather, he held that Israelite genres had their own character, differing from Greek or modern forms (1909b: 1192; 1917c: 265; 1927b: 8).[109] Still, he believed that, within Israelite culture, genres expressed the 'nature' of texts, expressing an inborn 'natural order' (1909b: 1192; 1913b: 1930; 1926: x; 1927b: 9-10; 1927d: 88). Some of the classifications of Israelite literature, he said, arise 'as though by themselves'[110] and are thus already widely accepted in biblical scholarship (1917c: 266; 1927b: 9).

On the basis of such an essentialist outlook, which implies that there can be only one proper classification, Gunkel sharply criticized some other typologies (1917c: 265f.; 1927b: 8-9). In contrast to his earlier recognition of a need to 'construct' a picture in historiography (1907b: 80), he came, especially in the 1920s, to seek a 'firm' ordering beyond 'the subjectivity of the individual scholar' in regard to classification (1926: viii-ix; cf. 1922: 3). Did he change his mind, or did he

---

108. De Wette was not cited by Gunkel, but he may be included among those who, according to Gunkel (1927b: 8), had presented a classification without seeing its 'significance' (*pace* Smend [1958: 108; 1991: 26], treating de Wette as a forerunner of Gunkel not known to him).

109. They are similar, however, to other Near Eastern genres (e.g. 1927d: 96).

110. Similarly, Uhland, *Schriften*, I: 14 ('by themselves'); III: 12 ('almost by themselves').

distinguish between history and genre analysis in regard to their objectivity?[111]

One point should be made clear. Gunkel distinguished between 'genres' and 'classes' (for psalms: 1913b, 1930). 'Genres', in his view, have a structure in which language, content and life role are integrally connected and which are, at least mostly, oral. Placed by him into an oral context which he could not observe, they were hypothetical. (Diverging from Gunkel, one might think of them as ideal forms.) In contrast, the 'classes' of which he spoke are groups of available texts, such as appear in the Bible; they do not exhibit a pure pattern.

Gunkel held that a genre is identified on the basis of the fact that 'specific (*bestimmte*) ideas are expressed in a specific [linguistic] form upon a specific [kind of] occasion' (1924b: 183). He formulated this triple perspective on genres systematically from 1921 on.[112] His three-fold view, however, had already been stated earlier (1906c: 32; 1917a: 109), although without explicit reference to mood, which later became a regular part of his description of content ('thoughts and moods').

He always listed content before linguistic form, just as the discussion of 'topics' or 'invention' (thought) preceded that of style in Aristotelian rhetoric. Linguistic form, nevertheless, was considered by him to be useful for the recognition of a genre (1921: 45; 1924a: 145-46; 1924b: 182-83; 1927b: 23). The practical life context, however, was treated as the logically primary one in a sequence that proceeds from the occasion to the content to the form of expression (1917a: 109). If one wishes to order psalms according to 'their inner nature', he said, one must do so 'according to the activities to which they belong' (1927b: 10, 19; similarly, Uhland).[113] His final formulations (in 1927b, 1927d, and 1930) accordingly listed the life-situation first.

The word 'form' is, of course, ambiguous. For a particularist, it

111. A factor perhaps contributing to Gunkel's outlook was a swing towards 'a new objectivity' in German art, literature, religion, etc., in the early and mid-1920s, oscillating with or opposing an irrational or sceptical line in part indebted to Nietzsche. (On an emphasis on objectivity in religion after World War I, see, for example, the report in *RGG*, II, 1929: 1697.)

112. 1921: 44-45; 1924a: 145-46; 1924b: 182-83; 1925: 109; 1927b: 22-23; 1927d: 88-89; 1930: 1677-79.

113. According to Uhland (III: 10), a viewing of literature in connection with its occasions allows one to enter into 'the inner life and nature of the people'. (Uhland expressly based his classification on occasion and content rather than on linguistic form [III: 10, 12]).

refers to a group of concrete phenomena; for others, it can refer to a holistic structure. When the term *Formgeschichte*, 'form-history', came to be used for a movement in New Testament studies stimulated by his approach, Gunkel expressed unhappiness about the use of the word 'form', since linguistic form (relatively external) was not the most important element in his analysis (letter of 1925 [Rollmann, 284]). Two years later, however, he made reference to a relevant statement by Goethe: 'The material [of a text] is obvious, the content [the thought] is found only by adding something [presumably: reflective analysis] and the form [organic aesthetic structure] is a secret to most'. Gunkel commented that this is a 'true word'—especially appropriate for a people who do not have an easy perception of form, presumably Germans (1927b: 23). 'Form' in a Goethean holistic, organic sense was, clearly, acceptable to Gunkel as a designation for his scholarly interest.

In fact, an integrated view of form probably represents the primary difference between Gunkel and his predecessors. De Wette had presented his classification of the psalms as an ordering by 'content' and had held that Hebrew poetry is 'formless'. Gunkel made no such cleavage between form and content. He did distinguish between verbal form and thought, but he saw a connection between them.

An important issue, then, is this: are the three aspects of a genre related to each other intimately so that the content is appropriate for the occasion and the linguistic form is appropriate for the content and perhaps also directly for the occasion or interactive context (for instance, a language of awe may be appropriate for addressing deity, no matter whether the content is one of joy or distress)? Gunkel gave at least some indications of such appropriateness, that is, a more-than-merely-accidental association between those aspects. For individual artistic works he asserted that 'the right form is the necessary expression of the content' (1904c: 23), 'the form must follow the content' (1917a: 107), or, more cautiously, that form and content are closely connected (1906b: 4). In analysing the genres of psalms toward the end of his life, he gave reasons for the employment of either second- or third-person language; for instance, he explained the use of 'you' with reference to God in psalms of lament on the basis of the fact that prayer is not a 'conversation with God' (about the world) but a (deeply felt) 'speaking to God', citing Heiler's study of prayer around the world.[114] He

114. 1927b (*Einleitung*, Part I): 122; 1933 (Part II, edn Begrich): 250, 268, 272,

described certain motifs in psalms of lament—such as the expression of pitiful suffering and a pointing out that God's concerns are at issue—as a way of providing God with motivations for coming to the aid of the one praying, in this way explaining the appearance of those motifs in the psalms.[115] To indicate the rationale of expressions, he used such expressions as 'according to its nature', 'it is self-explanatory' (*selbstverständlich*), 'humanly understandable', 'not accidental', 'no wonder', 'the reasons for this'.[116] Sometimes he connected a thought and expression with the special character of Israelite religion,[117] but often the grounds given were generally human.

The exploration of reasons, however, was not carried out fully; often, by not addressing the issue, Gunkel left undetermined the extent to which content or style is accidental or intrinsically appropriate.[118] On a theoretical level—although Gunkel did not expressly reflect on this—such caution is appropriate, for probably all phenomena, human and otherwise, embody both reasonableness, or law-likeness, and happenstance. In subsequent biblical form criticism, however, as it abandoned Gunkel's interest in theory, the exploration of a rationale was largely ignored and, indeed, forgotten.[119]

By giving attention to the interrelationship between life, content and linguistic form, Gunkel exhibited an affinity with Boeckh's theory of genres. According to Boeckh—continuing a classical outlook[120]—the central characteristic of a genre is its 'aim' (*Zweck*); thus 'the highest task of genre criticism (*Gattungskritik*) is to investigate whether content and form…are suitable (*angemessen*) for the inner aim of a genre' (250). Since in Boeckh's view aesthetic criticism similarly asks whether form and content fit an aim, genre analysis and aesthetic

---

313, etc. Gunkel's readiness to observe reasons for expressions can be seen earlier, for example in 1904b: 40.

115. 1927b: 125, 129; 1933: 236, etc.

116. 1927b: 1, 47; 1933: 233, 235, 250, 272, 312.

117. 1927b: 69; 1933: 234, 312.

118. In 1917a: 109, he said simply that certain matters and forms of expression were 'customary' for a certain occasion or aim.

119. I thought, in my formulation of 1969: 1, that attention to a rationale was a new aspect of form criticism, to be added to Gunkel's procedure; even in 1993: 76, I remained unaware (on a conscious level) of this feature of Gunkel's work.

120. See above, 4.1.d, for this tradition in biblical interpretation from the fourth century CE on.

criticism were understood by him to be fundamentally identical (156, 250). Gunkel mirrored this association in his insistence that a 'scientific' (scholarly) aesthetics involves attention to genres (1904c: 24; 1906c: 32-33; 1907a; 1907b: 83). He probably did so on the basis of an at least indirect knowledge of Boeckh's work.[121] In fact, in 1906 Gunkel described the situation of a genre as involving an effect to be achieved—in other words, an aim (1906c: 33). If a situation is thus conceived, there is an inner (intrinsic) connection between a genre and its life situation, a relation of appropriateness which can be considered aesthetic.

Unlike Boeckh, however—but like Uhland and Zimmern—Gunkel also conceived of the life context of genres in terms of externally described situations, for a picture of which he drew on information available in other texts, such as in narratives that report the use of a given genre (as Zimmern had done, see above). While that is indeed a social perspective, it was not in line with the sociology of his time. G. Simmel, one of the founders of sociology and Gunkel's colleague in Berlin, was in the process of developing a 'formal' sociology, describing social relationships he called 'life forms', such as exchange, conflict and domination (especially, in 1908). These represent *roles*, rather than external (more or less arbitrary) *settings*. Somewhat earlier, Durkheim had argued (perhaps one-sidedly)[122] that functions are prior to concrete organizations (1888: 45); furthermore, like others, he discussed the fact that functions and, especially, organizations become more specialized as a group increases in size (1893), so that specialized arrangements are not 'original', as Gunkel implied. These sociological analyses of roles and functions harmonized better with Boeckh's focus on aim—which was open in regard to specific organizational forms—than with one that connects literature with organized settings. Gunkel's knowledge of

121. Gunkel's rejection of dilettante exclamations over the beauty of a text (1904c: 23; 1906c: 32; 1906b: 3; 1909b: 1191) was very close to that of Boeckh (156). This and other similarities mentioned, including the correspondence in their conception of a 'history of literature' (1904c: 23; 1909b, title; etc.), indicate that Gunkel knew Boeckh, at the very least—but perhaps only—indirectly (e.g. through Lasson, see above). In Boeckh's spirit (although not necessarily in dependence on him for this point), Gunkel described a narrative as being constructed 'effectively' for its 'aim' (*Zweck*, 1901a: 263).

122. Durkheim himself apparently did not repeat his 1888 statement quite as sharply later.

sociology, however, was weaker than his acquaintance with a number of other fields.[123]

The notion of rigid (not merely probabilistic) connections between external settings and generic structures can be maintained only by assuming a heavy-handed rule of convention. Has there been such a rule of custom? Even a quick observation shows that ideas, forms of expression and external occasions do not stand together rigidly in any preserved literature. Gunkel, however, posited an oral condition in which the three aspects stand firmly together.

This conception involved a theory of 'pure forms'. (In this idea, Gunkel may well have been influenced by Jülicher, who had examined the parables of Jesus on the assumption that they originally exhibited a pure form.[124]) Specifically, Gunkel appears to have believed that in traditional oral life, only one kind of thing can be said in only one way on any given occasion so that genres appear in a 'pure manner'. Thus, he said that the oldest genres, which are actively related to life, 'are almost always completely pure' (1906a: 54) or even (omitting 'almost') 'always completely pure' (1906c: 36) or 'completely pure and simple' (1927b: 28).

Two kinds of consideration supported Gunkel in this position. One was a belief that ancient persons were more strictly bound by custom than are moderns (e.g. 1906a: 52; 1917a: 109). This thesis is doubtful, but he was not alone at that time in holding it.[125] Another consideration was his observation that 'still today' genres, such as that of the sermon or the children's story, have their own special location in life (1906c: 33).[126] As an amateur sociologist, Gunkel thus projected into the past the specialized arrangements of modern life. He reflected, with justification, that a given genre is often connected with a specific profession (*Stand*) that 'guards its purity' (1906a: 53), but he failed to consider that a smaller society has less of a division of labour and thus may well have less differentiated and, in that sense, less 'pure' genres than does a larger one.[127]

123. He cited a historical study of the family (1926: 45) but otherwise showed little acquaintance with sociological works.

124. Jülicher's impact on Gunkel has already been noted. Criticism of Jülicher will be reported below.

125. Olrik (1909: 11) can be interpreted along such a line.

126. Similarly, H. Schmidt (1903: 395—reflecting lectures by Gunkel), and P. Wendland in 1910 (Gercke and Norden, 448).

127. He did remark that individuals were less 'differentiated' in earlier times

In fact, Gunkel's assumption about an original purity of genres ran counter to the positions of most literary theorists at that time.[128] Thus one must indicate that Gunkel, despite his wide knowledge, had serious lacks as well. Specifically, W. Scherer, in an important work on poetics cited by Gunkel (1902: xxiv), argued that the oldest songs were not strict in form and that literary forms gradually differentiated from each other because of an increasing division of labour 'in life' (1888: 9-18). The thesis of a gradual differentiation of literature had already been developed in 1763 by John Brown, after observing conjoint biblical forms in 1751;[129] he believed that the roles of poet, musician and legislator were at first one and that poetry began as a 'rapturous mixture of hymn, history, fable and mythology' before dividing into genres (Wellek, I: 127-28).

The thesis of a gradual differentiation of genres became prominent at the end of the nineteenth century in systematic views of 'literary history', developed in greatest detail by Brunetière (1890) and also by ten Brink (1891: 6-7, already mentioned above). Uhland, like others, believed in an early lack of differentiation (III: 15) but also expressed a less unilinear view in saying that literary forms sometimes move towards greater elaboration with new interaction between them and sometimes back towards a simple ground (I: 404). It is not likely, however, that Gunkel was aware of the degree to which he diverged from these points of view.

Gunkel did know that in Mesopotamian psalms praise and lament were often combined; but he seems to have assumed, as did his student E. Balla (1912: 12), that the combination there was secondary. When F. Stummer (1924: 130) challenged that assumption, Gunkel left to the future the settlement of the question of whether there had at one time been separate forms in Mesopotamia (1927b: 85). Apparently, he could now see (late in his life) that his scheme was in doubt, but (perhaps understandably) he proceeded to fill in the details of his view of psalm genres. In the form in which that careful overview was completed by his student Begrich, it included extensive discussions of how one form

(1906a: 52; 1909b: 1192) but did not apply this perception to the question of specialization within society and culture.

128. Heiler, in his study of prayer which Gunkel knew at least eventually (by 1927b), argued for a relative freedom in simple prayers (40, 50).

129. Above, 5.3.

penetrated another on the assumption that they had at one time been distinct.

In close conjunction with Gunkel's notion of an original purity of genres stood his belief that early oral productions were very brief (1906a: 53-54). He asserted, without giving any evidence, that oral literature was very limited in extent[130] and imagined, it seems, that a short piece would have to embody a pure genre. He was probably unaware of the fact that this conception contradicted Goethe's opinion in 1819 that a union (not separation) of forms is especially characteristic of old and short poems and of oral improvisations (VII: 118-19).[131] In proposing that brevity is a sign of antiquity (1901a: xxii), Gunkel was also out of touch with nineteenth-century discussions of literary development which led A. Ludwig to say in 1876 that 'no one ought to assert nowadays any more that the older is equivalent to what is simpler'.[132]

Although Gunkel thus stood largely alone in his conception of literary development, he did accept one theory which had been held widely in the West from Graeco-Roman times on, as well as in other parts of the world, namely, that nations and literatures move through cycles. In Gunkel's view, the apex of Israelite literature ran from the eighth to the sixth centuries BCE. During this period, he believed, simple earlier forms were adapted and joined in creative ways, while thereafter 'mixtures' took place (1906a: 88, 93; 1909b: 1192-93; etc.). Unfortunately, he did not make clear how a creative adaptation differs from a presumably less valuable mixture. It appears, however, that he made

---

130. 1906c: 33. A different position appears in a statement by Gunkel, which represents a slip of his pen but contains an element of truth, declaring that listeners can deal with longer units than can readers (34; the opposite is assumed immediately thereafter). It is true, for very long epics only episodes are customarily performed at any one time (Flueckiger 1989: 11).

131. Gunkel generally knew Goethe's work well (Klatt, 142, 265), although evidently not in this respect. See below for a different statement by Goethe.

132. *Der Veda*, II: vii. One aspect of the nineteenth-century discussion concerned the relative primacy of popular and elite literature; for instance, Ewald was convinced that popular song had 'sunk' from higher art (*Die Dichter des Alten Bundes*, 2nd edn, I, 1866: 33). Gunkel was aware of at least some of this discussion; his statement 'a people (*Volk*) does not compose poetry' (1909b: 1193) echoes Gruppe (1887: 64—'the people as such [i.e. as a unit] cannot compose poetry'), and Christ (1898: 23—'the whole people, it is true, does not compose poetry'). (A survey of the question was given by Gummere 1894: xxvii-lx.)

the distinction in order to account for the sense, which he had from early on (1893: 242), that postexilic literature was less great in character than pre-exilic prophecy.[133] In his devaluation of mixtures, Gunkel may well have been influenced by Goethe's judgment during his classicist period shortly before 1800—later modified, as we have seen—that a mixture of artistic kind is a sign of decay.[134]

The idea that genres were adapted by profound individuals, especially in writing, meant that Gunkel contrasted the written products of the Hebrew Bible with Israelite collective and oral forms. In fact, he distinguished between 'cultic' and 'spiritual' songs (1904a: 240; 1913b: 1945; etc.)—a point to which we will return.[135] In making this distinction, he was influenced by a tradition within classical scholarship which observed a disjunction between display poetry and practical life in imperial Alexandrian and in other similar Hellenistic contexts.[136] Furthermore, A. Erman, with whom Gunkel was in personal contact, thought that Egyptian poetry was fresher, less stereotyped, after c. 1300 BCE than it had been earlier (1909: 98), and M. Jastrow, in a work Gunkel knew, wondered whether some of the Mesopotamian hymns were purely literary (1905: 421).

Whether or not Gunkel's analyses were altogether appropriate, his interpretations can be valued for recognizing both a difference between written texts (somewhat elitist in their art and reflection) and oral life (emotional-practical and populist)[137] and a connection between them. Some of his followers later became excessively enamoured of the oral character of the tradition (such as of psalms).[138] That was not true of

---

133. E.g. Wellhausen; cf. Klatt (186). That pre-exilic prophecy represents an apex is indeed likely, although Wellhausen and others have unduly devalued later literature.

134. XLVII: 22 (1798); letter to F. Schiller, 23 December 1797. Both of Goethe's judgments (the one of 1797/8 and the different one of 1819) were widely known, but especially so this earlier one.

135. Below, 13.2.c.

136. See above, for example, for Gruppe, and among more recent works, Gentili (1984). The difference between serious and entertaining uses of songs may have been exaggerated by scholars. According to the Greek Xenophanes (sixth century BCE), people 'who are about to make merry should first honour the gods with hymns' (Diels and Kranz, fragment 1; Wheelwright, 35); that does not indicate a sharp division.

137. Rightly, for Gunkel, Kirkpatrick (27).

138. For instance, Westermann (1996: 9-49) again limits form criticism to an

Gunkel, even while he avoided the opposite error of ignoring the oral side.

3. *Evaluation*

a. *Relationality?*

It is clear that Gunkel, like many others of his day, wished to acknowledge both generality and particularity. However, he had only a weak apprehension of the relational perspective in which these two dimensions are integrated.[139] Instead, he tended to deal with these two aspects separately. Especially, Gunkel associated generality with oral culture and particularity with written expressions. A more integral connection of these two aspects would have shown itself in an application of the concept of probability, which combines a degree of regularity with a degree of unpredictability, so that genres would constitute probabilistic complexes, not hypothetically pure structures that lie behind the text.

Not having readily available new conceptual tools with which to overcome nominalism, he adapted an older outlook, specifically Aristotelian essentialism, in his holding that general categories (genres) have a distinct ('pure') form. At the same time, he continued the external orientation typical of particularism in his associating genres with externally describable 'settings' (as Uhland had done) rather than with their 'purposes' (in line with a long tradition, voiced also by Boeckh). Although Aristotelianism and particularism differ in conception so that they stand in a tension within Gunkel's work, they do have a partial affinity for one another. According to Piaget, for example, classification—important for Aristotelianism—represents in itself no more than a 'concrete' way of thinking, not yet a 'formal' one (as he defined that), largely relational.[140]

For his philosophy, Gunkel may have relied not only on Troeltsch but also on his close philosopher friend Lasson, who believed Aristotle, Paul and Hegel to be fundamentally in harmony with each other.[141] That would help to explain why Gunkel's view continued or revived both essentialism and Idealist-Hegelian features.[142] Partly as a reflection

oral process.

139. For instance, he shows no knowledge of the relational thinker Cassirer, who published a major work in 1910 (on whom see *RFT*).

140. On Piaget, see *RFT*.

141. *Philosophen-Lexikon*, 1950, II: 24; see also *RGG*, 2nd edn, III: 1496.

142. On Hegelian elements, see above, 11.1.a.

of continuing nominalism and partly as an aspect of the newer relational thought, other scholars before or during Gunkel's days had a more flexible, less essentialist, view of genres. Specifically, the idea that genres are not rigidly demarked but flow into another was well established (e.g. Uhland, III: 288; Boeckh, 147; Nietzsche, XVIII: 157; Babbitt, 1910: 249).[143] In dealing with biblical literature, perhaps already reflecting relational thinking, König employed less external concepts for life than did Gunkel and made better room for overlaps in types.[144] With respect to narratives, in fact, Gunkel did use the notion of genres flexibly and employed them not so much for the purpose of classification as for characterization.[145]

Gunkel, as we have seen, distinguished between genres and classes, but he thought of the former as oral patterns and the latter as groups of written documents (which vary in characteristics). He would have been closer to 'formal' relational thinking if he had treated forms as theoretical structures or as possibilities, which are never actualized without modification or admixture.[146] One reason why forms do not appear in a pure manner, either in physical or in human phenomena, is that they interact with each other. This interaction can be described by saying that they cut across one another. Gunkel approached a cross-cutting view of forms in a public lecture in which he divided the psalms according to 'spheres', especially that of the king, the nation and the individual (1922: 4). If he had combined this division with one according to 'types of piety'—which he outlined a few years later (1926: x)— he would have reached a two-dimensional structure to which further considerations can be added. A multidimensional array in which considerations of size of group, mood, and so on, are more or less ideal 'factors', not rigid orders, would have provided a better view, indeed one more in line with what was, or came to be held, in other disciplines.[147]

143. Gunkel did give indications of the variability of genres (e.g. 1917b: 52) and of some difficulty in drawing lines between them (1917b: 7), but not with sufficient emphasis.

144. See the summary above. A classification like Gunkel's, but with an acknowledgment of overlaps, appeared in R. Kittel (1905: 189) (as also in Kittel's subsequent commentary on Psalms).

145. See the evidence presented by R. Moore (1990: 18, 63).

146. According to Piaget, 'formal' thought includes an increased ability to think of possibilities as such (see *RFT*).

147. See *RFT*.

Classification, however, was not Gunkel's major contribution. On the contrary, as has been mentioned, the genres of psalms with which he worked had largely been identified earlier. Furthermore, his specific classification (especially in the version edited, perhaps too mechanically, by Begrich) was quite complex and incoherent in terms of the primary criteria applied.[148] Rather, his contribution lay in providing a picture and rationale for each genre within a variegated social complex, including the community as a whole, royalty and individuals.[149] Perhaps most importantly, his discussion of the major genres conveyed the sense that they are general human structures in which one can participate. This is probably the main reason for Gunkel's electrifying impact.

It has been observed in twentieth-century anthropological studies that comparisons between cultures provide insight not so much by observing surface parallels as through recognizing correspondences in relationships (e.g. Evans-Pritchard 1951: 18, 27). On the basis of this recognition, it must be said that Gunkel's world-wide comparisons, although interesting, were not as significant as they might be. They often treated only similarities in ideas or arrangements rather than relational—structural or functional—equivalents. It is true, Gunkel repeatedly spoke of 'analogy', but this word is often used in German (as in English) somewhat loosely to designate a partial similarity, while, strictly understood, an analogy is concerned with a correspondence of relationships (A is to B as C is to D).

To be sure, an application of true analogy would have required a much better understanding of the cultures involved than was available to Gunkel. Surface comparisons, as they were prominent in the work of Frazer,[150] were not yet well superseded in anthropological procedure. Far too few ethnographic data had been analysed in their context (such as through field work) to permit extensive structural or functional

148. Hymns, Songs of Yahweh's Ascent to the Throne, Royal Psalms, Communal and Individual Laments, Communal and Individual Thanksgiving, Words of Blessing and Curse, Victory Song, Legend, Torah, Prophetic Psalms, Wisdom Poetry, Entrance Liturgies, etc. (These are genres appearing in, not necessarily classes of, psalms.) This is quite a miscellany.

149. See especially his essays in 1913b (2nd edn, 1930) and 1922, which are not overwhelmed by details. (However, the details of his Introduction [1927b, 1933] also constitute a very valuable contribution.)

150. *Golden Bough*, 1890, etc.; *Folklore in the Old Testament*, 1918. Frazer's comparisons are not altogether without value, especially for tracing the historical-geographic movement of motifs.

comparisons. To carry out systematic analyses along such lines would, in any case, have required the efforts of more than one person. Even in regard to his own kind of comparison, Gunkel rightly believed that it would constitute work for several generations of scholars (1910a: 14).

To describe what is involved in comparative study one can adapt a term coined by Saussure. For transtemporal phenomena, Saussure used the expression 'panchronic' (see *RFT*). A more cautious term is 'multi-chronic' or 'transchronic', since no structures appear at 'all' times; for instance, Saussure's 'panchronic' phenomena are limited to what he calls 'language' (this becomes circular, for he probably would not call 'language' anything that lacks those phenomena). According to Saussure, panchronic features of language consist of relations, for all languages contain no single specific phenomenon in common.

That Gunkel was at least partially sensitive to the relational character of a transchronic reality was indicated by his expectation that the melody of the psalms described by him will be transposed by the reader into the present (1904a: vii). This anticipation was in line, perhaps consciously, with observations by E. Mach and by C. von Ehrenfels by 1890[151] that reality is constituted not so much by its particular parts but by the relations between these, a situation which they illustrated by the fact that a melody remains the same even when it is transposed, although then each of its parts changes. Gunkel did not attempt as an exegete, he said, to do the transposing of the melody with an application to the present (i.e. to address current issues); but it was his aim to get the psalms 'to have their say' (*zum Reden bringen*, 1904a: vii; 1926: vii), in other words, to bring to the fore their dynamic structure, which is transhistorical.

One important aspect of relational theory is the affirmation that an object apprehended resonates with the perceiving subject. Gunkel accepted this in believing that 'true understanding' comes only through 'love', or, more generally, through a 'personal relationship' with the material. He illustrated this by saying that only one who has an ear for music can well describe it (1904c: 15-16). As we have seen, Gunkel's approach to a text was not a detached one but one that involved hearing (through time), seeing (of associations) and caring (for human beings). His style of writing had accordingly—together with analytic sharpness—a deeply emotional tone.[152]

---

151. See *RFT*. These observations reverberated widely in German culture.

152. Gunkel's empathetic approach (like that of Dilthey [Klatt, 122]) attempted

Positive contributions along relational lines were thus provided by Gunkel's simultaneous attention to social situation, content (thought and feeling) and language (although he exaggerated the rigidity of their association and envisioned the social situation more externally than is appropriate), by his consideration of intrinsic connections between these phenomena, by his worldwide perspective (even though it was superficial by focusing on phenomena themselves) and by the explicit personal-social dimension of his scholarship.

b. *Gunkel's Place in History*
Gunkel's genius—as is true for most great contributors—lay not in an isolated creativity but in an ability to create a rich synthesis on the basis of communication, an awareness of a variety of disciplines and issues. He gave simultaneous attention to social life, human thought and emotion, and language. He valued both generality and particularity. He brought together concerns with factuality (to a moderate extent), aesthetics and religion. He wedded scholarship with a sense for human issues that transcended professional preoccupations. It is true, his reach towards integration exceeded his grasp, but that is always true with a high reach.

Not only did Gunkel learn from disciplines other than biblical study, but he also desired to contribute to them. Specifically, he expressed the hope that his commentary on Genesis would aid the 'historian of art' (i.e. of literature), the aesthetician, the folklorist, the practical theologian and the teacher of religion (1901a, preface). Indeed, as stated by Gunkel (1904b: 1109), the religiohistorical movement in general was interdisciplinary in character and received 'much more understanding [i.e. appreciation] among historians, philologists and philosophers than among theologians'. In subsequent decades, in fact, he had a direct and indirect impact on a variety of disciplines (as mentioned in Chapter 7), especially through his emphasis on *Sitz im Leben*.

Gunkel's most important contribution lay in the fact that he overtly characterized genres as trimodal, with reference to their life situation, content and linguistic form. This represented a synthesis, but Gunkel was apparently the first to present such a formulation explicitly.

Gunkel's major error lay in believing that the connection between the

to reach the other with its own view and condition (1911: x), but it was not objective in the sense of detached or cold.

three aspects is a tight one in oral life. This misconception was due largely to the fact that his grasp of the scholarly scene was incomplete. Certainly, no one is perfect in knowledge. Furthermore, sometimes he made an unlucky choice in the scholar he followed, especially so in Wundt who, despite his great contribution to psychology and anthropology, remained within a particularist framework.[153] Such failures in knowledge illustrate the wisdom of standing in communication in so far as possible. Nevertheless, one can point out that if Gunkel had not envisioned a tight connection between the aspects of a genre, he might never have furnished his trimodal formulation, which turned out to be heuristically important for biblical and other studies. Even isolation, supporting peculiar formations, can contribute to communication in the long run.

The fact that Gunkel's programme belonged intimately to his historical context is shown by the phenomenon that the Bible as Literature movement shared his basic vision,[154] as did Jewish and Catholic writers. In fact, in many ways, these interpretive traditions were superior in their approach to that of Gunkel, for they did not share a number of his misconceptions, especially that of his belief in the rule of simple forms and rigid genres in oral speech. A major reason for this difference appears to be that they were, on the whole, even better integrated into the emerging scholarly ethos. Indeed, some of their most important contributors were not biblical specialists, a fact which also accounts for the limitations of those movements in making advances in technical matters, so that they often do not seem 'scholarly'.

In subsequent English-language scholarship, as elsewhere in the world, Gunkel's work was often appreciated for its sensitivity to the text and to human life,[155] while his assumptions about original forms were rejected or ignored. In contrast, in German Protestantism a different path was taken. Gunkel's aesthetic and religiophenomenological

153. See *RFT* for Wundt's acceptance of 'associationism' in psychology and above for ways in which Gunkel was or may have been misled by him.

154. See above for programmatic formulations by Moulton and Kent earlier than those of Gunkel.

155. Appreciation began early. For instance, T.K. Cheyne dedicated to him a 1904 commentary on the psalms; he clearly valued Gunkel primarily for his religiohistorical orientation (in 1914, Cheyne published *The Reconciliation of Races and Religions*). Appreciation continued (thus, again, Geller [1996: vii-viii], unhappy about Gunkel's followers).

vision was largely rejected, but much of his questionable developmental scheme was accepted as an aid for continuing historicist investigations.[156]

A factor contributing to the situation in Germany appears to be the insularity of theology there. In fact, the German university is really a 'multiversity'.[157] That has some advantages but also definite disadvantages. Much academic energy has been expended on guarding distinctions between disciplines, although the major great figures have been able to transcend those boundaries, as Adolf Harnack observed in a critique of the ideology of fragmentation (1906: 163 [1901]). Klatt's inability to relate Gunkel to his context in an otherwise excellent biography of him itself represents an example of that insularity. Unaware of relevant works in other fields, he claimed that Gunkel created the 'genre- or literary-historical method' by himself (112).[158]

It is better to see that Gunkel stood with limited communication only in those of his assumptions about genres that were erroneous. The fact that Gunkel, as an individual, had limitations in knowledge is understandable, but that his misconceptions were not recognized as such by a long list of followers can be explained only on the basis of a tradition of isolation. This tradition was already much in effect during Gunkel's own day; it rejected his aesthetic and religiohistorical orientation.

Gunkel's lack of fit with his immediate discipline was in part due to the circumstance that he needed to shift from New Testament to Hebrew Bible studies, for reasons reported earlier. That this factor was conscious for him appears from a report by Baumgartner (1963: 6); according to this, Gunkel once said that he looked for a new approach since he lacked some of the traditional training for Hebrew Bible studies. In any case, the importance of Gunkel's contribution supports the observation that major advances often arise from an interaction of disciplines and that they are therefore not infrequently provided by persons who enter into a field from the outside (T. Kuhn, 1962: 89). In contrast, the isolation of a discipline leads—as has been said by later

156. Cf. Klatt, 13, and below, 12.3. and 13.2.a.

157. Observed also by Albright (1964: 11).

158. The studies that have been mentioned as background were the most prominent ones in their fields during Gunkel's time. Clearly, Klatt was unable to identify them. He should not be blamed as an individual for this failure, however, for it appears to be typical of his academic tradition.

German classicists[159]—to 'unfruitful learnedness'.

In short, Gunkel's life and work included both a broad perspective (although it had limitations) and a personal independence that allowed and impelled him to go against what was considered normal in his immediate surrounding. Those two aspects, it should be noted, are not contradictory but rather support each other, for the wider one's vision is the more readily one can be independent in relation to one's immediate setting, and vice versa. This situation shows again that individuality is not opposed to interaction.

159. *Unfruchtbare Gelehrsamkeit*—Hentschke and Muhlack (1972: 142).

Chapter 12

FORM IN PROTESTANT NEW TESTAMENT SCHOLARSHIP,
C. 1875–1965

The field of the New Testament is the one in which the term *Form-geschichte*, commonly translated 'form criticism', was first used. The procedures associated with that term are of sufficient general interest that not only New Testament scholars but also those focusing on the Hebrew Bible can find it worthwhile to give attention to the developments of formal studies in relation to the New Testament.

1. *A Movement Towards Form near the Turn of the Century (before 1915)*

The period from 1775 to 1875 had witnessed a remarkable break-through of historical criticism, during which concerns with form were secondary. It is true, observations about 'myths', 'legends' and 'poetry' were made in that time, but they stood largely in the service of a reconstruction of historical developments, and 'form' could be set in contrast with a more important 'content'.[1] By about 1875, historical criticism had reached its approximate limits both in terms of what it can achieve and in terms of what is useful to know for an understanding of the New Testament.[2] Thus, when a new intellectual ethos was emerging towards the end of the century, it was appropriate for Protestant New Testament scholars to turn their attention again to formal issues, although they would do so now in a somewhat new manner conditioned by historical criticism.

A motto for the new outlook was furnished in 1882 by Franz Overbeck: 'A literature has its history in its forms; thus every real

1. E.g. F. Lücke, in his hermeneutics cited, 1817 (main part): 13; D.F. Strauss, *Das Leben Jesu*, II, 1836: 736-42.
2. E.g. the Introduction by H. Holtzmann (1885) represents a state in historical criticism not very different from the one that still obtains even today.

history of literature will be a history of forms' (*Formengeschichte*, 423). This declaration was often quoted, presumably since it expressed an outlook that was becoming widespread. The specific background of the statement lay in the emerging interest in forms in classical studies.[3] As a church historian, Overbeck was struck by the fact that the literary forms of the New Testament are quite different from those of subsequent Christian literature (426-28).[4] He judged that the New Testament contained an 'originating' or 'primal literature' (*Urliteratur*) that was independent of the world—specifically, of its literary structures—and was influenced by previous forms of religious literature only (443). Much of it, in his opinion, was not true 'literature'; for instance, Paul's letters, which were occasional, represented a 'literary non-form' (431). The form of the gospel was a special one created by Christianity and soon again disappeared (432, 443). In manuscripts published posthumously in 1919, he clarified his notion of an originating literature, saying that an origin embodying the rise of a movement cannot be described historically by participants in it, for they would be rendering a history of their present, a virtual self-contradiction (1-28); the Christian primal period is therefore dark and should be left in that state—in contrast to what is attempted in both conservative and liberal theology (20).[5]

In 1886, Carl Weizsäcker[6] presented in a work on the 'Apostolic Age of the Christian Church' a brief sketch of themes that came to be prominent in twentieth-century form criticism. He said that the gospels

3.   Cf. above, 11.2.a, c, d. Nietzsche, a friend of Overbeck, was a classicist by profession and himself contributed to the interest in a history of genres. Church history, Overbeck's speciality, had numerous points of contact with classics.

4.   Overbeck was anti-theological but retained a religious or quasi-religious veneration for the New Testament. His view of the difference between New Testament and patristic literature was modified by H. Jordan in a work carrying out the programme of a history of literary forms (1911). Jordan showed definite continuities between the New Testament and later writings (within a number of literary categories) and pointed out that although 'worldly' forms increased in the latter, they did not displace more strictly religious ones, which continued (495).

5.   Similarly, Ferdinand Baur had described the time of Jesus (a more limited time than that to which Overbeck referred) as a 'primal period (*Urperiode*) which lies beyond the sphere of historical development' (*Vorlesungen über neutestamentliche Theologie*, 1864: 122) and thus had not treated it historically.

6.   His field was historical theology (not far from Overbeck's specialization) with a special focus on the New Testament. (ETs of some of his and of others' writings can be found in Kümmel 1972.)

were written for practical use and surmised that the traditions on which they were based had assumed fairly 'firm forms', since they 'needed to serve definite aims of the community', not merely personal memory (383-84). In the epistles he observed reflections of church worship, including liturgical formulas, doxologies and blessings (602-605). The notion that the Gospels were designed to evoke and support faith had been presented many times in the preceding period but had typically been subordinated to a reconstruction of the events to which the Gospels refer.[7] Now, the role of the literature became more strongly a theme in its own right. Noteworthy in Weizsäcker's presentation, and in many to follow were the phenomena that the focus was on the community more than on individuals and that the theme of conflict, which had ideologically been important previously, was not emphasized as strongly as had been done earlier.[8]

The New Testament scholar C.F.G. Heinrici provided literary analyses of New Testament writings in several studies, including an essay in a volume honouring Weizsäcker (1892) and a comprehensive overview (1908). He recognized elements of classical rhetoric in Paul's letters. Such features were not regarded as simply external, for the 'content' and 'form' of a letter under discussion were thought by him to correspond to one another (1887: 81, 573). He observed that the letters followed established patterns but did so elastically (1892: 330). For the Gospels, he noted both similarities and differences in relation to Hellenistic literary forms, such as apothegms (pointed sayings) and biographics, and also conformities with Israelite wisdom (1892: 329f.; 1900: 80; 1913: 6-9).

As Heinrici saw it, the basis for the origin of New Testament literature lay in the needs of missionary preaching (with stories about Jesus and proofs from prophecy) and the instruction of believers, such as the ordering of church life in a way that transcends national, social-status and sexual differences (1908: 25-27, 125). The various kinds of activity of the early Church were often carried out by persons with different

---

7.   A notable exception to the historiographic interest had been D.F. Strauss, *Christliche Glaubenslehre* (1840–41), outlining the meaning of Christian faith apart from a belief in the historicity of events in Jesus' life; this analysis, however, did not deal with the functions of traditions in the Church.

8.   Conflict, as noted above, 6.1, is a major bourgeois emphasis. It was a major theme in the work of F. Baur (in studies from 1831 to 1864), who thought of it as leading, in a Hegelian manner, to a higher synthesis.

roles: apostles, teachers, evangelists, prophets, organizational leaders, etc.; for a picture of these, he drew on the New Testament and on Eusebius, whose report of church roles had been discussed by him earlier.[9] The complementary activities, according to his analysis, led to different literary types, which each had a definite basic impetus and principle (1908: 100). The literature of the New Testament, in turn, informed the life of the Christian communities (25).

Since the literature served religious functions,[10] it should not be judged by aesthetic standards, according to Heinrici (1908: 125). In fact, he believed that the aesthetic quality was not very high (125-26).[11] Still, he acknowledged that, as expressions of piety, many New Testament writings have their own beauty—including power, clarity and vividness (126)—and that some of the letters are rhetorical masterpieces in a special way that partially deviates from standard Hellenistic forms (1892: 330). Like others with a fairly strong orientation towards church functions, Heinrici was reserved towards a religiohistorical approach that undercuts the absoluteness of Christianity (1901: 1); nevertheless, an important aspect of his contribution lay in pointing to the Hellenistic background of New Testament styles.

A member of the religiohistorical school, Johannes Weiss, presented equally important analyses of New Testament literature. They were somewhat stronger on the aesthetic side and a little less concerned with ecclesiastical organization. In addition to furnishing more limited studies from 1895 on, Weiss covered the New Testament comprehensively twice: first in regard to the tasks of scholarship (1908) and then in an important overview of the literature 'in its forms and according to the motives of its rise' (1912: 2175, in *RGG*). He stated that although a scholar orientated towards the general study of religion is interested primarily in basic human forms that are reflected in the New Testament, the task of the historian is to recognize its peculiar form (1908: 51). In regard to Jesus he held that the 'forms of his speech' were very clear

9.   Also, 1902: 48-50. Somewhat similarly already de Wette, in his 'Introduction' to the New Testament (4th edn, 1842, §61).

10.   A sign of his interest in function was his characterization of the aim of hermeneutics as that of understanding the text in the way in which it was (actually) understood by its intended audience, together with a recognition of the author's aim and means toward that end (1899: 723f., with reference to Boeckh for the generic aspect of this).

11.   He accepted as 'proof' of this a less-than-enthusiastic evaluation of Paul's letters by the sixteenth-century humanist Pietro Bembo.

and aided the preservation of his words (1908: 44; 1912: 2182). He believed that Jesus' speeches, especially his parables, exhibit high art; that artistry extends beyond purely external matters. Specifically, he recognized in Jesus' teaching not only a graphic quality and oft-praised realism but, very importantly, a strong presence of paradox, expressing a deeply religious life (1908: 46; 1912: 2177). The sayings of Jesus, in his view, were preserved orally in a community which had a 'life interest' in their preservation (1912: 2182); this community had already begun before the death of Jesus and predated a belief in his resurrection (1910: 3). Its tradition, together with narratives about Jesus (the character and growth of which described in some detail)[12] led to the formation of the Gospels, which served practical missionary and instructional purposes (1912: 2175, 2190). Paul's letters were in many ways 'real' letters—addressed to specific individuals and groups—but they also contained 'treatises' and reflected the style of a public speaker, standing close to the genre of the ancient diatribe (1908: 12; 1912: 2202-206). A noteworthy feature of Weiss's analysis was that the personal roles of individuals (especially of Jesus, Paul and Peter, 1912: 2186; cf. 1914) received attention along with community interests, so that a balance was struck between individuals and community.

An important history of New Testament literature was presented in 1912 by Paul Wendland. One of his contributions, from 1886 on, had been a discussion of the Stoic-Cynic diatribe and of reflections of it in Philo's work. His work had encouraged Heinrici, Weiss and Weiss's student R. Bultmann (in 1910) to give attention to the relation of Paul's letters to the form of the diatribe.[13] Himself building on analyses by others, Wendland held that the aim of the gospel tradition was not to present history as such but to awaken and strengthen faith (1912: 261), that the oral tradition of Jesus' words and deeds largely reflected Christian preaching (260), and that the stratum Q in the Gospels was intended to present norms for the life of the community (286, with Wernle 1899). In miracle stories and the Gospel of John he saw the

---

12. For example, Weiss included a discussion of miracle stories (for which the Greek and Jewish backgrounds had been treated by R. Reitzenstein, *Hellenistische Wundererzählungen* [1906], and P. Fiebig, *Jüdische Wundergeschichten des neutestamentlichen Zeitalters*, 1911 [the latter work was perhaps not known to Weiss]).

13. Cf. Moffatt 1911: 45-47; Stowers, 7-25. Pfleiderer (1902: 30) observed parallels with the Stoic Seneca in both thought and style.

form of 'aretalogies' (glorifying accounts,[14] 307, 310). Paul's letters, in his view, have a 'liturgical frame' (345). Wendland had a major interest in style, but the content of the literature also played a role in the analysis, so that style, function and content were examined together.

After taking account of the comprehensive overviews of New Testament literature by Heinrici, Weiss and Wendland, it is appropriate to give attention to treatments of special issues by others. A good number of these analyses were presupposed by the more comprehensive views just discussed.

One major issue revolved around **the uniqueness and timeless validity** of the New Testament. The notion that Christianity is historically peculiar but has a potential universality was advocated by Albrecht Ritschl, probably the leading German theologian in the latter portion of the nineteenth century, with an influence also on Overbeck (Emmelius, 143). Ritschl's view of the uniqueness of the Christian revelation can be understood as a form of particularism; for instance, it denied natural revelation, which had traditionally been accepted by Jews and Christians along with special revelation. Ritschl's notion did include a social aspect, namely, a commonality within those affected by the reign of God; he and his followers supported both the Church as an organization and moderate social service.[15] Thus one can describe his view as coming close to 'group particularism', one that accepts generality within the group but not across its boundary.[16] An outlook of this sort became widespread in Protestant New Testament studies, although it was not the only one current. Others were either more conservative or moved towards a more inclusive religiohistorical perspective. Adherents of the inclusive view as a rule supported democracy and even social democracy.[17]

Following Ritschl in many respects but placing more emphasis on the teaching of Jesus, Adolf Harnack believed that this teaching (regarding the fatherhood of God, with a call to love) embodied the 'essence of Christianity', which constitutes 'timeless' truth (1900: 10, 94). In a

14. Reitzenstein used that term in the work just cited (1906).

15. An ET of essays with a social orientation (quite mild) by two Ritschlians appeared in A. Harnack and W. Herrmann, *Essays on the Social Gospel* (1907).

16. Ritschl did not completely deny religious commonality, but he moved in that direction (cf., e.g., Mueller, 25). For Ritschl, universality of a faith was a future possibility (perhaps to be limited in extent, 1870–74, III: 118), not a present reality.

17. See above, 11.1.c, in connection with Gunkel.

manner resembling that of Overbeck, he described postbiblical Christian literature as having become 'worldly', specifically, Hellenistic (1886-90). He believed that Roman Catholicism became unduly intertwined with the world but that Luther stripped off this contamination. Indeed, Harnack was correct in seeing that the Catholic tradition has, on the whole, been more regularly involved in the world than much of Protestantism, which has often followed nominalist philosophy, separating faith from reason. Harnack, usually considered 'liberal', thus adopted a strongly Protestant line. Like others who emphasized the uniqueness of New Testament literature, he was not greatly interested in aesthetic or specifically literary aspects but stressed a content that remains the same within varying forms throughout time (1900: 9).

Stimulated by Overbeck (Emmelius, 227) but diverging from him, Adolf Deissmann presented a sociological view of the special character of New Testament writing. On the basis of newly discovered papyri and inscriptions, he concluded that those writings reflected a culture that was popular and directed towards immediate problems; thus they were to a large extent not literary, either in the sense of being elitist or in that of having been produced for repeated use.[18]

Many analyses pointed to a high degree of commonality in viewpoints and expressions within the Christian community. According to Alfred Seeberg, the New Testament presupposed an early Christian catechism, covering both faith and ethics as distinct but related aspects of it, with the use of standardized 'formulas' (1903). Somewhat similarly, but with extensive reference to traditions in the surrounding world, the classicist E. Norden (a Jewish-background student of Usener, whose work had an impact on Gunkel)[19] described standardized forms ('formulas') of Christian preaching and prayer as they are reflected in New Testament literature. He used for this analysis Overbeck's term *Formengeschichte* ('history of forms'; 1913: vii) and connected linguistic form with content or psychology (for example, Orientals are, according to this analysis, interested in divine 'being', while Greeks and Romans focus on action).[20] Vincent Stanton argued that

---

18. *Bibelstudien* (dedicated to Weizsäcker and Heinrici), 1895: 192, 207; *New Light on the New Testament*, 1907: 48, 64; *Das Christentum und die unteren Schichten*, 1908: 23 (this work makes clear his interest in social issues); etc.

19. See Cancik and Cancik-Lindemaier (58-59), and above, 11.2.a.

20. 1913: 222f. This conclusion is virtually opposite to one drawn by many others.

resemblances within New Testament literature can be due to the fact that narrators shared purposes and followed common models furnished by church leaders (1909).[21] More cautious theologically than many, Ernest Parsons rejected a universal validity of the Bible, but he pointed to a 'persistence' of situations, at least within the early Church (1914).[22]

Jewish and Hellenistic parallels were commonly treated as antecedents of New Testament forms, although Hellenistic religions were usually thought not to have affected the heart of Christian faith. Comparisons with religions farther away—which might have provided more purely structural parallels (or 'analogies')—were conspicuous by their absence.

This absence was not accidental. Harnack, for instance, had argued influentially against the inclusion of the general history of religion in the programme of theology faculties, in good part on the grounds that 'Christianity in its pure form is not one religion alongside others but religion as such' (1906: 172 [1901]). His argument, to be sure, stood oddly in tension with his observation that major advances in scholarship typically come from a 'fusion of disciplines' (163). He did envision the possibility that 'perhaps after long, long work we will come to a comparative study of religion', and he expressed the wish that every theology student become familiar with another religion, a wish not widely fulfilled (177).

There were indeed voices more open to other faiths. Thus, Benjamin Bacon said in 1903 that God 'hath not left us without a witness in any age or among any people' (4, following Acts 14: 17). O. Pfleiderer, who had dealt with the general history of religion in 1878, stated that 'Christianity did not fall from the sky as something completely (*schlechthin*) new or unique' but that it provided a 'creative synthesis' with 'a peculiar character and continuing value' (1903: 103a, 108). Gunkel argued similarly, in greater detail, that 'Christianity is a syncretistic religion' (1903). Nevertheless, none of these works, nor others religiohistorically orientated, presented comparisons for the New Testament that were wide enough to cover historically unconnected phenomena, as Gunkel did for the Hebrew Bible.[23] Thus the element of

---

21. *The Gospels as Historical Documents*, 133.

22. *A Historical Examination of Some Non-Marcan Elements in Luke*, 9, 13.

23. Similarities between Buddhist and early Christian stories—known for some time and discussed, for example, by Pfleiderer (1903: 23-29)—raised the question of possible historical connections. G.A. van den Bergh van Eysinga, *Indische*

generality, which is important for form criticism, was limited, especially since careful attention to general psychology and sociology was also missing.

A specific issue that arose again and again was **whether the gospels were 'biographies'**. This question often had strong ideological connotations. One of them was the recognition that first-century writers did not have an interest in individual personality at all like that embodied in 'modern'—especially, nineteenth-century—biographies, an interest which was receding again with a decrease in individualism. Another consideration reflected the argument of Ritschl (1874: 2f.) that Jesus can only be known through his 'effect' in the faith of the Christian community and that an attempt to construct a biography of Jesus in a critical historical manner, which is itself not without presuppositions, destroys his significance, as, according to Ritschl, the work of D.F. Strauss demonstrates.

Issues of this theoretical sort, as well as analyses by scholars who for more technical historical reasons despaired of writing a biography of Jesus, stood in the background of literary judgments that the Gospels did not present biographies of Jesus. Such an opinion was expressed by Heinrici (1892: 330; similarly, 1913: 6-9), Bacon (1910: 41), O. Bauernfeind (94), and C. Bouma (154), among others,[24] although they also pointed to similarities between the gospels and Hellenistic biographies.[25] This position, or any concerning 'the' genre of the Gospels, presupposes an Aristotelian or quasi-Aristotelian essentialism, which does not see that any classification depends on a definition constructed with some purpose in mind. In fact, essentialism came to be widespread in twentieth-century biblical literary analysis. C. Votaw, however, responded to the question as to whether Gospels were biographies with the answer, 'No or yes, according to the connotation given

Einflüsse auf evangelische Erzählungen (1904—the German edition acknowledged aid by Gunkel) envisioned India as the originating place; the reverse position was also argued, or the question was left open. For Weinel in 1920, see below. Comparisons can, of course, also show differences.

24. Cf. Holtzmann (1907: 26-27); J. Robinson (1957: 9); and Dormeyer (1989), for views since 1888 concerning the 'religious' rather than 'historical' interest of the Gospels. See above for Lagarde in 1877 and A. Eichhorn in 1898 and below for J. Robertson, A. Menzies, and so on.

25. Similar opinions had been voiced sometimes before then, although less strongly. Renan placed the Gospels among 'legendary biographies' (Burridge 1992: 4).

to the term "biography"' (1915: 49); he considered them biographies 'in a popular sense' (49).

A related question was **whether, or to what extent, the Gospels furnished 'myths'**. Over a long period of time, the word 'myth' had been used with several different, although overlapping, meanings. Certainly, this word, like any other natural one, has no single 'correct' meaning, contra the many scholars in New Testament and other studies who have spoken as though 'myth' has an essence.

Frequently recurring meanings for the term have been as follows: (1) stories as such; (2) unreliable or untrue stories, which may, however, resemble or represent ('imitate') truth; (3) stories providing a frame of reference, especially an origin (it was known widely in the ancient world that origin stories are often inaccurate historically, so that meanings 2 and 3 overlap); (4) stories dating from an early ('original') period of humanity (this usage represented a historicist shift which modified meaning 3 [cf. above, 6.3.a]); (5) stories about gods (believed by a number of nineteenth-century writers, especially by the Grimm brothers, to represent the earliest kind of narrative and thus to coalesce with meaning 4); (6) indirect ways of speaking about deity (overlapping with meaning 2 ['not true'] in regard to rejecting a literal description); (7) narration central for a cult (readily involving meanings 3 [furnishing a frame of reference] and 5 [narration about deity]).[26] It is clear, and was indeed long known, that the Gospels represent myth at least in senses 1 (stories), 3 (concerning the origin of salvation), 5 (about divine activity) and 7 (with a crucial relation to ritual).[27]

A number of writers, especially outside professional biblical academia, used the notion of 'myth' in arguing for the non-historicity of Jesus. Notable among them were the historian J. Robertson (from 1900

---

26. See above for myths or origin stories in the views of Plato, Theon, Philo, Origen, Hadrian (prophecy of past and future), Augustine, Maimonides, Moses ben Naḥman, Colet, Cajetan, Flacius (on primary causation), Teller, Heyne, A. Eichhorn, Gabler, G.L. Bauer, G. Meyer, Hays, Jahn, Fries, de Wette, D. Strauss, George, Ewald, W. Müller, Gunkel (1895, 1901a, etc.), Wundt, Bethe and Malinowski, and below for those of W.R. Smith, Stauffer, Dodd, Wilder, Mowinckel, B.W. Anderson, M.-L. Henry, Hooke, Childs, Graves and Patai and others. (Cf. Rogerson 1974: 175-78; Doty 1986 [as well as other recent general surveys]; Oden 1987: 40-91.)

27. The connection with ritual—a theme important to anthropologists and classicists at this time—was highlighted in W. Bousset's study of Christ as the focus of the Christian cult (*Kyrios Christos*, 1913: 247, etc.).

on) and the philosopher A. Drews (1909).[28] Both of them related the image of Jesus to pre-Christian cults as well as to Christian ritual. The historicity of Jesus was denied, further, by the New Testament scholar Bruno Bauer (in 1877) and by several other authors without using the term 'myth' as such, but often for similar reasons.[29]

These denials of historicity were based in good part on an interest in a collectivity as the bearer of a cult, rather than in an individual Jesus (Kalthoff 1903: 93, with a 'proletarian' orientation; Drews 1909: 178-81). Furthermore, as is appropriate in relation to a cultic structure, it was repeatedly insisted that the object of faith is not a 'past' figure (e.g. Kalthoff, 94). Indeed, although some of the rejections expressed primarily a radical historical criticism (e.g. B. Bauer, Robertson), others embodied an anti-historical mood.[30]

These studies received sufficiently wide attention that New Testament specialists repeatedly provided responses to them. The central issue was regularly stated in terms of whether the Gospel account is mythical or historical. Thus, the essentialist assumption that a story cannot be both historical (based on fact) and mythical (in its structure and role) was widely made by both advocates and opponents of a mythical view of Jesus.

One way to avoid the ambiguity of the word 'myth' is to use another word with a clearer definition. A. Menzies, a general historian of religion (in 1901),[31] and Bacon, following him (from 1906: 878 on), did so by employing the term 'aetiology' for an account that furnishes an origin or basis for a phenomenon, such as a ritual.[32] Bacon called his

28. In 1906, he had presented a version of Christianity without Jesus, describing history as the tragedy (with salvation) of God/humanity.

29. Denials had begun in the eighteenth century. (See Goguel [1925] for an overview.)

30. At least one (Couchoud 1924) was based on religious psychology (visions, etc.), which to some extent transcends history. Strenski (1987: 196-97) argues that major twentieth-century theories of myth reflect disenchantments with history due to dislocations.

31. According to Menzies (*The Earliest Gospel*, 1901: 20, 23), the tradition consisted of short pieces, except that parts of the Passion narrative had been formed prior to the written Gospels. (This view, which had considerable antecedents especially for its first part, became widespread in twentieth-century criticism.)

32. The word 'aetiology' was used widely during the nineteenth century to indicate a kind (or aspect) of myth. In biblical studies, aetiological myths were mentioned by Nöldeke (*Die alttestamentliche Literatur*, 1868: 10) and Gunkel

procedure the 'method of "pragmatic values"' (1909: ix; 1910: 41; etc.);[33] such values are not purely historical but relate to our time (1903: 3, 11). In Bacon's view, the Gospel accounts provided a basis or model not only for rituals but also for other aspects of the faith and experience of Christians; for instance, he thought that the story of Jesus' baptism (and call) reflected the experience of conversion by new Christians (1910: 55). He saw extensive connections, however, of the accounts with rituals, both Jewish and Christian (1911: 374-75, 379, 393-94; 1921: 7: 'the sacraments came first, the literature came afterwards'; etc.).[34] Already prior to him, Eichhorn had come to the conclusion that the story of the Last Supper was 'very strongly influenced by the cult and dogmatics of the earliest church' (1898: 25).

One fundamental question concerned **the extent to which it is possible and advisable to go beyond the texts** towards the reality to which they refer (e.g. Jesus) or towards earlier stages of their tradition. Both of these traditional historical moves continued. Thus Bacon declared, with reference to both German- and English-language studies prior to 1909, that 'the real interest in our time lies no longer in the exact apprehension of the sense the writers of 70–90 AD may have given to the evangelic tradition' (accepting their words as historical truth); rather, the point of interest is now 'at least a generation earlier. What was the event which gave rise to the story? Through what phases has the tradition passed to acquire its canonical forms?' (1909: vii). This historical orientation, however, was by then controversial.[35] Bacon's colleague Frank Porter accordingly envisioned a three-step movement in scholarship: A first stage was one in which 'the past as the book records it is imposed on the present as an external authority';

(1895: 23-24 [creation as an aetiological myth is similar to other aetiological myths and sagas in Genesis]). Whether Menzies and Bacon knew Gunkel's work is unclear, but Bacon said that he perhaps 'came naturally' to his approach because of his early specialization in Hebrew Bible studies until about 1896 (1910: 43; Harrisville 1976b: 2, 11, 135).

33. The term 'pragmatic', it is true, was not new; it has been used, for example, by Heinrich Paulus, *Philologisch-historischer Kommentar über die drey ersten Evangelien* (2nd edn, 1804, xiv). Bacon related the concept to philosophical pragmatism (1914: 119).

34. Also and especially for the Fourth Gospel, in a number of studies, from *An Introduction to the New Testament* (1900: 258-29, on).

35. Bacon himself moved beyond it in publications and teaching (cf., e.g., Wilder 1991: 59).

then, in 'the stage through which we are passing' now, 'science, and particularly historical science, brings forcible deliverance from that bondage, and teaches us to view the past as past'. For the future, however, he said this: 'Then should follow a further stage, at which, while the rights and achievements of historical criticism are freely accepted, the power that lives in the book itself is once more felt' through 'religious feeling and imagination', bringing 'enjoyment' (1909a: 276).

Porter's outlook resembled that of Kähler (and others) in his emphasizing the role of 'the living Christ' for faith (1893: 461). But it differed from that of many colleagues by **highlighting the role of 'literature'**, with reference to Aristotle, Longinus, Lowth, Arnold, Coleridge, Bushnell, etc. Although literature can be considered to be a partially humanistic category, Porter believed that 'wherever heights of religion are reached, there is beauty'.[36] Deviating from the nineteenth-century use of the term 'literary criticism' for historical criticism, Porter had this to say: 'Literary criticism, in distinction from historical criticism, is an attempt to answer the question, what gives a book permanent power'; an important answer is that 'great books are known to be great by their effects'—above all, 'ecstacy and wonder', as the author of *On the Sublime* had said. Such ecstacy arises 'not only by the greatness of its thought, but also by the passion which creates for thoughts wonderful words, especially words concrete and boldly figurative in character'.[37]

Thought, feeling, expression and life were, clearly, all crucial for Porter's conception of literature. This combination of them was similar to Gunkel's trimodal view of genres, although the aspect which Gunkel called 'life' was treated as an effect of literature rather than as its background. Furthermore, Porter emphasized that poetic truth is 'general' (cf. Aristotle) or 'universal' (1909b: 264; Bainton 1957: 221-25), so that his work contained also the element of generality important for form criticism.

Although Porter's statement referred to the 'book itself', a sense for

36. Unpublished MS cited in Harrisville (1976a: 15).

37. 1909b: 263. In early writings and mostly also later, Porter affirmed the importance of historical study even though 'truth' transcends 'facts'. (In some MSS Porter questioned whether the historicity of Jesus is necessary for Christian faith, but one must consider the possibility that the MSS were left unpublished because he was unsure of the adequacy of their contents.) Theologically, Porter attempted to find a path between the particularism of the Ritschlians, who focused on Jesus, and the opposite emphasis on generality and naturality that was common among investigators with a religiohistorical orientation (1893: 445-54; Harrisville 1976a: 66).

literary patterning can be applied not only to texts as they stand but also to a hypothetical text, such as a prior tradition. In other words, the advisability of a structural 'literary' approach is an issue different from that of whether attention should be given to the final form.

Literary or stylistic analysis was indeed applied to several different levels of the New Testament writings, although, it is true, not very often by German Protestants.[38] Friedrich Blass devoted, in 1896, a section of his grammar to the employment of traditional rhetorical 'figures' of style and thought in various parts of the New Testament. Hermann von Soden pointed to high literary art both in the Gospels and in hypothetical earlier versions of them (1904, 1905).[39] The study of Jesus' art (including the art of life) by the non-specialist O. Frommel (1906) reached back to Jesus himself. (The value of this study was acknowledged by Gunkel [see above] and also by Heinrici [1908: 126] and J. Weiss [1908: 45; 1912: 2215].)

In 1888, Jülicher had presented a formal analysis of the parables of Jesus. That was an important study, but its view (developing one-sidedly a point of view set forth previously)[40] that the parables have only one point, without any allegorical aspects, was challenged in 1903 by C. Bugge[41] and Wellhausen.[42] They pointed to the Israelite-Jewish tradition of the *mashal*, in which no precise line can be drawn between stories with a single point and those that have allegorical elements. The same point was made in greater detail by Paul Fiebig. He criticized

38. For the Anglo-American Bible as Literature movement, out of which Porter arose as a student of Harper, see above and also Morgan and Barton (1988: 228). French interpretation, standing within or near the Catholic Church, was then strong in literary study. E. Renan (at one time a candidate for the priesthood) observed the literary 'beauty' of the Gospels (*Histoire des origines du Christianisme*, IV, 1877: 198-217). Firmin Nicolardot (a non-Catholic or lay Catholic?) noted 'the play of dialogue' in Luke (*Les procédés de redaction des trois premiers évangelistes*, 1908: 147-62). A. Loisy examined rhythmic prose in the New Testament in 1921 (etc.).

39. *Die wichtigsten Fragen im Leben Jesu*, 1904: 7-8, 15; *Urchristliche Literaturgeschichte*, 1905 (ET 1906).

40. Jülicher acknowledged two antecedents from 1850 on (1899: 317); Baird (98, 188, 302) lists three still older ones, the earliest being by J. Turretin in 1728 (did these interpreters deny all allegorical aspects?).

41. *Hauptparablen Jesu*, 1903. (Bugge had been encouraged by Gunkel's work to present a 'historical-theological' interpretation rather than a traditional 'historical-critical' one [iv].)

42. *Evangelium Marci*, 1903: 30-31. Jülicher admitted in a review of this study that his analysis had been 'perhaps somewhat one-sided' (*TLZ* 1904: 260).

Jülicher's rejection of 'mixed forms' on the basis of the appearance of such in rabbinic tradition and commented that 'life does not work according to pure schemes'[43]—in effect, countering Gunkel's notion of pure genres, which may well have been inspired by Jülicher, to whom, as we have seen, he acknowledged methodological indebtedness.

Heinrich Weinel, an early student of Gunkel, concerned himself with the poetic qualities of the teaching of Jesus by taking poetry in a profound sense. He pointed out that poets and dramatists deal with the 'great issues of life' (1903: 14); thus, 'if we understand by "poet" someone who...can give life and soul to things, who has eyes to see what we ordinary people do not see and ears to hear what we do not understand, then Jesus was a poet' (1904: 64). Furthermore, there is 'art in saying what is seen in such a way that others see and hearts move'; Jesus' parables exhibit this (1912: xxv). Following an old tradition, he believed that prophet and poet go together in directing attention to the 'life of life' (1904: 64-65; cf. 1912: xxv). Jesus' use of images shows that he was not a (dry) teacher but like a prophet, with power (1900: 18).

Although Weinel was interested in the organized Church—attended by very few (mostly conservative in outlook, 1903: 25)—he had a perspective that went beyond it. He implied that prophets were not limited to Christianity (1904: 64-65) and explicitly acknowledged values in other religions.[44] Observing that the Church expects from its adherents a sacrifice of the intellect and is, furthermore, 'now the protector of the strong and the oppressor of the weak' (1903: 7, 58), he had sympathy with its critics. He noted that artists and Social Democrats repeatedly had a high regard for Jesus even when they were hostile to the church (1903: 13, 31; 1914: 164-65). Just as he did not believe that Jesus was committed to a particular 'confession', he was politically critical of 'superpatriots' (1912: xvi). In short, he was clearly against group chauvinism.[45]

43. *Altjüdische Gleichnisse und die Gleichnisse Jesu*, 1904: 163; *Die Gleichnisreden Jesu*, 1912: 132.

44. Weinel placed Buddhism on a level of religious evolution equivalent to that of Christianity, although he clearly preferred Christianity; Judaism, Islam, Confucianism and Taoism received lesser acknowledgment (1920: 63-79; 1904: 71-72). Eventually, when he became a systematic theologian, he spoke of the 'morphology of religions' (1928: 5).

45. In 1932, before Hitler took full power, Weinel criticized antisemitism and anticipated that some persons would stand firm in the face of persecution by the

Accordingly, in opposition to 'modern orthodox' theologians who in his opinion exaggerated skepticism about Jesus in order to force congruence with apostolic faith (1903: 19), Weinel was ready to reconstruct the words of Jesus. For this procedure, he recognized that it is not valid to look for 'the smoothest, shortest and clearest text' (1904: 35). In this recognition he went counter to Gunkel's notion of pure oral genres; it is likely, however, that Weinel did not consciously oppose that idea, for he wrote prior to Gunkel's sharp formulation of it in 1906. Thus Weinel exhibited some of Gunkel's strength (especially aesthetics) while avoiding one of his weaknesses.

According to the definition of 'form criticism' accepted in the present study, only analyses that place forms of expression in relation to thought and life and that do so with a concern for generality fall under that rubric. Not all of the studies were sufficiently well-rounded to meet that standard. A good number of them, however, came close to fulfilling it.

The more well-rounded analyses resembled—often consciously[46]— the approach of Aristotle, who had welded together observations about different aspects of speech: context (problem and purpose), content and (with caution) style, each with attention to generality. A problem associated with this revival of Aristotle's perspective was that, repeatedly, it led to an essentialism in regard to genres, sometimes more rigid than Aristotle's.[47] Many of the stronger analyses, however, did allow for flexibility.

2. *The Situation after World War I*

a. *Sociocultural Conditions*
Soon after World War I, 'dialogical' and language-orientated versions

Nazis (in Klotz, I: 129, 134). Thereafter still, although excessively irenic in manner toward National Socialism—'one has to go along', he said (reported by K.L. Schmidt 1933a: 347); 'peace' is needed in the Church (1934: 172)—he supported democracy at least by implication, declared a readiness to make himself politically suspect, objected to state pressure toward creating a national Church and expressed the worry that active roles for women would be curtailed by a reorganization of the Church as that was already being done in the political realm (1933: 42, 60, 64-65, 81).

46. For example, Jordan made express references to Aristotle's view of form as an integrative structure (1911: 6).

47. Aristotle's analysis of genres was actually fairly open.

of relational thought emerged, developed largely by Jewish (or Jewish-background) thinkers, including Rosenzweig, Buber, Cassirer, Rosenstock-Huessy and Heschel, and by the Catholic Ebner.[48] This line had an attraction also for Protestant theologians, even if only as a subsidiary one.[49] Protestant thought, however, especially in Germany, remained heavily particularist, not by denying all generality (which would be difficult to do) but by giving priority to the particular.[50]

A reason for the continuation of, or reversion to, particularism in the German cultural context probably lay in the crisis atmosphere that prevailed there after World War I, for anxiety engendered by a crisis commonly leads to a narrowing of vision.[51] It is true, the crisis situation also opened eyes, namely, to the reality of evil, not sufficiently acknowledged by theologians prior to World War I (although world pessimism—including an emphasis on a world-ending eschatology in the New Testament—had begun before 1900).[52] Unfortunately, the crisis, with its sense of evil, contributed to further evil, above all, in Nazism. Thus the period of 1918–45 was a dark one in a number of ways.

With the new social sense arising near the turn of the century, particularity was readily taken as communal; that is, sharing was stressed within the circle, but commonality with others was denied or sharply downgraded. Such collective particularism, decrying both 'individualism' and 'cosmopolitanism' as false 'liberal' ideas,[53] was very widespread in Germany during the 1920s and the 1930s. The group

48. See *RFT* on these, in addition to references within the present volume.

49. Relational thought was especially strong in E. Brunner's theology. However, even he regarded God's reality as primarily particular, without an equal balance with commonality (1931: 19). Gogarten referred to a dialogical structure primarily in order to highlight 'opposition' or 'contrast', which is really only one of its aspects (1926: 36).

50. The nominalist-inclined Søren Kierkegaard was a hero.

51. The excessive nationalism in Germany, in fact, reflected an anxiety about the nation, which was still young (founded in 1871), now defeated and the recipient of an accusation of war guilt. Similarly, the excessive orientation toward the Church as an organization expressed an anxiety *vis-à-vis* the claims of other religions as well as against individualism.

52. See *RFT* and J. Weiss, *Die Predigt Jesu vom Reiche Gottes*, 1892.

53. See, for example, the very popular proto-Nazi A. Rosenberg, *Der Mythus des 20. Jahrhunderts* (1.2. 6, etc.), and P. Althaus, *Das Erlebnis der Kirche* (2nd edn, 1924: 5) (Althaus compared church consciousness with a national sense, so that it is not altogether surprising that he supported Nazism for a while).

highlighted could be the nation or the Church, or a combination of nation and Church. The last of these possibilities was stated especially sharply by E. Hirsch; he joined the exclusive truth of Christianity with the role of 'white ruler-peoples', led by Germany.[54]

Non-Christian particularism in politics lost the theoretical restraint which earlier versions (such as of Hobbes) had included, since it dropped the notion of universal (even though contingent) divine laws. The new version was called 'decisionism' by C. Schmitt (1922), who became the leading political theorist in Germany during the 1930s.[55] Theologians emphasizing 'decision' also omitted or downgraded the notion of universal laws.[56] Nihilism, a radical form of particularism fed by notations made by Nietzsche in his final (near-mad) years, was a part of the ensuing political madness. In any case, one must not assume monocausality in regard to Nazism. Along with severe antisemitism (Church- and folk-based), irrationalism played a role in its rise.[57]

b. *K. Barth*

When an outlook envisions an all-encompassing reality in which every-thing is unified, one has 'monism', or unitive universalism, a kind of particularism that recognizes only one reality.[58] A position approaching monism was taken by Karl Barth. As a student, he had learned from Gunkel that the Hebrew Bible has meaning, in other words, that it is not just a dead fact (Klatt, 77); thus he belongs in a sense to the circle of Gunkel's students. Barth's theory, in fact, provided a context in which many German post-Gunkel form critics moved, although they had either major or minor disagreements with it (see, for example, below, 13.2.b).

54. 1938: 22, 177-78. Hirsch allowed for generality, but only within the 'historical circle' of his time and place (4, 62; cf. Hirsch 1986: 50, 65, 81 [1936], 142 [1937]—contra Seebass 1974: 18).

55. C. Schmitt, who cited Hobbes as his own forerunner (32), believed that modern political theory adapted theological views in a secular form (without God). The larger antidemocratic, power-orientated, and 'nihilist' stream of decisionism (including Italian and French contributions) is sketched in Sontheimer (19, 327-30).

56. Gogarten spoke of 'decision' already in 1921, probably on the basis of a common background with C. Schmitt. It involved for him obedience to a 'finite' reality—apparently, Jesus—since only such obedience embodies an external com-mand, something that he valued! (1923: 39).

57. Goldhagen has appropriately pointed to a strong and pervasive anti-semitism, without denying other factors that shaped German actions (1996: 420).

58. Cf. above, 6.1.a, for Parmenides, Spinoza and Hegel in different degrees.

Barth, who continued Ritschl's particularism (although turning it into universalism), said that one can move only from the special to the general, not vice versa (1939: 679), and that, in fact, 'the general [humanity] exists for the sake of the special', God's confrontation in Jesus Christ, in which humanity finds its meaning and fulfillment (1942: 6).[59] These statements came in close conjunction with delineations of 'power' and 'sovereignty', themes important for nominalism. Barth was, however, careful to add in each case that one does arrive at the general; in other words, he included generality in his view, although as a subsidiary category.

Unlike Ritschl, Barth saw in the event of Jesus Christ the ground or primal history (*Urgeschichte*)[60] for the whole world, so that its significance is not limited to the historical stream within which it has a conscious impact. Accordingly, he spoke of Christ's comprehensive 'worldliness', *Weltlichkeit* (1924: 81, 84 [1920]), and criticized 'religion'—not 'other religions', but an equation of God's work with religiousness, including that of Christians.[61] For Barth, 'the revelation in Christ is not an "historical" event (in a limited sense) but the breakthrough of the power which *was* and *will be*' (1919: 75). He believed that all reality is focused on the event of Jesus Christ, which represents the fullness of time (1932: 119). Salvation history includes all other history (1940: 64). Although he could stress, especially for a number of years, the spatiotemporal singularity of the Christ event itself (1927:

59. Barth's giving 'priority to the particular' is well established (Cunningham, 70).

60. 1922: 5, 117; 1927: 43, 230 (with a reference to Overbeck, as in 1922: vii, 6, although 'primal history' had a different meaning for Barth); 1942: 6.

61. In 1919, he advocated 'universalism' against 'positive churchiness' (84, 90), supported human solidarity in contrast to the belief that one morality or religiousness has been supplanted by another (43) and spoke of a continuity which includes Moses, John the Baptist, Plato and socialists (46, 69); he rejected a 'fence' between Christians and others since a 'separated sanctuary is no sanctuary' (1924: 34 [1919]). In 1927, he said that 'absoluteness' is found not in Christianity but in revelation (250, allowing for revelatory truth outside the Bible; similarly, 1939: 360). That does not mean that he rejected the Church as such; in fact, in 1939, he described Christian 'religion' as 'true' by God's grace in the way that a sinner can be justified and sanctified (357-97). But he continued to believe in an invisible Church (231, 239) and held to the 'relativization also of Christian religion through divine revelation' (362f.), acknowledging parallels to Christian faith in Buddhism, Hinduism and elsewhere (230, 372-76). In 1955, he spoke of the Christ event as occurring whether it is recognized or not (119).

224; 1939: 13), he ended by describing the event more frequently as
one that occurs continually (1953: 829; 1955: 49, 119-25 [with reference to ritual actualizations in Barth's own early experience]).

In the early years after World War I, Barth differentiated sharply
between God and human beings,[62] but he came also to present strongly
a continuity between them, one based on divine reality and activity. All
of 'positive' (good) existence (1953: 867) was then viewed as being
patterned after God and Christ, according to what he called 'analogy' or
'similitude'[63] (1945: 207; etc.), with sexual relations, a universal human
structure, as a prime example (1951: 138, 143, 158). Barth's position,
accordingly, resembled Platonism,[64] except for the fact that the model
determining reality, Jesus Christ, has a dynamic—in some sense
'historical'—character (he rejected 'timeless' truth only in the sense
that for him the all-encompassing action of God involves time (1945:
64]). Since Plato's conception of forms as models represented a philosophical adaptation of religious thought, this partial congruence is not
altogether surprising.

Barth's view came close to monism, since he saw in evil something
that is not (*das Nichtige*, the null or nulling [e.g. 1919: 59; 1955: 250,
529]).[65] He did avoid a thoroughgoing monism by incorporating relational elements into his perspective. Central for his conception, for
example, was God's 'word', one to which human beings answer. This
relation, however, is a one-sided one. Although the human response
was called 'voluntary' or 'free' (1953: 112, 859), it was also described
as standing in awe before God's power (112). A legitimate human word
towards God was always seen as secondary, as a response; it thus provides no real tension or partnership. Furthermore, Barth said that God

62. In this sense, he was not monistic at that time (cf. W. Lowe 1993: 44).

63. He played with the literary term *Gleichnis*, 'parable', 'similitude' (1950: 57;
1953: 222, 860, 863, 867). Barth rejected an 'analogy of being', fearing that it provides a road from humanity to God, but he accepted an 'analogy of faith' (cf.
McCormack 1995).

64. Platonist characteristics of Barth's views, both early and late, have been
noted also by Balthasar (119—for 1940) and Fisher (273—for 1910). Barth (1919:
60) accepted the 'final words' (deepest truth) of Platonism; of course, he was not
fully Platonist.

65. A monistic tendency is implied also in the universal-particularist interpretation of Barth by Hunsinger, who rightly points out that Barth has repeatedly been
described as (close to) monist (14). For an express struggle with an approach to,
without arrival at, monism, see Barth 1942: 139-57.

has decided from eternity to 'want' to be with humanity but does not 'need' it (1940: 307; 1953: 824—differently in regard to need, Heschel 1962: 235).[66]

Barth's system indeed treated as fundamental the authority of God. That is understandable, for an appeal to authority constitutes a major option within particularist ontology as an alternative to chaos, which threatens within that ontology. (In fact, authoritarian or irrational fideism and scepticism have long gone together; thus, Barth's outlook has a certain affinity with irrational forms of postmodernism.[67])

Barth shared the appeal to authority with National Socialism, which constituted a rival to the Church when it came to power early in 1933.[68] Closely related to this commonality with his opponent was the fact that Barth's rejection of natural theology (similar to Ritschl's) implied that he rejected natural law, as had been done by the German 'historical school' of law, which began in the nineteenth century and was followed by the Nazis.[69] In fact, one can argue, contra Barth, that opposition to Hitler could have been stronger with an adequate theory of natural law;

66. Barth's very early view (before World War I) held to a correlation between God and humanity (H. Frei has called that view 'relationalism' [shortened to 'relationism' by Fisher: 182]; see *RFT* for 'correlation' in the thought of Cohen, about whom the young Barth was enthusiastic [Fisher, 2], and of Ebner). Subsequently, Barth—not unlike fourth-century Christian theologians—placed relations primarily within God, so that the roles of the three 'Persons' (personas) in relation to the world—Creator, Redeemer, Inspirer—are secondary, an 'overflow' (1940: 307). In such a perspective God has no needs (as was already held by Greek thinkers cited by Heschel). Differently, E. Brunner (1938: 33) regarded a relation to humanity as intrinsic to God, and a number of later theologians (including, in good part, K. Rahner) have done so, carrying through with a relational view more fully [E. Johnson 1992: 225, 231; T. Peters 1993: 81-187]).

67. See *RFT* on Lyotard (although Barth's universalism makes a major difference); Ward (1995); I. Andrews (1996).

68. The structural similarity between Nazism and Barthian theology, with an emphasis on imposed authority, was seen by Friedrich (1933: 1045); Mulert (1936: 165); and by the Swiss correspondent Arthur Frey, *Der Kampf der evangelischen Kirche in Deutschland* (1937). Barth, however, did not support human authoritarianism to the extent that this was done by F. Gogarten, *Wider die Ächtung der Autorität* (1930).

69. Torrance (1990: 147), however, is right in the observation that Barth opposed only an *independent* natural theology. In fact, Barth thought that 'natural theology', however problematic, is inevitable, for Christians are always 'citizens' (1940: 157).

those Christians who supported Hitler relied heavily on the theme of national peculiarity rather than on more general human ethics.[70]

Barth's inclusive tendency, to be sure, provided a basis for granting value to all human beings, not only to church members. Thus he was (at least for a while) a Social Democrat. When he returned to his native Switzerland, after being ousted from a German university in 1935, he became an active and open opponent of Nazism, although he was, especially at first, weak in championing the cause of Jews.[71]

Barth's monism was especially pronounced in his theory of Scripture. He insisted on the 'unity' of the whole Bible, which consists in its testifying to 'one thing' (1939: 537), the super-event of Jesus Christ. He considered that focus to be so strong that he thought that the whole of the biblical message can theoretically be found in any single part. In practice, 'an interpretation is adequate to the extent that it...at least implicitly also interprets all other texts' (537). This image of a cohesion is reminiscent of early Jewish and Christian interpretations but appears to be even more monolithic. Furthermore, he said that the Bible is 'the necessary form of [the revelational] content' (545); less strongly unifying would have been a judgment that the form is an 'appropriate' one.

Barth published exegeses of Paul's letter to the Romans (1919, 1922), lectured on the Gospel of John (1925/26 and 1933) and dealt with many biblical passages in his 'Dogmatics'. In all of these instances, he gave only cursory attention to the specific historical background of the text, since he wanted 'to see *through* the historical to the spirit of the Bible, which is the eternal spirit', for 'what was once serious is still so now, and what is today serious and not just an accident and whim stands in a direct connection with that which was once serious' (1919: v).

The declaration just cited expressed a desire, comparable to Gunkel's, to go beyond what is merely accidental. It did not harmonize, however, with the relational idea that not ideas in themselves but their relations to a context, which thus need to be investigated, are

70. Barth thought, at least at one time, that an acceptance of natural theology played into the hands of Nazism (e.g. Barth 1956: 69 [1937]); but a rejection of natural law may have constituted an even more serious problem, in that it undermined a social ethics and led to Barth's counselling against cooperating with non-Christians in political activity (e.g. 73-74 [1937]; Barr 1993: 10-11).

71. See Barth 1956: 34, 59, 64-65; Busch, 260-61, 274-87, 331; Süss (on Barth's slowness in this regard, relative to Bonhoeffer).

transchronically significant. A low interest in relationality appeared also in the fact that Barth's exegesis lacked structural analyses; in other words, relations within the text were also not carefully pursued.

Nevertheless, as has been seen, the concept of form was not entirely missing. At one point, Barth said that the divine 'form'—which he identified with God's inner 'relations' and which, he said, is determined by the divine 'content'—is *'einleuchtend...überzeugend'* ('providing light [= making sense]...persuasive'); it radiates joy and is beautiful (1940: 745-46). By granting to form, supporting insight, at least a subsidiary status, he indicated that divine authority is not purely arbitrary.[72]

This inclusive view should have allowed Barth to make free use of the human sciences; however, his nominalist outlook worked against his doing so. Especially his followers, who were often particularist in a less inclusive way, largely steered clear of anthropology and comparative religion. It is true, the evil that was rampant in Germany during the Nazi period justified, in a sense, a withdrawal from the 'secular' world. Still, one can point out that withdrawal also does not permit active social opposition.

c. *W. Temple*

A position rather different from Barth's was set forth by William Temple (five years his elder). Temple repudiated a distinction between the spheres of natural knowledge and revelation (1934: 16, etc.). 'Only if God is revealed in the rising of the sun in the sky' and 'in the history of Syrians and Philistines [cf. Amos 9.7]', he said, can God be revealed in Israel and in the rising of Jesus (306). In line with this idea, he accepted for theology the importance of 'psychology, anthropology and the comparative study of religions' and of 'reason' generally (15, 355, 396). He rejected an 'external' authority that does not reside in the nature of reality (355).

Although Temple recognized that the 'modern' era was drawing to a close (404), he continued an Idealist emphasis on mind as ultimate. He pointed, however, to the 'avowedly materialist' character of Christianity (478) and saw 'a kinship between mind and the world' (130). Politically, for several decades from near the beginning of the century on, he participated actively and thoughtfully in efforts toward providing social justice, nationally and internationally (Suggate). Under the guidance of

---

72. In fact, in 1919 he had stated that '"eternal truths of reason" for all' appear in faith (63).

his wife Frances Temple, his social orientation included support for women's roles in the Church (Iremonger, 257-58, 304-306, 452).

There is no information about any interaction between Temple and Gunkel (19 years older), but Temple's theology would have been much more congenial to Gunkel than was Barth's. Furthermore, his theology fitted closely the outlook of a number of subsequent form critics, especially outside Germany, whether or not it was known by them. Indeed, if it is the genius of form criticism to relate language, thought and life to each other and to do so with a general perspective, a broad interdisciplinary vision like his is virtually necessary.

3. *Gunkel's New Testament Students*

Gunkel's New Testament students M. Dibelius, K.L. Schmidt, R. Bultmann and E. Stauffer did not have Gunkel as their primary teacher; after all, he had been transferred early to Hebrew Bible studies. However, they were impressed by him in part because of the force of his ideas (and person) and, perhaps more importantly, because of the way his ideas fitted predilections current among those who adopted them.

That the disposition of the recipients was important becomes apparent when one notes which of Gunkel's ideas were accepted by them and which were not. His followers rejected for the most part his aesthetics and his general orientation towards religion, neither of which fitted the particularist temper of contemporary German Protestant theology. They adopted, however, his belief that ancient oral culture was collectivist and highly structured so that it took shape in 'pure' genres. The fact that this image of oral life went contrary to professional research in the relevant disciplines during the preceding 100 years was ignored.[73] Evidence that popular culture was not created by people en masse had, in fact, been available since about 1825 and had moved New Testament scholarship thereafter away from a concern with oral tradition as the background of the Gospels.[74] A focus on oral shaping, however, was

---

73. Gunkel was aware of some of that research (see above, 11.2.d, for him and Ewald). Gerhard Kittel reported in 1926 the situation in folklore studies, but his report was not heeded (see Riesner 1981: 13, following Güttgemanns 1970: 130). It is worth noting that the study by Jolles of 'simple forms' (1930) did not claim that they were 'pure' in oral tradition; in fact, R. Petsch, reviewing Jolles in 1932 (both of them were cited by M. Dibelius 1933: 6), spoke of a gradual differentiation together with an interaction of forms.

74. See C.H. Weisse, *Die evangelische Geschichte*, I, 1838: 11.

revived in the twentieth century in biblical studies, since it fitted an appreciation for lowly persons and a desire to transcend individualism.

While Gunkel's students rejected individualism even more than Gunkel himself did, they were, nevertheless, reluctant to abandon particularism. Rather—sharpening a pre-existing line—they moved the focus on particularity from the individual to the group (in this case, the Christian Church), giving little attention to larger, including international, cultural phenomena. This move paralleled what was happening in German society after World War I, reaching a climax in 'National Socialism'.

The move they made created an intellectual oddity that was called *Formgeschichte*, 'form-history'. This procedure adopted the new interest in 'form' that was then emerging but it made engagement with form subservient to history in its older nominalist sense. From the point of view of the history of scholarship, this constituted a regrettably mixed-up process, for the newer method adopted was not suitable for answering diachronic questions. However, scholarship after 1915 was not limited entirely to that problematic programme.

a. *Dibelius*

Martin Dibelius coined[75] the term *Formgeschichte*, 'form-history', in 1919 by shortening the word *Formengeschichte*, 'history of forms', which had been used by Overbeck and E. Norden. This modification reflected the fact that Dibelius sought not so much a history *of* forms as a history *based on* form, a form-derived history.

Contra Overbeck and Norden, who had focused on written literature, Dibelius believed that a form-historical programme[76] was especially appropriate for oral productions, since they are governed by 'firm

75. The term had already been used in 1822 by a biologist under the influence of Goethe's 'morphology' (Breymayer, 1972: 64). It is not likely that Dibelius was aware of this work. However, Goethe's morphology, which included the notion of integral organic development, was influential in German literary scholarship after World War I—perhaps already enough so in 1919 as to make an impact on Dibelius (cf. his statement about a 'law' which expresses an 'organic' development, 1919: 5).

76. Dibelius's programme was remarkably like that formulated by J. Weiss, cited above, i.e. to study the literature 'in its forms and according to the motives of its rise' (Weiss 1912: 2175; Dibelius also used the term 'motive' for the genesis of the literature, 1919: 6). Dibelius, however, executed the programme somewhat differently—it appears, more questionably.

forms' related to 'practical needs' (1919: 1; 1926, I: 16). The oral forms were, in his view, sufficiently fixed to serve as the basis for a history that is 'anti-individualistic and sociological' (1929a: 188). Specifically, he defined *Formgeschichte* as the study of the 'laws which make the rise of these small genres understandable' (1919: 3).

Dibelius based a reconstruction of history on the assumption that the life situation of a genre can be deduced from its structure. This assumption is a reasonable one if the life situation is understood, with Boeckh, in terms of a purpose (e.g. to praise or exhort) rather than externally in terms of concrete arrangements, which are less integrally related to literary form. Indeed, Dibelius believed that genres, in their styles and selection of content, reflect their 'purposes' or 'interests', so that one can, for instance, 'recognize the purpose of the stories from their styles' (1919: 16; 1929a: 212; 1935: 37).

A history carried out according to this principle is neither diachronic (sequential) nor simply descriptive, but is of the kind that was championed by Dilthey: a structural analysis with the recognition of a goal. That is, in fact, close to the way Dibelius described Gunkel's procedure (1929b: 18). It is true, Gunkel also attempted, by drawing on information found in other texts (e.g. narratives), to get a picture of the external arrangements that are customary in a group for a given genre; Heinrici had followed a similar procedure. Dibelius, however, was not very interested in the external circumstances of the gospel literature and spoke instead simply of 'relations to life' (1926, I: 7), 'functions of the community' (1929a: 202), or 'conditions for life and life functions of the first Christian communities' (1933: 9); he characterized *Sitz im Leben* as 'significance...in the life of the people' (1932: 147).

If Dibelius had done no more than this, he would not have been at all controversial, for the general lines of such literary analysis had been laid down before World War I (although he failed to give explicit acknowledgment of that in 1919, probably assuming it to be clear to German scholarly readers). He took, however, a further step and proposed debatable diachronic theses. One assumption on which these were based was Gunkel's idea that early forms of the tradition exhibited relatively pure forms of a genre.[77]

One of the relatively new theses set forth by Dibelius was that the various kinds of gospel literature differed in age and had different

77. E.g. Dibelius 1919: 25-26, 30 (discussed by Haacker, 55). This thesis became stronger in 1933 (2nd edn).

reliabilities in reflecting the life and teaching of Jesus.[78] Specifically, Dibelius believed that materials used for preaching and teaching (i.e. for seeking and instructing converts, respectively)[79] were the oldest and the most reliable, while those showing joy in narration (especially, miracle stories) were secondary. Relatively late also, in his view, were mythical elements. (He did not count the oldest accounts of the resurrection as mythical, since they told only of circumstances surrounding it, such as the discovery of an empty tomb.) He believed that this line of analysis shows that it is possible to reconstruct some features of the historical Jesus and that his figure was not grounded in myth even though it was taken up into a myth functioning in ritual (82-86, 95).

A ground for this developmental scheme lay in the assumption, resembling that of Harnack, that faith (believed to lie at the heart of the gospel) is not worldly.[80] Dibelius took joy in narration or, more generally, a profane character of stories as evidence for their lateness (42, 53). An important aspect of this view—no doubt deliberately ironic in relation to more traditional beliefs—was that the miraculous elements of the tradition were held to be relatively worldly.[81]

Thus the movement exhibited in the rise of gospel genres represented for Dibelius a transition from a 'world-foreign' faith to a 'worldly' existence (1919: 94, 100; 1926, I: 9, 28, 31; II: 107). He did not lament this transition, however, but connected it with a need for faith to become involved in the world both evangelistically and ethically (1925: 108; 1929b: 34; 1933: 301).

In regard to aesthetics, Dibelius held that the earliest believers were 'unliterary', following 'not a drive for artistic formation but the

78. However, he said in regard to traditions incorporated into the book of Acts that an assignment to a literary genre does not imply a judgment about historicity (in H. Schmidt 1923: 49).

79. A difference between 'preaching' and 'teaching', important for Dibelius, had been discussed by Heinrici, Wernle (followed by Wendland, among others) and Seeberg.

80. Harnack had bemoaned Christianity's involvement in the 'world' (specifically, in Hellenism, although he also rejected the Hebrew Bible) but had valued positively an evangelistic outreach and, for his own day, a social concern. Dibelius viewed the process of Hellenization a little more positively as a symbolic and (for its time) necessary aspect of an outreach.

81. The Catholic P. Benoit argued, more appropriately, that an interest in enjoyable and detailed narration is old (1946: 494). The antiquity of miracle stories has been well defended in recent years.

pressure of their life' (1919: 4, 15). Obviously, he assumed that life does not 'press' for art. Dibelius recognized no 'artistic aim' in short sayings and anecdotes of the Synoptic tradition (95), apparently because he identified art with elaborate or elite formulations, which he mentioned explicitly in 1926, I: 6.[82] (A. Deissmann also used the word 'unliterary', but he meant by this for the most part 'unlettered' and 'not artificial' rather than 'inartistic'.) Although Dibelius saw that Jesus' parables reflect features of 'folk poetry' (1919: 98), in his view 'the creative piety of original Christianity knew no values of this world, also no literary ones' (1926, I: 8).

Dibelius's reserve towards the art of literature is somewhat surprising in the light of his personal history. He reported having had an interest in theatre and literature during his early student days and that, at a teachers' seminar for women, he had chosen to teach German along with Religion, since issues of faith and life would be best understood in the light of their representation in literature (1929b: 5, 17-19).[83] To this autobiographical report, however, he added the telling observation that form criticism, from Gunkel on, stood under 'suspicion' by 'the older generation' that it is a 'praiseworthy but basically superfluous study of externals that diverts attention from what matters', an 'idle play of aesthetes' (1929b: 18). This was an old Protestant theme. In response to this hostility in his context, Dibelius defended attention to art and style only as a means to an end; he declared that his aim is an 'understanding of the content, not aesthetic enjoyment' (1929b: 18; similarly, 1926, I: 5).

In rejecting aesthetics, Dibelius joined a chorus emanating from Gunkel's students within a period of a few years. Bultmann had declared (1925a: 317) that the study of genres serves 'not aesthetics but the study of history'. Dibelius soon made the same point more explicitly: 'My fellow workers and I are not concerned with aesthetic appreciation but with understanding the process that led to the production of the gospels' (1927: 170). K.L. Schmidt, one of these 'fellow workers', said that style is not 'an aesthetic *Liebhaberei* [something one playfully loves to engage in], but a sociological fact' (1928: 639; the same words were used again by Dibelius 1933: 7). In an overview of form-critical

---

82. He knew that popular literature, too, is aesthetic (1929a: 188), but this recognition made an impact neither in 1919 nor in the second edition of this in 1933, which in some cases toned down the aesthetic element even further.

83. He even published in that area (1929b: 21).

studies (1929a), Dibelius warned against confusing this way with an aesthetic one, although the latter can serve as an 'additional' approach (188), and criticized P. Fiebig for presenting an aesthetic view of the narrative style of the Gospels (187). Fiebig, in response, sought to extricate himself from this (horrible?) charge by saying that Dibelius had 'misunderstood' him; he continued, however, to assert that form and content go closely together.[84] Bultmann stated again (1931: 4-5) that 'genre' or 'form' is 'a sociological, not an aesthetic concept', and criticized M. Albertz,[85] a student of Deissmann, for overemphasizing aesthetics.[86] (Soon thereafter, Fiebig and Albertz were quite active in the Confessing Church, as was the aesthetically orientated von Soden, mentioned earlier; thus their artistic sense was not contrary to an active engagement.[87])

Gunkel's students, in short, abandoned a major aspect of his approach by viewing aesthetics along superficial lines. One reason for the rejection appears to have been a reluctance to associate faith with joy and play, as is indicated by the references to enjoyment and of what one 'loves to do'. Another reason was probably a desire to avoid a perspective that is not limited to Christianity. Indeed, Dibelius saw that an aesthetic approach, if it is to be scholarly, needs to consider the forms of other religious literatures (1929a: 188).

In 1941 (*Why Theology?*), Dibelius returned to the issue in a somewhat complex manner. Within a fictional dialogue a young man says, 'Yesterday I read Faust [by Goethe]' (5). Although he expresses caution by adding that 'Faust is not pure poetry but a world-view poem', he goes on to declare that 'theology was, in the ancient world, the speaking of God as it was done by poets'. In Christianity, he observes, theology was done by the teacher rather than by the poet, although repeatedly there were those who emphasized that all speaking of God is inadequate and must be understood to be metaphorical (11).

---

84. *Rabbinische Formgeschichte und Geschichtlichkeit Jesu*, 1931: 6, 23-24.

85. Martin Albertz, *Die synoptischen Streitgespräche*, was largely completed by 1918 but not published until 1921, in time to include some references to Dibelius (1919); it used the unabbreviated term *Formengeschichte* and observed artistic strength (as well as some weakness along that line), together with practical (e.g. apologetic) aspects (80, 100, 109-10).

86. Somewhat later, Gadamer, who stood close to Bultmann, presented a less restrictive view of aesthetics, in which 'play' can have 'holy seriousness'.

87. See, for example, Fiebig's criticism of antisemitism in Klotz (1932: 29); Meier (III: 517); K. Herbert (232). For von Soden, cf. below, 13.1.a.

A profound view of poetry is thus acknowledged cautiously.

Dibelius did stand somewhat close to Gunkel in his transchronic (or transcultural) orientation. This orientation included attention to the intrinsic connection between data, for associations that are inherent are likely to appear more than once. In an early work on the ark of the covenant, which was suggested to him by Gunkel, he followed a 'religiohistorical procedure'; this, as he explained, seeks 'parallels', specifically, 'analogies' which 'have nothing to do with historical derivation' (1906: 60). Especially, he discussed phenomena of empty thrones, for example in India, without implying that there had been any historical derivation of one throne from another. His aim (as he later reported it) was to understand the connections between thrones and their uses; but he admitted that his limited knowledge of the societies in question meant that part of this work did not go beyond a collection of surface parallels (1929b: 13). For the genres of Synoptic literature, he sought to recognize 'laws' (1911: 4-6; 1919: 3; 1929a: 202), so that one can understand the 'reason' for their shape (1919: 27) and for their spread and development (1919: 5). Such laws imply intrinsic connections and at least a partial generality.

In 1931, he observed that 'a knowledge of cult formulas, songs and sayings of other religions of that time sharpens an observer's perception' of 'formal parallels' in the New Testament (1931: 211). The qualification 'of that time' may indicate that he referred to historically related traditions and not to more far-flung analogies. In 1941, however, he said in a more theoretical vein that, by his time in history, a knowledge of other religions has become highly appropriate for Christian theology (15). Previously, he had indicated that Christianity and Buddhism were then interacting with each other (1925: 105).

Dibelius did not himself engage in interreligious analysis, but he supported the ecumenical movement, which drew together Churches of different countries and cultures. He believed that the movement can aid 'reconciliation between nations' and can sharpen a sense for the Church's social mission (1930: 51-52). He gave it his support even though 'the young theologians' were initially inclined against it (in Gerstenmaier 1937: 193). Indeed, his international orientation stood in tension with a strong nationalism in Germany. At the same time, he said in regard to relations within a society that 'cooperation, even in a community of questionable composition…is always more Christian than a sanctimonious aloofness from the world' (1938: 42). In accord with this nationally and internationally irenic attitude, Dibelius appears to have written nothing either for or against National Socialism. This is a considerable feat, for in the years from 1933-41 he dealt repeatedly with social and political issues (often historically) in essays that were based on presentations both within Germany and abroad.[88]

In regard to social ethics, Dibelius pointed out that Christianity originated from the 'little people' (1925: 110). He acknowledged human equality, however, not on the basis of something positive expressed in natural law but on the negative ground of a common nothingness before God (169). He favoured Christian social service but not a world revolution based on an idea of 'general welfare' (1953: 203 [1934]). Still, he recognized in the ethical instructions of the book of James a 'certain international and interconfessional character' (1921, Introduction, 3). In regard to women's roles he was fairly liberal.[89]

Dibelius examined a number of New Testament literary forms (including parenesis, i.e. ethical instruction) and presented a fine comprehensive overview of early Christian literature in 1926. In this overview, he did not use the words 'form-history', which he had defined in H. Schmidt (1923: II, 27) as the study of small units lying behind the text. Instead, he called that work a 'history of literature', which presents 'Christianity's reaching form in its literary aspect' (1926, I: 5). Its programme was comparable to *Formengeschichte*, 'history of forms', according to the terminology of Overbeck and others, and stood on more solid ground than did the 'form-history', *Formgeschichte*, in which he had attempted to go speculatively beyond

88. This assessment reflects a perusal of most (but not quite all) of Dibelius's writings; he awaits a biography. Kümmel (1981: 726) reports that he was a democrat, that his passport was taken for a while in 1938 and that he gave support to women's roles (cf. below) Dibelius was the only one on his faculty who supported G. Dehn (another student of Gunkel [*TRE*, XIV: 298]) in 1931 against nationalistic students, but he also highlighted the involvement of Christians (including young theologians) in the war and compared the dynamics of Christianity with that of Nazism (1941: 77-78). The ecumenically minded Deissmann similarly played it safe politically.

89. Having earlier taught at a seminar for women teachers (Kümmel 1981: 726; cf. Gunkel's path), he directed (it seems) the dissertation of a woman, Grete Gillet, on the missionary character of Mark, completed in 1919 but not printed (Dormeyer, 84), and later supported women's participation in the pastorate (Kümmel 1949: 139).

the (largely legitimate) reconstructions that had already been made prior to World War I.

b. *K.L. Schmidt*

Karl Ludwig Schmidt—a student of Deissmann, besides taking at least one course with Gunkel—made several significant contributions before he was removed from his academic post by the Nazis. (His having a personality ready to fight [Cullmann 1956: 6]—as did Barth and, to some extent Bultmann—undoubtedly was a factor in his active opposition and consequent dismissal, perhaps more so than a specific theological position [contra Barth's claim that a certain kind of theology was crucial for opposition to Nazism; cf. below, 13.1.a].) In relation to gospel materials, he looked for 'analogies' rather than for 'genealogical' dependences upon other traditions (in H. Schmidt 1923, II: 75). The closest analogies he found were mediaeval and later Christian and Jewish ones (91-114). In his judgment, the lack of good classical parallels shows that Christianity 'did not, on the whole, enter into the world' (134). Later, in Switzerland, he dealt with questions of Church-state relations and with psychological dimensions of biblical literature, in conversation with Carl Gustav Jung (*Eranos-Jahrbuch* 1945–47 and 1950).

c. *Bultmann*

R. Bultmann recognized two tasks of what he called *Formgeschichte*. In relation to the gospels he characterized them as follows (1928: 418): one is 'to describe the literary character of the gospels as a whole' with regard to 'their position in the general history of literature'; this task properly belongs to a 'history of form(s)'.[90] The other is to reconstruct the antecedent history of the materials transmitted in the Gospels; it corresponds to the programme of 'form-history' as defined by Dibelius.

Bultmann saw that a history and analysis of forms, the first task, carries further a long tradition of interpretation. He pointed out that early and mediaeval Christian exegetes were concerned with biblical form primarily in the light of ancient rhetoric, that a sense for form was awakened by Herder, and that—after this interest was for a while overshadowed by historical criticism—it was renewed by Gunkel, Heinrici,

---

90. In Germanics, a little later, Böckmann (1949) and Prang (1968) used the term *Formgeschichte* in this sense, comparable to that of *Formengeschichte*, used by Overbeck and Norden (see *RFT* for Böckmann and Prang).

Deissmann, Norden, Wendland, J. Weiss and Dibelius (1929: 1682; cf. 1925a: 313). In his study of the diatribe, he referred in addition to Hadrian, Flacius, Glass, Wilke, Blass, Wilamowitz, König and a few others (1910: 1-2). Thus he clearly had in view the line discussed in the present volume (in so far as it was written in Greek, Latin or German). For this purpose, Bultmann did not distinguish in principle between oral and written literatures. He believed that both kinds have 'fairly firm forms' and that 'higher' individualistic literature, too, has forms and genres' (1925a: 317).[91]

The second task listed, that of reconstructive form history, was set forth on the basis of two assumptions. One of these was that the gospel materials consisted 'originally of individual pieces'; the other, that the history of these can be determined by examining their form (1928: 418). It is relevant to observe that both were problematic. For instance, the word 'original' (which appears in the first assumption) properly refers to a theological or philosophical rather than a historical category. It is true, 'original' can perhaps be defined as what was first said by Jesus or by a disciple in a manner resembling the surviving text. Yet Bultmann did not define it thus; rather, for him, the 'original' form can be older than Jesus, who may have presented a 'secondary' form by combining earlier materials (1921 ['History of the Synoptic Tradition']: 52). Without a limit in time, an 'origin' becomes ahistorical. (In practice, Bultmann regarded the origin of many traditions to be later than Jesus.) The imprecise use of the word 'origin' might be forgiven if it were not connected with a more serious problem, namely, Bultmann's questionable belief that earlier forms were regularly more simple than were later ones. Undoubtedly, in the very long-range history of humanity as it emerged from antecedent animal life, simpler (and less differentiated) forms of communication preceded the forms now known. However, such a long-range consideration is not relevant for a local history and especially not for a particular text.

Although Bultmann's search for originally simple forms resembled a similar one by Gunkel, a difference between them was expressed in the fact that Bultmann spoke of the *Sitz im Leben* of an individual text

91. For a non-theological model, he pointed to a history of the arts presented by J. Burckhart, *Weltgeschichtliche Betrachtungen* (1905: 69-80—1869 lectures), which gave a thumbnail sketch of the arts with their structural characteristics and relations to the society; he said that Burckhart's history shows that a form-historical analysis is appropriate not only for popular literature (1931: 5).

(1925a: 316), while for Gunkel a *Sitz im Leben* characterized a genre (in its hypothetical early purity). A reason for this difference may well lie in the fact that Bultmann was Gunkel's student in 1904/1905, at a time when Gunkel did not yet use the term *Sitz im Leben* but employed the term *Situation* to designate the location either of an individual text or of a genre. Although Bultmann was personally close to Gunkel in later years (Evang, 18, 71), he apparently did not take account of the development in conceptualization that went along with Gunkel's change in terminology.

It is true, Bultmann realized that the term *Sitz im Leben*, as coined by Gunkel, does not refer to a particular context, but to a 'general histori-cal situation' (1925a: 317), that is, to a 'typical situation or kind of behavior in the life of a community' (1931: 4 [in the 2nd edn of 1921, responding to discussion]; similarly, 1928: 418). The illustrations he furnished for that—war, harvest, cult, work and the hunt (1928: 18; 1931: 4)—are sufficiently universal to indicate that Bultmann had in mind general patterns of social life.[92] The abstract illustrations and his use of the phrase 'kind of behavior' show, furthermore, that he was not strongly interested in external aspects of the situation, which are rela-tively variable. However, by speaking of the *Sitz im Leben* of a text (as distinct from that of a genre), he related a (particular) text to a (general) kind of context, creating a mixture in conceptualization.

In contrast to Dibelius, who primarily pursued laws of formation that account for the basic structures of texts rather than for their change, Bultmann formulated 'laws of tradition' (1921: 3). He judged that they primarily involve expansion; in this belief he followed Herder, who had argued for the priority of Mark on the grounds of its greater simplicity (XIX: 391 [1797]). Incidentally, Bultmann did not consider the trans-mission of oral materials to be fundamentally different from the history of written ones.[93] On the contrary, he derived his laws of tradition largely from an examination of changes from Mark to the other Gospels.[94] He held, moreover, that the traditions lying behind the Gospels included written documents (1921: 24). Thus the goal of his

92. Of course, he also referred to the local forms of the Christian community, which yielded 'expressions of life' (1928: 420).

93. Seen rightly by Kelber (1983: 6).

94. The examination, however, was found wanting by Sanders (1969) and Key-lock (1975).

procedure is not accurately described as that of determining an 'oral prehistory'.

Bultmann's outlook, however, was strongly particularist. Just as philosophical nominalists seek the foundation of all reality in simple units, so he believed that gospel literature was derived from simple individual building blocks. In this he followed Wellhausen.[95] In fact, if 'form criticism' is thought to deal with individual small units, it is more in line with the historicism of Wellhausen than with Gunkel's theoretical conception, although it is true that Gunkel was also influenced by Wellhausen.[96] Bultmann's relative lack of interest in laws of form (in comparison with Dibelius) also reflects his strongly nominalist outlook.

Bultmann's nominalism had the consequence that he rejected essentialism, specifically the idea that a given unit is classified properly under only one heading. He recognized the possibility, and indeed value, of clear distinctions in theoretical construction, but he saw in actual reality a fluidity between types and a likelihood of mixtures and thus accepted the validity of multiple classification according to different considerations (1921: 107; 1925a: 317-18; 1931: 260-61). For instance, he could class a single story as a 'legend', as a 'dispute' and as a 'biographical apothegm'.

Bultmann, nevertheless, had an interest in generality that went beyond mere classification.[97] This was indicated by the way he used the term 'life-situation' (as has already been seen). Furthermore, a moderate interest in generality appeared in Bultmann's consideration of 'analogies' to the literature of the Gospels. He referred to both early and late European and Asian (including Buddhist and Muslim) parallels (1921: 21; 1928: 418f.). He accepted folkloristic parallels furnished by Baumgartner (1931, preface). The comparative materials, however, were treated as surface phenomena, not examined as dynamic equivalents (relationally parallel). The conclusion he reached about the genre of the Gospels was that it is unique (1921: 227-29).

Nominalism distinguishes reason (including what may be called 'culture') sharply from faith. Somewhat along this line, but in a nuanced way, Bultmann held that the relation between religion and

95. Wellhausen declared that the oral tradition of the Gospels contained 'only scattered material' (1905: 43).

96. See above, 11.1.a.

97. Classification is done also by particularists (as the designation 'nominalist' states) and represents part of what Piaget called 'concrete operation'.

culture—including aesthetics, ethics and 'science' (knowledge)—is a 'dialectic' one; that is, the two sides stand in a tension with each other.[98] Specifically, in 1920 he argued that religion and culture are fundamentally distinct, although they were at one time united, and stated that religion (including Christianity) has, in fact, often retarded the development not only of knowledge and art but also of law and ethics (1920a: 421). In his view, culture is basically general in character, based on 'necessity', while religion is what happens to the individual (421, 436). (A better relational perspective would make room for the two aspects in both culture and religion.)

In his dialectical view, Bultmann took dual positions (with both yes and no) in regard to the relation of religion to the three major aspects of culture. He acknowledged aesthetic values in popular literature—including the teaching of Jesus (1921: 52, 101)—but he refused to treat biblical form criticism as an aesthetic project. In regard to ethics, Bultmann held that love is integrally connected with faith but that it furnishes no ethical rules or principles, involving, rather, an encounter with one's neighbour in each moment.[99] With respect to history, Bultmann engaged in a continuation of historical criticism, but he believed that matters examined by historical study are 'only relative...part of a great relational complex', not 'absolute', as is faith (3, 5, 8 [cf. Jaspers and Bultmann 1954: 73]; similarly, 1948-53, Epilogue, 2). Thus he placed relationality (including relativity) within culture only.

Bultmann's dialectical (yes/no) view of ethics probably contributed to the fact that he defended the integrity of the Church but was largely—although not entirely—silent in matters of social critique, as

98. The term 'dialectic' was applied to the thought of several thinkers after World War I (including the early Barth and Gogarten).

99. 1926: 86f. [in his volume on Jesus]; 1933–65, I: 229-44 (1930); II: 59-78 (1940). He criticized 'kingdom-of-God work' and 'Christian socialism' (1933–65, I: 15 [1924]). Oral tradition has it that he voted (at an unstated time) Social Democratic (Evang, 78); that may be true, but why is there no indication in Bultmann's writings of this social view? (Rejection of the validity of asserting one's rights on the ground of justice, a rejection which he attributed to Jesus in 1936, is virtually the only reasonably concrete social principle mentioned by Bultmann. W. Kamlah ([1940: 36, 322]) used that principle, taken from Bultmann, to advocate individual self-surrender on behalf of a group; the group rather than the individual, he said, may and should assert itself—this group being, above all, the state [in the second edition of 1951, the reference to the state is dropped]).

were indeed most of his Christian compatriots.[100] His demythologizing programme—in the midst of war (1941)!—was, in fact, curiously unconnected with what was going on, especially in regard to its evil, unless the strong value it placed on modern thought implied acceptance of current processes.

In an essay directed to the World's Student Christian Federation, Bultmann cast doubt on the value of the literary study of the Bible (1960: 166-70 [1934]). A readiness to hear God's word in the Bible, he believed, leads by itself to an apprehension of it (167-68). Approaching the Bible as if it were an ordinary book diverts from hearing the divine speech (168). The reader, he said, 'has just as little time and reason to ponder over the *how* [of God's word] as has [a child] to submit the style of [its] father's words to theoretical examinations' (166). This assessment treats style as something unimportant, although it was based on a form-critical judgment, namely, that God's word in the Bible is 'in the form of God's address' and thus 'can only be listened to, not examined' (166). Bultmann's assessment clearly assumed that listening does not include examining. (Yet even a child can and needs to have at least an implicit theory about a parent's style, such as in distinguishing a

---

100. Bultmann defended the right of converted Jews to serve as pastors (1933b: 359-70), joined the Confessing Church and co-authored a statement opposing a radical wing of German Christianity in 1936. Beyond the Church, he criticized denunciations of Jews and others (1933a: 166, citing Hitler in support of such criticism), wrote a preface for a study by his Jewish student Jonas in 1934, and pointed out that national characteristics include not only virtues but also vices (1941a: 16); these steps went beyond what many others did, but he seems otherwise to have been silent in public on such issues. (The opinion of Lindemann [47] that Bultmann's exegesis on John 19.11 [1941b] denied statehood to the Nazi regime is probably in error; on the contrary, Bultmann's modification of this exegesis in a later edition was probably due to its having been too supportive of Nazism. In fact, Bultmann said in this work that 'the Jews' represent the devil's 'world' in the Gospel of John [242, 508]; if that is correct for John, a report of that view called for an express self-distancing of the interpreter from it or—if the intent is to give an interpretive twist to it—for an abstract rephrasing of it [e.g. as a critique of 'religious authorities' or of 'the local community'], neither of which was done by Bultmann in this existentialist, not just factual, commentary.) His later autobiographical reflections were oddly reserved in mentioning the greatest evils of Nazism (as noted by Adam, 207). See below for his religious exclusivism, as well as for his apparently learning from the Jew Jonas (persons who are prejudiced against a group often do accept its individual members). After the war, Bultmann supported social cooperation with non-Christians (1933–65, III: 61-75).

command from advice; although Bultmann was right in implying that such a theory need not be explicit, it is an important aim of a college education—the context which he addressed—to become aware of such considerations.) Bultmann's judgment about the role of the Bible, furthermore, assumed that a divine word to human beings is the only important structure in the Bible, without giving adequate attention to other biblical forms.[101]

In line with his advice to students, Bultmann's exegesis was engaged only to a very limited extent in questions of form in such a way as to reveal the dynamic structure of the text. Yet attention to literary questions was not altogether lacking. A notable formal analysis appeared in his treatment of Jn 1.1-18 as a speech of the Christian community (1941b: 1).[102] In 1950, he recognized a similarity between his exegesis and a recent way of approaching poetry, namely, that they point to possibilities of human life displayed in a text.[103]

In contrast to his reserve in regard to literary analysis, Bultmann opened exegesis to a philosophical perspective concerned with structures of human existence. He did so especially in conversation with Heidegger and Dilthey.[104] Heidegger did not deal with actual temporal phenomena (including evolutionary ones, which had been the topic of quite a few philosophers somewhat earlier), but with temporality as a structure. Dilthey, on his part, had been interested in textual structures as expressions of life; Bultmann learned from him (as well as, probably, from Gunkel) to speak of 'life relations' (1933–65, II: 211, 217-18 [1950]).

Romanticism, as later described by Bultmann, had denied the possibility of general reason and of truths with timeless value (1957: 9). In

101. Bultmann expressed reservation about the thesis of Dibelius that preaching stood at the beginning point of all early Christian expressions (1921: 32). In his *Theology* (1948-53), however, the *kerygma* (God's word) dominates, with little attention to other structures, including biblical 'wisdom'.

102. On the whole, however, in his exegesis of John, 'Bultmann abandons the language of aesthetics that pervades the fourth Gospel' (Riches, 87).

103. 1933–65, II: 221, 228. On this way—a twentieth-century modification of the older representational view set forth by Aristotle—see *RFT* for Dewey, Frye, Bloch, S. Langer, and so on.

104. Bultmann was involved with Dilthey's work already from about 1912 but had a fuller engagement with it from the 1940s on (Sinn, 142). His involvement with Heidegger began in 1923.

contrast to that, Bultmann, like the philosophers mentioned, acknowledged general understanding; he acknowledged it, however, only for the human realm. Divine truth was for him primarily particular, so that he was in this sense a 'romantic' in regard to faith.[105] For instance, he said, 'I cannot speak of God's action in general statements; I can speak only of what he does here and now with me' (1958: 66).[106]

Bultmann knew that the categories of generality and connectivity are needed for a 'free' decision, for this must be based on 'reasons' or 'grounds' if it is not a 'blindly arbitrary' one (1933–65, IV: 131 [1963]). Indeed, purely arbitrary reality would imply either chaos or an authoritarian structure in which someone's will is imposed. Bultmann believed that reasoned freedom obtains in the world outside of God (131), but he did not admit such a position of human beings vis-à-vis God. Specifically, he denied that Jesus' teaching and the Christian proclamation are generally *einleuchtend*, that is, persuasive by making sense (1926: 14; 1933-65, III: 170 [1957]). Rather, God's word is 'paradoxical' (III: 170). He did admit general truth, but only if it becomes particular and is applied not through insight but through 'authoritative address' (III: 166). According to Bultmann, an absence of generality within faith prevents human beings from having any claim on God (1926: 44); in other words, it keeps God clearly in command.[107]

True, Bultmann said that he rejected 'blind obedience' to God—accusing Judaism of that (improperly so, since the Jewish statement he cited [1926: 64-65] refers specifically to a ritual law and does not apply in the same way to all law)[108]—but he provided no alternative or supplement to relying on irrational or non-rational decisions.[109] Some sort of human freedom, not very well explained, was implied in Bultmann's speaking of a 'possibility' towards which one is directed (e.g. 1926:

105. Thus, rightly (also more generally in regard to Bultmann's procedure), K. Berger (66-67). (*Pace* Berger, the label is less appropriate for Dibelius.)

106. Similarly, 1926: 14; 1948–53, Epilogue, 1. However, some general truths can lose their generality and thus become revelational address (according to 1933–65, III: 170 [1957]).

107. Cf., for nominalism and Luther, Lorenz (47-48, 114, 117).

108. See above, 4.1.a; 4.2.a; 6.3.c. Furthermore, critiques of Judaism as a 'calculating' religion were voiced in Bultmann's seminars during 1933 and 1935, apparently either by him or with his tacit approval (Jaspert, 80, 93).

109. He spoke expressly of the authority of the text as integral to its application (1925c: 350). Furthermore, like Barth, Bultmann usually made assertions about the nature of faith in a doctrinaire manner.

15), a possibility which a human being 'is' (1933–65, I: 139 [1928]). This open possibility—in itself a valuable emphasis (Riches, 72)—approached chaos, according to a statement in 1926 (83) that temporal continuity is annulled in a true 'decision'.[110]

Bultmann modified his atomistic view after 1926.[111] Thus, in 1930, he pointed to an I-you relation and to a 'being with' (following Heidegger) in human life; this human relatedness represents, he believed, at least a preliminary version of the demand of love expressed in Christian faith (1933–65, I: 230-36). During that same year also—as Heidegger had done in 1927 (1978: 45-77)—he compared and contrasted a philosophical 'formal-ontological' description with an 'ontic' ('concrete and contingent') proclamation of faith (1930: 340). Heidegger and Bultmann both indicated that the formal-ontological-rational is a background for, and in that sense, at least, included in, the ontic-theological. Bultmann, however, with more reserve towards the formal-rational than Heidegger, emphasized not the role of the formal dimension as a part of faith but primarily its role as a background for it, in that it furnishes a 'preunderstanding' of what might be involved in revelation, expressing a 'life relation' for it (1933–65, II: 218, 228, 231 [1950]; 1958: 52).

Bultmann's notion of a preunderstanding was in line with the post-nominalist insight that perception does not begin with particularity but rather takes place against the background of prior general conceptions and questions. Neither Bultmann nor Heidegger, however, took note of the fact that the latter's philosophy was indebted to Christian and other life-commitments and was not existentially neutral.[112]

From about 1940 on—in large part stimulated by his student H. Jonas[113]—Bultmann proceeded to a formal existentialist analysis no

110. Cf. above for the 'decisionism' of C. Schmitt and the idea of decision held by Gogarten, both of which were particularist and authoritarian.

111. More precisely, after 1923, when his 1926 work on Jesus was written (and read to Heidegger).

112. Thus, already, Jaspers in Jaspers and Bultmann (1954: 15): 'There is no [purely formal] existentialist (*existential*) analysis...It is...at the same time [personally involved] existential (*existentiell*)'.

113. On Bultmann's relation to Jonas, see above. Jonas spoke of an *existenzial-ontologische Motiv* in *Augustin und das paulinische Freiheitsproblem* (1930: 68), and described his approach in *Gnosis und spätantiker Geist* (1934: 89), as *existen-tial*; in a preface to the latter work, Bultmann described it as engaging in 'existence analysis', a procedure that New Testament studies can also apply. For other aspects

longer only of a preunderstanding but of the structure of a committed perspective itself. This was an important step and prepared the way for his New Testament theology. The fact that Jonas was a Jew and thus perhaps more ready than were his Protestant compatriots to be open to postnominalist thinking probably contributed to this subtle but important shift.

Bultmann's first major work along a formal-existentialist line was a commentary on the Gospel of John (1941b). More comprehensively and systematically, he delineated 'formal structures' of 'human existence' in his analysis of the theology of the New Testament (1948–53, §16, end). In Bultmann's view, theology provides an 'explication' of faith (this view is similar to Gunkel's). Accordingly, he sought to 'interpret theological thoughts in their connection with the "act of life"' (Epilogue, 1). Some of the central categories discussed by him were 'body' as self-relatedness, the 'indicative' as basis for the 'imperative', the 'future' as a gift, and freedom from the 'world' and its powers (§§17, 38, 40). These structures were not thought of as purely particular, but as realities presupposed or present wherever there is faith. Because of their potentially general relevance, Bultmann's presentation of them had a tremendous appeal to many readers.

This existentialist analysis was closely allied with what Bultmann called 'demythologization' (1941a, etc.). 'Myth', according to Bultmann, pictures divine realities in outdated terms; indeed, he did not offer a structural or functional definition of myth but rather adopted a developmental view of it as an early kind of understanding[114] to be overcome. His programme was radical in some ways, but it also had a traditional side, for Bultmann did not abandon an exclusionist Christian outlook.

Bultmann's attention to the human dimension bore a similarity to Gunkel's notion of *Sitz im Leben*, but his conception of life did not utilize psychology, sociology or anthropology. In other words, it was not grounded in comparisons with other phenomena. This omission was deliberate, for Bultmann was convinced of the special uniqueness of the Christian truth, not merely in the sense that it is different—a

of Jonas's anticipation of (presumably, influence on) Bultmann, see R. Johnson. Bultmann may also have learned from van der Leeuw (1933), which he edited thoughtfully (viii).

114. See above on Heyne, the Grimm brothers and implicitly D.F. Strauss, important for Bultmann.

comparison would have shown that—but in the sense that it alone is true.

The stress on uniqueness was expressed prominently in the essay which first outlined the idea of demythologization (1941a) and was indeed an integral part of it, for demythologization assumed that statements of faith need not be inherently mythical.[115] Specifically, Bultmann regarded as historical and non-mythological (although, to be sure, 'analogical') the statement that Jesus, as presented in the proclamation, represents God's 'decisive action' (1941a: 68; 1954: 196).[116]

Although he credited human beings in general with the ability to ask questions about God, Bultmann believed that non-Christian answers are illusions (1941a: 10). He recognized that Paul spoke of natural revelation but argued that Paul used that category only as part of an accusation (23). He acknowledged a 'light of revelation' in nature and history only when these are placed in relation to Christ (26). On the whole, then, he followed Ritschl in his rejection of natural revelation and in his view of redemption as one that takes place in a historical line proceeding from Jesus.[117] (He differed from Ritschl, however, in that he interpreted this line not as an 'effect' but as a 'proclamation'.)

Bultmann's view clearly reflected the fact that he remained fundamentally particularist in matters of faith and thus hesitant about a form which might be shared.[118] Nevertheless, his work incorporated a

115. It is true, Bultmann did not wish to eliminate the myths themselves as they are presented in the New Testament (1941a: 38), but he believed that it is possible to do without a 'mythical way of thinking' (1954: 185). Differently, for example, Jonas: 'Myth taken symbolically is the glass through which we see darkly' (1964: 233).

116. He mentioned, but did not accept, a broader interpretation of this by Dilthey and Jaspers (Bultmann 1941a: 49). This was said during the time of a war against the Jews.

117. Bultmann's teachers included the Ritschlians Herrmann and Harnack, as well as J. Weiss (son-in-law of Ritschl), whose departure from that tradition was only partial. Bultmann's remark that Jn 4.24 excludes from consideration the portion of humanity that has not yet heard the Word (1941b: 257) might hint at a broader view (Painter, 221); yet in response to Jaspers he gave no indication of an open perspective but emphasized the historical line (Jaspers and Bultmann, 1954: 70). He reiterated the view clearly in answer to J. Macquarrie (Kegley, 1966: 275). His most accepting statement referred to Albert Schweitzer (who stood within the Christian stream) as an example of 'Christian love' (1933–65, III: 129 [1955]).

118. He called theology a 'historical' science (1930: 243). That did not mean that its object can be established by ordinary historical investigation, but Bultmann

number of relational elements (cf. Boutin). Especially significant among them was the close attention he gave to the relation of New Testament thought to patterns of life. In doing so, he treated reflectively a connection that had been stressed by Gunkel and furnished a profound, even though limited, contribution to the study of form.

d. *Gunkel's Reaction*

What did Gunkel himself think about the work of his students? From correspondence by Gunkel we know that he had a high opinion of Bultmann and that he arranged for the publication of the latter's study of the Synoptic traditions.[119] Yet, in a letter to Jülicher in 1925, he expressed unhappiness about the analyses of the Gospels by Dibelius, K.L. Schmidt and Bultmann: 'It appears to me that my New Testament students have effaced the clear lines which I reached through much effort' (Rollmann, 285). It is likely that part of the problem lay in the fact that they used certain aspects of his procedure in order to gain external diachronic information. Indeed, he disliked the term 'form criticism', since 'criticism' meant for him a concern with that kind of information (284).

Gunkel sketched an alternative to their route, in an informal letter style:

> Especially it seems to me that they have not yet found the real point at which they should have begun: it should be expected a priori that the words of Jesus—so finely hewn—are subject to definite laws of form which it should be possible to describe: if we were only able to see them! A similar situation must be true for the oldest stories. And the later ones, too, which are affected more or less by Hellenistic taste, must somehow show their deviation[120]... Such observations would lead...to a new, truly 'form historical method'.

Still, he was not highly critical: 'I do not see in such attempts a "dangerous error" but find fault only in the fact that this way...has not yet been taken. These matters, however, cannot be "forced"...such

believed that 'theology as science has the task of securing [the] proclamation [which] speaks of the act of God which occurred in a certain history' (1984b: 58 [1941]).

119. Evang, 18, 71 (the 'friendly' relations valued by Gunkel no doubt included Bultmann's admiration of him).

120. He pointed to Lk. 17.20 as reflecting 'the typical form of the philosopher anecdote'. Rollmann comments that Dibelius came closer to this point in the second edition of his 1919 work in 1933.

observations come as a gift—all of a sudden they appear' (285-86).

When one considers that the students mentioned omitted and even rejected the aesthetic and religiophenomenological dimensions of Gunkel's work, which represented its heart, their teacher's critique is not surprising. One must, however, also take account of the fact that Gunkel's 'clear lines' emerged only gradually and were not yet fully formed when these scholars were associated with him as students, c. 1905. In fact, his introduction to the Psalms, which gave attention to interrelationships between linguistic form, content and situation, was not published until after he wrote the letter.

e. *Stauffer*

E. Stauffer was a student of Gunkel (as well as of M. Kähler) in the 1920s. Thus, when Stauffer asked that one should learn from Gunkel what *Formgeschichte* truly involves (1952: 83), he could speak with awareness of Gunkel's mature approach.

In 1929, Stauffer presented what he called a 'morphology of New Testament thinking'. As he described it, this examines the 'formal interrelationship' of thoughts, with an 'organic connection' between them (9); the central elements for it are 'thought presuppositions' (11). Not merely the relations of thoughts among themselves are considered, but also their base in experience (11). Furthermore, 'style form' is viewed as related to 'thought form' in manifold mutual interactions (14). 'Laws of style' are held both to constitute and to reflect a 'genre', for even art has a logic (14). A movement of thought should thus be discernible from the movement of style (20). The view taken in regard to a life situation is that the organizational context of a genre can vary (including missionary preachings, sacramental practice and instruction) but that the basic connection of a genre is with a 'movement of life', including an 'aim' (15f.; cf. Boeckh). For instance, a prayer celebrates or requests, a sermon proclaims, and a letter (epistle) contains reflections more than do other forms (16-19).

After examining some specific patterns, Stauffer gave attention to a fundamental structure he called 'myth'. Mythical thinking—described by him with dependence on Usener, Wundt, Cassirer and Lévy-Bruhl— assumes the 'connectivity of things' and views individual objects as 'models' of the whole (51-53). Accordingly, New Testament thought is 'a form of primal mythical thinking' (53). This is true since myth does not deny or ignore factuality but sees a comprehensive significance in facts (54). In harmony with writers in the fields of art and philosophy, Stauffer believed that mythical thinking is 'original' in the sense of 'perennial'. (Bultmann, writing somewhat later, seems not to have taken account of Stauffer or of those he drew upon.)

The most basic experiential basis of New Testament thought was located by Stauffer in the figure of the martyr, represented by John the Baptist, Jesus and Aqiba. Martyrdom ('witness'), he said, is 'word supported by one's whole life, life in its entirety becoming word' (74). Since in this structure the word has an integral connection with life, Stauffer was critical of theologians who place the Gospels outside normal experience and knowledge (90-91). He believed that Jesus played a central role in reality, a reality which includes religion, art, ethics, folk wisdom, physical laws, history in general and personal life with its 'experiments' (95).

In 1941, Stauffer produced a New Testament theology that was based in part on morphological principles. He treated prayer which allows one to say 'you' to God (§44), liturgical and dogmatic formulas, missionary sermons and instructions (§§50, 60, 212-13). He described three major dimensions of understanding the way of Christ, each of which involves a relationship: the doxological deals of Christ in relation to God; the antagonistic, of Christ and anti-God; and the soteriological, of Christ and the world (§3). An important duality treated by him was that of indicatives and imperatives; their relation is aetiological, that is, the indicatives provide a ground for the imperatives (§45, etc.).

Stauffer's work thus represented an achievement that was at least partially in line with Gunkel's procedure and also interacted with the larger world. During the Hitler years he stressed involvement in an ambiguous world to the point of death, although this involvement could (did?) mean cooperation with the Nazis.[121] After the war, he advocated

121. In 1933, he compared the swastika with the cross, and tied this in with the Nazi call for sacrifice—on the side of the Nazis, it would seem (he was certainly willing to give that impression), but he cited Oliver Cromwell (a non-German) on the need to rebel against a state (35). He advocated participation in ambiguity to the point of doing nasty things—were those to be done against Jews or possibly against the state (as was true for Bonhoeffer later)?; he left practical applications ambiguous (12, 24-27). In 1936, he signed a statement by the Protestant faculty of Bonn, which supported Nazism and called for struggle with uncertainty, contra the clear ecclesiastical line drawn by the Confessing Church (cf. K. Meier, II: 229). In his *New Testament Theology* (1941), however, he rejected antisemitism and said that a Church needs to say 'No' to an authority that succumbs to demonic self-

a 'morality without obedience', probably in reaction to the strong authoritarianism prevalent in the preceding period (1959: 17-25).[122] He questioned male rule in the family, valued insights by non-Christians (including poets and Camus), and held that God may be accused (1961: 47, 59, 70-76), although he was conservative in historical matters.

f. *Summary*

Gunkel's influence was by no means the only factor in the work of these New Testament specialists, but its presence can be seen in their concern with the interrelationship between style, thought and life and to some extent in attempts to deal with the question of generality. Missing from all of their work, to be sure, was the aesthetic dimension.

Some important structural contributions were made, especially in those analyses in which the term 'form-history' (*Formgeschichte*) was avoided. The fact that this term is absent in the better studies of literary form might seem paradoxical. Yet it is not, for that term subordinated form to history; it designated a kind of history rather than a kind of formal analysis.[123] Specifically, the term referred to an attempt to treat formal observations as means to answer diachronic questions. Less problematic was a reverse procedure, which included history as an element within a recognition of relational forms. That appeared in Dibelius's 'history of literature' (1926), in Bultmann's formal existentialist analysis and in Stauffer's morphology. These were appropriate kinds of formal history, somewhat comparable to the profound studies by the Catholics Soiron and Schelkle,[124] which related literature to thought and life.

4. *Other Protestant New Testament Studies, c. 1915–1965*

Gunkel's students have been treated so far with special care. The remaining survey will be mostly concerned with issues rather than with

glorification, although with martyrdom rather than a holy war (§§47-49). In 1943, he was denounced by the dean of his faculty for criticizing Nazism. (See Vos [102], and for his own account of the history, Stauffer 1960: 294-98.)

122. His criticism of rabbinic ethics in that context is grating. Unfortunately, antisemitism in the sense of an unfair representation of Judaism continued to be not unusual.

123. K. Berger (67) and Baasland (183) rightly regard classical form history (especially that of Bultmann) as only very partially formal.

124. Described in Chapter 9, above.

scholarly individuals, although a few individuals—especially Dodd, Wilder and Fuchs—will be given detailed consideration.[125]

Form-history was greeted with both enthusiasm and criticism. Enthusiasm was based largely on the fact that the procedure related the Gospels closely to the life of the Christian community. Some interpreters, in fact, welcomed the implication that the ecclesiastical emphasis downgraded the importance of the historical Jesus.[126]

Criticism of form-history, as the attempt to construct history on the basis of form, in contrast, was based on four major theses: (1) *form in itself does not reveal history* (e.g. Fascher 1924: 226; Easton 1928: 80-81 ['form criticism may prepare the way for historical criticism, but form criticism is not historical criticism']; Büchsel 1939: 79, 425); (2) more specifically, *oral traditions do not form pure genres, so that mixed forms are not relatively late* (L. Köhler 1927: 22, for sayings; Easton 1928: 80);[127] (3) *literary forms and life settings are not tightly connected with each other* (Fascher 1924: 214; Goguel 1926: 159); (4) *form-historians excessively downgrade the significance of individuals, including especially that of Jesus*[128] (Goguel 1926: 159; Easton 1928: 116; Manson 1943: 27; Riesenfeld 1957: 8-30; Boman 1967: 10, 29, 49). These were very strong arguments,[129] but they were not taken seriously by some scholars.

A considerable number of studies identified church traditions in various parts of the New Testament.[130] Such traditions included ethical instructions and liturgical forms, such as hymns and creeds. The different genres could be considered to form together an 'organic whole' (Reicke, 1953: 160). Some interpreters connected one or more of the Gospels, as such, with liturgical use.[131] The general tendency was to emphasize the collectivity rather than individuals. However, E. Selwyn

125. See Doty (1969: 259-321) for further items.

126. See above for early expression of this attitude by Lagarde, Ritschl, Kähler, Eichhorn, Kalthoff, and so on.

127. Cf. the Catholics Tricot, Schick (both cited above) and Benoit (1946: 494: 'Real life is complex'). Similarly, Goguel 1926: 158.

128. The role of Peter, highlighted by J. Weiss, was downplayed also.

129. For some other critiques, see Stephen Neill, *The Interpretation of the New Testament 1861-1961* (1966: 251, 263).

130. Cf. overviews by A. Hunter, *Paul and his Predecessors* (2nd edn, 1961), and P. Vielhauer, *Geschichte der urchristlichen Literatur* (1975: 9-57).

131. E.g. G. Kilpatrick (1946) for Matthew; for a variety of opinions see Stendahl (21).

pointed in 1946 to an individual (Silvanus) as playing a major role in the formulation of a baptismal catechism he reconstructed. Furthermore, G. Moule raised a word of caution about assuming that liturgical-sounding passages represented fixed traditions, because of a likelihood that forms were fluid in relation to each other (1962: 25, 210).

In dealing with traditions, a central issue was that of their life situation. For this, there were terminological problems, which were connected with theoretical ones.

It was widely, although not uniformly, recognized (such as by Bultmann, see above) that the term *Sitz im Leben* in Gunkel's usage refers to a *type of situation* rather than to a particular one. Bultmann drew from this usage the conclusion that form criticism cannot deal with the historical Jesus (1925a: 316). However, Schürmann (Roman Catholic) pointed out that during Jesus' time, too, there were typical situations (1960: 351).

Although it was seen that a *Sitz im Leben* is general, it was not equally well recognized that for Gunkel this term referred to the life situation of a *type of text* (a genre) rather than to the context of a particular one. In fact, Bultmann and other New Testament scholars commonly spoke of the *Sitz im Leben* of a single text.[132] The divergence from Gunkel's usage had subtle but profound implications.

If *Sitz im Leben* refers to the role of a type, not of an individual text, the textual structure with which it is connected is placed on a level of generality which potentially includes the present reader or hearer. That is true even if only a single exemplar of a certain type is available for examination, for what constitutes a type or class is not the number of examplars but the way in which something is viewed. If an existing or hypothetical object is viewed as something (e.g. a request, command, or hymn), it is seen as representing a type, a 'form'. Indeed, there is good evidence that, from early on, human beings perceive or imagine objects *as* having a structure, with the implicit or explicit implication that they represent a type, even when they have only seen one or none at all.[133] Such a form can be said to have a *Sitz im Leben* or general life function, as a purely particular phenomenon can not.

---

132. E.g. Fascher 1924: 223; Dibelius 1933: 9 (not yet thus in the 1st edn, 1919); G. Bornkamm 1958: 1002; cf. Haacker, 51. (See above for Bultmann.)

133. This is an argument against nominalists, who think that perception is first particular and then generalized. Organisms in general are predisposed to react to stimuli of certain *kinds*.

An apprehension of a general form may indeed have been implicit in the mind of scholars even when they spoke of a single text. The explicit highlighting of such a form, nevertheless, would have provided the depth that was characteristic of Gunkel's analysis of the genres of psalms. It may be remembered that he envisioned the true thrust of psalms to be embodied in the structure of their genres. A major reason for Gunkel's impact probably lay in the fact that his view of texts *as* members or reflections of certain types (e.g. lament psalms) resonated with the reader. Similarly, the profound effect of Bultmann's 'Theology' (1948–53) was due to the fact that by the time it was written he had come (with the aid of Jonas) to see in the literature not just particular messages but existential structures of faith. Insight of this kind was often implicit, but typically not more so, in the work of other New Testament scholars.

A related issue was whether a setting should be conceived in terms of a specific organizational structure such as the Eucharist or baptism (e.g. Lohmeyer 1928: Selwyn 1946: Käsemann, 34-51 [1949]) or more broadly in terms of a function in the community, however concretized. Placing texts into a connection with ritual had special attraction not only to those Protestants who already had a strong liturgical tradition but also to others who were creating or reviving liturgical forms of worship in an attempt to overcome individualism (cf. Genthe, 245-55). To the extent that the association of a text with a certain ritual is not based on an integral relation between that rite and the form of the text, a connection between them (if there was such a one) is, however, usually not apparent from the text. Fortunately, an absence of such knowledge is not a major problem, for an accidental external setting has little human significance, so that there is little reason to be concerned about it.

A broad concept of 'cult', which focused on devotion to deity without specific attention to its accidental concrete aspects, appeared in the treatment of the passion story by G. Bertram.[134] 'Cult' meant for him (1922: 5) not a specifically organized liturgy but the inner relation of the believer to the cult-hero, as distinguished from dogma (official expressions of thought) and ethics (rules for behaviour). This abstract conception corresponded to an anthropological characterization of religion in terms of the trio of cult, creed and code. Within this trio,

---

134. Bertram was a student of Deissmann, who was clearly successful in moving his students toward sophisticated perspectives.

'cult' refers to one's explicit interaction with deity, including a so-called 'private' one (which, too, is social). A feature of this approach is that it focuses on the intrinsic nature of human life or faith; its purpose is not merely to describe (as is done by a particularist, who can recognize only accidental external form) but to understand. Accordingly, Bertram was interested in the 'inner logic' of the Passion story and in roles in which a community engages 'not accidentally' but 'necessarily' (8).

Bertram said that the central question in *Formgeschichte*, as he understood it in a non-historicist way, is the extent to which content and stylistic form 'correspond to' each other (1927: 165). Labelling his study 'literary-critical' (1922: 7), he compared some features of the Passion account with the use of contrast for relief by dramatists, observing that theatre and cult were not distant from each other at that time (81).[135] He was not interested in either defending or attacking the historical accuracy of the accounts but only in the way the presentation was shaped by religious interests, although historical implications of his analyses appeared as a side effect (7).

A still broader consideration of human life appeared in the work of Shailer Mathews and Shirley Jackson Case, whose teaching and writing reached well beyond the New Testament.[136] From 1897 on, Mathews wrote extensively on the social dimensions of the teaching of Jesus and of other portions of the New Testament (supporting, for instance, the equality of women, 1897: 96, etc.). He regarded religion, including that focused on Jesus, as 'a functional psychological expression of life', specifically, a 'living with the value-producing elements of the universe' (1924: 10, 373, 401). Chinese and biblical conceptions of ultimate reality are 'functionally... the same', in his view, despite their considerable differences and divergent origins (1931: 19). These propositions, however, were asserted rather than supported by evidence, so that they required a leap of faith as much as did contrary assertions by

135. The Passion story, as it appears in Mark, was praised highly for its art by the classicist Erich Bethe (*Griechische Dichtung*, 1924: 374-78).

136. Mathews taught rhetoric, history, and political economy before going to Chicago in 1894 to teach New Testament history; from 1906 on, he taught there historical and comparative theology. After receiving his PhD under Bacon and Porter, Case taught first history and philosophy of religion (1907–1908) and then, in Chicago, New Testament interpretation; beginning in 1917, he increasingly taught church history.

Barth and Bultmann. They also presented, undoubtedly, too positive a picture of religion (including Christianity).

Case saw in the book of Revelation both 'literary art' (1919: 130, 148-60) and a concern with 'solutions for the evils of the world' (1918: 228). He reflected on the 'functional values of the Lord's supper for the new society' of early Christians, who were at first largely lower-class people (1923: 79, 158). Building on the work of previous scholars, he referred to the 'life interests' of early Christianity (1927: 106); for a recognition of these, he applied a method that is not simply 'documentarian' but gives 'attention…to social orientation' (vi).

C.H. Dodd, in England, combined a wide perspective with close attention to the New Testament text. He participated in the form-historical tradition (especially in 1937, on 'apostolic preaching'). Most important for an appropriate kind of form criticism, however, was the fact that he drew together literary, ideational and existential (psychological and sociological) considerations, with at least some attention to general structures.

One of Dodd's prime interests was literary. He pictured the Gospels as 'an unfinished drama' (1920: 1)[137] and gave detailed attention to the symbolism of the Gospel of John (1953a). He believed that the 'widespread appreciation of the Bible as literature is…one of the most salutory results of the general change of outlook in the last two generations' (1929: 2). The Bible, he observed, is now 'sufficiently emancipated from dogmatic schemes' to be enjoyed by the humanist; its greatness, like that of dramatic literature, lies, of course, not in its style alone (2).

This approach to literature did not involve an automatic acceptance (or rejection) of past writings. Rather, Dodd—in his theology closer to Temple than to Barth—placed himself among those who no longer look for 'an infallible external authority' but who become convinced 'rationally' of what is 'true and important'; he quoted Jesus: 'Why do you not yourselves judge what is right?' (1929: 233-34; Lk. 12.57). He supported an intrinsic understanding of authority, as that of Pheidias in sculpture, Shakespeare in drama, Beethoven in music and of experts more generally (21-23). He did regard biblical writers as 'experts in the knowledge of God, masters in the art of living' (24), although he also

---

137. He overplayed the role of the Pharisees in this. He represented Paul's view as one that describes humanity's 'battle against Sin' (94).

believed that many items of biblical faith and morals cannot be accepted as they stand (13).

Dodd sought to combine particularity with generality. In Jesus, he said, 'history has become the vehicle of the eternal' (1935: 197). Truth is 'permanent' but not, in a Christian view of it, 'disembodied' or 'timeless', that is, without reference to time (1936: 38; 1938: 15). 'The particular historical' event of Jesus, as he put it, was interpreted by his followers 'in terms of a mythological concept, which had been made by the prophets into a sublime symbol for the divine meaning and purpose of history in its fullness' (1937: 147); this involves a beginning and an end in God, beyond time (1938: 171). Myth, he believed, is necessary to express a meaning and a purpose, although it is always inadequate; the 'least inadequate myth' moulds itself on the past historical action of God (1937: 167).[138] An unresolved tension appeared in his thinking, however, in that he did not want to reduce all events to 'a uniform process, governed by general laws' (1935: 208) but nevertheless held that 'religion...is one' despite its organizational variety (1937: 160).

The duality of the special and the general came to notable expression in Dodd's analysis of the parables of Jesus. He stressed 'their intense particularity as comments upon an historical situation' (1935: 195). Yet he said: 'They are works of art, and any serious work of art has significance beyond its original occasion' (1935: 195).[139] In fact, he observed that the form of the parables pointed in that direction; their realism 'assumes an inward affinity between the natural order and the spiritual order', the former being both non-human and human (1935: 21-22; 1951: 80).

On the personal level, Dodd referred to psychological studies of 'passivity or self-surrender as the means to a renewal of life and energy' (1920: 113). In regard to society, he believed the 'Divine commonwealth' transcends individualism and human divisions (145, 151) and leads towards reconciliation between nations (1952; he was a pacifist). He was open to cooperation with non-Christians, for he understood Scripture to indicate that God's relation to humanity is not

138. Dodd seems not to have known Stauffer's similar conception of myth in 1929; Bultmann took account of neither. In 1953a: 6, without use of the term 'myth', Dodd said that the *kerygma* (preaching) 'indicates the significance of the facts'.

139. Joachim Jeremias, *Die Gleichnisse Jesu* (1947), followed Dodd only in the particularist, not in the artistic-general, aspect of his analysis.

'restrictive or exclusive' (1947: 119). He supported involvement in social matters on the grounds that the law of Christ 'is not a specialized code of regulations for a society with optional membership' but is 'based upon a revelation of the nature of the eternal God' (1951: 81).

Much of Dodd's line was carried farther by Amos Wilder, after studying both with him and with Bacon and Porter (1991: 54, 58). While a student and thereafter as professor of New Testament, Wilder published four volumes of poetry and six books dealing with religious aspects of literature. Major studies devoted specifically to biblical studies included a scrutiny of the relation of eschatology and ethics in the teaching of Jesus (1939) and an analysis of 'the language of the gospel' (1964a). The latter work was late enough to utilize reflections by E. Fuchs.[140] Wilder also gave a brief survey of the Bible as Literature movement as an antecedent to his work (1971: xii-xxi).

Important for Wilder were human 'reason and imagination' (1964b: 209). He was disturbed by Bultmann's authoritarianism with its 'emphasis on obedience' (1939: 165) and believed that the basis of Christian ethics involves an appeal to 'reason and discernment... assisted by the witness of Scripture' (154). Like Dodd (1953b: 129-42 [1946]), he held that the New Testament contains something like 'natural law' (1946: 125-35). The fact that 'poetic and religious experience are...basically akin' implied, for him, 'a natural or universal salvation' (1952: 20). In speaking of reason, he obviously did not refer to unfeeling rationality; instead, he believed that psychology, sociology, anthropology and linguistics are important for literary analysis (1956: 9; 1964b: 207; 1969: 23).

With mixed feelings, Wilder noted that 'the custody and future of the Christian tradition has to a considerable degree passed over into the keeping of non-ecclesiastical and even secular groups', who often wrestle 'more profoundly' with Christian issues than do those inside the Church (1952: xii). To be sure, these outsiders are 'heretical', missing important elements of Christianity, but they 'continue its explorations' and are effective in 'protesting against the narrowing and stifling' of Christian faith (243-44).

Like Gunkel and Dodd, Wilder attempted to combine generality and particularity. Specifically, he held that art both 'transcends the time and

---

140. See, for him, below; Fuchs, however, appears not to have noted Wilder (1939); Wilder (1991: 54), further, reports an ethnocentric remark by Fuchs, that even the Swiss 'have very little of our German answers'.

place in which it was created' and bears the mark of its own setting (1940: xvii). He acknowledged 'the alien character of many basic assumptions and conceptions' of Jesus, Paul and John (1955: 166) but believed that the oldest narratives of the Hebrew Bible highlight 'elemental relationships of life', known also to the modern psychologist (1954: 32-36). The parables of Jesus are both 'unique' and 'universal' (1964a: 96). In his analysis of New Testament literary forms, he placed a major stress on their 'novelty' (1964a: 27, etc.); yet he also related those forms to general literary patterns, including dialogue, story, poetry and symbol. As he put it (1971: xxx): 'We recognize the novelty of early Christian discourse and language forms, as well as the transhistorical impulse which prompts such novelty and power and which continues to operate whenever these texts come to speech in new times'.[141]

In analysing literary structures, he operated on the assumption that 'form and content cannot long be held apart'; in fact, he did not wish to 'confuse form proper with externals' (1964a: 12, 32). Art forms, he believed, are 'connected with basic assumptions about existence' (1964a: 79). For instance, the structure of a narrative, including both fiction and history, reflects a 'sense of temporality and succession' (1969: 56; cf. 1964a: 79). In line with this, biblical writers understood God's dealing with the world as a drama, to which a human response is a doxology (1952: 20). Myth, with its comprehensiveness and mystery, he believed, is a necessary form of faith (1955: 46-56, 82, 165; 1964a: 128-29);[142] it is accordingly not only supportive of present reality but can provide a new orientation (1982: 20).

Wilder recognized that some forms of aestheticism present pure imagination in a way that avoids responsibility (1982: 168 [1971]). However, he held that an accusation of aestheticism is often designed to protect a conventional life (1976: 101). Although many writers on the literary scene have been involved merely in a 'cult of negation', he saw an exception to this in those concerned with 'social revolution' (1940: 178); he thus recognized a duality of negative and positive critique that has run throughout the twentieth century. In his own work,

141. Uniting novelty with generality—each formulated in a rather extreme manner—he said (1964a: 136), less cautiously, that in Christian speech 'a new *genus homo*' arose in such a way that humanity 'broke through into universality' (136).

142. As a soldier in World War I, Wilder had experienced 'occult agencies and *phantasmata*' (1982: 23f.), which he represented in his poetry.

by understanding apocalyptic forms of speech (with the help of social psychology) as 'symbolic', he countered Bultmann's individualistic conception of New Testament eschatology (1939: 235; Crossan 1981: 22).[143] Indeed, both through such writing and through his contribution to discussions that led to the influential volume on social ethics edited by G.E. Wright in 1954 (1991: 71), he helped shape theological thought about politics and thus politics, itself. He said that 'salvation has to be political', although there is a 'deeper liberation' reflected in the texts (1978: 56).

In 1982, Wilder expressed the opinion that some studies in the 1970s had been 'overconverted' to literary analysis so that they ignored 'social-historical dynamics' (1982: 19, 30). Certainly, his own work was one in which language, thought and life were related to each other. Like Weinel and Dodd, thus, he stood close to Gunkel while avoiding some of the questionable assumptions that were pursued by form-historians.[144]

Some interpreters—probably a majority—adopted an attitude less open to the world beyond the Church. Paul Minear, a prominent representative of the Biblical Theology Movement (Childs 1970), can be cited as an example. He highlighted the fact that form criticism directs readers of the Bible to the 'situations of worship, moral decision, inward opening of the heart toward God' within the Church (1946: 47) and considered that biblical forms which had been effective at one time—story, parable, proverb, poetry—might still be 'appropriate' for the preacher and teacher (55). By giving attention to these forms, he expressed a continuity with the past, without repeating the details of the tradition or accepting the precise historicity of stories, which, according to form-critical analysis, he said, was not their point (48). At the same time, however, Minear held that form criticism, by showing the radicalism of sayings by Jesus emphasized by Bultmann, 'inhibits me from trying to establish them as the basis of international law, as the rationale for a new economic system, as the pattern for scientific psychology'; they are not, he said, 'universal laws' but have authority only for Christians (51).

143. Wilder had encountered the social gospel in 1919, while still an army officer, in a French Protestant seminary (1991: 53).

144. Although Wilder did not follow form-history, he has been discussed as a form critic by H. Köster (1983: 288) and V. Robbins (1992: 843).

Ernst Fuchs, a student of Bultmann, initially followed his teacher in rejecting revelation outside Christianity. Thus, in 1946 he declared that Christianity is 'essentially for all human beings' and 'therefore cannot recognize any other religion alongside itself' (6). This statement shows again that universalism often represents large-scale particularism, in this case identifying true religion with a peculiar form. Ten years later, he said that theological significance lies not in what is general in the Bible—shared with its surroundings—but in what is special within it (1959: 180 [winter 1955/56]).

Very soon thereafter, however, Fuchs moved in a different direction. He pointed out that faith in Christ is older than Paul's doctrine of justification (1959: 54 [spring 1956]), implying by that observation a perspective wider than Bultmann's. Bultmann had noticed that Jesus' words shared much with other cultures and had concluded that Jesus was less religious than was Paul, so that Paul should be preferred to Jesus for representing faith (1920b: 741); Fuchs clearly did not agree with that conclusion. He went on to say in the same essay that faith is 'according to its structure, love', so that 'the church is inherently related to the world'; since the world is a 'structural aspect of faith', today's 'social question', placed at some distance from faith by Bultmann, is proper for it (63).[145] A few years later Fuchs declared that faith 'deepens...human wisdom' (the latter is thus not considered religiously irrelevant)[146] and that 'God speaks to us not only through Jesus' (1965: 137, 272 [1961]).

Love, Fuchs believed, is what makes human beings human (1965: 381 [1962]. It seems that he was not inclined to deny the presence of love (equated with faith) in human beings generally. In fact, he said that his existential analysis was more radical than Bultmann's demythologization, by analysing the 'love of Jesus' as the 'movement of our own existence' (1958: 13). Instead of Bultmann's rather consistent 'no'

145. In 1933 (as an assistant to K.L. Schmidt [Busch, 214]), Fuchs had been dismissed by the Nazis, in part since he was a Social Democrat. In 1946, he said that 'true socialism is Christianity' (26). One can wonder whether his politics contributed to his being blocked from a position and defrocked not long after that, in 1951 (cf., e.g., the sociopolitical factor in the case of C. Briggs). Richard Soulen (in Hayes, forthcoming) mentions a combative disposition (cf. Wilder 1982: 27) as a (further?) factor in his difficulties, as was true similarly for W.R. Smith, Gunkel, K.L. Schmidt, and others.

146. He said that he learned this from the relatively conservative Adolf Schlatter.

to humanity, Fuchs said emphatically 'yes'.[147] Since the word 'love' can be replaced by 'God', 'faith in God is the most natural thing that can be'; it is *einleuchtend* (makes sense) for practical reasoning (1965: 171 [1961], as was denied by Bultmann but in a sense accepted by Barth).

Existentialist interpretation meant for Fuchs a consideration of the 'structure of existence' (1959: 67 [1952]). Unlike Bultmann, who contrasted human 'existence' sharply with non-human 'nature',[148] Fuchs raised the possibility that the concept of 'existence' should cover all beings and reflected that (in any case) being-as-such lies in the background of the human reality with which interpretation deals (67f.), following in this the later Heidegger. Especially characteristic of human existence, he said, is language or speech (68), which goes with love (1960: 302 [1959]; 1965: 172 [1961]). In his hermeneutics, accordingly, Fuchs outlined speech movements in the New Testament' (1954: 211-65). These include 'analogy' (metaphor, simile, allegory and parable), 'dialectics' (paradox and a Christological grounding with a call to love), and 'talk' (sermon, instruction and song).

For Fuchs, human existence is constituted by relations (1971: 129). Specifically, the 'word' does not stand alone but is related to a 'situation', an 'existential geography'—a *Sitz im Leben*, he could have said—so that its transchronic significance is expressed not in a similarity of concepts but in an 'analogy of existence' (1955: 16).

The 'speech event' (*Sprachereignis*) occurring in a text is, according to Fuchs, not merely an individual 'speaking event' (*Sprechereignis*, as Bultmann proposed for him to say). That is, it constitutes the communicative structure of reality ('speech'), not just a particular utterance within it (1960: 425 [1960]).[149] Thus, in interpretation not the past but the present is interpreted; the text opens a window into the hearer's or reader's reality (1953: 44; 1960: 430 [1960]; 1965: 131 [1959/60]). This outlook was in line with one common in non-theological disciplines, which Bultmann had described—somewhat one-sidedly, but in

147. Bultmann had said that 'God means the radical negation' of humanity (1933–65, I: 2 [1924]); even God's grace, as he pictured it, keeps human beings down. Fuchs, in contrast, affirmed that God says 'yes', the 'word of all words' (1960: 428 [1960]); in fact, Fuchs rarely referred to the negative aspects of life.

148. Thus, still, in 1933–65, IV: 129 [1963].

149. *Sprachereignis* refers to what Saussure called *langage*, speech or language as such, in contrast to *parole*, a particular utterance (*Sprechen*)—to 'being', not to 'a being' (Fuchs, 1960: 425).

part correctly—as having a concern with generality. Most anthropological, sociological and psychological studies examine phenomena with the hope that they will furnish insight into human existence, including the investigator's own, by suggesting or testing theories. Some kinds of literary analysis, too, bring to light structures of life—for instance, if they follow Dilthey's philosophy, to which Fuchs pointed (1968: 25; 1979: 9). According to Fuchs, 'the poet brings the word to its proper truth in the verbal structure' (1955: 15); theology, as 'knowledge of God's word', is 'knowledge of life' (13).

Reflection on the fittingness of a text in relation to reality, called 'meditation',[150] had long stood as a step between an exegesis and a sermon. Fuchs observed that this step has been abandoned to a large extent and that preachers attempt to move directly from historical exegesis to proclamation. To remedy this problem, he advocated an expansion of the exegetic process so that it would include, as an intermediate, reflective 'meditation' (1960: 405; see also 1979: 9). Wilder urged Fuchs to give attention to psychology and sociology in his reflections (1964b: 207). In view of the similarity between reflective 'meditation' and theoretical consideration in the human sciences, Fuchs should have been ready to do so; however, his analysis moved on the level of principle, which left open specific matters. Certainly, his work can be seen as a profound statement of the interrelationship of word and human life.

One scholar who regularly furnished a reflection at the end of his studies, by including a chapter on 'the permanent value' of what had been discussed, was E.F. Scott (from 1907 on). Scott did not believe that Christianity had a 'unique inspiration' (1907: 223) but held that Christian hope had 'its springs in needs and aspirations which are common' to human beings (1931: 189); indeed, he proposed the thesis, difficult to verify, that 'perhaps of all religions Christianity has borrowed the most' (1928: 13). He believed that the principal defect of the historical method is that in its emphasis on diachronic genesis 'it leaves out of sight the profounder origins of religious ideas and beliefs' (1928: 12). Convinced that 'much labor is now wasted on doubtful historical investigations', he urged attention to psychology and 'a more penetrating study of the records themselves in their inner purport and mutual relations' (14-16).[151] In regard to gospel traditions, he argued that a

150. See above for Hugh of St Victor.
151. He praised Porter and Bacon, to whom the volume to which he contributed

'fixed form would act as a safe-guard' for their preservation (1938: 141). He analysed the book of Revelation as 'great literature', creatively adapting conventions (1939: 180, 187). As he described it, the book expressed 'faith in God' (175), pointing to a higher order widely acknowledged by human beings (168). Although it was 'one-sided' in its negative view of society, it saw evils that have since re-emerged (175-77; he was writing just before World War II).

One final issue needs to be discussed briefly. Should an analysis of form be a step on the road to a study of history, or should a recognition of form be an end towards which historical investigation makes a contribution? Presumably, both paths are legitimate in principle, as long as proper procedures are followed; for instance, it is probably not appropriate to use form as a basis for a speculative history, contra traditional form-history.[152]

A good example of a proper (rather than improper, speculative) use of formal analysis in the service of historical study was furnished by H.J. Cadbury in *The Making of Luke–Acts* (1927). He examined the motives and forms of the materials used, common methods of expression (language, popular forms, patterns of writing) as they affect the work, the author's personality as it is revealed in the text (without settling the author's precise identity!) and the work's purpose. Equally well executed was Paul Schubert's study of the 'Form and Function of the Pauline Thanksgivings' (1939). With a knowledge of the generic pattern of thanksgiving occurring at the beginning of letters, Schubert showed how variations in this pattern anticipate a letter's subject matter, stylistic qualities, the degree of intimacy, etc. (77). Formal features were thus observed as an aid to understanding Paul's writings.

Schubert's study reflects a major change in dealing with the thanksgiving in Paul's letters. Most exegetes prior to 1600 had treated it as a rhetorical structure that has an intrinsic value in creating a friendly atmosphere. Thereafter it was widely viewed as a genuine expression of Paul's subjectivity. (See above, 5.3.) Now the thanksgiving came to be

---

was dedicated, for moving in that direction, beyond purely historical study (1928: 15, 18).

152. An assumption stated by A.T. Cadoux, *The Parables of Jesus* (1930: 60)— 'The story that is better as a story, more convincing and self-consistent, will probably be nearer to what Jesus said'—is tenable (if at all) only because of the qualification 'probably'.

regarded as a historically conditional social convention, which is adapted to particular purposes.

Interest in form itself—not as a means for historical assessment—also appeared in a number of studies. Thus, Alan Richardson showed, in 1941, that 'The Miracle Stories of the Gospels' are not 'dead records of wonders of an age that is past...but parables of the dealing of the living Christ with those who trust Him and obey His Word' (136-37); he affirmed the accounts as faith-interpreted history. Fuchs's student Eta Linnemann described the parables as a word event with a continuing meaning, although the original historical situation—not easily reconstructed—must be considered.[153] Another student of Fuchs, Eberhard Jüngel said that the parable form shows the nature of God's rule *as* a parable, standing in a tension with the world (1962: 135, 138). Geraint Jones, dealing with 'The Art and Truth of Parables' (1964), argued that, as art, some of the parables are relevant to humanity's 'enduring experience' and that the 'human situation' is both illuminated and illustrated by them (xi-xii). In describing this human aspect, Jones sought to go beyond the what he called the parables' *Sitz-im-Leben* (165), but he meant by this term their historical setting, not what Gunkel meant by it. Gunkel's conception pointed to a recurring human situation, which Jones also highlighted in his own way.

It is clear from this brief overview that, just as Dibelius and Bultmann themselves moved beyond speculative form-history towards more valid and meaningful formal studies, so New Testament scholarship on the whole matured by giving attention to the living forms present in those writings. The interpreters who have been discussed accepted a distance between past and present but also saw structural continuities. By showing continuities, they counterbalanced the earlier drive to achieve freedom from the Bible, which was a necessary precondition for modern society with its individualism, nationalism (each nation having a peculiar character diverging from ancient Israel) and capitalism (as well as Marxism and Fascism). Thus, quite a few expressed a concern for social welfare transcending sheer competitiveness.

By seeking to go beyond individualism in an emphasis on the Church, many Protestants moved in the direction of Catholicism, just as Catholics opened themselves at this time to particularist historical

---

153. *Die Gleichnisse Jesu*, 3rd edn, 1964: 35-36 (1st edn, 1961; ET 1966). She later turned against historical criticism.

criticism, which had been nurtured especially by Protestants. *Rapprochement* also went further in that a number of interpreters favoured interaction with the human sciences. Thus, somewhat like Gunkel, they pursued contact not only between past and present but also between themselves and non-Christians, including among these putatively secular persons.

Chapter 13

FORM IN SPECIALIST PROTESTANT STUDIES
OF THE HEBREW BIBLE, C. 1915–1965

1. *The Social and Intellectual Situation*

In moving towards formal analysis, Protestant Hebrew Bible studies often continued procedures and assumptions set forth by Gunkel. Very rarely did they reject older historical approaches. Rather, one of the major challenges of this period concerned the question of how form and history are properly combined.

A number of useful overviews of publications prior to 1965 are available. Very detailed ones include Introductions to the Hebrew Bible by O. Eissfeldt (1965) and G. Fohrer (1965) and a volume edited by J. Hayes devoted specifically to works commonly classed form-critical, by about 500 twentieth-century scholars (1974).[1] The present analysis will not focus on the many substantive observations made in these, but will concentrate on principles that were inherent in them and on their intellectual and social context. For simplicity of presentation, reference will be made only to a small number of writers.

Although individual writers were, on the whole, quite interested in the social implications of what they were saying, it must not be assumed that there is a precise fit between social and intellectual commitments and specific investigations, for individual scholars are affected by many different involvements and are not always aware of discrepancies in their engagements. Since, furthermore, data about most of the scholars' lives and thought are limited, a primary focus will be on the larger currents of life, thought and investigation.

a. *Social and Personal Involvements*

A major theme in these years was a need to overcome individualism. A.S. Peake, for instance, observed that social reformers of his day

1. Less detailed are Hahn (1954/66), Kraeling (1955), Kraus (1969) and Clements (1976).

found support in the 'passion for righteousness' in the Hebrew Bible (1922: 148 [1912], 193 [1907]; 1923). H. Wheeler Robinson pointed out the 'social righteousness' and 'social values' of that literature (1913: 229; 1946: 163)—concerned with the poor and weak members of society (1936: 60)—and described the close interplay between individual and society in what he called the notion of 'corporate personality' (1936).[2] George Barton, a Bible scholar with a broad perspective, called God, as represented in the literature, a 'social Being' (1919: 358; 1934: viii, 95). R.B.Y. Scott wrote a volume on the prophets in order to underscore 'the responsibility of religion in the struggle for justice, freedom and human solidarity' (1944: vii). Others expressed similar concerns.[3] G.E. Wright stated that 'social reform' is characteristic of Judaeo-Christianity (1950: 46) and edited a cooperative study on biblical social ethics (to which Wilder contributed, 1954). In the US an emerging concern was the relation between the races (Albright 1964: 316;[4] Wright 1960: 40).

Of course, ideas about the social dimension of faith varied. T.H. Robinson, who wrote repeatedly on Amos, regarded the 'true greatness of Amos' as lying in the fact that 'he did not denounce the system as system [but] said that it must be worked on principles which Israel had received from Yahweh in the desert', and called for an application of 'healing and saving power' (1922: 155, 157). With a different emphasis, G.E. Wright described God as a warrior for the sake of justice (1962: 57) and declared that a 'concern for the needy and for justice to the oppressed may involve the active use of power that cannot be described in every instance as non-violent' (1969: 149). Louis

2.   This essay was presented at a conference in Germany and appeared in a largely German volume—circumstances favouring its becoming well known in Germany.

3.   E.g. J. Peters, near the beginning of the century, advocated social reform as a parish priest in New York City, supporting labour (M.P. Graham in Hayes, forthcoming). According to F. James, 'the successors of Moses were ever championing the poor, the oppressed, the foreigner' (1954: 17). Muilenburg (1961: 68f.) spoke of the Bible's 'prevailing concern for the oppressed, the disinherited, the weak, the poor and afflicted'.

4.   In 1913, Albright, with youthful enthusiasm, characterized prophets as 'largely social reformers' (letter cited by Long [1996: 153; 1997: 132]); later, he continued to describe them as 'social reformers' inveighing against 'oppression,' but he expressly disavowed their anticipating 'socialism' or 'communism' (1940b: 135).

Wallis wanted the Church to be 'the inspiration of social justice' (1942: 295 [1918]) but pointed out soberly that a perfect social order in the future will be too late for 'countless millions' living before then; however, for him (as for others), the 'struggle for justice' had a 'transcendental' meaning, projecting into eternity (1935: 311).

On the continent of Europe, definite—although largely moderate— social concerns were expressed by a number of prominent scholars, not all of whom can be mentioned. A quite pronounced concern was that of Antonin Causse in France. His writings on the sociology of Israel were orientated towards 'social Christianity', which he partially put into actual practice on his family land (Kimbrough, 4-12).

The Norwegian Sigmund Mowinckel became interested in 1934 in the Moral Rearmament movement of F. Buchman, seeking—as Mowinckel described it[5]—a transformation of society towards greater social justice and stronger brotherhood. Buchman sought to achieve that goal through the exercise of 'absolute love, honesty, purity and unselfishness' by individuals, but he also said that his group 'under-stands Labour', with the implication that it was not without sympathy towards the need for structural changes of society (1953: 33 [1936], 80 [1938]). In applying the message of the Psalms to current life, Mowinckel interpreted the 'enemies' mentioned in them as including the evils that are the opposite of Buchman's ideals, such as dishonesty (1959: 127 [1938]). Earlier, Mowinckel had acknowledged, for the historical meaning of the Psalms, some reference to socioeconomic contrasts (1921: 17; similarly, 1962, II: 91 [1951]). At least after 1940, however, he pursued primarily an interest in church activities (see N. Dahl, 9, 18), an orientation that was probably implied already in his cultic interpretation of the Psalms from early on.

After World War I, Denmark and Sweden were governed largely by Social Democrats; in Norway, the Labour Party was dominant from 1935. How biblical scholars related to these governments is unclear. Nevertheless, it is noteworthy that a belief in a high role for Israelite kings was strong in these countries and in Great Britain, where royal lines continued to represent national unity, while in Germany, France and the US—without royalty—there was considerable reserve toward that emphasis.[6]

5.   *Afterposten*, 22 January afternoon (1935: 3).
6.   Scholars emphasizing the role of Israelite kingship included the Norwegians Mowinckel (from 1916 on) and Birkeland (1933, etc.), the British A.R. Johnson (in

The Swiss Walther Eichrodt examined sociopolitical issues over a long period of time. In 1925, he described Israelite 'national religion' as one for which a sense of justice was important. An interest in society was integral to the theme of 'covenant' in his 'Theology of the Old Testament' (1933–39). In 1944 (as co-author) and in 1948 he wrote on the social message of the Hebrew Bible.[7] However, he also believed that 'there is in the present situation the danger that the Christian church, in her zeal to make up for her former neglect...will over-estimate her abilities and will imagine that the setting up of a just social order lies in her power' (1949: 398). His younger compatriot Walther Zimmerli—teaching in Germany from c. 1950 on—continued this social interest. He observed unhappily that Christianity lives in an 'isolated manner', limited to a 'narrow inner realm', and pointed out that 'the people of the Old Testament understood all the orders of its life—which are in many ways akin to the orders of its surroundings—as personal address of its one Lord' (1961: 193, 198, 208).[8]

In Germany, the political context of biblical scholarship was wrenching. The Weimar Republic (from 1918 to early 1933) was superseded by Nazi rule, followed in 1945 by another republic. German pastors were largely hostile to the 'liberal' Weimar Republic;[9] thus their opposition to theological 'liberalism' had its political counterpart. Unfortunately, a number of those who had engaged in social mission near the turn of the century (e.g. Adolf Stöcker) had joined with this mission an antisemitic orientation, which was accentuated in Nazism.

Several Hebrew Bible scholars, including Hans Bruppacher[10] and

Hooke 1935, etc.), the Swedes Engnell (1943, etc.) and, his teacher, Widengren (publishing his own version in 1955), and the Dane Bentzen (especially, 1948b). For a fuller bibliography, cf. Eissfeldt (1965: 51). In the US, J. Peters placed a definite emphasis on Israelite royalty in 1922.

7.   For these and several other important essays see his bibliography in *TLZ* (85, 1960: 629-34; 95, 1970: 955-58). One of them (in 1963) was directed against an acceptance of homosexuality; on the whole, he was moderate.

8.   Similarly, Zimmerli (1964a: 16 [1959]). Although he was himself hardly radical in politics, he was later sympathetic toward university student protests in 1968 (Smend 1989: 296), referred to the prophetic message 'with its revolutionary No to often religiously sanctioned inhumanity' (1968: 177), and criticized Bultmann's emphasis on 'unworldliness' (1971: 148).

9.   See, for example, Mulert (1937a: 366); Herbert (19).

10.   Bruppacher (vii) lists several socially concerned German studies written near the beginning of the century.

Gunkel's students Hans Schmidt and Emil Balla, showed social concerns. For Schmidt that meant especially an opposition to alcohol (to
the imbibing of which by German soldiers on French soil he attributed
their defeat in 1918 [1924a]); he viewed favourably its prohibition in
the US (1924b: 32).[11] Balla said that Amos 'saw with horror' the reality
of social contrasts (1927: 309). In association with Schmidt, Johannes
Hempel sympathized with a pastor's movement towards abstinence
from alcohol (1926a). In 1932, further, he saw in the growing National
Socialism a judgment on the Church for having failed in inculcating a
social sense in middle and upper levels of society (in Klotz, 46). This
social orientation, moderate as it was, helps to explain why Schmidt
and Hempel (like most Germans) came to support the Hitler regime.[12]
Indeed, they supported Nazism more than was morally defensible or
Christian, although they also insisted that God needs to be held higher
than the nation.[13]

Other German Old Testament scholars who supported the Nazi state
to a considerable degree included Anton Jirku, Adolf Wendel, Artur
Weiser and Hartmut Schmökel. Their positions, it is true, were complex. In 1934, Wendel (a student of Gunkel) preached a sermon that
remembered gladly Hitler's coming to power a year earlier (1936: 9-

11. Schmidt wrote two small volumes on the alcohol question (one of them
dealing with the Hebrew Bible) in 1919 and 1924.

12. In its positive goal (national cooperative welfare) National Socialism
resembled the outlook of the Hebrew Bible, as was pointed out repeatedly, for
example, by Herntrich (1933) and Schuster (1935); cf. Nicolaisen (1966: 121, 216)
for Wendel, etc.

13. In 1935, Schmidt reported (12) Luther's view that a 'true prince', provided
by God, should 'fear God' and not praise himself; in 1940, he expressed support for
'Hitler's state' (164). In 1931, Hempel argued that Israel was far from a racial unit,
that a people ('folk') is higher than a state, and that higher still is God (1931: 171-
74). Two years later (according to a report, K.L. Schmidt 1933b: 348), Hempel
welcomed the Hitler revolution because it brought many Germans into the Church.
In 1938a, he placed greater value than before on 'blood' (6, 78) and made it a point
to describe hostile actions by Jews (30—a description even further extended in its
second edition in 1964, without reference to the far greater destruction Jews had
suffered!). In 1938b, he emphasized 'historical ambiguity', probably to justify support for Nazism with its nasty deeds. In the journal *ZAW* edited by him, he published in 1942/43 a quite pro-Nazi MS written in 1939, which described the Third
Reich and Judaism as involved in a fight to the death, before proceeding with
reflections on the role of the Old Testament, 209-12). See, further, Scholder, I: 402;
K. Meier, II: 409; Smend 1988: 17-20.

15), but in 1935 he insisted that God stands above a nation (even though nationality is important, as it is in the Hebrew Bible) and expressed the hope that the Church would act as *Führer*, leader (8, 15, 18-20, 29).[14] Weiser believed that German life should not be disturbed by a 'foreign' (i.e. Jewish) nature (1934: 48); yet he pointed in an exegesis of Psalm 110 to the dangers that are present 'in a connection between religion and politics if the political will seeks to subordinate faith' and referred to Amos's criticism of making 'God a party-supporter of an overbearing national self' (1935: 198).[15] Schmökel supported his nation's fight against Jews, who have 'lorded it over us' for 14 years (in the Weimar Republic)—quoting Luther's reference to 'Jewish poison'—but also said that for biblical prophets 'all nations are equal' before God's judgment (1936: 7, 11, 23, 25, 28).[16]

It should be pointed out that so-called 'German Christians' (this term is not an altogether clear one) by no means always divinized race[17] and that, unlike advocates of a German Church and German pagans, most of them accepted the Old Testament as having at least a partial value, often as a model of national religion.[18] One of their more radical leaders (and perhaps others) thought that Christian Germans continued the role of Israel in God's plan—Jews having rejected it by failing to accept Jesus (Leffler 1935: 33 [a similar view of one's own nation as a new Israel has appeared in Anglo-American culture]). Quite conservative theologians also were associated with this group. Indeed, Nazis soon lost interest in 'German Christians' since they constituted rivals to their authority (K. Meier, III: 16f.).

14. Cf. K. Meier, III: 305-306. In 1932: 60, Wendel had observed ironically that Jew-haters exhibit the very attitude (hate against foreigners) for which they criticize Judaism. However, in 1937, he said that 'one can be an antisemite without rejecting the Old Testament' (see Nicolaisen 1966: 120).

15. Weiser, like many others, resigned from an early radical organization of 'German Christians' toward the end of 1933. However, he implied support for the war (not unusual for a German) in 1941: 80.

16. In 1934, he wrote a work on 'Yahweh and Foreign Nations', affirming 'God's all-encompassing love of humanity' (124).

17. See especially a theological declaration in 1936 (Herbert, 170). A 'worship of race' was rejected by Leffler (1935: 48).

18. See n. 12 above; Althaus 1933: 16; Hutten 1937; similarly, the Catholic Kaupel 1933: 37-39; cf., further, Nicolaisen 1966: 66-87; 1971. To grant the 'Old Testament' a partial value is, in fact, a standard Christian stance. See on this, further, below, 13.1.b.

On the whole, theologians who accepted the designation 'liberal' were—unlike most of the scholars mentioned so far—at least in a cautious manner critics of Nazi politics.[19] (Those who supported Nazism in good part were largely 'moderates'; such persons are not likely to go against the stream.) Critiques by liberals are not surprising, since Nazism, both in its politics and in its rhetoric, was strongly antiliberal (i.e. against both individualism and internationalism and in favor of authority). The critics with university positions, however, were dismissed from their posts, so that liberals, who had already been few in number, largely disappeared from the academic scene.[20] The New Testament scholar H. von Soden (cf. above)—more active in the politics of the Confessing Church than his friend Bultmann, although liberal theologically—was for a while excluded from university service.[21] The fairly liberal Hebrew Bible scholar Gustav Hölscher, who cooperated with K. Barth in church elections, was subjected to a punitive move.[22]

Some professors joined the Confessing Church, largely inspired by Barth. This group opposed the Nazi state for the most part not so much for its social politics as for its attempt, early on, to gain control over the Church.[23] The group's relative lack of criticism of general political

19. See, for example G. van Norden, 315; Scholder, I: 402: in some detail, Graf, 151-85 (liberal Christian opponents included A. von Zahn-Harnack, chair of the union of German feminists, 156). W. Schubring, liberal editor of the *Protestanten-blatt*, denied to the Third Reich 'its fundamental basis, trust' and declared all its statements 'lies' (in his Berlin church, 1933 or early 1934; see Scholder, II: 52). H. Mulert and M. Rade, editors of the liberal *CW*, expressed criticism cautiously, although sometimes fairly clearly (e.g. Mulert 1933: 384; 1937b: 807; Rade 1935: 997), until stopped. (Cf. Gerlach, 161-63, 175, on Rade's mixed position.) A co-editor of *CW* was deported in 1933 for giving aid to Jews, something Rade and other liberals did also (Graf, 163, 172f.). Earlier voices against antisemitism had come almost exclusively from 'culture-Protestants' (T. Rendtorff, 69). Schubring, Mulert and other liberals stood with the Confessing Church, despite theological differences with Barth (K. Meier, I: 46; Feige, 168; Stegemann, 49, 53; Graf, 166).

20. They included P. Tillich, Rade and Mulert, along with some professors more conservative than these (see, e.g., Herbert, 157).

21. See Dinkler and Dinkler-von Schubert; Lindemann 1989: 34, 51.

22. For a list of dismissals, punitive moves, etc., cf. Niemöller, 340-42 (although this list may contain some errors, as has been charged, it shows that the state did not take outright opposition lightly).

23. Partial criticism of social policies is reported, for example, in Stegemann (51-56). The liberals who joined the Confessing Church did so primarily for reasons of politics.

policies was due in part to the fact that many of its members supported those policies (including, when it came, the war)[24] and in part to a sense that politics is not the sphere of the Church, as well as in part to circumspection, since the group was already under pressure. The Confessing Church must be admired for its insight, courage and perseverance in maintaining its relative independence; but Barth (who, as a Swiss, could add an external perspective) increasingly criticized it for its failure to engage in political critique. The Nazi party, on its part, established a policy of separating itself from the Church (K. Meier, III: 17-26, 134-38, 604). The party tolerated the Church as long as it did not engage in political opposition, and even welcomed its confessional disunity.[25] (Its long-range plans included the destruction of the Church after the war.)

Old Testament specialists who took part in the Confessing Church included Joachim Begrich (Gunkel's student), Friedrich Horst, Gerhard von Rad, Hans Walter Wolff and Claus Westermann, the latter two as pastors, before entering academia after the war (cf. K. Meier, III: 639). In close association with this circle stood Albrecht Alt (von Rad's teacher) and Martin Noth (another student of Alt).

Among these, Horst had a strong 'will for the right in church, state, and community' (Wolff 1963a: 315); as a result of some of his oppositional activities, limited as they were, he was removed from his academic position from 1935–45. Westermann, entering academic life after the war (with Zimmerli as a teacher), highlighted biblical concerns for society (1952/53a: 143; 1956a: 343; 1957a: 198 99 [although

---

24. See, for example, reports by G. van Norden, 242, 244, 246, 299, 308 (including a telegram supporting Germany's withdrawal from the League of Nations, signed by M. Niemöller and others); Mulert 1937a: 366 (saying that many Confessing Church members were then, as already before 1933, National Socialists); Baumgärtel 1958: 4-10, 21-26, 31; Feige, 187; and, for the war, J. Beckmann (in Ginzel, 128); K. Meier, III: 608; Gerlach, 391-92. But the support was not unanimous; see Scholder, II: 60; K. Meier, III: 143, 601-603; Herbert, 222-31; and Stegemann, 55, 61 (reporting a judgment—not made public—that the war does not meet 'just war' criteria).

25. See, for example, K. Meier, III: 23, 603; Herbert, 222. The sharpest criticism made by the Confessing Church—with reference also to the treatment of Jews—was presented to Hitler privately in 1936 (but leaked to the international press); it led to the death of the Jewish-Christian F. Weissler in charge of handling the document (Herbert, 167-69).

defending a 'normal coexistence of rich and poor']; etc.).[26]

Otherwise, however, members of the group were characterized by a lack of involvement or relative neutrality in state politics.[27] For instance, von Rad recommended as especially good a pro-Nazi defence of the Old Testament,[28] although he also criticized that same year an 'idolatry of eros and state' (Alt, Begrich and von Rad 1934: 58).[29] A posthumously published memoir describing his military service in 1945 (written in 1960) gives no hint of a sense that the war was unjust (1976). During the war, he met with a circle that included the poet Ricarda Huch, whose members were at least partially opposed to Nazism;[30] but his report of this circle does not refer to such opposition but says that in 1944 they anticipated 'with heaviness' the end of a period (1964: 18).

Alt (1934) and Noth (1940) drew a line between sacred and secular law.[31] This position undercut both an alignment and a conflict between Church and state. Alt appears to have been critical of the Nazis, but his opposition was less than clear and may have been limited to specific theological and scholarly points (e.g. that Jesus was most likely a Jew, in opposition to the view of some Germans).[32] Indeed, these academicians would not have been teaching if they had opposed Nazism politically (unless a widely concerted opposition would have had an effect). As it was, their lack of political engagement gave them time and mental

26. Westermann's expression of social concern was stronger later (1975a: 117, 120 [1969], 135 [1972]).

27. For Begrich's apparent modification of Gunkel's view of the 'poor' in the Psalms, see above. To be sure, some references to social righteousness were made, e.g. by H.W. Wolff in a sermon (in Westermann 1958: 105 [1956]).

28. 1934: 188, on V. Herntrich, a theological conservative supporting Nazism enthusiastically, although within limits.

29. An essay on creation faith (1958: 136-47 [1936]) opposed 'German Christianity'.

30. On Huch's at least partial opposition, see Bendt *et al.*, 367, 376, 394-95.

31. See below further for both of these writings. Noth was associated with the Confessing Church (K. Meier, I: 286; III: 285) and thus was not at one time recommended for a more prestigious university (Beyschlag, 285), but he was not inclined towards politics, including church politics (Smend 1989: 259). His 1940 study had (like many others) an anti-Jewish thrust (not well supported, as F. Crüsemann [1989: 2] indicates).

32. See Smend 1989: 184; the joke referred to there (n. 4) was (intentionally?) unclear. Cf. also Gerstenberger in Mommer *et al.* (11-13) for Alt's relation to his context, but much remains uncertain.

space for scholarship for which they came to be well known.

After the war—as far as is known—German Old Testament special-ists who had taught prior to 1945 neither claimed to have engaged in political opposition nor expressed regret about failing to have done so; in fact, they said nothing in regard to the horror of what had been done.[33] This silence would seem to support the impression that, like most of their compatriots, they had lacked active, and perhaps inward, opposition to the political aspects of Nazism. However, Hans-Joachim Kraus (a younger scholar, prior to 1945 a member of the Confessing Church) and Zimmerli (who had given some aid to Jews before 1945)[34] confessed Christian and, in the case of Zimmerli, Swiss guilt for acts of commission and omission.[35] On the whole, clearly, German scholars were—like others—too caught up in their own society to transcend it in a major way.

Most of the Protestants who were not strongly orientated towards the state focused instead on another group, the Church. Indeed, the Church as an organization appears to have been a major interest among Protes-tants worldwide, countering individualism. The liturgical movement, strong during the period under discussion (1915–65), clearly expressed this interest and undoubtedly contributed to a highlighting of collective cult (ritual) in Hebrew Bible studies. Interestingly, two of the most prominent British voices in support of the cult—A.R. Johnson and (more moderately) H.H. Rowley—had a Baptist heritage, which is not known for its emphasis on liturgy; quite likely, these two writers were seeking to provide for their tradition a better balance.[36] This situation shows that it is erroneous to envision a precise correspondence between a person's social location and what that person says, as is done in an approach known as 'vulgar Marxism' (see *RFT*), for human beings do in part transcend their immediate location, as they interact with others.

Those who emphasized ritual structures—probably most biblical specialists—tended to be conservative or moderate in their larger social

33. Thus, Kusche 1991: 167. M. Andrews (1971/72: 296) has reported that von Rad was also privately (in relation to him) silent on the war. However, R. Rend-torff, a student of von Rad, was to take a major interest in the Holocaust; other younger scholars have also come to deal with this.

34. Smend 1989: 288.

35. Kraus 1956: 210; Zimmerli 1964a: 32 (1953), 9 (1959). Those who do the most are often most aware of their shortcoming.

36. R. Ackerman (43) has also noted a sharp contrast between W.R. Smith's interest in ritual and his 'puritanical' religious background.

orientation, in line with a correlation of this sort that has been observed by psychologists of religion (e.g. Neal, 332). After all, ritual involves a constant order and usually a delimitation from outsiders.[37]

At the same time, individualism was not altogether dead. It remained alive in the US more than elsewhere, perhaps. Thus, Fleming James dealt with 'personalities of the Psalter' against the 'background of Gunkel's type-study' (1938, subtitle). He sought to avoid both an exaggeration and a minimizing of individual roles (245-46).

Very slowly, academic contributions by women entered into the picture, although only a few of them obtained positions in higher education. Three women students of Gunkel published scholarly studies.[38] Across the ocean, Emilie Briggs co-authored a commentary on the Psalms with her father (1906–1907). Caroline Breyfogle was probably the first woman to receive a doctorate in Hebrew Bible, in Chicago (1912). Laura Wild, Margaret Crook, and Louise Pettibone Smith—all of them with literary interests—held biblical posts in women's colleges.[39] Two Swiss dissertations by women appeared in 1948 and 1949; one of them, by Irene Lande, was stylistic, supported by L. Köhler and by Gunkel's student Baumgartner.[40] After 1950, Eva Osswald, Barbara Hornig,[41] and Marie-Louise Henry had academic success in East Germany.

In some (many?) cases, women contributed within family contexts, without primary credit as authors, since their scholarly education did not lead to individual appointments for them. For instance, J. Hempel

37. That is not to say that some traditions with a strong social outlook (e.g. the Catholic) cannot combine this with a cultic emphasis.

38. Cf. above. Biblical studies by Jahnow and Zurhellen-Pfleiderer will receive specific attention below. For Jahnow's writings on women's roles and on the teaching of religion in public school (her profession), see Buss in Hayes, forthcoming. Biblical studies by Plath appeared in 1901, 1905, 1912 and 1916. A philosophy dissertation on the Samaritan targum by Leah Goldberg (to judge by the name, Jewish) was accepted in Bonn in 1935.

39. For several of these—and for Houghton, Innes and Chase—see above, 10.5 and 10.6. (Crook also published *Women and Religion*, 1964, with special regard to biblical roles.) See also listings in Eissfeldt (1965), especially studies, largely on psalms, by Helen Jefferson from 1949 to 1963.

40. Earlier, when positioned in Marburg, Baumgartner had similarly aided Jahnow, who wrote her 1923 study while teaching at a women's school in that city. The other dissertation was by Rosa Riwkah Schärf (apparently, Jewish), on the figure of Satan.

41. With a dissertation on postexilic prose prayer (1958: 644-46).

was aided by his sister (1914: 1-2) and from the 1920s on by his wife Maria Hempel-Kolbe, to whom, as 'co-worker', he dedicated a major overview of Hebrew literature (1930). He told me in 1962[42] that it is an advantage to have an academically educated wife and that his own productivity would have been impossible without her working with him.[43] Similarly, C. Westermann told me in 1962 of the cooperation he received from his wife Anna in preparation for his Genesis commentary. In the preface to the second volume of this (1981), he said that the commentary had become their 'common work' because of their 'manifold working together'.[44] W. Irwin gave credit to his wife for important 'insights' and helpful 'critical judgment' (1952: xii-xiii). It may never be known what specific intellectual contributions were made by these family members, but the fact of their contribution should be kept in mind.

In addition to the social context of scholarship, the personal dimension must be acknowledged. Naturally, this involves many varied considerations, which remain largely hidden. It is known, however, that Mowinckel, like Gunkel, suffered major mental stress. His first monograph, on Jeremiah, was written during confinement to a sanitorium (1914: 66). For some time after that, he experienced religious tension; as reported, he hoped (in vain) for a match between personal experience and what, according to his scholarship, is characteristic of living religion (N. Dahl, 9, 18). In fact, we have seen that major contributions in most disciplines (even in physics and mathematics) are grounded in deep commitments; work done merely for the sake of academic advancement probably can lead to no more than minor insights.

Since scholarship and life are not separated for major thinkers, it is not surprising that leading biblical scholars indicated by word, or showed in practice, a desire to reach a broad public. Such a public included, but was not always limited to, a church audience. For instance, Bernhard Duhm expressed a desire to reach also non-theolo-

42. On a trip with an eye towards the history of scholarship.

43. Formal acknowledgment of her contribution (outside the dedication mentioned) was for her preparing indexes to at least five of his studies; these included topical indexes, which require an understanding of the subject.

44. The fact that she was not on the title page (or even called by name in the preface) reflects the fact that women remained largely in the background; W. Irwin also did not name his wife. (Westermann spoke of his wife's role without being asked.)

gians (1916, preface)[45] and Emil Kraeling addressed 'students of religion, literature, philosophy and art, who have encountered the Book of Job' (1939: vii). Leroy Waterman asked provocatively, 'What has biblical study done to make available as a present resource the best moral directives of the Bible?' (1947: 13). R.B.Y. Scott, besides addressing social issues, indicated with care that the Psalms give guidance by showing how one 'may speak to God' (1958: 12).

Showing an interest in human service, both Mowinckel and Westermann wrote extensively for general audiences, sometimes speaking to practical issues. For instance, a privately distributed paper by Mowinckel in 1928 'applied the genre criticism of biblical psalms to the use of various types of hymn in services of worship within the Contemporary Church of Norway, and used this as a critical review of the revised Hymnal' (N. Dahl, 16). Westermann contributed to both general-theological and non-theological journals, especially early in his writing career (in the 1950s). Most of his subsequent biblical analyses clearly have a contribution to the life of human beings in mind.

b. *International and Interreligious Perspectives*
We have seen that an attempt to overcome individualism led to an interest in the significance of groups, both national and religious. Beyond such a group-orientation lies a still larger perspective towards humanity as a whole; this was unevenly developed in the decades under discussion. (A still broader view that deals with humanity's place in nature was virtually absent.)

Specifically, international issues were discussed by the Swiss scholars Eichrodt (1920, on peace) and Köhler (1953: 170 [1931]), by the English Peake (1923: 5, etc.), by W.F. Albright in the US,[46] and by the Canadian R.B.Y. Scott (1944: 207). Otherwise, however, these issues appeared only rarely in Hebrew Bible scholarship.

Germans under Hitler, in particular, were 'tired of the ideal of reconciliation of peoples and regarded as unbelievable a message concerning the "equal rights of peoples" and of international brotherhood'

45. This work appeared within the series *Lebensfragen*, edited by Weinel.
46. He pictured a 'progressive world sweep of the West' (1940a: 83), without an adequate recognition of African and Asian contributions to the West (although some reference to these is made in 1964: 253). He urged, however, 'toleration without indifference' for the sake of the survival of civilization (in Bryson 1960: 321).

(Baumgärtel 1958: 30).[47] The academic side of national introversion can be seen in the fact that German scholarship developed for a number of years in a relatively isolated fashion.[48] This tendency appears notably in von Rad's writings published between 1930 and the early 1950s;[49] von Rad did take a wider perspective after that—in part perhaps as a result of serving as guest professor outside the country more than once from 1949 on—certainly, more so then than did many younger scholars.[50]

More extensive than involvement in international issues were inter-religious engagements. Yet they were limited in the extent to which they considered religious traditions outside the Near East.[51]

47. It must be noted that non-German countries had contributed to this attitude, through their sense of moral superiority (they had earlier—together with Germany [an important colonial congress took place in Berlin]—been aggressive towards non-whites) and through being unrealistic in the Treaty of Versailles (with an indemnity similar to one placed by Prussia on France in 1871 and by Germany on Bolsheviks in 1918!). This observation does not in any way exculpate German actions, but it does show that others, too, have to admit guilt, as well as lack of wisdom. W. Temple was one who recognized wide guilt and saw that sharp retribution would lay the groundwork for another fight (Suggate, 178); Reinhold Niebuhr, too, expressed for himself and for other 'liberals' a deep disappointment with the treaty, in part for this reason (1919: 218). Victors in World War II learned a lesson from their mistake after World War I, but the US has moved only gradually towards admitting its own earlier misdeeds in conquest and slavery. Certainly, moral judgments need to be made. Unfortunately, second thoughts by the victors in regard to the Versailles treaty, not well applied, encouraged Hitler.

48. Others, too, were limited in their vision, although usually to a lesser extent. Dodd did not know Bultmann's commentary on John (1941b) 'as a whole', when writing his own study of the Fourth Gospel some time before 1950 (1953a: vii, 121); however, he cited prior work by Bultmann and the volume's motto, a quotation from Goethe, was German. (The assertion by Köster [1994: 293] that E. Massaux did not know works by Dibelius and Bultmann may well be incorrect; he certainly knew studies based on these and may have assumed awareness of them.)

49. Cf. Crenshaw 1978: 172. Studies reprinted in von Rad (1958) contain no references to non-German biblical scholarship other than that of Mowinckel; richer references, however, appeared before 1930 (Welch's work on Deuteronomy was important for him) and later on, especially in his *Theology* (1957-60).

50. See below, 13.1.c; 13.2.b. International in their scholarly orientation were also the major figures Hempel, Eissfeldt (especially in later years) and Fohrer. It is, of course, more difficult for relatively young scholars to have a wide range.

51. See Hahn (44-118); Rogerson (1974, 1978); and Leach (1983—judging that

Broad interreligious perspectives, although often not related in detail to biblical literature, were present in the work of a number of North American scholars, including George Barton (Canadian), Millar Burrows, William Graham, and Herbert May.[52] John Peters compared the Psalms occasionally with the Atharva Veda of India and with Persian Gathas that 'exalt the poor' and inculcate care for them (1922: 21, 103, 174). Albright had become interested in comparative mythology and the history of religion (1964: 308), although he focused most of his attention on the ancient Near East. C. McCown briefly acknowledged 'analogous developments' in different parts of Asia (1958: 306).[53] Born in China of German missionary parents, the present writer began, in 1961, a series of form-critical studies that gave consideration to the general history of religion.[54] Wolfgang Roth, a German-born citizen of Canada (and later of the US) who taught in India for a while, examined 'Numerical Sayings in the Old Testament' with attention to Indian parallels (1965).

Comparison could lead to a devaluation of other groups. Albright judged that 'most features of Hinduism are simply survivals of ancient polytheism' and that Hindu and Buddhist scriptures are not 'on a level' with the Bible (1964: 252f., 315 [1948]), although he considered 'Indic metaphysics' to be sophisticated (92). His student G.E. Wright set the Hebrew Bible into a sharp contrast 'against' the environment (1950) and held that 'Israelite faith...was an utterly unique and radical departure from all contemporary pagan religions' (1952: 19). This judgment was not based, of course, on an examination of 'all' religions, if only because that is impossible.

Knowledge of other cultures was facilitated in Great Britain by its dominating an empire and, in a certain connection with this, by a

'no mutual communication' between biblical studies and anthropology has taken place, 8), for information about relevant studies. Few of these, however, dealt with the religions of India and China or with African or native American traditions as such, instead of with 'primitive' culture. (Even discussions of this were very limited [Eilberg-Schwartz, 2-4]).

52. See below. R.H. Pfeiffer (1961: 125) compared Amos with the Romans Horace and Juvenal, satirizing upper classes.

53. These have been discussed by historians of religion since the nineteenth century.

54. My teachers included Burrows; my dissertation director, although not a formal teacher, was B.D. Napier. Important for my outlook were interests in philosophy, anthropology, psychology and sociology.

far-flung missionary movement. For instance, W.O.E. Oesterley, who had been born in India, described 'The Sacred Dance' as it was practised in Israel and elsewhere (1923). A.R. Johnson indicated that prophecy 'is no isolated phenomenon' in human history (1936: 314); A. Guillaume showed that to be so, in greater detail (1938). S.A. Cook spoke of the value of comparative study—recognizing both remarkable similarities and remarkable differences—and anticipated that it may lead to a new stage in thought (1914: 372; 1938: 13, 203, 206). H.W. Robinson acknowledged revelation in various religions, although he held that Jesus is 'far more' than other major figures (1942: 161, 174).

How does one explain congruences? G.R. Driver accounted for similarities in prayers on the basis of 'common' human inclinations (in D. Simpson 1926: 173). R. Abba (and some others) believed that biblical myths drew on a 'collective unconscious', since some images appear in widely separated contexts (1958: 111). The anthropologically trained historian of religion E.O. James took a more relational position by pointing to general human requirements (or 'functions') met by religious, such as biblical, phenomena (1933: vii; 1958: 17, 305-306; cf. 1935: 85-89).

According to Rowley, it was well known that 'the religious quality and value of the teachings of non-Christian religions finds a fuller appreciation in the Church than formerly' (1944: 78). In fact, as a former missionary in China (1922–24), he asserted—presumably speaking for his own culture—that 'few missionaries would today advocate an unsympathetic approach to other religions' (1946: 12).[55] He sought 'to develop a truly comparative method', which does not consist in an 'unfavourable' view nor in a 'collection of superficial similarities' but, rather, gives attention to contexts and basic structures (1951: vii-viii)—in other words, to external and internal relations. Along such a line he compared themes of suffering and social criticisms in India and China with biblical ones (1951, 1956a). He believed that Chinese figures are 'worthy to stand beside the Israelite prophets' and recognized 'a genuine prophetic character' in Confucius, the

---

55. In 1899, S. Kellogg, a missionary from the US to India, said that 'all Christians, and missionaries especially, recognize and heartily acknowledge such truths as they may find more or less clearly admitted in the religions of those among whom they labor' and found important truths in Islam, Hinduism and Buddhism, although he went on to say that 'as systems of religion, we must pronounce them false' (167-74).

Buddha, Zoroaster and Muhammad (1956b: 39). This view did not contradict the fact that Rowley was in many ways traditionally Christian[56] (cf. a similarly broad Roman Catholic outlook); indeed, one can ask whether a different position is compatible with Jewish and Christian views of God as just and loving. The *rapprochement* between religions towards which Rowley reached was not unlike a movement towards mutual acceptance of Christian Churches, which he observed (1953: 3).

In Scandinavia, the organization of universities favoured close cooperation between biblical studies and other disciplines, such as the general history of religion. Accordingly, a wide awareness entered into important formal studies, although these did not necessarily make express reference to materials outside of the ancient Near East. They involved analyses of psalms by Mowinckel (from 1916 on), of prophecy by J. Lindblom (1924, etc. [see 1963]), of both psalms and prophecy by Geo Widengren (in 1936, 1948, etc.), and of biblical literature as a whole by Ivan Engnell (1945, etc.).[57] Mowinckel, in fact, used cultic structures of the Hebrew Bible as a model for discussing cult generally (1953).

Berend Gemser, who had spent some time teaching in South Africa, referred to African and other worldwide parallels in the Dutch version of his commentary on Proverbs (I, 1929: 18-20). These references were eliminated in the briefer German form of the commentary (1937)[58] and thus have often been overlooked.

In Switzerland, the general history of religion was known—and sometimes discussed—by both Eichrodt (cf. the internationally orientated studies, already cited) and Zimmerli, among others. Zimmerli, whose teaching duty from 1935 to c. 1950 included the history of religion, contrasted an element of the biblical creation account with a Chinese theme (1943a: 60) and, more positively, acknowledged

56. Rowley said that he had become 'more conservative' by 1944 (vii).

57. A wide knowledge can generally be assumed for Scandanavian scholars. The discussion of 'honour' and 'soul' by Grønbech were among anthropological analyses presupposed by Pedersen (1926–40). Ringgren published quite widely in the history of religion.

58. This was done presumably either by himself or by his editor Eissfeldt (see 1937, preface), probably since these references were not expected to be a matter of high interest for its particular public. The Dutch version presented a relevant bibliography, including S.C. Malan, *Original Notes on the Book of Proverbs* (3 vols., 1889–93)—a resource not to be overlooked.

Muhammad as a prophet, although as one with limitations (1943b: 137-47, 168-79). Alfred Bertholet pursued the general history and phenomenology of religion with a special focus on Hebrew Scripture.[59] He derived from this Scripture some insights that contribute to an understanding of religion in general for example, a recognition that different perspectives can exist side by side (1923: 12).

In Germany, two rather different approaches were in effect—one, more or less open; another, virtually closed.

The first was carried out by several religiohistorically inclined friends of Gunkel. They included Hugo Gressmann—saying that 'since God is for me a living reality, I must think of [God] as universal' (1926: 1051)[60]—and Willy Staerk, utilizing Heiler's worldwide study of prayer (1920).

Most of Gunkel's students moved along this line. H. Schmidt engaged in a fairly extensive search for parallels, although he limited it for the most part to historically connected cultures (1907) and was reserved toward using analogies (1927: 4). Jahnow presented a comprehensive study of expressions of mourning, with a consideration of mourning as a human universal (1923). Her work is perhaps the only available study of a biblical genre that includes most of the appropriate elements, including comparative ones. An important study of Israelite lay prayer by Wendel (1931) referred extensively to other traditions. Baumgartner believed that worldwide similarities in proverbs reflected a continuing human nature and similar cultural circumstances (1933: 13). Georg Fohrer, a student of Gunkel's student Balla, received his doctorate with a science-of-religion dissertation on 'The Holy Way' in 1939 and expressed himself in favour of cooperation with adherents of other religions for the sake of human welfare (1969: 21 [1965]). His broad orientation probably aided his correcting form-historical aberrations from c. 1960 on (see below, 13.2.a).

In less personal connection with Gunkel stood Hempel, a student of the fairly conservative Rudolf Kittel (whose work paralleled that of Gunkel in some ways)[61] and eventually a teacher of Zimmerli. Hempel

59. For an awareness of his work in the Bakhtin circle, see *RFT*.

60. Is this not an inescapable sense? Even Barth and Brunner, with whom Gressmann had a dispute (Smend 1988: 15f.), did not deny it. Gressmann's examination of wisdom reached towards India (1925: 33). His warm relationship with Jews led to a visit in the US, where (unfortunately) he died.

61. Cf. above. Kittel did not deny all significance to ancient religions, but

believed that the history of religion reveals differences against a back-ground of common features (1922: 5, on prayer). He reasoned that when a comparison is done 'from the point of view of the love of God' (*sub specie amoris Dei*) rather than from a humanistic standpoint, the 'relative' truth of other faiths does not threaten the 'absoluteness' of Christianity; on the grounds that it is necessary to begin with one's religion, he used Christianity as a 'structural paradigm for other reli-gions' (1924a: 13, 15). With considerable irony, he noted that the failure (!) of Mongols to receive the Christian missionaries they had requested had the result of removing a threat from predominantly Christian Europe, since the Mongols were pacified by turning to Buddhism instead of to Christianity (1938b: 47).

A very different, closed line was followed by other German scholars. Friedrich Baumgärtel stated that 'God's law speaks to us only in the Bible, not outside it' (1934: 35; in its context, this statement served as a laudable guard against the idea of a people's special law apart from the Bible, a conception used to support Nazism). Members of the Alt circle took a similar position; although they made repeated reference to geo-graphically adjacent areas, with which historical connections can be assumed, the rest of the humanity was on the whole ignored by them.[62]

A contributing factor to this isolation was an opposition to human endeavours, including 'religion', thought to stand in contrast with Christian faith. This position resembled Barth's perspective; but it was not identical to it, for in Barth's view 'religion' includes Christianity as a religious system while true 'faith' holds to God who rules in so far as there is being. The closed position, however, could serve as a defensive measure against an evil state.

A notable exception to the isolation of this group was the attention given by members of it to the thesis of the fairly conservative August Klostermann (1900) that there is a similarity between the promulgation of Israelite law and mediaeval proclamations of Icelandic law. This 'analogy' was used to illustrate the presumed operation of a cultic pre-sentation of law in Israel.

After World War II, a moderate openness appeared among younger Germans. Especially, Westermann, son of an Africanist (and student of Zimmerli), showed good knowledge of the general history of religion in encyclopaedia articles on images, angels, folk tales, blessing/curse and

considered Israel to be their 'flower' (1921: 96-97).

    62. That was largely true also for Eissfeldt.

temple.[63] He asserted that biblical history does not represent a 'sector history', in the form either of a 'salvation history' (forming a special activity of God) or of a 'history of religion' (separating religion from other aspects of life (1960a: 25 [1955]). He believed that God works outside as well as inside the Church (1975a: 17 [1958]).

Westermann raised the question whether, if one's own religion is regarded as one among many, one has something with which one can live or for which one can die (1960a: 21 [1955]). That is certainly an important question, but there is no evidence that persons with a broad orientation are less committed to life or less ready to risk life and limb than are those more narrowly focused. It seems, however, that those with a wider view are more ready to give service beyond their own group; as we have seen, liberals were relatively high in opposition to Nazism (including aid to Jews).[64] Later, in 1980, Westermann said that an 'unconditional affirmation of one's own religion' is 'no longer possible and responsible in a time of worldwide communication' (154).

Rolf Rendtorff, who was primarily a student of von Rad but was also associated with von Rad's colleague Westermann, argued that according to a Hebrew Bible standpoint revelation is not limited to one human circle.[65] Otto Kaiser, a student of Weiser, advised individuals exegeting texts to take into account religious parallels to them (without overlooking important differences); he said that doing so would aid the recognition of basic structures of existence embodied in texts and thus indicate the relevance of these to their own lives (1963: 31-32).

In making comparisons, a major problem was how to evaluate different faiths. One option was to envision them as forming a set of steps, which might follow each other in a historical sequence. Christianity,

---

63. *Evangelisches Kirchenlexikon*, I, 1956: 518-21, 1071-75; II, 1958: 1238-41; III, 1959: 916-19, 1324-28.

64. See above for Rade and others. In a study of those who gave often quite dangerous aid to Jews during the Hitler years, the following factors (together with a few others) were found to correlate with such aid: family closeness (probably engendering care); a childhood moral education based on reasoning, rather than on authoritarian punishment; and a universal ethics (Oliner and Pearl, 160, 165, 179, 184). The church of the fairly liberal A. Trocmé (who, like Bonhoeffer, had broadened his outlook by presence at Union Seminary in New York) saved many Jews (Haillie).

65. In Pannenberg (1961: 39), K. Koch, another student of von Rad, called for a consideration of the history of religion but rejected a general phenomenology and stressed the 'uniqueness' of Israel and Christianity (1962: 117-18, 122-23).

from early on, believed in a progressive sequence in its relation to the 'Old Testament' and to prior revelation, and expected for the future a glorious denouement even while also believing in a growth of the power of evil; it thus contributed to a more generalized idea of progress, which reached its height in the nineteenth century. Although the idea of progress began to wane in European culture at the end of that century as people became disenchanted with capitalist modernity, it continued—at least in regard to the period BCE—in biblical studies. A belief in progress, then, held true not only for scholars who can be labelled more or less 'liberal'[66] but also for others. For instance, von Rad envisioned a 'growth' in special divine revelation towards the New Testament (1938a: 17, etc.).

Christianity accepted the Hebrew Bible as part of its own eventual canon on the assumption that Christ fulfilled it. In line with this tradition, Protestant (and Catholic) scholarship in all countries for the most part continued to hold that the 'Old Testament' led integrally into the New[67] and that Judaism represented a deviation from its thrust. This was said also by Eichrodt (1933–39, I, §4, B, ii, 5; 1937: 26) and Zimmerli (1941: 10), although these two had a definite—within limits, positive—interest in Judaism.[68] Rowley thought that Israel failed in its mission to the world, even though he expressed appreciation towards Judaism (1952a: 161). Defences of the Old Testament published during the 1930s in Germany did not counter antisemitism but—like most earlier Christian writings—claimed the Hebrew Scripture for Christianity,

---

66. E.g. Gunkel's student Zurhellen-Pfleiderer (influential in public education—1916: viii); G.A. Barton (1918: 1—progressive revelation and evolution are, respectively, a divine and a human way of looking at the process), etc.; Oesterley and Robinson (1930); W. Graham and May (1936); Burrows (1931—rejecting here an attempt 'to demonstrate the superiority of one [religious] founder over another', 223; 1938: 87-88); S.A. Cook (1938); Albright (1940a, barely liberal); and Matthews (1947).

67. E.g. Vischer 1935; Baumgärtel 1937: 107; Noth 1969: 52 (1937); von Rad 1938a: 15; Rowley 1939: 98f. (acknowledging modifications); again, 1946: 295; Albright 1942: 5; Wright 1951: 228. Antisemitism, in fact, was far from limited to, or perhaps even unusually pronounced in, Germany (thus also Bacharach, 46); it was a precondition for the Shoah.

68. See the bibliographies in *TLZ* (85, 1960: 629-34) and in the Zimmerli Festschrift (1977). Zimmerli spent two days at a kibbutz in 1937 (1964a: 45) and was later at least partially supportive of the state of Israel, where Judaism can practice the 'social justice' of Scripture (1954: 8); cf., on him, above.

distinguishing the Hebrew Bible sharply from later Judaism without mentioning that the New Testament differs similarly from later Christianity.[69]

Against this outlook it must be said that, although it is difficult to measure distances between faiths, from an ordinary history-of-religions standpoint it would seem natural to regard the Hebrew Bible as standing closer to Judaism than to Christianity.[70] It is, of course, possible to believe—as both Christians and Jews have done—that Christianity carried the revelation of the Hebrew Bible to the world (to be sure, with modifications).[71] From one point of view, this extension can be seen as a fulfilment; from another, as an attenuated version. (Christianity's universalism does not mean that it is less particularist than is Judaism, for, as we have seen, universalism can be particularism writ large. In fact, Christians have repeatedly been less willing to admit God's activity outside their own circle than Jews have been.[72])

69. E.g. Volz (1932: 27—pointing out that already the Hebrew Bible was highly critical of its people, 6; similarly, others); Alt, Begrich and von Rad (1934: 12-13, 46, 67); Weiser (1934: 50); H.W. Hertzberg (1934); Schmökel (1936: 28); among church leaders and systematic theologians, cf. Faulhaber (1934: 5) (Catholic) and Gloege (1937: 419-20), and see further Nicolaisen (1966: 120, 148; 1971: 218-19). (But Procksch [1936: 4-5] and Weiser [1939: 7] described the Hebrew Bible as Jewish confession or scripture without apology.) The first four volumes of the 'Theological Word Book of the New Testament' (1933–42), which stressed the Hebraic background of the New Testament, were edited by R. Kittel, who was antisemitic (not alone in this). For similar earlier views (from Reuss in 1850 to Sellin in 1932), see Kusche; for others, Smid (225-42); for critiques: Kraus (1991: 4-5 [1963], 243-44 [1986]); Nicolaisen (1966: 119, 148); C. Klein (1975); R. Rendtorff (1980; 1991: 92).

70. As implied also in Matthews (1947). Cf. Buss 1967: 153. Christianity reflects a process of differentiation—i.e. between believing and more 'ordinary' social life—that permitted its spread, since it could coexist with different local patterns. A similar process took place in Buddhism. In neither case, to be sure, did the non-missionary tradition (Judaism, Hinduism) stand still, to constitute a 'fossil' (contra Toynbee, I: 35, etc.). H.W. Robinson (1946: 282) called Israel the 'mother' of both Judaism and Christianity.

71. So, expanding earlier views, F. Rosenzweig (letters to R. Ehrenberg, 1 November 1913, and to E. Rosenstock, October 1916), and W. Herberg (1953: 67-78).

72. It is true, there were Jewish apocalypses that anticipated the destruction of Gentiles, but these were not accepted as canonical by Jews and were, for the most part, transmitted by non-Jews. See Buss 1979: 6 (with n. 7); 1989: 52; Coward 1988: 31-33 (for postbiblical Jewish views). Not without some justice, Rowley

Significance in its own right—not merely as a 'preparation for the New'—was recognized for the Old Testament by some, perhaps most notably by Rowley. He held that it has its own contribution to make, especially in its emphasis on ethics and concrete history (1939: 105, 111; 1946: 13; 1953: 120).[73] Similarly, Wright argued that a 'trinitarian hermeneutics' (contra Barthian 'Christomonism') allows for a role of the first person of the Trinity, without exclusive reference to the revelation given in Jesus.[74] The revelation presented in the Hebrew Bible, according to Wright, involves 'a social and political message', which includes 'natural law ethics' (1951: 238-39; more fully, 1969).

W. Irwin called the Hebrew Scripture 'the keystone of human culture' (1952, subtitle).[75] Such appreciation of the Jewish Bible represented, at least potentially, a moderation of the idea of progress and, with it, a greater recognition for Judaism than before. Albright was one who respected Judaism more highly than had earlier Christians.[76] H.J. Kraus, too, thought it was time for excessive Christian pride to die (1956: 217).

These issues are relevant to form criticism, for this endeavour (according to almost any definition) involves attention to generality. In fact, the contribution made by form-critical studies has been almost directly proportional to their breadth of vision, as will be seen. Nevertheless, one-sided group particularism was widespread among Protestants. Many of them struggled to reach an appreciation for other Protestants and for Catholics and Jews but were not ready to go further afield.

c. *The Particular and the General: Developments in Theory*
It is appropriate, then, to look at the theoretical (philosophical) outlook that was presupposed in critical approaches, especially in regard to the

spoke of Israel's 'aggression [on the world] through Christianity' (1939: 72).

73. Similarly, Eichrodt (1925—see above); (in a sense) some of the 'German Christians' (see below); the Dutch A. van Ruler (1955) and K. Miskotte (1956), with salvation-historical views focusing on the Hebrew Bible (see Reventlow 1986b: 54-60); H.W. Wolff (1956: 366).

74. It must be remembered that without some distinction, relations—however metaphoric they may be for the Trinity—disappear.

75. Produced 'at the crossroads of the ancient world', it included 'natural law' (18, 136).

76. See, for example, 1944: 85-86. He was quite active on behalf of Jewish refugees from 1933 on and supported the state of Israel.

issue of generality. At least two kinds of generality are relevant for the process of interpretation. One is transcultural comparability—a sharing of features by two different streams of tradition. (Attention to such comparability, limited as it was, has already been surveyed.) Another kind of generality is the repetition of an earlier form of life within a single continuous tradition (e.g. Jewish or Christian). These two versions have a common conceptual base, namely, the assumption that two events or beings can share a structure.

As will be remembered, nominalism denies the possibility of sharing, and a major aim of historical criticism has been to free the present from a need to repeat the past. The historical perspective largely carried the day by 1900 in anthropology and sociology, with an evolutionary perspective, but an important question came to be whether any sharing—even only partial sharing—with the past is still possible or advisable. An answer widespread thereafter was that older cultures, including so-called 'primitive' ones, should be valued at least in some respects. For this emerging perspective, one can use the term 'post-historical'; it accepts the historical dimension of change but does not accord this dimension exclusive legitimacy.

In a post-historical manner the following scholars—who also made transcultural comparisons—believed in the abiding value of biblical expressions: H.W. Robinson (1913: 212), Staerk (1920, Introduction: 4), and Rowley (1944: 15, 122; 1946: 11). For instance, Rowley, who did not limit true faith to the Bible, described what he called the 'newer attitude' as follows:

> It accepts substantially the work of Biblical criticism, but beyond the desire to know the date and authorship of the books of the Bible and the meaning they had for their first readers, it seeks the abiding significance of the Bible, and in particular its significance for this generation (1944: 15).

Some writers appealed to the character of great literature as something that transcends specific temporal circumstances (H.W. Robinson 1955: 15 [1916]; Muilenburg 1923: xxxv).[77] Albright held that the 'generic' form of psalms, without specific temporal references, is what 'makes them so universally valid…for all subsequent times' (1950a: 2).

Several voices, however, were heard in opposition to the notion of

---

77. As did the Jewish Jastrow (1919: 8). Muilenburg, however, later said that the revelation contained in the Bible 'does not present itself to us in terms of permanently valid principles or ethical norms' (1951: 214).

general truth. Hempel said that Israelite ethics is not 'timeless-theoretical' and that one cannot legitimately abstract general principles from Old Testament ethical judgments without constantly keeping in mind their historical reality (1938a: 89-90). This formulation, unfortunately, is ambiguous, for 'timeless' can mean either 'non-temporal' (not related to time) or 'transtemporal' (not limited to one time).[78] Somewhat clearer was a statement by Zimmerli that the biblical message of the reign of God is not a 'general' idea, for that statement said explicitly that the message is bound to a place and time and is not available to all human beings as an insight (*einsichtig* [1940: 135]). Zimmerli did acknowledge a 'wisdom' aspect of the Bible, which presents general truths and has the 'authority of persuasiveness by insight (*Einsicht*)', but he believed that this does not form the 'centre' of biblical revelation (1949b: 369-75; 1963: 308; cf. 1971: 19).

Von Rad declared that a treatment of biblical narratives as expressions of 'general religious truths' should be opposed as resolutely as possible; he gave as a negative example the religious education texts by Zurhellen-Pfleiderer, which had a pronounced historical perspective but did not hold to a salvation history with a limited extent (von Rad 1942: 48). Similarly, the fairly conservative Swiss J. Stamm stated that the Hebrew Bible does not present basic principles but rather a special history not subject to general laws (1956: 393). Wolff also questioned the applicability of 'generally valid anthropological principles' to the Bible (1963b: 5).

In large part on the basis of form-critical observations, von Rad gave major attention to structural correspondences, but these operated, in his view, only within the biblical circle. Like Barth, he saw the history told in the Old Testament as a prerepresentation of Christ, a 'shadow' of what is properly real (*des Eigentlichen*), a 'prototype';[79] but, unlike Barth, he rejected analogies outside of that circle.[80]

---

78. For example, when Barth said that 'creation is not a timeless truth, although...it involves all time' and that God's actions are both 'eternal, covering all time' and 'concretely temporal' (1945: 64), he clearly meant by 'timeless' something that is 'not related to time'; he did not reject transtemporality.

79. 1936: 276; 1943: 232; 1952/53: 17-33 (saying that 'typology' as a form of thinking is general-human, 1953: 413); 1957–60, II: 398 (citing Barth).

80. 1957–60, II: 377, 382; in later editions, he made clear that he was not referring to 'external', superficial, analogies. (Barth, as we have seen, saw analogies in other faiths and in love between the sexes, etc.). Von Rad did allude to 'simpler' versions of biblical structures in extra-Israelite (earlier?) texts (1963: 416) and

In his 'Theology of the Old Testament' (1957–60), von Rad developed the following scheme: past structures represented in narratives were projected into the future by Israelite prophets; thus, there is a correspondence between two major complexes within the Hebrew Bible, differing in their temporal direction. The prophetic projection, according to von Rad, points towards Christ, who is the true goal of the Old Testament, which lacks a 'centre' in itself (II: 376).[81] Von Rad, further, indicated that the literary structures of the New Testament correspond to those of the Old Testament; they fulfil the prophetic projection and provide both a past and a future for Christians. This pattern analysis may very well be correct in major ways (such as regarding a sacred past and a sacred future), but it is questionable whether it should be limited to the biblical tradition. Von Rad did not discuss—and may not have been familiar with—alternative positions developed by Rowley (and others) on the relations of the Hebrew Bible to the New Testament[82] and to other faiths, although by 1957 von Rad's perspective had become more international than it had been earlier.

Von Rad, in fact, moved gradually into the direction of accepting reasonableness (and thus generality) as an aspect of faith. In 1938, he had denied that there are many biblical passages that 'persuade by making sense' (*einleuchten*, 1938a: 12); furthermore (in 1951b: 145), he had contrasted Israelite faith with religions that refer to 'universal laws'. In 1957, however, he allowed Gemser's study of motivations in biblical law to show him that they have the goal to make laws 'understandable' (in the sense of understanding 'why') so that human beings can 'affirm them from within'. Although there are non-rational aspects of biblical law, the Bible's God (he said) asks for 'mature [free] obedience' expressing love and thanksgiving.[83] He noted that the tendency to provide motivations—apparently a growing one in Israel—was not present in ancient Near Eastern law codes and concluded that

referred to 'the universality of the Old Testament faith in creation' (1957–60, II: 401). Nevertheless, von Rad was more 'historical' than Barth (Koch 1966: 485).

81. In 1960, he regarded Christ's fulfilment of the Old Testament as being obvious (1957–60, II: 387); in later editions, this statement disappeared.

82. E.g. in regard to the independent value of the Hebrew Bible, which a purely typological approach undermines (despite von Rad 1943: 232; 1957–60, II: 344), as was recognized by R. Rendtorff (1959: 48).

83. 1957–60, I: 199, 202 (4th edn, 211, 213); German words used were *begreiflich, verstehen, innerlich bejahen, mündig*. (Similary, Plato, *Laws*, 720-23.)

the providing of reasons was a special biblical feature.[84] He pointed out, further, that Israelite wisdom sought rational insight (1957–60, I: 423, 432, 449; 1970: 366). In 1970, he came to say that Israel did not differentiate between rational and religious apprehensions (86).

Finally, in an article on Christian wisdom shortly before his death, von Rad observed that Jesus' words 'swarm with conclusions based on reason and experience' (1971: 153). Thus, he raised the question whether Christian faith should perhaps furnish truths that are 'evident'; he asked whether experience is only a lottery (as would be suggested by a theology stressing God's arbitrariness) or whether there are connections that have a logic. He indicated that 'we can learn much from today's human sciences' and that, in fact, there is a great need for 'catching up' in dealing with them. Speaking for the circle in which he moved, he said that 'we teach life without the nearness of God' and that this distance of theology (including biblical studies) from the world has led to a 'terrible muteness' (in an 'equally terrible...loquaciousness'). He called for a 'helpful conversation with the other' (154). Such a conversation presumably includes listening, for in a 1964 sermon von Rad had indicated that challenging words now come especially from outside the Church, from poets and philosophers acting as prophetic voices (1972: 136). Von Rad's late statement in 1971 in many ways furnished a model for the future, since it represented a break with what he and others who stood close to him had done earlier. Among factors that led von Rad in this direction, one can consider the circumstance that he had spent time outside Germany and, probably even more so, the political events of the late 1960s.[85]

Prior to 1965, a denial of generality was especially (although not exclusively) prominent in German-speaking Protestant scholarship. It loosened attachments to old ways (in that sense it was anti-traditional), but it also formed the theoretical base for excluding attention to other religions and for being reserved about the use of humanistic disciplines

84. This comparison is, perhaps, not quite fair, since so-called 'law codes' in Mesopotamia represent a narrower genre, but von Rad is not the only one to have observed a special tendency towards rationality in Israelite law/ethics (among these was Hempel 1926b: 209f.).

85. In 1960/61, von Rad taught at Princeton Theological Seminary. My work having been stimulated by him, I paid a visit to him there and during that argued (as perhaps others did) for the importance of the discipline of anthropology for form criticism. See also below, 13.2.b, for von Rad's development c. 1950 after spending time on the British Isles. Truly, scholarship can gain from exchanges.

(in this way it was conservative). The rejection of generality was characteristic not only of Barthians but also of 'German Christians'. Among these, the doctrine of divine creation was called upon as a basis for valuing a folk or race, for creation was not thought by them to involve generality—as has been held to be the case by others—but to ground particularity. This position was in line with Ockham's theory that God creates particulars rather than general structures.

To review the historical development of this outlook, it is useful to mention that since the end of the eighteenth century, on the whole increasingly until the 1930s, a major emphasis was placed by Germans on the nation as a particular unit; this outlook continued and perhaps sharpened earlier non-German views concerning national differences.[86] In a similar way, German Protestant biblical scholarship emphasized particularity for Israel increasingly during the nineteenth century (Smend 1991: 117-27) and in the first half of the twentieth, intensifying historical criticism which had begun in other countries. Nominalism indeed came to be characteristic of German thought during the period under discussion, but it did not originate in that time and place and was, in fact, not limited to it.

Specifically, a particularist position was expressed by denying the presence of 'abstractions' in the Bible (Wright 1944: 66 [more cautiously 1952: 85]; Zimmerli 1964b: 17) and, going further, by rejecting even the legitimacy of abstracting principles from the Bible (Westermann 1954b: 305; von Rad 1957–60, II: 385). A denial of the presence of abstraction is appropriate if by 'abstract' one means 'lacking concreteness', for biblical representations are usually not purely abstract. It is, however, not accurate to say that biblical language is only concrete. Characteristic of biblical speech, rather (as Stauffer saw [see above, 12.3.e]), is a union in which a particular person or event represents a general reality (e.g. Jacob as Israel and David as a prototype for individuals praying).[87]

---

86. See above for Dryden and other non-Germans; Tilgner (1966) for German Protestants; also, G. van Norden (229); Oden (12-15, 38); Barr (1993: 112). The 'German Christian' J. Hossenfelder said that religion must be *artgemäss*, according to national kind (1933: 15).

87. This union was still largely intact in early Protestant thought (called 'realistic' by H. Frei). Applicable to it is Albright's phrase 'empirical logic'— although it is far from clear that this succeeds an earlier 'proto-logical' thinking (contra Albright 1964: 319 [1948], etc.), for it seems to be present in non-human animals. (At the same time, Albright [1964: 72] underestimated developments in

The term 'abstraction' is, strictly, a nominalist term; it was used by mediaeval and later nominalists to denote the 'drawing out' of general terms from particular objects believed to be primary.[88] For biblical writers, as for other ancient and most current thinkers, 'abstractions' are not really necessary, for a perception of an object is never without a theoretical pattern; one always sees an object 'as' something. In fact, particularist theory has usually been held only in the moderate ('conceptualist') form, which accepts general terms on a secondary basis as abstractions. To deny the use of general terms even for readers, to serve as interpretive abstractions from the concrete data, constitutes a very radical nominalism. (In contrast, 'liberation' came later to be a widely used general term for a biblical theme.)

We have noted (in Chapter 7) that purely concrete thinking is transcended in relational formal thought; this often, again, employs 'models' to exhibit relations.[89] That kind of thinking was slow to make inroads into Protestant theology. Nevertheless, steps were gradually taken towards it. For instance, Wright became more thoroughgoing than he had been (1952: 32) in recognizing the symbolic nature of speech about God, in which concrete symbols point beyond themselves (1960, 1969).

A significant theoretical statement combining particularity with generality was presented by Mowinckel already in 1938 (ET 1959). He held that the Hebrew Bible implies the presence not only of 'special revelation', but also of '"common revelation" in nature, intelligence, consciousness, and history' (1959: 54). He believed that they are not two independent paths towards truth, for 'reason and revelation are not opposites' (81-82). In his opinion, 'honest thinking' wants to know not only 'that' something happened but also 'how and why' (65). He recognized individuality *and* generality—*both* in humanity *and* in non-human nature—and saw that the phenomenon of probability joins these two aspects (65-66).

formal logic after Aristotle.) H. Knight thought that 'under the abstracting operation of intellectual analysis, the character of reality as experienced simply evaporates' (1947: 16); yet it is likely that Israelite faith contained an intellectual dimension.

88. See above, 4.3.c.

89. Cf. Gerhart and Russell 1984 (with bibliography): 'There are many things we know that have the same form' (111)—thus, extended knowledge and understanding are possible. Rosch (see above, 1.2) has stressed the use of models in human categorization (not just in formal thought).

Mowinckel argued against a then-widespread sceptical relativism, pointing out that it is 'hostile to life' and leads to a 'cry for authority' in politics in order to avoid anxiety (64-65—accurately describing what was happening in Germany as well as elsewhere). This statement by him implies a critical attitude towards authoritarianism. Mowinckel nevertheless accepted an element of external authority in theology, for he asserted without much reason that the eternal fate of humanity rests upon the 'one Jesus'. Employing a phrase popular in theological circles at that time, he said that God 'has broken vertically into history' to plant something absolute (67), although, shortly before that, he had stated that '*everything* stands in a natural continuity' (51). Thus he did not carry through fully with a relational view.[90]

Mowinckel indicated that 'it is both biblical and "Christian"'[91] to acknowledge a divine revelation, a contact with God, a spiritual light, even though broken and unclear, among the great religious heroes of other religions' (117). He did not make equally clear at that point that biblical expressions, too, are broken and unclear, although he quite probably believed that to be the case. Mowinckel, however, said that Israel 'purified' myth without removing it altogether, for—contra Bultmann—'mytho-poetic' form is necessary for religion (1959: 104-106).[92]

Concerning form criticism, Mowinckel said that Gunkel-type genre criticism (*Gattungsforschung*) had from its beginning worked with sociology and psychology. Understanding the special in the light of what is general and typical, that path reaches 'a more living and organic picture' of prophets and of their message than would otherwise be possible (1938: 10).

A large number of studies, with a high point in the 1950s, declared that history is the primary medium of revelation in the Bible. The word

90. In the Norwegian original, 'has broken vertically' is placed in quotation marks—an obvious allusion to a Barthian (quasi-Barthian?) theme.

91. In line with early Church 'apologetes', whose openness to (Greek) reason was rejected by Ritschl and (in his train) by Harnack, Barth and Bultmann. For instance, Justin (second century CE) characterized those who 'lived by reason'—including leading Greek and pre-Christian biblical figures—as 'Christians' (*Apology* 1.46).

92. A response to Bultmann—with use of the term 'mytho-poetic' (in quotes, probably alluding to Wilder [1955: 82, 122, 165])—was added in the ET of 1959, but the general position was already clear in the Norwegian, 1938. See also 1953: 135.

'history', however, was used with a wide range of meanings. The fact that the word was used even though there was little agreement on its sense probably reflects the fact that scholars held on to an older tradition in which this term was central, although this tradition was waning outside Protestant theology and was losing its cultural importance.[93] 'History' referred sometimes to particularity[94] and sometimes (especially in the 'existentialist' tradition) to the human as distinct from the non-human world; it could refer to both contrasts at once, since some thinkers continued the view that had begun in the preceding period that human reality is not bound by natural laws. Alternatively, the word could designate—often against Bultmann—connectedness,[95] especially social existence (Wright 1952: 49). For many scholars, explicitly or implicitly, the emphasis on history meant a downgrading of the role of law in contrast to the importance which this had for Judaism.[96]

Most interpreters, however, did not identify history as the only relevant category for biblical thought. That became especially true towards the end of the period under discussion, but balanced statements had already appeared earlier. Specifically, Weiser affirmed as significant both one-time events and an eternal message (1931: 1). H.W. Robinson held that 'history...is one form or aspect of the eternal' (1942: 171), since 'time is in God, and not God in time' (1939: 155). Wright spoke of the 'revelation of the eternal in the temporal' (1944: 104).

Although some scholars contrasted biblical 'history' with 'myth', others accepted for the Hebrew Bible a mythical dimension.[97] B.W. Anderson referred to biblical 'myths' of beginning and end, for which the language of history must be used (1951: 244, 254-55, with a reference to Wilder). Ringgren asserted that 'to the Israelite myth and

93. This waning was recognized in the 1960s also by scholars who favoured 'history': Wolff (1960: 218); Koch (1962: 177-78); Westermann (1963: 269-70).

94. H.W. Robinson 1942: 176; Wright 1952: 13, 42; Noth, 1952/53: 14; von Rad, 1952/53: 21; 1957–60, II: 330.

95. Zimmerli, 1952/53: 40; Albright 1964: 318.

96. That was explicit already in Noth (1969: 47 [1928]).

97. Mowinckel spoke of the Exodus 'myth', because it is cultic and has 'salvation-historical' significance (1922: 45). Childs (1960), differently, expressed a largely (although not entirely) negative attitude toward myth, one that was criticized by the Catholic J. McKenzie (1960: 338). M.-L. Henry described myth as an expression for the transcendent, which goes also beyond oneself (1992: 41, 56 [1961]). On the whole, 'myth' was rejected by those who stressed the difference between biblical and other faith.

history are not essentially distinct from each other' (1963: 107 [1957]); in this he was followed by Engnell (1970: 205 [1962]).[98] Indeed, virtually all interpreters saw that the biblical view was transtemporal in the sense that the narrated history had relevance for the present of the biblical writer. L. Köhler held, for this reason, that 'the Hebrew spirit has hardly a past or history' (1953: 126).

Graves and Patai (the latter a Jew) retold stories of the book of Genesis together with later Jewish variations of them in *Hebrew Myths* (1964). They characterized myths as 'dramatic stories that form a sacred charter either authorizing the continuance of ancient institutions, customs, rites and beliefs...or approving alterations' (11 [the criticizing aspect of myths is often overlooked, but their legitimizing function relates not only to what is already established]).

In regard to a much-discussed contrast between history and nature, Weiser believed that for the Hebrew Bible they form a 'unity' (1934: 53), although history is primary (1931: 49). Albright viewed them as 'one' (1940a: 87). According to S.A. Cook, the 'ultimate processes in the Universe cannot be external to us', since we are part of it (1938: 304), and the Bible did not 'sever' God, humanity and nature (1945: 185). H.W. Robinson saw in the 'symphony' of nature, humanity and history 'the unity of Revelation amid all its diversity' (1946: 279).[99] Samuel Terrien considered that the Psalms did not make a clear distinction between nature and history (1952: 85). The thesis that in the Hebrew Bible God is lord of both of these was affirmed by Zimmerli (1963a: 299 [1959]) and Westermann (1960b: 102).[100] Von Rad, too, believed that Israel did not divide nature from history as 'deeply as we are used to do' (1957–60, II: 350), although—like H.W. Robinson (1946: 123) and perhaps more so—he held that history is primary (as he stated in 1936 [1958: 146]).

In one of his intercultural comparisons, Rowley pointed out that history is not a category unique to biblical faith: 'The Chinese Sages also believed that God was active in history' (1956a: 136). This observation by him undercut a line of argument (then quite common) which pro-

---

98. Hooke (1963) used the term 'myth' for large aspects of biblical traditions (e.g. concerning Elijah and Elisha, 156), as E.O. James had done.

99. Similarly, Rowley (1956b: 47): God is revealed 'in many ways'.

100. In 1964 Westermann projected a path that avoids both pure history and pure (generalized) phenomenology (191); he used the word 'blessing' to designate the steady aspect of divine activity (210, as already in 1957b: 525).

ceeded from an assertion that the Bible is unique in its emphasis on history[101] to the conclusion that God acted primarily in the sphere of biblical history. (A more logical conclusion of the initial assertion would have been that Israel was uniquely aware of the historical aspect of revelation.)

The notion of history itself underwent a change, especially well represented in the writings of H.W. Robinson. Most important, perhaps, was the fact that 'we are no longer sure that history spells progress' (1942: xxv). Rather, 'the contingency of history is…one aspect of its actuality' (xviii); presumably, then, it does not contain a movement towards an inevitable goal. Furthermore, 'the relativity of truth' is inherent in revelation to particular persons (1942: 84-85).[102]

Robinson rejected the possibility of speaking of 'bare events', that is, of a history without a subjective element (1942: xx-xxi, 183). The same position was taken by John Marsh (1952: 160-62). Earlier already, as has been mentioned, Eichrodt had drawn attention to the subjective element in history, as well as to the fact that historians need general concepts for their understanding (1929: 86); a similar emphasis had been made by Weiser (1931: 20), known to Marsh. Von Rad acknowledged, at least from 1960 on (with a knowledge of Marsh, etc.),[103] that all history is 'interpreted' (1957–60, II: 9) and that there are no 'brute facts' (1964b: 393).[104] Westermann (1960a: 26 [1955]) and Zimmerli

---

101. E.g. Wright 1952: 38; R. Rendtorff 1959: 48 (expressing a widespread opinion).

102. Westermann observed (1964: 190) that in England and Scandinavia the relation between what is common and what is special was a matter of widespread concern and that little attempt was made to establish the 'absoluteness' of Israel's faith.

103. Von Rad cited Marsh (in 1957–60, II: 112-13). If H.W. Robinson (1942) in part stood behind Marsh (although Marsh did not refer to it), that would mean at least an indirect impact of this work on von Rad. Von Rad did cite H.W. Robinson (1946) in 1957–60, II: 113 (indeed, von Rad [1957-60, II: 424] echoes Robinson [1946: 282] in the relational thesis that biblical theology needs to be rewritten for each generation).

104. In 1938a: 14f., von Rad had still spoken of the 'facticity' of Christ (with a 'real presence' in the Old Testament); in 1957–60, I: 117, he had mentioned 'exact historiography' as different from biblical history writing. (A distinction between 'fact' and interpretation reappeared in 1963: 412, 414.) Differently from H.W. Robinson, however, he rejected the 'modern' view of history as relative (1957–60, II: 117). Von Rad's students did not accept his literary understanding of history.

(1962b: 25) held, at least for the point of view of the Hebrew Bible, that history and word belong together. (Temple had located revelation in 'the coincidence of event and appreciation' [1934: 315].)

Albright's theory of history placed major emphasis on analogy (1964: 73-74). He regarded biblical history as 'humanly speaking, the outcome of normal processes' (1964: 318 [1948]).

Applying the historical perspective to itself, Westermann pointed out that historical criticism is itself '"temporally conditioned"—needed, but not the only possible method' (1960a: 20 [1955]). For a different path which can be taken, Barr pointed to the rise of 'sciences like the social sciences, anthropology, economics, linguistics', etc. Their methods 'are only in part historical', he noted; 'they show us that human life...can be and must be studied with transhistorical as well as with historical approaches' (1963: 203).

In fact, a number of scholars had employed these human disciplines by then. True, some used them as means for reaching historical conclusions,[105] instead of deriving from the Bible insight into social order and experience. However, that was by no means the case for all, as will be seen. One, for instance, who stood relatively high in theory and was also concerned with major genres was H.W. Robinson. He interacted with psychology (from 1911 on),[106] sociology (e.g. 1946: 163) and anthropology (e.g. African jurisprudence, 1936: 49).[107] Since the human sciences had incorporated a relational perspective, this thus began to enter into biblical study.

2. *Major Paths in Form Criticism: Form-History, History of Form, Form Analysis and Theory of Form*

It is useful to distinguish within form criticism four major phases by means of the following terms: 'form-history', 'history of form(s)', 'analysis of form' and 'theory of form'. (The first three of these have already been discussed for New Testament studies in Chapter 12.) What these approaches have in common is that they incorporate the

---

105. Cf. Kraus 1969, §§75-76. Primarily historical was, for example, Noth (he had theological interests but did not spell them out; cf. 1940: vi).

106. See 1942: ix. He discussed psychological beliefs by Israelites and the experiential psychology of language, prophecy and sacrifice (1923: 1-15; 1925; 1942: 41) and treated the literature's wrestling with suffering (1939).

107. Similarly comprehensive was J. Pedersen (1926–40).

interest in form that emerged in a new way in the twentieth century. They differ in the way they relate this interest to the historical orientation that was dominant in the preceding period, as follows.

The procedure of *'form-history'* (history determined by form) attempts to reconstruct the history of literature through an examination of its forms. It does so on the basis of assumptions that convert formal-structural observations into diachronic-historical ones, as will be seen. Quite differently, a *'history of form(s)'* is a sequential examination of literary forms, after their times and places have been individually determined on the basis of such historical criteria as allusions to events or actual attestations (e.g. archaeological locations). *'Form analysis'*, differently again, utilizes diachronic information, such as that a text was written during the first millennium BCE, but its aim is the recognition of form; it is 'historical' not in a developmental sense but in the sense that it lays bare structures of human existence synchronically, for synchrony, too, is a kind of history. Finally, *'theory of form'* does not just treat a particular text but moves towards principles, asking transtemporally what factors play a role in, behind, or in response to, texts.

Of these four approaches, the first one is, in principle, flawed. The other three procedures, however, are legitimate and indeed valuable phases of form criticism. The four will be treated in turn, as they were pursued between 1915 and 1965.

a. *Form-History and History of Forms*
Although 'form-history' and 'history of forms' can be distinguished, in practice they often intertwine. In fact, the German word *Formgeschichte* frequently covers both approaches.[108] Studies devoted to these two paths will thus be treated together.

'Form-history' in Hebrew Bible studies rested on several assumptions that had been set forth by Gunkel in what must be regarded as the problematic aspect of his work. Neither Gunkel nor those who followed him in these assumptions provided adequate supporting evidence for holding them; indeed, the general opinion in other disciplines ran contrary to them. This discrepant situation is probably best explained on the basis of a fairly strong isolation of the biblical scholars who

---

108. Thus, Bultmann (1928—see above) and Koch (1964—the latter with primary emphasis on the 'history of forms' but adhering to some of the assumptions commonly used in form history).

practised that procedure after Gunkel; the isolation was due in part to an academic tradition separating disciplines, already discussed,[109] and in part to a 'neo-orthodox' theological tradition which—according to a possible definition of that designation—was sceptical of engagement with secular disciplines (this tradition stood close to Barth, but, since individual thinkers vary, it was not strictly Barthian). Separation from the secular world had a side to be welcomed, in that it prevented some of the scholars from being heavily involved in Nazism. Yet the separatist perspective itself reflected a philosophy that resembled Nazism in its particularism, and the group's work suffered from a lack of insight that might have come through interaction with others.[110] Scholars outside Germany, as well as Catholic German scholars,[111] rarely accepted the questionable assumptions, probably because they were better connected with other fields. Within Protestant German scholarship, adherence to them began to collapse in the 1960s, although it continues even today. Opinions on both sides will be cited.

One of the primary assumptions was that **early stages of literature contained short units**. This idea was applied to Second Isaiah by Gressmann in 1917, Köhler in 1923, Mowinckel in 1931, and Begrich in 1938.[112] Gressmann thought that the shorter a story, the older it was (1913: 375).[113] Wendel believed that 'old' prayers were brief, for they appear thus in narratives and he judged that reports of extended prayer sessions reflect later times (1931: 127). He did not make clear why quotations (which might easily be condensed) should be accepted as full reports, while references to early extended sessions should be disbelieved. Westermann radicalized Wendel's conception by holding that hymns, vows and laments each grew from a single sentence (1954a: 52; 1984: 145).[114]

109. See 11.3.b; 12.1 (together with Harnack's responses to it).

110. One might judge that biblical studies between 1933 and 1945 suffered from what Wehrli (18), with reference to Germanics during this period, termed a 'psychosis'. Nevertheless, some aspects of that work remain valuable.

111. See Tricot (1939), Schick (1940) and Benoit (1946), mentioned above, and A. Szörényi (1961: 133, 138, opposing an original purity of genres.).

112. See Muilenburg (1956: 384), opposing this assumption.

113. A. Lods believed that brevity and antiquity correlate 'on the whole' (150: 145). It is, of course, possible that such a sequence happens to hold for biblical writings.

114. For long oral prayers in Africa, cf. Evans-Pritchard (1956: 22). Westermann has noted that in the Bible long prose prayers are late (1973: 84), but that sequence

Von Rad believed that the Hexateuch (Genesis to Joshua) grew out of a 'credo' (Deut. 26.5-10), primarily on the grounds that this was a ritual presentation and brief (1938b). Fohrer (1961a: 16), however, gave good reasons to believe that the 'credo' was a relatively late formulation, probably a 'concentrated summary'; in this he was soon followed by others. Albright (1950b: 163) undermined the idea that early works were concise by referring to Ugaritic texts.[115]

A second presupposition was that **forms were more rigid in ancient times than they are now**. This was stated, for example, by Mowinckel (1962, I: 25) and K. Koch (1964: 13). Contra this view, one can say that while deliberate individualism is indeed largely modern, that does not necessarily mean that ancient formulations were rigid. The one example of rigidity that Koch gave hardly represented a 'proof' of such a state. The sayings of Confucius, for instance, are varied, and ethnographic accounts of oral forms since early in the century have reported flexibility.[116] Wisely, Engnell held that the 'so-called literary categories' were not 'real and conscious patterns' according to which psalms were composed (1960: 28). G.W. Ahlström, his student, held that genres are not 'finished schemes' which secondarily 'break up' (*Psalm 89*, 1959: 10).

A third important form-historical assumption was that **'original' oral forms were clearly distinct from one another** and that these were only secondarily joined ('mixed') together, especially in writing. (Thus again C. Kuhl [1958: 998]: 'The genres, which originally were cleanly separated from each other, became complicated and were modified; they affected each other and became more strongly mixed'.) Gunkel's friend Staerk, for instance, thought that a mixture of styles reveals a 'lack of feeling for style, which, apparently became pronounced as time went on' (1920: 1). Weiser, however, pointed out that a mixture of styles appears already in the Song of Deborah, so that a purity of genres was not standard during the Israelite period (1950: 12).

One version of the assumption of originally distinct forms was the belief that many forms which now appear in several kinds of speech originated in only one of these kinds. Thus, Begrich held that the oracle

probably reflects only the history of written literature.

115. He was cited by C.H.W. Brekelmans, one of the critics of von Rad's theory (1963: 3). Cf., further, J. Durham (1976: 197-99).

116. For ethnographic views, see *RFT* and the report by G. Kittel noted above, 10.3.

of salvation was a priestly form 'imitated' by prophets (1934: 90) and that *torah*, 'instruction', was originally priestly even though the term *torah* also occurs frequently in wisdom (in Hempel *et al.* 1936: 64). Zimmerli held that the 'self-introduction' formula 'I am Yahweh' moved from priestly to prophetic speech, since he believed that the formula must have started out belonging to one or the other tradition in its 'pure' version (1963a: 26, 34 [1953]).[117]

Such judgments about originally separate forms ignored the fact that societies tend towards a division of labour with a larger number of specialities as they grow in size; in fact, the examples of distinct genres given by Koch (1964: 3-6) come from 'our present' time. Mowinckel, more appropriately, pointed to an early union of priestly and prophetic roles (1923: 9; 1962, II: 56).[118] Similarly, Engnell (1945: 69-70) argued against a sharp distinction between priestly and prophetic oracles in Israel.

In his analysis of the 'credo' (1938b), von Rad judged that the absence of a reference to the Sinai tradition is attributable to its being originally independent of it.[119] Weiser (1949a: 68-70) and Fohrer (1964: 122), however, rejected this view. The issue is similar to a question in New Testament studies: whether, or to what extent, narratives and ethical instructions (sometimes called *kerygma* and *didache*, respectively) form independent traditions or are part of a larger whole.[120]

---

117. R. Rendtorff argued that the simplest form here represented a secondary 'reduction...to extreme consiseness' (1960: 836). Zimmerli further assigned to the formula 'that you may know that I am Yahweh' (or similarly) an old priestly 'home' (1963a: 89 [1954]); the antiquity of relevant passages, however, is in severe doubt (thus already Fohrer [1965: 449]; the occurences in Exodus may well be exilic).

118. To be precise, Mowinckel connected the priestly role primarily with a non-ecstatic seer role (following Hölscher); a more generalized connection (including the ecstatic) was made by Haldar (1945: 199). It is, in fact, quite possible that early Levites were relatively undifferentiated in providing religious/social leadership; cf. von Rad (1947: 143); Buss (1969: 82); Schulz (1987: 95).

119. That may, of course, be true even though the appearance of separate formulations can have other reasons; cf. the use of different songs at Christmas and Easter, referring to different parts of a single story.

120. Cf. above. A. Seeberg (1903) argued for a single, although differentiated, catechism; others, including Wernle (1899), Heinrici (1908), Wendland (1912), M. Dibelius (1919) and Dodd (1937), highlighted at least a relative independence for these forms.

The assumptions concerning rigid and separate genres at an early time appeared together in an oft-cited statement by Alt in his study of law:

> Genre- or form-historical study rests on the insight that in every individual genre, as long as it lives its own life, specific contents are firmly connected (*fest verbunden*) with specific forms of expression…since they corresponded to the special, regularly recurring events and needs of life out of which the genres each individually arose (1934: 11).

The statement reflects ideas of Gunkel but goes a step beyond them in picturing ancient persons almost as automatons in a highly differentiated social order.

Alt, like a number of others, held that early groups of prescriptions were each distinct in content and formulation before they were joined with each other. In contrast, R.H. Pfeiffer stated—probably more correctly—that the union of different kinds of regulations in a single body of law continued a comprehensive tradition that is older than the formation of specialized codes in Mesopotamia (1941: 31).[121] Scandinavians who argued for the antiquity of non-pure legal and other forms included Gunnar Hylmö (1938: 111) and, especially, Aage Bentzen (1948a: 111).

Mowinckel vacillated. In response to Alt's formulation in 1934, he stated that 'strict formal uniformity is almost always a result of an extensive development and of a conscious cultivation of a genre; the whole history of culture seems to show that at the beginning is multiplicity and that systematization is an end result' (1937: 219). Later he reiterated this point and argued—against Gunkel—that it is a 'law of evolution' that the unmixed, simple forms are later than the composite and undifferentiated ones, pointing out once again that the oldest known songs were impure in style (1962, I: 96-97). He believed, nevertheless, that secondary mixtures also occur (96-97). This possibility must indeed be recognized, but his assertion that such mixture was done 'without any real comprehension' and represented 'a disintegration of the style' (II: 111) went counter to the principle he had stated earlier.

In Mesopotamian psalm literature—older than the Israelite—praise and lament often stood together. As we have already seen (above,

121. Cf. a similar union, with comparable stylistic variations, in the Roman Twelve Tables (Buss 1977: 61).

11.2.d), Stummer, in 1924, challenged Gunkel's idea that this conjunction represents a secondary mixture and suggested, rather, that there was a movement toward differentiation. C.C. Cumming, comparing 'The Assyrian and Hebrew Hymns of Praise' (1934), took Stummer's position further by referring also to ancient Indian and other hymns in which praise and petition are regularly (even if not always) joined; he believed that in Israel the praise motif was secondarily 'developed into an independent hymn of praise' (18). (This conclusion, however, referred only to the relative frequency of such independent hymns and needs to be further modified.)[122]

Westermann oscillated between recognizing a tendency towards differentiation (probably because of his knowledge of anthropology) and assuming an original purity of genres. A complicated picture may be correct; his analysis, however, wavered between these two different paradigms, adding a speculative form-history to a history of forms based on datable texts, as follows.

For psalms as they appear in the Bible, Westermann observed that petition or lament never appears alone, without praise or an expression of confidence (1954a: 51), although lament appears alone in narrative reports of early prose prayer (reports which he took to be complete).[123] Furthermore, he insisted that petition and praise imply each other in principle; that means that even though a short (non-liturgical) expression contained, in his view, only one of these two themes, it operated as part of a larger complex which involved both, a 'polarity' (1954a: 15, 51-52, 113).[124] For use in repeated ritual, he believed, the psalms combined the small elements that were spoken separately in informal contexts (1973: 84; 1984: 19-20). He held, however, that at an advanced stage in Israel's history a differentiation occurred both within psalms of

122. Some 'pure' or nearly 'pure' hymns of praise written in Mesopotamia and Egypt did not become accessible until after 1934. Hindu commentators recognized both distinctions and connections between 'praise' of a deity and a statement of 'desire' for something deity can provide (Patton: 72f.,105-35).

123. 1954c: 66-71; he suspected that a report that was more than very brief had been elaborated beyond its original short form (68)—why?

124. This analysis stands in some contrast with the positive valuation Westermann placed on Israel's producing independent psalms of praise, as Babylon, according to his report, did not (1954a: 25). His reference to Egyptian hymns (30-35), however, shows that he was at least partially aware that Israel was not peculiar in having 'pure' hymns. (An 'alternation between lament and thanks' in the life of the 'pious' was mentioned by Gunkel and Begrich [1933: 284].)

praise (1954: 98) and within psalms of petition and lament (1964: 292-305 [1954]); he claimed that the newer separate laments (without petition) were different from the older separate laments. However, since he had only narrative reports for the older prayers, there was inadequate evidence for such a conclusion.[125] Probably better grounded—especially in light of the general history of religion—was Wendel's judgment that both simple and combined forms ran parallel to each other for a long time (1931: 13).

Westermann envisioned an early time when religion was not yet separated from politics, law, art, etc. (1960b: 25), so that there was not yet even a separate religious language (1975b: 77-86). Specifically, he believed that the notion of a constant 'blessing' belonged to a pre-theological period, in which there was still an undifferentiated relation to God (1957b: 536). He also said, however, that the idea of blessing is sufficiently different from Israel's historical confession that it has 'nothing to do' with it (525). Similarly, he thought that the relatively humanist 'seer' word had in its root 'nothing to do' with divine speech in prophecy, although these two styles were mixed early (1960a: 30).[126] These judgments do not harmonize well with the idea of an early unity.

A special type of differentiation is a distinction between strictly religious or 'cultic' and other aspects of life. As has already been mentioned, Noth distinguished between 'state law' and 'sacral law' during the Israelite monarchy (1940: 36).[127] Furthermore, like von Rad (1938b: 44-45), he believed that the traditions of the Pentateuch began to a large extent in a cultic context prior to the monarchy—in the 'mouth of the priest' or of the 'celebrating community'—and then passed beyond that context (1948: 215, etc.). That view assumes a hiatus between cult and non-cultic life that is hardly warranted; indeed, Noth himself said that the subsequent popular stories were 'not profane' (214).

125. Similarly, his thesis that complaints against God were primarily early (1954: 49, etc.) is questionable, especially for Israelite-Jewish tradition as a whole (cf., e.g., 1954: 78; the dates for Pss. 44 and 74 are not certain), and he appears to be correcting this point in an essay in honour of W. Brueggemann.

126. According to Westermann, a *description* of salvation to come (which has its 'origin' in wisdom-orientated blessing) is 'fundamentally different' both from a general (priestly) *declaration* that salvation is on the way and from a specific (properly prophetic) *announcement* that it will arrive (1974a: 236 [1963]; 1987: 87).

127. Bentzen thought that this contrast was too strong (1948a: 233).

In 1951, von Rad described the concepts and operations of 'holy war', a union of politics and religion. He assigned this union primarily to the premonarchical period (in which 'cult' and 'life' did not diverge [30]), but he described also a new version of the union in prophecy, Deuteronomy and 1 Maccabees. He did not, it seems, give sufficient attention to the prevalence of the notion of holy war in royal ideology,[128] a fact which would indicate that the notion was continuous in time. Characteristically for a form-historian, he attempted to reconstruct an early pattern on the basis of later attestations treated as out of place.

A fourth assumption that played a major role in form history was that **aetiologies formed the foundation for many of the narratives**. Alt believed that Joshua 1–11 was based on independent aetiological stories (1953: 182 [1936]) and argued that the account of Jacob's travel from Shechem to Bethel in Gen. 35.1-4 was designed to justify a ritual pilgrimage reflecting a move of the central sanctuary from Shechem to Bethel (1953: 79-88 [1938]). Von Rad thought that the original aetiological point of Genesis stories had repeatedly disappeared (1949: 12). Little attention was given to the finding in folklore studies that aetiological elements are often secondary, nor to Gunkel's corresponding observations (1902, etc.), until the Jewish scholar I. Seeligmann (1961: 151) referred to folklore studies and Westermann (1964: 41) to Gunkel's observation.

Albright personally observed among Arabs that what might look like an aetiology was a mnemonic device (1939: 13).[129] His student John Bright vigorously argued for the secondary nature of aetiologies (1956: 91-100, although it should be noted that the historicity of accounts is by no means established thereby). Brevard Childs (1963: 279-92) and his student Burke Long (in 1968) took such observations further.

Not all speculative reconstructions of the history of form proceeded on the basis of the four assumptions mentioned. Better founded were attempts at reconstruction that referred to comparable phenomena in the ancient world. Even among these attempts, however, the notion of an

---

128. Pointed out already by F. Schwally in 1901, known to von Rad, and later by Weippert (1972: 460-93). (For the whole history of the discussion of holy war, see Ben Ollenburger in the ET of von Rad's study.)

129. Gressmann (1914b: 10) held that stories (*Sagen*) are like vines which need to attach themselves to something. Such a view underlay some of Noth's observations, besides his locating the source of some stories in aetiologies (e.g. 1948: 127). Noth could see an aetiology as secondary (1948: 135).

early pure structure made itself felt. Thus, Hooke argued (from 1933 on) that a Near Eastern pattern underlay biblical phenomena, where it appears in broken form.[130] Following another line, several German scholars (especially Alt, Noth, von Rad, Weiser) reconstructed an early covenantal structure with an amphictyonic organization comparable to that of confederacies in the surrounding world.[131] This view received support through a comparison with the structure of Hittite treaties by George Mendenhall (1954a, b). The comparison was soon followed widely. Questions about the antiquity of the idea of a covenant between God and Israel emerged, however, in the 1960s.[132]

In a different way, Albright and his students Frank Cross and David Noel Freedman[133] sought to establish a history of literary forms. They placed poems into a sequence with attention to orthographic, grammatical and stylistic features. In so far as such a historical placement is based on stylistic features, this procedure must be considered to be speculative, an inappropriate 'form-history' deriving history from form.[134] However, if the dating of individual texts is based on historical allusions in the texts or on other valid historical criteria, then the sequence of styles which emerges from such dating can represent a sound history of forms.

Noteworthy is the fact that the general tendency of form-histories in

130. Hooke followed a 'diffusionist' position, emphasizing the historical spread of customs and ideas; he was indebted to a theory which placed the source of this pattern in Egypt (Hooke 1958: 1-2), although he did not accept Egypt as the source. (Before c. 1930, Hooke had studied with C.G. Jung—rejected by him thereafter?)

131. The notion of a premonarchial organization comparable to ancient Greek confederacies, including amphictyonies, had been developed by Ewald; Noth's comparison failed to take into account the varied nature of such confederacies (see already 'Amphictyonia', in *Paulys Realencyclopädie der classischen Altertums-wissenschaft* [new edn by G. Wissowa, 1894], and more recently de Geuss [61-65], with studies listed).

132. See McCarthy 1972; W. Clark in Hayes 1974: 118-22; Nicholson 1986; and below (Eichrodt, etc.).

133. See Albright 1922: 69-86; Cross and Freedman 1975; and Freedman in the second edition of G. Gray.

134. A sequencing of styles is in some ways similar to the sequencing of pottery forms. However, pottery sequences are recognized on the basis of objects that are stratigraphically datable; furthermore, stylistic textual variations appear to be more flexible and thus less datable than those of pottery, in part since texts live longer so that various forms are continued (creating, for instance, uncertainty about what is 'archaic', i.e. old, and what is 'archaizing').

Hebrew Bible studies was to argue for the antiquity of forms and traditions, while in the field of New Testament form-histories tended to be sceptical historically (especially, about Jesus). In either context, the diachronic positions that were set forth may indeed not have been wrong in every instance; yet the formal analysis on which they were based did not truly provide support for them.

In sum, form-historians took the examination of form to be a new tool for solving spatiotemporal questions, in relative isolation from formal studies in other fields. In this procedure, it was the misfortune of many of them to follow Gunkel in three doubtful assumptions that can be attributed to limitations in his knowledge of other disciplines—namely, his belief that forms were originally brief, rigid and separate—and to depart from his procedure in two respects in which his analyses had been in good contact with other fields, by ignoring his recognition that aetiologies are often secondary and by discontinuing attention to aesthetic and anthropological aspects of form. For instance, in Koch's introduction to form criticism the problematic assumptions were highlighted, but aesthetics appeared hardly at all and anthropology not very much (1964). (Koch [xiii] reported an objection that 'form-history is idle, aesthetically tinged play', but such an objection certainly was not valid with respect to 'form-historical' works).[135]

Nevertheless, the studies in question contained formal analyses which can contribute insight quite apart from the diachronic conclusions which they drew. For instance, von Rad's analysis of the Hexateuch (1938b) highlights a cultic pattern which forms the foundation of a community, just as, in Malinowski's terminology (1926), a 'myth'—usually connected with a ritual—provides a 'charter'. This insight is independent of the date for the start of the pattern, which continues in Judaism and Christianity to the present day. Mendenhall's view of a combination of historical and ethical dimensions in a covenant structure is helpful for an understanding of one side of biblical faith,[136] no matter when or how that union arose. Zimmerli's and Westermann's structural

---

135. The fairly conservative H. Lampartner thought that an overemphasis on genres militates against seeing psalms as works of art (1958: 9). For Westermann's and von Rad's aesthetic analyses (in works not labelled 'form-historical'), see below.

136. It did not cover the legal, as distinct from ethical, dimension; in fact, Mendenhall—rejecting the legal aspect of the Hebrew Bible—was critical of 'liberation' politics (see, e.g., 1975: 170).

examinations provide for a sensitive understanding, not strongly affected by the details of a history of forms.[137] Similarly, Cross and Freedman's description of the language of poems as 'rich and exuberant' (1975: 3 [1950]) is appropriate apart from the assignment of a specific date for them.

b. *Form Analysis*
Somewhat different from form-historical studies were those that had form analysis, for its own sake, as a primary aim.

One kind of formal focus was aesthetic. This included an interest in what had traditionally been called 'style'—'figures' of speech and thought, including repetitions of various sorts. In line with the usage of the particularist/Ramist tradition, a narrow sense of 'rhetoric' as dealing with style was continued by Muilenburg ('A Study of Hebrew Rhetoric: Repetition and Style', *Congress Volume 1953* [VTSup, 1]: 97-111). Important studies of metre, rhythm and parallelism (all of them kinds of repetition) appeared from 1875 to 1915, as well as thereafter;[138] the fact that there was no rigid differentiation between 'prose, rhythmic prose and poetry' was widely recognized (e.g. S.A. Cook 1945: 63). Stylistic phenomena, to be sure, have significance only if they are seen in connection with a content or function, as took place in the following analyses.

Taking a comprehensive view, F.C. Eiselen said that 'true poetry' requires: a 'substance that grips the emotion', 'imagination' and an 'emotional, exalted style' (1918: 13). T.H. Robinson, similarly, held that greatness in literature requires an 'intense passion for truth' and the 'courage' that emanates from it, together with a rich style (1947: 67). Muilenburg believed that 'literature is concerned with matter as well as with manner' (1933: 22),[139] as well as, conversely: 'Not only *what* is said is important but also *how* it is spoken' (1961: 18). Tying these two aspects together, E. Kraeling asserted that 'great literature' must present 'a new thought or experience...in a suitable form' (1939: 4-5).

---

137. This does not mean that a historical view makes no contribution to a recognition of form, but for such a view one probably needs to think in terms of millennia, rather than centuries, and to adopt a comprehensive comparative perspective.

138. See Gray, both editions.

139. In 1961: 13, he said that 'more than any others of our age, it is poets, dramatists and tellers of stories who penetrate most deeply into the mind and heart' of human beings; they 'engage us in that interior conversation where the walls of our isolation and self-centeredness are broken down'.

Since content relates to life, Israelite prophets, according to Irwin, had the 'sensitiveness and understanding... which is the distinguishing feature of every great artist', especially an interest in the 'fine art of living' (1941: 321). H.W. Robinson found a union of style, content and life concerns in the Hebrew Bible. In listening to it, he said, 'we are never made to feel that metaphor and simile are an artificial embellishment of prophetic truth' (1946: 16); on the contrary, 'the poetic form of the Bible is essential to its truth, for religion itself is the poetry of life' (1955: 132).[140] Reflections of this sort were, however, often not supported in detail.

In contrast to some other German scholars who were reserved toward aesthetics, Hempel held that both the form and the content of images reflect experiential processes (1924b: 104) and that biblical pictures have a 'revelatory' function, making 'existential' statements about relations with God (1957: 34-35). On behalf of 'biblical aesthetics', Westermann called an 'I-you' relation 'beautiful', since in Israel 'good' and 'beautiful' were not separated (1950: 278). He said that poetry (or literature, *Dichtung*) has 'its origin where human beings listen and hear at the horizon of existence' (1955b: 921).

Von Rad developed a literary form-analytic perspective strongly from about 1950 on.[141] In his 'Old Testament Theology' (which is largely a literary structural analysis, the plot of which has already been outlined) he stated: 'Literature (*Dichtung*)—especially for ancient peoples—is much more than aesthetic play; rather, an incisive will to know is active in it' (1957–60, I: 115). He cited Dilthey's view of

---

140. Earlier, the Swiss Lucien Gautier described Hebrew poetry (with attention to its major genres) as 'admirably adapted to religious subjects' (*Introduction à l'Ancien Testament*, 1906, II: 8).

141. Earlier formal analyses appeared (in 1936: 265-76), on Jeremiah's confessions; on early history writing (1958: 148-88 [1944]); briefly in a sermon of 1949 (1972: 31); and to some extent in his exegesis of Genesis, with attention to its final form (1949). Thereafter, the formal interest became quite pervasive (cf. Crenshaw 1978: 104-37). Contributing factors were a longstanding personal interest and literary contacts (see von Rad 1964a; Crenshaw 1978: 175; Smend 1989: 226, 241; 1997: 89), as well as, possibly, a knowledge of non-German writings as a stimulus for his movement after 1950. (Before 1950, his works had been largely 'form-historical', subordinating form to history; the last of these, his study of the holy war, was basically completed when he presented it in 1949 as a guest professor in Bangor, Wales [1951: 4]. One can speculate that his spending time in Wales may have helped to open him to new possibilities in biblical study.)

literature as an 'organ for understanding life' and as a creative power (1957–60, I: 115, 117). Thereafter, he continued to move further in the direction of seeing aesthetic structures as significant. Thus, play was related by him to 'earnest' content (1963: 410), with the aid of a traditional Latin saying to that effect. In 1964 he mentioned poets among God's current 'warners' (1972: 136). In advice for Bible-based preaching (1973: 9 [1965/6]), he declared that poetry is not 'rhetorical ornamentation' but 'a quite specific form of recognizing and expressing reality... not interchangeable with another'.[142]

The fact that literary form involves more than embellishment and reflects structures of content and life was shown in studies that spoke of 'drama', 'tragedy', 'irony' and 'paradox'.[143] Thus, Terrien, in his analysis *Job: Poet of Existence* (1957), thought that 'the supreme irony of the human situation' is that despair is both necessary for, and detrimental to, faith (41).[144] His student Edwin Good reached the conclusion that true irony represents 'liberating faith' (1965: 244).

Although G.E. Wright asserted that 'in Biblical faith everything depends on whether the central events actually occurred' (1952: 126), he described biblical faith as 'history interpreted by faith' (128). His description of biblical theology as 'recital' was literary–structural and was perceived that way by the scholarly community then. Muilenburg—whose literary interest had a strong personal dimension[145]—pointed out that Wright's formulation was 'allied to the current existentialist approach', which 'takes very earnestly the relationship between the interpreter and the original speaker in Scripture' (1958:

---

142. Further, in 1970: poetic form is not 'an insignificant external matter' but expresses an intensive meeting with realities or events (39); 'gnomic apperception' is a 'specific kind of recognition' bound to 'a specific linguistic form' (46)—citing non-theological theorists.

143. P. Humbert (1936: 220): drama, tragedy; von Rad (1936: 269 and 1972: 31 [1949]): tragedy; J. Hyatt, *Jeremiah* (1958: 16-17, 43-46): 'dramatic' symbols and parables; E. Haller, *Die Erzählung von dem Propheten Jona* (1958: 15, 19): 'sharp dissonance', 'paradox', 'lightly ironizing'; W. Stinespring, 'Irony and Satire' (*IDB*, II, 1962: 726-28); W. Holladay (1962: 47): irony.

144. Terrien considered 'the irony of love and faith', viewing 'irony as a device of revelation' and concluding that Job 'finds in the divine irony a hint of love to which he responds by the irony of faith' (243, 248-49).

145. Buechner (21) reports that Muilenburg said in 1950s lectures that 'until you can read the story of Adam and Eve, of Abraham and Sarah, of David and Bathsheba, as your own story you have not really understood it'.

21). Muilenburg appreciated much in such existentialist interpretation, but he saw as one of its dangers that 'in its insistence upon the existential appropriation of the event, the historical and *sui generis* and concrete reality of the original text may be lost' for 'we are sometimes told that all we need is a *sense* of history, not a knowledge of its concrete content. The givenness of the historical revelatory event may thus be dissipated into a psychological state' (1958: 21). While this perceived danger did not apply to Wright's view as such, it is nevertheless certainly true that Wright was interested in the structure of faith and of its expression and not only in sheer facticity.

Similarly theoretical, Hempel saw a 'realistic' inclination in narratives which give attention to both details and the whole (1930: 85). Other scholars—for example, Leonhard Rost (1926)—also described narrative art, although not expressly in its relation to structures of thought or life.

Until the early 1920s, literary expression was often set in relation to the person of the poet,[146] but later writers pushed the author into the background. When psychological analyses were made, they referred to the character of the text rather than to that of the author.[147] For instance, G. Gerleman showed how the style of the Song of Deborah, with hardly a metaphor, deals with 'emotional qualities and contrasts' (1951: 174).

Pure individualism was transcended through attention to genres. Thus, S.A. Cook described the effect of biblical literature according to its types transhistorically:

> Here are passages so powerful for consolation and encouragement, for warning, threat, or discernment of the future, that on countless occasions they have answered the mood of the West as surely as they did the not dissimilar occasions which first called them forth (1936: 167).

Comprehensive studies that treated literary patterns in terms of genres included Hempel (1930—a systematic overview in a general literary series), Pfeiffer (1941—as part of his Introduction, 23-40), Lods (1950—historically organized), Napier (1955—on myth, legend, history, prophecy, law), and Muilenburg (1961—referring to vocatives, questions and commands, as well as to larger patterns, 20-30).[148]

146. E.g. Duhm (1897: ix) on Job; Volz (1922: xxxvi-xxxvii) and Skinner (1922: 46, 215-18) on Jeremiah.

147. Thus already *Alttestamentliche Lyrik* by the non-specialist P. Fleischmann (1916).

148. Causse (1926: 25-26, 167-72) held that early biblical songs brought about a

Connections between the different aspects of a literary genre—style, content and life—were formulated by Mowinckel with the help of the notion of 'aim' (which had already been central for Boeckh, as well as in older conceptions of genres): 'The content was determined by the aim, and the aim...was dictated by the situation'; the stylistic form, he believed, was an outgrowth of all three of these factors (1962, I: 28 [1951]). He said that the form used was the one which 'was felt to be the most natural and most suitable means'.

In regard to the question of suitability, Mowinckel gave less attention than Gunkel had to whether phenomena in the Psalms are 'natural' intrinsically, but referred simply to 'rules governed by a long tradition', with the implication that the forms were at least in part only conventional (28). Zimmerli (1963b: 24), however, reported with approval Gunkel's pointing to an 'inner necessity' of the relation between life and word, while also recognizing that conventions play a major role in shaping it.[149]

Even though there are both natural and merely conventional relations between style, content and context, it is clear in existing literature that these aspects do not always cohere firmly.[150] Gunkel knew that, but he envisioned a unity of these aspects in the oral speech that lay behind the written word. Mowinckel's student H. Birkeland (1955: 27) said that his rigid view, as it was restated sharply by Alt, is 'simply wrong'. K.-H. Bernhardt (1959: 34), too, denied a unity of style and content. It can be noted that the idea of strict connectivity runs counter to twentieth-century rhetoric, which recognizes primarily probabilistic patterns, and is indeed contrary to relational theory, for relations involve both a degree of connectivity and a degree of independence.

On a level below genres in terms of comprehensiveness lie formulas and verbal symbols.[151] I. Lande presented a survey of formulaic expressions that were used in recurring situations (1949). It was her sense that they began as expressions 'appropriate' (*gemäss*) for a certain kind of situation and became conventional (ix). To judge from her

'collective enthusiasm...social unity'.

149. In dealing with a literary structure in Qoheleth, Zimmerli said that 'it lies in the nature of the case' that it falls into the two parts he described (1962a: 129).

150. Thus, Bentzen wanted to make style (alone) the criterion for classification (1948a: 109, 233).

151. This is a rough analysis. Actually, the concept of what is an 'entire act of speech' is elastic; a simple one can coincide with a formula, for example, 'thank you'.

report of biblical usages, they did not change greatly during the biblical period; that fact encourages caution towards hypothesizing historical developments. Symbols (such as water), which are to some extent, but not altogether, arbitrary in nature, were discussed by quite a few scholars, including the Dutch A.J. Wensinck (from 1916 on).[152]

One of the relations explored widely was a connection of basic features of language (grammar and vocabulary) with thought. A large number of works dealt with peculiar concepts expressed by key Hebrew words (e.g. Snaith 1946). T. Boman believed that fundamental differences between Greek and Hebrew ways of thinking (which he took to be not conflicting but complementary) were reflected in differences between the respective languages, including grammar (1952). This view of the significance of language was attacked by Barr in 1961. The attack was indeed well-based in many respects (especially in regard to grammar); but, as should be noted, it represented a one-sided view of linguistics. Words, for instance, do furnish a 'culturally shared...cognitive map' (Givón 1984: 31, according to a longstanding view). Their meanings correlate—although not rigidly—with cultural perspectives.[153]

A number of structural views focused primarily, although not exlusively, on content (one aspect of form, taken as a complex of relations). That was true for Hempel's structural analysis of ethics (1938a). It was also true for those who sketched a high degree of unity in biblical theology. As Rowley recalled, diversity within the Bible had been emphasized in theological training towards the beginning of the century (1953: 1). Thereafter, however, at least in some circles, the pendulum swung for a while in the other direction in an emphasis on unity. When the theme of a strong unity within the Bible was joined with that of a sharp difference in relation to other traditions, a one-sided group particularism resulted, as was often the case in the so-called Biblical

152. See, for example, references in B.W. Anderson (1962) and Buss (1969: 83-115) and by H.G. May in the 1970 edition of Farbridge (1923—Jewish; an updated version is needed!).

153. See *RFT* on linguistics, as well as Brinkman for a discussion of Barr. Barr, who drew heavily on a critique of the 'Whorf hypothesis', acknowledged briefly that he was representing only one line (1961: 294-95). He made some contrasts which he may now doubt himself: God's revelation versus group process (recognizing a linguistic impact only for the latter, 248) and Christianity versus 'Hellenistic ethos' (saying that they were 'largely foreign' to each other even though they used similar vocabulary, 249).

Theology Movement. (Rowley himself—treated by Childs [1970: 14, etc.] as a major figure in this movement—was fairly well balanced, having not only a wider view but also holding that 'the diversity must not be forgotten' and that biblical unity is dynamic, found 'within a process' [1953: 2, 20].) It should be noted that this movement, envisioning a coherent structure in the Bible, ran parallel to structural movements in other fields, in reaction (sometimes overreaction) against a preceding emphasis on evolution.

An especially important structural analysis was presented by Eichrodt, who was well acquainted with other disciplines (1933–39).[154] Eichrodt adopted relationality as his basic principle. He dealt with three relations (God–Israel, God–world, God–human beings), as they are treated in biblical writings, and described them in active, not merely intellectual, terms. The notion of a 'covenant' for the God–Israel relation fitted this procedure well, since it constituted a relationship and had organizational features, such as laws and several kinds of leaders (prophets, priests, kings). The organizational aspects were treated carefully so that the work furnished a comprehensive picture of Israel.[155]

In evaluating the appropriateness of this analysis, one must keep in mind that the appearance and meaning of the word 'covenant' as such is not crucial.[156] More important is the question whether Eichrodt overemphasized one kind of relation for that of God to Israel to the exclusion of others which also played a role, such as more natural ones (cf. McCarthy 1963), and whether he or some scholars following him treated the covenant pattern not as an open and flexible one but as an (Aristotelian) 'essence' of Israelite faith. One sign that Eichrodt followed a relational line is that he saw that there is a subjective element in what he called 'historical' study, which was more structural than diachronic (1929: 86).

The relation of the covenant idea and organization to literary structure was highlighted by Mendenhall's reference in 1954 to Hittite treaties. Since these contain narration, injunctions and threats, a comparison between biblical and treaty forms showed how historical and

154. Cf. 1929: 83-91. Eichrodt rejected 'historicism' but thought of his work as 'historical'; in fact, he gave attention to development within each topic he treated.

155. Covenant had been a central category for a sociological analysis of Israel by M. Weber, first published in 1917–19. It should be noted that 'covenant' was Eichrodt's central category only for the God–Israel relation.

156. As Eichrodt rightly said (1974: 193-206). Thus also McCarthy (1978: 21).

legal aspects of Israelite faith can be integrally related to each other—with gratitude as a major factor—and how prophecy may be related to other genres (Huffmon 1959: 285-96, etc.). In many ways, this analysis is reminiscent of Philo's, according to which God's action, past and future, forms a framework for a persuasive call.[157]

It is quite possible that, following Mendenhall, many studies referred too specifically or exclusively to treaties between nations rather than to covenantal structures more generally; the notion of covenant need not be taken so narrowly.[158] Comparison with non-Israelite patterns—either for the purpose of gaining structural insight or the sake of historical placement, or both—usually did not range far afield, but Götz Schmitt, (1964: 325-27) referred to Mitra ('covenant' or 'bond'), a deity which was worshipped in Persia and India and was not unknown in Shechem, a centre for the use of that concept in Israel.[159]

Equally relational, and perhaps better in some ways, was the notion of a dialogue (I–you) between God and human beings. Its pattern was described by a number of biblical scholars in terms of its literary form, content and connection with life. The theoretical structure of dialogue had been highlighted by notable, largely Jewish thinkers from Cohen on.[160]

In his 1920 study, *Poetry and Religion*, the Jewish thinker and critic Israel Abrahams said that the Psalms (and, by extension, the arts as a whole) represent a 'response' to God's speaking through the prophets (54, 58, 80).[161] This view was cited by H.W. Robinson (1946: 262). Robinson commented that the Psalms are not only response but have become revelation, since they aid in the interpretation of that to which they respond (265).

Developing the dialogical view, Robinson observed that the Hebrew Bible describes humanity in its relation to God and God in relation to humanity, so that they are 'mutually related' (1946: 49-50).[162] For the

---

157. Other Jewish interpreters, as noted, also related narratives to the law, but they usually placed greater emphasis on law as such, while Christians tended to downgrade law.

158. See references above for Mendenhall, etc.; further, Buss (1966: 502-504; 1969: 82—wisdom is included as an aspect of covenant; for instance, treaties, if they are relevant, were handled by scribes).

159. Koch (1991: 60) has recently cited also Hurrian and Phoenician parallels.

160. See *RFT* and above, Chapter 8 (M. Bakhtin learned from Cohen).

161. Abrahams made no reference to Cohen's slightly earlier work.

162. Relationality (between God and humanity and between human beings) was

divine side of the dialogue, Robinson pointed to revelation given by the prophet (who, among other things, 'looks forward'), by the priest (the 'guardian of tradition'), and in wisdom (reflecting 'experience' [1946: 199, 231]). His analysis thus treated biblical theology in terms of concurrent genres that closely match the canon. Specifically, it dealt with what Robinson called 'form' (type of inspiration and basic questions) in contrast to 'content' (281).

In thus matching genres with the structure of the canon and in seeing them as part of a dialogue, Abrahams and Robinson continued and carried further a long tradition in exegesis, of which much has already been reported.[163]

A very similar line, pursued by Zimmerli and Westermann, was stimulated by Rosenstock-Huessy, a Jew who stood close to the Cohen circle but converted to Christianity. This wide-ranging scholar had constructed a general theory of literature on the basis of a 'higher grammar' displaying discourse patterns that often correspond to sentence structures, especially to a use of the three 'persons': I, you, s/he/it (1924, etc.).[164]

According to Zimmerli, 'humanity lives on the basis of a call to it' (1949a: 15-22)—a statement that resembles Rosenstock-Huessy's word (1924: 36): 'God has called me, therefore I am'. That does not mean that humanity is docile; rather, in Zimmerli's view, human beings have 'nobility' in that God expects an 'answer' to the calling word (1949a: 22). Furthermore (in 1963a: 217 [1950]), he said that a 'meeting with the person of the neighbour'—for which language is the vessel—is a human being's 'most noble encounter'.

Zimmerli gave close attention to the function and history of the phrase 'I am Yahweh', which is prominent in assurances of aid—especially in response to a request—and has firm ties to legal promulgations (1963a: 34, 40 [1953]). The phrase highlights the use of divine speech in priestly and prophetic proclamations different from the more humanistically expressed 'wisdom'.[165] Since Israel shared the divine self-

---

stressed also by Vriezen (1954) and Muilenburg (1961: 56-60).

163. For earlier instances of this tradition, see the biblical canon itself implicitly (above Chapter 2), Jewish and Catholic views concerning different degrees or kinds of inspiration, Protestant discussions of 'special hermeneutics' (usually related to canonical divisions), Flacius, Harper, etc.

164. Zimmerli referred to Rosenstock-Huessy expressly in 1963a: 299 (1959).

165. See above for his view that the phrase is basically priestly.

presentation form with its neighbours, Zimmerli saw it as expressing a continuity ('solidarity') with Canaanite speech; he rejected the idea of a special biblical 'holy language' (1963a: 299 [1959]). In regard to 'wisdom', he had said in 1933 (192) that it focuses largely on human individuals' self-centred concerns, but later he softened this point by saying that wisdom is not 'wholly profane' (1963: 303). In 1956, he presented an overview of the threefold canon according to these genres with their different uses of divine or human speech (62-76).

Westermann held that there is no divine word 'absolutely' without a human answer (1955a: 108-109).[166] In this, he was indebted to Rosenstock-Huessy's view that a word is not 'completed' without an answer.[167] Accordingly, he regarded the Hebrew Bible as a dialogue that contains the human response present everywhere within it—as had also been said by H.W. Robinson[168]—although the third division of the canon (with wisdom and Psalms) represents more especially an answer (1957: 260). But are wisdom, Psalms, etc., only an answer, without their own initiative? Taking a human view, Westermann said that 'God is within the realm of human questions' (1974a: 189 [1959]). Perhaps stimulated by Rosenstock-Huessy's argument for the sequence 'cry, answer, thought',[169] Westermann observed that God's rescue in the exodus is depicted as a response to a human cry, so that prayer is not merely an answer to God but also that to which God responds (1974b: 21).

More elaborately than his antecedents had done, Westermann gave attention to the dynamic structure of different forms of speech: from God, to God, about God, etc. These different forms furnish the bases of genres that constitute the Hebrew canon (1957: 260; 1958; 1960c: 64; 1962). Within a single genre, too, he could observe a pattern reflecting the three grammatical persons; specifically, psalms of lament include first-person lamentation, third-person complaints against enemies and

---

166. He did not reprint in 1960a the part of the essay in which he said this.

167. Cited by Westermann in a review of the work in which that statement appeared (1954b: 303).

168. H.W. Robinson (1946) was not cited by Westermann in his general-audience volume of 1957, with no reference to secondary literature, but was it known to him? (It was known to von Rad at least soon after this and arguably should have been known also to Westermann.) On Westermann's knowledge of English work by 1964, see above, 13.1.c.

169. See Westermann's review (1954b: 304). Westermann referred to Rosenstock-Huessy more than once thereafter.

second-person words to God with requests, reproaches for failure to act, and expressions of confidence (1954: 45-46, etc.). Along this line, he interpreted the book of Job as a 'dramatized lament'; only the secondary speeches of Elihu speak really 'about God' (1956b: 12, 115).[170]

(Westermann had good acquaintance with the theory of language.[171] This fact helps to explain the schematic character of his approach similar to that of French structuralism, inspired by twentieth-century linguistics. Furthermore, his use of charts for representing the organization of biblical books, for example in 1962b, is comparable to that typical of Bible studies in the traditions emanating from Harper and White according to a process that is useful for posthistorical study by lay people.)

Von Rad, too, included a dialogical dimension in his 'Theology' (1957–60), treating major biblical portions with their genres, in roughly canonical order. Unlike H.W. Robinson, Zimmerli or Westermann, he followed the order of the canon that was standard for Christians rather than that accepted by Jews. (This is not necessarily a problem for Jewish readers, however, since Christian faith does not lie very much on the surface in his often fine literary-descriptive presentation.)

Von Rad's analysis resembled that of H.W. Robinson (1946), such as in describing the prophet as one who points forward.[172] Much of the plot of his work, furthermore, was already present in Zimmerli (1956).[173] However, von Rad[174] and Westermann,[175] at least in some of

170. Comparisons between Job and psalms of lament had been made, for example, by Marschall (1929: 95). The Protestant theologian E. Schlink (1957: 252-60) distinguished between God's word, prayer (to 'you' from 'I'), doxology (focusing on God), witness (addressing a neighbourly 'you' on the basis of God's word), doctrine (with little of 'you' or 'I'), and 'confession' (all together).

171. He reviewed two books on the theory of language (W. Luther, *Weltansicht und Geistesleben* [1954]; F. Tschisch, *Weltbild, Denkform und Sprachgestalt* [1954]) in *Zeitschrift für Phonetik und allgemeine Sprachwissenschaft* (9, 1956: 187-89, 276-77); probably relevant is the fact that his father was a linguistic anthropologist.

172. Von Rad knew H.W. Robinson (1946), at least by 1960 (see above).

173. Presumably, this particular study came too late to have much of an impact on von Rad's conception in 1957, although it may have had an impact on his vol. II. Yet relevant earlier work by Zimmerli (in part itself influenced by still earlier studies by von Rad) was known to von Rad in 1957.

174. See the heading in 1957-62, I: 352; but the treatment of wisdom in the section with this heading stands in some tension with it.

175. 1957a: 260; 1958: 135; with more reserve, 1962: 138.

their statements, treated 'wisdom' (formulated in the Bible predominantly as human, rather than divine, speech) as an answer, whereas Robinson had considered it to be revelation and Zimmerli had given it an almost independent humanistic status. This view of all of human speech as an 'answer' takes the divine–human dialogue to be strongly unequal, as was done by Barth (cf. Mathys, 244-45), in contrast to Robinson's concept of a 'mutual' relationship between God and human beings.[176]

c. *Life Situation as a Concern of Form Analysis*

A full form analysis gives attention not only to relations between linguistic phenomena (style, for example: repetition) or to relations between elements of thought (logic, how they fit together conceptually), nor only to relations between these two levels, but also—very importantly—to the relation of these to human life. The technical term for this connection is *Sitz im Leben* or, since this term has been burdened with questionable assumptions, perhaps better: life situation.

To anticipate some of the major findings, it can be said that many studies had an interest—more so even than Gunkel[177]—in determining specific describable settings, rather than in pursuing a theoretical apprehension of life. This interest should probably be evaluated as 'misplaced concreteness'[178] since it was not well supported by the data and often led away from, rather than towards, an understanding of the verbal structures. Not every concrete view is erroneous, of course, but Western thinking after c. 1300 CE had become more concrete ('literalist') than earlier thinking had been, and accordingly did not mesh very well with the concerns represented in a traditional text. The particularist emphasis on concreteness was being superseded widely after 1900, but not equally so in all fields; Protestant theology, which stood close to nominalism, was in this regard a holdout for a while, at least in some circles. We will see, however, that most of the problematic concrete proposals were abandoned in the 1960s and that more strictly formal

176. Cf. above for views by Heschel and Brunner, more strongly relational than Barth's.

177. Thus, R. Rendtorff (1991: 30—it seems, approvingly); G. Wallis (251—1962 lecture, pointing to the Alt school as the circle in which this process took place especially).

178. Thus, Alter (1987: 247), employing a term coined by A.N. Whitehead (1925: 75, 85).

thought had begun to enter into biblical studies before then.

It is convenient to trace the topic by type of literature, beginning with a detailed view of the treatment of **psalms**.

Gunkel observed that the life situation expressed in psalms of lament was 'not overly concrete' (1927d: 89). He estimated that for individual cultic psalms, which, in his opinion, have not survived, the main problem was sickness (1906a: 65; 1913b: 1937; 1927b: 174).[179] In the psalms that are preserved in the Bible, he believed, the causes of lament involve literal or figurative poverty or trouble of various sorts, as was true in the 'songs of the poor' presented in Egypt not long from the time of Moses.[180] Gunkel did not attempt to date the Israelite use of the poverty theme precisely but presented evidence that it began before the exile (e.g. 1906a: 89). He also indicated the transtemporal character of oppression: 'in this world, the poor and lowly...are everywhere oppressed and mishandled by the rich and mighty' (1904a: 133). His Swiss student Baumgartner believed that the theme of the 'righteous poor' was presupposed already in Amos 2.16 and 5.12 (1917: 51).

Another one of his students, Hans Schmidt, identified within individual laments psalms that are concerned with a defence against accusations and suggested that they were presented at the temple by persons brought to it for a divine judgment (1928 [anticipated in 1912: 18]). The reply of Gunkel and Begrich (1933: 253f.) was that the image of false accusation may be metaphoric. G. Marschall viewed the legal process of the psalms as one that involves the sufferer's moral standing before God and in the community, with the requested healing constituting a justification (1929: 98).[181]

In regard to the theme of poverty, a number of scholars from the end of the nineteenth century on, including Gunkel (1906a: 77; 1913b: 1945; etc.), believed that the 'poor' in the Psalms formed not a miscellany of individuals but a group or party within Israel that was both relatively poor economically and, especially, 'poor' in spirit (i.e. humble).

179. Begrich, however, who edited the continuation of this analysis, seems to have viewed some of the preserved biblical psalms as standing in connection with the 'cult' (Gunkel and Begrich 1933: 175-80). In 1927d: 89f., Gunkel said that at a 'later' time various kinds of problems, not just sickness, were brought to the temple.

180. See above, 11.1.c. In Egyptian 'psalms of the poor', with which Gunkel was familiar, poverty was semiliteral (one speaker was an official who lost his position [Erman 1909: 98]).

181. That meaning appears to apply in Egyptian psalms (Roeder 1923: 46-51).

Commonly, this social group was thought to begin during the monarchy and to be important after the exile.[182]

Mowinckel rejected the notion of opposing parties (1921: 111-13, although he continued elements of it). Having become aware of the relevance of Mesopotamian literature already before becoming Gunkel's student, he argued that in Israel, as in Mesopotamia, evil magic (by human beings or demons) was blamed for illness (1921). Enemy curses, according to his interpretation, could take advantage of misdeeds by the sufferer that leave the sufferer unprotected by deity or could by themselves produce a condition of 'sinfulness'; a ritual of cleansing or vindication would then be appropriate (1921: 86, 141-49; 1962, II: 6,12-13).[183] According to Mowinckel, the actual suffering that formed the basis of complaint ranged from sickness to a wide variety of other problems, including tension with rich or worldly persons. He thought that the hated rich or despisers of law often simply furnished a stylized way of speaking about sorcerers but that sometimes a sufferer would assume that the unknown sorcerer was one of the rich (1921: 119; 1924: 64).

Mowinckel's student Birkeland concluded (1933a) that 'poverty' or 'affliction' referred to a variety of ordinary problems experienced by many different people. Soon thereafter, however, he identified the 'I' speaking in the Psalms primarily with the king or the community and the enemies with outside forces (1933b).[184] Mowinckel accepted the royal interpretation in part; he came to think that sickness described may, in some cases, be a metaphor for, or the mental consequence of, a political defeat (1962, II: 17 [1951]).[185]

---

182. See N. Lohfink 1986: 157-65; Chang, 1-34. Perhaps best, without reference to 'groups' or 'parties', was the belief of A. Kirkpatrick (1901) that some psalms refer to wealthy and powerful persons who oppress the poor, before and after the exile (on Pss. 10, 51, 94, 109, etc.).

183. In a variation of this view, Albert Brock-Utne proposed in 1929 that at least some demons were conceived as accusers before God (Norwegian 1929 MS, reported in Birkeland 1933b: 15). Accusing demons play a role in later Jewish liturgy (cf. Feinberg 1959: 218; perhaps also Heinemann 1977: 202).

184. Even more emphatically in 1955.

185. The fellow Norwegian P. Munch, however, continued the group theory by holding that the tension in the Psalms reflected class contrasts arising with the monarchy (1936: 13-26). He referred, further (1937: 41), to the lower priesthood, pushed down by centralization. Graetz (1882—see above) had pointed to Levites after Hezekiah as psalmists.

More generalized solutions were offered by others. Widengren pointed out that in Akkadian psalms it is impossible to disentangle images of internal and external enemies, personal or demonic (1936). Ringgren thought that the 'enemies' represent mythical powers imping-ing on individual and collective wellbeing in various ways (1963: 46). George Anderson expressed what came to be a fairly widespread opin-ion: 'The conventional monotony' of psalms is 'appropriate' for their use 'on many different occasions, which were of the same general char-acter, but which did not correspond to each other in every particular'; their language 'allows for a wide range of national and individual experience' (1965: 28).

While these generalized interpretations of the external setting may be largely correct, they do not highlight the Psalms' internal theory—the way in which they perceive reality. H.J. Francken (Dutch) pointed out that a cultural pattern '"recognizes" a situation' (1954: 60); that is, a physical context is not yet a 'situation' until it is interpreted as such with the aid of a perceptual pattern.[186] This does not imply that actual legal or economic strife is irrelevant, but only that there is an interpre-tive dimension to be considered.

In regard to the interpretive schemes used, Birkeland believed that legal/moral judgments were rationalizations of self-interest comparable to or even more blatant than those of twentieth-century countries at war (1933b: 63-64) and that the self-designation 'poor' expressed a 'slave mentality' stronger in Israel than elsewhere (320). Closer to the view of the psalmists themselves, Mowinckel had observed that 'the sufferer—the socially oppressed as well as the sick person struck by sorcerers—is, in old Israelite conception, "righteous"... in relation to the oppres-sor' (1921: 116). He located a major source of the theme of God's aid to the weak in the cultic–personal 'experience of God as the holy, judging and overwhelming one', as a result of which 'the pious will instinctively react against whatever may be proud and lofty and rich and mighty and self-sufficient'; in his view, 'psalmists merged these religious elements... with their antagonism to the rich and mighty' (1962, II: 92 [1951]).

How old were these ideas? Mowinckel thought that they were pre-exilic (1921: 114, 116) but denied that criticism of the rich was made already in 'oldest Israel' (1924: 62-63). In contrast, Marschall argued,

186. Similar positions by W. Thomas (1918), Voloshinov (1973 [1929]), Lipps (1938) and Vatz (1973), etc., will be mentioned in *RFT*.

more confidently than Gunkel, that conceptions of God as the judge of all wrong and as the helper of the weak and poor were held in Israel from its 'oldest period' on, in part because those conceptions were present already in Babylonia and Egypt (1929: 65).[187] He explained that 'in the Orient' (only there?) the rich frequently misuse their power (112). Gemser (1955: 126) pointed to Babylonian requests that God judge one's controversy with hostile forces as a background for Israelite tradition. The circumstance that Israel arose largely from oppressed or marginal persons came also to be discussed as a factor that contributed to Israel's ideology, especially so by Mendenhall (1962: 66-87).[188]

A major controversial issue in the interpretation of the Psalms was whether most of those preserved in the Bible were cultic. Gunkel said 'no'; Mowinckel, 'yes'. Such statements are not very meaningful until it is clear what is meant by 'cult'. Gunkel regarded a text as cultic only if it was accompanied by a non-verbal ritual, such as sacrifice (1904a: 240; 1913a: 147 [1912]).[189] Furthermore, Gunkel usually conceived of rituals and their texts as being directly connected with a temple.[190] Mowinckel admitted a somewhat broader conception of cult, at least in his later work; there he noted that the Passover ritual at home 'was something in the nature of cult' (1962, II: 88 [1951]) and that 'cult'—as in the synagogue, Islam and Christianity—can be without sacrifice (21). Nevertheless, he meant by 'cultic psalms' those that were used in temple services (1924: 28) in close conjunction with sacrifices.[191] Gunkel and Mowinckel thus had a similarly narrow view of cult, but they differed on whether biblical psalms were a part of it. Their focus

187. For Egypt, cf. Erman (1909: 98); Roeder (1923: 46-59), in part already cited.

188. Earlier scholars who emphasized the Mosaic liberation of oppressed persons as a central factor in Israelite faith included Kent and F. James (see above). (Alt 1953: 170 [1939] discussed a marginal status but not its contribution to ideology.)

189. In this last reference, Gunkel characterized certain Egyptian songs as 'non-cultic'—even though their aim was to remove cultic evil—since they were not accompanied by sacrifice.

190. For instance, he imagined that a sick person goes 'into the sanctuary' (1906a: 65; 1913b: 1938; 1922a: 81; 1930: 1618; thus also Balla 1912: 14).

191. Mowinckel excluded from cult (in a 'specific' sense) prayers and other religious acts in 'ordinary daily life', even if they were done or assisted by religious specialists (1923: 11).

on public ritual undoubtedly reflected a widely debated issue, namely, how much of a value to place on organized worship—Gunkel being reserved towards this and Mowinckel definitely in support, contra the 'individualistic liberal' and 'individualistic spiritual' disparagement of the cult that Mowinckel had known as a student (Rian, 230).[192]

From a scholarly standpoint, Gunkel's and Mowinckel's identification of cult with sacrificial or temple ritual is somewhat surprising. It is true, historians of literature (e.g. Greek) contrasted socially useful, including cultic, productions with others that are more purely literary and more strongly individual.[193] Yet virtually everyone acknowledged a sphere of 'private cult'—ritual practised at home or in a variety of contexts, often without what is normally called 'sacrifice'.[194] Such ritual was discussed in writings dealing with the religions of Greece, Egypt, Mesopotamia, India, China, Persia, etc. (such as in Erman 1885: xiv, 369-71, well known to Gunkel [see 1904a: 252-60], and in works by H. Oldenberg, which Gunkel used [see above]). Wellhausen discussed the cult of home and clan in ancient Israel (1901: 99-102).[195]

In most phenomenological treatments of religion, the word 'cult' designates an aspect (not a separable part) of religion. It does so, for instance, in the formulation that religion has three aspects: cult, creed and code—that is, overt religious acts and expressions, the content of what is believed, and the social behaviour inculcated or fostered. As we saw, the New Testament scholar Bertram (1922) referred to this trio—termed 'cult', 'dogma' and 'ethics'—and in line with that conception

192. N. Ridderbos (1950: 3) referred expressly to the 'liturgical movement'. (Catholics, too, had a 'liturgical movement' after World War I [Seidel, 174]).

193. See above, 11.2.d, on Xenophanes (with a critical query), and Heiler (1919: 183).

194. In 1973: 91 (Swedish 1967), Ringgren described the location of incantations as being 'in a special sanctuary' ('ablution house') or 'in the home, in the sick-room, or in any other place in case of need', but he did not apply this pattern to Israelite laments in 1963 (Swedish 1957).

195. See further, for example, Boeckh (1877: 415); Pfleiderer (1878: 153); Chantepie de la Saussaye (1905, I: x, 238; II: 150, 204); Langdon (1909: vii, ix); W. Grube (1910: 163); Stummer (1922: 6, 111). Later studies have described a wide-ranging cult in Africa (e.g. Idowu 1962: 107-43). In 1904/5 lectures taken down by Bultmann, Gunkel presented an extensive discussion of Israelite cult (with references to Wellhausen and Chantepie de la Saussaye, among others); he evidently included attention to small-scale cult (De Valerio, 65-67), but may have assumed that 'sacrifice' was an integral part of it (see note 187 above).

used the word 'cult' broadly.[196] Mowinckel pointed to the same three dimensions (which he called 'cult', 'myth' and 'ethos') from 1950 on, expressly saying that the three are 'aspects' rather than 'separate spheres' of religion (1953: 7 [1950]; similarly 1962, I: 15 [1951]). If, however, cult is not a separate sphere within religion, then there is little sense in speaking of 'non-cultic' prayer, as Mowinckel had (1962, II: 109), for prayer is an instance of overt religious expression.[197] To give an analogy: in anthropology or sociology, the 'family' is discussed as an aspect of a group, that is, not as a separate part or object but as a set of relations in which all persons are involved. Certainly, cult is inherently social; but that is true of all human activity, including private prayer (Mowinckel himself pointed to the social character of this, 1962, II: 108).

What is at stake in this methodological question is not terminology (which can legitimately vary) but whether a social reality is described concretely as a set of facts (perhaps even reified as an object)[198] or whether it is understood formally in terms of relations.[199] Mowinckel moved only partially towards the latter procedure. Specifically, Mowinckel learned from Grønbech to recognize the creative character of cult in the eyes and experience of participants. However, he unduly limited this character to large collective cults; Grønbech himself did not do so, although he focused primarily on festivals.[200]

Mowinckel recognized better than Gunkel that established processes can allow for personal creativity (1922: 7; 1962, II: 57), but he did not see clearly that the interplay between what is established and what is individual can have many gradations, both physically near and away from the temple. (Not yet well-known in biblical studies at that time was the fact that oral productions often proceed by improvization using

196. As did the Swedish New Testament scholar B. Reicke (1953: 133) and the German practical theologian O. Haendler (1957: 148).

197. For Mowinckel, prayer is not in itself cultic (1962, I: 22); but since prayer is not 'myth' (belief as such) or 'ethos' (social behaviour), what is it within religion?

198. E.g. Hermisson (1965: 151), among many speaking about 'the cult'.

199. See Buss (1964), with more detail. 'Understanding' is here not limited to an 'inside' empathetic view but designates any grasping of a relationship.

200. See Grønbech (II: 141, 144, 163, 297) on sacred space (the whole country), sacred objects and sacred meals, even apart from the temple hall and from the great festivals. The groups he described were, in fact, too small to have significantly diverging public and private cults (cf. Chantepie de la Saussaye, II: 547).

established forms;[201] such a process provides opportunity also for non-professionals.)

For determining the external circumstances of a genre, the principle had been established (by Zimmern, Heinrici, Gunkel) that one should give attention to narrative reports of the use of texts of a given type, as well as to directions given in association with texts. This principle was followed only partially. C.C. Keet pointed to Nehemiah 8 to show that even public worship was not limited to the temple (1928: 137). Some scholars referred to the fact that Hebrew Bible narratives have accounts of psalms sung by Miriam and the people as a whole after passage through the Red Sea (Exod. 15), by Levites before battle (2 Chron. 20.21), by King Hezekiah on his sick bed (Isa. 38.3) and by Jonah in the belly of the fish;[202] but different conclusions were drawn from these reports. Begrich (like others) thought that they show that there were 'cult-free' psalms, on the assumption that psalms away from a sacred precinct are not cultic (1926: 67).[203] Weiser (and others) said that they show that 'originally cultic' psalms could come to be used privately (1935: 17). Bentzen, however (again like others), discounted the narrative evidence by saying that in some respects, at least, narrators 'no longer understood' the psalms (1948a: 163).[204] Relying on the theme of forgetfulness, Mowinckel said that the temple healing rituals he hypothesized were largely forgotten by the end of the second temple period, for which instead private rituals are attested (1921: 167).

More closely in line with the textual evidence, B.D. Eerdmans (Dutch) took the numerous references in psalms and in their super-scriptions which indicate that psalms were sung outside the temple

---

201. See Culley (1967). Thus also, at least often, in ancient Greek festival hymns (Burkert 1994: 12). This pattern continues in Christian worship services in so far as they do not have written liturgies, and it plays a role in Christian private prayer as well.

202. 2 Sam. 22, attributed to David, has no express reference to cult in a narrow sense; in Dan. 2.20-33, such a setting appears not to be involved.

203. Begrich referred to the songs of Hezekiah, Jonah and the three men in the fiery furnace (Daniel, longer version). Gunkel and Begrich (1933: 183) admitted 'various transition forms'.

204. Bentzen thought so for Hannah's use of a royal psalm (1 Sam. 2) and for Jonah's song. However, the account of Hannah may show that ordinary people could sing royal psalms (cf. now Watts 1992: 29-40, citing Gottwald). Jonah's psalm is not inappropriate in its location, as has been indicated by G. Landes (3-31).

area, such as on a sick bed or while travelling or hiding in a cave,[205] as reflecting normal practice. Indeed, he distinguished psalm singing from the priestly temple cult (1947: 8-9, 47, 51). In this, without knowing it, he stood close to the Jewish scholars Kohler (1897 [see above, Chapter 8]) and Kaufmann (who assigned non-sacrificial aspects of worship to 'popular, not priestly, cult', 1960: 305 [1945]).

Gunkel allowed for private singing by conceiving of most of the individual psalms as 'spiritual songs'.[206] Causse (1922) thought similarly of the songs of the postexilic 'poor of Israel'. Somewhat differently, a few Protestants conceptualized 'cult' broadly and placed at least some of the psalms in a private form of cult, without a necessary connection with a temple (Weiser 1935: 17;[207] Rowley 1956b: 147, using the word 'worship'; Holm-Nielsen, 1960: 10, discussing wisdom psalms; Buss 1963: 392; 1964: 319-21).[208] Such a perspective was taken up widely after 1965, with a recognition of different kinds and levels of cult.[209]

It is, of course, possible that some psalms were non-cultic in the sense that they were not used for interaction with deity but only for instruction. (Cf. Saadia Gaon's view of biblical psalms as Word of God for instruction, including a modelling of prayer, rather than as actual

---

205. For Ps. 57.1 and 142.1 (David praying in a cave), cf. prayer inscribed some time before the end of the first temple in a cave at Khirbet Beit Lei (recently discovered).

206. Little express attention was given by Gunkel and others to the effect of the cessation of sacrifices outside Jerusalem. However, if Gunkel considered 'cult' to involve sacrifice, then postexilic songs outside of Jerusalem were, of course, by definition non-cultic.

207. But in 1950: 54, Weiser held that biblical psalms did not belong to private cult processes.

208. Thus perhaps already Erbt (1909: 260-61) and Gressmann (in D. Simpson 1926: 12, 20), i.e. if they envisioned private worship (*Gottesdienst*) as taking place outside the temple. Ridderbos considered a prayer in the home to be 'cultic' only if it is a preformulated one from the temple archive presented by a professional singer (1950: 4). R. De Vaux (Catholic) included some parts of private cult (1960: 351). My comments covered individual and small-group acts and expressions, whether they take place at a sanctuary or at home and whether or not they are assisted by a professional. (In China I had witnessed a professional home healing ceremony.)

209. The causes for a change in perspective are unclear, but there may have been connections with one or more of the antecedents listed, as, in fact, there should have been.

human words to God.) Furthermore, orientations toward God ('cult') and towards fellow human beings (testimony) are frequently combined, as appears to have been the case especially in those psalms that were not laments.[210] Accepting such a dual angle of vision, Mowinckel thought of 'learned psalms' as real 'prayers', although, in his terminology, non-cultic ones (1962, II: 106-109).

In relating psalms to the central cult, special attention was given to the psalms celebrating Yahweh's kingship. Somewhat like Moulton, Duhm, Gressmann and Volz,[211] Mowinckel hypothesized for the autumn New Year festival a ritual of Yahweh's throne ascension at which these psalms were presented; he thought it likely that this rite came in close conjunction with a ritual renewing human kingship (1916: 7; etc.). More specifically, H. Schmidt located the divine kingship psalms in the early morning of the first day of the autumn festival (1927: 25,27). The Norwegian S. Aalen believed, more cautiously, that those psalms should not be connected with only one occasion and associated them with morning ceremonies beyond the New Year festival (1951: 61-63). Differently, Snaith argued that they belonged to the Sabbath afternoon ritual of the second temple (1934: 88).

It should be noted that there was a certain amount of vagueness in Mowinckel's discussion regarding the external circumstances of presentations; indeed, he was primarily interested in the structural character of psalmody as constituting a creative drama of renewal.[212] A characterization of ritual as renewal in such a way that it was not

---

210. H.L. Jansen indicated such a combination in postbiblical Jewish psalms (1937: 112-19, 145); J. Corvin did so later for prose prayers in biblical narratives (1972). G. Quell had pointed out an 'educative' function for the cult (1926: 14). W.G. Lambert referred to the presence of ethical injunctions in Sumerian hymns (1960: 118).

211. Moulton (see above) did not identify a specific festival as occasion. Duhm (1899: 133-34, 234) connected at least two of the relevant psalms with cultic processes at the autumn festival, without speaking of a throne ascent. Gressmann (1905: 297 [inadequately recognized in Mowinckel's acknowledgment of indebtness to him, 1922: xi]) and Volz (1912: 14, without tying in the psalms of Yahweh's kingship) referred to a similar ritual in Babylon. Gressmann knew Duhm's analysis; did he or Duhm know that of Moulton? (They referred to other Anglo-American work; for example, Gressmann cited Chicago-based J.M.P. Smith. However, the Babylonian parallel may have led to independent conclusions.)

212. A certain lack of interest in external aspects appears, for instance, in his response to Kraus, who pressed him on the dramatization envisioned (1962, I: 170).

limited to a major festival—although related to it—was furnished by Hooke. For Semitic ritual, Hooke noted not just one, but rather two, New Year festivals (spring and autumn) and concluded (probably somewhat one-sidedly) that rituals throughout the year re-enacted elements of the New Year ceremonies (1938: 20-21, 51).

A focus on an external context was involved in the somewhat widespread hypothesis that expressions of confidence in psalms of lament either took the place of, or came in response to, a ritual oracle (Balla 1912: 26; Gunkel 1913b: 1939; Mowinckel 1921: 149, 154; Gunkel and Begrich 1933: 178; etc.). The appearance of an oracle in response to a lament is indeed well attested. Yet a more purely rhetorical interpretation of the expression of confidence is possible and was given by Gunkel before 1913.[213] Indeed, rabbinic tradition had explained the expressions of praise at the beginning and end of biblical prayers (and in the Eighteen Benedictions, in which no oracle is presupposed) by the practice of a rhetor.[214]

Westermann downgraded the importance of 'cult' as a separately organized institution. His reasons were in part scholarly and in part theological. On the scholarly level, he had, like Mowinckel (1962, I: 22), enough knowledge of anthropology to realize that early prayers and blessings were not dependent on 'the cult' in the sense of a special organization (1954a: 13; 1957b: 536).[215] Theologically, he was in a sense humanistic. Specifically (not unlike Barth), he believed that the Church should 'not be intent on cultivating its own separate community' (1952/53a: 143).[216] An openness of the Church towards the

213. 1904a: 46, on Ps. 22 (repeated in the 3rd edn, 1911). E. Albert (1964: 38) reports an African form of petition directed towards a human superior employing expressions of praise and hope near the beginning and at the end. (Albert's essay is one on the 'ethnography of communication', influenced at least indirectly by Gunkel; see *RFT* on Hymes)

214. *Sifre* on Deut. 33.2; *b. Ber.* 32a (cf. Bickerman 1962: 167; Heinemann 1977: 203). The same pattern appears, presumably without an oracle, in Qumran psalms (Morawe, 48).

215. Westermann, however, varied in his terminology; in 1959/60: 18, he referred to the 'house community' as 'the oldest cultic unity'—thus using 'cult' in a fairly broad sense—and he later described the religion of Gen. 12–50 as an early, not professionally organized, form of cult (1975b: 79; 1981: 123-25 [1977]).

216. Westermann wrote an essay with the title 'A Fence Around the Church?—The Pastor is not a Cult Official' (in *Sonntagsblatt* 1956, Nr. 44, not available for examination).

outside was supported by his view that lament and praise[217] are general-human modes (1954: 112, cf. 14-15; 1956c: 165, 167). In his words, 'the praise of God in Israel was never a cultic process separated from the rest of existence'; the real '*Sitz im Leben*' of psalms is the process of 'entreating' and 'praising' (1954a: 113). For an understanding of this process, he was interested in receiving aid from psychology (1952/53b: 239).[218] Later, he said that theology, psychology and sociology should once again cooperate in a perspective on human life (1974b: 28 [=1974a: 258]).

Some of the theoretical questions about the meaning of psalms for life were addressed in works directed toward the general public. That is not surprising, since a general audience requires theory if it is to be enlightened. R. Walker, quoting a statement by Alice Meynell[219] that words 'not only express...but enhance' thought, said that the Psalms provide words that are needed (1938: 12). He found in the Psalms 'the stir of life' and saw them as 'the product of the busy onrush and strife of life' (12). Since they 'faced frankly...disconcerting facts' and thus counter 'repressions', he believed them to have 'immense therapeutic value' (7, 96).[220]

Terrien, too, sought to show the Psalms' 'meaning for today' (1952). He characterized the worship of the psalmists as 'the acknowledgment...of God's infinite worth' with a tension between God's 'transcendence' and 'cultic immanence' (xi, 24). Specific observations pointed to the 'boldness' of the Psalms in expressing anguish and hope (xii) and to the intellectual content provided for 'religious emotions which would otherwise vanish into sterile sentimentalism' (95).[221]

217. Westermann thought that 'praise' describes more accurately an elementary human outlook—including especially that of Israel—than does 'thanksgiving' (1954a: 16-17).

218. In this review of Jung's *Antwort auf Hiob* (ET: *Answer to Job*), Westermann observed that in this work a biblical theme was highly important to someone outside theology (i.e. Jung), but he expressed disappointment that the volume did not give to a biblical scholar much psychological insight into lamenting.

219. Meynell wrote poetry and essays near the turn of the century.

220. In Walker's judgment, the Psalms have a 'permanent hold' upon humanity since 'they voice universal human experience' and through them people 'find the living God' (11, 13). In other work he highlighted the social concerns of major prophets.

221. More briefly and less directed to the public, Buss (1963) attempted to outline, besides the external circumstances, the 'inner meaning and structure' of

Furthermore he said, with stark realism, that poverty, as it is reflected in the Psalms, 'creates not only spiritual receptivity and produces a sensitiveness to great social justice' but 'also tends to warp' an outlook with bitterness (268).

Views concerning the situations of genres other than psalms must be surveyed more briefly. (References to psalms will reappear in connection with this survey.)

To begin with, one can observe that a number of **festivals or ritual contexts** were postulated for the presentation and even origin of **a variety of texts**. The folklorist P. Saintyves (= Emile Nourry) thought that many biblical stories or at least story motifs were based on rituals (1922). John Peters assigned quite a few psalms to liturgies in Jerusalem, Shechem, Dan and Bethel (1922). J. Pedersen viewed the exodus story as the 'legend' of the Passover festival by which it was shaped (1934: 161-75). Mowinckel proposed that prescriptive decalogues and rules stating conditions for entry were presented at the autumn festival in Jerusalem which celebrated a renewal of the covenant (alongside Yahweh's enthronement) and that, indeed, the Sinai narratives of the Bible were reflections of that festival (1927). Modifying this position, Alt thought that a covenant renewal with legal/ethical inculcation had taken place every seven years during the premonarchical period at Shechem (1934: 65).[222] Von Rad accepted a connection of the Sinai tradition with a Shechem ceremony and believed that the historical credo of Deut. 26.5-10—which makes no reference to Sinai—was associated with an early summer festival (Feast of Weeks) at Gilgal (1938b).

A fairly comprehensive view of festivals was given by Kraus as follows: in the premonarchical period there was a land-entry festival in the spring at Gilgal featuring a procession with an ark (1951b: 181-99) and a 'tent festival' in the autumn eventually held at Shiloh (1954: 23-37). During the time of the first temple, a 'royal Zion festival', uniting local traditions with those of the tent and ark, was celebrated in the autumn at Jerusalem (1951a: 50-98;1954: 37). In the postmonarchical period, the Zion festival (now without an ark) highlighted God's kingship (1951a: 112-43).

Israelite cult, with attention to both closeness and distinction between God and humanity.

222. See Deut. 31.10-11 for the seven years and Deut. 27 for Shechem. (A periodic ceremony at Shechem had already been suggested by Ernst Sellin.)

These reconstructions were often not unreasonable but were speculative, especially for the early period. In fact, Kraus himself became less
definite about his concrete organizational proposals later on, at which
time he came to place more stress on the relational theme of liberation
of the poor and weak (1978: 108-11; cf. 1975). The tendency to postu-
late festivals or to connect given traditions with specific festivals was
criticized by Fohrer (1961a: 16) and was widely questioned after
that.[223]

An analysis of ritual that was both external and internal in its focus
was F. Hvidberg's discussion of 'weeping' and 'laughter' in Canaanite
and Israelite ritual and literature (1962 [Danish 1938]). Weeping and
laughter are indeed visible and can even be staged, but they express
not-strictly-visible ('internal') and not-merely-arbitrary ('intrinsic')
human feelings of sorrow and joy.

Gunkel's threefold view of a genre—life situation, content and linguistic form—was gradually applied to **'law'** (including ethical injunctions). This took place in a series of steps.

A division of biblical regulations into *types* had been common for
some time (above, 4.1.a). In Christian tradition, a distinction between
'moral' (or 'natural'), judicial (or political) and ceremonial law was
standard. Jewish distinctions did not differ altogether from those made
by Christians, but were less sharp.

The fact that differences in *linguistic form* are significant in correlation with divergences in types of *content* was observed in 1888 by
J. Rothstein.[224] Specifically, he distinguished religious and moral
'words' (*debarim*) given in the second person[225] from judicial regulations (*mishpatim*) formulating a condition with 'if...' or a participle;
the words, he said, are directed immediately and unconditionally
towards the recipient as a 'person' and include demands for which vio-
lations are usually not publicly known (4). This contrast was elaborated
by B. Baentsch (1892, 1903); however, he used the label 'apodictic'
both for the second-person 'words' (1903: 1i) and for the participial

223. Thus, for Psalms, already the Catholic P. de Vaux (1960: 350).

224. In his 1867 commentary on Exodus, C.F. Keil had commented on the correlation between form and content, but without reflecting on the significance of the
styles used.

225. The biblical basis for the use of the term *debarim* in this sense is Exod.
20.1.

judicial form (1903: xlvii).[226] Similar analyses, differing in detail, were made around the turn of the century by other scholars in Germany and in the English-speaking world.[227] Budde (1906: 96) called all conditional judicial laws (using either 'if' or a participle) 'casuistic'.

Gunkel (1906a: 22-23) went on towards a reconstruction of the *social location* of the different kinds of law. He held that the 'categorical' you-shall laws were taught by priests and that the others were spoken by a variety of leaders (priests, elders, kings, officials). Gressmann, somewhat more concretely, located the operation of judicial law under a sacred tree or near a city gate and considered that the you-shall laws were presented like a 'catechism' by priests, especially in connection with admitting persons to the cult (1921: 230).[228] Mowinckel connected the you-shall laws specifically with an annual covenant festival in Jerusalem (1927). These reconstructions became increasingly concrete and externally descriptive and thus not only more speculative but also less expressive of human (including social) significance.

Alt took three further steps. First, he grouped together second-person and participial laws; he called these two forms 'apodictic' (as Baentsch had done for both without placing them explicitly together) and termed only the 'if' laws 'casuistic' (narrowing this term from Budde's usage). Secondly, he regarded thus-defined apodictic law as Israelite–Yahwistic and the other tradition as having been taken over from Israel's neighbours. Thirdly, he placed the apodictic tradition into a covenant-renewal festival held at Shechem every seven years, whereas 'casuistic' law was taken to represent dispute settlements customarily made at city gates.

All three of these steps were shown by subsequent discussion to be problematic.[229] Alt's emphasis on apodictic law, however, appealed to

---

226. Baentsch also described those with direct address as 'categorical' (1903: 188).

227. Including Staerk (1894: 38, already referring to the 'customary' distinction between 'cultic'—i.e. 'religious–moral'—*debarim* and judicial *mishpatim*), C. Briggs (1897: 242-55), H. Holzinger (e.g. *Exodus*, 1900: 98), and I. Benzinger and G. Gray in *Encyclopedia Biblica* (III, 1902: 2716, 2734).

228. Like Holzinger and Benzinger, Gressmann referred to the Roman distinction between *ius* and (religious) *fas*.

229. See W.M. Clark in Hayes (1974: 105-28) where also information about Alt's immediate predecessors can be found; Osumi (1991: 3). Alt's antecedents prior to 1925 have been largely forgotten, presumably in good part since he did not refer to them, as perhaps too well known (a number of them, including M. Weber,

many students of the Bible by its drawing attention to the I–you character of second-person 'words', which had been noted by Rothstein and
previously by Philo (see above).

A structural–functional analysis of laws without Alt's questionable
steps was made by the Catholic Cazelles in 1946. He pointed out that
Israelite 'if' laws constitute (for the most part) what in Europe is called
'private law'—when one person sues another—while the participial
laws provide for the exclusion of an individual from the life of the
people (110, 124).[230] The life situations are thus conceived in terms of
operations or *functions*, not, as for Alt, in terms of historical derivations
(native versus non-Israelite) and external settings.

In another divergence from Alt, E. Gerstenberger argued that second-
person words arose from a 'clan ethos' (1965), in which the sacred and
the secular—'revelation' and human cognition—were not yet separated. In fact, Gerstenberger concluded that a 'dialectic of revelation
and reason' (i.e. a tension between them) was 'foreign' to the Hebrew
Bible (1965: 147; that conclusion may, however, not be accurate for the
available canon, which at least partially differentiates between Mosaic
or prophetic revelation and wisdom).

While scholars who stood consciously in the tradition emanating
from Gunkel gave extensive discussion of the correlation of style with
content and setting, they gave relatively little attention to the relation
between content and life, that is, to the way in which the injunctions
dealt with problems of human existence. This aspect of texts was
treated by other scholars who were interested in sociological issues.
These included—besides the sociologists M. Weber and L. Steffens[231]
and the Polish-Jewish social theorist A. Menes (1928)—the biblical
specialists Causse (with work culminating in 1937), L. Wallis (1935,
1942), and Graham and May (1936). In somewhat varying ways, they

were mentioned by A. Jirku, cited by Alt). For the political situation of the analysis,
see above. Alt did not deal with the form of detailed ritual legislations, which came
to be treated by others.

230. Cazelles's view was adopted and somewhat modified in Buss (1977; 1989:
60).

231. Steffens, a Christian, saw 'the revolt of Israel as a typical revolution' (1926,
subtitle), in part since the revolutionary leader, in this as in other cases, had had
special advantages that facilitated a leadership of those who had been down (57).
The latter observation had already been made by Abraham ibn Ezra, pointing out in
his exegesis of Exod. 2 that Moses avoided a slave mentality by being raised in the
palace.

valued both cooperative order and creativity.[232]

A number of works took account of the verbal forms of a **'controversy'** (*rib*) which may or may not be brought before a court (e.g. an assembly of persons at the city gate). Gunkel and others believed that biblical writers of various kinds 'imitated' such forms (Gunkel 1915: lxv;[233] Gunkel and Begrich 1933: 364; Begrich 1938: 22). This belief implied that the legal–moral sphere was at one time separate from other realms of life. Differently, Köhler, on the basis of the roles of such forms in Second Isaiah and Job, held that 'the Hebrew person thinks in the forms of law' (1953: 170 [1931]), as a pervasive pattern. Following him, Gemser (dealing widely with psalms, prophets, Job, etc.) said that the *rib* pattern is 'not ... a purely literary style-motif, but ... a form of thinking and feeling, a category, a frame of mind' (1955: 128); it implies an ethical view of the world (136).[234]

In 1952, Weiser's student Ernst Würthwein discussed evidence in the Psalms that God had a role as judge in Israelite ritual (as Mowinckel had done earlier in 1922: 65-77). He believed that the regular ritual included a judgment directed against Israel in so far as it has violated covenantal demands and that the uses of legal forms by biblical prophets were drawn from this background (1952: 1-16). Already a little earlier, Bentzen (1950: 85-99) had pointed to an Egyptian ritual

232. See above for their political orientations, which were fairly egalitarian. (Fortunately, Wallis dropped the unfair anti-Judaism expressed in his earlier work of 1912 [cf. 1935: 304-11]). Somewhat more highly descriptive (less theoretical) was the work of Lods in the 1930s. For overviews of sociological studies, see Hahn (157-84); Schottroff (1974: 46-66); Mayes (1989). Hahn (212) and Schottroff (55) thought that Graham & May and Causse, respectively, were too constructive in theory; but a theory should be replaced by a better one rather than by none.

233. *Einkleidung*. Gunkel argued in this essay (and elsewhere) that most of the genres used by prophets were 'not originally prophetic' (il). Shamanic speech, however, has been quite rich in its forms.

234. In the train of Köhler, H. Richter analysed the book of Job as arguing a basically legal point of view, although a negative one, namely, that human beings lack a legal claim before God (1955). Also following Köhler, Westermann incorporated the controversy pattern into his analysis of Job as a lament (1956b). If he had known Gemser's work of 1955, Westermann might have made even clearer than he did that the legal–moral pattern was a part of Near Eastern lament structure. The recognition that legal speech and lament belonged together would also lead to at least a modification of Richter's conclusion; for if an accusation of God was a common part of the Israelite lament structure, it must have been considered to be legitimate in principle.

directed against both external and internal enemies of the national order as a model for a background for Amos's words.[235]

Against Würthwein, H.J. Boecker argued that the prophetic uses of controversy forms were adapted from 'profane' legal processes (1960: 400-12). One of his arguments was that a self-defence by Yahweh, which appears in a number of prophetic words, is difficult to imagine in a cultic process (409). That may be true if 'cult' is taken as a rigid, unvarying process. However, an appropriate response to a ritual complaint brought against deity is a divine self-defence, which may have been uttered by a prophet in more or less close association with such a ritual.[236] Furthermore, ordinary controversies between human beings were not thought of at that time as merely secular, and religious ritual expressions were imbued with a forensic spirit already in Egypt and Mesopotamia, as Gemser and others had already pointed out;[237] in short, judicial and cultic processes were not separate entities.

Like Boecker, Westermann envisioned a secular background for prophetic announcements of judgment, but he considered a legal style to be the one that best corresponds to the thrust of these words, which furnishes a divine reaction to human action (1960c: 143)[238]—without concerning himself with the organizational contexts of such words. Similarly, a number of scholars connected the theme of judgment with the notion of a covenant between God and Israel, without specifying external circumstances for either controversies or prophetic expressions (Weiser 1949b: 250; Mendenhall 1954: 42; Huffmon 1959: 285-95; Wright 1962 and others).[239]

235. All of these analyses have been challenged since then, not surprisingly.

236. H.E. von Waldow (1953—known to Boecker; 1960) envisioned such a situation for Second Isaiah.

237. The Arabic seer-priest was also a settler of disputes, according to Pedersen (in Rowley 1950: 135), underscoring an early union of roles.

238. As a reaction, the divine act is neither unmotivated nor simply automatic. In this opinion, Westermann differed both from Wolff, who argued that the reasons given by prophets for the disaster announced were secondary, stated by them in order to produce a desired religious effect in the hearers (1934: 1-22), and from Koch, who advocated the interpretation that inherent consequences were 'put into force' by God (1955: 1-42, clarified/modified in 1991: 106). More recent discussions (including Buss 1969: 124) cannot be reported here.

239. E.g. von Waldow (1963—modifying 1953 and 1960 somewhat); others include some Catholics, such as J. Harvey (see McCarthy 1972: 37-40, 69, 78). Würthwein himself had left open the actual circumstances of the prophetic words

In 1964,[240] Boecker described controversy forms in detail. He treated forms of expression used prior to the presentations of a controversy to a court separately from those used before an assembled court. There is much overlap between these two stages, however; for instance, expressions of accusations and defence are basically the same at each stage. Furthermore, many controversies reported in the Bible using those same forms were never brought before a court. What Boecker described, then, were to a large extent not strictly 'legal' forms in so far as these involve a court, but, more broadly 'controversy' forms. In other words, the basic life situation of a *rib* was not the gate—although some controversies were settled there—but a certain kind of interaction, what Simmel called a 'life form', specifically, a controversy, which, like most ancient (and modern?) struggle, included an appeal not merely to power but to 'rightness'.[241]

Considerable attention was given to the connection of **prophetic speech** with rituals. A large number of scholars held that prophets had a recognized role in association with holy places.[242] Many of them discussed ways in which prophets utilized forms and traditions believed by those scholars to be embedded in ritual presentations. Quite a few, in fact, were convinced that prophets played an expected role within, or in close connection with, established proceedings; associations with rituals were suggested especially by texts patterned as a liturgy with an interplay between several types of speech, such as prayer and oracle.[243]

In discussions of the relationship between 'prophets' and 'cult' there were terminological problems, since the meanings of these two words were unclear. The Hebrew word *nabi'*, usually translated 'prophet', refers in the Bible to an inspired person who stands in a specially close personal relation to deity and who thus can furnish a word from God or can pray in a powerful manner.[244] The verb *nb'*, cognate with that noun,

preserved in the Bible (1952: 15). K. Baltzer placed at least some words of judgment in connection with (not necessarily as a part of) specially organized fasts which may lead to covenant renewal ceremonies (1960: 62-68).

240. In dissertation form, 1959.

241. See further Buss (1969: 76-77, nn. 98-99); that includes war as a controversy (thus, for Hittites, A. Goetze, *Kleinasien*, 2nd edn, 1957: 129, and now P. Bovati, 7.1. 1.5a, and others).

242. Thus, W.R. Smith 1882: 85. That was probably not a new idea then; J. Skinner's reference to a 'theocratic' office (1922: 218) sounds traditional.

243. For twentieth-century views, see Rowley (1967: 144-75).

244. That the word 'prophet' in Gen. 20.7 designated someone with 'effectual

covers not only oracle-giving but also singing or chanting, including both pleading and praising (1 Sam. 10.5; 1 Kgs 18.29; 1 Chron. 25.1-3). It is, however, not known whether singers were regularly called 'prophets'. Mowinckel assumed that they were not and held that singers and cult prophets, although they were closely associated and even overlapped, were not simply identical (1923, 1924). Specifically, he attributed to cult prophets the role of presenting oracles. These could be designed for a repeated ritual (1923: 41-51) or address a particular situation (1923: 22, 27; 1962, II: 56).[245]

Another problem concerned the word 'cult'. By intending a narrow meaning for the term in the designation 'cult prophet', Mowinckel implied that there were other prophets who were not cultic.[246] If, however—probably best for a phenomenology of religion—'cult' is conceived broadly to refer to overt religious action and expression, a prophet such as Jeremiah is brought within the realm of cult by the very fact that prayer is 'definitely a cult-act' (Welch 1953: 48) and the prophetic role is inherently cultic.[247] Reventlow gave voice to this broad conception of cult (1962: 168), but in practice he followed a narrow one; for instance, he supposed Jeremiah was commissioned in an 'ordered liturgical ordination ceremony' (1963: 76).[248]

One heavily debated scholarly issue was how to understand prophetic

intercession' was known to S.R. Driver (1891: 111) (and by others before him?). The role of intercession was discussed by von Rad (1933: 114), among others; it was important also for the shaman of a tribe in India described in Elwin, 134-35.

245. For prophets addressing a particular situation, Mowinckel referred to 2 Chron. 20.14 and Neh. 6.7, 12, 14. According to A.R. Johnson, the role of the pre-exilic temple prophet was absorbed by that of temple singer after the exile (1944: 62), but prophets who were not singers may well have continued. A differentiation between general and particular oracles—the former presented by, and the latter quoted by, singers—was made explicit in Buss (1963: 389). That particular oracles could be spoken in connection with rituals is supported by the story of Wen-Amun in ancient Phoenicia and by twentieth-century processes (Buss 1964: 324). Oracles in several psalms, however, are quoted and thus do not need to be spoken by a 'prophet' in a precise sense of that word (*pace* Mowinckel 1923: 40).

246. Probably wisely—to avoid this implication?—Mowinckel did not use the phrase 'cult prophet' in a general study of prophetic tradition (1946).

247. Thus R. Hentschke (1957: 1-2, 128, 145), although he preferred not to use this broad 'phenomenological conception'.

248. In 1986a: 118, discussing prayer, Reventlow described the contrast between 'cultic' and 'profane' as a 'modern prejudice'; by that time, he also moved away from his narrow view in practice.

words which rejected overt religious actions and expression and identified genuine service of God with concern for the weak.[249] A widespread opinion was that these words were hyperbolic and were not intended as a rejection of overt cult altogether.[250] Indeed, a major motivation for connecting the prophetic role with what was called 'the cult' was to defend the continuing relevance of organized ritual for present-day faith (Mowinckel 1921: v; 1924: 24; Welch 1953: 30); often, it is true, this was done at the cost of de-emphasizing the prophets' social message, thus in a sense confirming their criticism of ritual.

A number of scholars discussed the connection between prophecy and the tradition of law. A. Kapelrud (1953/54: 26, 30), Robert Bach (1957), and Kraus (1957) pointed out that ethical standards of the great prophets were closely related to 'apodictic law' in you-shall(-not) form and argued that this tradition was presupposed by, and thus older than, the prophets. Kapelrud thought that it was a part of royal cult ideology (1953/54: 31) or, as he subsequently stated, that it constituted a generally known ethic, in any case one that was not yet connected with the name of Moses (1956: 66, 68). Bach and Kraus, however, accepted the thesis of Alt that apodictic law was an old-Israelite and especially-Israelite cultic tradition.[251]

A crucial aspect of prophetic oracles was that they were believed to come from God if they are indeed 'true' oracles. The psychological state corresponding to this belief was one of receptivity and ego-tran-

---

249. It is theoretically possible to include in 'cult'—or identify with true cult—ethical activities, as Isa. 58.6 did in saying that the 'fast' God has chosen is to 'let the oppressed go free'. Rowley incorporated this perspective in stating that, for Israelite prophets, 'the essence of worship consisted in a personal relationship' with God 'which might be renewed in the shrine, but which must be continued outside the shrine' (1956a: 116). To use the word 'cult' so broadly as to include all human interaction inspired by religion, however, does not serve a scholarly purpose, for it then becomes identical with 'religion'.

250. Würthwein (1947: 145-49) made a case for interpreting them as declarations that God refuses to accept ritual approaches (as in God's non-acceptance of Cain's sacrifice in Gen. 4.5) at a particular time; such an interpretation, according to which God does not always reject ritual, may give comfort to persons who favour normal cult processes, but since there is no reason to think that Israel was then worse than people have been at other times, even such a refusal has a radical implication.

251. It is possible that the truth lies between the two divergent positions (thus, for example, N. Porteous, in Rowley 1950: 148-54). The fact that prophetic words related especially to apodictic, rather than to 'if'-styled law, makes sense in the light of Cazelles's observations of Israelite law.

scendence, some versions of which have been labelled 'ecstatic'. This state, with its many variations as a worldwide phenomenon, was discussed by a number of scholars.[252] Analysed, too, were representations of it in literary forms, such as reports of auditions and visions, the use of the message formula ('thus says…') and God's speaking in the first person in oracles.[253] Little attention, however, was given to the connection of ego-transcendence with the content of what was said, such as to a strong social ethic and to the announcement of a divine victory over human evil.[254] Thus, the form-critical procedure that attends to connections between life, content and style was not completed.

Among other types of speech, **love poetry** can be mentioned briefly as an object of similar investigation. During the early part of the century, a number of scholars were convinced that the poems of the Song of Songs were sung at wedding festivals. Especially from 1922 on, T.J. Meek and others held that the Song of Songs reflected a sacred ritual. Both of these views of an organizational setting, however, appeared to many to lack adequate evidence; thus, neither one was held widely by 1965.[255] An intensive study of the literature of the Song in terms of the psychology and relational sociology of love did not come until later in Protestant scholarship, except in such as was relatively traditional.

Finally, it is appropriate to look at the question of a life setting in a **general theoretical** way. Two terms that were used frequently from 1950 on to indicate an established organization were 'office' (*Amt*) and 'institution'.[256] Fohrer (among others) objected to both of these terms, especially to what they had come to mean in biblical scholarship (1961b: 312; 1965: 27). It should be noted, however, that in sociology the word 'institution' is often used fairly loosely (e.g. T. Parsons [1937: 407] for 'a body of rules governing action'; and Jameson [1981: 106]

252. See Rowley 1952b: 89-128; Lindblom: 219, 423-24—for their own views and for others they report (e.g. Skinner 1922; Seierstad 1946, Norwegian; Knight 1947).

253. See G. March in Hayes 1974: 141-77.

254. Buss (especially 1965: 46-53) did discuss self-transcendence, but only in relation to the sense of an 'End', not clearly in relation to ethics.

255. See Rowley 1952b: 187-234; Elliott 1989: 1-32, for scholarly views.

256. See Muilenburg (1984: 130-31 [1965]), for scholars who used the word 'office', including Alt (in 1934), and, from 1950 on, Noth, Würthwein, Zimmerli, Kraus, Reventlow, Boecker, Waldow. 'Institution' was used by von Rad (1951: 29); Reventlow (1961: 282); Boecker (1964: 9; etc.). (The earlier use of these two words by Skinner [1922: 215-16, 218] was somewhat looser.)

for literary genres).[257] In fact, Fohrer *et al.* spoke of language as an 'institution' (1973: 82).

A life situation that does not depend on a specific organizational setting was envisioned not only by Westermann (e.g. on psalms) but already a little earlier by H.W. Robinson, thus: 'The great formative ideas…have constantly to be brought back to their *Sitz im Leben*, their functioning in actual experience, in order to retain their vital truth'; specifically, they need to be considered in terms of a two-way relationship between God and human beings (1946: 49). Similarly, Muilenburg spoke of a genre's 'function in the life of the community or individual' and said that the various genres have 'different aims in view' (1951: 209), thus relating them to aims rathers than to organized contexts.

When Fohrer (1983: 66 [1959]) and Koch (1964: 43-45) said that a speech form can change its life situation, they had in mind a quite concrete view of this and accepted Gunkel's assumption that various aspects of life were separate before they came to interact. 'Life situation', however, is probably best viewed (as by H.W. Robinson, Westermann and some others) in terms of the functioning of a speech form, which is often older than a specific setting; examples of such functiong are instructing, praising, accusing and requesting. Indeed, in most cases, a special organization (e.g. school, temple, court, bank) is later than an operation or role (education, cult, strife, economic exchange).[258] The function of a particular text (Fohrer 1983: 76-77 [1959]) can then be seen as a special version or application (possibly a metaphorical one) of a general speech role[259] In fact, Fohrer (in 1965: 54-109)

257. For instance, a pattern of economic exchange constitutes an institution in a wide sense, while a bank with a building is an institution in a narrow sense. The list of 'institutions' given by Jepperson (1991: 144) includes both 'marriage' and 'sexism'.

258. Cf. above for Durkheim's view (similarly, Mann, I: 15). Durkheim also pointed out that a structure—that would include a literary form—can change in its function, but not without, in some important respect, itself undergoing a change; accordingly, it is problematic to say that a genre can change its social location.

259. Thus, Muilenburg, in describing the roles of literary forms in Second Isaiah, said that 'exclamations, commands, direct address, dialogue, question and answer…all reflect the functions which words perform in life' (1956: 386). Not infrequently, a text exhibiting one genre can play a subsidiary role within a text exhibiting another (Fohrer 1983: 77). To express this situation, Koch distinguished between a comprehensive 'frame genre' and the literary types of its parts (1964: 26-30).

arranged biblical genres according to their general operation (requesting, instructing, narrating, etc); that is an appropriate, although not the only legitimate, arrangement.

A focus on human life (that is, on process rather than on organizational phenomena such as particular festivals) was pushed into the background by von Rad in 1957. The testimony of the biblical writings, he said, was about Yahweh—specifically, about Yahweh's actions towards Israel and to the world—not about the believer, such as the believer's faith in God (1957–60, I: 112, 117). Thus, he failed to carry through with a full form-critical approach, for which a life situation is crucial. A consequence of von Rad's restraint was that his *Theology*—which was strong in regard to literary and ideational structure—was low in existential significance, that is, in meaning for human life, as he himself came to see.

A stronger affirmation of human life was made by some who believed that divine inspiration heightens rather than negates human perception and expression (Peake 1922: 152 [1912]; J.M.P. Smith 1922: 80; G.A. Smith 1927: 10).[260] Yet one can wonder what, in such a formulation, is meant by 'divine'. In a relational point of view, one needs to specify the nature of the relation between human beings and deity, since neither party—including deity—may have any characteristics in itself.[261]

One possibility is to take activity and receptivity as two different, but partially complementary, relations of existence.[262] These two ways of relating may not be purely human (versions of them may appear in non-human existence), but they must have human forms if they are to be expressed and understood by human beings. Specifically, the biblical dialogue is stated in human language. When God speaks in the first person in biblical literature, a human being is the one who says that,

260. Quite differently, Bultmann (1933-65, I: 2 [1924]): God is 'the radical negation' of humanity (particularism emphasizes conflict; for example, Tanner [126-62] shows how 'modern' nominalist thinking set forth a conflict between divine and human agency). See above for sophisticated views by the Catholics Schell (1889) and Lévesque (1895/96); the Protestant Cunliffe-Jones (1945: 19) echoed these in holding that an infinite God does not restrict but enhances freedom.

261. See *RFT*.

262. Thus, Buss (1961, inspired by Zimmerli and others; 1969: 139, etc.). (A specific stimulus for a concern with the distinction between divine and human speech in Hosea came to me from von Rad in a letter of 1956, prior to my dissertation [1958, revised in 1969]).

giving voice to the dimension of receptivity. The active side of life, in contrast, is represented in the Hebrew Bible by other styles and contents, especially when God is not said to be speaking. Biblical literature thus expresses human 'life' in two forms. That does not necessarily mean that God is not real, for a physicist does not normally deny the reality of something identified operationally, but it does mean that what is called 'God' can be spoken of significantly only as one relates to that being in a certain way. One might say (although this is too simple) that God is the reality that appears in a receptive relation; the fact that limited realities (human beings, trees) have a god-like quality (they 'speak' to one or 'grab' one) when approached in such openness has ethical implications.

Such an analysis implies that faith, including that of the Bible, can be examined by the human sciences (anthropology, including psychology and sociology). I have pursued this possibility since c. 1960, receiving stimulus from a number of scholars mentioned, especially from Zimmerli and von Rad, but giving greater attention to the human sciences than these did and thus coming into the proximity of H.W. Robinson and others, who preceded them. An effect of following this line is that language (such as, God represented as speaking) is related to content (in this form to ultimate matters, such as Origin and End)[263] and to human existence (which may voice existence as such).

d. *The Interrelation of Style, Content and Life: Theory of Form*

Attention to the nature of relations within a textual world leads to a theory of form. With this aim, a form-critical analysis not merely describes the linguistic form, content and life situation of a genre but reflects on the nature of connections between these aspects. Such connections are more likely to be intrinsic (not merely accidental) if the life situation is understood in terms of a human operation rather than in terms of an organizational setting.

When relations are understood in terms of their effect and logic, one has 'insight'. As was seen, Gunkel (especially in his analysis of the genres of psalms), Dibelius in 1919, Dodd in 1929, Mowinckel in 1938 and 1951, Fuchs in 1961, Zimmerli in 1963 and von Rad increasingly from 1957 to 1971, expressed an interest in rationale (reasons for style and content) and thus in a rationality that constitutes insight (*Einsicht*). In the area of law, Gressmann held that the 'if' form of casuistic style

---

263. See above, 2.2.

lay in 'the nature of the material' and that it has been used in European laws for this reason from ancient times to the present (1921: 227). Alt asserted an intrinsic (*wesenhaft*) connection between style and content, on the one hand, and the 'events and needs of life', on the other (1953: 284 [1934]); in fact, he took this view so far that he assumed that connections operated rigidly in oral life. I. Lande envisioned similarly (although not necessarily as rigidly) an 'appropriateness' of formulas in their setting (1949). Mowinckel thought that relational insight was contained in cultic structures themselves: 'The rules and forms of the cult are "wisdom", "insight" into the deepest reality; they are revelations of its connections' (1953: 122 [1950]).

A concern for rationale, however, was not apparent in most of the studies commonly labelled 'form-critical',[264] which were predominantly nominalist (only externally descriptive). Accordingly, this issue played no role in Koch's introduction to the method (1964), nor in other surveys.[265] Many of the affirmations of connections between language, thought and experience, as they have been cited above, were made outside of this tradition.[266] One example was furnished by Heschel; he thought that the presence of human speech to God in the Bible, together with divine speech, symbolizes the fact that 'the belief of the people of Israel was not an act of blind faith of acceptance of dogmas but rather the result of insight, the outcome of their being exposed to the power and presence of God in the world' (1996: 255 [1956]).

Relevant for insight is attention to generality. Local commonality of expression in a historically circumscribed literary genre reflects, to be sure, a large degree of arbitrary conventionality. If, however, an association of a certain form of expression with a certain content or of a certain content with a certain life situation appears in more than one cultural context, the possibility must be considered that the relation is not accidental but one which has a reason. That is true even for the most mysterious aspect of faith. For it 'makes sense' that one needs to

264. Surveyed in Hayes (1974). Even Mowinckel did not develop a rationale, but relied largely on convention (as was seen above).

265. Even in 1993: 76-77 (having stressed rationale in 1969: 1), I was not conscious of the earlier interests of Gunkel (and others) along that line.

266. Such affirmations or implications were made by most of the Jewish and Catholic and many of the Protestant interpreters cited in Chapters 8, 9, 10; further, among others, by Stauffer (1929), H.W. Robinson (1955) and Wilder (1964a); and, on Psalms, by Walker (1938), Terrien (1952) and Westermann (1954a, etc.).

relate to an infinite or ultimate reality to a large extent—although not purely—receptively or 'non-actively' (non-assertively), as happens in a number of religions.[267] The symbol of divine speech is an appropriate (although not a necessary) one for expressing this dimension of existence.

A comparative perspective which would draw attention to such issues was not altogether absent, especially from the work of the more notable contributors, but it was hardly well developed. Indeed, when von Rad in 1938, Zimmerli in 1940, and Bultmann as late as 1957, rejected insight, a major concomitant of that rejection was a belief that the scope of revelation is limited. Barth, who allowed for *Einleuchtung* (persuasive rationality) in 1940, was more inclusive, as has been seen.

Comparison, of course, shows not only commonality but also differences. This duality is affirmed by relationism, which requires particularity along with generality. Local and translocal divergences are characteristic especially of the surface level. Yet even on a deeper level, that of relations rather than of phenomena, variety exists. (In fact, not every relation is 'good' in the sense that one will want to approve it; rather, there can be evil ones—such as 'oppression'—with which one has to learn to deal.) Transcultural variations in structure, however, were analysed even less well—that is, less carefully in detail and in terms of larger questions—than were commonalities, perhaps since some theoretical framework (however tentatively held) is needed for seeing differences.

The position that insight into relationships is challenging without being coercive, since the structures and operations laid bare open up transtemporal possibilities for the reader or hearer, was stated by A.A. Anderson. In his words:

> A theology of Relationships...is both descriptive and normative. By 'normative' we do not mean a dogmatic system which is above all criticism but rather a challenge which demands our decision; it offers...the possibility of hearing the living word of God, which may be accepted or rejected but not ignored (1963: 19).

Rowley had said (in regard to history) that, because of the presence of rationality in faith, revelation does not use the 'bludgeon of authority', although faith involves an intuition beyond reason (1963: 6-7 [1949]).

---

267. Caution: receptivity (or, for that matter, non-action) is not identical with passivity (H. Knight 1947: 16; Fackenheim 1968: 140-45).

Relationism, by accepting both a partial independence and a partial connectivity for realities, combines insight with mystery.[268] Much of biblical scholarship, however, had room only for mystery, for many of those who consciously stood in the tradition of Gunkel adhered to an authoritarian and exclusivist theology and some, perhaps (e.g. Birkeland), envisioned no basic or intrinsic order at all for the world.

Thus, if 'form' is taken as a system of relationships and form criticism is, accordingly, understood as a study of the relations between life, thought and word, much work, even now, still lies ahead for this endeavour. Nevertheless, it is possible to say that an important beginning has been made.

268. Some who object to authoritarianism seem to imply that the alternative is an arbitrary judgment (as is, in fact, the case within a particularist philosophy).

Chapter 14

CONCLUDING REFLECTIONS

1. *Acknowledgment and Transcendence of Past Biblical Scholarship*

As one surveys studies of the Bible during the last 200 years, a notable impression is that they have been, on the whole, of remarkably high sophistication in dealing with form,[1] although they are associated with theologies and ideologies that one may reject. It is true, there have been many differences of opinion; for this reason alone, the analyses cannot all be accurate in their presentations. Yet most of the more important differences in positions were due to differences in basic perspectives. Specifically, the divergent allegorical meanings which Jews and Christians derived from texts reflected their different beliefs about reality, such as that of the Messiah. Furthermore, variations in philosophical assumptions have had profound effects.

As has been indicated, philosophical perspectives are regularly connected with corresponding social orientations. In somewhat schematic terms: (1) a one-sided emphasis on generality favours an aristocratic order; (2) a one-sided recognition of particularity favours the middle class, for, in supporting competition, it undercuts both hierarchical tradition and the need to consider the welfare of all (including the 'weak'); and (3) a combination of the general and the particular is required for a solidarity that covers those who would otherwise constitute a 'lower' or oppressed stratum, such as economic or sexual. (Whether thought or social structure is primary in relation to the other—they may be reciprocally related—and how transitions came about are issues that are not discussed here.[2])

A caution, however, needs to be expressed about the self-serving

---

1. J. Barton (1996: 18) is unduly impressed by the advance of twentieth-century form criticism over earlier steps; in fact, twentieth-century versions are weak in reflectiveness.

2. They are discussed in *RFT* (cf. Chapter 7 above).

nature of interpretation.[3] It is a truism that one favours that with which one identifies, but the object of identification can be highly varied; it can be onself as an individual, one's family, one's social class or 'race' or gender, one's nation, a religious group, a profession (e.g. biblical studies), an idealistic line (e.g. civil rights), humanity, all organic life, all of existence, etc. One of the most important features of human life is that such varied identifications are possible, for good or ill. Capitalist theory is based primarily on the identification with oneself, although it makes generous allowance for allegiance to the family and some allowance for other commitments.[4] Marxism focuses especially on class identification, but it considers a simplistic outlook that recognizes only this to be 'vulgar Marxism'. The present study has focused especially on perspectives associated with social strata, for the relative prominence of classes is a major element that has changed during the two millennia covered. Occasionally, however, there has been mention of individuals' transcendence of their limited group.[5]

An example of group transcendence is given in the fact that the present work, by a US citizen with a German background, is appreciative of investigations by British scholars[6] but sceptical of form-history as it has been practised in Germany and to some extent in the US,[7] whereas

---

3.   Contra what appears to be a sweeping assumption of some (e.g. Penchansky [65]: 'The issue is...who benefits from that ideology'. Penchansky, however, implies that he himself has an interest in 'a society characterized by the just treatment of its weakest members' [91], although he is probably himself not one of the weakest ones.) With appropriate caution, Clines has observed that 'issues of power, of self-identity and security, of group solidarity, of fear and desire, of need and greed...have *also* played a role in the production of the text, *sometimes* a leading role' (24; italics added).

4.   In opposing laws supporting the poor, Thomas Malthus argued as follows: 'By making the passion of self-love beyond comparison stronger than the passion of benevolence, [God] has at once impelled us to that line of conduct which is essential to the preservation of the human race... [under present conditions]. He has enjoined every man to pursue as his primary object his own safety and happiness and the safety and happiness of those immediately connected with him' (*An Essay on the Principle of Population*, 3rd edn, 1807, Appendix).

5.   E.g. for Plato, Philo, J. Peters, Rowley, Kraus (all of them in more than one respect).

6.   Such as, among those covered in some detail, Lowth, Moulton, Innes, H.W. Robinson, Rowley, Dodd, Daube and Wilder.

7.   In the US, there have been attempts to date poems on the basis of their form (see 13.2.a).

the English Rogerson can speak well of German scholarship but be critical of the intellectuality of English people.[8] Furthermore, although Protestant, male, Eurocentric, professional biblical scholarship is highlighted here, other work is covered also, even perhaps more favorably. As scholars, we seek such a balance, despite inevitable prejudice, and should give similar credit to others, past and present (contra 'vulgar Marxism').

The major social and philosophical orientations which have been described have varied in history especially in terms of what is dominant at any one time. There have always been different orientations at any given time, but some of the perspectives have not been recorded in writing or have been muted. The muted ones often occupied a low position within the social hierarchy, but they could be aristocratic within a predominantly non-aristocratic society. It is easy to focus primarily on interpretations which are the most prominent ones at any one time. Such a procedure, however, gives an exaggerated impression of change, since the relative prominence of strata has changed more than have the strata themselves. Some attention has thus been given in the present study to non-prominent lines, including women's interpretations and those which continued formal-literary views during the heavily historicist nineteenth century. A fuller history will need to uncover more of such submerged interpretations of biblical form, perhaps as they are implicit in sermons, songs, etc.

Although much that has been done is of high sophistication, a major problem area must be indicated for the twentieth century. The predominant ethos of this century—one that has been only partially accepted by Protestantism—includes a sense that both particularity and generality are important for intellectual as well as for social endeavours. Accordingly, a major issue for biblical scholarship has been how to combine these aspects of existence. One attempt to combine them appeared in the procedure known as 'form-history'. This, however, was based on questionable assumptions and continued to give priority to (particularist) history. Other formal analyses were more fruitful, but an exploration of appropriate ways to combine particularity and generality—as is done in relational theory—continues to present a challenge to the field.

What has been done well does not have to be repeated. Thus the point of the history of scholarship is not to furnish models for the future

8.   E.g. in 1995a: 69, 74-93, and in Johnstone, 134.

but to provide a springboard for further work with a knowledge of what has already been accomplished. One thus needs to ask, were there after 1965, and are there still now, new vistas to be opened? A full discussion of new possibilities must be reserved for another context. Nevertheless, one can indicate a few of them—although one cannot predict the future, for the future is, perhaps inherently, that which is partly open (if that were not so, there would be no point in making an effort towards it).

A major new path is a fuller participation of women in public discourse. Movement in this direction has undoubtedly been the most important development in biblical studies since 1965. Although this movement falls outside the time-frame of the present work, it is worth noting that feminist studies have been largely relational in character, explicating literary and social relations rather than refining the diachronic placement of texts.

While much of this is new, it is important to remember that women had made significant contributions earlier. The women who did so often relied heavily on experience, especially inner experience.[9] One reason for the reliance on interiority (which is not the same thing as individualism) was probably the fact that women were largely excluded from the kind of education males received and from public life generally.[10] Indeed, one of the factors in the modern drive towards social equality for the sexes was the spread of formal education to women, which proceeded slowly over several centuries from the High

9. See above for Hadewijch of Brabant, Teresa of Avila, Guyon, Lead, Lee, Beecher, Gestefeld and Chandler. Further, Mary Astell (Anglican), in a *Serious Proposal to the Ladies* (1697), relied on 'reason' (including experience), of which she thought 'revelation' to be 'a more perfect' form (135; Selvidge, 133). Quite a few women leaders were Quakers, who follow an inner light (Selvidge, 23). Joanna Southcott said: 'I am but a simple woman, and was never brought up to high learning'; in any case, she would rather not read what others say—in fact, they contradict one another—but 'I...write by the Spirit as I am directed' (*Letters, &c.*, 1801: 9, 11; *The Second Book of Visions*, 1803: 65 [Selvidge, 179-80]). Among writers after 1875, the following are some who stressed interiority: Christina Rossetti on the Apocalypse (1892; cf. A. Wainwright, 209-11), Mary Baker Eddy, *Science and Health, With Key to the Scriptures*, 1894 (e.g. on Gen. 3.1-3); Anna Kingsford (with E. Maitland), *The Perfect Way* (1923, 1.1.1-6).

10. Whether also a biological or developmental–psychological factor supported interiority remains controversial. (In any case, cultural conditioning can have a biological effect, if only because the brain adapts to usage even within an individual's life.)

Middle Ages on.[11] Whether women will want to retain in the future a strongly experiential orientation, not as an exclusive but nevertheless as an important dimension of their thinking (perhaps together with involvements in it by men)—so that there would be some continuity between past and future—is a question that must be left open here, if only since I myself am not a woman.

Another beckoning line, besides a new role for women, is an interreligious and intercultural perspective. It is part of a postcolonial process.[12] A major phase of this process reflects the desire of members of different colonized groups to explore their own perspectives. Such an exploration is necessarily transcultural at least to some extent, since it involves interaction with an ancient culture, in so far as it deals with the Bible, and since it takes place in reaction against a previously (and in many ways still) dominating Eurocentric culture.

Scholars who stand primarily in the Eurocentric tradition also need to be attuned to interreligious and intercultural engagement, for—although they should recognize that such investigation must be shared, with non-Europeans playing crucially important roles—a lack of willingness to learn from or even about other traditions (common in neo-orthodoxy) may imply a profound disrespect for them. Not everyone needs to be engaged in overt comparison, but interpretation is affected in subtle ways if one is aware of other traditions, and one should know enough about these so that one can appreciate explicit connections made by others, such as by non-Westerners, so they are not treated as marginal. On the practical level, which cannot be dissociated from the theoretical, non-dominating intercultural politics is now important for the good of humanity.

There have already been important moves in an inclusive direction. In fact, quite a few major Western scholars have had a wide knowledge of religious traditions, and a number of Asian, African and other scholars have addressed cross-religious and cross-traditional issues. Repeatedly, non-Europeans have written in their own language, so that more has been done than is known in the West.[13] Nevertheless, work along a

11. Cf. the observation by C. Beecher, cited above.

12. Even Foucault, who once insisted that all knowledge is local, changed his mind in this (see *RFT*).

13. See above, 13.1.b, and Martey (for Africa), H. Goodman (for India) and Kwok (for Asia, especially China), referring to works in both European and other languages.

transcultural line is still limited in extent. The written traditions of India and China, for instance, have been given very little consideration by Western biblical scholars.

Consequently, there is probably room for several hundred comparative monographs, as well as for larger syntheses or probes. Individual studies might well focus on genres, as did that of H. Jahnow on the dirge and a recent one by E. van Wolde on creation stories. Thus one might look at narratives (histories, epics, etc.), laws (including ethical and ritual injunctions), proverbs, hymns or love poetry. The nature of the structure and function of these genres—together with their place in the larger history of humanity—can become clearer through such investigations. For biblical scholars now, a comparative engagement is unfamiliar, it is true, but current pursuits of 'intertextuality' can furnish valuable experience for it, although efforts along this line have so far been limited in their spatial range.[14]

On the theoretical level, comparisons are useful since they can help to show in what way relations between phenomena are intrinsic (which does not necessarily mean that they are good) and to what extent the actualities are a matter of free play. In fact, it is likely that most processes involve a combination of reason and play. Especially if something (such as a relation) recurs either within a group or in different groups there may well be a reason for it, although not necessarily an admirable one, but sheer contingency, grounding particularity—which is a part of the richness of existence—is important also.

With respect to formal analysis, non-European literary classifications and hermeneutical considerations can both sharpen procedures already used in biblical studies and open up new angles. For instance, Hindu analyses of canonical materials include descriptive classification with attention to ritual situations in a way that is similar to twentieth-century biblical form criticism.[15] Perhaps especially intriguing, however, are ways of dealing with texts that differ from those now current in biblical study.[16]

14. Cf. E. Wainwright (1997: 455): 'Intertextuality...is not simply concerned with the influence or borrowing from sources...it seeks to address the intersection of texts from not only Jewish but also Greco-Roman literary contexts as well as myriad oral contexts'. To be sure, two major considerations are important for comparison: (1) differences as well as similarities need to be noted, and (2) phenomena should be seen in relation to their contexts (thus, for both points, Hallo, 23).

15. See Patton, 91-135 (cited above, 13.2.a).

16. Cf. Sanskrit and Chinese stylistic typologies mentioned above, 3.5.

Comparative study that reaches beyond an immediate context constitutes, of course, an opening up of a transchronic (including trans-
spatial) view.[17] In fact, it is likely that an adequate form criticism is
neither primarily diachronic nor simply synchronic, but rather transchronic, as the work of—among others—Gunkel, Mowinckel, Jahnow,
Westermann, Dodd and Wilder, all with wide views, has already
indicated.[18]

2. *Relational Form Criticism: Future Possibilities*

Pursuing a transchronic perspective is not in principle new. In fact, it is
impossible to do anything without holding one implicitly. Specifically,
if one examines a past phenomenon (all phenomena are past!) while
one stands in the present (one cannot stand anywhere else!), one must
somehow transcend time (without leaving it). So far widely neglected
within professional biblical scholarship, however, is an open and disciplined facing of this situation.[19] An overt transchronic perspective
brings biblical study within the realm of anthropology, the general
history of religion, sociology and psychology (although interaction
with up-to-date psychology is so far weakly developed). That means
more than 'using' these disciplines while one remains within a factual
realm; it means actually participating in a discussion of issues that are
raised by them.[20] That these sciences are somewhat comparable to the

17. As was indicated above, 11.3.a, 'transchronic' is a term preferable to Saussure's 'panchronic'.

18. After 1965, when it became generally clear that the use of form criticism for
diachronic questions is problematic, quite a few theorists came to consider the
genius of form criticism to be synchronic (thus, for example, E. van Wolde 1989:
3); yet that is still an inadequate characterization. (Van Wolde, in fact, ended her
study transchronically, bridging past and present, although without using the word
'form criticism' in connection with that step; furthermore, she furnished a worldwide perspective in 1996, which was at least implicitly form-critical, since she
focused on the genre of creation stories.)

19. Of course, much is done intuitively by biblical scholars and others (e.g. by
clergy), and that is not necessarily less adequate than what would be done in a more
'disciplined' way. Still, J. Barton has apparently felt a need to go beyond the field
in treating the classicist Martha Nussbaum as a model for transchronic interpretation (1995).

20. W. Jeanrond (largely following the Catholic D. Tracy) calls for a 'readiness
to participate in the wider human conversation' (1991: 175), but it is hard to find a
biblical scholar doing so.

physical sciences should not be disconcerting if one does not place humanity in radical opposition to the rest of existence.

All of the sciences—human or otherwise—deal with relations. Thus it is helpful at the present time that the best available outlook is, apparently, a relational (including communicational) perspective. This view recognizes simultaneously connection and distance, conflict and cooperation, variety and a degree of commonality. (S.J. Samartha [1994] accordingly proposed a 'relational hermeneutics' because relations both distinguish and connect.)

Human beings evince more variability than do others that are less complex. Nevertheless, one can to certain extent 'understand' human phenomena—for example, in clothing, music and ritual—if one sees the relations into which they enter; in many ways, these relations recur in different groups.[21] (In fact, Saussure held that the only aspects of language that are 'panchronic' are relations.) To recognize the relations specifically of literary structures is the task of form criticism.

Such an approach represents not so much a method that one chooses at will but rather a way of looking at things.[22] If one believes that both particularity and generality—both a degree of separateness and a degree of connectivity—are aspects of what is real, certain practical implications follow almost of themselves. Some of these implications are social; they include a simultaneous affirmation of one's more immediate circles, of humanity at large and of existence beyond that. Other implications are intellectual, relevant for scholarship.

In the realm of scholarship, connectivity implies the possibility both of comparison between cultures and of interaction between disciplines. Gunkel's work was strong in these respects, making worldwide comparisons and pursuing far-flung interdisciplinary interests. Furthermore, his belief that every genre involves a certain connection with life, a definite range of content (including feeling) and typical linguistic forms implied that there is an interrelation between these three aspects; sometimes he explicitly reflected on the nature of this interrelation.[23]

21. Dewey, who (like others before him) considered the object of science to be relations, regarded these as 'invariant' (1929: 163); that may be too strong a term, but relations certainly recur.

22. 'Method' became a favourite term from the sixteenth century on, expressing an incipient form of calculating reason (cf. Ong, 225-69; Gilbert; Hagen 1990; V. Kahn, 107, 280). It appeared frequently in Ramist biblical interpretation (see above, 5.3); in 1637, Descartes published his *Discourse on Method*.

23. See above, 11.2.d; 13.2.d.

In observing connections between aspects of literary form, biblical scholarship can go further than Gunkel did, for he reflected on their nature only intermittently. One can ask on a more regular basis, 'How does this language go with certain thoughts and feelings, and how do these go with a given kind of situation?' For instance, there is a well-known correspondence between narrative form and certain aspects of the structure of experience.[24] Similarly, many other linguistic phenomena—including the use of the question 'why' in accusations—have good reasons besides a certain arbitrariness.[25] Even more importantly, thoughts and feelings are at least somewhat appropriate in relation to given situations, such as an accusing complaint in a condition of unjust suffering or, in ethics, respect and care for a limited other (including the weak other) when one faces receptively a mysterious but encompassing Other. (Whether this 'Other' should be affirmed is not directly a form-critical question, but the 'life' of receptivity is.[26]) Since there are different kinds of situations and problems in life, there are different genres, each with its characteristic shape.

Attention to this kind of issue would mean a revival of the notion of 'aptness'. This notion was important in Graeco-Roman rhetoric at a time when societal order was a major value, but it was downplayed in postmediaeval particularist aesthetics. A relational view would take a nuanced position. It would reject necessity[27]—that is, the idea that certain ideas or style elements are required[28]—but it would also reject exclusive arbitrariness, or sheer unconnectedness.

A major implication is that biblical data are approached neither as

24. Cf., e.g., Wilder, above.

25. Cf. I. Lande, above, 13.2.b. The oft-mentioned 'arbitrariness' of language relates primarily to details, not to larger language patterns, such as the three 'persons' (I, you, s/he/it). A 'why' question puts the accused person on notice that the speaker does not consider the action described to be morally justified but (in theory, at least) also allows for a possibly valid defence; it thus sets the complaint into the framework of a moral discussion, calling for a response.

26. See above, 13.2.c (near end).

27. Differently, Lonergan has said that insight grasps 'necessity' (1980: 41, 46); for, in an Aristotelian framework (which he accepted), 'essential' features are 'necessary'.

28. That has been held or implied in a number of traditional theories of canon, for example, in Hindu views that the structure of the Vedas underlies that of the cosmos (B. Smith, 68), in Jewish Torah mysticism, and in Barth's judgment, cited above, that the canon's form is necessary.

dry data nor as an external authority but are explored in terms of their reasons. Such an investigation not only leads to understanding but may also genuinely persuade the reader of the significance of a text (although that does not always imply acceptability), so that a faith one lives by is not blind or slavish—although ultimate reality goes beyond understanding (a fact that is intrinsic to ultimacy). Indeed, an affirmation of 'liberation' and critique of 'oppression' implies that what is sought is not an entirely arbitrary exercise of force, for that would be oppression.

Among others, Gunkel, Dodd, Temple and Rowley have spoken in favour of a non-authoritarian faith. Recently, authoritarianism has been frequently rejected by women writers.[29] For instance, Kathleen Jones rejects a kind of authority that is equated with what she calls 'sovereignty'; rather, she says, 'we need to remember always to ask "Why?"'. For 'WHY is the question the sovereign does not want to hear. "Why?" invites reflection, it invokes memory, it keeps the conversation going' (1991: 119). Along the same line, Alice Laffey concluded her *Introduction to the Old Testament: A Feminist Perspective* (1988) with a call for seeing 'why' certain concerns are reflected in the Bible', specifically for 'understanding and explaining both the patriarchy of the Old Testament and also the feminist impulses that the culture produced' (221-22). As this call makes clear, understanding reasons for phenomena can lead to a rejection of their continued applicability—the reasons may no longer apply, or they may not have been appropriate to begin with, or may now be more effectively answered in other ways—as well as for a positive appreciation of them.[30] The African American Wimbush has said that 'to the extent that reasons for' an experiential 'world', such as of the Bible, 'are discernible, it is possible to understand and translate' it (1985: 13, 19).[31] Translation implies modification along with application.

29. E.g. Sölle, 43. (That does not mean that some kind of 'authority' may not be relevant; for example, McFague [1982: 183] spoke of a friend's authority, in a 'mature' relationship of respect.)

30. Cf. above, on reason (not purely calculating), M. Astell (1697) and C. Beecher (1860). Some twentieth-century women philosophers' similar views on reason are cited in *RFT*.

31. Similarly, Boff (1987: 143-50) (in a Latin-American tradition that champions 'liberation' not in terms of competitive individualism but in terms of human fulfillment) has argued for a 'correspondence of relationship' instead of a 'correspondence in terms'.

That does not mean that a discerning of reasons for biblical phenomena is sufficient for assessing their significance. Quite a few other considerations need to come into play for that, including intuition (with a receptive dimension), which has an inescapable role in any dealing with questions of meaning and ethics. But it does mean that reflection, such as is possible in biblical scholarship, can contribute to theology and ethics.[32]

Mediaeval and Renaissance Jewish thinkers, following the lead of the Hebrew Bible itself, moved far, perhaps sometimes too far, in the direction of discerning reasons for biblical themes and forms.[33] Differently, Protestant thinking (including secular thinking with a Protestant stamp), which has been heavily particularist, has tended to oscillate between the alternatives of arbitrary authoritarianism ('despotism') and an attitude that 'anything goes'. (There are important exceptions to that, for example, in Mowinckel's and Traina's works and in others cited above, 13.2. b-d.) During the twentieth century, Catholicism has learned from Protestant particularist-historical scholarship. Conversely now, Protestantism needs to learn from Catholicism (which has a tendency towards generality, as its name indicates) and from Judaism, so as to become less one-sidedly particularist, although there is a value, not to be despised, in having a tradition that makes sure that particularity is not overlooked.

Besides connectivity, indeed, relationality involves an element of distance and contingency. This fact implies that 'aptness' should not be pressed, for there are a great variety of ways in which one can respond to a given problem, and a certain response can be expressed in different ways. Furthermore, it implies that it is possible, indeed likely, that there are tensions within a text and that some thoughts and expressions must be judged inappropriate or even evil (the Bible is not perfect!). With regard to genres, a looseness in connections means—contra Gunkel— that generic patterns are normally probabilistic rather than rigid and that, since any object enters into a multiplicity of relations, classifications can be made in different ways through the application of different criteria.

Interestingly, a separation between disciplines, too, can serve a useful purpose, even for communication. Gunkel's scholarly situation in this

32. Cf. above, 2.1.a, and, in greater detail, *RFT*.
33. See above for Saadia, Maimonides and Azariah de' Rossi. Cf. also later Jewish interpreters, including Heschel.

regard was paradoxical. He gained from extensive interaction but also made major mistakes by failing to interact as fully as he might have done. This situation might indicate that perfect interaction should be an ideal in so far as it is attainable. Yet Gunkel's idea of rigid genres that are tightly connected with concrete oral settings—a misconception which resulted from his shortcoming in interaction and which misled much of biblical scholarship—had a positive side, for it provided a sharply etched position which challenged and stimulated members of other disciplines, who then modified his view appropriately.

One of the partially valid reasons for neo-orthodoxy's keeping distant from the rest of the world, with its disciplines,[34] was the fact that there was a good deal of evil active in the world. Neo-orthodox theology, however, had a weakness in that it assumed too readily that evils lie outside the Church. (For instance, antisemitism was rampant within the Church and was indeed fostered by it.[35]) This line also failed to see that only contact makes possible a countering of destructive forces and a contribution to the growth of oneself and the other. Thus, von Rad, who stood within that tradition, saw in 1971 that his circle had much catching up to do in this respect, both for the sake of biblical scholarship itself and for what it has to say, for only when one is in contact with others can one contribute to them. In other words, distance alone is not an adequate stance. As long as biblical scholarship remains one-sidedly particularist (whether diachronic or synchronic[36] in operation), as is still largely true today especially within Protestantism, it can neither receive nor give adequately.

That biblical scholars can rightly have some confidence in their being able to make a contribution in other fields is indicated by the fact that Gunkel, who desired to furnish observations valuable to others, succeeded in doing so at least in part. W.R. Smith did so similarly,[37] and others had been influential earlier.[38] Gunkel's impact on other disciplines lay in the area of method. There is no reason why there cannot

34. As stated above, keeping distant from the world can be a defining characteristic for neo-orthodoxy.

35. Cf. above, 11.1.b, on O. Dibelius.

36. Van Wolde (1995) well describes a 'chronistic' (group-particularist) synchrony, which has a valid place in scholarship but needs to be distinguished from transchrony.

37. Cf. now discussions of Smith's impact in Johnstone.

38. They include D.F. Strauss and B. Bauer, the latter a teacher of Marx (Baird, xx, 278).

also be substantive interdisciplinary contributions by biblical scholarship, as long as one does not think of the Bible as being 'wholly other'.[39]

Interaction, then, is possible for the mutual benefit of groups.[40] Already now there are important contributions to a study of the Bible by persons without an express religious commitment.[41] Perhaps in the not too distant future Muslim, Hindu, Buddhist and other religious scholars will also become part of a communicating network. Members of various traditions already engage to some extent in biblical scholarship within their own groups. Perhaps they are willing to engage in interaction. The image 'network', just employed, is useful in this context, since it symbolizes both a semi-independence for the 'nodes' of the network and the existence of connections between them.[42] None of the participants in the discussion need to forsake their own commitments; in fact, relationality to the observer is an important factor and should be acknowledged.

In sum, form criticism, as it was defined at the beginning of the present volume, observes interrelationships between thoughts and moods, linguistic forms, and the experiences and activities of life on the basis of giving attention to more than one text; ideally, this involves a knowledge of more than one culture. A relational understanding of form does not envision that connections are rigid and thus universal in a monistic way[43] but rather sees and values variety. At the same time, it

39. Minear, in 1946, rejected taking the sayings of Jesus as a 'pattern for scientific psychology' (see above, 12.3). There is no reason, however, to think that psychology might not learn from biblical themes (as has indeed happened in the work of David Bakan, among others). An example of transchronic analogy is given by Overholt (1982: 73): 'having learned something about the underlying similarities of two specific prophets, Jeremiah and Handsome Lake, we have, I believe, gained at least some understanding of all other prophets as well'. (Learning from the Hebrew Bible, however, is not developed in Overholt [1996].) See above, 13.1.b, for a religiohistorical insight Bertholet gained from the Bible.

40. Thus also Blount, 184.

41. For example, an atheist can make sensitive analyses of the Bible, not simply rejecting it (cf. Exum 1992; 1993: 11). Some non-theistic philosophers value major elements of biblical ethics.

42. See *RFT* on Hesse, Foucault (in one of his themes) and a trend in sociology.

43. As has been pointed out repeatedly above (Chapters 6, 12, 13), monistic universalism is (or at least can be) particularism writ large, while generality involved actual or potential transparticularity; those two categories are thus quite different.

believes that phenomena are not altogether arbitrary but reflect shared, although contingent, processes. It thus seeks an insight into form that looks for (moderate) appropriateness or likelihood[44] rather than for either necessity or pure randomness. It is grounded, in other words, in the belief that reality exhibits together with a degree of separateness and conflict a mutual belonging. In such a duality of separateness and connection—indeed, only with that conjunction—communication can occur; this is not an unalloyed good,[45] but it furnishes a potential for joy.

44. Not all phenomena are 'appropriate' in a positive sense. For instance, oppression is 'likely', rather than 'appropriate', when a person with an advantage encounters a weaker one.

45. Already ancient wisdom valued restraint in speech.

BIBLIOGRAPHY

Editorial note: With special permission of the publisher, the present work dispenses with a regular bibliography. For the convenience of the reader, many book titles are given in the discussion itself (in italics or, if their content is part of the flow of the sentence, with capitalization and quotation marks); to save space, they are not repeated here. Some works, furthermore, are not cited with their formal titles, but are described in the text as 'Commentary on . . . ', or similarly. The index of authors provides a guide to all works.

Aalen, Sverre
 1951   *Die Begriffe Licht und Finsternis.*
Abba, Raymond
 1958   *Nature and Authority of the Bible* (new edn 1992).
Ackerman, Robert
 1991   *The Myth and Ritual School.*
Ackerman, Sonja
 1997   *Christliche Apologetik und heidnische Philosophie im Streit um das Alte Testament.*
Ackroyd, Peter
 1984   *T.S. Eliot.*
Adam, A.K.M.
 1995   *Making Sense of New Testament Theology.*
Adams, Marilyn McCord
 1987   *William Ockham.*
Ahlwardt, Wilhelm
 1856   *Über Poesie und Poetik der Araber.*
Aichele, George
 1997   *Sign, Text, Scripture: Semiotics and the Bible.*
Albert, Ethel M.
 1964   ' "Rhetoric", "Logic", and "Poetics" in Burundi: Culture Patterning of Speech Behavior', *American Anthropologist* 66, No. 6, Part 2: 35-54.
Albright, William F.
 1922   'The Earliest Forms of Hebrew Verse', *JPOS* 2: 69-86.
 1939   'A Hebrew Letter from the Twelfth Century B.C.', *BASOR* 73: 9-13.
 1940a *From the Stone Age to Christianity.*
 1940b 'The Archaeological Background of the Hebrew Prophets of the Eighth Century', *JBR* 8: 131-36.
 1942   *Archaeology and the Religion of Israel.*

1944   'The Place of Minorities in Our Civilization', *The Jewish Forum* 27, April: 85-86.
1950a   'A Catalogue of Early Hebrew Lyric Poems (Psalm LXVIII)', *HUCA*, XXIII/I: 1-39.
1950b   'Some Oriental Glosses on the Homeric Problem', *AJA* 54: 162-76.
1964   *History, Archaeology, and Christian Humanism*.
Alonso Schökel, Luis
1960a   'Genera litteraria', *VD* 38: 1-15.
1960b   'Die stilistische Analyse bei den Propheten', *Congress Volume, Oxford 1959* (VTSup, 7): 154-64.
1963   *Estudios de poética Hebrea*.
1966   *La palabra inspirada* (ET 1967).
1988   *A Manual of Hebrew Poetics*.
Alt, Albrecht
1934   *Die Ursprünge des israelitischen Rechts* (reprinted in 1953: 278-332).
1953   *Kleine Schriften,* I (partial ET 1967).
Alt, Albrecht, Begrich, Joachim, and Gerhard von Rad
1934   *Führung zum Christentum durch das Alte Testament*.
Alter, Robert
1987   'Psalms', in R. Alter and F. Kermode (eds.), *The Literary Guide to the Bible*: 244-62.
Althaus, Paul
1933   *Die deutsche Stunde der Kirche*.
Althusser, Louis
1974   *Eléments d'autocritique* (ET 1976).
Anderson, A.A.
1963   'Old Testament Theology and its Methods', in F.F. Bruce (ed.), *Promise and Fulfilment*: 7-19.
Anderson, Bernhard W.
1951   *Rediscovering the Bible*.
1962   'Water', *IDB*, IV: 806-10.
Anderson, George W.
1965   'Enemies and Evildoers in Psalms', *BJRL* 48: 18-29.
Anderson, R. Dean, Jr
1996   *Ancient Rhetorical Theory and Paul*.
Andrews, Isolde
1996   *Deconstructing Barth*.
Andrews, M.E.
1971/72   'Gerhard von Rad—A Personal Memoir', *ExpTim* 83: 296-300.
Angela of Foligno
1993   *Complete Works*.
Arieti, J., and J. Crossett, (eds.)
1985   *Longinus: On the Sublime*.
Armour, Michael Carl
1992   *Calvin's Hermeneutic and the History of Christian Exegesis*.
Armstrong, D.M.
1978   *Nominalism and Realism*.

Arnold, Matthew
1960–77 *Complete Prose Works* (11 vols.).
Auerbach, Erich
1946   *Mimesis* (ET 1953).
Austin, J.L.
1975   *How To Do Things with Words* (2nd edn [1st edn 1962]).
Ayers, Robert H.
1979   *Language, Logic, and Reason in the Church Fathers*.
Baasland, Ernst
1992   *Theologie und Methode*.
Babbitt, Irving
1910   *The New Laokoon*.
Bach, Inka, and Helmut Galle
1989   *Deutsche Psalmendichtung vom 16. bis zum 20. Jahrhundert*.
Bach, Robert
1957   'Gottesrecht und weltliches Recht in der Verkündigung des Propheten
     Amos', in W. Schneemelcher (ed.), *Festschrift für Günther Dehn*: 23-34.
Bacharach, Walter Zwi
1993   *Anti-Jewish Prejudices in German-Catholic Sermons* (Hebrew 1991).
Bacher, Wilhelm
1889   *Aus der Schrifterklärung des Abulwalîd Merwân Ibn Ganâh*.
1892   'Die Bibelexegese der jüdischen Religionsphilosophen des Mittelalters
     vor Maimûni', in *Jahresbericht der Landes-Rabbinerschule in Budapest
     für das Schuljahr 1891–1892*: iii-156 (reprinted 1972).
1894   'Die Bibelexegese (Vom Anfange des 10. bis zum Ende des 15. Jahrhun-
     derts)', in J. Winter and Aug. Wünsche (eds.), *Die jüdische Litteratur seit
     Abschluss des Kanons*, II (reprinted 1965): 237-339.
1902   'Bible Exegesis: Jewish', in *The Jewish Encyclopedia*, III: 162-74.
Bacon, Benjamin W.
1903   'Ultimate Problems of Biblical Science', *JBL* 22: 1-14.
1906   'Gospel Types in Primitive Tradition', *HibJ* 4: 877-95.
1909   *The Beginnings of the Gospel Story*.
1910   'The Purpose of Mark's Gospel', *JBL* 29: 41-60.
1911   'The Resurrection in Primitive Tradition and Observance', *AJT* 15: 373-
     403.
1914   *Christianity Old and New*.
1921   *Jesus and Paul*.
Baentsch, Bruno
1892   *Das Bundesbuch*.
1903   *Exodus-Leviticus-Numeri*.
Baethgen, Friedrich
1880   *Anmuth und Würde in der alttestamentlichen Poesie*.
Bainton, Roland H.
1957   *Yale and the Ministry*.
1963   'The Bible in the Reformation', in *The Cambridge History of the Bible*:
     1-37.
Baird, William
1992   *History of New Testament Research*, I.

Balla, Emil
    1912   *Das Ich der Psalmen.*
    1927   'Amos', *RGG*, 2nd edn, I: 306-9.
Balthasar, Hans Urs von
    1951   *Karl Barth.*
Baltzer, Klaus
    1960   *Das Bundesformular* (ET 1971).
Barner, Wilfried
    1970   *Barockrhetorik.*
Baron, Salo Wittmayer
    1958   *A Social and Religious History of the Jews*, VI (2nd edn.).
Baroway, Israel
    1935   'The Hebrew Hexameter', *ELH: A Journal of English Literary History* 2:
                66-91.
Barr, James
    1961   *The Semantics of Biblical Language.*
    1963   'The Interpretation of Scripture. II. Revelation Through History in the
                Old Testament and in Modern Theology', *Int* 17: 193-205.
    1982   'Jowett and the Reading of the Bible "Like Any Other Book"', *Horizons
                in Biblical Theology* 4 No. 2: 1-44.
    1993   *Biblical Faith and Natural Theology.*
Barrow, John D.
    1988   *The World Within the World.*
Barth, Karl
    1919   *Der Römerbrief.*
    1922   *Der Römerbrief*, 2nd edn (cited according to reprints from 1923 onward;
                ET of 6th edn: 1933).
    1924   *Das Wort Gottes und die Theologie.*
    1927   *Die Christliche Dogmatik im Entwurf.*
    1932   *Die Kirchliche Dogmatik* (ET 1936–62), I/I.
    1939   *Die Kirchliche Dogmatik*, I/II.
    1940   *Die Kirchliche Dogmatik*, II/I.
    1942   *Die Kirchliche Dogmatik*, II/II.
    1945   *Die Kirchliche Dogmatik*, III/I.
    1950   *Die Kirchliche Dogmatik*, III/III.
    1951   *Die Kirchliche Dogmatik*, III/IV.
    1953   *Die Kirchliche Dogmatik*, IV/I.
    1955   *Die Kirchliche Dogmatik*, IV/II.
    1956   *Karl Barth zum Kirchenkampf.*
Barton, George A.
    1918   *The Religion of Israel.*
    1919   *The Religions of the World* (2nd edn).
    1934   *Christ and Evolution.*
Barton, John
    1992   'Form Criticism: Old Testament', *ABD* II: 838-41.
    1995   'The Use of the Bible in Ethics and the Work of Martha C. Nussbaum:
                Reading for Life', in J. Rogerson *et al.* (eds.), *The Bible in Ethics.*
    1996   *Reading the Old Testament* (2nd edn).

Bauer, Uwe F.W.
1991   *Kol had-devarîm ha-elle* [*All diese Worte*].
Bauernfeind, Otto
1915   *Die literarische Form der Evangelien.*
Baumgärtel, Friedrich
1934   'Die Zehn Gebote in der christlichen Verkündigung', in *Festschrift Otto Procksch*: 29-44.
1937   'Das Alte Testament', in Künneth and Schreiner: 97-114.
1958   *Wider die Kirchenkampflegenden.*
Baumgartner, Walter
1917   *Die Klagegedichte des Jeremia* (ET 1988).
1932   'Hermann Gunkel', *CW* 46: 386-92.
1933   *Israelitische und altorientalische Weisheit.*
1959   *Zum Alten Testament und seiner Umwelt.*
1963   'Zum 100. Geburtstag von Hermann Gunkel', in *Congress Volume, Bonn 1962* (VTSup, 9): 1-18.
Bayer, Oswald
1988   'Vernunftautorität und Bibelkritik in den Kontroversen zwischen Johann Georg Hamann und Immanuel Kant', in H. Reventlow (ed.), *Historische Kritik und biblischer Kanon in der deutschen Aufklärung*: 21-46.
Bea, Augustinus
1930   *De inspiratione Scripturae Sacrae* (2nd edn, with revised title, 1935).
1964   *Unity in Freedom.*
Beattie, D.R.G.
1977   *Jewish Exegesis of the Book of Ruth.*
Beaucamp, Evode
1959   *La Bible et la sens religieuse de l'univers* (ET 1959).
Begrich, Joachim
1926   *Der Psalm des Hiskia.*
1934   'Das priesterliche Heilsorakel', *ZAW* 52: 81-92.
1938   *Studien zu Deuterojesaja.*
Beidelmann, T.O.
1974   *W. Robertson Smith and the Sociological Study of Religion.*
Ben-Amos, Dan
1969   'Analytic Categories and Ethnic Genres', *Genre* 2: 275-301.
Bender, Thomas (ed.)
1992   *The Antislavery Debate.*
Bendt, Jutta, *et al.*
1994   *Ricarda Huch, 1864–1947.*
Benoit, Pierre
1946   'Réflexions sur la "Formgeschichtliche Methode"', *RB* 53: 481-512.
Benrath, Gustav Adolf
1966   *Wyclifs Bibelkommentar.*
Bentzen, Aage
1948a   *Introduction to the Old Testament*, I.
1948b   *Messias, Moses redivivus, Menschensohn* (ET 1955).
1950   'The Ritual Background of Amos i 2—ii 16', *OTS* 8: 85-99.

Berger, Klaus
1987   *Einführung in die Formgeschichte.*
Berger, Morris Bernard
1982   'The Torah Commentary of Rabbi Samuel ben Meir', (dissertation Harvard).
Berlin, Adele
1991   *Biblical Poetry through Medieval Jewish Eyes.*
Berlin, Isaiah
1976   *Vico and Herder.*
Berman, Harold J.
1983   *Law and Revolution.*
Bernard, Wolfgang
1990   *Spätantike Dichtungstheorien.*
Bernfeld, Simon
1921   *Die jüdische Literatur*, I.
Bernhardt, Karl-Heinz
1959   *Die gattungsgeschichtliche Forschung am Alten Testament als exegetische Methode.*
Bertholet, Alfred
1923   *Der Beitrag des Alten Testaments zur allgemeinen Religionsgeschichte.*
Bertram, Georg
1922   *Die Leidensgeschichte Jesu und der Christuskult.*
1927   'Glaube und Geschichte, das Problem der Entstehung des Christentums in formgeschichtlicher Beleuchtung', *TBl* 6: 162-69.
Bethe, E.
1905   'Mythus, Sage, Märchen', *Hessische Blätter für Volkskunde* 4: 97-142.
Betti, Emilio
1967   *Allgemeine Auslegungslehre als Methodik der Geisteswissenschaften* (Italian 1955).
Beyer, C. [Konrad]
1883   *Deutsche Poetik*, II.
Beyschlag, Karlmann
1993   *Die Erlanger Theologie.*
Bible and Culture Collective, The
1995   *The Postmodern Bible.*
Bickerman, Elias J.
1962   'The Civic Prayer for Jerusalem', *HTR* 60: 163-85.
1967   *Four Strange Books of the Bible.*
Birkeland, Harris
1933a   'ani *und* 'anaw *in den Psalmen.*
1933b   *Die Feinde des Individuums in der israelitischen Psalmenliteratur.*
1955   *The Evildoers in the Book of Psalms.*
Birt, Theodor
1913   *Kritik und Hermeneutik nebst Abriss des antiken Buchwesens.*
Bitter, Stephan
1975   *Die Ehe des Propheten Hosea.*
Bittlinger, Ernst
1905   *Die Materialisierung religiöser Vorstellungen.*

Bizer, Ernst
1966   *Texte aus der Anfangszeit Melanchthons*.
Blass, Friedrich
1892   'Hermeneutik und Kritik', in I. von Muller (ed.), *Handbuch der klass-ischen Altertumswissenschaft*, I: 147-295.
Blöchle, Herbert
1995   *Luthers Stellung zum Heidentum*.
Bloom, Harold
1989   *Ruin the Sacred Truth*.
Bloomfield, Maurice
1886   'Seven Hymns of the Atharva-Veda', *The American Journal of Philology* 7: 466-88.
Blount, Brian K.
1995   *Cultural Interpretation*.
Blumenberg, Hans
1966   *Die Legitimität der Neuzeit* (2nd edn 1976; ET 1983).
Blumenthal, David R.
1980   'An Illustration of the Concept of "Philosophic Mysticism" from Fif-teenth Century Yemen', in *Hommage à Georges Vajda*: 291-308.
Bobbio, Norberto
1993   *Thomas Hobbes and the Natural Law Tradition* (Italian 1989).
Bodin, Jean
1992   *On Sovereignty* (ed. J. Franklin).
Boecker, Hans Jochen
1960   'Anklagereden und Verteidigungsreden im Alten Testament', *EvT* 20: 398-412.
1964   *Redeformen des Rechtslebens im Alten Testament*.
Boeckh, August
1877   *Encyklopädie und Methodologie der philologischen Wissenschaften* (abbreviated ET of pp. 1-253: 1968).
Boehner, Philotheus
1958   *Collected Articles on Ockham*.
Boer, Roland
1996   'Green Ants and Gibeonites', *Semeia* 75: 129-52.
Boff, Clodovis
1987   *Theology and Praxis* (Portugese 1978).
Boman, Thorleif
1952   *Das hebräische Denken im Vergleich mit dem griechischen* (ET 1960).
1967   *Die Jesusüberlieferung im Lichte der neueren Volkskunde*.
Bonamartini, Ugo
1925   'L'epesegesi nella S. Scrittura', *Biblica* 6: 424-44.
Borgen, Peder
1984   'Philo of Alexandria', in *Jewish Writings of the Second Temple Period*: 233-81.
Bornkamm, Gunther
1958   'Formen und Gattungen II. Im NT', *RGG*, 3rd edn, II: 999-1005.
Bornkamm, Heinrich
1948   *Luther und das Alte Testament* (ET 1969).

Bouma, Cornelius
1921   *De literarische vorm der Evangeliën.*
Boutin, Maurice
1974   *Relationalität als Verstehensprinzip bei Rudolf Bultmann.*
Bovati, Pietro
1994   *Re-Establishing Justice* (Italian 1986).
Bowen, Francis
1885   *A Layman's Study of the English Bible.*
Boyarin, Daniel
1990   *Intertextuality and the Reading of Midrash.*
Boyle, Marjorie O'Rourke
1985   'Luther's Rider-gods: From the Steppe to the Tower', *JRH* 13: 260-82.
Brändle, Rudolf
1979   *Matth. 25, 31-46 im Werk des Johannes Chrysostomos.*
Bray, Gerald
1996   *Biblical Interpretation: Past and Present.*
Brecht, Martin
1995   *Augewählte Aufsätze*, I.
Brekelmans, C.H.W.
1963   'Het "historische Credo" van Israël', *Tijdschrift voor Theologie* 3: 1-11.
Bremmer, Jan N.
1990   'Herman Usener', in W. Briggs and W. Calder (eds.), *Classical Scholar-*
            ship, III: 462-78.
Brewer: see Instone Brewer.
Breyfogle, Caroline M.
1910   'The Religious Status of Women in the Old Testament', *The Biblical*
            World 35: 405-19 (a sequel to 106-16, which dealt with women's social
            status).
Breymayer, Reinhard
1972   'Vladimir Jakovlevič Propp (1895–1970)—Leben, Wirken und Bedeut-
            samkeit', *LB* 15/16: 36-90.
Briggs, Charles A.
1882   'The Literary Study of the Bible', *The Hebrew Student* 2: 65-77.
1883   *Biblical Study.*
1897   *The Higher Criticism of the Hexateuch* (2nd edn).
Bright, John
1956   *Early Israel in Recent History Writing.*
Brink, Bernhard ten
1891   *Über die Aufgaben der Litteraturgeschichte.*
Brinkman, Johan
1992   *The Perception of Space in the Old Testament.*
Brody, Jules
1958   *Boileau and Longinus.*
Brown, Dennis
1992   *Vir Trilingus.*
Brown, Francis
1908   'Introduction', in R. Harper *et al.* (eds.), *Old Testament and Semitic*
            Studies in Memory of William Rainey Harper, I: xiii-xxxiv.

Brueggemann, Walter
1980   'A Convergence in Recent Old Testament Theologies', *JSOT* 18: 2-18.
Brunetière, Ferdinand
1890   *L'évolution des genres dans l'histoire de la littérature. I. Introduction* (only volume published).
Brunner, Emil
1931   *The Word and the World.*
1938   *Wahrheit als Begegnung.*
Bruns, Gerald L.
1992   *Hermeneutics Ancient and Modern.*
Bruppacher, Hans
1924   *Die Beurteilung der Armut im Alten Testament.*
Bryson, Lyman
1960   *An Outline of Man's Knowledge of the Modern World.*
Buber, Martin
1923   *Ich und Du* (cited with reference to page numbers in 1962, I: 79-170; ET 1937).
1962   *Werke* (partial ET in *Scripture and Tradition*, 1994).
Buchholz, Armin
1993   *Schrift Gottes im Lehrstreit.*
Buchman, Frank N.D.
1953   *Remaking the World* (2nd edn).
Büchsel, Friedrich
1939   *Die Hauptfragen der Synoptikerkritik.*
Budde, Karl
1882   'Das hebräische Klagelied', *ZAW* 2: 1-52.
1883   'Die hebräische Leichenklage', *ZDPV* 6: 180-94.
1893   'Das Volkslied Israels im Munde der Propheten', *Preussische Jahrbücher* 77: 460-83.
1898   *Die fünf Megillot.*
1902   'Poetry (Hebrew)', *HDB*, IV: 2-13.
1906   *Geschichte der althebräischen Literatur.*
1907   'Erinnerungen an William Rainey Harper, Präsident der Universität von Chicago', *Internationale Wochenschrift für Wissenschaft, Kunst und Technik*, 28 September: 823-36.
Buechner, Frederick
1983   *Now and Then.*
Bühlmann, Walter
1976   *Vom Rechten Reden und Schweigen.*
Bullmore, Michael A.
1995   *St Paul's Theology of Rhetorical Style.*
Bultmann, Christoph
1995   'Creation at the Beginning of History: Johann Gottfried Herder's Interpretation of Genesis 1', *JSOT* 68: 23-32.
Bultmann, Rudolf
1910   *Der Stil der Paulinischen Predigt und die kynisch-stoische Diatribe.*
1920a   'Religion und Kultur', *CW* 34: 417-21.
1920b   'Ethische und mystische Religion im Urchristentum', *CW* 34: 738-43.

1921	*Geschichte der synoptischen Tradition* (ET of 3rd edn, 1958: 1963).
1925a	Review of Fascher 1924 in *TLZ* 50: 313-18.
1925b	*Die Erforschung der synoptischen Evangelien* (ET in F. Grant [ed.], *Form Criticism*, 1934).
1925c	'Das Problem einer theologischen Exegese des Neuen Testaments', *Zwischen den Zeiten* 3: 334-57.
1926	*Jesus* (ET 1934).
1928	'Evangelien, gattungsgeschichtlich (formgeschichtlich)', *RGG*, 2nd edn, II: 418-22.
1929	'Literaturgeschichte, biblische', 1, 3, *RGG*, 2nd edn, III: 1675-77.
1930	'Die Geschichtlichkeit des Daseins und der Glaube. Antwort an Gerhardt Kuhlmann', *ZTK* 11: 339-64.
1931	2nd edn of 1921.
1933a	'Die Aufgabe der Theologie in der gegenwärtigen Lage', *TBl* 12: 161-66.
1933b	'Der Arier-Paragraph im Raum der Kirche', *TBl* 12: 359-70.
1933-65	*Glauben und Verstehen*, 4 vols. (ET of I: 1-25 134-52 in *Faith and Understanding* 1969: 28-52 134-52; of II: 59-78, 211-35 in *Essays*, 1955: 67-89, 234-61; etc. [cf. e.g. 1984b]).
1941a	*Offenbarung und Heilsgeschehen.*
1941b	*Das Evangelium des Johannes* (ET 1971).
1948-53	*Theologie des Neuen Testaments* (later editions 1958, etc.; ET 1951-55).
1954	'Zum Problem der Entmythologisierung', in H.-W. Bartsch (ed.), *Kerygma und Mythos*, II: 179-208.
1957	*History and Eschatology* (= *The Presence of Eternity*; German 1958).
1958	*Jesus Christ and Mythology* (German 1964).
1960	*Existence and Faith* (ed. S. Ogden).
1984a	*Die Exegese des Theodor von Mopsuestia* (ed. H. Feld and K.H. Schelke; original MS 1912).
1984b	*New Testament and Mythology and Other Basic Writings* (ed. S. Ogden).

Burckhart, Jacob
| 1905 | *Weltgeschichtliche Betrachtungen.* |

Burke, Kenneth
| 1961 | *The Rhetoric of Religion: Studies in Logology.* |

Burkert, Walter
| 1992 | *The Orientalizing Revolution* (revised from German, 1984). |
| 1994 | 'Griechische Hymnoi', in W. Burkert and F. Stolz (eds.), *Hymnen der alten Welt*: 9-17. |

Burridge, Richard A.
| 1992 | *What are the Gospels?* |

Burroughs, George S.
| 1891 | *The Study of the English Bible in College.* |

Burrows, Millar
| 1931 | *Founders of Great Religions.* |
| 1938 | *Bible Religion.* |

Burtchaell, James Tunstead
| 1969 | *Catholic Theories of Biblical Inspiration since 1810.* |

Busch, Eberhard
| 1976 | *Karl Barths Lebenslauf* (2nd edn; ET 1976). |

Buss, Martin J.
1961 'The Language of the Divine "I"', *JBR* 29: 102-7.
1963 'The Psalms of Asaph and Korah', *JBL* 82: 382-92.
1964 'The Meaning of "Cult" and the Interpretation of the Old Testament', *JBR* 32: 317-25.
1965 'Self-Theory and Theology', *JR* 45: 46-53.
1966 'The Covenant Theme in Historical Perspective', *VT* 16: 502-04.
1967 'The Meaning of History', in J. Robinson and J. Cobb, Jr. (eds.), *Theology as History* (German 1967): 135-54.
1969 *The Prophetic Word of Hosea: A Morphological Study.*
1974 'The Study of Forms', in Hayes 1974: 1-56.
1977 'The Distinction Between Civil and Criminal Law in Ancient Israel', in *Proceedings of the Sixth World Congress of Jewish Studies*, I: 51-62.
1978 'The Idea of *Sitz im Leben*—History and Critique', *ZAW* 90: 157-70.
1979 'Understanding Communication', in M. Buss (ed.), *Encounter with the Text*: 3-43.
1989 'Logic and Israelite Law', *Semeia* 45: 49-65.
1993 'Form Criticism', in S. McKenzie and S. Haynes (eds.), *To Each its Own Meaning*: 69-85.
1996 'Hosea as a Canonical Problem', in S. Reid: 79-93.
Calinescu, Matei
1987 *Five Faces of Modernity.*
Campion, Edmund J.
1995 *Montaigne, Rabelais, and Marot as Readers of Erasmus.*
Cancik, Hubert, and Hildegard Cancik-Lindemaier
1994 'Formbegriffe bei Eduard Norden', in *Eduard Norden (1868-1941)*: 47-68.
Carabelli, Giancarlo
1995 *On Hume and Eighteenth-Century Aesthetics* (Italian 1992).
Carroll, Robert P.
1991 *Wolf in the Sheepfold* (= *The Bible as a Problem for Christianity*).
Case, Shirley Jackson
1918 *The Millennial Hope.*
1919 *The Revelation of John.*
1923 *The Social Origins of Christianity.*
1927 *Jesus.*
Cassel, David
1872 *Geschichte der jüdischen Literatur*, I.
1922 *Das Buch Kusari des Jehuda ha-Levi.*
Cassuto, Umberto
1934 *La questione della Genesi.*
Causse, Antonin
1922 *Les 'pauvres' d'Israël.*
1926 *Les plus vieux chants de la Bible.*
1937 *Du groupe ethnique à la communauté religieuse.*
Cazelles, Henri
1946 *Etudes sur le Code de l'Alliance.*

Chadwick, H. Munro, and N. Kershaw
1932-40   *The Growth of Literature* (3 vols.).
Chambers, Talbot W.
1891   'The Inaugural Address of Professor Briggs', *The Presbyterian and Reformed Review* 2: 481-94.
Chancellor, William E.
1888   'The Literary Study of the Bible', *The Old Testament Student* 8: 10-19.
Chang, Yang Ihl
1987   *The Theme of Oppression in the Psalms in Relation to its Occurrence in Prophecy and Ritual* (Ann Arbor, MI: Dissertations Abstract International).
Chantepie de la Saussaye, P.D.
1905   *Lehrbuch der Religionsgeschichte* (3rd edn).
Chesnut, Glenn F.
1977   *The First Christian Historians*.
Childs, Brevard S.
1960   *Myth and Reality in the Old Testament*.
1963   'A Study of the Formula, "Until This Day"', *JBL* 82: 279-92.
1970   *Biblical Theology in Crisis*.
1994   'Biblical Scholarship in the Seventeenth Century', in *Language, Theology, and the Bible: Essays in Honour of James Barr*: 325-33.
Chomarat, Jacques
1981   *Grammaire et rhétorique chez Erasme*.
Christ, Wilhelm von
1898   *Geschichte der griechischen Litteratur* (3rd edn).
Christiansen, Irmgard
1969   *Die Technik der allegorischen Auslegungswissenschaft bei Philon von Alexandrien*.
Christopher, Georgia
1982   *Milton and the Science of the Saints*.
Churgin, Pinkhos
1927   *Targum Jonathan to the Prophets*.
Clements, Ronald E.
1976   *A Hundred Years of Old Testament Interpretation* (= *A Century of Old Testament Study*).
Clines, David J.A.
1995   *Interested Parties*.
Cohen, Hermann
1924   *Jüdische Schriften*, I.
Cole, Thomas
1991   *The Origin of Rhetoric in Ancient Greece*.
Coleman, Will
1991   '"Coming through 'Ligion"', in D. Hopkins and G. Cummings (eds.), *Cut Loose Your Stammering Tongue*: 67-102.
Colish, Marcia L.
1985   *The Stoic Tradition From Antiquity to the Early Middle Ages*, I.
1994   *Peter Lombard*, I.

Collado, Vicente, and Eduardo Zurro
1983   *El misterio de la palabra.*

Collins, Adela Yarbro (ed.)
1985   *Feminist Perspectives on Biblical Scholarship.*

Congreso de Ciencias Eclesiásticas
1957   *Los generos literarios de la Sagrada Escritura.*

Cook, Silas P.
1891   'Bible Study in the Colleges of New England', *The Old and New Testament Student* 12: 155-62.

Cook, Stanley A.
1914   *The Study of Religions.*
1936   *The Old Testament.*
1938   *The 'Truth' of the Bible.*
1945   *An Introduction to the Bible.*

Cooke, Paul D.
1966   *Hobbes and Christianity.*

Cooper, Alan Mitchell
1976   'Biblical Poetics: A Linguistic Approach' (dissertation Yale).

Copleston, Frederick
1946-63   *A History of Philosophy* (9 vols.).

Coppens, J.
1938   'L'histoire critique de l'Ancien Testament', *NRT* 65: 513-50, 641-80, 769-808 (also published as a volume, 1938; ET, revised, 1942).

Cornill, Carl Heinrich
1896   *Zur Einleitung in das Alte Testament* (3rd edn).

Corvin, Jack W.
1972   'A Stylistic and Functional Study of the Prose Prayers in the Historical Narratives of the Old Testament' (dissertation Emory).

Couat, Auguste
1882   *La poésie Alexandrine sous les trois premiers Ptolémées.*

Couchoud, P.-L.
1924   *Le mystère de Jésus* (ET 1924).

Coward, Harold
1988   *Sacred Word and Sacred Text.*

Cowley, Roger W.
1985   *Ethiopian Biblical Interpretation.*

Craig, Kenneth M.
1993   *A Poetics of Jonah.*

Crenshaw, James
1978   *Gerhard von Rad.*
1985   'Education in Ancient Israel', *JBL* 104: 601-15.

Croll, Morris W.
1966   *Style, Rhetoric, and Rhythm.*

Crosby, Donald A.
1975   *Horace Bushnell's Theory of Language.*

Cross, Frank Moore, Jr, and David Noel Freedman
1975   *Studies in Ancient Yahwistic Poetry.*

Crossan, John Dominic
1981   *A Fragile Craft: The Work of Amos Niven Wilder.*
Crüsemann, Frank
1989   'Tendenzen der alttestamentlichen Wissenschaft zwischen 1933 und 1945', *Wort und Dienst* 20: 79-103.
Culley, Robert C.
1967   *Oral Formulaic Language in the Biblical Psalms.*
Cullmann, Oscar
1956   'Karl Ludwig Schmidt 1891-1956', *TZ* 12: 1-9.
Cunliffe-Jones, Hubert
1945   *The Authority of the Biblical Revelation.*
Cunningham, Mary Kathleen
1995   *What is Theological Exegesis?*
Curtius, Ernst Robert
1948   *Europäische Literatur und lateinisches Mittelalter.*
Dahl, George
1933   'Kent, Charles Foster', *Dictionary of American Biography*, X: 343.
Dahl, Nils A.
1988   'Sigmund Mowinckel', *SJOT* 1988, No. 2: 8-22.
Dähnhardt, Oskar
1898   *Naturgeschichtliche Volksmärchen.*
Daly, Lowrie, J.
1961   *The Medieval University, 1200-1400.*
Daniélou, Jean
1957   'Les genres littéraires d'après les Pères de l'Eglise', in Congreso de Ciencias Eclesiásticas 1957: 275-83.
Danker, Frederick W.
1988   *A Century of Greco-Roman Philology.*
Darwin, Charles
1859   *On the Origin of Species by Means of Natural Selection.*
Daube, David
1949   'Rabbinic Methods of Interpretation and Hellenistic Rhetoric', *HUCA* XXII: 239-64.
Davidson, Edward H., and William J. Scheick
1994   *Paine, Scripture, and Authority.*
Davidson, Samuel
1843   *Sacred Hermeneutics.*
Davies, Philip R.
1995   *Whose Bible is it Anyway?*
Davis, Brion
1975   *The Problem of Slavery in the Age of Revolution 1770-1823.*
Davis, Ellen F.
1995   *Imagination Shaped.*
Davis, Gerald L.
1985   *I Got the Word in Me and I can Sing it, You Know.*
Dawson, David
1992   *Allegorical Readers and Cultural Revision in Ancient Alexandria.*

De, Sushil Kumar
1960 *History of Sanskrit Poetics* (2nd edn, 2 vols.).
1963 *Sanskrit Poetics as a Study of Aesthetic*.
Dechent, H.
1904 *Herder und die ästhetische Betrachtung der heiligen Schrift*.
De Giorgio, Michela
1993 'The Catholic Model', in *A History of Women in the West*, IV (Italian 1991): 166-97.
Demers, Patricia
1992 *Women as Interpreters of the Bible*.
Derrida, Jacques
1967 *L'écriture et la différence* (ET 1978).
Desmond, Adrian, and James Moore
1991 *Darwin*.
De Valerio, Karolina
1994 *Altes Testament und Judentum im Frühwerk Rudolf Bultmanns*.
De Vries, Simon John
1968 *Bible and Theology in the Netherlands* (2nd edn, with an appendix, 1989).
Dewey, John
1929 *The Quest for Certainty*.
1938 *Logic*.
Dhorme, Edouard
1931 *La poésie biblique*.
Dibelius, Martin
1906 *Die Lade Jahwes*.
1911 *Die urchristliche Überlieferung von Johannes dem Täufer*.
1919 *Formgeschichte des Evangeliums* (2nd edn 1933).
1921 *Der Brief des Jakobus*.
1925 *Geschichtliche und übergeschichtliche Religion im Christentum* (= *Evangelium und Welt*, 1929).
1926 *Geschichte der urchristlichen Literatur* (ET: *A Fresh Approach*, 1936).
1927 'The Structure and the Literary Character of the Gospels', *HTR* 20: 151-70.
1929a 'Zur Formgeschichte der Evangelien', *TRu*, NS 1: 185-216.
1929b 'Zeit und Arbeit', in E. Stange (ed.), *Die Religionswissenschaft der Gegenwart in Selbstdarstellungen*, V: 1-37.
1930 'Zwei Vorträge zur ökumenischen Bewegung der Gegenwart', *TBl* 9: 49-54.
1931 'Der Formgeschichte des Neuen Testaments', *TRu*, NS 3: 207-42.
1932 'Herman Gunkel', *Forschungen und Fortschritte* 8: 146-47.
1933 2nd edn of 1919 (ET 1934).
1935 *Gospel Criticism and Christology* (German in Dibelius 1953).
1938 'The Message of the New Testament and the Orders of Society', in N. Ehrenstrom *et. al.* (eds.), *Christian Faith and the Common Life*: 17-43.
1941 *Wozu Theologie?*
1953 *Botschaft und Geschichte*, I.

Dibelius, Otto
　　1961　　　*Ein Christ ist immer im Dienst.*
Diels, Hermann, and Walther Kranz
　　1951-52　　*Die Fragmente der Vorsokratiker* (6th edn).
Diestel, Ludwig
　　1869　　　*Geschichte des Alten Testamentes in der christlichen Kirche.*
Dieterich, Albrecht
　　1902　　　'Über Wesen und Ziele der Volkskunde', *Hessische Blätter für Volks-kunde* 1: 169-94.
　　1903　　　*Eine Mithrasliturgie.*
　　1904　　　'Vorwort zum siebenten Bande', *ARW* 7: 1-5.
　　1905a　　'Hermann Usener', *ARW* 8: i-xi.
　　1905b　　'Griechische und römische Religion', *ARW* 8: 474-510.
Diettrich, Gustav
　　1901　　　*Eine jakobitische Einleitung in den Psalter.*
Dijk, Teun A. van
　　1977　　　*Text and Context.*
Dilthey, Wilhelm
　　1921-　　*Gesammelte Schriften.*
Dinkler, Erich, and Erika Dinkler-von Schubert (eds.)
　　1984　　　*Theologie und Kirche im Wirken Hans von Sodens.*
Dinsmore, Charles Allen
　　1931　　　*The English Bible as Literature.*
Dodd, C.H.
　　1920　　　*The Meaning of Paul for Today.*
　　1929　　　*The Authority of the Bible.*
　　1935　　　*The Parables of the Kingdom* (cited according to a virtually unchanged reprintings from 1936 on).
　　1936　　　*The Present Task in New Testament Studies.*
　　1937　　　*The Apostolic Preaching and its Development.*
　　1938　　　*History and the Gospel.*
　　1947　　　*The Bible Today.*
　　1951　　　*Gospel and Law.*
　　1952　　　*Christianity and the Reconciliation of the Nations.*
　　1953a　　*The Interpretation of the Fourth Gospel.*
　　1953b　　*New Testament Studies.*
Domanyi, Thomas
　　1979　　　*Der Römerbriefkommentar des Thomas von Aquin.*
Donohue, James J.
　　1943　　　*The Theory of Literary Kinds.*
Dormeyer, Detlev
　　1989　　　*Evangelium als literarische und theologische Gattung.*
Doty, William G.
　　1969　　　'The Discipline and Literature of New Testament Form Criticism', *ATR* 51: 259-321.
　　1986　　　*Mythography.*
Douglas, Ann
　　1977　　　*The Feminization of American Culture.*

Downing, F. Gerald
1992   *Cynics and Christian Origins.*
Drazin, Israel
1994   *Targum Onkelos to Leviticus.*
Drews, Arthur
1906   *Die Religion als Selbst-Bewusstsein Gottes.*
1909   *Die Christusmythe* (ET 1909).
Driver, S.R.
1891   *Introduction to the Literature of the Old Testament.*
Droge, Arthur J.
1989   *Homer or Moses?*
Droysen, Johann Gustav
1943   *Historik* (2nd edn).
Duhm, Bernhard
1897   *Das Buch Hiob.*
1899   *Die Psalmen.*
1916   *Israels Propheten.*
Dünzl, Franz
1993   *Braut und Bräutigam.*
Dupont, Jacques
1960   *Les sources du livre des Actes.*
Dupré, Louis
1993   *Passage to Modernity.*
Durham, J.I.
1976   'Credo, Ancient Israelite', *IDBSup*, 197-99.
Durkheim, Emile
1888   'Cours de science sociale', *Bulletin universitaire de l'enseignment sec-ondaire* 15: 23-48.
1893   *De la division du travail social* (ET 1933).
Dyck, Joachim
1966   *Ticht-Kunst.*
Easton, Burton Scott
1928   *The Gospels before the Gospels.*
Eaton, J.H.
1995   *Psalms of the Way and the Kingdom.*
Ebeling, Gerhard
1951   'Die Anfänge von Luthers Hermeneutik', *ZTK* 48: 172-230.
1959   'Hermeneutik', *RGG*, 3rd edn, III: 242-62.
1962   *Evangelische Evangelienauslegung.*
Eberhardt, Charles Richard
1949   *The Bible in the Making of Ministers.*
Ecker, Roman
1962   *Die arabische Job-Übersetzung des Gaon Saadja ben Josef al-Fajjumi.*
Edwards, Mark U., Jr
1994   *Printing, Propaganda, and Martin Luther.*
Edwards, Robert L.
1992   *Of Singular Genius, of Singular Grace.*

Eerdmans, B.D.
1947   *The Hebrew Book of Psalms.*
Efros, Israel
1938   *Maimonides' Treatise on Logic.*
Eichhorn, Albert
1898   *Das Abendmahl.*
Eichrodt, Walther
1920   *Die Hoffnung des ewigen Friedens im alten Israel.*
1925   *Ist die altisraelitische Nationalreligion Offenbarungsreligion?*
1929   'Hat die alttestamentliche Theologie noch selbständige Bedeutung inner-
            halb der alttestamentlichen Wissenschaft?', *ZAW* 47: 83-91.
1933-39   *Theologie des Alten Testaments* (3 vols.; ET 1961–67).
1937   'Gottes ewiges Reich und seine Wirklichkeit in der Geschichte nach
            alttestamentlicher Offenbarung', *TSK* 108: 1-27.
1949   'Revelation and Responsibility: The Biblical Norm of Social Behavior',
            Int 3: 387-99.
1974   'Darf man heute noch von einem Gottesbund mit Israel reden?', *TZ* 30:
            193-206.
Eilberg-Schwartz, Howard
1990   *The Savage in Judaism.*
Eiselen, Frederick Carl
1918   *The Psalms and Other Sacred Writings.*
Eissfeldt, Otto
1930   'Religionsgeschichtliche Schule', *RGG*, 2nd edn, IV: 1898-1905.
1965   *The Old Testament* (updated ET of *Einleitung*, 3rd edn, 1964).
Eliot, T.S.
1975   *Selected Prose.*
Elliott, M. Timothea
1989   *The Literary Unity of the Canticles.*
Ellison, Julie
1990   *Delicate Subjects.*
Elwin, Verrier
1955   *The Religion of an Indian Tribe.*
Emerton, Norma E.
1984   *The Scientific Reinterpretation of Form.*
Emmelius, Johann-Christoph
1975   *Tendenzkritik und Formengeschichte.*
Engnell, Ivan
1943   *Studies in Divine Kingship.*
1945   *Gamla Testamentet.*
1960   'Methodological Aspects of Old Testament Study', *Congress Volume,
            Oxford 1959* (VTSup, 7): 13-30.
1970   *Critical Essays on the Old Testament* (=*A Rigid Scrutiny*).
Enos, Richard Leo
1993   *Greek Rhetoric Before Aristotle.*
Erbt, Wilhelm
1902   *Jeremia und seine Zeit.*
1909   *Handbuch zum Alten Testament.*

Erman, Adolf
1885   *Aegypten und aegyptisches Leben im Altertum* (ET 1894).
1909   *Die ägyptische Religion.*
Eskenazi, Tamara C.
1995   'Perspectives from Jewish Exegesis', in Smith-Christopher: 82-103.
Evang, Martin
1988   *Rudolf Bultmann in seiner Frühzeit.*
Evans, G.R.
1984   *The Language and Logic of the Bible: The Earlier Middle Ages.*
Evans-Pritchard, E.E.
1951   *Social Anthropology.*
1956   *Nuer Religion.*
Exum, J. Cheryl
1992   *Tragedy and Biblical Narrative.*
1993   *Fragmented Women.*
Fackenheim, Emil
1968   *Quest for Past and Future.*
Farbridge, Maurice H.
1923   *Studies in Biblical and Semitic Symbolism* (new edn 1970).
Fascher, Erich
1924   *Die formgeschichtliche Methode.*
Faulhaber, His Eminence Cardinal
1934   *Judaism, Christianity and Germany.*
Faur, José
1969   'The Origin of the Classification of Rational and Divine Commandments in Mediaeval Jewish Philosophy', *Augustianum* 9: 299-304.
1986   *Golden Doves with Silver Dots: Semiotics and Textuality in Rabbinic Tradition.*
Feige, Franz G.M.
1990   *The Varieties of Protestantism in Nazi Germany.*
Feinburg, Charles L.
1959   'The Accuser and the Advocate in Jewish Liturgy', *BSac* 116: 212-20.
Feld, Helmut
1977   *Die Anfänge der modernen biblischen Hermeneutik in der spätmittelalterlichen Theologie.*
Felder, Cain Hope (ed.)
1991   *Stony the Road We Trod.*
Ferguson, Wallace K.
1962   *Europe in Transition 1300–1520.*
Ferré, Frederick
1996   *Being and Value.*
Ferry, Luc
1984   *Philosophie politique.* I. *Le droit* (ET 1990).
Feuillet, A.
1949   'Jonas', *DBSup*, IV: 1104-31.
Finnegan, Ruth
1967   *Limba-Stories and Story-Telling.*

Fisch, Harold
    1988   *Poetry With a Purpose*.
Fischel, Henry A.
    1977   *Essays in Greco-Roman and Related Talmudic Literature*.
Fishbane, Michael
    1985   *Biblical Interpretation in Ancient Israel*.
Fisher, Simon
    1988   *Revelatory Positivism?*
Flacius Illyricus, Matthias
    1968   *De ratione cognoscendi sacras literas* (ed. L. Geldsetzer [with German tr.]).
Floeckner, Karl
    1898   *Ueber den Charakter der alttestamentlichen Poesie*.
Flueckiger, Joyce Burkhalter
    1987   'Land of Wealth, Land of Famine: The Sua Nac (Parrot Dance) of Central India', *Journal of American Folklore* 100: 39-57.
    1989   'Introduction', in S. Blackburn *et al.* (eds.), *Oral Epics in India*: 1-11.
Fogarty, Gerald P.
    1989   *American Catholic Biblical Scholarship*.
Fohrer, Georg
    1961a   'Tradition und Interpretation im Alten Testament', *ZAW* 73: 1-30.
    1961b   'Remarks on Modern Interpretation of the Prophets', *JBL* 80: 309-19.
    1964   *Überlieferung und Geschichte des Exodus*.
    1965   *Einleitung in das Alte Testament* (ET 1968).
    1969   *Studien zur alttestamentlichen Theologie und Geschichte*.
    1983   *Studien zum Buche Hiob (1956-79)*, 2nd edn.
Fohrer, Georg *et al.*
    1973   *Exegese des Alten Testaments*.
Foucault, Michel
    1966   *Les mots et les choses* (ET 1970).
Fowler, Henry T.
    1912   *A History of the Literature of Ancient Israel from the Earliest Times to 135 B.C.*
Fox, Marvin
    1990   *Interpreting Maimonides*.
Fox-Genovese, Elizabeth
    1991   *Feminism Without Illusions*.
Fraade, Steven D.
    1991   *From Tradition to Commentary*.
Fraisse, Geneviève
    1993   'A Philosophical History of Sexual Differences,' in *A History of Women in the West*, IV (Italian 1971): 48-79.
Francken, H.J.
    1954   *The Mystical Communion with JHWH in the Book of Psalms*.
Frank, Douglas
    1986   *Less than Conquerors*.
Frank, Günter
    1995   *Die theologische Philosophie Philipp Melanchthons (1497–1560)*.

Fraser, Russell
1970   *The War Against Poetry.*
Frei, Hans
1974   *The Eclipse of Biblical Narrative.*
Freiday, Dean
1979   *The Bible—its Criticism, Interpretation and Use—in 16th and 17th Cen-*
     tury England.
Freytag, Hartmut
1982   *Die Theorie der allegorischen Schriftdeutung und die Allegorie in*
     deutschen Texten besonders des 11. und 12. Jahrhunderts.
Friedrich, H.
1933   'Zur kirchlichen Lage', *CW* 47: 1045-46.
Frischer, Bernard
1991   *Shifting Paradigms.*
Froehlich, Karlfried
1984   *Biblical Interpretation in the Early Church.*
Frommel, Otto
1906   *Die Poesie des Evangeliums.*
Frye, Northrop
1957   *Anatomy of Criticism.*
Frymer-Kensky, Tikva
1990   'The Sage in the Pentateuch: Soundings', in G. Gammie and L. Perdue
     (eds.), *The Sages in Israel and in the Ancient Near East*: 275-87.
Fuchs, Ernst
1946   *Christentum und Sozialismus.*
1953   *Was ist Theologie?*
1954   *Hermeneutik.*
1955   *Begegnung mit dem Wort.*
1958   *Ergänzungsheft for Fuchs 1954.*
1959   *Zum hermeneutischen Problem in der Theologie.*
1960   *Zur Frage nach dem historischen Jesus.*
1965   *Glaube und Erfahrung* (136-73: ET in J. Robinson and Cobb 1964).
1968   *Marburger Hermeneutik.*
1971   *Jesus: Wort und Tat.*
1979   *Wagnis des Glaubens.*
Gadamer, Hans-Georg
1960   *Wahrheit und Methode* (3rd edn 1972; ET 1975).
Ganoczy, Alexandre, and Stefan Scheld
1983   *Die Hermeneutik Calvins.*
Gardiner, Alan
1932   *The Theory of Speech and Language* (2nd edn, with 'Retrospect', 1951).
Gardiner, J.H.
1906   *The Bible as English Literature.*
Garrett, Duane A.
1992   *An Analysis of the Hermeneutics of John Chrysostom's Commentary on*
     Isaiah 1-8.
Gay, Peter
1969   *The Enlightenment*, II.

Gayley, Charles Mills, and Fred Newton Scott
   1899   *An Introduction to the Methods and Materials of Literary Criticism.*
Geller, Stephen A.
   1996   *Sacred Enigmas: Literary Religion in the Hebrew Bible.*
Gemser, Berend
   1929–31   *De Spreuken van Salomo* (2 vols.).
   1937   *Sprüche Salomos.*
   1955   'The *rîb-* or controversy-pattern in Hebrew mentality', in *Wisdom in Israel and in the Ancient Near East* (VTSup, 3): 120-37.
Genthe, Hans Jochen
   1977   *Kleine Geschichte der neutestamentlichen Wissenschaft.*
Gentili, Bruno
   1984   *Poesia e pubblico nella Grecia antica* (ET 1988).
Genung, John Franklin
   1904   *Ecclesiastes, Words of Koheleth.*
   1919   *A Guidebook to the Biblical Literature.*
Gercke, Alfred, and Eduard Norden (eds.)
   1910   *Einleitung in die Altertumswissenschaft,* I.
Gerhart, Mary, and Allan Russell
   1984   *Metaphoric Process.*
Gerlach, Wolfgang
   1987   *Als die Zeugen schwiegen.*
Gerleman, Gillis
   1951   'The Song of Deborah in the Light of Stylistics', *VT* 1: 168-80.
Gerstenberger, Erhard
   1965   *Wesen und Herkunft des 'apodiktischen Rechts'.*
Gerstenmaier, Eugen (ed.)
   1937   *Kirche, Volk, und Staat.*
Geuss, C.H.J. de
   1976   *The Tribes of Israel.*
Gilbert, Neal W.
   1960   *Renaissance Concepts of Method.*
Ginsburg, Christian D.
   1857   *The Song of Songs.*
Ginzel, Günther B. (ed.)
   1980   *Auschwitz als Herausforderung für Juden und Christen.*
Givón, T.
   1984   *Syntax,* I.
Gloege, Gerhard
   1937   'Die Deutschkirche', in Künneth and Schreiner: 403-21.
Glover, Willis B.
   1984   *Biblical Origins of Modern Western Culture.*
Goethe, Johann Wolfgang von
   1887–   *Werke.*
Gogarten, Friedrich
   1923   'Die Entscheidung', *Zwischen den Zeiten* 1, No. 1: 33-47.
   1926   *Ich glaube an den dreieinigen Gott.*

Gögler, Rolf
 1963   *Zur Theologie des biblischen Wortes bei Origenes.*
Goguel, Maurice
 1925   *Jésus de Nazareth: Mythe ou histoire?* (ET 1926).
 1926   'Une nouvelle école de critique évangélique', *RHR* 94: 114-60.
Goldhagen, Daniel Jonah
 1996   *Hitler's Willing Executioners.*
Goldman, Solomon
 1948   *The Book of Books.*
 1949   *In the Beginning.*
Goldstein: see Saiving Goldstein
Gómez Aranda, Mariano
 1994   *El comentario de Abraham Ibn Ezra al libro del Eclesiastés.*
Gonzalez, Francisco J. (ed.)
 1995   *The Third Way.*
Good, Edwin M.
 1965   *Irony in the Old Testament.*
Goodman, Hananya (ed.)
 1994   *Between Jerusalem and Benares.*
Goodman, L.E.
 1988   'Saadiah's Poetics', in Saadiah ben Joseph al-Fayyumi (ed.), *The Book of Theodicy*: 415-26.
Goodspeed, Edgar J.
 1946   *How to Read the Bible.*
Gorday, Peter
 1983   *Principles of Patristic Exegesis: Romans 9-11 in Origen, John Chrysostom, and Augustine.*
Gordis, Robert
 1971   *Poets, Prophets, and Sages.*
Gordon, Lynn D.
 1990   *Gender and Higher Education in the Progressive Era.*
Gossai, Hemchand
 1993   *Justice, Righteousness and the Social Critique of the Eighth-Century Prophets.*
Gossett, Thomas F.
 1963   *Race: The History of an Idea.*
Gottcent, John H.
 1979   *The Bible as Literature: A Selective Bibliography.*
Gottwald, Norman
 1996   'Ideology and Ideologies in Israelite Prophecy', in S. Reid: 136-49.
Graetz, H.
 1882   *Kritischer Commentar zu den Psalmen*, I.
Graf, Friedrich Wilhelm
 1988   '"Wir konnten dem Rad nicht in die Speichen fallen"', in J.-C. Kaiser and M. Greschat (eds.), *Der Holocaust und die Protestanten*: 151-85.
Graham, William C., and Herbert Gordon May
 1936   *Culture and Conscience.*

Graves, Robert and Raphael Patai
1964   *Hebrew Myths: The Book of Genesis.*
Gray, George Buchanan
1915   *The Forms of Hebrew Poetry* (new edn 1972).
Green, Peter
1990   *Alexander to Actium.*
Green, Yosef
1986/7   'Tiles and Bricks in Biblical Poetry', *Dor le Dor* 15: 160-62.
Greene, Dana (ed.)
1980   *Lucretia Mott.*
Greenstein, Edward L.
1989   *Essays on Biblical Method and Translation.*
Grelot, Pierre
1992   *What are the Targums?*
Greschat, Martin (ed.)
1985   *Im Zeichen der Schuld.*
Gressmann, Hugo
1905   *Der Ursprung der israelitisch-jüdischen Eschatologie.*
1913   *Mose und seine Zeit.*
1914a   *Albert Eichhorn und die religionsgeschichtliche Schule.*
1914b   *Die Anfänge Israels.*
1921   *Die älteste Geschichtsschreibung und Prophetie Israels*, 2nd edn.
1925   *Israels Spruchweisheit im Zusammenhang der Weltliteratur.*
1926   'Der Bibel als Wort Gottes: Ein Antwort an E. Brunner', *CW* 40: 1050-
            53.
Grønbech, Vilhelm
1930–31   *The Culture of the Teutons* (Norwegian 1909–12).
Grube, G.M.A.
1965   *The Greek and Roman Critics* (reproduced in 1995).
Grube, Wilhelm
1910   *Religion und Kultus der Chinesen.*
Gruppe, Otto
1887   *Die griechischen Culte und Mythen in ihren Beziehungen zu den oriental-
            ischen Religionen.*
Guillaume, Alfred
1938   *Prophecy and Divination.*
Gummere, Francis B.
1894   *Old English Ballads.*
Gunkel, Hermann
1888   *Die Wirkungen des heiligen Geistes, nach der populären Anschauung der
            apostolischen Zeit und nach der Lehre des Apostels Paulus: Eine
            biblisch-theologische Studie* (2nd edn 1899; ET 1979).
1892a   review of *Vorträge über die Offenbarung Gottes auf alttestamentlichem
            Boden*, 1891, by August Bender, in *TLZ* 17: 155-58.
1892b   'Frieden', *CW* 6: 541-42.
1893   'Nahum I', *ZAW* 8: 223-44.
1895   *Schöpfung und Chaos in Urzeit und Endzeit*, with contributions by
            H. Zimmern.

1899	2nd edn of 1888.
1900a	'Ein Notschrei', *CW* 14: 58-61.
1900b	'Das Vierte Buch Esra', in E. Kautzsch (ed.), *Die Apokryphen und Pseudepigraphen des Alten Testaments*, II: 331-401.
1900c	*Der Prophet Esra*.
1901a	*Genesis* (ET of the introduction: *The Legends of Genesis*, 1901).
1901b	'Die beiden Hagargeschichten', *CW* 15: 141-45, 164-71 (ET in *The Monist* 11, 1901).
1902	2nd edn of 1901a.
1903	*Zum religionsgeschichtlichen Verständnis des Neuen Testaments* (ET 'from the author's MS'—probably a slightly earlier version—in *The Monist* 13, 1903: 398-455).
1904a	*Ausgewählte Psalmen* (2nd edn 1905 [see 1905b]; 3rd edn 1911).
1904b	review of *Theologie und Religionsgeschichte*, 1904, by Max Reischle, in *Deutsche Literaturzeitung* 25: 1100-10.
1904c	'Ziele und Methode der alttestamentlichen Exegese', cited according to 1913a: 11-29.
1905a	'Das Alte Testament im Licht der modernen Forschung', in A. Deissmann *et al.*, *Beiträge zur Weiterentwicklung der christlichen Religion*: 40-76.
1905b	2nd edn of 1904a.
1906a	'Die israelitische Literatur', in P. Hinneberg (ed.), *Kultur der Gegenwart*, I/VII: 51-102 (see 2nd edn 1925).
1906b	*Elias, Jahve und Baal*.
1906c	'Die Grundprobleme der israelitischen Literaturgeschichte', cited according to 1913a: 29-38 (ET in 1928: 57-68).
1906d	'Waffensegen', *CW* 20: 649.
1907a	review of Frommel 1906, in *CW* 21: 67.
1907b	'Neue Ziele der alttestamentlichen Forschung?', *CW* 21: 78-84, 109-14.
1907c	review of Budde 1906, in *CW* 21: 850-51.
1909a	'Arme und Armengesetzgebung bei den Hebräern', *RGG*, I: 693-95.
1909b	'Bibelwissenschaft: Literaturgeschichte Israels', *RGG*, I: 1189-94.
1910a	*Die Religionsgeschichte und die alttestamentliche Wissenschaft* (ET in C. Wendte [ed.], *Fifth International Congress of Free Christianity and Religious Progress*, Berlin, August 5-10, 1910, Proceedings and Papers: 114-25).
1910b	*Genesis*, 3rd edn (ET of the introduction: *The Stories of Genesis*, 1994; of the whole: 1997).
1910c	'Dichtung, profane, im Alten Testament', *RGG*, II: 47-59.
1910d	'Gleichnisse im AT', *RGG*, II: 1461-62.
1911	*Die Urgeschichte und die Patriarchen* (Die Schriften des Alten Testaments, I/I).
1912	'Individualismus und Sozialismus im Alten Testament', *RGG*, III: 493-501.
1913a	*Reden und Aufsätze*.
1913b	'Psalmen', *RGG*, IV: 1927-49 (ET: see Gunkel 1930).
1913c	review of H. Schmidt 1912, in *Deutsche Literaturzeitung* 38: 2641-42.

1914a   'Was will die "religionsgeschichtliche Bewegung"?', *Deutsch-evange-lisch* 5: 385-96 (ET, modifying the original: *ExpTim* 38, 1926/27: 532-36 [references to troubled families and to Africa are quite offensive in this translation]).

1914b   'Jesus weint', *Deutsch-evangelisch* 5: 661-63.

1915   'Die Propheten als Schriftsteller und Dichter', in H. Schmidt (ed.), *Die grossen Propheten*: xxxvi-lxxii.

1916a   *Israelitisches Heldentum und Kriegsfrömmigkeit im Alten Testament.*

1916b   *Esther.*

1917a   *Die Propheten.*

1917b   *Das Märchen im Alten Testament* (ET 1987).

1917c   'Formen der Hymnen', *TRu* 20: 265-304.

1917d   'Wir Deutschen', *Der Stosstrupp* 1, No. 68: 2.

1920   'Psalm 133', in W. Nowack (ed.), *Karl Budde zum siebzigsten Geburts tag.*

1921   'Die Lieder in der Kindheitsgeschichte Jesu bei Lukas', in *Festgabe für D. Dr. A. von Harnack*: 45-66.

1922   'Die Frömmigkeit der Psalmen', *CW* 36: 2-7,18-22,79-83, 105-9 (ET in 1928: 69-114).

1924a   'Der Micha-Schluss', *Zeitschrift für Semistik* 2: 145-78 (ET in 1928: 115-49).

1924b   'Jesaia 33, eine prophetische Liturgie', *ZAW* 42: 177-208.

1925   'Die israelitische Literatur', in P. Hinneberg (ed.), *Kultur der Gegenwart*, I/VII, 2nd edn: 53-112 (pp. 53-104 = 1906a [except that page numbers are higher by two]; reprinted separately, 1963).

1926   *Die Psalmen.*

1927a   'Biblische Theologie und biblische Religionsgeschichte', *RGG*, 2nd edn, I: 1089-91.

1927b   *Einleitung in die Psalmen*, Part I (Part II: see 1933).

1927c   ' "The Historical Movement" in the Study of Religion', *ExpTim* 38: 532-36.

1927d   'Alttestamentliche Literaturgeschichte und die Ansetzung der Psalmen-dichtung', *TBl* 7: 85-97 (ET in Society for Old Testament Study, *Old Testament Essays*, 1928).

1928   *What Remains of the Old Testament and Other Essays.*

1929   'Literaturgeschichte, biblische', *RGG*, 2nd edn, III: 1677-80.

1930   'Psalmen', *RGG*, 2nd edn, IV: 1609-27 (ET of this, compared with the 1st edn, 1967).

1933   *Einleitung in die Psalmen*, Part II, completed by Joachim Begrich (Part I: see 1927b).

Güttgemanns, Erhardt
1970   *Offene Fragen zur Formgeschichte des Evangeliums* (2nd edn 1971; ET 1979).

Haacker, Klaus
1981   *Neutestamentliche Wissenschaft.*

Haendler, Otto
1957   *Grundriss der praktischen Theologie.*

Hagen, Kenneth
1990   ' "De exegetica methodo" ', in *The Bible in the Sixteenth Century*: 181-96.
1993   *Luther's Approach to Scripture as seen in his 'Commentaries' on Galatians 1519-1538.*
Hägglund, Bengt
1958   'Die Bedeutung der "regula fidei" als Grundlage theologischer Aussagen', *ST* 12: 1-44.
Hahn, Herbert F.
1954   *Old Testament in Modern Research* (2nd edn 1966).
Haillie, Philip P.
1979   *Lest Innocent Blood Be Shed.*
Halbertal, Moshe
1997   *People of the Book.*
Haldar, Alfred
1945   *Associations of Cult Prophets among the Ancient Semites.*
Halivni, David Weiss
1991   *Peshat and Derash.*
Hall, Vernon
1964   *A Short History of Literary Criticism.*
Hallo, William W.
1991   *The People of the Book.*
Hamburger, Margarete
1915   *Das Form-Problem in der neueren deutschen Ästhetik und Kunsttheorie.*
Handelman, Susan A.
1982   *The Slayers of Moses: The Emergence of Rabbinic Interpretation in Modern Literary Theory.*
Hannay, Margaret
1990   *Philip's Phoenix.*
Hardesty, Nancy A.
1984   *Women Called to Witness.*
Hardison, O.B., Jr
1962   *The Enduring Moment.*
1974   'Medieval Literary Criticism', in A. Preminger *et al.* (eds.), *Classical and Medieval Literary Criticism*: 263-490.
Harnack, Adolf
1886-90   *Lehrbuch der Dogmengeschichte* (3 vols.).
1900   *Das Wesen des Christentums.*
1906   *Reden und Aufsätze*, II.
Harper, William Rainey
1890   'Editorial', *The Old and New Testament Student* 10: 262-64.
1891   'Editorial', *The Old and New Testament Student* 13: 4-5.
1893   'Editorial', *The Biblical World* 1: 243-47.
1899   'The Use of the Story in Religious Teaching', *The Biblical World* 14: 87-92.
1905   *A Critical and Exegetical Commentary on Amos and Hosea.*
1916   *Work of the Old Testament Priests.*
Harris, Errol E.
1995   *The Substance of Spinoza.*

Harrison, Jane Ellen
1913   *Ancient Art and Ritual.*
Harrisville, Roy A.
1976a   *Frank Chamberlain Porter.*
1976b   *Benjamin Wisner Bacon.*
Harrisville, Roy A., and Walter Sundberg
1995   *The Bible in Modern Culture.*
Harveson, Mae Elizabeth
1969   *Catharine Esther Beecher.*
Hausammann, Susi
1970   *Römerauslegung zwischen Humanismus und Reformation.*
Hayes, John (ed.)
1974   *Old Testament Form Criticism.*
1995   'A History of Interpretation', in *Mercer Commentary on the Bible*: 23-52.
forthcoming   (ed.), *Dictionary of Biblical Interpretation.*
Heichelheim, Fritz M.
1970   *An Ancient Economic History*, III (partially revised from the German 1938).
Heidegger, Martin
1978   *Wegmarken* (2nd edn).
Heiler, Friedrich
1919   *Das Gebet* (2nd edn [=1923; 1st edn 1918]).
Heine, Ronald E.
1995   *Gregory of Nyssa's Treatise on the Inscriptions of the Psalms.*
Heinemann, Joseph
1971   'The Proem in the Aggadic Midrashim—A Form Critical Study', in J. Heinemann and D. Noy (eds.), *Studies in Aggadic Folk-Literature*: 100-22.
1977   *Prayer in the Talmud.*
Heinrici, C.F. Georg
1887   *Das zweite Sendschreiben des Apostels Paulus an die Korinthier.*
1892   'Die urchristliche Ueberlieferung und das Neue Testament', in *Theologische Abhandlungen Carl von Weizsäcker ... gewidmet*: 321-52.
1899   'Hermeneutik, biblische', *RE*, 3rd edn, VII: 718-50.
1900   *Die Bergpredigt.*
1901   *Dürfen wir noch Christen bleiben?*
1902   *Das Urchristentum.*
1908   *Der literarische Charakter der neutestamentlichen Schriften.*
1913   *Die Bodenständigkeit der synoptischen Überlieferung vom Werke Jesu.*
Helferich, Christoph
1985   *Geschichte der Philosophie.*
Hempel, Johannes
1914   *Die Schichten des Deuteronomiums.*
1922   *Gebet und Frömmigkeit im Alten Testament.*
1924a   'Religionsgeschichte und Theologie', *Deutsche akademische Rundschau* 6: 12-15.
1924b   'Jahwegleichnisse der israelitischen Propheten', *ZAW* 42: 74-104.
1926a   *Mystik und Alkoholekstase.*

1926b	*Gott und Mensch im Alten Testament.*
1930	*Die althebräische Literatur und ihr hellenistisch-jüdisches Nachleben.*
1931	'Altes Testament und völkische Frage', *Monatsschrift für Pastoraltheologie* 27: 165-78.
1938a	*Das Ethos des Alten Testaments.*
1938b	*Politische Absicht und politische Wirkung im biblischen Schrifttum.*
1942/43	'Chronik', *ZAW* 59: 209-15.
1957	*Das Bild in Bibel und Gottesdienst.*

Hempel, Johannes, *et al.* (eds.)
1936   *Werden und Wesen des Alten Testaments.*

Hengel, Martin
1969   *Judentum und Hellenismus* (ET 1974).

Henn, T.R.
1962   'The Bible as Literature', in M. Black and H.H. Rowley (eds.), *Peake's Commentary on the Bible*: 8-23.
1970   *The Bible as Literature.*

Henninger, Mark G.
1989   *Relations: Medieval Theories.*

Henry, Marie Louise
1992   *Hüte dein Denken und Wollen.*

Hensley, Jeffrey S.
1991   *John Calvin's View of Natural Theology and its Late-Medieval Influence.*

Hentschke, Ada, and Ulrich Muhlack
1972   *Einführung in die Geschichte der klassischen Philologie.*

Hentschke, Richard
1957   *Die Stellung der vorexilischen Schriftpropheten zum Kultus.*

Hepworth, Brian
1978   *Robert Lowth.*

Herberg, Will
1953   'Judaism and Christianity: Their Unity and Difference', *JBR* 21: 67-78.

Herbert, Karl
1985   *Der Kirchenkampf.*

Herder, Johann Gottfried
1877-1913   *Sämmtliche Werke* (ed. B. Suphan).

Hermisson, Hans-Jürgen
1965   *Sprache und Ritus im altisraelitischen Kult.*

Herntrich, Volkmar
1933   *Völkische Religiösität und Altes Testament.*

Herring, Basil
1982   *Joseph Ibn Kaspi's Gevia' Kesef: A Study in Medieval Jewish Philosophic Bible Commentary.*

Hertzberg, H.W.
1934   *Der Deutsche und das Alte Testament.*

Heschel, Abraham
1936   *Die Prophetie.*
1962   *The Prophets.*
1996   *Moral Grandeur and Spiritual Audacity.*

Hessler, Bertram
1992   'Zur biblischen Hermeneutik', *Wissenschaft und Weisheit* 15: 63-66.
Hill, Christopher
1972   *The World Turned Upside Down.*
Hinsley, F.H.
1963   *Power and the Pursuit of Peace.*
Hirsch, Emanuel
1938   *Leitfaden zur christlichen Lehre.*
1986   *Das Alte Testament und die Predigt des Alten Testaments* (expanded
                reissue).
Hirschfeld, Hartwig
1918   *Qirqisani Studies.*
Hirshman, Marc
1996   *A Rivalry of Genius.*
Hirzel, Rudolph
1895   *Der Dialog,* I.
Ho, Ahura
1991   *Ṣedeq and Ṣedaqah in the Hebrew Bible.*
Hoburg, Ralf
1994   *Seligkeit und Heilsgewissheit.*
Hodge, M.J.S.
1991   *Origins and Species.*
Hoffmann, Manfred
1994   *Rhetoric and Theology.*
Hoffmann, R. Joseph
1994   *Porphyry's Against the Christians.*
Holladay, William L.
1962   'Style, Irony and Authenticity in Jeremiah', *JBL* 81: 44-54.
Holland, John
1843   *The Psalmists of Britain.*
Holm-Nielsen, Svend
1960   'The Importance of Late Jewish Psalmody for the Understanding of Old
                Testament Psalmodic Tradition', *ST* 14: 1-53.
Hölscher, Gustav
1948   *Das Gedicht von Hiob und seinen Freunden.*
Holtz, Barry W.
1984   *Back to the Sources.*
Holtzmann, H.
1907   'Die Marcus-Kontroverse in ihrer heutigen Gestalt', *ARW* 10: 18-40, 161-
                200.
Hooke, S.H.
1933   (ed.), *Myth and Ritual: Essays on the Myth and Ritual of the Hebrews in
                Relation to the Cultic Pattern of the Ancient East.*
1935   (ed.), *The Labyrinth.*
1938   *The Origins of Early Semitic Ritual.*
1958   (ed.), *Myth, Ritual and Kingship.*
1963   *Middle Eastern Mythology.*

Hooykaas, R.
1984   *G.J. Rheticus' Treatise on Holy Scripture and the Motion of the Earth*.
Höpfl, H.
1934   'Critique biblique', *DBSup*, II: 175-240.
Horkheimer, Max
1947   *Eclipse of Reason*.
1968   *Kritische Theorie*, I (ET 1972).
Horkheimer, Max, and Theodor W. Adorno
1947   *Dialektik der Aufklärung* (ET 1972).
Hornig, Barbara
1958   'Das Prosagebet der nachexilischen Literatur', *TLZ* 83: 644-46.
Horst, Pieter W. van der
1984   'The Interpretation of the Bible by Minor Hellenistic Jewish Authors', in
            M. Mulder and H. Sysling (eds.), *Mikra*: 519-46.
Hösle, Vittorio
1987   *Hegels System*.
Hossenfelder, Joachim
1933   *Unser Kampf*.
Howlett, D.R.
1995   *The Celtic Latin Tradition of Biblical Style*.
Huffmon, Herbert B.
1959   'The Covenant Lawsuit in the Prophets', *JBL* 78: 285-95.
Hülsebus, Tina
1997   '"Freundin unter Dornen wie die Rose": Hedwig Jahnow', in E. Röhr
            (ed.), *Ich bin was ich bin*: 136-62.
Humbert, Paul
1936   'Les prophètes d'Israel ou les tragiques de la Bible', *RTP*, NS 24: 209-51.
Hume, David
1955   *Writings on Economics*.
Hummelauer, Franz von
1904   *Exegetisches zur Inspirationsfrage*.
Hunsinger, George
1991   *How to Read Karl Barth*.
Hunter, Archibald M.
1960   *Interpreting the Parables*.
Husserl, Edmund
1950–   *Husserliana*.
Hutchison, John A.
1956   *Faith, Reason, and Existence*.
Hutten, Kurt
1937   'Die nationalkirchliche Bewegung', in Künneth and Schreiner: 444-73.
Huygens, R.B.C.
1970   *Accessus ad auctores, Bernard d'Utrecht, Conrad d'Hirsau*.
Hvidberg, Flemming Friis
1962   *Weeping and Laughter in the Old Testament* (Danish 1938).
Hylmö, Gunnar
1938   *Gamla Testamentets litteraturhistoria*.

Hymes, Dell
1964   'Introduction: Toward Ethnographies of Communication', *American Anthropologist* 66, No. 6, Part 2: 1-34.
Idel, Moshe
1989   *Language, Torah, and Hermeneutics in Abraham Abulafia.*
Idowu, E. Bolaji
1962   *Olódùmarè: God in Yoruba Belief.*
Ijsseling, Samuel
1976   *Rhetoric and Philosophy in Conflict.*
Instone Brewer, David
1992   *Techniques and Assumptions in Jewish Exegesis before 70 CE.*
Iremonger, F.A.
1948   *William Temple.*
Irwin, William A.
1941   *The Prophets and Their Times* (revision of a volume by J.M. Powis Smith).
1952   *The Old Testament.*
Jackson, Bernard S.
1981   'On the Problem of Roman Influence on the Halakah and Normative Self-Definition in Judaism', in E.P. Sanders (ed.), *Jewish and Christian Self-Definition*, II: 157-203.
Jacobs, Louis
1973   *Jewish Biblical Exegesis.*
Jäger, Gerhard
1975   *Einführung in die klassische Philologie.*
Jahnow, Hedwig
1923   *Das hebräische Leichenlied im Rahmen der Völkerdichtung.*
Jahnow, Hedwig, *et al.*
1994   *Feministische Hermeneutik und Erstes Testament.*
James, E.O.
1933   *Christian Myth and Ritual.*
1935   *The Old Testament in the Light of Anthropology.*
1958   *Myth and Ritual in the Ancient Near East.*
James, Fleming
1938   *Thirty Psalmists.*
1954   *Personalities of the Old Testament.*
Jameson, Fredric
1981   *The Political Unconscious.*
Jansen, H. Ludin
1937   *Die spätjüdische Psalmendichtung.*
Japhet, Sara, and Robert B. Salters
1985   *The Commentary of R. Samuel ben Meir* Rashbam *on Qoheleth.*
Jarick, John
1995   'Theodore of Mopsuestia and the Interpretation of Ecclesiastes', in M. Carroll R. *et al.* (eds.), *The Bible in Human Society*, 306-16.
Jaspers, Karl
1948   *Der philosophische Glaube.*

Jaspers, Karl, and Rudolf Bultmann
1954   *Die Frage der Entmythologisierung.*
Jaspert, Bernd
1996   *Sachgemässe Exegese.*
Jastrow, Morris, Jr
1898   *The Religion of Babylonia and Assyria.*
1905   *Die Religion Babyloniens und Assyriens,* I.
1919   *A Gentle Cynic.*
Jeanrond, Werner G.
1991   *Theological Hermeneutics.*
Jebb, R.C.
1893   *The Attic Orators,* I (2nd edn).
Jeffrey, David Lyle
1985   'John Wyclif and the Hermeneutics of Reader Response', *Int* 39: 272-87.
1992   *A Dictionary of Biblical Tradition in English Literature.*
Jepperson, Ronald L.
1991   'Institutions, Institutional Effects, and Institutionalism', in W. Powell and
            J. DiMaggio (eds.), *The New Institutionalism in Organizational Analysis:*
            143-63.
Jeremias, Alfred
1887   *Die babylonisch-assyrischen Vorstellungen vom Leben nach dem Tode.*
1891   'Izdubar Nimrod', in W.H. Roscher (ed.), *Ausführliches Lexikon der*
            griechischen und römischen Mythologie, II: 773-823.
1918   *Die soziale Aufgabe der Kirche.*
Johnson, Aubrey R.
1936   'Some Outstanding Old Testament Problems. VI. The Prophet in Israelite
            Worship', *ExpTim* 47: 312-19.
1944   *The Cultic Prophet in Ancient Israel.*
Johnson, Elizabeth A.
1992   *She Who Is.*
Johnson, Roger A.
1974   *The Origins of Demythologization.*
Johnstone, William (ed.)
1995   *William Robertson Smith.*
Jolles, André
1930   *Einfache Formen.*
Jonas, Hans
1964   'Heidegger and Theology', *Review of Metaphysics* 18: 207-33.
Jones, Kathleen B.
1991   'The Trouble with Authority', *Differences* 3, No. 1: 104-27.
Jones, Scott J.
1995   *John Wesley's Conception and Use of Scripture.*
Joos, Martin
1962   *The Five Clocks.*
Jordan, Hermann
1911   *Geschichte der altchristlichen Literatur.*
Josipovici, Gabriel
1988   *The Book of God.*

Jülicher, Adolf
    1888   *Die Gleichnisreden Jesu.*
    1894   *Einleitung in das Neue Testament.*
    1899   *Die Gleichnisreden Jesu, I* (2nd edn).

Jüngel, Eberhard
    1962   *Paulus und Jesus.*

Junghans, Helmar
    1985   *Der junge Luther und die Humanisten.*

Kadushin, Max
    1987   *A Conceptual Commentary on Midrash Leviticus Rabbah.*

Kähler, Martin
    1883   *Die Wissenschaft der christlichen Lehre* (2nd edn 1893, 3rd edn 1905).
    1892   *Der sogenannte historische Jesus und der geschichtliche, biblische Christus* (ET 1964).
    1937   *Zur Bibelfrage.*

Kahn, Charles H.
    1979   *The Art and Thought of Heraclitus.*

Kahn, Victoria
    1994   *Machiavellian Rhetoric.*

Kaiser, Otto
    1963   *Einführung in die exegetischen Methoden.*

Kalthoff, A.
    1903   *Das Christusproblem* (2nd edn [1st edn 1902]).

Kamesar, Adam
    1993   *Jerome, Greek Scholarship, and the Hebrew Bible.*

Kamlah, Wilhelm
    1940   *Christentum und Selbstbehauptung* (2nd edn: *Christentum und Geschichtlichkeit*, 1951).

Kannengiesser, Charles (ed.)
    1984-89   *Bible de tous les temps* (8 vols.).

Kapelrud, Arvid S.
    1953   'Israels profeter og retten', *SEÅ* 18/19: 17-31.
    1956   *Central Ideas in Amos.*

Karpeles, Gustav
    1886   *Geschichte der jüdischen Tradition*, I.

Käsemann, Ernst
    1960   *Exegetische Versuche und Besinnungen*, I (ET of item cited in *Essays*, 1982).

Kathan, Anton
    1970   *Herders Literaturkritik.*

Kaufman, Gordon
    1972   *God the Problem.*

Kaufmann, Yehezkel
    1960   *The Religion of Israel* (fuller Hebrew 1937-48).

Kaupel, Heinrich
    1933   *Die antisemitische Bekämpfung des Alten Testaments.*

Kautzsch, E.
    1902   *Die Poesie und die poetischen Bücher des Alten Testaments.*

Keegan, John
    1993   *A History of Warfare.*
Keet, C.C.
    1928   *A Liturgical Study of the Psalter.*
Kegley, Charles W. (ed.)
    1966   *The Theology of Rudolph Bultmann.*
Kelber, Werner H.
    1983   *The Oral and the Written Gospel.*
Keller, Evelyn Fox
    1985   *Reflections on Gender and Science.*
Kellogg, S.H.
    1899   *A Handbook of Comparative Religion.*
Kelly, J.N.D.
    1995   *Golden Mouth.*
Kennedy, George A.
    1980   *Classical Rhetoric and Its Christian and Secular Tradition from Ancient to Modern Times.*
    1989   (ed.), *The Cambridge History of Literary Criticism*, I.
    1994   *A New History of Classical Rhetoric.*
Kenny, Anthony
    1985   *Wyclif.*
Kent, Charles Foster
    1895   *The Wise Men of Ancient Israel and Their Proverbs.*
    1902   *The Messages of Israel's Lawgivers.*
    1904   *The Student's Old Testament.* I. *Narratives of the Beginnings of Hebrew History.*
    1906   *The Origin and Permanent Value of the Old Testament.*
    1917   *The Social Teachings of the Prophets and Jesus.*
Kepnes, Steven
    1992   *The Text as Thou.*
Kerrigan, Alexander
    1952   *St Cyril of Alexandria: Interpreter of the Old Testament.*
Kertsch, Manfred
    1995   *Exempla Chrysostomica.*
Kessler, Martin
    1994   *Voices from Amsterdam.*
Keylock, Leslie R.
    1975   'Bultmann's Law of Increasing Distinctness', in G. Hawthorne (ed.), *Current Issues in Biblical and Patristic Interpretation*: 193-210.
Kilpatrick, G.D.
    1946   *The Origins of the Gospel According to St. Matthew.*
Kimbrough, S.T., Jr
    1978   *Israelite Religion in Sociological Perspective.*
King, Leonard W.
    1896   *Babylonian Magic and Sorcery.*
Kirkpatrick, A.F. (ed.)
    1901   *The Book of Psalms.*

Kirkpatrick, Patricia G.
1987   *The Old Testament and Folklore Study.*
Kittel, Rudolf
1905   'Psalmen', *RE*, 3rd edn, XVI, 187-214.
1921   'Die Zukunft der alttestamentlichen Wissenschaft', *ZAW* 13: 84-99.
Klatt, Werner
1969   *Hermann Gunkel.*
Klein, Charlotte
1975   *Theologie und Anti-Judaismus* (ET 1978).
Klein, Michael L.
1981   'The Translation of Anthropomorphisms and Anthropopathisms in the Targumim', *Congress Volume, Vienna 1980* (VTSup, 32): 162-77.
Klocker, Harry
1992   *William of Ockham and the Divine Freedom.*
Klopsch, Paul
1980   *Einführung in die Dichtungslehren des lateinischen Mittelalters.*
Klostermann, August
1900   *Deuteronomium und Grágas.*
Klotz, Leopold (ed.)
1932   *Die Kirche und das dritte Reich* (2 vols.).
Knight, Harold
1947   *The Hebrew Prophetic Consciousness.*
Knott, John R.
1980   *The Sword and the Spirit: Puritan Responses to the Bible.*
Koch, Klaus
1955   'Gibt es ein Vergeltungsdogma im Alten Testament?', *ZTK* 52: 1-42.
1962   'Der Tod des Religionsstifters', *KD* 8: 100-23.
1964   *Was ist Formgeschichte?* (2nd edn 1967, ET 1969; 3rd edn 1974; 4th edn 1981 [in this: 325-41, 271-324 = 3rd edn: 271-87, 289-342]).
1966   'Gerhard von Rad', in *Tendenzen der Theologie im 20. Jahrhundert*: 483-87.
1991   *Spuren des hebräischen Denkens.*
1994   'Das Hohe Lied unter kanonischer Perspective', in *Gottes Ehre erzählen* (Festschrift for H. Seidel): 11-23.
Koegel, Rudolf
1894   *Geschichte der deutschen Literatur.*
Koester, Helmut [= Köster, H.]
1995   *Introduction to the New Testament*, I (2nd edn).
Kohler, K.
1897   *The Psalms and their Place in the Liturgy.*
Köhler [Koehler], Ludwig
1927   *Das formgeschichtliche Problem des Neuen Testaments.*
1953   *Der hebräische Mensch* (ET 1956).
König, Eduard
1900   *Stilistik, Rhetorik, Poetik in Bezug auf die biblische Literatur.*
1907   *Die Poesie des Alten Testaments.*
1916   *Hermeneutik des Alten Testaments.*
1927   *Die Psalmen.*

Kopper, Joachim
1979   *Einführung in die Philosophie der Aufklärung.*
Köster, Helmut [= Koester, H.]
1983   'Formgeschichte/Formenkritik II. Neues Testament', *TRE* XI: 286-99.
1994   'Written Gospels or Oral Tradition?', *JBL* 113: 293-97.
Kraeling, Emil G.
1939   *The Book of the Ways of God.*
1955   *The Old Testament Since the Reformation.*
Krašovec, Joze
1984   *Antithetic Structure in Biblical Hebrew Poetry.*
Kraus, Hans-Joachim
1951a   *Die Königsherrschaft Gottes im Alten Testament.*
1951b   'Gilgal', *VT* 1: 181-99.
1954   *Gottesdienst in Israel* (2nd greatly expanded edn 1962, ET 1966).
1956   'Juden fragen Christen', in H. Giessen *et al.* (eds.), *Der mündige Christ*: 210-18.
1957   *Die prophetische Verkündigung des Rechts in Israel.*
1969   *Geschichte der historisch-kritischen Erforschung des Alten Testaments* (2nd edn).
1975   *Reich Gottes: Reich der Freiheit* (revised: *Systematische Theologie*, 1983).
1978   *Psalmen* (5th edn; ET 1988).
1991   *Rückkehr zu Israel.*
Krause, Gerhard
1962   *Studien zu Luthers Auslegung der Kleinen Propheten.*
Krinetzki, Leo
1965   *Israels Gebet im Alten Testament.*
Krusche, Werner
1957   *Das Wirken des Heiligen Geistes nach Calvin.*
Kuczynski, Michael P.
1995   *Prophetic Song.*
Kugel, James L.
1981   *The Idea of Biblical Poetry: Parallelism and its History.*
1990   (ed.), *Poetry and Prophecy.*
1997   *The Bible as it Was.*
Kugel, James L., and Greer, Rowan A.
1986   *Early Biblical Interpretation.*
Kuhl, C.
1958   'Formen und Gattungen I. Im AT', *RGG*, 3rd edn, II: 996-99.
Kuhn, Thomas
1962   *The Structure of Scientific Revolutions* (2nd edn 1970, slightly revised or reset—page numbers are sometimes higher by one—and with postscript).
Kuist, Howard Tillman
1947   *These Words Upon Thy Heart* (=*Scripture and the Christian Response*, 1964).
Kümmel, Werner Georg
1949   'Martin Dibelius als Theologe', *TLZ* 74: 129-40.

1972   *The New Testament: The History of the Investigation of its Problems* (German 1958, 1970).
1981   'Dibelius, Martin', *TRE*, VIII: 726-29.
Künneth, Walter, and Helmuth Schreiner (eds.)
1937   *Die Nation vor Gott.*
Kusche, Ulrich
1991   *Die unterlegene Religion.*
Kustas, George L.
1973   *Studies in Byzantine Rhetoric.*
Kwok Pui-lan
1995   *Discovering the Bible in the Non-Biblical World.*
Lagarde, Paul de
1920   *Deutsche Schriften*, 5th edn.
Lagrange, Marie-Joseph
1895   'Une pensée de Saint Thomas sur l'inspiration scriptuaire', *RB* 4: 563-71.
1903   *La méthode historique* (ET 1905).
1911   *Evangile selon Saint Marc.*
1928   *L'évangile de Jésus-Christ.*
Lamb, Jonathan
1995   *The Rhetoric of Suffering.*
Lamb, Mary Ellen
1990   *Gender and Authorship in the Sidney Circle.*
Lambert, W.G.
1960   *Babylonian Wisdom Literature.*
Lampartner, Helmut
1958   *Das Buch der Psalmen*, I.
Lampe, G.W.H.
1982   'Athens and Jerusalem: Joint Witnesses to Christ?', in *The Philosophical Frontiers of Christian Theology*: 12-38.
Lande, Irene
1949   *Formelhafte Wendungen der Umgangssprache im Alten Testament.*
Landes, George M.
1967   'The Kerygma of the Book of Jonah: The Contextual Interpretation of the Jonah Psalm', *Int* 21: 3-31.
Langdon, Stephen
1909   *Sumerian and Babylonian Psalms.*
Lapointe, Roger
1970   'Les genres littéraires aprés l'êre gunkélienne', *Eglise et Théologie* 1: 9-38.
Lausberg, Heinrich
1960   *Handbuch der literarischen Rhetorik.*
Lazarus-Yafeh, Hava
1992   *Intertwined Worlds: Medieval Islam and Bible Criticism.*
Leach, Edmund
1983   'Anthropological Approaches to the Study of the Bible During the Twentieth Century', in E. Leach and D. Aycock (eds.), *Structuralist*

Interpretations of Biblical Myth (reprinted from G. Tucker and D. Knight [eds.], *Humanizing America's Iconic Book*, 1982): 7-32.

Leeuw, G. van der
1933   *Phänomenologie der Religion.*

Leffler, Siegfried
1935   *Christus im Dritten Reich der Deutschen.*

Lempicki, Sigmund von
1968   *Geschichte der deutschen Literaturwissenschaft* (2nd edn).

Lerner, Gerda
1993   *The Creation of Feminist Consciousness.*

Levenson, Jon D.
1993   *The Hebrew Bible, the Old Testament, and Historical Criticism.*

Levie, Jean
1958   *La Bible, Parole humaine et message de Dieu* (ET 1961).

Lewalski, Barbara
1979   *Protestant Poetics and the Seventeenth-Century Religious Lyric.*

Lewis, C. Day
1948   *The Poetic Image.*

Lewis, C.S.
1950   *The Literary Impact of the Authorized Version* (reprinted with minor editing in 1963).

Lieberman, Saul
1950   *Hellenism in Jewish Palestine.*

Liedke, Gerhard
1971   *Gestalt und Bezeichnung alttestamentlicher Rechtssätze.*

Lindblom, J.
1963   *Prophecy in Ancient Israel* (2nd edn).

Lindemann, Andreas
1989   'Neutestamentler in der Zeit des Nationalsozialismus', *Wort und Dienst*, NS 20: 25-52.

Lindhardt, Jan
1979   *Rhetor, Poeta, Historicus.*

Lipps, Hans
1938   *Untersuchungen zu einer hermeneutischen Logik.*

Lipshitz, Abe
1988   *The Commentary of Rabbi Ibn Ezra on Hosea.*

Lochrie, Karma
1991   *Margery Kempe and Translations of the Flesh.*

Lockshin, Martin I.
1993   'Truth or pešaṭ', in B. Halpern and D. Hobson (eds.), *Law, Politics and Society in the Ancient Mediterranean World*: 271-79.

Lods, Adolphe
1950   *Histoire de la littérature hébraïque et juive.*

Lohfink, Gerhard
1973   *Jetzt verstehe ich die Bibel: Ein Sachbuch zur Formkritik* (ET 1979).

Lohfink, Norbert
1983   review of *The Wisdom Literature*, 1981, by R. Murphy, in *TP* 58: 239-41.

1986 'Von der "Anawim-Partei" zur "Kirche der Armen". Die bibelwissenschaftliche Ahnentafel eines Hauptbegriffs der "Theologie der Befreiung"', *Biblica* 67: 153-76.

Lohmeyer, Ernst
1928 *Kyrios Jesus.*

Lohse, Bernhard
1995 *Luthers Theologie.*

Loisy, Alfred
1901 *Les mythes babyloniens et les premiers chapitres de la Genèse.*
1902 *L'évangile et l'église* (2nd edn 1903; ET 1903).
1903 *Etudes bibliques.*

Lonergan, Bernard J.
1957 *Insight.*
1980 *Understanding and Being.*

Long, Burke O.
1996 'W.F. Albright as Prophet-Reformer', in S. Reid: 152-72.
1997 *Planting and Reaping Albright.*

Lorenz, Rüdiger
1973 *Die unvollendete Befreiung vom Nominalismus.*

Lowance, Mason I., Jr
1980 *The Language of Canaan: Metaphor and Symbol in New England from the Puritans to the Transcendentalists.*

Lowe, Donald M.
1982 *History of Bourgeois Perception.*

Lowe, Walter
1993 *Theology and Difference: The Wound of Reason.*

Lowy, S.
1977 *The Principles of Samaritan Bible Exegesis.*

Lubac, Henri de
1959-64 *Exégèse Médiévale* (ET in progress).

Lüdemann, Gerd, and Martin Schröder
1987 *Die religionsgeschichtliche Schule.*

Lüder, Andreas
1995 *Historie und Dogmatik.*

MacGregor, David
1992 *Hegel, Marx, and the English State.*

Macintosh, A.A.
1995 'Hosea and the Wisdom Tradition', in *Wisdom in Ancient Israel: Essays in Honour of J.A. Emerton*: 124-32.

MacIntyre, Alasdair
1984 *After Virtue* (2nd edn).

Mack, Burton L.
1990 *Rhetoric and the New Testament.*

Mack, Peter
1993 *Renaissance Argument.*

Magonet, Jonathan
1994 *A Rabbi Reads the Psalms.*

Malherbe, Johannes Stefanus
    1993   'Abravanel's Theory of Prophecy' (dissertation Stellenbosch).
Malinowski, Bronislaw
    1926   *Myth in Primitive Psychology.*
Mann, Michael
    1986–93   *The Sources of Social Power* (2 vols.).
Mannheim, Karl
    1929   *Ideologie und Utopie* (ET 1936).
Mansbridge, Jane J.
    1980   *Beyond Adversary Democracy.*
Manson, William
    1943   *Jesus the Messiah.*
Margerie, Bertrand de
    1980-90   *Introduction à l'histoire de l'exégèse* (4 vols.; ET of vols. I, III: 1993, 1994).
Marrou, Henri-Irénéé
    1948   *Histoire de l'éducation dans l'antiquité* (ET 1956).
Marschall, Gerhard
    1929   *Die 'Gottlosen' des ersten Psalmenbuches.*
Marsh, John
    1952   *The Fulness of Time.*
Martey, Emmanuel
    1993   *African Theology.*
Marti, Karl
    1906   'Eine neue Prophezeiung', *CW* 20: 1058-63.
Martin, Josef
    1974   *Antike Rhetorik.*
Mathews, Shailer
    1897   *The Social Teaching of Jesus.*
    1924   (ed.), *Contributions of Science to Religion.*
    1931   *The Growth of the Idea of God.*
Mathys, Hans-Peter
    1994   *Dichter und Beter.*
Matsen, Patricia P., *et al.*
    1990   *Readings from Classical Rhetoric.*
Matter, E. Ann
    1990   *The Voice of the Beloved: The Song of Songs in Western Medieval Christianity.*
Matthews, I.G.
    1947   *The Religious Pilgrimage of Israel.*
Maurer, Wilhelm
    1967   *Der junge Melanchthon*, I.
Mayer, G.
    1966   'Exegese II (Judentum)', *RAC*, VI: 1194-1211.
Mayes, A.D.H.
    1989   *The Old Testament in Sociological Perspective.*
McCarthy, Dennis J.
    1963   *Treaty and Covenant* (considerably expanded 2nd edn 1978).

1972   *Old Testament Covenant.*
1978   2nd edn of 1963.
McCormack, Bruce L.
1995   *Karl Barth's Critically Realistic Dialectical Theology.*
McCown, Chester C.
1958   *Man, Morals and History.*
McFague, Sallie
1982   *Metaphorical Theology.*
McGrath, Alister
1986   'John Calvin and Late Medieval Thought', *ARG*, 77: 58-78.
1987   *The Intellectual Origins of the European Reformation.*
1993   *Reformation Thought* (2nd edn).
McKane, William
1995   *A Late Harvest.*
McKenzie, John L.
1960   review of Childs, in *CBQ* 22: 337-38.
McKnight, Edgar V.
1988   *Postmodern Use of the Bible.*
Megivern, James J.
1978   *Bible Interpretation.*
Meier, Kurt
1984   *Der evangelische Kirchenkampf* (3 vols., 2nd edn; vols. I and II=1st edn).
Meissner, Henriette, M.
1993   'Grammatik und Rhetorik in Gregors von Nyssa Exegese', in Gregory of
            Nyssa, *Homilies on Ecclesiastes*: 203-48.
Mencken, H.L.
1930   *Treatise on the Gods.*
Mendelssohn, Moses
1971–   *Gesammelte Schriften.*
Mendenhall, George
1954a   'Covenant Forms in Israelite Tradition', *BA* 17: 49-76.
1954b   'Ancient Oriental and Biblical Law', *BA* 17: 26-46.
1962   'The Hebrew Conquest of Palestine', *BA* 25: 66-87.
1975   'The Conflict Between Value Systems and Social Control', in H.
            Goedicke and J. Roberts (eds.), *Unity and Diversity*: 169-80.
Menes, Abram
1928   *Die vorexilischen Gesetze Israels.*
Meyer, Ben F.
1994   *Reality and Illusion in New Testament Scholarship.*
Meyer, Gottlob Wilhelm
1802–1809   *Geschichte der Schrifterklärung.*
Miller, J. Hillis
1968   *The Form of Victorian Fiction.*
Minear, Paul
1946   'Form Criticism and Faith', *Religion in Life* 45: 46-56.
Minnis, A.J.
1984   *Medieval Theory of Authorship.*

Mitchell, Gordon
1995   'War, Folklore and the Mystery of a Disappearing Book', *JSOT* 68: 113-19.
Mitchell, Henry H.
1970   *Black Preaching*.
Moffatt, James
1911   *An Introduction to the Literature of the New Testament*.
Mogk, E.
1897   'Zur ätiologischen Sagenbildung', *Verein für sächsische Volkskunde* 1: 10f.
Mojsisch, B.
1992   'Relation. II. Spätantike, Mittelalter und Renaissance', *Historisches Wörterbuch der Philosophie*, VIII: 586-95.
Mommer, Peter, *et al.* (eds.)
1993   *Gottes Recht als Lebensraum*.
Monk, Samuel H.
1935   *The Sublime: A Study of Critical Theories of XVIII-Century England*.
Moor, Johannes C. de (ed.)
1995   *Synchronic or Diachronic?*
Moore, Rick Dale
1990   *God Saves*.
Morawe, Günter
1960   *Aufbau und Abgrenzung der Loblieder von Qumran*.
Morgan, Robert, and Barton, John
1988   *Biblical Interpretation*.
Moser, Simon
1932   *Grundbegriffe der Naturphilosophie bei Wilhelm von Ockham*.
Moule, C.F.D.
1962   *The Birth of the New Testament*.
Moulton, Richard G.
1885   *Shakespeare as a Dramatic Artist*.
1896   *Deuteronomy*.
1899   *The Literary Study of the Bible* (2nd edn [1st edn 1885]).
1901   *A Short Introduction to the Literature of the Bible*.
Moulton, Richard G. *et al.*
1896   *The Bible as Literature*.
Moulton, W. Fiddian
1926   *Richard Green Moulton*.
Mowinckel, Sigmund
1914   *Zur Komposition des Buches Jeremia*.
1916   *Kongesalmerne i det Gamle Testamente*.
1921   *Psalmenstudien*, I.
1922   *Psalmenstudien*, II.
1923   *Psalmenstudien*, III.
1924   *Psalmenstudien*, VI.
1926   *Zur Komposition des Buches Jeremia*.
1927   *Le décalogue*.
1937   'Zur Geschichte der Dekaloge', *ZAW* 55: 218-35.

| 1938 | 'Neuere Forschungen', *Acta Orientalia* 16: 1-40. |

1938   'Neuere Forschungen', *Acta Orientalia* 16: 1-40.
1946   *Prophecy and Tradition*.
1953   *Religion und Kultus* (Norwegian 1950; ET 1981).
1959   *The Old Testament as Word of God* (Norwegian 1938).
1962   *The Psalms in Israel's Worship* (2 vols.; revised from the Norwegian, *Offersang og Sangoffer* 1951; new edn 1992).

Mueller, David L.
1969   *An Introduction to the Theology of Albrecht Ritschl*.

Muilenburg, James
1923   *Specimens of Biblical Literature*.
1933   'The Literary Approach—The Old Testament as Hebrew Literature', *Journal of the National Association of Biblical Instructors* 1, No. 2: 14-22.
1951   'The Interpretation of the Bible', in Richardson and Schweitzer: 198-218.
1956   'The Book of Isaiah. Chapters 40-66, Introduction and Exegesis', *IB*, V: 381-773.
1958   'Preface to Hermeneutics', *JBL* 77: 18-26.
1961   *The Way of Israel*.
1984   *Hearing and Speaking the Word*.

Mulert, Hermann
1933   'Lagarde und der heutige Antisemitismus', *CW* 47: 384.
1936   'Theologie der Krisis, Religionen, Christentum', *CW* 50: 165-68.
1937a   'Die deutschen Christen zwischen Bekenntniskirche und Deutschglaube', *CW* 51: 363-68.
1937b   'Theologie und Politik', *CW* 51: 803-809.

Mullaney, Steven
1983   'Strange Things, Gross Terms, Curious Customs', *Representations* 3: 40-67.

Müller, Hans Peter
1983   'Formgeschichte/Formenkritik. I. Altes Testament', *TRE*, XI: 271-85.

Müller, Wilhelm
1889   *Zur Mythologie der griechischen und deutschen Heldensage*.

Munch, P.A.
1936   'Einige Bemerkungen', *Le monde orientale* 30: 13-26.
1937   'Das Problem der Reichtums in den Psalmen 37. 49. 73', *ZAW* 55: 36-46.

Muños Iglesias, Salvador
1968   *Los generos literarios y la interpretación de la Biblia*.

Murphy, James J.
1974   *Rhetoric in the Middle Ages*.

Nagy, Gregory
1989   'Early Greek Views of Poets and Poetry', in Kennedy 1989: 1-77.

Nakamura, Hajime
1975   *Parallel Development*.

Napier, B. Davie
1955   *From Faith to Faith*.

Neal, Sister Marie Augusta
1978   review of *The Ultimate Values of the American Population*, by W.C. McCready with A.M. Greeley, in *JSSR* 17: 330-32.

Nelson, Benjamin
1969   *The Idea of Usury.*
Nelson, William
1973   *Fact or Fiction.*
Nemoy, Leon
1952   *Karaite Anthology.*
Neusner, Jacob
1987   *What is Midrash?*
1989   *Writing With Scripture*, with W. Green.
1991   *Judaism as Philosophy.*
1994   *Introduction to Rabbinic Literature.*
Newman, Barbara
1990   'Introduction', in Hildegard of Bingen, *Scivias*: 9-53.
Nichols, Stephen G.
1992   'Prophetic Discourse', in B. Levy (ed.), *The Bible in the Middle Ages*: 51-76.
Nicholson, Ernest W.
1986   *God and his People.*
Nicolaisen, Carsten
1966   'Die Auseinandersetzungen um das Alte Testament im Kirchenkampf 1933-1945' (dissertation Hamburg [MS]).
1971   'Die Stellung der "deutschen Christen" zum Alten Testament', in *Zur Geschichte des Kirchenkampfes*, II: 197-220.
Niebergall, Friedrich
1912-22   *Praktische Auslegung des Alten Testaments* (3 vols.)
Niebuhr, R[einhold]
1919   'The Twilight of Liberalism', *The New Republic*, June 14: 218.
Niemöller, Wilhelm
1956   *Die evangelische Kirche im Dritten Reich.*
Nietzsche, Friedrich
1967-   *Werke* (ed. G. Colli and M. Montinari).
Norden, Eduard
1898   *Die antike Kunstprosa.*
1913   *Agnostos Theos.*
Norden, Günther van
1979   *Der deutsche Protestantismus im Jahr der nationalsozialistischen Machtergreifung.*
Norton, David
1993   *A History of the Bible as Literature* (2 vols.).
Noth, Martin
1940   *Die Gesetze im Pentateuch.*
1948   *Überlieferungsgeschichte des Pentateuch.*
1952/53   'Die Vergegenwärtigung des Alten Testaments in der Verkündigung', *EvT* 12: 6-17.
1969   *Gesammelte Studien zum Alten Testament*, II.
Obbink, Dirk (ed.)
1995   *Philodemus and Poetry.*

Oberman, Heiko Augustinus
    1967   *Forerunners of the Reformation.*
O'Brien, Julia M.
    1995   'On Saying "No" to a Prophet', *Semeia* 72: 111-21 (appeared in 1997).
Ockham [William]
    1957   *Philosophical Writings*, ed. Philotheus Boehner.
O'Connor, Daniel, and Oakley, Francis (eds.)
    1969   *Creation: The Impact of an Idea.*
Oden, Robert A.
    1987   *The Bible Without Theology.*
O'Donnell, James J.
    1979   *Cassiodorus.*
Oesterley, W.O.E., and Robinson, Theodore H.
    1930   *Hebrew Religion.*
Oey, Thomas Geoffrey
    1991   'Wyclif's Doctrine of Scripture Within the Context of his Doctrinal and Social Ideas' (dissertation Vanderbilt).
Oliner, Samuel P., and Pearl M.
    1988   *The Altruistic Personality.*
Olrik, Axel
    1909   'Epische Gesetze der Volksdichtung', *Zeitschrift für deutsches Altertum und deutsche Literatur* 51: 1-12.
O'Neill, J. C.
    1991   *The Bible's Authority: A Portrait Gallery of Thinkers from Lessing to Bultmann.*
Ong, Walter J.
    1958   *Ramus, Method, and the Decay of Dialogue.*
Opitz, Peter
    1994   *Calvins theologische Hermeneutik.*
Orsini, G.N.G.
    1965   'Form', in *Encyclopedia of Poetry and Poetics*: 286-88.
O'Sullivan, Neil
    1992   *Alcidamas, Aristophanes and the Beginnings of Greek Stylistic Theory.*
Osumi, Yuichi
    1991   *Die Kompositionsgeschichte des Bundesbuches Exodus 20, 22b—23, 33.*
Otto, Eckart
    1988   'Vorwort', in Klaus Koch, *Studien zur alttestamentlichen und altoriental-ischen Religionsgeschichte*: 5-6.
Overbeck, Franz
    1882   'Über die Anfänge der patristischen Literatur', *HZ* 48: 417-72.
    1919   *Christentum und Kultur.*
Overholt, Thomas W.
    1982   'Prophecy: The Problem of Cross-Cultural Comparison', *Semeia* 21: 55-78.
    1996   *Cultural Anthropology and the Hebrew Bible.*
Ozment, Steven B.
    1980   *The Age of Reform, 1250–1550.*

Pagels, Elaine H.
1973   *The Johannine Gospel in Gnostic Exegesis.*
Painter, John
1987   *Theology as Hermeneutics.*
Pannenberg, Wolfhart (ed.)
1961   *Offenbarung als Geschichte.*
1990   *Metaphysics and the Idea of God* (German of chs. 1-6: 1988).
Pappas, Nicholas
1995   *Plato and the Republic.*
Parker, T.H.L.
1993   *Calvin's New Testament Commentaries* (2nd edn).
Parsons, Talcott
1937   *The Structure of Social Action.*
Patte, Daniel
1975   *Early Jewish Hermeneutic in Palestine.*
Patton, Laurie L.
1996   *Myth as Argument.*
Paul, Hermann
1891   *Grundriss der germanischen Philologie*, I (2nd edn 1901).
Peake, Arthur Samuel
1922   *The Nature of Scripture.*
1923   *Brotherhood in the Old Testament.*
Pedersen, Johannes
1926-40   *Israel.*
1934   'Passahfest und Passahlegende', *ZAW* 52: 161-75.
Penchansky, David
1995   *The Politics of Biblical Theology.*
Perkell, Christine G.
1989   *The Poet's Truth.*
Peters, John B.
1922   *The Psalms as Liturgies.*
Peters, Ted
1993   *God as Trinity: Relationality and Temporality in Divine Life.*
Pfeiffer, Robert H.
1941   *Introduction to the Old Testament.*
1961   *Religion in the Old Testament.*
Pfeiffer, Rudolf
1968   *History of Classical Scholarship From the Beginnings to the End of the Hellenistic Age.*
Pfleiderer, Otto
1878   *Geschichte der Religion.*
1902   *Das Urchristentum* (2nd edn [1st edn 1887]).
1903   *Das Christusbild des urchristlichen Glaubens in religionswissenschaftlicher Beleuchtung.*
Pipes, William H.
1951   *Say Amen Brother!*
Pizzolato, Luigi Franco
1978   *La dottrina esegetica di sant'Ambrogio.*

Plath, Margarete
 1901 'Zum Buch Tobit', *TSK* 1901: 377-414.
 1905 'Der neutestamentliche Weheruf über Jerusalem', *TSK* 78: 455-60.
 1912 'Joel, der Prophet', *RGG*, III: 582-84 (2nd edn, III, 1929: 311-13).
 1916 'Warum hat die urchristliche Gemeinde auf die Überlieferung der Judaserzählungen Wert gelegt?', *ZNW* 17: 178-88.

Platte, Ulrich
 1995 *Ethos und Politik bei Ernst Troeltsch.*

Pobee, John S.
 1979 *Toward an African Theology.*

Polzin, Robert M.
 1976 *Late Biblical Hebrew.*
 1977 *Biblical Structuralism.*

Popkin, Richard H.
 1987 *Isaac La Peyrère.*

Porter, Frank C.
 1893 'The Liberal and the Ritschlian Theology of Germany', *The Andover Review* 19: 440-61.
 1909a 'The Bearing of Historical Studies on the Religious Use of the Bible', *HTR* 2: 253-76.
 1909b 'The Place of the Sacred Book in the Christian Religion', *Yale Divinity Quarterly* 5: 257-66.

Prang, Helmut
 1968 *Formgeschichte der Dichtkunst.*

Pratt, Louise H.
 1993 *Lying and Poetry from Homer to Pindar.*

Preminger, Alex, and Edward L. Greenstein
 1986 *The Hebrew Bible in Literary Critisicm.*

Preus, James Samuel
 1969 *From Shadow to Promise.*

Prickett, Stephen
 1986 *Words and The Word: Language, Poetics and Biblical Interpretation.*
 1991 (ed.) *Reading the Text.*

Prior, Michael
 1997 *The Bible and Colonialism.*

Procksch, Otto
 1936 *Das Bekenntnis im Alten Testament.*

Puckett, David L.
 1995 *John Calvin's Exegesis of the Old Testament.*

Quell, Gottfried
 1926 *Das kultische Problem der Psalmen.*

Quinones, Ricardo
 1972 *The Renaissance Discovery of Time.*

Rabenau, Konrad von
 1970 'Hermann Gunkel auf rauhen Pfaden nach Halle', *EvT* 30: 433-44.

Rabinowitz, Isaac
 1993 *A Witness Forever.*

Rad, Gerhard von
1933   'Die falschen Propheten', *ZAW* 51: 109-20.
1934   review of Herntrich 1933, in *Christentum und Wissenschaft* 10: 188.
1936   'Die Konfessionen Jeremias', *EvT* 3: 265-76.
1938a   *Fragen der Schriftauslegung.*
1938b   *Das formgeschichtliche Problem des Hexateuch* (reprinted in von Rad, 1958).
1942/46   'Das hermeneutische Problem im Buche Genesis', *VF* 3: 43-51.
1943   'Grundprobleme einer biblischen Theologie des Alten Testaments', *TLZ* 68: 225-33.
1947   *Deuteronomiumstudien* (ET 1953).
1949   *Das erste Buche Mose.*
1951a   *Der heilige Krieg im alten Israel* (ET 1991).
1951b   'Man and the Guidance of the Hidden God in the Old Testament', *The Student World* 44: 140-47.
1952/53   'Typologische Auslegung des Alten Testaments', *EvT* 12: 17-33.
1953   'Verheissung: Zum gleichnamigen Buch Fr. Baumgärtels', *EvT* 13: 406-13.
1957-60   *Theologie des Alten Testaments* (2 vols; ET 1962–65).
1958   *Gesammelte Studien zum Alten Testament*, I (ET 1966).
1963   'Offene Fragen im Umkreis einer Theologie des Alten Testaments', *TLZ* 88: 401-16.
1964a   'Erinnerungen an Ricarda Huch', *Radio Bremen Hausbuch 1964.*
1964b   'Antwort auf Conzelmanns Fragen', *EvT* 24: 388-94.
1970   *Weisheit in Israel* (ET 1972).
1971   'Christliche Weisheit?', *EvT* 31: 150-55.
1972   *Predigten.*
1973   *Predigt-Meditationen* (ET 1977).
1976   *Erinnerungen aus der Kriegsgefangenschaft Frühjahr 1945.*
Rade, Martin
1935   'Zur deutschen Judengesetzgebung', *CW* 49: 994-97.
Raeder, Siegfried
1977   *Grammatica Theologica.*
1991   'Matthias Flacius als Bibelausleger', in J. Matesic (ed.), *Matthias Flacius Illyricus—Leben und Werk*: 13-42.
Rahn, Helmut
1969   *Morphologie der antiken Literatur.*
Rahner, Karl
1958   *Über die Schriftinspiration.*
Ramsey, Ian T.
1957   *Religious Language.*
Randall, John Herman, Jr
1963-65   *The Career of Philosophy*, 2 vols. (preliminary version of vol. III: *Philosophy after Darwin*).
Rashkow, Ilona N.
1990   *Upon the Dark Places.*
Ray, Paul H.
1997   'The Emerging Culture', *American Demographics* 19, No. 2: 28-34, 56.

Ray, Roger
1982   'What Do We Know About Bede's Commentaries?', *Recherches de théologie ancienne et médiévale* 49: 5-20.
Reicke, Bo
1953   'A Synopsis of Early Christian Preaching', in A. Fridrichsen *et al.* (eds.), *Root of the Vine*: 128-60.
Reid, Mary Esson
1959   *The Bible Read as Literature.*
Reid, Stephen Breck (ed.)
1996   *Prophets and Paradigms: Essays in Honor of Gene M. Tucker.*
Reill, Peter Hanns
1975   *The German Enlightenment and the Rise of Historicism.*
Reines, Alvin Jay
1970   *Maimonides and Abrabanel on Prophecy.*
Reitzenstein, Richard
1893   *Epigramm und Skolion.*
Reller, Jobst
1994   *Mose bar Kepha und seine Paulinenauslegung.*
Rendtorff, Rolf
1959   *Das Werden des Alten Testaments.*
1960   '"Offenbarung" im Alten Testament', *TLZ* 85: 833-38.
1980   'Die jüdische Bibel und ihre antijüdische Auslegung', in R. Rendtorff and E. Stegemann (eds.), *Auschwitz—Krise der christlichen Theologie*: 117-39.
1991   *Kanon und Theologie* (ET 1993).
Rendtorff, Trutz
1991   *Theologie in der Moderne.*
Reuss, Edouard
1856   'Hebräische Poesie', *RE*, V: 600.
1874–79 *La Bible* (German version: *Das Alte Testament*, 1892-94).
Reventlow, Henning Graf
1961   'Prophetenamt und Mittleramt', *ZTK* 58: 269-84.
1962   *Wächter über Israel.*
1963   *Liturgie und prophetisches Ich bei Jeremiah.*
1984   *The Authority of the Bible and the Rise of the Modern World* (revised from the German 1980).
1986a   *Gebet im Alten Testament.*
1986b   *Problems of Biblical Theology in the Twentieth Century* (revised from the German 1983).
1990-   *Epochen der Bibelauslegung.*
Rhees, Rush (ed.)
1984   *Recollections of Wittgenstein.*
Rian, Dagfinn
1994   '"The Insights I Have Gained": Professor Sigmund Mowinckel as he Saw Himself', in A. Tångberg (ed.), *Text and Theology*: 228-36.
Richardson, Alan
1961   *The Bible in the Age of Science.*

Richardson, Alan, and Schweitzer, W. (eds.)
1951   *Biblical Authority for Today*.
Riches, John K.
1993   *A Century of New Testament Study*.
Richter, Heinz
1955   *Studien zu Hiob*.
Ridderbos, Nic. H.
1950   *Psalmen en cultus*.
Riesenfeld, Harald
1957   *The Gospel Tradition and its Beginnings*.
Riesner, Rainer
1981   *Jesus als Lehrer*.
Ringgren, Helmer
1963   *The Faith of the Psalmists* (Swedish 1957).
1966   'Literarkritik, Formgeschichte, Überlieferungsgeschichte', *TLZ* 91: 641-
            50.
1973   *Religions of the Ancient Near East* (Swedish 1967).
Rist, John M.
1994   *Augustine*.
Ritschl, Albrecht
1870–74   *Die christliche Lehre von der Rechtfertigung und Verkündigung* (ET
            1872–1900).
Robbins, Vernon K.
1992   'Form Criticism: New Testament', *ABD*, II: 841-44.
Robert, A.
1934   'Les attaches littéraires bibliques de Prov. I-IX', *RB* 43: 42-68, 172-204,
            374-84.
Robert, A., and A. Tricot
1939   *Initiation biblique* (3rd edn 1954; ET, revised, 1960).
Robertson, John M.
1900   *Christianity and Mythology*.
Robinson, H. Wheeler
1913   *The Religous Ideas of the Old Testament*.
1923   'The Psychology and Metaphysics of "Thus Saith Yahweh"', *ZAW* 41:
            1-15.
1925   'Hebrew Psychology', in A. Peake (ed.), *The People and the Book*: 353-
            82.
1936   'The Hebrew Conception of Corporate Personality', in Hempel *et al.*
            (eds.), 1936: 49-62 (reprinted in *Corporate Personality in Ancient Israel*,
            1981).
1939   *Suffering: Human and Divine*.
1942   *Redemption and Revelation*.
1946   *Inspiration and Revelation in the Old Testament*.
1955   *The Cross in the Old Testament*.
Robinson, James M.
1957   *The Problem of History in Mark*.
Robinson, James M., and John B. Cobb, Jr (eds.)
1964   *The New Hermeneutics* (German 1965).

Robinson, Theodore H.
1922 'The Message of Amos and its Bearing on Modern Problems', *Baptist Quarterly* 1: 148-57.
1947 *The Poetry of the Old Testament*.
Roebuck, Janet
1974 *The Shaping of Urban Society*.
Roeder, Günther
1923 *Urkunden zur Religion des alten Ägypten*.
Rogers, Jack B., and McKim, Donald K.
1979 *The Authority and Interpretation of the Bible*.
Rogerson, John W.
1974 *Myth in Old Testament Interpretation*.
1978 *Anthropology and the Old Testament*.
1985 *Old Testament Criticism in the Nineteenth Century: England and Germany*.
1988 'The Old Testament', in J. Rogerson *et al.* (eds.), *The Study and Use of the Bible*: 3-150.
1992 *W.M.L. de Wette: Founder of Modern Biblical Cristicism*.
1995a *The Bible and Criticism in Victorian Britain*.
1995b 'Synchrony and Diachrony in the Work of DeWette and Its Importance for Today,' in de Moor: 145-58.
Rollmann, Hans
1981 'Zwei Briefe Hermann Gunkels an Adolf Jülicher', *ZTK* 78: 276-88.
Rondeau, Marie-Josèphe
1985 *Les commentaires patristiques du Psautier*, II.
Rosch, Eleanor
1978 'Principles of Categorization', in E. Rosch and B. Lloyd (eds.), *Cognition and Categorization*: 27-48.
Rosenberg, Bruce A.
1988 *Can These Bones Live?* (2nd edn).
Rosenblatt, Jason P.
1994 *Torah and Law in Paradise Lost*.
Rosenbloom, Noah R.
1965 *Luzzato's Ethico-Psychological Interpretation of Judaism*.
Rosenstock-Huessy, Eugen
1924 *Angewandte Seelenkunde*.
Rosenthal, Erwin I.J.
1971 *Studia Semitica*, I.
Rosenzweig, Franz
1921 *Der Stern der Erlösung* (ET 1972).
1937 *Kleinere Schriften* (cf. ET *Scripture and Tradition*, 1994).
Rost, Leonhard
1926 *Die Überlieferung von der Thronnachfolge Davids* (ET 1982).
Røstvig, Maren-Sofie
1994 *Configurations*.
Roth, Cecil
1965 *The Jews in the Renaissance*.

Rothstein, J.W.
    1888   *Das Bundesbuch.*
Rottzoll, Dirk U.
    1996   *Abraham ibn Esras Kommentar zur Urgeschichte.*
Rowley, H.H.
    1939   *Israel's Mission to the World.*
    1944   *The Relevance of the Bible.*
    1946   *The Re-Discovery of the Old Testament.*
    1950   (ed.), *Studies in Old Testament Prophecy Presented to Professor
                Theodore H. Robinson.*
    1951   *Submission in Suffering and Other Essays on Eastern Thought.*
    1952a   *The Biblical Doctrine of Election.*
    1952b   *The Servant of the Lord and Other Essays.*
    1953   *The Unity of the Bible.*
    1956a   *Prophecy and Religion in Ancient China and Israel.*
    1956b   *The Faith of Israel.*
    1963   *From Moses to Qumran.*
    1967   *Worship in Ancient Israel.*
Runia, David T.
    1995   *Philo and the Church Fathers.*
Russell, Bertrand
    1945   *A History of Western Philosophy.*
Russell, D.A.
    1981   *Criticism in Antiquity.*
Russell, D.A., and Wilson, N.G.
    1981   *Menander Rhetor.*
Russell, Paul A.
    1986   *Lay Theology in the Reformation.*
Sæbø, Magne (ed.)
    1996   *Hebrew Bible/Old Testament: The History of its Interpretation,* I.
Sáenz-Badillos, A.
    1987   'The Biblical Foundation of Jewish Law According to Maimonides', in
                N. Rakover (ed.), *Maimonides as Codifier of Jewish Law*: 61-73.
Saintyves, P. [Nourry, Emile]
    1922   *Essai de folklore biblique.*
Saiving Goldstein, Valerie
    1960   'The Human Situation: A Feminine View', *JR* 40: 100-112.
Samartha, S.J.
    1994   'Religion, Language and Reality: Towards a Relational Hermeneutics',
                BibInt 2: 340-62.
Sandbach, F.H.
    1975   *The Stoics.*
Sanders, E.P.
    1969   *The Tendencies of the Synoptic Gospels.*
Sarna, Nahum M.
    1971   'Hebrew and Bible Studies in Mediaeval Spain', in R.D. Barnett (ed.),
                The Sephardi Heritage, I: 323-366.

1993   'Abraham Ibn Ezra as an Exegete', in I. Twersky and J. Harris (eds.), *Rabbi Abraham Ibn Ezra*, I: 1-27.

Sawyer, John F.A.
1967   'Context of Situation and *Sitz im Leben*', *Proceedings of the Newcastle upon Tyne Philosophical Society*, I: 137-47.

Schade, Ludwig
1910   *Die Inspirationslehre des heiligen Hieronymus.*

Schäublin, Christoph
1974   *Untersuchungen zu Methode und Herkunft der antiochenischen Exegese.*
1992   'Zur paganen Prägung des christlichen Exegese', in J. van Oort and U. Wickert (eds.), *Christliche Exegese zwischen Nicaea und Chalcedon*: 148-73.

Schelkle, Karl Hermann
1949   *Die Passion Jesu in der Verkündigung des Neuen Testaments.*

Schell, Herman
1889   *Katholische Dogmatik*, I.

Scherer, Wilhelm
1887   *Geschichte der deutschen Literatur* (4th edn).
1888   *Poetik.*

Scherpe, Klaus R.
1968   *Gattungspoetik im 18. Jahrhundert.*

Schiappa, Edward
1993   'The Beginnings of Greek Rhetorical Theory', in D. Zarefsky (ed.), *Rhetorical Movement*: 5-33.

Schick, Eduard
1940   *Formgeschichte und Synoptikerexegese.*

Schlageter, Johannes
1975   'Hermeneutik der Heiligen Schrift bei Wilhelm von Ockham', *Franziskanische Studien* 57: 230-83.

Schleiermacher, Friedrich
1959   *Hermeneutik.*

Schlieben, Reinhard
1979   *Cassiodors Psalmenexegese.*

Schlink, Edmund
1957   'Die Struktur der dogmatischen Aussage als oekumenisches Problem', *KD* 3: 251-306.

Schmid, Hans Heinrich
1968   *Gerechtigkeit als Weltordnung.*

Schmid, J.
1959   'Exegese', III, 6, *Lexikon für Theologie und Kirche*, III: 1287-90.

Schmidt, Hans
1903   review of Erbt 1902, in *Deutsche Literaturzeitung* 24: 393-97.
1907   *Jona.*
1912   *Die religiöse Lyrik im Alten Testament.*
1923   (ed.), *Eucharisterion* (Festschrift for H. Gunkel), II.
1924a   *Warum haben wir den Krieg verloren?*
1924b   'Das Alkoholverbot in Amerika und die Kirche', *TBl* 3: 31-34.
1927   *Die Thronfahrt Jahves.*

1928   *Das Gebet des Angeklagten im Alten Testament.*

1935   *Führer und Gefolgschaft nach dem Regentenspiegel Martin Luthers vom Jahre 1534.*

1940   'Georg Wobbermin zum 70. Geburstag am 27. Oktober 1939', *ZKG* 19: 163-64.

Schmidt, Johannes

1967   'Karl Friedrich Stäudlin—ein Wegbereiter der formgeschichtlichen Erforschung des Alten Testaments', *EvT* 27: 200-18.

Schmidt, Karl Ludwig

1928   'Formgeschichte', *RGG*, 2nd edn, II: 638-40.

1933a   'Allerlei Stimmen' *TBl* 12: 345-47.

1933b   'Luther und Hitler' (a report on essays), *TBl* 12: 347f.

Schmitt, Carl

1922   *Politische Theologie* (2nd edn 1934).

Schmitt, Götz

1964   'El Berit-mitra', *ZAW* 76: 325-27.

Schmökel, Hartmut

1934   *Jahwe und die Fremdvölker.*

1936   *Altes Testament und heutiges Judentum.*

Schnackenburg, Rudolf

1963   'Zur formgeschichtlichen Methode in der Evangelienforschung', *ZKT* 83: 16-32.

Schneider, John R.

1990   *Philip Melanchthon's Rhetorical Construal of Biblical Authority.*

Schoeps, Hans-Joachim

1977   *Deutsche Geistesgeschichte der Neuzeit*, I.

Schökel: see Alonso Schökel.

Scholder, Klaus

1977–85   *Die Kirchen und das Dritte Reich* (2 vols.; ET 1977).

Schottroff, Willy

1974   'Soziologie und Altes Testament', *VF* 19, No. 2: 46-66.

1984   'Goethe als Bibelwissenschaftler', *EvT* 44: 463-85.

Schreckenberg, H.

1966   'Exegese I (heidnisch, Griechen u. Römer)', *RAC*, VI: 1174-94.

Schreiner, Susan E.

1994   *Where Shall Wisdom Be Found?*

Schultz, Hermann

1869   *Alttestamentliche Theologie*, I (ET 1892).

Schulz, Hermann

1987   *Leviten im vorstaatlichen Israel und im mittleren Osten.*

Schürmann, Heinz

1960   'Die vorösterlichen Anfänge der Logientradition', in H. Ristow and K. Matthias (eds.), *Der historische Jesus und der kerygmatische Christus*: 342-70.

Schuster, Hermann

1935   *Das Alte Testament heute.*

Schwarzbach, Bertram Eugene

1971   *Voltaire's Old Testament Criticism.*

Scott, Ernest F.
 1907   *The Apologetic of the New Testament.*
 1928   'The Limitations of the Historical Method', in S. Case (ed.), *Studies in Early Christianity*: 3-18.
 1931   *The Kingdom of God in the New Testament.*
 1938   *The Validity of the Gospel Record.*
 1939   *The Book of Revelation.*
Scott, R.B.Y.
 1944   *The Relevance of the Prophets.*
 1958   *The Psalms as Christian Praise.*
Seebass, Horst
 1974   *Hermeneutik.*
Seeberg, Alfred
 1903   *Der Katechismus der Urchristenheit.*
Seeligmann, I.L.
 1953   'Vorraussetzungen der Midraschexegese', in *Congress Volume, Copenhagen 1953* (VTSup, 1): 150-81.
 1961   'Aetiological Elements in Biblical Historiography' (Hebrew), *Zion* 26: 141-69.
Segal, M.H.
 1971   *Parshanut ha-Miqra'* (2nd edn).
Segovia, Fernando F., and Mary Ann Tolbert, (eds.)
 1995   *Reading From this Place* (2 vols.).
Sehmsdorf, Eberhard
 1971   *Die Prophetenauslegung bei J. G. Eichhorn.*
Seidel, Hans Werner
 1993   *Die Erforschung des Alten Testaments in der katholischen Theologie seit der Jahrhundertwende.*
Seierstad, Ivar P.
 1946   *Die Offenbarungserlebnisse der Propheten Amos, Jesaja und Jeremia.*
Sellars, W.Y.
 1889   *The Roman Poets of the Republic* (3rd edn).
Selvidge, Marla J.
 1996   *Notorious Voices: Feminist Biblical Interpretation, 1500-1920.*
Selwyn, Edward Gordon
 1946   *The First Epistle of Saint Peter.*
Seybold, Klaus
 1990   *Introducing the Psalms* (revision of the German 1986).
Shapiro, Barbara J.
 1983   *Probability and Certainty in Seventeenth-Century England.*
Sharif, M.M. (ed.)
 1963-66   *A History of Muslim Philosophy.*
Shelley, Bryan
 1994   *Shelley and Scripture.*
Shepard, Robert S.
 1991   *God's People in the Ivory Tower: Religion in the Early American University.*

Shuger, Debora K.
   1988   *Sacred Rhetoric.*
Shunary, Jonathan
   1982   'Salmon ben Yeruham's Commentary on the Book of Psalms', *JQR* 73:
             155-75.
Shupak, Nili
   1993   *Where can Wisdom be Found?*
Simmel, Georg
   1908   *Soziologie.*
Simon, Uriel
   1991   *Four Approaches to the Book of Psalms* (revision of the Hebrew 1982).
Simonetti, Manlio
   1994   *Biblical Interpretation in the Early Church* (Italian 1981).
Simpson, D.C. (ed.)
   1926   *The Psalmists.*
Simpson, James
   1995   *Sciences and the Self in Medieval Poetry.*
Sinn, Gunnar
   1941   *Christologie und Existenz.*
Skinner, John
   1922   *Prophecy and Religion.*
Smalley, Beryl
   1952   *The Study of the Bible in the Middle Ages.*
Smend, Rudolf
   1958   *W.M.L. de Wette's Arbeit am Alten und Neuen Testament.*
   1988   'Die älteren Herausgeber der Zeitschrift für die alttestamentliche Wissen-
             schaft', *ZAW* 100, No. 3, Supplement: 2-21.
   1989   *Deutsche Alttestamentler in drei Jahrhunderten.*
   1991   *Epochen der Bibelkritik.*
   1994   'Karl Budde (1850-1935)', in *Language, Theology, and the Bible: Essays*
             in Honour of James Barr: 357-69.
   1997   'Rad, Gerhard von', *TRE*, XXVIII: 89-91.
Smid, Marikje
   1990   *Deutscher Protestantismus und Judentum 1932/1933.*
Smith, Brian K.
   1994   'The Veda and the Authority of Class', in L. Patton (ed.), *Authority,*
             Anxiety, and Canon: 67-93.
Smith, George Adam
   1927   'The Hebrew Genius As Exhibited in the Old Testament', in E. Bevan
             and C. Singer (eds.), *The Legacy of Israel*: 1-28.
Smith, J.M. Powis
   1922   *The Religion of the Psalms.*
Smith, Jonathan Z.
   1985   'What a Difference a Difference Makes', in J. Neusner and E. Frerichs
             (eds.), *'To See Ourselves as Others See Us'*: 3-48.
Smith, Theosophus H.
   1994   *Conjuring Culture: Biblical Formations of Black America.*

Smith, W. Robertson
  1881   *The Old Testament in the Jewish Church.*
  1882   *The Prophets of Israel.*
  1889   *Lectures on the Religion of the Semites.*
Smith-Christopher, Daniel (ed.)
  1995   *Text and Experience.*
Snaith, Norman H.
  1934   *Studies in the Psalter.*
  1946   *The Distinctive Ideas of Old Testament.*
Snyder, Jane McIntosh
  1989   *The Woman and the Lyre.*
Soiron, Thaddaeus
  1925   *Das Evangelium als Lebensform des Menschen.*
Sokolow, Moshe
  1984   'Saadia Gaon's Progelomenon to Psalms', *PAAJR* 51: 131-74.
Sölle, Dorothee
  1973   *Leiden.*
Sontheimer, Kurt
  1964   *Antidemokratisches Denken in der Weimarer Republik* (2nd edn).
Spellman, Lynne
  1995   *Substance and Separation in Aristotle.*
Sperling, S. David, *et al.*
  1992   *Students of the Covenant.*
Spicq, P.C. le
  1944   *Esquisse d'une histoire de l'exégèse latine au Moyen Age.*
Staerk, Willy
  1894   *Das Deuteronomium.*
  1920   *Lyrik* (2nd edn [1st edn 1911]).
Stamm, Johann Jakob
  1956   'Jesus Christus und das Alte Testament', *EvT* 16: 387-94.
Stanton, Elizabeth Cady, *et al.*
  1895–98   *The Woman's Bible.*
Stanton, William
  1960   *The Leopard's Spots.*
Staub, Jacob J.
  1982   *The Creation of the World According to Gersonides.*
Stauffer, Ethelbert
  1929   *Grundbegriffe einer Morphologie des neutestamentlichen Denkens.*
  1933   *Unser Glaube und unsere Geschichte.*
  1941   *Theologie des Neuen Testaments* (ET 1955).
  1952   'Der Stand der neutestamentlichen Forschung', in L. Hennig (ed.), *Theologie und Liturgie*: 35-105.
  1959   *Die Botschaft Jesu damals und heute.*
  1960   'Offener Brief von Erlangen nach Erlangen', *Deutsches Pfarrerblatt* 60: 294-98.
  1961   *Jesus, Paulus und wir.*
Steffens, Lincoln
  1926   *Moses in Red.*

Stegemann, Wolfgang (ed.)
1992   *Kirche und Nationalsozialismus* (2nd edn).
Stegmüller, Friedrich
1950-61   *Repertorium biblicum medii aevi* (7 vols.)
1951   'Ein neuer Johanneskommentar—des Petrus Aureoli', *Franziskanische Studien* 33: 207-19.
Stein, Edmund
1935   *Alttestamentliche Bibelkritik in der späthellenistischen Literatur.*
Steinberg, Theodore L.
1995   'The Sidneys and the Psalms', *Studies in Philology* 92: 1-17.
Steiner, Heinrich
1989   *Das Verhältnis Tertullians zur antiken Paideia.*
Steinitz, Wolfgang
1934   *Der Parallelismus in der finnisch-karelischen Volksdichtung* (FF Communications, 115).
Steinsaltz, Adin
1976   *The Essential Talmud.*
Stendahl, Krister
1954   *The School of Matthew.*
Sterling, Gregory E.
1992   *Historiography and Self-Definition.*
Stern, David
1988   'Midrash and Indeterminacy', *Critical Inquiry* 15: 132-61.
Stevenson, Rosemary J.
1993   *Language, Thought and Representation.*
Stinespring, W.F.
1962   'Irony and Satire', *IDB*, II: 726-28.
Stock, Brian
1996   *Augustine the Reader: Meditation, Self-Knowledge, and the Ethics of Interpretation.*
Stowers, Stanley Kent
1981   *The Diatribe and Paul's Letter to the Romans.*
Strafforello, Gustavo
1883   *La sapienza del mondo* (3 vols.).
Strauss, Gerhard
1959   *Schriftgebrauch, Schriftauslegung und Schriftbeweis bei Augustin.*
Strenski, Ivan
1987   *Four Theories of Myth in Twentieth-Century History.*
Strickman, H. Norman
1988   'Foreword', in H. Strickman and A. Silver (eds.), *Ibn Ezra's Commentary on the Pentateuch: Genesis (Bereshit)*: x-xxii.
Stuermann, Walter E.
1962   *Logic and Faith.*
Stuhlmacher, Peter
1986   *Vom Verstehen des Neuen Testaments* (2nd edn).
Stummer, Friedrich
1922   *Sumerisch-akkadische Parallen zum Aufbau alttestamentlicher Psalmen.*

1924 'Die Psalmengattungen im Lichte der altorientalischen Hymnenliteratur', *Journal of the Society of Oriental Research* 8: 123-34.

Stylianopoulos, Theodore
1975 *Justin Martyr and the Mosaic Law*.

Suggate, Alan M.
1987 *William Temple and Christian Social Ethics Today*.

Sullivan, Mark W.
1967 *Apuleian Logic*.

Süss, René
1991 *Een genadeloos bestaan*.

Swearingen, C. Jan
1991 *Rhetoric and Irony*.

Sweet, Louis Matthew
1914 *The Study of the English Bible*.

Szörényi, Andreas
1961 *Psalmen und Kult im Alten Testament*.

Talmage, Frank Ephraim
1975 *David Kimhi*.

Tanner, Kathryn
1988 *God and Creation in Christian Theology: Tyranny or Empowerment*.

Taylor, Charles
1989 *Sources of the Self*.

Temple, William
1934 *Nature, Man and God*.

Terrien, Samuel
1952 *The Psalms and their Meaning for Today*.

Thadden, Rudolf von (ed.)
1978 *Die Krise des Liberalismus zwischen den Weltkriegen*.

Thrams, Peter
1986 *Die Morallehre Demokrits und die Ethik des Protagoras*.

Thurman, Robert A.
1988 'Vajra Hermeneutics', in *Buddhist Hermeneutics*: 119-48.

Tilgner, Wolfgang
1966 *Volksnomostheologie und Schöpfungsglaube*.

Tirosh-Rothschild, Hava
1991 *Between Worlds*.

Tobin, Thomas H.
1983 *The Creation of Man: Philo and the History of Interpretation*.

Torjesen, Karen Jo
1986 *Hermeneutical Procedure and Theological Method in Origen's Exegesis*.

Torrance, Thomas F.
1990 *Karl Barth, Biblical and Evangelical Theologian*.

Toulmin, Stephen
1990 *Cosmopolis*.

Traina, Robert A.
1952 *Methodical Bible Study: A New Approach to Hermeneutics*.

Treip, Mindele Anne
1995 *Allegorical Poetics and the Epic*.

Trible, Phyllis
    1984   *Texts of Terror.*
Trigg, Joseph Wilson
    1983   *Origen.*
Troeltsch, Ernest
    1912–22   *Gesammelte Schriften* (vol. I, ET: *The Social Teachings of the Christian Church*, 1950).
Tsevat, Matitiahu
    1955   *A Study of the Language of the Biblical Psalms.*
Tuana, Nancy
    1992   *Woman and the History of Philosophy.*
    1994   (ed.), *Feminist Interpretations of Plato.*
Tucker, Gene M.
    1971   *Form Criticism of the Old Testament.*
Turner, Denys
    1995   *Eros and Allegory.*
Twersky, Isadore
    1972   *Maimonides Reader.*
    1980   *Introduction to the Code of Maimonides (Mishneh Torah).*
Ueding, Gert, and Bernd Steinbrink
    1986   *Grundriss der Rhetorik* (2nd edn).
Uhland, Ludwig
    1866-73   *Schriften zur Geschichte der Dichtung und Sage.*
Urbach, Ephraim E.
    1975   *The Sages.*
Vajda, Georges
    1971   *Deux commentaires Karaïtes sur l'Ecclésiaste.*
Vatz, Richard E.
    1973   'The Myth of the Rhetorical Situation', *Philosophy and Rhetoric* 6: 154-61.
Vaux, Roland de
    1960   *Les institutions de l'Ancien Testament*, II.
Vawter, Bruce
    1972   *Biblical Inspiration.*
Vellanickal, Matthew
    1995   'A *Dhvani* Interpretation of the Bible', in Smith-Christopher: 195-209.
Vermes, Geza
    1983   *Scripture and Tradition in Judaism* (2nd edn; virtually equal to the 1st edn 1961).
Vischer, Wilhelm
    1935   *Das Christuszeugnis des Alten Testaments.*
Vogelsanger, Peter
    1994   *Zürich und sein Fraumünster.*
Volz, Paul
    1912   *Das Neujahrsfest Jahwes.*
    1922   *Der Prophet Jeremia.*
    1932   *Der Kampf um das Alte Testament.*

Vos, J.S.
1984   'Antijudaismus/Antisemitismus im "Theologischen Wörterbuch zum N. T."', *NedTTs* 38: 89-110.
Votaw, Clyde Weber
1915   'The Gospels and Contemporary Biographies', *AJT* 19: 45-73, 217-49.
Vriezen, Th. C.
1954   *Hoofdlijnen der theologie van het Oude Testament* (2nd edn; [ET 1958]).
Wach, Joachim
1926-33   *Das Verstehen* (3 vols.).
Wainwright, Arthur W.
1993   *Mysterious Apocalypse.*
Wainwright, Elaine
1997   'Rachel Weeping for her Children: Intertextuality and the Biblical Testaments', in A. Brenner and C. Fontaine (eds.), *A Feminist Companion to Reading the Bible*: 452-69.
Waldow, Hans Eberhard von
1953   'Anlass und Hintergrund der Verkündigung des Deuterojesajas', (dissertation Bonn).
1960   '*...denn ich erlöse dich*'.
1963   *Der traditionsgeschichtliche Hintergrund der prophetischen Gerichtsreden.*
Walker, Rollin H.
1938   *The Modern Message of the Psalms.*
Waller, Gary
1994   *Edmund Spenser.*
Wallis, Gerhard
1994   *Mein Freund hatte einen Weinberg.*
Wallis, Louis
1912   *Sociological Study of the Bible.*
1935   *God and the Social Process.*
1942   *The Bible is Human.*
Walsh, P.G. (ed.)
1990–91   *Cassiodorus: Explanation of the Psalms* (3 vols.).
Wan Sze-Kar
1995   'Allegorical Interpretation East and West', in Smith-Christopher: 154-79.
Ward, Graham
1995   *Barth, Derrida and the Language of Theology.*
Waterman, Leroy
1947   'Biblical Studies in a New Setting', *JBL* 66: 1-14.
Watson, Francis
1994   *Text, Church and World.*
Watson, George
1973   *The Literary Critics* (2nd edn).
Watts, James W.
1992   *Psalms and Story.*
Wehrli, Max
1951   *Allgemeine Literaturwissenschaft.*

Weinberg, Bernard
1961   *A History of Literary Criticism in the Italian Renaissance.*
Weinel, Heinrich
1900   *Die Bildersprache Jesu.*
1903   *Die Nichtkirchlichen und die freie Theologie.*
1904   *Die Gleichnisse Jesu.*
1912   *Jesus.*
1914   *Jesus im 19. Jahrhundert* (covering also the early part of the twentieth century).
1920   *Die Bergpredigt.*
1928   *Biblische Theologie des Neuen Testaments* (4th edn).
1933   *Die deutsche evangelische Kirche.*
1934   'Thüringen und der Friede in der Kirche', *CW* 48: 169-72.
Weippert, Manfred
1972   '"Heiliger Krieg" im Israel und Assyrien. Kritische Anmerkungen zu Gerhard von Rads Konzept des "Heiligen Krieges im alten Israel"', *ZAW* 84: 460-93.
Weiser, Artur
1925   *Die Bedeutung des Alten Testaments für den Religionsunterricht.*
1931   *Glaube und Geschichte im Alten Testament.*
1934   'Das Alte Testament in der christlich-völkischen Gegenwart', *Deutsche Theologie* 1: 47-56.
1935   *Die Psalmen* (considerably revised in 1950, less so in 1959, very little thereafter; ET 1962).
1939   *Einleitung in das Alte Testament.*
1941   'Paul Volz', *Deutsche Theologie* 8: 79-89.
1949a   2nd edn of 1939 (ET: *The Old Testament*, 1961).
1949b   *Das Buch der zwölf kleinen Propheten*, I.
1950   3rd edn of 1935.
Weiss, Johannes
1908   *Die Aufgaben der neutestamentlichen Wissenschaft in der Gegenwart.*
1910   *Jesus im Glauben des Urchristentums.*
1912   'Literaturgeschichte des Neuen Testament', *RGG*, III: 2175-215.
1914   *Das Urchristentum* (ET 1937).
Weiss, Meir
1961   'Wege der neuen Dichtungswissenschaft in ihrer Anwendung auf die Psalmenforschung', *Biblica* 42: 255-302.
1963   'Einiges über die Bauformen des Erzählens in der Bibel', *VT* 13: 456-75.
Welch, Adam C.
1953   *Prophet and Priest in Old Israel.*
Wellek, René
1955–86   *A History of Modern Criticism: 1750–1950* (6 vols.).
Wellhausen, Julius
1889   *Die Composition des Hexateuch* (2nd edn).
1897   *Israelitische und jüdische Geschichte* (3rd edn).
1901   4th edn of 1897.
1905   *Einleitung in die drei ersten Evangelien.*

Wendel, Adolf
 1931   *Das freie Laiengebet im vorexilischen Israel.*
 1935   *Glauben und Volkstum im Alten Testament.*
 1936   *Predigten zu nationalen Tagen und Fragen.*
Wendland, Paul
 1896   'Die Therapeuten', *Jahrbücher für classische Philologie*, Suppl. XXII: 693-772.
 1904   'Soter', *ZNW* 5: 335-53.
 1912   *Die urchristlichen Literaturformen* (bound together with *Die hellen-istisch-römische Kultur...*, 2nd edn).
Wengert, Timothy J., and M. Patrick Graham
 1997   *Philip Melanchthon (1497–1560) and the Commentary.*
Werblowsky, R.J. Zwi
 1976   *Beyond Tradition and Modernity.*
Wernle, Paul
 1899   *Die synoptische Frage.*
Westermann, Claus
 1950   'Biblische Ästhetik', *Zeichen der Zeit* 4: 277-89
 1952/53a 'Bruderschaft im alten Gottesvolk', *Quatember* 17: 136-43.
 1952/53b 'Christus als Antwort auf Hiob', *Quatember* 17: 238-39.
 1954a   *Das Loben Gottes in den Psalmen* (ET 1965 etc.).
 1954b   'Das Totenliebespaar', *Zeichen der Zeit* 8: 303-05.
 1954c   'Struktur und Geschichte der Klage im Alten Testament', *ZAW* 66: 44-80.
 1955a   'Zur Auslegung des Alten Testaments', in H. Urner (ed.), *Vergegen-wärtigung*: 88-100.
 1955b   'Wort und Dichtung im Neuen Testament', *Neue deutsche Hefte* 55: 912-22.
 1956a   'Das Alte Testament—höchst aktuell', in H. Giessen (ed.), *Der mündige Christ*: 338-45.
 1956b   *Der Aufbau des Buches Hiob* (ET 1981).
 1956c   'Die Klage', *Zeitwende* 27: 164-71.
 1957a   *Tausend Jahre und ein Tag* (ET 1962).
 1957b   'Der Segen Gottes', *Zeitwende* 28: 525-36.
 1958   (ed.), *Verkündigung des Kommenden.*
 1959/60   'A Jewish and Christian Book', *LW* 6: 11-27 (German in *Wenn man dich fragt*, 1958).
 1960a   (ed.), *Probleme alttestamentlicher Hermeneutik* (ET 1963).
 1960b   *Umstrittene Bibel* (ET 1969, 1991).
 1960c   *Grundformen prophetischer Rede* (ET 1967, new edn 1991).
 1962   *Abriss der Bibelkunde* (4th edn 1966, ET 1967).
 1963   'God and His People: The Church in the Old Testament', *Int* 17: 259-70.
 1964   *Forschung am Alten Testament*, I.
 1973   'Anthropologische und theologische Aspekte des Gebets in den Psalmen', *Liturgisches Jahrbuch* 23: 83-96.
 1974a   *Forschung am Alten Testament*, II.
 1974b   'The Role of the Lament in the Theology of the Old Testament', *Int* 28: 20-38.
 1975a   *Predigten.*

| 1975b | 'Religion und Kult', *Zeitwende* 46: 77-86. |

1975b   'Religion und Kult', *Zeitwende* 46: 77-86.

1980   'Die Zukunft der Religionen', in T. Sundermeier (ed.), *Fides pro mundi vita*: 151-58.

1981   *Genesis*, II (ET 1985).

1984   *Ausgewählte Psalmen* (ET 1989).

1987   *Prophetische Heilsworte im Alten Testament* (ET 1991).

1996   *Das mündliche Wort*.

Westermarck, Edward

1912   *The Origin and Development of Moral Ideas*, I (2nd edn.).

Wheeler, Alice Jacoby

1966   'Society History in Eighteenth-Century Scotland' (dissertation Emory).

Wheelright, Philip (ed.)

1966   *The Presocratics*.

Whitehead, Alfred North

1925   *Science and the Modern World*.

Whitman, Walt

1961–   *The Collected Writings*.

Whyte, Lancet Law

1951   *Aspects of Form*.

Wians, William (ed.)

1996   *Aristotle's Philosophical Development*.

Wicks, Robert

1994   *Hegel's Theory of Aesthetic Judgment*.

Widengren, Geo

1936   *The Accadian and Hebrew Psalms of Lamentation as Religious Documents* (revised 1937).

1948   *Literary and Psychological Aspects of the Hebrew Prophets*.

1955   *Sakrales Königtum im Alten Testament und im Judentum*.

Wieman, Henry N.

1926   *Religious Experience and Scientific Method*.

Wilamowitz-Moellendorff, Ulrich von

1900   'Asianismus und Atticismus', *Hermes* 35: 1-52.

1905   *Die griechische und lateinische Literatur und Sprache* (*Kultur der Gegenwart*, ed. P. Hinneburg, I/VIII).

1959   *Euripides Herakles* (3 vols.; = 1895, but with different arrangement).

Wilder, Amos N.

1939   *Eschatology and Ethics in the Teaching of Jesus* (2nd edn 1950).

1940   *The Spiritual Aspects of the New Poetry*.

1946   'Equivalents of Natural Law in the Teaching of Jesus', *JR* 26: 125-35.

1952   *Modern Poetry and the Christian Tradition*.

1954   *Otherworldliness in the New Testament*.

1955   *New Testament Faith for Today*.

1956   'Scholars, Theologians, and Ancient Rhetoric', *JBL* 75: 1-11.

1964a   *Early Christian Rhetoric* (= *The Language of the Gospel*; see 2nd edn 1971).

1964b   'The Word as Address and the Word as Meaning', in J. Robinson and J. Cobb: 198-218.

1969   *The New Voice: Religion, Literature, Hermeneutics*.

1971   reissue of 1964a (page numbers are lowered by eight; new 'Introduction').
1976   *Theopoetic.*
1978   *Imagining the Real.*
1982   *Jesus' Parables and the War of Myths.*
1991   *The Bible and the Literary Critic* (51-72 = *JR* 64, 1984: 432-51).
Willi, Thomas
1971   *Herder's Beitrag zum Verstehen des Alten Testaments.*
Williamson, Ronald
1989   *Jews in the Hellenistic World: Philo.*
Wilson, Gerald Henry
1985   *The Editing of the Hebrew Psalter.*
Wimbush, Vincent L.
1985   'Biblical-Historical Study as Liberation: Toward an Afro-Christian Hermeneutic', *JRT* 42, No. 2: 9-21.
Winckler, Hugo
1901   *Himmels- und Weltbild der Babylonier.*
Wittenmyer, Annie
1885   *The Women of the Reformation.*
Wittgenstein, Ludwig
1953   *Philosophical Investigations.*
Wogue, L.
1881   *Histoire de la Bible et de l'exégèse biblique.*
Wolde, Ellen J. van
1989   *A Semiotic Analysis of Genesis 2-3.*
1995   'Telling and Retelling,' in de Moor: 227-44.
1996   *Stories of the Beginning* (Dutch 1995).
Wolf, Hans Heinrich
1958   *Die Einheit des Bundes.*
Wolff, Hans Walter
1934   'Die Begründungen der prophetischen Heils- und Unheilssprüche', *ZAW* 52: 1-22.
1956   'Zur Hermeneutik des Alten Testaments', *EvT* 16: 337-70.
1960   'Das Geschichtsverständnis der alttestamentlichen Prophetie', *EvT* 20: 218-35.
1962   *Frieden ohne Ende.*
1963a   'Das wissenschaftliche Werk von Friedrich Horst', *TLZ* 88: 313-18.
1963b   'Das Alte Testament und das Problem der existentiellen Interpretation', *EvT* 23: 1-17.
Wölfflin, Heinrich
1932   *Principles of Art History.*
Woodbridge, John D.
1982   *Biblical Authority.*
Wright, G. Ernest
1944   *The Challenge of Israel's Faith.*
1950   *The Old Testament Against its Environment.*
1951   'From the Bible to the Modern World', in Richardson and Schweitzer: 219-39.

1952	*God Who Acts*.
1954	(ed.), *The Biblical Doctrine of Man in Society*.
1960	*The Rule of God*.
1962	'The Lawsuit of God: A Form-Critical Study of Deut. 32', in *Israel's Prophetic Heritage* (Festschrift for J. Muilenburg): 26-67.
1969	*The Old Testament and Theology*.

Wundt, Wilhelm

| 1905 | *Völkerpsychologie*. II. *Mythus und Religion*, I. |

Wünsche, August

| 1906a | *Die Schönheit der Bibel*. I. *Die Schönheit des Alten Testaments* (vol. II on the New Testament did not appear). |
| 1906b | *Die Bildersprache des Alten Testaments*. |

Würthwein, Ernst

| 1947 | 'Amos 5, 21-27', *TLZ* 72: 143-51. |
| 1952 | 'Der Ursprung der prophetischen Gerichtsrede', *ZTK* 49: 1-16. |

Wyatt, Peter

| 1996 | *Jesus Christ and Creation in the Theology of John Calvin*. |

Yeo, Eileen Janes

| 1996 | *The Contest for Social Science*. |

Young, Frances M.

| 1993 | *Virtuoso Theology*. |
| 1997 | *Biblical Exegesis and the Formation of Christian Culture*. |

Zimmerli, Walther

1933	'Zur Struktur der alttestamentlichen Weisheit', *ZAW* 51: 177-204.
1940	'*Ein* Gotteswort, zwei Testamente', *Grundriss* 2: 129-37.
1941	'Vom Auslegen des AT. in der Kirche', *VF* 2: 7-22.
1943a	*1. Mose 1-11*.
1943b	'Der Prophet im Alten Testament und im Islam', *Evangelisches Missions-Magazin* 87: 137-47, 168-79.
1949a	*Das Menschenbild des Alten Testaments*.
1949b	'Wem gehört das Alte Testament?', *Zeichen der Zeit* 3: 369-75.
1952/53	'Verheissung und Erfüllung', *EvT* 12: 34-59.
1954	'Das neue Israel: Israel als gemeinsames Werk westlichen und östlichen Judentums', *Deutsche Universitätszeitung* 9: 6-10.
1956	*Das Alte Testament als Anrede*.
1961	'Gott—Schicksal oder Anrede?', *EvT* 21: 193-208.
1962a	*Prediger*.
1962b	'"Offenbarung" im Alten Testament', *EvT* 22: 15-30.
1963a	*Gottes Offenbarung: Gesammelte Aufsätze* (partial ET in *I am Yahweh*, 1982).
1963b	'Die historisch-kritische Bibelwissenschaft und die Verkündigungsaufgabe der Kirche', *EvT* 23: 17-31.
1964a	*Israel und die Christen*.
1964b	*Was ist der Mensch?*
1968	*Der Mensch und seine Hoffnung im Alten Testament* (ET 1971).
1971	*Die Weltlichkeit des Alten Testaments* (ET 1976).

Zimmern, Heinrich

| 1885 | *Babylonische Busspsalmen*. |

1905   *Babylonische Hymnen und Gebete.*
Zippert, Thomas
   1994   *Bildung durch Offenbarung.*
Zucker, Moshe
   1984   *Saadya's Commentary on Genesis.*
Zurhellen-Pfleiderer, Else
   1916   *Biblische Geschichten und Persönlichkeiten.*

INDEXES

INDEX OF REFERENCES

OLD TESTAMENT

NEW TESTAMENT

JEWISH WRITINGS

INDEX OF NAMES